# A Patriot's History® of the Modern World

# A Patriot's History®
## of the
# Modern World

From America's Exceptional Ascent
to the Atomic Bomb: 1898–1945

Larry Schweikart and Dave Dougherty

SENTINEL

To Andrew Brietbart, for whom the lion's den was a party invitation.

SENTINEL
Published by the Penguin Group
Penguin Group (USA) Inc., 375 Hudson Street,
New York, New York 10014, U.S.A.
Penguin Group (Canada), 90 Eglinton Avenue East, Suite 700,
Toronto, Ontario, Canada M4P 2Y3
(a division of Pearson Penguin Canada Inc.)
Penguin Books Ltd, 80 Strand, London WC2R 0RL, England
Penguin Ireland, 25 St. Stephen's Green, Dublin 2, Ireland
(a division of Penguin Books Ltd)
Penguin Books Australia Ltd, 250 Camberwell Road, Camberwell,
Victoria 3124, Australia
(a division of Pearson Australia Group Pty Ltd)
Penguin Books India Pvt Ltd, 11 Community Centre, Panchsheel Park,
New Delhi – 110 017, India
Penguin Group (NZ), 67 Apollo Drive, Rosedale, Auckland 0632,
New Zealand (a division of Pearson New Zealand Ltd)
Penguin Books (South Africa) (Pty) Ltd, 24 Sturdee Avenue,
Rosebank, Johannesburg 2196, South Africa

Penguin Books Ltd, Registered Offices:
80 Strand, London WC2R 0RL, England

First published in 2012 by Sentinel,
a member of Penguin Group (USA) Inc.

10   9   8   7   6   5   4   3   2   1

Map illustrations by Philip Schwartzberg, Meridian Mapping, Minneapolis

Library of Congress Cataloging-in-Publication Data

Schweikart, Larry.
    A patriot's history of the modern world / Larry Schweikart and Dave Dougherty.
        p. cm.
    Includes bibliographical references and index.
    Contents: [v. 1.] From America's exceptional ascent to the atomic bomb : 1898–1945
    ISBN 978-1-59523-089-8
    1. United States—History—20th century. 2. United States—History—21st century. 3. United
States—Foreign relations. 4. United States—Influence. I. Dougherty, Dave. II. Title.
    E741.S247 2012
    973.91—dc23
                                    2012027033

Printed in the United States of America
Set in Janson Text
Designed by Spring Hoteling

# CONTENTS

# Introduction

It was only six o'clock in the morning, but the desert cool was already yielding to solar rays that in a few hours would reach scorching temperatures. Blowing sand swept the face of a young lieutenant in the British 21st Lancers as he and his troops waited patiently behind a wall of khaki for the assault massing at the formation's front. British and Egyptian riflemen stood and kneeled in double ranks, interspersed with Maxim guns and heavy artillery. It was an impressive sight, even for Lieutenant Winston Churchill, who had seen his share of action. Now, in September 1898, he jotted down notes he would use in his moonlighting job as a war correspondent, incomplete as they necessarily were from his vantage point inside the British square and behind the bristle of Enfield rifles.

In the distance, a massive dust cloud drifted his way. But it was no typical desert sandstorm: instead, the first of 80,000 supposedly unstoppable "Ansar" Muslim forces under the command of Abdullah al-Taashi (called "Khalifa" or ruler) poured out of the hills and from the plain in a headlong charge at the Anglo-Egyptian ranks. Once known as "Mahdists" for their allegiance to the dead self-proclaimed "Mahdi" (the "Guided One") the Ansar warriors were known by a different name by the British: "dervishes," for their whirling mystic religious dances and their perceived scorn for Western-style firepower. This day destroyed that reputation as torrents of artillery shells, Maxim machine gun bursts, and ordered rifle volleys mowed down the Ansars by the hundreds. None got closer than fifty yards to the British-Egyptian lines. Half of the Muslims were killed almost instantly, the rest circling to regroup. When the Khalifa retreated to re-form his army, General Horatio Herbert Kitchener (later Lord Kitchener) advanced his columns, sending the 21st Lancers and young Churchill forward to clear away stragglers. The 21st rode into an ambush of 2,500 Ansar infantry, yet charged repeatedly until the

Muslim forces ran. By 11:30, after additional futile dervish charges, the Khalifa's forces were shattered and the British celebrated Omdurman—their last magnificent victory of the Age of Imperialism. In just five short years, many of the same units that so easily dispatched an enemy force more than double their size would struggle mightily to defeat smaller Boer forces in South Africa. There, an enemy coming from a European culture not only equipped with modern weapons but also practicing the "Western way of war" would stifle the mighty British Empire for half a decade.

Just eleven years after Omdurman, the torch of world leadership and influence passed from England in another symbolic way. Literally at the other end of the earth from the Sudanese desert—90 degrees North latitude—American Navy Commander Robert E. Peary, his lungs aching from the freezing air, took latitude sightings and, convinced he was at his destination, planted the American flag at the North Pole. His ascension to the most northerly point on earth, despite subsequent controversy about how far north Peary actually went, seemed figuratively to elevate the United States as a nation. At the other end of the globe, British explorer Captain Robert Falcon Scott of the Royal Navy would launch his ill-fated Terra Nova expedition the following year. Scott led four others on a quest to attain 90 degrees South—the South Pole—in a race against Norwegian explorer Roald Amundsen. Whereas Amundsen used dog sleds, Scott employed a complex and fatally flawed combination of motorized sleds, dogs, and horses. The motor sledges broke down, and ponies proved a disastrous choice as they ate more than they could pull. Yet Scott was reluctant to kill and eat them along the way. Although Scott and his companions managed to reach the South Pole on January 17, 1912, they found that Amundsen had arrived there five weeks earlier and seized the glory. Worse, as they retreated to their base, Antarctic blizzards plowed into them, trapping the desperate group eleven miles short of a food cache. Scott's food, fuel, and heat ran out as he wrote in his diary, "Last entry. For God's sake look after our people."[1] It was an obituary as much for the British Empire as it was for Robert Falcon Scott.

Like almost all European countries, between 1900 and 1950, England lurched toward socialism, forced into currency devaluations, forgiven its enormous debts by the United States after both world wars, and eagerly accepted American aid through the Marshall Plan. The pound sterling was replaced as the world's reserve currency, as it underwent three devaluations: in 1931, 1949, and 1967.[2]

Meanwhile, a new superpower arose across the Atlantic. America's ascent to global dominance was unavoidable after the First World War, but the unrelenting shift in power between the Battle of Omdurman and Peary's polar journey made it apparent even before the Great War that the American eagle would supplant the British lion—at least to non-European observers. Certainly the acquisition of overseas territories by the United States in the Spanish-American War made America a world power in the most literal sense of the word. Beyond that, the nation had matured, grown up, and filled out. The continental United States was complete, and following the explosive economic growth of the Gilded Age, the nation had few superiors in the international market. Even the defeat of Spain in 1898—accomplished with an ill-equipped army (but a modern navy) and a less than full wartime mobilization—caused the Europeans to take notice. If one of their own could be bested so easily, perhaps Uncle Sam had muscles after all.

Yet America's rise to global power came as the nation still struggled with its character, and its vision of its own future. A fierce battle for the type of society the United States would be had partially ended in 1896, when William McKinley won the presidency over the pro-silver faction of William Jennings Bryan. McKinley, running on the gold standard (which stipulated that the only reserve currency of the nation should be gold and should not include silver), had struck a blow for fiscal conservatism. In essence, he insisted that the dollar be "as good as gold." The gold standard reassured business that it would not be ravaged by rapid price increases in raw materials, and that the value of money would remain stable. The country agreed, much to the chagrin of farmers, who found that large-scale agriculture was making the family farm increasingly obsolete. But there were also inflationists who wanted to use the free silver movement to artificially reward debtor groups; as prices for farm goods rose, for example, farmers would receive more income while their single largest expense—their long-term mortgage on the farm—would remain locked in at lower rates. But McKinley's death in 1901 left Theodore Roosevelt as president, and drastically redirected the government's efforts toward what would later be called "economic justice."

From that point through the beginning of the next century, the struggle between Progressive liberals in both major parties who wanted redistribution of wealth and more government involvement in all aspects of society and, for want of a better term, "Constitutionalists" who believed that the individual is responsible for himself and his family, that the political system existed for the people, not for politicians to reshape their constituents like so much clay, would dominate the American political narrative. Often obscured by traditional partisan conflict, the real battle was far deeper, with more profound implications than which party held the White House. This is the first major theme of *A Patriot's History of the Modern World*: which of the two visions of America that existed in 1900 would emerge victorious— the nineteenth-century Progressive worldview, whatever its modern accessories and recasting, or the Constitutional view of government and society. Roosevelt, clearly a Progressive, pushed the United States toward the former; Calvin Coolidge and Ronald Reagan, both Constitutionalists, would attempt to nudge the nation back toward the latter.

A second theme of this work is that the United States is, and has always been, "exceptional" in its founding and national character. That perspective remained common throughout much of the twentieth century, but by 2009, President Barack Obama seemed to lump the United States together with every other nation: "I believe in American exceptionalism, just as I suspect that the Brits *believe in British exceptionalism and the Greeks believe in Greek exceptionalism* (emphasis ours)."[3] Obama's comment indicated that he lacked even the most basic understanding of what is meant by the term "American exceptionalism." It is more than the simplistic belief that one's country has its advantages, appealing characteristics, and specific national identity. Nor is it the creature of "biased" Eurocentric or Amerocentric historians. At root, American exceptionalism is the confluence of four factors that collectively do not exist in any other country in the world. Some possess one or two; England possesses three and at one time had all four—but no longer. These are: 1) a heritage of common law; 2) a Christian and predominantly Protestant religious tradition; 3) a free-market economy; and 4) property rights, especially land rights. The common-law heritage held that the law was given to the people (later this was modified to include "by God") and that the ruler merely enforced the law that everyone observed and understood as divinely inspired. Thus, in common law, authority moved from the people upward, not the other way around, as with "Divine Right" and civil law, in which rights came from the monarch down. America inherited the common-law tradition from England, where it had migrated from Germany, but virtually the rest of the world adopted civil law, with its top-down, autocratic approach. By the mid-twentieth century, even England had started to drift from its common-law moorings. And at no time were the American-style checks and balances present in the European social democracies. Prime ministers were usually part of the majority party, not an independent chief executive. Moreover, none of the civil-law countries had the same inherent respect for a written constitution so prominent in the U.S. system.

Much of Europe has had a Christian religious tradition, but only parts had a distinctly Protestant background (Holland, parts of Germany, England, Scandinavia), leaving the United States in a rather small community of Protestant nations. Even then, several of those nations had state churches, which never developed in America due to the First Amendment. But Protestantism brought with it a heavy dose of individuality. Calvinist teachings insisted that each man read and understand the Bible for himself; Puritans and Quakers in America practiced congregational church government, which was exceptionally democratic and local; and the entire tone of Protestantism was antiauthoritarian.

While much of Europe, England, and, after the Second World War, Asia and even Latin America have at one time or another had free-market economies (to one degree or another), few have been as unfettered as the capitalist system practiced in the United States. The American variant of capitalism, again with its Protestant overtones, relied heavily on individual entrepreneurship and eschewed state involvement. Failure was considered a learning tool, not a source of public embarrassment, and bankruptcy laws reflected that. Laws provided extreme ease with which to start, sell, or terminate businesses. And finally, American property rights, emerging from the Land Ordinance of 1785 and the Northwest Ordinance, not only closely linked political rights to land ownership, but also established the principle that individual land ownership was a social goal to be advanced by government. Following Thomas Jefferson's model, the early United States made it easy and relatively inexpensive for anyone not only to acquire property but also to gain legal title deed to that property—a characteristic that was rare in Europe and is still unseen and not even understood in much of the rest of the world. Therefore, American exceptionalism was in fact unique, consisting of four "legs" not found anywhere else in the world by the mid-twentieth century.

What has often served as a source of confusion is that the Europeans claim some of the same heritage, but often use similar terms to mean entirely different things. Americans have often been guilty of failing to understand that Europeans do not see the world through American eyes—they have their own perspective that firmly places Europe in the center of the universe even during periods of American military and economic dominance. Until World War I and even later, Europeans often looked upon the United States as a large country with great potential suffering from an excess of liberty leading to irresolution, naïveté, and international impotence. European concepts of a "free market" have been from the late 1800s on dramatically different from those of Americans, integrating heavy regulation, socialized labor unions, and far more interference from government.

A certain snobbishness by Europe remained well entrenched throughout the 1900s. Culture and refinement were often viewed on the Continent as strictly European attributes—recalling the French Abbé Raynal's comment in 1770 that "America has not produced a good poet, one able mathematician, one man of genius in a single art or a single science"—and it was generally held that Americans understood little of politics and foreign affairs.[4] American egalitarianism in politics and the lack of a large professional military caste led Europeans to think the United States was hopeless in prosecuting wars. Even as late as the 1960s, many Germans believed that the United States was controlled by women's clubs. These views were reinforced by the reports of European visitors who traveled past the East Coast cities, where they found a people who were simply good-hearted, but uncultured, and whom they looked upon as "childlike" in their trust of strangers, and easily misled or manipulated—even politically.[5]

Americans, on the other hand, hewed to the proposition that the United States was an exceptional nation, the shining city upon a hill, containing more virtue than all of Europe put together. Many of the Founders had disdained the European cities as cesspools and swamps, and therefore understood the longing by poorer immigrants to reach American shores. Americans generally welcomed waves of immigrants—with some backlash against the Catholic Irish—and absorbed them with relative ease and without conflict until the 1880s. Only then—when the majority of European immigrants began to come from southern Europe or the Balkans—did the influx of so many non-English-speakers who practiced religions other than Protestantism strain the American social fabric.

Exacerbating the difficulties of absorbing these immigrants was the problem that, contrary to the American mainstream, many arrived having internalized radical socialist and communist doctrines. Many failed to distinguish the difference between a tyrannical, autocratic European monarch and an American president. The reaction came in the form of nativism during the influx of Irish Catholics 1840–1860, which morphed into isolationism, and the persecution of Jews, Mexicans, and Asians occurring alongside Jim Crow–sanctioned separatism late in the nineteenth century . Yet this, too, was another element of America that virtually no other nation faced: a polyglot mix of people, ethnicities, religions, and cultures. For the first time, American exceptionalism had to be explained and taught, not merely taken for granted by those who had come from an English or Germanic background, and to be cherished as a foundational principle. However, the Progressive movement in the United States began to erode these principles and the value of an exceptional America, steering her to become a member of the international community and following Europe's lead.

European countries, with their oligarchic governments and more homogenous populations, never developed the concept of freedom as Americans lived it. To a large degree, even in democratic European countries, the notion of freedom was limited to "freedom to serve the state." This European failure to understand the American character—its definitions of liberty, its reliance on personal responsibility, and its emphasis on land ownership—constituted a difference in the definitions of freedom that proved profound.

America's ascent to power from 1898 to 1945 not only reflected the "exceptional" traits that made her distinct from the Europeans, it *embodied* those traits. From the failed attempt at Prohibition—and its repeal, admitting a major national mistake—to the G.I. "can-do" attitude in World War II, the United States dared greatly. Her projects such as the Panama Canal seemed daunting to the point of impossibility, yet they were built where others failed. Her heroes such as Teddy Roosevelt, Robert Peary, Sergeant Alvin York, Charles Lindbergh, and Babe Ruth all seemed giants whose exploits were incomparable. (Ruth's single-season home run record stood until 1961.) Her artistic, business, and intellectual titans such as Frank Lloyd Wright, Henry Ford, A. P. Giannini, and Walt Disney, often augmented by immigrants such as Albert Einstein and Enrico Fermi, pushed America to world preeminence in architecture, industry, finance, film, and science. And by 1945, not only was it clear that the United States would be a superpower, but it seemed that her best years still lay well into the future.

*A Patriot's History of the Modern World* follows the history of the last century to the end of World War II along three thematic lines: the struggle between Progressivism and Constitutionalism within America; the rise of American global power and its corollary in the decline of European constitutionalism and international influence; and the rise of new, non-Western powers challenging the United States for world leadership (or, perhaps, dominance).

What, then, constitutes the "modern" world in this context? We define it as the period after the United States stepped onto the world stage up to the present day. The year 1898, when the United States went to war with Spain over Cuba, marks the beginning of this era, as it was the first time America proved it could be an international power. Before then, the United States had confined itself to punitive expeditions against the Barbary Pirates and actions in the Western Hemisphere, mostly dealing with its neighbors Mexico and Canada. All European nations expected Spain to make short work of the impudent Americans and wreak utter havoc on the U.S. fleet. Only Great Britain was at all reserved in her judgment of the probable outcome, having been wrong three times (the Revolution, the War of 1812, and the Mexican War) in her assessment of her Atlantic cousins. But when Spain was utterly defeated in a series of astounding victories in Manila Bay and the waters off Cuba, respect for American diplomats, soldiers, and sailors took a giant leap forward.

With the defeat of Spain, the United States broke the bonds that shackled her to the rest of the Western Hemisphere and limited America to a provincial, internal outlook. The limited national government soon found itself replaced by a federal colossus, requiring an income tax to provide the necessary revenues, a massive bureaucracy to manage its affairs, and a European-style central bank to control the economy. Like its European counterparts, the Federal Reserve, created under President Woodrow Wilson, was a private corporation, unaccountable to and uncontrolled by elected officials yet all too often seemingly in cahoots with the administration currently in office.

Yet even as the United States stepped onto the world stage as a world leader, she refrained from active involvement. The war with Spain was confined to Cuba, only ninety miles from American territory, and a single naval battle in the Philippines. The Islands of Hawaii were annexed in 1898, and America's participation in suppressing the Boxer Rebellion in China and the Philippine Insurrection quickly followed, but these were seen as little more than police actions. Even after World War I, the U.S. Army was reduced to 150,000 men (only 50 percent larger than the size of the army permitted Germany by the Versailles Treaty).[6] The Navy, however, while not gutted, remained in line with the Washington Naval Conference agreements of 1921–22. While Spain fought a civil war, which attracted participants from Italy, Germany, and Russia, the United States carefully stayed out. Italians conquered Africans and the Japanese brutalized the Chinese, but except for sanctions, America stood down. Only the immediate threat of Britain's collapse against Hitler sparked enough concern to start Lend-Lease, and only a direct attack by Japan brought the United States into World War II. Yet by 1945, when no fewer than eight empires had been destroyed—the Ottoman, Austro-Hungarian, German, Russian, French, Dutch, British, and Japanese—America steadfastly refused to secure any of those territories as colonies, even to the point of denying aid to allies seeking to hold their lands. Instead, the United States, perhaps overconfident that the institutions so central to its exceptional character would be readily accepted throughout the world, insisted on open, Western democracies as the most just and efficient means to resist the new threat of Soviet communism. Often the conversion problems proved insurmountable in countries that lacked all of America's pillars of democracy—common law, Protestant Christianity, a free-market capitalistic economy, and the sanctity of private property—but the United States cannot be faulted for not trying to spread the American Way.

But the American Way was not just democratic government. There is nothing magical about democracy. After all, a democratic nation produced Adolf Hitler, and phony democracies in the twentieth century have repeatedly given murderous thugs such as Saddam Hussein and Kim Jong-il "majorities" in faux elections. In contrast, some Middle Eastern kingdoms, whether through intimidation, fear, or resignation, function with a minimum of violence and some level of economic progress. International aid agencies have learned that merely imposing democratic systems in utterly undeveloped parts of Africa or Asia did not automatically yield peace, stability, or progress. Rather, America's ascent to world power demonstrated that so long as the essence of American exceptionalism remained at the core of all efforts foreign and domestic, the likelihood of success was nearly guaranteed. Because that exceptionalism, as has been noted, consisted of more than merely democratic government; nations wishing to emulate America's progress could not simply pick and choose one or two parts of the package. Rather, the elements reinforced one another in a mutually supporting relationship—a fact that would be made clear in the Second World War when America and her allies defeated two powers that had adopted some, or most, of the "Western way of war" but which still resisted the critical elements of liberty and free speech that completed the circle. Thus, for a writer such as Niall Ferguson to assert, for example, that the United States at the end of the Second World War "was still much less powerful than the European empires had been forty-five years before" is misguided, reflecting a certain nineteenth-century understanding of "empires."[7] That view also rested on a European-style understanding of colonialism, which, as historian Paul Johnson said, "was a highly visual phenomenon [abounding] in flags, exotic uniforms, splendid ceremonies, Durbars, sunset-guns, trade exhibitions at Olympia and Grand Palais, postage stamps and, above all, coloured maps."[8] The fact that American overseas expansion in the early twentieth century lacked precisely these "highly visual" trappings, but by World War II would export a much different type of symbol—Coca-Cola or Ford trademark images, for example—testified to the real influence the United States wielded.

America's astounding success in World War II, and her preeminent position among all free nations in the decades afterward, meant that U.S. products, goods, services, and ideas would increasingly expand into Europe and Asia. Over the ensuing half century, Americanism would become global: Marriott would have hotels virtually everywhere; McDonald's hamburgers and Disney movies would reach even remote areas of the world, and nations would define themselves largely in relation to their amity toward, or hostility to, the United States. Yes, Belgian chocolates, French cheeses, Japanese anime, Mexican cuisine, Canadian hockey, European soccer, and Korean cars would all carve out spots in American markets and culture. Yes, by 2012 one could find an (east) Indian actor or actress prominently featured on network television, or a Hong Kong Chinese turning out popular action movies, or an occasional foreign film that connected with the U.S. moviegoing audience.

But by and large what Victor Davis Hanson has repeatedly said of non-Western militaries—that the British were in Zululand, but it was impossible to imagine the Zulu on the Thames—applies to American influence worldwide. Whether through its products, its democratic processes, or its self-confidence, America remains the world's sole "exceptional" nation, which is to say, it alone has a self-written narrative that explains why the United States should—not just "could"—influence others. That self-definition remained alive, but largely contained within the Western Hemisphere between 1898 and 1941, with the exception of the brief foray into European conflict and the subsequent disastrous diplomatic solution America allowed to be imposed on a large part of the globe at Versailles. While the United States had the potential to become the world's superpower in 1919, it had neither the desire nor the focus, and indeed in the immediate postwar aftermath, the tension between prewar Progressivism and the newly revived Constitutionalism of Warren Harding and Calvin Coolidge took center stage. Their emphasis on limited government, business growth, and restrained foreign interventions lasted a mere eight years, and stood out in sharp relief from the Progressive-dominated period that lasted from William McKinley's death in 1901 through World War II.

Meanwhile, the Europeans, almost all possessed of democratic constitutions adopted long after the U.S. Constitution, but not modeled on it, had spread their version of democracy around the world through their colonies. Yet with no understanding of common law and its central role in expressing the will of the people, almost all of the European governments and their colonial clones drifted into constitutional autocracies, and in the Third World those governments quickly disintegrated further into dictatorships covered by fig-leaf constitutions.

The American ascent to superpower status that began innocuously with the rapid defeat of Spain in 1898 and culminated in the difficult and bloody victory over Nazi Germany and Imperial Japan in 1945 had been accomplished largely because the Progressives stood aside at the right moments and permitted America to be America. Franklin Roosevelt's antipathy to business during the Great Depression yielded to a commonsense liberating of the titans of industry from 1941 to 1945. While his misguided views of Joseph Stalin led him to make repeated concessions to the communists, he stopped short of ceding world supremacy. Harry Truman quickly righted the scale after Roosevelt's death, and the nature of Soviet intentions was not seriously questioned by another American president until 1976 by Jimmy Carter. In short, having hamstrung aspects of American exceptionalism in the 1930s, Roosevelt restored them during the time of ultimate crisis.

What remained in 1945 was a stark contrast of free and unfree societies, one led by an exceptional American republic and culture, one dominated by communist tyranny. While it is likely that the war itself prolonged Soviet communism by decades (allowing Stalin to both appeal to Russian patriotism and simultaneously purge threats), by the end of the war there were few rosy-eyed visionaries outside of the hard-left Progressives and academicians who still advocated Soviet-style communism for the United States.

The "Harvest of Sorrow" and the mass executions of the 1930s had shattered many illusions among fellow travelers as the truth about Stalin's regime leaked out. Thus, across the American political spectrum in 1945 there was a sense that right had prevailed, that the path followed by the United States was the correct and moral one, and that American exceptionalism was indeed worth celebrating. America's story from 1898 to 1945 is therefore nothing less than the triumph of American exceptionalism over liberal Progressivism, despite a few temporary victories by the latter. Few Americans who heard of Robert Peary planting the flag on the North Pole, or who knew of Charles Lindbergh's astounding flight, or who watched Babe Ruth pound home run after home run ever thought another nation was capable of such greatness. No one who witnessed the atomic bombs could doubt the power of America's wrath if turned on an enemy. The American ascent to *world* influence was the fastest in human history. Whether it was the best remained a question of how true the United States could stay to its founding values, and whether it would decide to remain . . . exceptional.

# CHAPTER ONE

# American Emergence
# Amid European Self-Absorption

## Time Line

1898: American battleship *Maine* blown up in Havana harbor; Spanish-American War; Battle of Omdurman (British Sudan); French submarine sinks stationary battleship; U.S. annexes Hawaii

1899: Boxer Rebellion begins (ends 1901); Philippine Insurrection begins (ends 1913); Second Boer War begins (ends 1902)

1900: U.S. population reaches 70 million; first Zeppelin flight; quantum physics born

1901: Commonwealth of Australia formed; Spindletop gushers begin Texas oil production; Hay-Pauncefote Treaty; William McKinley assassinated, Theodore Roosevelt assumes presidency

1902: Roosevelt Corollary

1903: Wright brothers successfully demonstrate controlled flight; first World Series played

1904: Entente Cordiale allies Britain and France; Trans-Siberian Railroad completed; Russo-Japanese War (ends 1905)

1905: Russian revolution; First Moroccan Crisis (Germany and France); Norway formed; Treaty of Portsmouth ends Russo-Japanese War

1906: HMS *Dreadnought* launched; Germany launches first submarine (U-boat); San Francisco earthquake; first feature film released in United States

1907: Panic of 1907 (U.S.); Dominion of New Zealand formed; triode amplifier starts birth of electronics industry

1908: Boy Scouts formed; oil discovered in Middle East; Young Turk revolution in Turkey; Henry Ford produces Model T; Bulgaria declares independence from Ottoman Empire

1909: Anglo-Persian Oil Company (British Petroleum, or BP) founded; U.S. Supreme Court upholds right of city government to regulate height of buildings in *Welch v. Swasey*; corporate income tax passed by Congress; Robert Peary reaches North Pole

1910: George V becomes king of England; Union of South Africa created; Japan annexes Korea; Montenegro gains independence; Portugal declares itself a republic; Mexican revolution against Porfirio Díaz; Norman Angell writes *The Great Illusion*

1911: Agadir Crisis (Germany and France); Wuchang Uprising (China) ends Qing (Manchu) Dynasty; Italy declares war on Ottoman Empire, annexes Tripoli; Roald Amundsen reaches South Pole

1912: *Titanic* sinks; Republic of China established; France imposes protectorate for Morocco; First Balkan War (Montenegro, Greece, Bulgaria, Serbia vs. Turkey)

1913: U.S. income tax amendment ratified; Federal Reserve Act passed; President Francisco Madero assassinated in Mexico; three-way struggle for power in Mexico between Victoriano Huerta, Venustiano Carranza, and Pancho Villa; Igor Stravinsky's *Rite of Spring* ballet performed in Paris

1914:     Woodrow Wilson intervenes in Mexico; United States
          occupies Veracruz; Kiel Canal deepened, allowing transit
          of German battleships between North and Baltic seas;
          Gavrilo Princip assassinates Austrian Archduke Franz
          Ferdinand (June 28), sparking World War I; Antoni
          Gaudí creates Parc Güell

The Pacific moon hung like a fat lemon, an ironic symbol marking what would become the dawn of the American global era, at 11:30 on the night of April 20, 1898. Eight ships of Admiral George Dewey's Asiatic Squadron slipped into the Boca Grande Channel in Manila Bay, where the crew intended to lay waste to the Spanish vessels in the harbor. Although Dewey, the son of a Vermont doctor, had a reputation as a practical joker and low-level troublemaker at the Naval Academy in Annapolis, this evening he stood grimly, watching his column silently plow through the Pacific waters en route to its deadly rendezvous. Feeling all of his sixty-one years, with his droopy white mustache and wise eyes, Dewey could have passed for a manager of one of the new American baseball teams, or a doctor, which would have made his father proud. He could barely remember his mother, dead at a young age from tuberculosis, but he expected she too would have gushed over her brave son, now leading a flotilla into battle. Now it was his turn to be proud.[1]

Having survived the academy—one of only fifteen out of the sixty who had entered with him as "plebes"—Dewey had commanded the USS *Mississippi* during the short combat in 1862 that led to the surrender of New Orleans by Confederate forces. He then quite literally barely survived his next assignment, when a Rebel shell exploded on the quarterdeck of the *Monongahela*, where he was the executive officer. The explosion killed the captain and four other officers, but Dewey walked away unharmed. With the end of the Civil War, Dewey marched through a series of tedious assignments: lighthouse inspector, commander of a rickety steam sloop headed for Asia, Washington bureaucrat. His role in several innovations related to electric searchlights and signaling apparatus led to his appointment to the Board of Inspection and Survey, where he was responsible for inspecting all new warships. Though he remained desk-bound, it was here that he became familiar with the latest naval technology, including newfangled gadgets such as John Holland's submarine. A promotion to commodore seemed hollow, until the post of commander-in-chief of the Asiatic Squadron opened up in May 1896.

Some might have balked at the prospect of leaving the nation's political power center for an isolated position in the Far East, but Dewey relished the autonomy. He sought the post after McKinley took office, then was given a boost by the new assistant secretary of the Navy, the bombastic Theodore Roosevelt, at whose urging McKinley appointed Dewey toward the end of the year. The new commander reported to his flagship, the *Olympia*, in anchorage at Nagasaki, Japan, and in February 1898 sailed for Hong Kong, where the squadron rendezvoused. It entered a period of hectic detailed preparation for battle, and the ships were repainted with new gray battle camouflage replacing admiralty white.[2] Sailing from the British colony on April 24, Dewey turned north for thirty miles, before resuming a southerly course to engage the Spanish.

The circumstances that led the United States and Spain to war could be described as romantic and high-minded by some, or manipulated and contrived by others. To a certain extent, both descriptions are true. Cuba had been chafing under the Spanish leash for years, and going as far back as the Ostend Manifesto in 1854, some Americans had wanted to either purchase or seize Cuba as an American territory. So real was the possibility of obtaining Cuba due to its proximity and Spain's weakness that all that was needed was a push from Southern politicians. Instead, they obsessed over acquiring Kansas as a slave state, leading historian David Potter to artfully describe the South as having "sacrificed the Cuban substance for a Kansan shadow."[3] By the 1890s, as the United States turned its attention from Reconstruction to its western frontiers and burgeoning presence in the world, the tensions in Cuba seemed all the more relevant. Spain, after all, was a sagging European nation, hardly possessing power to tell Cubans what to do. American sugar and other business interests in Cuba felt directly threatened by insurrectionist activities, which would disappear if Spain was gone. Finally, the "Yellow Press," sensing a new age of American influence on the globe, incessantly cranked out propaganda portraying brave Cuban freedom fighters battling the oppressive Spanish overlords. Perhaps none of this would have reached a boiling point without the De Lôme letter of February 9, 1898, wherein Enrique Dupuy de Lôme, the Spanish minister in Cuba, sent a personal letter that was (illegally) intercepted by Cuban revolutionaries and made public. In it, he referred to U.S. president William McKinley as "weak and catering to the rabble" and as standing well with "the jingos of his party."[4] When the battleship *Maine* was ordered to Havana as a show of America's interest in the island—and remained there peacefully for more than a week—the crisis seemed to dissipate. But on February 15, the *Maine* was rocked by an explosion, obliterating the forward third of the ship. A naval board of inquiry, which lacked technical expertise, conducted a four-week investigation that concluded a mine had destroyed the ship. Blame flew in all directions, but mostly it landed in the lap of the Spanish. Meanwhile, Assistant Secretary of the Navy Theodore Roosevelt anticipated the moment when the United States would step onto the world stage.[5] While his superior, Secretary of the Navy John D. Long, took four hours off on the afternoon of February 25 to visit an osteopath for a massage, Roosevelt ordered Commodore Dewey at Hong Kong to concentrate his squadron and prepare for war with Spain. The United States Navy owed Roosevelt a great deal, as well before hostilities with Spain, Long had acquiesced to Roosevelt's energetic rebuilding of the fleet. On April 11, McKinley asked Congress for a war declaration, but Congress delayed for two weeks until Spain made the matter moot by declaring war on the United States.

Based on the principles of Alfred Thayer Mahan, naval historian and president of the Naval War College, which called for a new blue-water navy capable of taking on the Europeans and the Japanese in a decisive battle of massed firepower, the doctrine Roosevelt and Dewey subscribed to emphasized long-range gunnery focused on capital ships. Dewey would soon reap the rewards not only of Mahan, but of Benjamin Harrison's Navy secretary, Benjamin F. Tracy. From a distance, Tracy could have been mistaken for Andrew Carnegie with his short-cropped beard and white hair. Like Roosevelt, he was a New Yorker, possessing great energy and vision. Working with Mahan, Tracy had supported construction of modern warships funded in the Navy Bill of 1890. The resulting battleships *Indiana*, *Massachusetts*, and *Oregon* were authorized and, two years later, joined by the *Iowa*.

Dewey had none of those ships under his command, but the overall improvement of the force he did have could be traced in a straight line from Tracy to Mahan to Roosevelt. The squadron Dewey took to the Philippines consisted of the *Olympia*, a cruiser, the *Boston*—one of the famous "A, B, C, D" protected cruisers that had kicked off a new era of American naval power—the *Baltimore* and *Raleigh*, two more protected cruisers, the *Petrel* and the *Concord*, both gunboats, and the *McCulloch*, a Treasury Department revenue cutter. Hardly the equal of some of the powerful squadrons that had sailed in previous eras, Dewey's Asiatic force represented a substantial part of the American fighting ships at the outbreak of hostilities. The nation counted 5 battleships, 2 cruisers, 12 protected cruisers, 3 unprotected cruisers, and some 45 miscellaneous vessels (including Civil War–era monitors and an "armored ram") in its arsenal. Added to that, slightly over 120 other yachts, cutters, tenders, tugs, and colliers made up the "auxiliary navy."[6]

Despite its inferiority to England's Royal Navy, the American fleet had staged a remarkable resurgence since the Civil War, when hundreds of vessels were mothballed or scrapped. Engineer-in-chief Benjamin Isherwood had presided over the last burst of innovation when he shepherded through the construction process the USS *Wampanoag* (launched in 1864). With its advanced technology, including a geared steam engine, full iron plating, iron turrets, and two 100-pounder guns, the *Wampanoag* bested almost any ship in the world. Isherwood's propulsion gear turned a screw that endowed the *Wampanoag* with blazing speed—almost 18 knots (33 miles per hour) on its sea trials in 1868. Yet that year she was decommissioned, renamed, and condemned due to heavy coal consumption and concerns about her length-to-breadth ratio. Put into a pier to rot in 1874, the *Wampanoag* signaled the end of an era, for it would be more than twenty years before another American warship would attain such speeds. The U.S. Navy became a punch line in Oscar Wilde's *Canterville Ghost*. Americans were boring, said Virginia, who befriends the ghost, because "we have no ruins or curiosities." The ghost replies, "You have your navy and your manners."

It was a remarkable combination of technological breakthroughs and the literary success of an obscure captain teaching history and tactics at the Naval War College that revived America's fortunes at sea. Alfred Thayer Mahan, whose father Dennis had been a professor at West Point, had commanded several vessels in the Civil War (many of which were involved in collisions, leading to questions about his judgment as a commanding officer). Appointed lecturer at the War College, Mahan received a full year at the instruction of college president Rear Admiral Stephen B. Luce to focus his attention on the historical uses of sea power. Assembling research, Mahan produced a radical new doctrine that served as the intellectual bête noire of the land-oriented "Heartland of Eurasia" concepts advocated by British geographer Halford Mackinder.[7] As both Imperial Germany, then later, Nazi Germany, then finally, the Soviet Union marched to military dominance, strategists obsessed over figuring out which view—Mahan's or Mackinder's—was right.

Whereas Mackinder would stress control of the "Heartland of Eurasia," consigning the ocean powers to lesser importance, Mahan saw ocean-going commerce as critical to fighting wars. An advocate of mass firepower from heavy ships, Mahan advocated consolidating the fleet for a great, decisive sea battle, where victory would open up enemy coasts for invasion. Within a few years, Mahan was the equivalent of a literary star, but only across the oceans, where both the Japanese and British lionized him. A prophet without honor in his own land, Mahan's reputation grew steadily abroad until it was impossible to ignore at home. That his ideas fit well with the muscular expansionism championed by Theodore Roosevelt was so much the better for him.

What gave substance to the prospect of a deep-water American navy, however, was not the bespectacled Roosevelt's rousing interventionist speeches but the steelmaking genius of an immigrant Scotsman, Andrew Carnegie. Arriving penniless in the United States at age thirteen, Carnegie worked as a bobbin boy, telegrapher, and general go-fer for J. Edgar Thomson of the Pennsylvania Railroad. Possessed of an uncanny sense of "the next big thing," Carnegie seamlessly moved from railroads to the bridges that supported them to the iron that built the bridges. Willing to share his rewards with keen managers and the practical inventor-engineers he employed, Carnegie nevertheless kept his eye on obtaining complete control over his business through the "Iron Clad Oaths" each partner was required to sign, allowing Carnegie Steel (that is, Carnegie himself) to have the first shot at purchasing the partner's shares should one decide to sell or otherwise leave the company.

Carnegie didn't invent anything, but he employed the top minds and managers—fellow immigrants, such as the Kloman brothers, or Civil War veterans, such as "Captain" Bill Jones. A master motivator, Jones once inspired his division to out-produce a rival simply by writing the steel output of the rival's plant on the floor. During the Johnstown Flood of 1889, Jones personally provisioned an entire trainload of relief supplies. He, the Klomans, Julian Kennedy, and others in the Carnegie stable were hands-on innovators who refined Carnegie's product through their ceaseless improvements, both technical and managerial. Julian Kennedy, who managed Carnegie's blast furnaces, typified Carnegie's hands-on executives; he had 150 patents during his career with the company, more than half in operation somewhere in Carnegie's mills.

What Carnegie's company produced, however, was nothing less than the finest steel in the world, every bit the equal of any of the British yards. Obsessed with driving costs down and production up, Carnegie pushed his men and mills to turn out the best, cheapest steel in the world, though not for the U.S. Navy. Having seen his Bessemer furnaces force the cost of making rails down from $28 a ton to $11.50 a ton between 1880 and 1900, Carnegie nevertheless backed away from bidding for ship armor plate. The Scotsman's pacifism dovetailed nicely with his opinion that the profits were too low in ship plating until 1889, when the construction of two new battleships, the *New York* and the *Maine*, suffered delays due to insufficient plating. Sniffing an opportunity, Navy Secretary Benjamin Tracy appealed to Carnegie to rethink his involvement with the Navy. "There may be millions for us in armor," Carnegie concluded, yet still he dawdled, hoping for an even better arrangement.[8] Finally in 1890, Tracy threatened to purchase steel from the British, forcing Carnegie to build a new plant near Homestead, Pennsylvania, and win the contracts for three new battleships.[9]

Even with the efforts of steel men like Carnegie and his protégé Charles Schwab (who left Carnegie Steel after it was sold to J. P. Morgan to lead a successful turnaround of Bethlehem Steel), American ships still lagged behind the best British designs. But they were catching up fast, and in 1898 they didn't have to fight the British. Dewey knew his ships were decidedly better than those of the Spanish. Whether he had enough firepower and skill to defeat the Spanish fleet remained to be determined, but the commodore brimmed with confidence, thanks to information provided by both the American consul, Oscar F. Williams, who had remained in Manila as long as possible to scout enemy strength, and the *Olympia*'s own Ensign Frank B. Upham, who donned civilian dress and cavorted with sailors arriving in Hong Kong from Manila. It was from Upham that Dewey learned the Spaniards claimed to have mined the Bay. Finally, Dewey had information from a business acquaintance in the Philippines that powder supplied by contractors to the Spanish fleet was of such uneven quality as to render Spanish gunnery poor, which, combined with the reports of Williams and Upham, led him to believe he could easily best the Spaniards. By the time he sailed from Hong Kong, Dewey had obtained and assessed information on the Spanish fleet, forts, mines, the depths and locations of channels and entrances to Manila and Subic bays, the state of the tides, currents, and winds, and his personnel were fully ready for battle. Dewey later credited the intense training and intelligence gathering in Hong Kong for his victory, saying, "This battle was won in Hong Kong harbor."[10]

## "Drunken, Canting, Lying, Praying"

Europeans watching from afar were confident that exactly the opposite would happen and America's military would prove inadequate. They saw the war through a kaleidoscope of class, national, and religious lenses, all reflecting not only what they *thought* would happen but also what some *hoped* would transpire. For the European socialists, all three parties to the conflict—the Spanish, the Americans, and the Cuban elites leading the revolution—were agents of "capitalist exploitation."[11] Catholics in general sided with the Spanish, as did the French, with their heavy investments in Spanish bonds. Everywhere the war was analyzed and sides were taken based on national self-interest. Nations such as Austria, with its Hungarians, Germans, Gypsies, Slovaks, Serbs, Slovenes, Croats, and Romanians, took a dim view of revolutionary rhetoric, no matter what the underlying circumstances, and Austrian emperor Franz Josef had family connections to the Spanish royal family. But Austria had no overseas colonies and did not particularly care to support nations that did, so it favored the United States. Some monarchs such as Kaiser Wilhelm II of Germany, whose "first romantic impulse was to fly to the aid of Maria Cristina [of Austria] in defence of the monarchical principle," supported Spain, but this did not carry over to the population as a whole, especially among Protestants.[12] Moreover, Germany's main foreign policy objective was to neutralize France, a goal in which the war served no end.[13] The Kaiser did possess some colonial ambitions in Asia, but in the end Germany would follow a policy of strict neutrality, expressed in a poem in the German satirical journal *Kladderadatsch:* "Uncle Sam I Cannot Stand, for Spain I Have No Sympathy."

France, on the other hand, not only retained a strong monarchical streak, but cultivated a strain of anti-Americanism over the French failure to maintain colonies in the Caribbean. This, combined with the concern that revolutionary fervor in one part of the world might, to paraphrase American socialist historian Charles Beard, cause democratic feelings in other French colonies to foam perilously near the crest, inspired France to support Spain.[14] France was not alone in its fears: three Russian volunteers managed to reach Cuba, for which Soviet historians would later lionize them as warriors in the "Cuban War of National Liberation."[15] Only Britain, whose interests in the Caribbean benefited from the Monroe Doctrine, concluded that the threats posed by an independent Cuba or a Cuba controlled by the Americans were outweighed by a victory by monarchist

Spain, since a principal beneficiary of a Spanish victory would be Imperial Germany, which might try to wrest control of Pacific colonies away from Spain. Thus the British, while officially neutral, surely sided with Uncle Sam, even if their military experts continued to view American fighting prowess with condescension.[16]

England's "experts" were in good company with their skepticism about U.S. military power. Many Europeans found themselves embracing contradictory and mutually exclusive views. Continental newspapers routinely blared condemnations of the Monroe Doctrine (which was never invoked as a casus belli by the United States). The Dutch press warned that a victorious United States would turn its eyes toward Dutch possessions in the Caribbean.[17] Further, they predicted the United States would need 70,000 troops to establish order in the Philippines, estimating the number of the rebels there under Emilio Aguinaldo at 40,000. The Dutch journalists were slow learners. Even as the remnants of the Spanish fleet in Manila were surrendering, Dutch papers prophesied that the "real" Spanish fleet was on its way to Cuba and would teach the Americans a lesson.[18]

Certainly Spanish newspapers exuded confidence in the war's outcome, with some calling for outright invasion of the United States. *El País* roared, "The Cuban problem will not be solved unless we send an army to the U.S.," and *El Correo Español* called for war.[19] When the results of the American commission investigating the sinking of the *Maine* concluded it was a planned explosion instead of an accident, Spaniards marched in the streets shouting "To New York!" Most Spanish Republican presses adopted anti-American rhetoric, referring to the United States as "a nation of immigrant outcasts and avaricious shopkeepers, without culture, without honour, without a soul . . . brutal pigs, weak and stupid drunkards, arrogant and immoral cowards. . . ."[20]

Overconfidence, on the part of Europeans when it came to fighting Americans, persisted for over a century, most of it originating from the low military budgets of the young republic and disdain for an army built overwhelmingly on citizen soldiers.[21] Spain merely echoed the British, who had consistently dismissed Americans since their first defeats in the Revolution. One English surgeon sneered at the "drunken, canting, lying, praying, hypocritical rabble without order, subjection, discipline, or cleanliness" who opposed his red-coated regulars.[22] Opinion had scarcely improved by the War of 1812, when an Englishman described American regulars' movements as "loose and slovenly," nor in the Mexican War, where the major

British papers predicted a Mexican victory.[23] As a military power, America "is one of the weakest in the world . . . fit for nothing but to fight Indians," a view shared by the Mexicans and their dictator, Santa Anna, who promised to plant the Mexican flag in Washington, D.C.[24] The British minister in Texas in 1845 doubted that U.S. soldiers could "resist artillery and cavalry," and the London *Times* agreed, stating that Mexican forces were "superior to those of the United States."[25]

In addition, snobbishness afflicted European elites to the point where they could not imagine tactless and uncultured Americans defeating a Continental power. Germany's landed classes, the Junkers, who dominated the officer corps and the vaunted German General Staff, expected that the war with Spain would be decided at sea, and after looking at the balance of power, Emperor Wilhelm II concluded, "The Hidalgo surely will beat up Brother Jonathan because the Spanish navy is stronger than the American."[26] Germany's Admiral Alfred von Tirpitz, who also thought the Spanish navy superior, nevertheless argued that a long war favored the United States, but he was nearly alone. Most of the conservative German voices, including the journal *Grenzboten*, proclaimed that Spanish military professionalism would be the decisive factor. Once again, the Europeans mistook pomp and ceremonial drill for genuine fighting capabilities, though the Germans can be partly excused for inaccurate assessments because they had no journalists sending firsthand information. After the war, however, most German observers still failed to read the results properly, claiming that the Americans had not faced a serious opponent who would have exposed her military weaknesses.[27] Professionals, especially the Prussians, doubted Americans could perform in battle against a European foe. When the New York *World* blared in its headlines, "WE ARE READY," the Austrian *Wiener Journal* scoffed, "Sam may be prepared but he is not ready."[28]

Europeans' misunderstanding and mistrust of volunteer armies afflicted their judgment when it came to the Spanish-American War. By 1900, almost every European country had adopted compulsory military service. Among the major powers, only the United States retained a substantially volunteer army. To Republicans in Spain, where the wealthy could buy their way out of service, volunteer armies did not represent freedom but class abuse, the corollary of which was a preferred compulsory draft. Therefore, as one Spanish Republican editorialized, "do not expect the American army to equal the inspirations, the ideas, the customs, the patriotism, inherent to Latin armies."[29] The misperceptions of what republicanism en-

tailed for the Americans led to repeated analyses that were deeply flawed.
Observers asked why American working men, "who enjoy fabulous wages
and a general comfort unheard of even in our richest rural towns," would
not "avoid exposing themselves to die by the bullet? . . . Republic and war
are incompatible, as can be seen right now in the Yankee camps."[30] Hence,
from different ends of the spectrum European aristocrats and republicans
both derided American martial capabilities as overly (and unreliably) democratic.

Perhaps the most astounding misjudgments (at home and abroad) were
those that predicted American intervention in Cuba would lead the United
States into bankruptcy. Spanish Republican politician Emilio Castelar
prophesied that war would be "an immediate disaster for the Saxon republic. . . . America would have to arm itself to the teeth. . . . it would have to
increase its budget to the level of Caesarist budgets; it would have to convert
its creative legions of workers into legions of exterminators. . . . it would
have to lose its liberty. . . ."[31] Austria's *Wiener Tagblatt* echoed the "greedy
American" theme, claiming, "The Americans would lose money fighting
against Spain and that was something the clever Anglo-Saxons would never
want."[32]

Only a few journalists discerned that the American way of war, with its
citizen soldiers, produced *better* fighters because of republican values. "The
Yankees," wrote one,

> those "pigs," without patriotism, without ideals, with no other God
> than the dollar [who seem to have] no other object in life than to
> get rich, go voluntarily to war against Spain. And not only penni-
> less adventurers go voluntarily but young men belonging to the
> richest families of Washington and New York go to war and have
> fallen as its first victims. Aristocratic and mesocratic Spanish youth
> should not ignore *this example* that the enemy is setting us. Let it
> not be said that the stinking rich Yankees give lessons of patrio-
> tism, courage, [and] nobility, to young Spaniards.[33]

Another observed, "*Spaniards* have not gone to this war of their own
free will. . . . By contrast the Yankees have all gone voluntarily . . . there are
entire regiments of volunteers who, instead of receiving money, give it, offering their lives and their wallets to their country." That was, he concluded,
"truly a nation in arms . . . [and] moreover, a patriotic nation."[34] Monarchy

was the enemy, he wrote—an enemy that had "killed patriotism." An Austrian writer, in a similar vein, saw only "a disaster for the unhappy Iberian peninsula" to come from a war.[35] Indeed, most conservative papers in Austria agreed that a long war would favor the Americans and end badly for Spain.

By 1898, a small handful of British journalists had begun to draw different impressions of American volunteers from those offered a century earlier or from the majority of their colleagues. "Bronzed out-of-door, healthy looking fellows, of enormous physique," as one writer described Americans, "looked individually capable of going anywhere."[36] The men once portrayed as undisciplined now seemed "a more professional style," and the American light cavalry were "as fine as any in the world."[37] Roosevelt's "Rough Riders," of course, attracted the most attention, although evaluating both the regulars and the volunteers, the British correspondents thought the latter were "amateurs." Europeans still assessed the Americans as lacking in discipline: morning drill was "an almost intolerable thing," partly due to the heat and humidity; American discipline was "above average," though still too casual.[38] The American supply organization, another snorted, was "run upon a higgledy-piggledy system which it is impossible to describe."[39]

## Dewey, Roosevelt, and Victory

Enough disparity in the opinions of experts remained that Spain clung to the hope that the "real" Americans—the ones whom Europeans kept predicting would falter—would show up. The war, after all, would be fought at sea, where despite the obsolescence of Spain's fleet, a single lucky shot could sink an enemy. But other realities concerned Spanish war planners. In neither Cuba nor the Philippines did the Spanish have a loyal population to support them, but if American ships could be lured into range of shore-based batteries, and those combined with the firepower of the Spanish navy, then the fleet might have a chance. Dewey and Rear Admiral Winfield Scott Schley, who commanded the flying squadron off Florida, knew that as well. Spanish shore batteries and ships were hopelessly outranged by superior American guns, so the Americans only needed to remain at a distance. Dewey lacked only one thing while preparing for war in Hong Kong—sufficient ammunition—but even that showed up at the last possible moment with the *Baltimore*, which arrived only forty-eight hours before the British ordered Dewey to leave Hong Kong. The squadron moved thirty miles up the Chinese coast to Mirs Bay, where the ammunition was distributed throughout the ships on April 25.

Consequently, following the explosion and sinking of the USS *Maine* in Cuba, on February 15, and the subsequent declaration of war against Spain, both the American and Spanish squadrons were on the move, Dewey heading from Mirs Bay to the Philippines, while Admiral Patricio Montojo y Pasarón, a seasoned officer who had been awarded some of Spain's highest honors, sailed out of Manila Bay for Subic Bay and the protection of its shore batteries. He soon learned that the large guns that were to have been installed around the bay still sat on the beach and his mines were unreliable, so he was forced to return to Manila Bay.

The *Castilla*, which was completely unmaneuverable, was turned into a floating battery with sand barges brought up to surround her. Montojo also hurriedly placed guns all around the entrance of Manila Bay, well aware of the dubious track record of fixed shore batteries in combating mobile cruisers. He had done his best, but when Dewey said to the captain of the *Olympia*, "You may fire when ready, Gridley," the Spanish fleet was quickly annihilated at the cost of one American sailor, the victim of heatstroke.

On the other side of the world, American volunteers flocked to the recruiting stations, many clamoring to join the famous Rough Rider regiment of cavalry. Theodore Roosevelt, who had done so much to prepare the nation for the war, had resigned his office as assistant secretary of the Navy to become the second-in-command of the regiment as a lieutenant colonel, under Colonel Leonard Wood. Roosevelt's volunteers consisted of scoundrels and outlaws, Apaches and Mexicans, dandies and New York polo players. Sheriff Buckey O'Neill, one of Arizona's most famous lawmen, had also joined, perhaps to keep an eye on all the ruffians who sought refuge there. When the Rough Riders arrived in Tampa, however, they found only one ship—reserved for another regiment. Roosevelt impulsively commandeered the vessel, although it lacked space for the mounts, so the Rough Riders, some of the "finest light cavalry in the world," embarked for Cuba . . . as infantry.

An orange-gold Cuban sun, occasionally streaked by sea mist and humidity, beat down on American units disembarking at Daiquirí. This was a much different army from the forces that had made up the Union and Confederate armies thirty-five years earlier. Professional units had spent much of their career battling Indians on the Plains, and large-scale infantry operations had not been seen since 1865. While some of the Plains cavalry had first-class weapons, the troops wading ashore at Daiquirí were armed with inferior Krag-Jørgensen rifles with a slow reloading rate (to help conserve ammunition, according to the Ordinance Department), putting them at an extreme disadvantage to the Spaniards and their superior charger-loaded German-made Mausers. Even tactics had been tailored to defeat Sioux, Cheyenne, and Apache combatants, not European-style foes with artillery. When Americans did employ traditional infantry tactics, they were from the Civil War, against a toughened enemy who had fought guerrillas and learned to use cover instead of massed lines. Nevertheless, Americans began to develop suppression fire covering advancing squads.

General William Shafter had established the base for his corps at Siboney, east of Santiago, and sent General Joseph Wheeler, a former Confederate cavalry general, to attack the Spanish rearguard. Wheeler walked into an ambush, and while the Americans were bloodied at Las Guásimas, the Spanish continued their retreat. By the first of July, 15,000 Americans, including cavalry and four black regiments, assaulted entrenched Spanish positions at El Caney and San Juan Hill outside Santiago.

After Leonard Wood was promoted to command a brigade, Roosevelt assumed command of the regiment with the rank of colonel, and shortly thereafter the Rough Riders, the 10th (Colored) Cavalry, and the 3rd Cavalry regiment launched their assault on foot against the Kettle Hill portion of San Juan Heights on July 1. The Buffalo Soldiers carried the brunt of the fighting—aided by the timely arrival of a pair of Gatling guns—and with the Rough Riders took Kettle Hill. A British correspondent described the soldiers as "ants" sweeping up the ridge: "It was incredible but it was grand. The boys were storming the hill. . . . But we knew that it had cost them dear."[40]

Cuban insurgents considered the victory to be theirs, but the American triumph was obvious. Even the British correspondents who had once derided their American cousins esteemed them differently. Douglas Macpherson of the *Daily Graphic* wrote, "I have the most unqualified admiration for the American regular soldier. There is no better fellow anywhere."[41] Spanish forces consolidated and resisted at Fort Canosa, followed by an American siege of the city, aided by Cuban forces.

But already a much more deadly enemy had descended on the Americans: malaria and yellow fever, which caused five times more casualties than Spanish bullets. The Spanish, too, were afflicted with disease, having only 55,000 men available to fight out of their 230,000-man force. Despite the

Spaniards' advantage in numbers and weaponry (the rapid-firing Mauser versus the American fixed-magazine Krag-Jørgensen single-shot rifles and black powder Springfield "Trapdoor" also adopted to force American soldiers to economize on ammunition with a slow rate of fire) and decimated by the ravages of disease, the American forces pushed inland. The Spanish fleet, which remained in the safety of the bay, finally sortied out on July 3 and lasted just hours. Five of the six Spanish ships were destroyed or grounded, and 1,600 Spanish sailors, including Admiral Cervera, were captured.

Even before the smoke cleared, Congress adopted a joint resolution that stated the United States could not annex Cuba and had to leave "control of the island to its people." Certainly some racism was involved: Americans did not want an invasion of cheap labor, particularly if it was brown-skinned. More significantly, however, Americans truly did not want an empire. They had seen what empires had done (and were doing) to Europe, and while subtle influence over local Latin American governments was most desirable, colonization was not. In 1869, when Santo Domingo "effectively offered itself up for annexation . . . the proposal was defeated in Congress."[42] While a strong element of paternalism tainted Americans' efforts in Latin America (most notably the Platt Amendment of 1901), America was generally on a "civilizing mission." Under the interpretations of modern liberal historians, every island, every jungle became a persimmon to be plucked by the imperialistic Americans. But to turn-of-the-century Americans, Cuba represented a jalapeño—digestible, no doubt, but with acidic side effects.

Whether the newly acquired territories would be better off beneath the American flag was not in question, even for the Spanish. One Spanish writer noted that "everyone who is reliable and serious in Cuba prefers the Yankees a thousand times over to separatism" (that is, independence), and a Russian journalist predicted the "joy of the Philippine insurgents" in securing American aid would secure liberty and peace there.[43] The first evidence of American policies could be seen in Cuba, where the United States introduced education and fiscal reforms. When Congress undertook an investigation of the war, European republicans were astounded at the openness of the system. Although a few Europeans looked dimly on Spain's ouster at the hands of a money-centered United States (the Austrian *Wiener Journal*, certainly not alone, claimed "the Yankees are businessmen and nothing else"), this view remained in the minority, with most glumly admitting that progress and freedom tended to follow in the Americans' wake.[44] One Spanish writer prophesied that "in all the colonies they have just acquired the Yankees will do in a few years what we have been unable to do in centuries. . . . that will be our greatest shame."[45] German commentators agreed, viewing the American victory as "a triumph for progress and a gain for mankind"; while a Russian newspaper predicted the U.S. victory would transform the political balance of the world.[46] To a few, the American victory marked the end, as one American prelate wrote to Rome, "of all that is old & vile & mean & rotten & cruel & false in Europe. . . . When Spain is swept [from the oceans] much of the meanness & narrowness of old Europe goes with it, to be replaced by the freedom & openness of America." He added, "This is God's way of developing the world."[47] German intellectuals and writers condescendingly snarled that Spain had shrunk "to the rank of a small Asiatic people, decadent and mummified."[48]

Not long after the Spanish surrender, Cuban officials met General Leonard Wood on a steamer in Havana harbor. Wood's goal was to create "a republic modeled closely upon the lines of our great Anglo-Saxon republic."[49] That Cuba possessed none of the attributes that were necessary for an American-style republic was simply not recognized at the time. Wood, the son of a physician, attended Harvard Medical School, then served with the U.S. Army fighting the Apaches. In 1886, after carrying dispatches one hundred miles through Indian territory, Wood was awarded a Medal of Honor. Later, he became a star football player at Georgia School of Technology (now Georgia Tech), before organizing the Rough Riders with Theodore Roosevelt. Far from seeking to "colonialize" Cuba, Wood set out to educate the Cubans (by 1902, some 250,000 students passed through the schools he established), and oversaw a massive reform of public works, including sewer projects, drainage of swamps, street repairs, and construction of hospitals. Americans under Wood translated textbooks into Spanish, trained 1,300 Cuban teachers, opened thousands of schools (modeled on Ohio's public school system), and diligently sought to "infuse new life, new principles and new methods of doing things" into the island. He also imposed judicial reforms, especially those that emphasized private property rights.[50] American soldiers distributed food, waged a sanitary campaign, rooted out corrupt officials, built roads and bridges, and dredged Havana harbor. But the greatest achievement under Wood's tenure involved Dr. Walter Reed's discovery in 1900 that a particular mosquito transmitted yellow fever. Through the efforts of the Army Medical Corps, mosquito netting was put up in sleeping quarters, standing bodies of stagnant water were drained, and fumigation became commonplace. By 1902 not a single case of yellow fever was reported in Havana, whereas 1,400 cases had been reported in 1900.[51]

Cuban sugar planters, who had suffered mightily during the insurrection, bordered on bankruptcy. Wood put a moratorium on the collection of debts from the planters, which lapsed in 1902. Critics therefore could attack Wood regardless of his policies: if he kept the moratorium, he was merely propping up the "imperialist puppets," and if he allowed the moratorium to lapse, he was sounding the "death knell for much of the island's planter class."[52] When American corporations bought the bankrupt Cuban sugar plantations, Wood was accused of acting for "U.S. interests." Americans acquired about 15 percent of Cuban land, bringing in new technology and infrastructure. The Platt Amendment gave the United States long-term leases on bases in Cuba, leading to the construction of the naval base at Guantánamo Bay (made permanent by the Cuban-American Treaty of 1903), and prohibited Cuba from transferring land to any power other than the United States, or engaging in any treaty with another country "which will . . . impair the independence of Cuba." At that point, the Army withdrew.

## America's First Guerrilla War

Although the Spanish-American War ended with the United States in official possession of the Philippines, actual control required America to engage in its first foreign war against guerrilla forces. McKinley sent Dewey against the Spanish and provided land forces to take control of the islands primarily to obtain a bargaining chip with Spain for negotiations over Cuba.[53] Step by step, however, McKinley was drawn into a situation neither foreseen nor desired—namely, America's first foray into imperialism. The Germans and British were interested in the islands, and McKinley built up his forces with the apparent intent to provide, as in Cuba, an orderly transition to self-rule. Emilio Aguinaldo, the leader of an army of Filipino irregulars, proclaimed the independence of the Philippines on June 12, 1898, followed by the announcement of a revolutionary government eleven days later. General Wesley Merritt arrived in July to take command of the American forces, with an order from McKinley to issue a proclamation declaring that the United States came to protect the inhabitants and their property and to guarantee their individual rights.[54] The Spanish governor agreed to surrender his men to the Americans, who in turn promised to keep the Filipino irregulars out of Manila. In June, the 15,000 American soldiers who had gone ashore to mop up Spanish resistance against a Spanish commander putting up token resistance to avoid a court martial back in Spain now faced Aguinaldo, who felt betrayed by his American allies. Negotiations with the Filipinos kept them at bay for a time, but on August 17, the War Department declared there would be no joint occupation between the Filipinos and the United States and that the "insurgents and all others must recognize the military occupation and authority of the United States."[55] When Spain and the United States signed the Treaty of Paris on December 10, officially handing over the Philippines to American control, the situation became irretrievable. McKinley stated that "the mission of the United States is one of benevolent assimilation, substituting the mild sway of justice and right for arbitrary rule."[56] Others had a slightly less noble view of the affair. Speaker of the House Thomas Reed quipped, "We have bought ten million Malays at $2.00 a head unpicked, and nobody knows what it will cost to pick them."[57]

Fighting with Aguinaldo, who had set up a republic at Malolos, broke out in February 1899, pitting some 15,000 actual U.S. combat forces against twice that number of *insurrectos*. It took only a month for the Army to slice through the Filipino resistance, capturing Malolos in March. But General Elwell Otis found that he could not extend his forces too far from the cities due to the monsoons and disease that eroded the fighting capabilities of units by up to 60 percent. When the state volunteers left in September 1899, Otis had only 27,000 men, and actual fighting units of perhaps half that. Resupplied and regrouped, Otis's forces set out in the fall and defeated Aguinaldo's troops again and again, though the leader himself always escaped. In November 1899, Aguinaldo dispersed his soldiers as organized forces and sent them into the jungles to engage in guerrilla warfare.

The United States added 34,000 more troops over the next two years, although an average of 24,000 to 44,000 were actual combat troops. Predating the tactics of al-Qaeda in Iraq over a century later, Aguinaldo quickly ascertained that he could not defeat the American military—even in guerrilla war—rather, he had to "sour Americans on the war and ensure the victory of the anti-imperialist William Jennings Bryan in the presidential election."[58] Filipino general Francisco Macabulos said the objective of the *insurrectos* was "not to vanquish the [U.S. Army] but to inflict on them constant losses" so as to affect public attitudes in the United States.[59] The strategy failed with the application of a carrot-and-stick response from American commanders, who steadily separated villages from the guerrillas, then sequestered them so that the "fish," as Mao Zedong would later put it, would have no "sea" to swim in. Regiments lived among the villagers, maintaining regular and reliable intelligence. They drew another 15,000 Filipinos to the U.S. side—the famed Philippine Scouts and the Philippine Constabulary.

At the same time, to win the confidence, respect, and loyalty of the population, Americans engaged in a great deal of what is today called "nation building." English was added to Spanish as an official language in the islands, while Army engineers constructed dams and irrigation canals, cleared roads and ports, reformed the currency and laws, and produced medical near-miracles, including the elimination of cholera and smallpox and a drastic reduction in malaria. Perhaps the charge that the United States sought coaling stations or bases has a kernel of truth, as certainly Mahan's doctrine had by then convinced most knowledgeable naval minds that ready access to coal was essential to protecting American interests. Not surprisingly, the United States—like the European colonizers—poured far more into the territories it acquired than it took out.

Rebel leaders, dispirited both by American advances in the islands and by McKinley's reelection in 1900, surrendered. Aguinaldo himself was captured personally by Brigadier General Frederick Funston, who posed as a prisoner of war to find the rebel chief. Funston won a Medal of Honor by courageously rafting across the Pampanga River under fire, and after the war was picked by Woodrow Wilson to head the American Expeditionary Force if needed in Europe after World War I broke out. But Funston died of a heart attack before the U.S. declaration of war.

A new American commissioner, William Howard Taft, arrived in late 1900, setting up a Filipino political party and preparing the country for democratic institutions and elections. The last resistance was crushed on the Fourth of July, 1902, although the Muslim "Moros," who still practiced slavery and polygamy, continued to resist until 1913. Placed under the military control of Governor General John "Black Jack" Pershing, the economy revived and employment rose—hemp and lumber exports increased more than 150 percent in Pershing's tenure. Pershing did respect Islam, donating government land for the construction of mosques, but he also insisted on complete disarmament. When he handed control over Southern Mindanao to the Moros in 1913, Pershing had quashed the tribes' martial inclinations (killing ten Moros for every American soldier lost). Pershing's local civilian administration gained enough respect from the Moros that they made him a *datto* (tribal chief). In 1903, at age forty-five, Pershing left the Philippines with a case of malaria and a reputation as one of America's best officers and most available bachelors. He returned a married man in 1907 as head of the Department of Mindanao and the civilian governor of the Moro Province for another tour that lasted until 1913 and solidified both American control of Mindanao and Pershing's military reputation.

## A Fighting Quaker in a Banana Republic

For several decades following the Spanish-American War, the United States would intervene in the affairs of Caribbean islands and Latin American countries. Santo Domingo (the Dominican Republic) was already in danger of being overrun by the Europeans for failing to pay its debts, and in 1903, rebels there fired on a U.S. ship, killing a sailor. When President Theodore Roosevelt dispatched troops to keep an eye on the rebellion, critics claimed the United States had designs on the island, whereupon Roosevelt retorted, "I have about the same desire to annex [Santo Domingo] as a gorged boa constrictor might have to swallow a porcupine wrong-end-to."[60] A year later, confronted with Europeans demanding debt repayments from Venezuela, Roosevelt sent the fleet under Dewey to demonstrate in the eastern Caribbean, and invoked the Monroe Doctrine to keep the Europeans out. But Roosevelt realized that "If we intend to say 'hands off' to the powers of Europe, then sooner or later we must keep order ourselves," as he told Secretary of State Elihu Root. Disorder and chaos in Central America, South America, or the Caribbean *did* affect American interests—and not just businesses—and could easily spill over into revolutions that might spread through Mexico. Recognizing the danger, TR later told Congress, "Chronic wrongdoing, or an impotence which results in a general loosening of ties of civilized society, may in America, as elsewhere, ultimately require intervention by some civilized nation. . . ." The Monroe Doctrine could force the United States, "however reluctantly, in flagrant cases of such wrong-doing or impotence, to the exercise of an international police power."[61]

Thus, the United States sent troops to Cuba in 1906 when the government fell apart (and withdrew them again in 1909 when a new government was stabilized); broke up a coup backed by the United Fruit Company in 1924 in Honduras; and governed Haiti and the Dominican Republic for several years prior to World War I. In 1917, the United States landed troops again in Cuba to quell a rebellion. About 3,000 troops remained in the Dominican Republic throughout World War I, patrolling and battling guerrillas, until finally, in 1922, the guerrillas agreed to surrender. By then there was a new flare-up in Haiti, sparked by the reinstitution of the French cor-vée ("forced work"). Although this resulted in the construction of almost five hundred miles of roads, it was a practice deeply resented by the Hai-tians and a source of much anti-Americanism. Local bandit-militias, the *Cacos*, led by Charlemagne Masséna Péralte, fought a series of battles with the Americans throughout 1919. Whereas in the past, the Marines had eas-ily routed such groups, the new rebellion was more widespread and had greater popular support. A Marine sergeant, Herman Hanneken, who had been commanding a group of local gendarmerie as a "captain," hired his own *Cacos* and conceived a brilliant ruse to infiltrate Péralte's camp. Dress-ing Marines as *Cacos*, he managed to get into the camp, whereupon Hanneken shot the rebel leader himself. A few *Cacos* battled on, but by 1920, the Second Caco War was over. A few thousand Marines had succeeded where 27,000 of Napoléon Bonaparte's troops had failed.

Major Smedley Butler, the "fighting Quaker" who had deep reserva-tions about the benefits of military involvement in the region and who later in life became an outspoken critic of military adventurism, typified the Amer-ican involvement in Latin American missions. Never lacking courage under fire, Butler won two Medals of Honor, his first in 1914 in Veracruz, after he led his men in a door-to-door battle to occupy the city.[62] A year later, in Haiti, Butler and his patrol of 44 mounted Marines were ambushed by 400 *Cacos*. After holding their perimeter throughout the night, the Marines un-der Butler charged the larger enemy force from three directions the follow-ing morning and, convinced they were nearly surrounded, the *Cacos* fled. Notably, Butler's exploits came when medals were seldom awarded for po-litical purposes and when great bravery was common on the field of battle.

## Sudan's Jihad

Just a month before Dewey stunned the Spanish, in May 1898, England had mounted a powerful expedition to move up the Nile River to subdue the forces of Abdallah al-Taashi, known as the Khalifa. The Khalifa had emerged from a three-way struggle among the successors of the Mahdi ("expected one")—whose men had killed British hero Charles "Chinese" Gordon, former governor of Sudan (though the Mahdi himself claimed credit). Gordon had suppressed the slave trade in Sudan from 1874 to 1875, earning him the title "Pasha." Revered on two continents, Gordon was a larger-than-life figure who occasionally counted on his reputation to

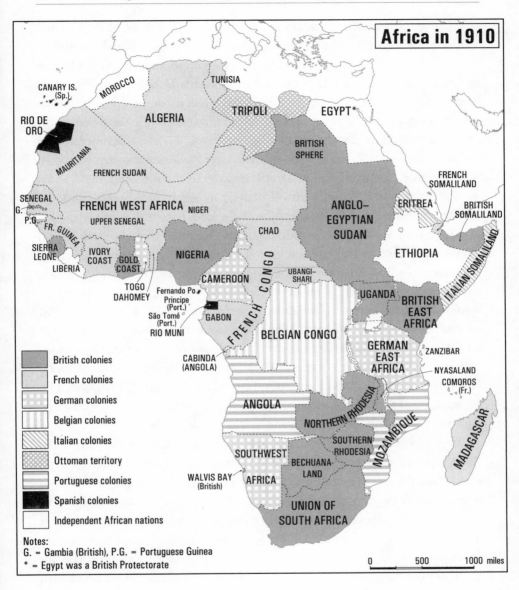

**Africa in 1910**

CANARY IS.
(Sp.)

MOROCCO

TUNISIA

RIO DE
ORO

ALGERIA

TRIPOLI

EGYPT*

BRITISH
SPHERE

MAURITANIA

FRENCH SUDAN

FRENCH
SOMALILAND

SENEGAL

G.

P.G.

FR. GUINEA

FRENCH WEST AFRICA

NIGER

UPPER SENEGAL

CHAD

ANGLO–
EGYPTIAN
SUDAN

ERITREA

BRITISH
SOMALILAND

SIERRA
LEONE

IVORY
COAST

GOLD
COAST

NIGERIA

ETHIOPIA

LIBERIA

TOGO

DAHOMEY

CAMEROON

UBANGI–
SHARI

ITALIAN SOMALILAND

Fernando Po
Principe
(Port.)
São Tomé
(Port.)
RIO MUNI

GABON

FRENCH CONGO

UGANDA

BRITISH
EAST
AFRICA

BELGIAN CONGO

GERMAN
EAST
AFRICA

ZANZIBAR

CABINDA
(ANGOLA)

NYASALAND

COMOROS
(Fr.)

ANGOLA

NORTHERN RHODESIA

MOZAMBIQUE

MADAGASCAR

SOUTHERN
RHODESIA

SOUTHWEST

BECHUANA-
LAND

WALVIS BAY
(British)

AFRICA

UNION OF
SOUTH AFRICA

British colonies
French colonies
German colonies
Belgian colonies
Italian colonies
Ottoman territory
Portuguese colonies
Spanish colonies
Independent African nations

Notes:
G. = Gambia (British), P.G. = Portuguese Guinea
* = Egypt was a British Protectorate

0      500      1000 miles

supersede reality. Often, it worked. In 1883, the Khedive (viceroy) of Egypt had undertaken a campaign against the fanatical Islamic sectarian Muhammad Ahmad bin Abd Allah, who called himself the Mahdi. Unmoved by oceans of blood and contemptuous of all non-Sudanese, the Mahdi viewed himself as a redeemer and strict adherent of the Koran, called to spread the word to Cairo, Damascus, and Constantinople; anyone who rejected him was to die.

The British sent an expedition of Egyptians commanded by Colonel William Hicks, which the Mahdi annihilated, killing all but about 300 of the 10,000 men.[63] Lord Edmond Fitzmaurice said in a speech to the House of Lords that an "army has not vanished in such a fashion since Pharaoh's host perished in the Red Sea." While Hicks was incompetent and put his overconfident forces at extreme risk in a march through the desert with insufficient supplies, by the time he was attacked he was outnumbered four to one by the Mahdi's men, some of them equipped with modern weapons. Subsequently, two more Egyptian armies were likewise routed.

Egypt ordered the withdrawal of its garrisons from Sudan, and the British government requested that Charles Gordon go to Egypt and supervise the operation from Khartoum. England doubted that even the Mahdi would make war on England by killing a British citizen of such visibility. Gordon arrived in Khartoum in 1884, but instead of evacuating the city, chose to stay and fight. After early successes, Gordon found himself surrounded inside Khartoum and under siege from the Mahdi's forces. Finally, a relief force under Sir Garnet Wolseley set out from Cairo, but it reached Khartoum three days after the city fell on January 22, 1885. When two steamers Wolseley sent ahead arrived at the city, they found a massacre. Gordon's head, which had been displayed on a pike, was already gone. The Mahdi died of typhus shortly after taking Khartoum; Gordon was honored with statues in Trafalgar Square and at the Gordon School in Surrey.

Britain's Sudanese experiences, while perhaps superficially similar to the American struggles with the Plains Indians, were of a different type altogether, for this was an enemy whose religious fanaticism united large numbers of tribes and regions. Whereas the Sioux under Sitting Bull were fortunate to unite several of their own bands, plus the Cheyenne, the Mahdi had assembled massive armies all driven by a fanatical version of Islam. The Americans had experienced an early "War on Terror" with the Muslim Barbary pirates, but the Mahdist uprising constituted the West's first brush with Islam as a unifying military force on a widespread basis since the 1500s.

Another contrast existed in the almost exclusively American tendency to make citizens out of all those in subjugated or colonized areas (although Indians were excluded for a long span). Virtually none of the Egyptians or Sudanese had any connection to the British Empire, and certainly little loyalty. It is a misperception that the British Empire was, in fact, "British" in any sense save that of purely military and political control. Subjects were not encouraged to "become British"—on the contrary, they were derided and scorned by the English when they attempted to do so. This proved all the more remarkable in that several of Africa's loudest voices for independence came from natives educated in the British system, who had been viewed by fellow African revolutionaries as traitors.[64]

Nevertheless, elite Africans such as James Davies of the *Nigerian Times* and Ghanaian lawyer J. E. Casely Hayford "commonly believed as much as their European mentors in Western civilisation [sic], and commonly thought that disseminating it was what Africa urgently needed."[65] They were products of "the missionary movement upon whose arguments of the correlations between Western civilisation and Christianity rested the foundations of their outlook [and they] saw Christianity as the essential preliminary to the building in West Africa of a nation whose society would be modelled [sic] on that of the Western world."[66]

Regardless of the services they performed for the Empire, and regardless of the European power in question, natives were never considered potential citizens. In 1918, after thousands of Africans and soldiers from other European empires had died on the Western Front, Senegalese writer Lamine Senghor observed, "When we are needed, to make us kill or make us work, we are French; but when it comes to give us rights, we are no longer French, we are *Nègres*."[67]

Americans, on the other hand, thanks to the Land Ordinance of 1785 and the Northwest Ordinance, rapidly made new settlers and those of newly colonized areas citizens. At first, these were mostly whites, although there are records of freed African indentures not only voting but, in one case, serving in the Maryland assembly in the colonial era. Even later when races such as southwestern Hispanics were denied full social and economic equality for a time, in the eyes of the law they were as American as the Vanderbilts. Had such a system been in place in Egypt or Sudan, the Mahdist armies might never have grown to such size, and local support for the British army would have differed substantially.

After the death of the Mahdi, the Khalifa took control over the desert tribes, and the British, having withdrawn most troops, could no longer ignore Egypt and Sudan. Sir Horatio Herbert Kitchener led a new expeditionary force, including 8,000 British regulars and 17,000 native troops from Sudan and Egypt, southward along the Nile. Unlike Hicks fifteen years before, Kitchener had no intention of separating himself from his supply line along the river, or from the additional firepower of his gunboats.

Like Lord Chelmsford at Ulundi in 1879, Kitchener forced the Khalifa to attack him on ground of his choosing.

## The Western Way of Victory

By the late 1890s, Westerners were beginning to realize that their style of fighting against non-Westerners, not just their technology, gave them a critical edge in battle. Americans had seen this on the frontier against the Indians, and would see it again in the Philippine campaigns against the *insurrectos* and the Moros, and it was already recognized by the British. The Europeans had perfected their military techniques over two centuries of conquest in Africa, India, and Latin America, but historians had downplayed the impact of military history in the Age of Imperialism, especially in the early 1800s before steam and rapid-fire weapons were available. This was a mistake, however. As early as the 1500s, Cortés in Mexico and Pizarro in Peru demonstrated that a handful of well-trained, decently armed Europeans could defeat a hundred *times* their number of natives, who lacked the basic concepts of volley fire, rank and order drill, and individual autonomy of the warriors. Even when cultures did encourage fighters to act independently—such as among some of the Plains Indian tribes in North America—the result was not autonomous soldiers willingly subjecting themselves to the greater discipline of the unit, but a ragtag, helter-skelter approach to fighting.

Certainly, even the best European units, poorly deployed or ineptly led, could be overwhelmed, and ultimately overwhelming numbers could prevail. Yet Europeans, who take perverse satisfaction in romanticizing their few defeats, have overplayed such debacles as Isandlwana, where 1,800 British troops (including 850 Natal Kaffirs) were overwhelmed by Zulus, or Balaclava, where the Light Brigade charged emplaced cannons on horseback. These glorious defeats have often been depicted in works of art. *Charge of the Light Brigade*, by the painter Richard Caton Woodville, immortalized the "Noble six hundred" men of the 17th Lancers as most of them rode to their deaths at Balaclava. And the only memorable painting of Kitchener's victory at Omdurman is one celebrating the charge of the 21st Lancers—a near disaster.

While stirring, paintings and heroic poems such as Alfred, Lord Tennyson's famous 1854 verse "The Charge of the Light Brigade" failed to capture the reality of Western warfare that was evidenced at Omdurman, or at the final obliteration of the Muslim forces at the Battle of Umm Diwaykarat in November 1899. There, relatively equal British/Egyptian and Mahdist forces squared off; only *three* British troops were killed while Mahdist warriors suffered 1,000 casualties, mostly to Maxim machine guns, and another 3,000 were captured.[68] Osman Digna, the last of the Mahdist rebels, was captured the following year. By then, the British were already hip-deep in the Second Boer War, which, for all its illumination about the carnage enabled by mass firepower and long-range artillery, obscured the utter dominance the European style of war demonstrated over those using any other combat formula.

What the Age of Imperialism showed was that Europeans and Americans could easily subdue native peoples because their firepower was augmented and vastly enhanced by a culture of fighting that emphasized volunteer and well-trained armies that prized individual initiative to the benefit of the unit. Those traits came from the Western system of individual rights, free expression (including about tactics and strategy), and civilian control of the military. In American conquests, a common-law structure gave everyone a stake in the survival and expansion of the society—a factor sadly absent in most conquered countries and tribes, even after the colonizing powers left. A similar shallow approach afflicted those countries, including Mexico (another civil-law country), that had won independence from Spain during the nineteenth century. They failed to develop the political and cultural structures necessary for a free people to thrive. Survive they could, but prosper? Not with the primitive Old World economic systems they adopted.

Western military tactics could not be easily grafted onto African, Asian, or Islamic societies, making it more difficult for them to compete with the West by simply picking up Western arms. Merely introducing free markets did not prove a solution either unless the societies wanted to embrace open trade and less regulation—indeed, to adopt the entirety of Western culture, which they were often loath to do. The problem was, whether in rifles or railroads, the non-Western world had not constructed the scaffolding of private property rights crystallized into title deeds and paper certificates of ownership that already had catapulted the United States ahead of the rest of the world. It took until the late twentieth century for a Peruvian economist, Hernando de Soto, to realize that Latin American nations (and by implication, the decolonized states of Africa and Asia) were poor not because they had no wealth, but because the wealth they had could not be leveraged through loans and collateral inherent in titles and deeds. Moreover, the absence of a paper trail of deeds and titles that could be cited in court cast the entire process of making, buying, and selling into a giant vat of corrupt molasses, slowing everything down by years, exhausting owner and worker alike. Applied on a state level, the effects were a grinding poverty at worst and a lethargic economy at best.

In fact it was production, itself the result of creative juices and investment, that vaulted the Western world into military dominance. Marxists and those steeped in the leftist drivel of "Eurocentric oppression" and imperialism answer that it is inherent in capitalist nations to expand, and to an extent, they would be correct. Yet the Zulus and Mahdists (for entirely less noble reasons) themselves wanted to expand, as seen in their conquests of Sudan and South Africa, but they did not go farther nor could they defeat the Europeans. Why? One answer is that by the late 1900s, only the West could make mistakes and still recover. Capitalism provided a culture of instant replacement, yes, even for soldiers lost in combat. When troops were lost, more soldiers could immediately take their place in a rifle line, operate a Maxim gun, or shovel coal into furnaces that powered the *Olympia* and similar ships. Virtually no native army, anywhere, could or did recover from a debacle such as the Americans suffered at Little Bighorn or the British at Isandlwana, but the U.S. Army and the British Empire hurled new forces into the field in each case within months and achieved victory in their campaigns. Western capitalist structures, and the systems of free citizens voting themselves into wars, provided a nearly bottomless pit of manpower and machines, even for nations with relatively small populations like England. Because of this technology multiplier, and the resilience of the economies, Great Britain at one point in the nineteenth century ruled more than one third of the globe with a regular army smaller than that which the United States sent into Iraq in 2003.

## Economics and Empires

For England, the economic and strategic necessity of holding on to its colonies was apparent, and worth the cost (although studies have shown, overall, that the British invested far more in the colonies than they took out).[69] Despite the Zulu Wars (1879), the Second Afghan War (1878–81), the Egyptian/Sudanese Expeditions (1883), another Zulu rebellion (1887), the Third Ashanti War (1893–95), the Fourth Ashanti War (1895–96), the wars against the Mahdi (1893–99), the Ugandan Mutiny (1897–1901), the Ekumeku Resistance in Nigeria (1883–1914), two Boer Wars (1880–81 and

1899–1902), the Anglo-Pathan War (1897–98), and the "Mad Mullah" jihad in Ethiopia (1899–1905), in which the British emerged victorious everywhere but Afghanistan, there was little departure from the orthodoxy that the Empire was necessary to England's well-being. At its peak, the British Empire covered 13 million square miles and ruled over about 23 percent of the earth's surface (contrasting sharply with the United States, which controlled approximately 6.5 percent of the land surface and 5 percent of the population by the 1990s). The very fact that England could mount so many expeditions, in widespread provinces around the world, and emerge victorious in nearly all of them was less impressive than the fact that, for the most part, British civilians barely noticed. Only when the reports of an Isandlwana made headlines did anyone remember there was any conflict at all. British newspapers were more concerned with unrest in Ireland, which eventually staged its own mini-rebellion during Easter Week, 1916.

England's rising standard of living (the number of registered paupers fell to fewer than 100,000 in 1900 out of a population of more than 38 million people), her amelioration of class conflicts through a century's worth of reforms, the dwindling power of the House of Lords, and the steadying

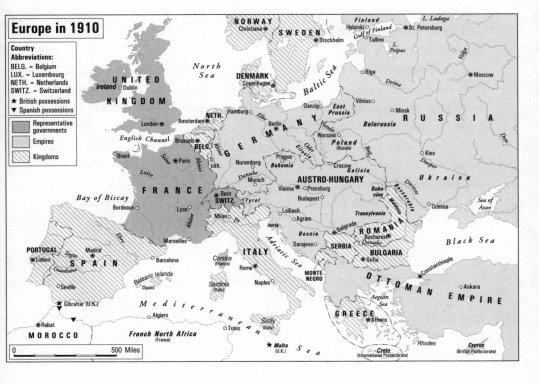

influence of the monarchy minimized social upheaval in England itself.[70] The Lords had made themselves even more irrelevant by their continued opposition to Irish Home Rule, which they rejected twice. Ireland's Easter Rising was crushed in a week, and most of the ringleaders hanged, although in the long run rebels under the Sinn Fein banner gained substantial support from the executions. Some have viewed the Easter Rising as the first true socialist revolution in Europe, but most rebels rejected any explanation of their intentions, save creating an independent nation of Ireland. Possibly the illegitimate son of a Jewish father, Éamon de Valera, the most prominent of the Rising's leaders, was born in New York in 1882 and was taken to Ireland three years later, where he benefited from a solid education resulting in a scholarship to Blackrock College. Appointed to a mathematics position at Rockwell College, he worked at a number of university positions over the next few years. Active in the Irish Republican Brotherhood, he helped plan the Rising. When it collapsed, Valera's American citizenship likely saved him from the gallows, as England wanted the United States to enter the Great War and did not want to alienate Americans by executing one of her citizens. At any rate, continued problems with Ireland further pushed England away from an American-style true bicameral legislature of balanced powers and fully into the European mode. And the English system took on all the more importance with London's dominance in international finance.

Although a few European cities still vied for preeminence with London, neither Amsterdam nor Paris had both the financial and transportation hubs to dominate the world stage. Steam and railway lines were now joined by the age of telegraphy and transoceanic cables, linking Hamburg and Berlin with Vienna, New York, and Istanbul. Britain and the United States also benefited in this new transportation/communication nexus from the global gold standard, formalized in 1896 by McKinley's election. With the firm commitment to the gold standard undergirding a relatively unregulated banking system and a burgeoning industrial base, the United States caught up to England, and New York threatened to surpass London as the world's money center.

The gold standard constituted one leg of an economic triad managed and made permanent by the Republicans from 1877 to 1900, with the other two being the tariff and the integration of a national market. During that era, voter participation was high, "political opinion was informed, organized insurgency was common, and people felt that the outcome of elections mattered."[71] Political conventions, even at the state level, were well attended. The state Democratic convention in Mississippi, for example, drew 1,200 delegates in 1895, and in Colorado in 1898, "fusionists" (those Democrats and Populists who wanted to join pro-silver Republicans) literally battled antifusionists in an opera hall, where 150 shots were fired and one man was killed.

Republicans had carefully balanced the tariff, the least economically essential of the triad, against the more serious establishment of a national set of rules for the market and the necessary, but often painful, gold standard. The tariff, a popular political issue that could be hammered out among constituent districts, was entrusted to Congress, while the courts handled the more difficult rate and regulation issues. As political scientist Richard Bensel noted, "The Constitution did provide a fairly flexible framework within which the Republican party forged its developmental regime, but there is little in the American experience that suggests that a properly designed constitution is all a nation needs to guarantee that democracy and development will be compatible."[72] This truth would be learned anew by European colonies during the decolonization process.

By 1900, the United States had emerged from a period of robust, even revolutionary, capital and investment expansion, and unparalleled prosperity. Ordinary Americans, and often even poorer Americans, enjoyed a rising standard of living that had already caught up to or passed those of most other developed nations, and the overall magnitude of the abundance in the nation defied perception. "Everything was on a grand scale. A single chicken [on a dinner table] does not exist," wrote one history of American eating.[73] The explosion in prosperity was due in great part to the nature of Republican dominance after the Civil War, and certainly came at a cost. Groups that might have resisted industrialization—whites in the South, farmers, those on the losing end of the tariff debates—were the most disenfranchised and least politically powerful groups in the country. Hence debates were fought out in the West and the industrializing North, where the Republicans dominated. While the West (and parts of the South) rebelled against the gold standard, and while elements in both sections lobbied for regulation of railroads, elevators, and other "public" utilities, the West especially had already benefited (and would benefit still more) from the vast mileage of iron rails increasing the volume—if lowering the price, due to the gold standard—of farm goods.

Complaints by agrarians were real, the pain they suffered was genuine, but it was also, in context, far less than others were enduring. Prices across the board fell after the Civil War, and study after study has confirmed that the farm sector was hurt the least by these declines. Meanwhile, as industry surged and wages elsewhere rose, consumers had more money than ever to purchase products.[74]

Otherwise, the gold standard had been closely managed by the executive branch, both Democrat and Republican. This reinforced the trust in the U.S. government, reassured foreign and domestic investors, and allowed the vast profits from American industrialization to be plowed back into the economy. The gold standard imposed a strict discipline on federal spending that also eliminated uncertainty. It was, as two prominent economists called it, the "Good Housekeeping Seal of Approval" for government finances.[75] In June of 1896, J. P. Morgan, in a rare public policy stand, told reporters, "European investors are watching the situation here closely. They will not invest in American securities until they know in what kind of money we propose to pay our debts."[76] The voting public agreed, electing McKinley by a 271–176 electoral college margin and a half million popular vote advantage. Bryan's defeat reflected a genuine plebiscite over the gold standard as a symbol of a wide range of economic policies, and McKinley's victory marked a major shift in the margins of support garnered by Republicans.

From the late 1800s on, attempts by various groups—sharecroppers, silverites, wage laborers, agrarians—to leverage government to extract rents from the fast-growing industrial economy proved futile. While these groups complained, and ultimately nominated Bryan for the 1896 Democratic presidential campaign, they made little headway in seizing others' wealth until Theodore Roosevelt became president. Southerners could largely be ignored, but the demands of unions and Westerners could not. When the regulatory regime began to constrain railroads and banks—two industries that, for all the caterwauling, benefited farmers enormously—growth in the western United States began to attenuate somewhat. Not one of the top thirteen industrialized counties was in the West, and outside of San Francisco, there were only two other western counties in the top twenty.[77] All of them lay along major railroad routes. Likewise, the South was overwhelmingly agricultural, and not surprisingly, just as before the Civil War, most patents were issued in the industrial northern states. But the Old South was hit hardest by Republican "hard money" policies, and the states of Mississippi, Alabama, Georgia, Arkansas, and Virginia ranked at the bottom in economic growth.[78] Virtually all of the least-developed counties in the United States lay in what used to be the Confederacy, and multiple generations of southern solidarity with the Democrats were assured. The West, on the other hand, benefited from a rapid transfer of capital through the national bank system, which showed a dense concentration of banks in the frontier/mountain West.[79] Complaints that there was "no money in Kansas," while accurate, obscured the fact that there were plenty of banks in Kansas, but that the money-creation powers of the national banking system were inadequate, especially without a national branch banking system.

Even restrained by those imperfections, the U.S. capital market linked together Laramie and London, San Francisco and Shanghai, Boston and Berlin, bringing an unprecedented wave of investments into the United States. Not all was monetized—hence the ongoing complaints about the elasticity of money—but it was all used, absorbed into the massive industrial explosion of the late nineteenth century.[80] British investors, in particular, had committed heavily to railroads, most notably the Atchison, Topeka and Santa Fe, the Baltimore and Ohio, the Louisville and Nashville, the Central Pacific, the New York Central, the Pennsylvania, and the Union Pacific.

The railroad networks sprawled across the United States because of a revolution in how businesses were run, and this too involved the banks. Beginning in the 1850s, the size, scale, and scope of railroads exceeded that of the next largest business enterprise by several orders of magnitude. Selling stock as their primary means of raising capital, railroads became ten, twenty, or even fifty times larger than other "big businesses." With thousands of stockholders, a separation of ownership and management occurred whereby professionals were hired to run the companies. Evolutionary change in the railroads toward this "managerial revolution" was made revolutionary by the Panic of 1873, when many leading railroads failed. Large banks took them over, imposing on them an administrative structure that looked like . . . a bank.[81]

## Teddy Roosevelt Assaults Business

As managerial hierarchies spread to other large firms, competition drove down prices; and in an effort to stabilize prices, virtually every sector of large-scale industry experimented with ways to reduce competition. Among the tactics tried and discarded were cartels, pools, and "gentlemen's agreements." John D. Rockefeller at Standard Oil had come up with another gimmick, the "trust," whereby shares of the newly created Standard Oil Trust would be exchanged for an equal number of shares in a company Rockefeller wanted to control or acquire. The targeted refiner, while losing control of his operation, nevertheless retained value (and, indeed, likely increased the value of his company by its affiliation with Standard). Other industries—paint, whiskey, sugar—soon followed, and trusts were demonized as "controlling" Congress, prompting the near-unanimous passage of the Sherman Antitrust Act to rein them in. Instead of reducing the power of big business, however, Sherman *increased it* by forcing businesses out of inefficient mergers, pools, cartels, trusts, and informal monopolies, and into more efficient vertical combinations. While some could claim Sherman legislated "more competition," in fact it forced all American—and soon, the world's—companies to join the managerial revolution.

Therefore, instead of dealing with a handful of inefficient trusts that struggled to control a portion of the market, the nation was handed by default a system that refined corporate power and turned sluggish, bloated companies into lean, mean enterprises that had to compete with one another. Almost immediately upon assuming office as president, Theodore Roosevelt recognized the power of the new firms, especially if they combined, leading him to sic his Justice Department on the Northern Securities Company for "restraint of trade." Roosevelt, of course, had been searching for a vehicle to test his view of muscular regulation. Following the E. C. Knight sugar refining case of 1895, in which the Supreme Court said that regulation of a manufactured good was a state responsibility unless it crossed a state line, Roosevelt dispatched his attorney general, Philander C. Knox, to file a suit against the Northern Securities holding company that enfolded the Northern Pacific, Great Northern, and Chicago, Burlington, and Quincy railroads into a single umbrella company worth nearly half a billion dollars. Yet the holding company had not charged higher rates, and therefore no harms from this monopoly actually existed. Nevertheless, the Court ruled against the combination in light of possible future restriction of commerce, obliterating the concept of "innocent until proven guilty" when it came to the corporation.[82]

Business—how it ran, what motivated entrepreneurs, why profits were critical—escaped TR, becoming his most glaring weakness as president. Disagreeing with Roosevelt was easy, but disliking him was impossible. Harry Thurston Peck, a literary critic, once described him as "a stream of fresh, pure, bracing air from the mountains, to clear the fetid atmosphere of the national capital."[83] William Allen White described him as having "a shoulder-shaking assertive, heel-clicking, straight-away gait, rather consciously rapid as one who is habitually about his master's business."[84] Wealthy, Roosevelt spent much of his presidency railing against combinations of industry; frail as a youth, he took up boxing and bulked up to two hundred pounds of muscle—one opponent described him as a "strong, tough man; hard to hurt and harder to stop."[85] A portrait in contradictions, TR reasoned that whatever he had overcome, others could as well, and whatever offended him surely must offend the public, too. No comments better encapsulated Roosevelt's view of life than the classic "Man in the Arena" speech:

> It is not the critic who counts: not the man who points out how the strong man stumbles or where the doer of deeds could have done better. The credit belongs to the man who is actually in the arena, whose face is marred by dust and sweat and blood, who strives valiantly, who errs and comes up short again and again, because there is no effort without error or shortcomings . . . [for] at least if he fails while daring greatly . . . his place shall never be with those cold and timid souls who knew neither victory nor defeat.[86]

Roosevelt's positive contribution to American history lay not in his flawed business policies but in his commitment to American strategic power and his support for American interests abroad. Above all, TR loved America—not as she might be when properly "reformed," but as she was. He certainly intended to improve the United States (he was a Progressive after all), but Roosevelt lacked the self-loathing that afflicted so many post–World War II liberals and Progressives. If anything, Roosevelt went overboard from time to time, essentially arguing that America was great and she owed it to other peoples to insist that they be great, too.

Few Europeans shared his views, although for over a century the question of who the American was had been debated. Alexis de Tocqueville praised Americans' love of freedom and equality. British eugenicist Francis Galton, in the 1850s, had described Americans as "enterprising, defiant, and touchy; impatient of authority; furious [with] politicians; very tolerant of fraud and violence; possessing much high and generous spirit, and some true religious feeling, but strongly addicted to cant."[87] TR, possessing an eye for the press and public relations, realized he governed a nation that had already become an international power, impossible to overlook or ignore, exactly as the irrepressible Roosevelt himself was to everyone.

## Progressivism and Its Debilitations

At home, however, Roosevelt headed a movement that soon emerged as one of the most destructive forces since slavery, Progressivism. Infused with a liberal interpretation of Christianity that redirected the individual toward helping his fellow man with material blessings, rather than pointing him toward the salvation of Christ, the Progressives became far more dangerous to American liberty than any previous movement. While they shared the objective of redistributing wealth with the Populists, Progressives shifted their focus from controlling particular forms of economic endeavor (trains, grain elevators, factory owners) toward gaining power over broader swaths of American society, most notably the newly emerging middle class. This group became the Progressives' target because it had both wealth, which the government could tap as a source of revenue, and political power, which could allow Progressives to obtain control of the federal government without a revolution.

Although many Progressives emerged from the upper class and educational elites and saw the wealthy as having an obligation to help support the poor, not all believed they should be compelled to do so by government. But the temptation was great: here, in America, for the first time was a large collective entity (the federal government) with a potential for a bloodless revolution that redistributed wealth, and the perfect mechanism for that revolution was an income tax. Needless to say, the concept of an income tax so troubled the Founders that they had specifically prohibited a direct tax in the Constitution (Article 1, Section 9), thus forcing the Progressives to pass an amendment. That, in turn, required creating a national consensus that depended entirely on selling the concept to the large swath of middle-class voters. Political leaders began with a modest proposal, initially targeting the Northeast, where they expected the most opposition. Some of the wealthy already supported the tax out of fear that without it, more radical and painful alternatives might emerge. Few advocates championed the tax as a means to generate revenue: Democratic congressman Cordell Hull from Tennessee, the primary drafter of the 1913 and 1916 income tax bills, as well as the 1916 inheritance tax bill, was far less concerned about the revenue-producing capabilities of the tax than about advancing "economic justice."[88] To that end, the form was simple (one page, in most cases), the rates were phenomenally low by today's standards (6 percent on the ultra-wealthy, and half a percent on most of those who paid taxes at all), and the exemptions so numerous that only 2 percent of all Americans paid income taxes.[89] This was good strategy for the pro-tax people, too, as the smaller the number of people who actually paid taxes, the easier it would be to raise them in the future. It was the classic case of the camel putting his nose in the tent—soon the entire camel would follow.

And then there was the tariff, which required constant revision of "schedules" (rates). Most congressmen never examined a single schedule other than as applied to outside goods produced in their own district. A Louisiana congressman might, for example, have some interest in the sugar rates, but none in the iron rates; a Pennsylvanian might care about iron, but not tar. Republican House leaders, then, were entrusted by their parties with organizing the messy schedules into a vote that passed easily and with almost no dissension within the party.[90] Merely the potential of haggling over hundreds of rates for everything from rope to cheese to timber led Congress to see the income tax as a replacement for the cumbersome tariff structure, even when it was not generating a large percentage of the nation's revenue.

These concerns over tariff revisions, "economic justice," and the Progressive desire to start federalizing more money culminated in the income tax amendment of 1913. There was no withholding: all taxes were paid on April 15, a date seemingly deliberately chosen for its remoteness from the November elections. With the passage of income tax withholding from wages during the New Deal, the noticeable and immediate burdens of the tax system were further diluted, making it easier than ever to raise taxes incrementally. Opposition arose only when the burden of taxes reached a tipping point, as occurred in the late 1970s.

## The First, Failed Canal

By the time the income tax passed, Roosevelt's light had dimmed. He had lost the 1912 presidential race, splitting the ticket with fellow Progressive William Howard Taft and allowing the Democratic Progressive, Woodrow Wilson, to gain the White House. But his legacy endured, and the most fantastic project of the early twentieth century was created in large part due to Roosevelt's support and vision. The Panama Canal "bore stark witness to the enormity of American industrial might and the ability of Americans to project that power overseas."[91] It represented one more example of how Americans seemed to accomplish what other nations could not.

Springing from the futuristic dream of Ferdinand de Lesseps, a French lawyer-turned-engineer, the ambitious Panama Canal project was deemed possible namely due to de Lesseps's success at constructing the Suez Canal (opened in 1869). In many ways, de Lesseps was France's first nonmilitary celebrity technocrat, surpassing Gustave Eiffel (whom de Lesseps later dragged into the Panama Canal muck, eventually sending the hapless builder of the Eiffel Tower to jail for his role in the exorbitant expenditure of funds and for his complicity in fleecing the French public).[92] De Lessups had no real connections, no official capacity, no background in finance, no particular engineering skill. He did have an education at the École Poly-technique—but so did thousands of others with more talent. Like today's celebrities, who feed off one another by appearing together, so too did Jules Verne and Victor Hugo associate with de Lesseps and he with them to fur-ther the image of a powerful cadre of revolutionary thinkers. Hugo encour-aged de Lesseps, that he might "astonish the world by the great deeds that can be won without a war!"[93] Nor was de Lesseps without good sense—he had stayed out of the French effort to build a railway across the Sahara Des-ert from Algeria to Timbuktu, which ended in a disaster both for its pro-moters and for the French forces sent to survey the route in 1881. Historian David McCullough labeled de Lesseps "the *entrepreneur extraordinaire*; con-temporaries called him the 'the first promoter of the age.'"[94] English prime minister Lord Palmerston had a different view, labeling him a "swindler and a fool."

In fact, de Lesseps had virtually no building experience in any project anywhere comparable to the Suez—yet he pulled it off thanks to new, large French digging machines. The success at Suez embedded in de Lesseps an inflated opinion of the capabilities of technology to solve any problem.

Essentially nominating himself to lead the Panama project, de Lesseps summoned a congress of financiers, engineers, and politicians, and sought both to boost stock sales in the enterprise and to forge a consensus on the route he (and France) had already chosen, one running alongside the Pan-ama Canal Railroad. Money was raised, and digging commenced, but no one had a clue how to deal with the Chagres River, which would have to be redirected or somehow incorporated into a canal. More important still, no one had come to grips with the deadly disease of yellow fever. Malaria had a preventative (quinine), but was still extremely common. De Lesseps remained unmoved, possessing a "jaunty disregard of technical problems, the inability to heed, to *trust* the views of recognized authorities if those views conflicted with his own, the faith that the future would take care of itself, that necessity would give rise to invention in required proportions and at the proper moment, the unshakable faith in his own infallibility [emphasis in original]."[95]

Needless to say, Panama was vastly different in geography and cultural attitudes from Cairo: Panama at both ends (Panama City and Colón) was among the most despicable places on earth. Unequaled in "swindling and villainy," as one English historian put it, nowhere else was there

> so much foul disease, such a hideous dung-heap of moral and phys-
> ical abomination as in the scene of this far-famed undertaking of
> nineteenth-century engineering. . . . Everything which imagina-
> tion can conceive that is ghastly and loathsome seems to be gath-
> ered into that locality.[96]

Dead cats and horses were not uncommon sights in the streets of mid-century American cities, but this combined with the garbage piled high only exacerbated the filth and disease. So much liquor flowed in Panama that the bottle dumps at Colón rose as tall as a house and the streets were literally paved with wine bottles turned upside down.

Upside down also aptly described the digging situation under de Lesseps's supervision, where the contractors found that the more they dug, the more rainfall washed mud into the cuts. The lock system that would be required proved far beyond de Lesseps's abilities and financial whim-whammery. He finally declared the Compagnie Universelle du Canal Interocéanique de Panama closed and bankrupt in February 1889.

## America Picks Up the Shovel

With France's exit from Panama, two paths to building a canal still remained for the United States to consider: the failed Panama route (which most engineers still preferred) or a route through independent Nicaragua, for which many prominent senators lobbied. Two events coalesced to shift sentiment to Panama. First, in April 1902, a volcano erupted on the Caribbean island of Martinique, annihilating the city of St. Pierre and obliterating nearly 30,000 people. Suddenly the assessments of Nicaragua as a state riddled with volcanoes looked more sobering. Second, in June 1902, Senator Mark Hanna—McKinley's onetime right-hand man and campaign manager—delivered a highly organized address to the Senate, in which he laid out nine key advantages of the Panama route. The speech swayed several votes and led some to refer to the project as the "Hannama Canal." Less than two weeks later, newspapers reported that Roosevelt had settled on the Panama route, and warned Colombia to agree to a treaty quickly or face unnamed threats from the U.S. government.

Efforts to direct American interest toward Panama were greatly enhanced by Philippe Bunau-Varilla and William Nelson Cromwell, a pair known in Washington as the "Panama lobby." Bunau-Varilla, physically small, proud, a former soldier and engineer whose serious but youthful countenance boasted a full red mustache, arrived in Panama in 1884 with de Lesseps's company. Patriotically French to the core and personally courageous, Bunau-Varilla came from limited means, yet impressed canal administrators on the journey over to Panama, eventually becoming the quartermaster of the organization. He observed firsthand the intervention of the Americans in the so-called Prestan uprising, which greatly reoriented him toward U.S. power. Historian David McCullough dismisses notions that Bunau-Varilla was a flim-flam artist, or a schemer who somehow interposed himself into Panamanian politics. Quite the contrary, Bunau-Varilla's writings and books, such as *Panama: The Past, Present, and Future* (1892), proved pivotal in keeping the dream alive, and his excellent English allowed him to effectively convey his vision to American audiences during his 1901 speaking tour.

But in 1888, when de Lesseps's company began to run out of money, Bunau-Varilla found himself stranded in Panama with dashed hopes and few prospects except for a great deal of canal company stock, which someone could ostensibly buy to build the canal. He journeyed back to France in 1898 and enlisted the New York firm of Sullivan & Cromwell for the New Panama Canal Company (founded 1894). The fast-talking Cromwell bore a resemblance to a graying Mark Twain. Working his way up the legal ladder, he became part of the corporate restructuring wave of the late 1800s pioneered by J. P. Morgan, and even worked with Morgan on the U.S. Steel purchase. His corporate activities put him in contact with the captains of industry, from Alfred Gwynne Vanderbilt to Edward H. Harriman to Collis Huntington, and it was through the Panama Canal Railroad Company that he came to represent, and later serve as lobbyist for, the new canal company. Cromwell dove into the new task ferociously, mailing materials to

Capitol Hill, buttonholing congressmen in Washington, negotiating with the Colombians, and ultimately becoming the driving force behind the formation of the Canal Commission, providing the members with all of the evidence they would need to make a decision in favor of the Panama route.

For all their common interests, Bunau-Varilla was contemptuous (or possibly jealous) of the attorney, referring to him as "the *lawyer* Cromwell." The two did not meet in person until 1902; nevertheless, they were linked by destiny. They were arrangers, people who "knew people," string pullers, and with Cromwell working in the shadows and Bunau-Varilla in the spotlight, they dragged the canal back to life.

It was William Nelson Cromwell who circulated a Nicaraguan postage stamp that featured a belching volcano in the background, underscoring the testimony before the Morgan commission about the dangers of building in the region. The stamp affected the votes of at least three senators, who voted for the Panama route after receiving the stamps, and the Senate voted $40 million for the new Panama Canal Company in the Spooner Act of 1902.[97] But one condition had to be met for the Spooner Act to go into effect: a treaty had to be negotiated with Colombia. Two previous agreements—the Clayton-Bulwer Treaty (between the United States and Britain in 1850, in which the parties agreed that any canal built would not be militarized, but that each would protect rail or canal shipping in the region) and the 1901 Hay-Pauncefote Treaty (in which the same nations modified Clayton-Bulwer and recognized American rights alone to build and control a canal in Central America, provided all nations would be allowed transit)— governed any construction in the region.

In the ensuing mini-revolution, Panama declared independence from Colombia, and, thanks to the presence of nearby American gunboats and Marines, Colombia was unable to reinforce its garrisons and restore the isthmus to its previous condition. David McCullough admits that without America's military presence, "the Republic of Panama probably would not have lasted a week."[98] An equally accurate observation would have been that had the people of Panama viewed themselves as Colombians, or had Colombia maintained a serious presence in Panama, the Republic wouldn't have been born. Criticized for encouraging a revolution, Roosevelt's characteristic reply was "Tell them I'm going to make the dirt fly!"[99] And so he did. Purchasing the French holdings—the largest real estate deal in history up to that point, at roughly $40 million paid to J.P. Morgan & Company, the agent for the transaction—the United States set up an Isthmian Canal

Commission to run the ten-mile Canal Zone as a U.S. territory. The Zone was complete with hotels and bars playing ragtime music, married housing, bachelor quarters, country clubs, and the YMCA, which had gymnasiums, bowling alleys, and billiards, movie theaters, and every touch of Americana. Tourists by the thousands flocked just to see the work in progress, and nothing was more awe-inspiring than the Culebra Cut, a nine-mile swath chopped through the mountains.

The man chosen to actually dig the canal, John Frank Stevens, came at the recommendation of railroad genius James J. Hill, who called him the best construction engineer in the United States. Burly, rough, and handsome, Stevens was admired by Teddy Roosevelt as well; his approach to great projects resembled that of Andrew Carnegie, whose faith in ordinary men doing extraordinary things was a cornerstone of his empire. While working for Hill, Stevens had cut the Marias Pass through the Continental Divide, personally scouting the path alone, staying alive in the freezing cold only by marching back and forth at night. Likewise, he discovered another pass in the Cascades, named for him, and would eventually tunnel through that mountain range, cumulatively building over one thousand miles of railroad. He liked to work without interference, and expected his job would speak for itself. This classical American entrepreneurial attitude was exactly the kind Roosevelt liked, telling Stevens only "get busy and buttle like hell!"[100] Arriving in Panama in 1905, Stevens found the project mired in indecision—no final plan had been drawn up yet, and indeed the review board hadn't even convened!—and debt, having spent $120 million with little to show for it.

Stevens could be found on the work lines daily, noting that there were three diseases in Panama, yellow fever, malaria, and cold feet, the worst of which was cold feet. Told no collisions had occurred on the railroad line, he scoffed that it just meant nothing was moving. Perhaps Stevens's most impressive act involved a general halt to all work on the Culebra Cut to organize a sensible plan of work. He even sent some steam shovel and crane men back to the United States.

A quick assessment revealed that, before any real work could be done, yellow fever needed to be dealt with. Stevens's main ally in the war against the disease was Dr. William Gorgas, a devout and modest Christian who had learned from Dr. Walter Reed and Dr. Carlos Finlay in Cuba, who had already proven that mosquitoes transmitted yellow fever. Gorgas, and the prior Yellow Fever Commission, had issued reports and published their work, yet the Army and Congress ignored it, even after a scientific congress in Paris the following year declared Walter Reed's conclusions about the transmission of the disease to be "scientifically determined fact." "What's that [mosquito] got to do with digging the canal?" Gorgas was asked.[101] Nevertheless, with the patience of Job, Gorgas forged ahead, insisting that defeating the mosquito remained a key to a successful canal.

After his assessment, Stevens broke the Washington logjam and ensured that the doctor got everything he needed. Panama City and Colón were fumigated; soap, brooms, garbage cans, and other essentials were brought in by the thousands; oil was applied to cisterns and cesspools; and the major cities were all outfitted with running water. Stevens wisely didn't get caught up in the squabbles over what *caused* yellow fever, and made no public endorsements of Gorgas's positions. Rather, he simply de jure implemented Gorgas's solutions. Theodore Shonts, the new head of the Panama Canal Commission, opposed Gorgas, and the issue finally landed in Roosevelt's lap. "You must choose between Shonts and Gorgas," Dr. Alexander Lambert, a hunting pal of TR's, told the president.[102]

And so he did. Roosevelt sided with Gorgas, Shonts fell in line, and suddenly the Panama doctor had millions of dollars at his disposal to fight the disease. It took a year and a half to eradicate yellow fever in Panama, but as quickly as water supplies were cleaned up, the situation improved from area to area, enabling work to begin. By December 1906, the last death from yellow fever was reported in Panama. Next, Stevens—a railroader—decided the old Panama line was too light, some four times smaller than what he worked with on the Great Northern. Setting up new warehouses, telegraph lines, and shops along the route, Stevens replaced the existing track with new and heavier stock. He hired a whole new force of trainmasters, superintendents, dispatchers, and mechanics, all trained in the Great Northern's techniques. Quickly, a healthy symmetry unfolded: as the tracks moved forward next to the cleaned-up, disease-free towns, fresh food arrived, and within six months the construction force had tripled. At one point, Stevens had 12,000 men constructing only buildings. Agents recruited in New York, New Orleans, and Caribbean islands, offering jobs for over 4,000 skilled workers available in the first year alone. Transportation to Panama was free, as was housing and medical, and the average pay for a skilled worker was $87 per month in an age when a men's suit was only $10 and a steak dinner, at most, a quarter.

Even so, applications fell behind labor force requirements, with many of those who showed up being unsuitable for the necessary machinist and plumbing jobs. Barbados proved one of the major suppliers of laborers, particularly at the wages the Americans offered. At one point, 20 percent of the Barbadian population, and some 40 percent of the adult males, were employed in Panama, sending back nearly $300,000 a year. It was devilishly hard work, loading and unloading, pouring cement in the steamy Panamanian climate, cutting brush, cutting lumber, and above all, digging. Supposed "laziness" among the West Indians disappeared with better diets—particularly more meat—impressing even the skeptics. Above all, Stevens appreciated the need to create in Panama working conditions equal to those for industrial laborers and tradesmen in the United States. Yet throughout, he considered it a basic engineering calculation of moving dirt from one location to another, mostly via train.

Looming ahead, however, was the Culebra Cut, the most difficult engineering obstacle for the project. Stevens and his associates considered massive hydraulic mining via water blasts, or using compressed air that would send the dirt to the sea through giant pipes. Stevens ultimately preferred a simple assembly line of dirt, disposed of by the railroad, using the excavated soil to fill in for the locks. The most important aspect of the operation, as Stevens saw it, was not the distance from excavation to dumping, but rather that the dirt kept moving. He envisioned an endless chain of rail cars in constant motion. Devising a remarkable network of tracks, Stevens kept empty cars poised next to the massive shovels, while filled cars rolled out on a downgrade.

Stevens also had to wade into the political fray, helping swing the decision from a sea-level canal to one with locks, and in stark opposition to the report delivered to the White House in January 1906 called *Report of the Consulting Engineers for the Panama Canal*. A minority report called for a canal built with a series of locks, creating a larger Gatún Lake out of Lake Bohio, and in February, the Isthmian Canal Commission chose the lock design. Roosevelt personally visited the canal project in November, climbing into one of the massive steam shovels for a photo opportunity: it was classic TR, with a giant banner greeting him at the Culebra Cut reading, "WE'LL HELP YOU DIG IT." But it would be dug without Stevens, who resigned in 1907 for reasons that were never disclosed. He was replaced by Major George Goethals, a silver-haired, messy chain smoker who "detested fat people."[103] But Goethals met with everyone, talked to everyone, and listened to virtually anyone, allowing private meetings on Sundays with workmen or any other person who had a gripe.

Work did not suffer under Stevens's replacement. Goethels had the operation carving out the equivalent of the Suez Canal every three years, ultimately excavating a pile that would, if shaped as a pyramid, reach 4,200 feet high. About half of the workforce at the Culebra Cut was involved in dynamiting, with a single ship bringing in one million pounds of dynamite at a time. By March 1909, sixty-eight giant mechanized shovels chopped out two million cubic yards in a month, with a single shovel excavating 70,000 yards in a twenty-six-day period. More than seventy-five miles of railroad track was laid within the nine-mile canyon, not counting the Panama Railroad itself, allowing 160 trains a day to run in and out of the Culebra Cut.

An endless stream of visitors, many of them influential, toured Panama during construction of the canal, including the son of President John Quincy Adams, Charles Francis Adams, Jr. (then seventy-six years old). Adams expressed astonishment at the transformation of a handful of disease-ridden jungle outposts into "civilization." Congressmen made regular junkets to "inspect" the work, enjoying a tropical vacation most of the time. At its peak, the Panama workforce numbered over 45,000, including 2,500 women and children—the families of American workers who moved to the Canal Zone. Overwhelmingly, however, Panama was a region full of men, and as such, it featured 220 saloons in Panama City and another 131 in Colón. Incentives to get married (an immediate grant of a rent-free, four-room apartment) combined with the prevalence of brothels meant more than a few men married prostitutes. But the finer side of life was present, too. Cities sported bakeries, excellent shopping, libraries, restaurants; regular social events included dances, bowling clubs, dramatic and theater presentations, and a variety of exclusive men's clubs. Taboga Island, in the Bay of Panama, could be reached through a three-hour boat trip, and offered a close vacation resort with sheltered beaches. Historians, scientists, and archeologists began to trickle into the Zone, conducting research.

All the while, still more industry and infrastructure permeated Panama. Another railroad was built, along with a hydroelectric plant. The military began placing sixteen-inch guns, with a range of twenty miles, at Toro Point and on the islands in the Bay of Panama. In 1910, with the completion of the West Diversion channel, the lake began to take over the jungle. The mighty locks rose as structural marvels, all of which was reported with enthusiasm back home, and their massive size (about five blocks long and six stories high), if stood on end, would have exceeded the height of the Eiffel Tower. The entire project employed some five million sacks of cement shipped from New York and made use of the newest concrete and toughest American steel, becoming the largest concrete structures built by Americans until the Boulder Dam was built in the 1930s. Despite what by modern standards would be considered primitive technology, the locks stood up amazingly well over time, and best of all, the plan called for the falling water of the Gatún spillway to furnish all the electrical power needed to open and close the locks. More impressive still, intermediate gates were built so that if a smaller vessel came through (at its maximum, a lock could hold the world's largest ship, the *Titanic*), a smaller chamber could be used to speed up the flooding or release process. To ensure that out-of-control ships didn't damage the locks, a massive chain "catch" device stood ready to restrain the vessel before it could do any damage.

On September 26, 1913, the Gatún locks underwent a test run with a tug, and in a painfully slow process (because the lake had not yet reached its highest level), the tug finally emerged through the locks onto Gatún Lake. The following month, in a clever publicity scene, President Woodrow Wilson, elected in 1912, transmitted the signal to Panama by telegraph wires that blew up the dike in the Culebra Cut, and the waterway was filled. When a crane boat, the *Alexander La Valley*, went from the Pacific to the Gulf side without fanfare in January, it marked the first actual transit of the isthmus. Seven months later, an equally undistinguished vessel, the cement boat *Christobal*, became the first oceangoing vessel to cross through the Panama Canal, draining all the pomp from the official opening on August 15, 1914. Yet the canal that would in theory unite the world was already a distraction from the real events in Europe, which would soon come apart in the Great War.

## The Unpacific Pacific

Matching the American presence in the Caribbean was an expansion in the Pacific that came through the American presence in the Philippines and possession of other island territories, which threatened the British. England now faced potential opponents on both oceans, not the least from the rising empire of Japan, which posed a growing naval threat. With the Meiji constitution of 1890, Japan had adopted a constitutional monarchy model that resembled the government of Prussia, allowing power to be shared between the emperor and the parliament, called the Diet. Many quipped that Japan had a Prussian government, a British navy, and a French education system—an Occidental façade that nevertheless concealed a decidedly Oriental mind-set. Japan intended to apply *Yamato-damashii* ("Japanese spirit") to modernization. *Yamato-damashii* soon took on overtones of Bushido (a code of samurai warrior conduct), or military nobility propaganda. The emperor was a deity, and all Japanese were descended from the gods. Other races, however, were not, and were treated as distinctly inferior. All foreigners were *gaijin*—barbarians. Bushido stressed honor in its most extreme form—loyalty to the emperor, to family, and to Japan. Death was preferable to dishonor; "saving face" was a hallmark of all interactions, public and private. After the Japanese victories in the Sino-Japanese and Russo-Japanese wars, Bushido took hold as a catchphrase for progress. It was the Japanese naval victories at Port Arthur and Tsushima that caught British (and American) attention, though, for here was a supposedly backward Asian nation defeating a theoretically superior Western power. Admittedly, Russia was viewed as barely ahead of the Ottoman Empire by Britain and France—its population had only recently emerged from serfdom, and still lagged far behind other European countries and America when it came to industrialization. Yet Japan defeated a "white" nation vastly larger than itself, and at sea no less.

When war broke out in 1904 over a Korean border dispute with Japan, Russians derided their enemies as "yellow monkeys," the "Asiatic horde," or the "yellow danger." Dismissing both Japanese land and sea forces as inferior—despite their recent shellacking of China—the Russians learned firsthand how advanced the Imperial Navy was when one night a surprise torpedo attack by a squadron of Japanese destroyers disabled two battleships and a cruiser, eliminating Russia's superiority in battleships in the Far East. Admiral Heihachiro Togo foolishly followed up in daylight on February 9, engaging virtually the whole Russian fleet. After a few minutes of blasting away, Togo fortunately escaped with his fleet intact.[104] Three months later, however, when the Russian Baltic Fleet arrived in the Pacific after a tedious voyage, having been dispatched on October 15, a much different outcome resulted. Possessing faster battleships with superior high-explosive shells, Togo "crossed the 'T'" of the Russian line (in which the Japanese fleet turned at a 90-degree angle to the oncoming line of Russian ships). This maneuver brought to bear most of his guns and rained shot on the Russians. The commander of the *Suvorov* recalled, "Shells seemed to be pouring upon us incessantly one after another. The steel plates and superstructure on the upper decks were torn to pieces. . . . Iron ladders were crumpled up into rings, and guns were literally hurled from their mountings."[105] Within hours, the Russian battleships were crippled or sunk; that night, Japanese torpedo boats and destroyers swarmed around the survivors, forcing the scuttling of four more battleships or heavy cruisers. In all, Russia lost twenty-one ships, including virtually all of her nineteen battleships and heavy cruisers, and her killed, wounded, or captured numbered almost 10,000, against 700 Japanese dead or wounded, the latter including a young officer named Isoroku Yamamoto who later was the architect of the Pearl Harbor attack and commanded the Combined Fleet in World War II. He lost two fingers and came within an ace of having his career terminated by the maiming.

Tsushima enabled Japan to annex Korea in 1910 without opposition and served notice to the West that Japan was, if not its equal, a legitimate power in the Pacific. But neither the Japanese, nor the Russians, nor the Germans fully understood the new dynamic of naval power. Simply building ships wasn't enough. Sir John Fisher's radical new battleship, the *Dreadnought* (1906), with steam turbines and "all big gun" armament, seemed to confirm his unofficial title as the "genius incarnate of technical change."[106] Contrary to the notion that, because of its revolutionary design, the *Dreadnought*

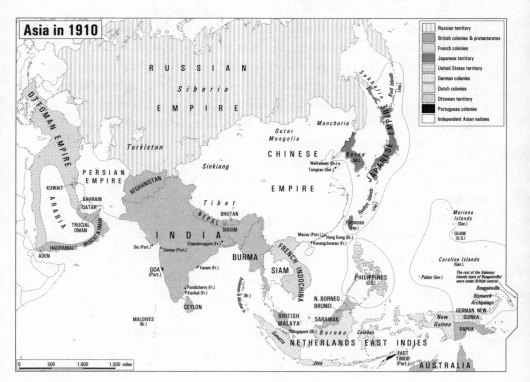

"leveled the playing field" for aspiring naval powers such as Germany (which embarked on its own version of the ship and widened the Kiel Canal to permit passage of larger vessels), Fisher's advances showed how once again true power came from culture. Britain's naval culture had produced Fisher, after all, not vice versa. As in any technology—and battleships were no different—the most significant changes come from incremental, relentless improvements possible only in a cultural milieu in which engineering and technology are fostered. The same principle kept the Chinese from turning gunpowder into a culture of volley-fire muskets, and prevented the Iranians from applying the stirrup to mounted shock combat horseback charges. Lacking a strong, innovative naval culture, none of the second-tier aspirants could really hope to compete at sea with England or America.

## Poles Apart

A final, and fitting, event marked America's entrance onto the world stage when a naval officer, Commander Robert E. Peary, reached the North Pole in 1909 with a small expedition of Eskimos, dog sleds, and his sidekick Matthew Henson. Peary's claim to be the first at the Pole was initially controversial, mainly because yet another American, Dr. Frederick A. Cook, said he had reached the coveted 90-degree North latitude much earlier. (Cook's claims were later shown to be fraudulent.)[107]

Peary, a naval officer most frequently photographed in polar gear and sporting a massive, dense mustache, had been involved in polar exploration for years: in a 1906 expedition, he was separated from his companions by a storm and the warming of polar ice suddenly presented him with the possibility of becoming trapped without food. In a mad dash, he negotiated the ice and reunited with his party. Considered to be the best dead-reckoning navigator in history next to Christopher Columbus, Peary suffered his share of criticism, much of it by Cook supporters, and some of it brought on by his own sense of megalomania. But he accomplished more than any other polar explorer up to that time. His "Peary System" of traveling with dog sleds over the ice, establishing food caches, and using "icebreaker" teams to cut the trail ahead while the main party followed the somewhat easier route behind, constituted a major improvement over previous approaches to polar travel and would prove far superior to the British mish-mash of ponies and engine-driven devices used in the fatal Antarctic expedition of Robert Falcon Scott.[108]

After establishing a final base camp using the Peary System, Peary and

Henson set off with four Eskimos on the final dash for 90 degrees north on April 2, 1909, from an estimated distance of about 133 miles away. On April 6, they camped at a place that Peary calculated was at or near the Pole, and after remaining in the area for thirty hours making observations and taking pictures, the party returned to their ship, the *Roosevelt*, docked on Ellesmere Island at the edge of the polar ice cap on April 27. Although they made what many consider unrealistic speeds, Peary and Henson were traveling back over trails that had already been broken once and stayed in igloos already built. Peary's diary, released by his family in the 1980s for public examination for the first time since the early 1900s, revealed that Peary's daily observations of ice conditions, weather, speed, and distance covered correlated almost exactly with those of Matthew Henson, even though the two barely spoke after returning to the *Roosevelt*.[109] Additional confirmation came when later explorers on similar expeditions reported similar conditions to Peary's and made comparable speeds.

When he planted the flag at the Pole on April 6, Peary staked America's place in the world of exploration, symbolically eclipsing the British, whose Robert Falcon Scott reached the South Pole in 1912 only to find that a party led by Norwegian Roald Amundsen had beaten him. Scott and his four comrades died in a freezing storm, eleven miles away from a food depot that was originally planned for a location twenty-four miles closer. Leaving his heart-wrenching "Message to the Public"—in which he avoided all personal blame—Scott in death temporarily snatched world attention away from Amundsen's remarkable achievement.[110] But even Amundsen could not overcome the contrast of images: the American flag flying victoriously, while Scott froze tragically, a victim of a society past its prime, and most of all, of his own ego, which itself had only recently come under scientific scrutiny.

## The World of the Mind

At the turn of the century, exploration and investigation were not limited to the earth's physical and geographical expanses, but spread to the human mind. Psychology and the study of human behavior emerged before World War I as people sought to understand the functioning of normal and abnormal human personalities. The center of this new activity was Vienna, more specifically Sigmund Freud, who drew around him such notables as Alfred Adler, Carl Jung, Wilhelm Stekel, and Lou Andreas-Salomé, all impressive intellects, who over time went their separate ways like bees spreading pollen throughout the flowers of European medical practices and universities.

Originally trained to be a neurologist, Freud dabbled in hypnotism, but finding that ineffective in explaining and altering human behavior, developed a technique called "talking out" or "free association" wherein patients would talk themselves out of their problems. Freud's background lent itself to this aloof methodology, since being a Jew in an anti-Semitic society, he was already considered different and even strange. Freud capitalized on this factor, as it allowed him to be and remain on the outside looking in at his patient without being fettered by preconceived ideas concerning faith and spiritual interference. Employing a secular, scientific view, Freud developed theories heavily influenced by Ernst von Brücke, the director of the physiology laboratory at the University of Vienna, who believed that humans were living organisms in a dynamic system in which the laws of chemistry and physics applied.[111] Freud applied this idea to personality, as affected by transformations and energy according to science as much as the human body. Later he wrote, "My life has been aimed at one goal only; to infer or to guess how the mental apparatus is constructed and what forces interpret and counteract in it."[112]

His first literary production, *The Interpretation of Dreams*, was published in 1899. Although the work was very poorly received, Freud remained convinced he was on the right track since he believed dreams were caused by unconscious forces indicative of personality and the dynamic changes occurring in a person's life. In 1904, he followed with *The Psychopathology of Everyday Life*, in which he furthered this thesis by attributing daily errors, memory lapses, and slips of the tongue to these same unconscious forces. From here, he published a trilogy of works, *A Case Study of Hysteria*, *Wit and Its Relation to the Unconscious*, and perhaps the most important, *Three Essays on Sexuality*. With this last work, he gained a large popular audience, as humans everywhere were fascinated by anything concerned with sex, especially when it stressed the power of sexuality and sexual experience. Whether he intended to or not, Freud precipitated a profound shift in the way people viewed sex and contributed to the modern focus on sexual dysfunction and the idea that sex was the most important factor in determining one's happiness.

In terms of its general psychological theory, Freud's work presented a combination of the hormic driving forces and the hedonistic pleasure-pain theory, seasoned with a light sprinkling of Schopenhauerean and Nietzschean philosophy.[113] In contrast, Carl Jung, the son of a Protestant minister, departed from Freud over the importance of sexuality, even questioning if there was some unconscious factor at work in Freud himself that caused him to elevate sex to such a dominant position. Jung experimented with word associations in patients, and rather than seeing universal sexual forces at work, he detected cultural and ethnic-historic influences that were important. Myths were important for an ethnic group, as were the symbols in use and understood by one group but not another. Dealing with historical patterns of symbols, Jung discerned aspects that were not individual in orientation, but were group-based. While this allowed social and historical variables to be added to the mix, and behavior was at least partially socially determined, it put Jung at odds with Karl Marx, the founder of communism, whose theories of economic determinism were in vogue. Marx assumed that individual psychological motivations of all humans were the same, remaining unaltered throughout history. He missed the historical and ethnic context, and would never have understood the concept of synchronicity as a hypothesis of revolution (an acausal connecting principle) as Jung developed it.

These masters of the mind contended with the human psyche as it formed, or even dictated, human behavior. Others, however, were content to merely express humanness in the most elementary of surroundings, the buildings people lived and worked in. And just as Freud and Jung came to wildly different conclusions about what constituted the human mind and motivation, so too did three giants of architecture arrive at vastly different interpretations of man's physical surroundings.

## Human Nature in Steel and Stone

Less than two weeks after German forces slammed into Belgium, triggering the bloodiest war in Western history to that time, a fire swept through the idyllic Wisconsin home of architect Frank Lloyd Wright, Taliesin. It was not accidental: a servant hired by Wright a few months earlier not only locked all the doors and windows and set the blaze, but then rampaged through the house with an ax after the fire started, killing Wright's live-in lover, Mamah Cheney, and her two children and finally entering a dining room where six workmen were having lunch to kill four of them. The killer, Julian Carlton, hid in a basement furnace, attempted to commit suicide by swallowing acid—which only seared his mouth and esophagus so he could not eat—then was captured. Carleton died of starvation soon thereafter.

Wright, so stunned that he later claimed to have gone blind from trauma, finally emerged from seclusion to promise that Taliesin would be

rebuilt.[114] The home, characteristic of Wright's designs of that period, featured large, wall-less open areas, with the entire house integrated into the
hillside. Furniture was built in—a manifestation of the organic architecture theory which allowed the occupant to interact with the outdoors while
remaining protected from outside elements.[115] Glass was decorative, functional, and abundant, and Wright borrowed heavily from the cathedral
stained glass designs his mother had introduced him to as a child. Organic
architecture employed local, natural building material—stone and wood
from the area where the building was constructed—and demanded that a
building become a part of its surroundings. The most famous of his organic
buildings, the awe-inspiring Fallingwater (completed in 1939) near Bear
Run, Pennsylvania, sat atop a waterfall, which cascaded forth seemingly out
of the house itself.[116]

For all the serenity Wright's designs possessed, his personal life was a
series of chaotic tragedies and self-inflicted wounds. Eight years after the
fire and murders at Taliesin, he married a morphine addict named Maude
Noel, but that marriage dissolved, whereupon Wright took up with Olga
Lazovich and married her. Throughout his romantic turmoil, Wright continued to design and build fabulous residence towers, offices, administration buildings, apartments, hotels, and, from 1943 to 1959, the Solomon
Guggenheim Museum in New York City, one of the first museums to be
intended as a work of art in itself. Its round design permitted art to be
viewed in a constant motion, with embedded lights and geometric floor
shapes accentuating the interior of the structure and enhancing the experience. Embodying the term "ahead of his time," Wright designed buildings
that the technology of his time could not sustain—some of the designs,
indeed, the Petra Island house in Mahopac, New York, with its seventy-
eight-foot overhanging deck, would have collapsed if built with materials
available when Wright designed it.[117] Other Wright-designed structures,
especially many of those in California built in the Mayan Revival style to
resemble ancient block temples, eroded and nearly disintegrated. Critics
took these as examples of Wright's flaws, but his supporters cited them as
evidence of genius.

As Wright was refining one modernistic style, across the Atlantic, in
Barcelona, Spain, Antoni Gaudí was reaching his creative pinnacle in his
garden complex at Parc Güell, completed in 1914, the Church of Colònia
Güell, completed 1916, and Palau Güell in Barcelona (1890–96). The Catalan had already impressed Wright's teacher, Louis Sullivan, although Gaudí

was in no way like the Americans. Whereas Wright bathed his work in the ecology of architecture as expressed in the natural elements—wood, stone, and plants—Gaudí immersed himself in the history and culture of the area in which he built. Part of the *Renaixença* movement, reviving Catalan identity, Gaudí didn't just borrow from the past, he rebuilt it. Wright's first trip for a project was to the site to examine the landscape; Gaudí's, to a library to investigate a location's character. In sharp contrast to Sullivan's brass and mahogany, or Wright's lumber and rock, Gaudí splashed color and decorative tile abundantly. His wild shapes and uneven surfaces, combining Gothic and Muslim designs, made his structures as likely to appear in a twenty-first-century Disney theme park as a twentieth-century Spanish street.

Antoni Gaudí embodied paradox. Predictable to a fault, he embraced poverty with the admonition, "Elegance is the sister of poverty but you must never muddle poverty with misery."[118] Gaudí was determined to escape the world of materialism, yet his major patrons were the leading industrialists of Catalonia. A devout Catholic who inspired the Alan Parsons Project to produce an entire rock album eighty years later, a self-denier and pessimistic opponent of Spanish liberalism, whose work grew more grand and glorious the further he moved from his youthful idealism, Gaudí was to architecture what his fellow Spaniard Pablo Picasso was to painting. For a man who once wrote, "Ornamentation has been, is, and will be polychrome," Gaudí dived into depths of architectural decorating unseen since the Renaissance.[119]

The ornate Casa Batlló in Barcelona (1907), for example, featured rounded, curving edges akin to a pastry or a dinosaur. In contrast to Wright, whose layers and often blocky, square approaches offered a sense of anal-retentive order, Gaudí's buildings lack symmetry or sharp edges at all. One critic described the style as "fish scales": "even the walls are rounded in undulations and have in essence the feel of the smooth skin of a sea serpent about them."[120] Yet just as Wright's Fallingwater incorporated the beauty of a waterfall, Gaudí's serpentine bench at Parc Güell was doubly functional as a channel for rainwater on rainy days and a bench on dry ones. Both men demanded an active architecture that enlisted the occupant in the experience—Wright by looking out through the broad vistas of Taliesin, Gaudí through the mystical feeling of rolling along his balconies and benches that would strike the conscience of the observer. Wright wanted a sense of awe for the landscape; Gaudí, a marvelous humility before God. As eccentric as Wright,

Gaudí's devout Catholicism infused his creations with overt spiritual themes, none grander than La Sagrada Familia (The Sacred Family) cathedral in Barcelona.

Called "God's Architect," Gaudí routinely cited miracles and divine inspiration for his stunning cathedral design, all paid for with private funds. La Sagrada Familia in fact resembles a crown that represented the birth, death, and resurrection of Christ, enhanced by eighteen towers that symbolized the twelve apostles, the four evangelists, Mary, and Jesus. Gaudí designed the details of La Sagrada Familia with a higher purpose in mind, from the corners of the cathedral (representing the periods of Catholic fasting) to the giant fountain and massive lantern that symbolized the purification of the soul. Begun in 1883, the cathedral combined the sense of the sacred with the sensual shock of the unusual, virtually Gothic-on-psychedelic-drugs, though like a powerful drug, some loved it and others hated it. Louis Sullivan called it "the greatest piece of creative architecture in the last twenty-five years. It is spirit symbolized in stone!"[121] George Orwell, in *Homage to Catalonia*, described it as "one of the most hideous buildings in the world, [its spires] exactly the shape of hock bottles. . . . I think the anarchists showed bad taste in not blowing it up when they had the chance."[122] When Eusebi Güell, a Barcelona construction magnate who was Gaudí's major patron, died, it caused a marked change in the architect's attitudes. He refused to have his picture taken, or to talk to reporters; he was a vegetarian, and while wealthy, like modern celebrities who fancy themselves in "solidarity with the poor," dressed like a pauper. While at work on La Sagrada Familia in 1926, Gaudí was run over by a tram. He died three days later, leaving the cathedral incomplete. For seventy years, others attempted to finish the work, although their progress was interrupted by the Spanish Civil War, parts of the church were destroyed by Catalan anarchists, and plans for a high-speed underground train threatened to undermine the foundation.

As Gaudí toiled away on La Sagrada Familia and Wright struggled with the horror of the Taliesin murder/fire, a third architect with revolutionary ideas, Walter Gropius, completed the Fagus Werk shoe-shaping factory in Alfeld an der Leine, Germany. Unlike his contemporaries Wright and Gaudí, Gropius was called to duty in World War I and saw action as a reservist, fighting on the Western Front, where he was wounded. He returned to architecture after the war to found the Bauhaus ("House of Building") school, generally considered the first true modernist architectural style. In a Europe where Gaudí's excesses inspired love and hate, the clean and sterile modernist style of Gropius offered a simple alternative antidote. With generous use of glass and metal, Gropius was completely unlike the environmentally sensitive Wright—yet later Wright would borrow from (though never copy) the large flat surfaces and jutting floors that characterized Gropius's "Glass Chain" or "Crystal Chain" style.[123] Gropius, with his steel and glass, was nevertheless an expressionist, whose rounded turrets, transparent walls, and asymmetry had much in common with both the American and the Spaniard. Leaving Nazi Germany in 1934, Gropius soon moved to America. Ironically, in their later years, both Wright and Gropius designed structures for Iraq, Wright creating what would become Arizona State University's Grady Gammage Auditorium (intended for Baghdad) and Gropius laying out the University of Baghdad (later built by his colleagues at the Architects Collaborative in Cambridge, Massachusetts). By 1914, through grossly different styles, the three architectural revolutionaries of the modern age reflected different aspects of the tripartite nature of the human condition, man (Gropius), nature (Wright), and God (Gaudí).

It was left to a much different artist to express the conflict among the three. Thousands of miles to the east, Igor Stravinsky, coming off the international success of his ballet *The Firebird* in 1910, grappled with the nature of man in his new ballet. Obsessed with a project based on pagan ritual in which a "sacrificial virgin dances herself to death," Stravinsky's *Rite of Spring* pitted the beauty of the human form in the dance with the violence and conflict of nature as captured in a Russian spring.[124] That moment of upheaval "that seemed to begin in an hour . . . was like the whole earth cracking," he noted, and it was "the most wonderful event of every year of my childhood."[125] Obsessed by the polar opposites of Eros and Thanatos, Stravinsky epitomized the attitudes in Europe, where a new liberation of the possible stood on the precipice of a volcanic eruption of martial carnage such as the world had never seen. Perhaps it was fitting, then, that when *The Rite of Spring* was performed at the Théâtre des Champs-Elysées in 1913, it sparked a brawl inside the opera house. Catcalls led to heated arguments inside the theater, followed by a general riot in which Stravinsky partisans and critics pounded each other, ladies with their handbags and men in tuxedos rolling in the aisles.[126] Yet it was only a hint of the violence about to sweep Europe. Some men, such as Wright and Gaudí, would skate along its outside fringes, never dipping into the horror—Stravinsky, in fact, would move to Switzerland, briefly visit Russia in July 1914, and leave again for

Switzerland just before the borders were closed. Others, like Gropius, would narrowly avoid death in the conflagration.

In many respects the embodiment of art during this period was not the astounding architecture of the three giants, but the work of a painter—a Spaniard named Pablo Picasso. Born in 1881, Picasso dominated art in the twentieth century, and no artist was able to escape his influence. Whereas other artists, such as his friend Henri Matisse, tended to stay within certain bounds of their schools and techniques, Picasso forged ahead, entering new periods, developing new techniques, and innovating throughout his long life (he died at the age of ninety-one). A child prodigy, Picasso entered art school at thirteen, but at the age of sixteen went out on his own. His early works were divided into distinct periods: the Blue Period (1901–4), Rose (1905–7), African-influenced (1908–9), Cubism (1909–12), and Synthetic Cubism (1912–19). No sooner would an artist join Picasso in a period and follow his style than Picasso moved on to another one. A man of many contradictions, a scandalous personal life, and socialist/communist views, Picasso seemed to be the universal representative of those plying his craft and setting the standard of behavior, political involvement, and bohemianism for artists throughout Western Europe and even America. Not unsurprisingly, he remained neutral during World War I, sat out the Spanish Civil War, remained in Paris under the Nazis where he was unmolested, but toward the end of his life joined the Communist Party and took a hostile stance toward the United States. That much of his prosperity in fact derived from America and American patrons, and was repaid with antipathy, no doubt would have greatly interested his contemporary, the psychologist Sigmund Freud. Picasso was decadent and bourgeois to the core, refusing a divorce to protect his fortune, and running through a succession of young mistresses, then younger mistresses, until at last his energy gave out. His life acutely encapsulated the story of Europe in the first decades of the new century.

## Grand Illusions

Virtually no artists, architects, or musicians in 1914 anticipated what would happen that August, and in their views of a challenging but largely peaceful future they were scarcely different from most, for whom the prosperity of the age, combined with the seeming deep appreciation for the horrors of modern weapons, rendered future warfare inconceivable. Voices of the "war-is-impossible" view are well known. The leading proponent, Norman

Angell, saw his book *The Great Illusion* (1910) attain cult status. Angell clubs and organizations, more than forty in the major universities, took root and *The Great Illusion* was translated into eleven languages. Lectures on Angell's thesis resounded in the halls of Cambridge and the Sorbonne, although whether Angell's influence extended to kings and ministers remains a matter of debate. There could be no new war, Angell insisted. The cost was simply too great, even for the winner. National conflict would result in "commercial disaster, financial ruin and individual suffering," and the major powers knew it. So "pregnant with restraining influences" and so intertwined were the economies of Europe that war "becomes every day more difficult and improbable."[127]

Angell was lauded for his revolutionary views, except they were hardly revolutionary. Almost a decade earlier, a young member of Parliament, Winston Churchill, had likewise predicted that "a European war can only end in the ruin of the vanquished and the scarcely less fatal commercial dislocation and exhaustion of the conquerors."[128] Churchill noted that in previous ages, such factors as undeveloped transportation and the length of growing seasons limited conflicts, but in the modern age, he dourly warned, there could be no winners. Even with the recent memory of the Boer War fresh, "We do not know what war is. We have had a glimpse of it [and even] in miniature it is hideous and appalling."[129] (Twenty-first-century readers should remember Churchill whenever someone tries to use economic interdependence as an argument for why another world war is not possible.) No less than the highly respected economist John Maynard Keynes had claimed European interconnectedness had reached such remarkable levels that war was inconceivable. Should it come, however, he prophesied that such a war would not last more than a year after the first shots were fired. International bankers, however, trembled at the thought of markets torn asunder and debtors unable to repay.

The bankers were right. After August 1914, when the first shots of World War I were fired, the Rothschilds, the hardest hit firm in the world, lost 1.5 million pounds sterling and watched the company's capital fall by half over the next four years. Nor was the United States immune from the economic disaster war posed to the financial markets. Upon the Austrian declaration of war against Serbia, Wall Street values fell by 3.5 percent; the London market had to close on July 31, not reopening until the following January. The fact that the markets dropped so suddenly has led some to contend that capitalists were surprised, deluded by the prospects of peace.

Were they? The evidence points to businessmen and financiers being overtaken by politics and events beyond their control, and the answer must be a very qualified yes.

Moreover, while military spending made up a smaller share of the state budget, the state sector of the developed nations' economies had grown substantially large, and was increasing rapidly. In Germany, it was 18 percent of GNP in 1913; in Britain, 13 percent; and in Russia, Japan, and France, even more. Russia, hoping to force-feed industrialization, had two thirds of the railroads under government control, along with most of the gold and coal fields, factories, agriculture, and a state bank. Long before Japan had its Ministry of International Trade and Industry (MITI), Czar Nicholas II had a Ministry of Trade with agents on the boards of all trading companies and which dictated freight charges and set profits. One could say that long before the Communists took over, Russia was where the Progressives in America wanted to be.

As the winds of war grew irrepressible, the sense that nothing so terrible could happen to the Continent continued to reassure nations that some last-minute agreement would magically materialize. A dark, conspiratorial version of the "Dell Theory" also emerged: a handful of money men just would not allow a war to interrupt their profits. According to German banker Walther Rathenau in 1909, "Three hundred men, all of whom know one another, direct the economic destiny of Europe and choose their successors from among themselves."[130] (This view would prove quite durable: in 1921, the *Financial Times* still maintained that "half a dozen men at the top of the Big Five Banks could upset the whole fabric of government finance by refraining from renewing Treasury Bills."[131]) Whether because of the notion that people would never sacrifice their material pleasures to larger ideas, or because a handful of nefarious bankers controlled "the system," it was easy for Europeans to delude themselves into thinking war would not come.

Looking around Europe's major cities, the thought that anything would—*could*—interrupt the prosperous, relatively carefree lifestyle that had emerged in the late nineteenth century seemed ridiculous. John Maynard Keynes commented on this first era of "globalization" in 1901, noting that an upper-class Londoner could order food, products, and entertainments from around the world and expect they would be delivered to him. He could, as Keynes observed, "secure forthwith . . . cheap and affordable means of transit to any country or climate without passport or other formality," could send his servant "to the neighbouring office of a bank for such supply of the precious metals that might seem convenient," and could order by telephone "the various products of the whole earth [for] delivery upon his doorstep."[132] And with England at nearly full employment (there were only 100,000 registered paupers, mostly in London), it seemed all material needs were met.

The conquest of the poles left man dominant over all the globe; the death of poverty placed him above such mundane issues as daily existence. Through architecture and dance, art and song, it seemed as though man had transcended mud and blood, moving into a golden age. And yet disturbing evidence abounded that showed the harsh realities of war, political strife, revolution, poverty, and inadequacy not only remained, but had bubbled to the surface with jarring frequency. Whether through the steady buildup of great power alliances, the continued fracturing of the Ottoman Empire and the Young Turk revolution, or the cauldron boiling in the Balkans, "old" Europe was crumbling.

No nation was in more desperate straits than Russia. Despite attempts to modernize and create a Duma (the Russian parliament) in 1905 with a constitution that could pave the way for change, the Russian colossus had drifted too far behind its European cousins, leaving an opening for radicals to short-circuit a peaceful evolution. Count Sergei Witte, who advanced from stationmaster to the minister of finance from 1892 to 1903, had worked feverishly to bring Russia into the modern world. His greatest achievement, the Trans-Siberian Railroad, ran over 6,300 miles from the Polish border to Vladivostok. Constructed between 1891 and 1905, the railroad greatly facilitated the reinforcement of Moscow in 1941 when the Nazis were at the gates. Thus, it is a high irony that the Soviet Communists owed their survival to the man most responsible for bringing capitalism to Russia. By the time Witte was finished, railroads bound together one sixth of the earth's surface into a single—if dysfunctional—political unit.

Attempts by the Czars to push Russia into the modern age resulted in massive exports of such products as sugar, where Russian per capita consumption of 10.5 pounds per year compared with England's 92 pounds. Russia exported one quarter of its sugar in 1900 and 12 million pounds of cotton, even though its domestic per capita consumption was only 5.3 pounds compared with England's 39 pounds. Thus, the Russian monarchy was busy distorting the market as badly as the Communists would. The nation exported 60 percent of its domestic production of kerosene, and showed the folly of obsessing over a "favorable balance of trade," because the Russians constantly had a trade surplus, yet their people were falling further behind. Czars did encourage the growth of corporations—whose dollar value nearly doubled, thanks to foreign investment; and coal production rose more than twenty-fold from 1870 to 1900. But mechanical power remained almost unknown, standing at 1.6 horsepower per 100 persons in 1912 to twenty-five times that in the United States or twenty-four in England. Government-sanctioned cartels also kept production down: a dozen iron and steel firms controlled three quarters of all Russian production. In short, Russia abandoned free trade in 1891, and it was a smaller step to communism economically in Russia than was generally thought by most Westerners.

Russia's leading intellectuals did not help, either. The "slavophile" Russian writers, such as Alexei Khomiakov (1804–60), rejected reason completely, regarding it as "the mortal sin of the West." Fyodor Dostoyevsky (1821–81) wished to destroy all logic (and all arithmetic), seeking to "free humanity from the tyranny of two plus two equals four." Sex, many thought, was sinful. Leo Tolstoy (1828–1910) "considered all property and sex to be evil." Tolstoy denounced "most art and literature, including his own novels, as vain, irrelevant, and satanic." Tolstoy hated his own wife, "whom he came to regard as an instrument of his fall from grace," but he praised marriage without sex while other Russian authors praised sex without marriage![133]

Russia's precarious structure was set on course for a revolution, a destination virtually ignored by the rest of the world, which similarly paid no attention to the Eurasian giant's alliances and connections with other hotbeds of unrest, particularly in the Balkans. The golden age dreams and the grand illusions of 1900 turned sourly dark by 1910 for those who chose to look. Expressions of optimism and unity that had fallen so effortlessly from so many lips and dripped so easily from the ink of so many pens began, in the second decade of the twentieth century, to appear hollow. Instead, by 1914, Europe stood on the edge of a precipice, while American Progressives busied themselves attempting to manipulate, reform, and perfect what was already the world's preeminent nation. Even the cataclysm that followed would not deter them from attempting to remake society. Instead, they would expand their horizons to remake the world.

# CHAPTER TWO

# Cataclysm

## Time Line

1914: Archduke Franz Ferdinand assassinated; World War I begins (August 3); Battle of the Marne; Russians defeated at Battle of Tannenberg; United States declares neutrality

1915: Stalemate and trench war in the West; poison gas first used; Gallipoli campaign against Ottoman Empire; Italy joins allies, Bulgaria joins Central Powers; *Lusitania* sunk; Henry Ford sells Model T for under $500

1916: Battles of the Somme and Verdun; Brusilov Offensive on the Eastern Front; Battle of Jutland

1917: Zimmermann note; Czar Nicholas abdicates; Russian (March) Revolution; United States declares war on Central Powers; Russian (October) Revolution; Bolsheviks seize power

1918: Russia leaves war; last German offensives; French and American offensives in Ardennes; November 11 armistice; worldwide flu epidemic; Russian civil war

1919: Versailles Conference; Prohibition passed in United States

America emerged at a time when Europe, pacific and stable on the outside, was fraying on the inside. The internal upheaval, which would soon overtake the entire world, unfolded in many ways because European society and government lacked the traits that made the United States—for all its flaws—"exceptional" and different. The American abhorrence of titles and nobility, the widespread availability of property to all who had even the smallest savings, and social strata that permitted easy ascension (and fall) provided the United States with moorings that European nations not only lacked, but which, by their absence, created tensions that could not be mitigated except by violence on a massive scale. Given the still-dominant and inbred system of monarchs, along with militaristic aggressiveness by second-rate countries, both exacerbated by invisible alliances that could suck a great power into a mortal struggle with an enemy of equal might, the stage was set for a European cataclysm.

## The Future of War

Few doubted the biblical-level destruction that war threatened to wreak on Europe. A sobering portrait of such a landscape came from Ivan S. Bloch, a Polish Jew, banker, and railroad financier obsessed with modern warfare. Still clinging to the Norman Angell/Winston Churchill position that war was obsolete, Bloch produced a six-volume analysis called *La Guerre Future* (1898), which was condensed and translated into English as *Is War Now Impossible?* Armed with the new Maxim gun (soon improved upon with Browning's light air-cooled machine gun), long-range artillery, smokeless powder, and rifled barrels, military forces could decimate units moving in open ground. The bayonet charge was now a thing of the past; cavalry, hopelessly out of date as an offensive force (although it would take multiple military disasters to prove the point). Defensive forces, dug in behind earthworks and entrenchments, fronted by the new barbed wire and acres of land mines, would have a massive advantage. Perhaps war was not impossible, but had not the previous century shown that "civilized powers" rarely fight one another? Between 1879 and 1917, of the 270 wars recorded, fewer than a third of them were fought in Europe, although those that did occur always threatened to engulf the major powers. Another indicator of belligerence, military spending, was also down among the Western nations. Russia, the leader, spent 4 percent of national product on its military, but Germany and Britain spent only 3 percent, and only France and Germany had even 1 percent of their populations in the armed forces (France at 1.5 percent was the leader).[1] And, as we have seen, the U.S. Army was minuscule compared with the Europeans' land forces.

This in no way invalidates the arguments that "militarism," however one defines it, did not contribute significantly toward the war. But the proliferation of weapons didn't dictate the rise of militaristic attitudes—the process is vice versa. Germany had implemented a reserve system that allowed quick access to vast manpower pools, a factor in both the strategic planning of the German General Staff and the belligerence of the Kaiser at opportune times. Many hoped, however, that the hostile attitudes and aggressiveness of the military leadership, particularly in Germany, could be curbed by marriages between Europe's royal families. But in the end, these blood relationships mattered little. None of Old Europe's leaders were "men of the people," few commanded widespread personal loyalty, and in any event, the monarchs of 1914 could not veto war plans drawn up by their military high commands. Kaiser Wilhelm II would argue for redirecting the German war effort away from France, but in vain. In Russia, the Czar was insulated from public audit, while at the same time fearing a democratic uprising on the one hand and aristocratic backstabbing on the other.

Important pockets of optimism could be found across Europe—the Germans had an annual growth rate of almost 3 percent in their GDP—but in many cases this represented a recent burst, not as in the United States, where the GDP had averaged almost 4 percent growth annually since the Civil War and occasionally approached 7 percent. Nevertheless, European growth constituted a continuing trend. Land reform had begun in Russia, slowly, to be sure, but significant in its potential. Inflation in the West was low due to the gold standard, business—especially American business, after the Panic of 1893—was prospering, and wages were rising. Cities, though dirty and crowded, had an air of expectation and hope.

No city denied the approaching storm clouds of chaos and blood more than Paris, which (aside from Brussels) had the most to lose in a continental conflagration. Paris had recovered from the Prussian invasion of 1870 to stake its claim as the "New Jerusalim," [sic] although it was hardly holy. To many the city seemed to embody urban perfection by human hands, thanks to its art, culture, and fashion. Journalist William Shirer called the French capital "as near to paradise on this earth as any man could ever get," and writer Harold Rosenberg described Paris in 1940 as "the Holy Place of our time. The only one."[2] Thomas Appleton said Paris was where good Americans went when they died. By 1900, Paris was not only architecturally interesting, with its Eiffel Tower and Sacré-Coeur, but also morally provocative. Its lenient censorship laws "permitted entertainment and publications that would have had little chance of survival elsewhere in Europe," and its "ambiguous morality" encouraged brothels, cafés, low-level drugs, and saloons, all mixing with the contradictory odors of fine perfume, auto exhaust, and horse dung.[3]

Others saw an emptiness, a *mal*, a cynicism that "gnaws at us," as Georges Clemenceau observed, a Paris that drifted into lethargy, spreading a malaise that affected the rest of the country. Nevertheless, France still carried a Napoleonic longing for achievement, grandeur, and accomplishment that it would never achieve again. For despite an affinity with foreign artists, dancers, and composers at the turn of the century—especially Strauss and Mussorgsky (who died in 1881 but remained quite popular)—France seemed to rebel against anything French.

One critic, decrying that domestic art had descended into chaos and spectacle, complained that foreign styles were "barbarism," and in frustration concluded, *"Plus d'école, mais une poussière de talents; plus de corps, mais des individus"* ("No school any longer, only a smattering of talent; no group any longer, only individuals")[4]. In short, France suffered from a crisis of confidence concealed by bursts of artistic energy in a decaying edifice of French culture and past glories, a few real, but most imagined. There was no industry or entrepreneurship, leaving wags of the day to joke, "Three Englishmen start a business, three Germans start a war, three Frenchmen start five political parties."

## Condescension and Self-Doubt

France's *mal* was a source of contempt for aristocratic Germans, who did not suffer France's lack of self-esteem. The Second Reich was willpower on steroids: "Since we have no Bismarck among us," complained liberal historian Friedrich Meinecke, "every one of us must be a piece of Bismarck."[5] No concept more penetrated the average intellect typified by Wilhelm II than that of will. Of course, along with will came power and triumph. No one—at least until Western liberals, especially American, of the late twentieth century came on the scene—set out to undermine their own societies and cultures. Even the liberal Left accepted the proposition that in Germany, "there is a single will in everyone, the will to assert oneself."[6] One student announced, "We will conquer! . . . With such a powerful will to victory nothing else is possible."[7] That *Kultur*—that self-esteem—derived in large part from war, a "life-giving principle," as General Friedrich von Bernhardi labeled it in 1911. The author Ludwig Thoma, writing from Munich on the eve of the conflict, recorded, "I was struck by the impression of how this courageous and industrious people has to purchase with its blood the right to work and to create values for mankind."[8] Students in Bavarian universities were summoned to arms in August 1914 with the call, "Students! The muses are silent. The issue is battle. . . . [German *Kultur*] is threatened by barbarians from the east . . . and the holy war begins."[9] The "desire for peace has rendered most civilized nations anaemic," wrote von Bernhardi, an aspiration which was "directly antagonistic" to universal laws.[10]

But even Germany possessed a powerful internal counterweight, a large number of socialists and working-class who did not always buy into the call of "will." Kaiser Wilhelm sensed these undercurrents, and struggled to make sufficient incremental reforms to appease the more radical elements, while at the same time not threatening the established landed classes. The Second Reich suffered from deep structural problems and had seen chancellors come and go with increasing regularity, each unable to substantively address Germany's internal tensions. Germany had been united for less than forty-five years, and the nation was still young, vigorous, and finding itself with some difficulty in structure and means, but not in determining the ultimate goal.

At the outbreak of World War I, all across Europe, the young clamored for war, leaving for the front with enthusiasm as the older generation accepted the conflict with grim resignation and helplessness. Young French writers Charles Péguy, Henry de Montherlant, and Pierre Drieu La Rochelle joined Germans Walter Flex, Ernest Wurch, and Ernst Jünger and Brits Robert Nichols and Rupert Brooke (who would die in action) in describing war as "purgative," a "marvelous surprise," "a fine thrill," "a privilege," or a "holy moment."[11] In contrast to later intellectuals, musicians, and celebrities of the Vietnam era, who pompously declared war vile and pointless, the European opinion makers wanted, as Arthur van den Bruck put it, "an insurrection of the sons against the fathers," precisely *for* war. Afterward, when the casualty lists and endless graves blasted them with reality, these same energetic belligerents would sing a different tune—or rather, write a different verse. British writers and poets, especially, immersed themselves in the senselessness of the carnage, losing all enthusiasm for causes and even alternative outcomes. R. C. Sherriff, Robert Graves, Isaac Rosenberg, Maurice Baring, and the aforementioned Nichols all turned to defeatism, nihilism, and gloom.

But that was only after four years of the most grotesque combat the

world had seen. Earlier, in 1914, attitudes were different. This was especially true in Germany, where belligerence was fueled by perceptions that
others did not respect Germany properly, an attitude strengthened by alliances between the British and French. Affronts had piled up in the German
mind. France had built the Suez Canal with virtually no German assistance: at first, even Britain opposed it until changes in the proposed tonnage rates convinced British investors to agree to a new protocol in 1873.
But Germany, still organizing itself as a nation, played almost no role in the
Canal and policies were dictated to her until the First World War. In 1903,
Germans experienced a new slight when, after partnering with the British
to collect Venezuelan debts, President Cipriano Castro had refused to
honor his country's obligations, whereupon England, Italy, and Germany
imposed a blockade. Castro gave in, but Germany emerged a loser when the
British press ripped English politicians for "allying" with her. That incident
was followed by a British insult involving the Baghdad Railroad in 1911.
The project, designed to link Turkey and the Tigris-Euphrates Valley, was
too large for German capitalists. When London investors seemed sympathetic—needing only government assurances—Parliament backed down in
another public firestorm. German capitalists, thinking their financing was
assured, had already laid two hundred miles of track when the financing
was pulled, leaving investors with a train to nowhere.

## Stumbling to Global Conflict
Both the Boer War, in which Germany supported the Boers behind the
scenes, and the Moroccan Crisis (1905–6), where former antagonists Britain and France reached an accord, shocked the Germans and convinced the
Kaiser that he was aligned against a constellation of enemies. "We shall be
unable to make any overseas acquisitions," he noted after the accord.
"Against France and England an overseas policy is impossible."[12] German
resentment toward France and Britain was reignited with the Agadir Crisis
of 1911, when a German attempt to gain a foothold in Morocco through
"gunboat diplomacy" was thwarted high-handedly by the French (with
quiet and reluctant support from Britain). After a settlement in which Germany gained territory in the former French Congo in exchange for territory near Cameroon and an acknowledgment of the French protectorate in
Morocco, many Germans felt the game was rigged. The deal received sharp
criticism from the German press.

Such developments were taken as insults to the German character. "We must secure to German nationality and German spirit throughout the globe that high esteem which is due them . . . and has hitherto been withheld," insisted Prussian general and military historian Friedrich von Bernhardi.[13] German resentment toward England, Russia, and France continued to build until 1914. After Austria delivered an ultimatum to Serbia, demanding an end to all anti-Austrian propaganda, a crackdown on Serbian dissidents, and the removal of anyone from military or government service who had anti-Austrian sentiments, the Kaiser received a telegram from his ambassador in Russia indicating Russia would support Serbia. Looking at it, he responded, "I have no doubt left about it: England, Russia and France have agreed among themselves—after laying the foundations of the *casus foederis* . . . through Austria—to take the Austro-Serbian conflict as an *excuse* for waging a *war of extermination* against us."[14] Thus German paranoia, seemingly fully justified due to political, moral, and physical assaults from a perceived strangling circle of enemies, pushed the country over the brink.

The combination of insult and the alliance of Britain and Russia with France spurred even German intellectuals to build a case for war, viewing it as an unpleasant but inevitable instrument of national policy, which could spark national revival, even the resurrection of Europe. Although later many of them would sing a different tune, in 1914, observers looked forward to a time when "after the pain of this war there would be a free, beautiful, and happy Germany."[15] War was like childbirth: bloody, but necessary to create new life. German writers described the onset of bloodshed as "liberation from bourgeois narrowness and pettiness" and "a vacation from life."[16] Hermann Hesse lectured that struggle was "good for many Germans" and that "a genuine artist would find greater value in a nation of men who have faced death and who know the immediacy and freshness of camp life."[17] Emil Ludwig, later a critic of martial sentiments such as these, harbored no such doubts at the moment of the first German offensive, when he was unabashed in his support for war: "even if a catastrophe were to befall us such as no one dares to imagine, the moral victory [of August 1914] could never be eradicated."[18] Another novelist, Ernst Glaser, wrote of the world around him, "The war had made it beautiful."[19] Art, poetry, philosophy—these were what the war was fought over, claimed another. "An aesthetic pleasure without compare," said a character in a German novel, describing combat.[20] War was an effort on behalf of Europe itself. "Let us remain soldiers even after the war," said Franz Marc, "for this is not a war against an eternal enemy. . . . it is a *European civil war*, a war against the inner invisible enemy of the European spirit."[21] Where the British waged war to preserve traditional social values and civilization, Germany aspired to spiritual greatness as the protector and propagator of the "true European Spirit" much like it had been during the Holy Roman Empire. Germany was "propelled by a vision, the British by a legacy."[22]

Even then, the Kaiser and his advisers were cautious. Desperate to avoid being the odd man out of a European alliance system, Germany had blustered and bullied, foolishly allowing nonaggression pacts with Russia to expire. Even worse, the infamous Schlieffen Plan to sweep through the flat plains of Belgium into France ensured that two more enemies—Belgium and Britain (because of her traditional concern about access to northern European ports)—would be aligned against her. Whereas Germany's national inferiority complex propelled her in one direction, France, having solidified the Russian alliance, drifted in another, overconfident of her military abilities.

French bellicosity swelled in the years before the war as the nations quietly prepared for conflict. Subscribing to concepts of the *offensive à outrance* and *élan* ("offense to excess," or "hit 'em with everything you got," and "fighting spirit"), the French developed a mirror strategy to the one they knew Germany would most likely employ in the event of war, namely a sweep from the north through Belgium, even if the Belgians denied them free passage. Thus the French response would be to blast through the Ardennes on the German left flank—just as Germany was swinging around the French left flank—meaning that in both cases, strategy would to a great degree determine policy rather than vice versa. All in all, the respective war plans had put all Europe on a hair trigger of mobilization, made worse by the German plans to disregard Belgium's neutral rights if and when war came. In previous wars, nonbelligerent nations had frequently allowed foreign armies passage through their territory, provided they pay for damages. German planners still clung to their hope that Belgium would relent and not resist.

The wood and tinder were firmly in place and all that was needed was the proverbial spark. That came on June 28, 1914, in Sarajevo, when Gavrilo Princip, part of a group of six high-school-aged South Slav nationalists, nervously waited for the car carrying Austrian Archduke Franz Ferdinand, guns and grenades in hand.

## Assassination by Accident

History is rife with seemingly minor incidents that turn the course of the world. Soldiers from General George McClellan's army found General Robert E. Lee's battle orders with a package of cigars before the battle of Antietam. Abraham Lincoln's assassin succeeded only because a guard was away from his post at Ford's Theatre. Theodore Roosevelt, running for president in 1912, was in point-blank range of John Schrank's gun when a bystander deflected the bullet's path just enough so that Roosevelt's folded, fifty-page speech absorbed the shot and stopped the bullet short of his heart. The impact of any of those turns of fate is debatable, though one would be hard pressed to argue that any were more earth-shattering than the chain of events that followed the death of the archduke and his wife, Sophie, in Sarajevo in 1914.

While on his way to make a routine diplomatic speech, Franz Ferdinand, the Hapsburg heir apparent, rode with his wife Sophie Chotek, a low-ranking Bohemian aristocrat whom he had married out of love, down the avenue bordering the Miljacka embankment of Sarajevo, unaware that it was lined with assassins. While the couple was en route, four of the would-be killers got cold feet. One who did not hurled a grenade at the party: it blew out a front tire on the following car, slightly wounding the military governor's aide-de-camp. After stopping to look after the wounded officer, Franz Ferdinand doggedly continued to city hall. The military governor prevailed on him to forgo the remaining events, and the archduke decided to alter his course and drive to the hospital to inquire about the aide-de-camp on his way back to his train. As the procession started toward the hospital, the lead chauffeur turned in error to follow the scheduled route, and the military governor told the cars to stop. They did, leaving the archduke less than ten feet away from Princip, who was standing on the sidewalk. The assassin fired two shots at point-blank range, killing both the archduke and Sophie.

Immediate reaction was restrained—after all, political assassinations were common at the time, and at least a dozen Austrian leaders had been shot at in the previous few years. Not only had President William McKinley been assassinated in 1901, but between 1898 and 1913 no fewer than forty political figures had been killed, including six prime ministers and four kings, among them King George I of Greece. Almost all of the assassinations had been carried out by leftists or anarchists. The Balkans alone had seen eight successful assassinations, but this one in particular was directly tied to the expanded influence of a Serbian state working for the independence of southern Slavic states from Austria-Hungary, which the Austro-Hungarians felt could not be permitted out of fear that a Slavic-Serbian state might ally with Russia. And there were larger forces at work than the Austro-Serbian conflict: the Balkan states had fought several successful mini-wars against the Ottoman Empire to greatly diminish its power in Europe, while both Russia and Austria suddenly faced restless nationalities inflamed by the success of the Bulgarians and Serbs in evicting the Turks. Russia, having failed in 1908 to support Serbia against Austria, could not abandon a Slavic ally a second time, while the Austrians wanted to institutionalize their informal protectorate over Serbia. The subsequent ultimatum issued to Serbia was so strong as to constitute a virtual declaration of war. Backed by its allies the Germans, Austria delivered its message to Belgrade on July 23 (hence its name the "July ultimatum") and began mobilizing. Serbia had forty-eight hours to comply with Austrian demands. Immediately, however, the Serbs received another secret telegram—of support from Russia. Wheels of war rapidly spun, with no one any longer in control of the throttle. European military leaders, politicians, and monarchs suddenly realized what had been set in motion. French premier René Viviani, a Socialist, called for his country to pull back from the borders by ten kilometers, terrified that "war might burst from a clump of trees, from a meeting of two patrols, from a threatening gesture . . . a black look, a brutal word, a shot!"[23] Another powerful antiwar voice, Socialist Jean Jaurès, had opposed France's Three-Year Law, which required young Frenchmen to serve three years in the military. Modern romantic notions that Jaurès alone could have halted the acceleration to war are unrealistic, but forever unanswered, as on July 31, 1914, a nationalist assassin killed Jaurès in a Paris café. The president of the Chamber of Deputies eulogized Jaurès, saying, "There are no more adversaries here, there are only Frenchmen."[24] Indeed, the entire French Socialist movement had joined the "establishment" over the previous twenty years; now, to prove their loyalty, Socialists had to support the war—a position most regretted within the year, and one which permanently reversed the movement's willingness to engage in a compromise of convenience.

Miscalculations abounded on both sides. France and Russia assumed that the obvious weight of populations aligned against Germany would forestall hostilities—especially if England and Belgium were thrust into the Allied camp. Britain dallied to embarrass the Germans, all the while appearing resolute in her support for France and Belgium. The war speech by the foreign secretary, Sir Edward Grey, when it finally came, began with such conciliation to Germany that a Tory minister whispered to another, "By God, they are going to desert Belgium!"[25]

Confidence in both German and French militaries led the main belligerents to conclude that each could defeat the other, and indeed, do so quite rapidly. Had most of the leaders truly believed they were in for a war of four years and deaths in the millions, they might well have redoubled their efforts for peace. But this wasn't the only monumental miscalculation: a string of incomprehensible smaller errors compounded juvenile attachments to cavalry on both sides and, in the case of the French, outrageously silly uniforms with red pants. When some wiser heads attempted to replace the garish French colors with camouflage gray or khaki, they were shouted down with thunderous derision. Bright uniforms, claimed the *Echo de Paris*, were mainstays of French "taste and military function," and a former war minister during a hearing on adopting different uniforms exclaimed "Eliminate the red trousers? Never! *Le pantalon rouge c'est la France!*"[26]

Major General Sir Henry Wilson, commander of Britain's IV Corps in France, confidently wrote in his diary that his forces would be in Germany in three weeks—an astonishing statement in retrospect, but no less detached from military reality than Santa Anna's rash prediction that he would lead Mexican armies into Washington, D.C., during the Mexican War. Horrific initial losses hardly changed opinions: as late as January 1915, General Douglas Haig said the Allies could "walk through the German line at several places" as soon as they got sufficient artillery ammunition.[27]

To be sure, there were voices of caution, men who knew combat up close and had tasted the murderous fire of modern guns. Germany's corpse-like Field Marshal Helmut von Moltke (the elder) had predicted in 1890 that a future war could last for years. His thinking wore off on his nephew, von Moltke the younger—cited for bravery as a grenadier, but by 1906 the German chief of staff—who instructed the Kaiser that the next war "will be a national war which will not be settled by a decisive battle but by a long wearisome struggle . . . which will utterly exhaust our own people, even if we are victorious."[28] Britain's Lord Horatio Herbert Kitchener, appointed as secretary of state for war in August 1914, also knew the lethality of modern weapons all too well. He had seen rapid-fire guns up close in the Franco-Prussian War where, at age twenty, he fought with the French army as a volunteer, then witnessed his own Maxim guns and artillery shred the Mahdi army at Omdurman, and experienced heavy losses at the Battle of Paardeberg at the hands of the Boers. Suddenly placed in charge of the British military effort, Kitchener stunned the Imperial Staff when he told them to "be prepared to put armies of millions into the field and maintain them for several years."[29] Britain originally had planned to send six infantry and one cavalry division, scarcely 150,000 men, to support the French but cut that almost immediately to an anemic four infantry divisions out of concern that Britain herself might be invaded. Now Kitchener was instructing the government that victory would require a British army of *seventy divisions*, and mobilization could not attain those levels for three years, "implying," as historian Barbara Tuchman noted, "the staggering corollary that the war would last that long."[30] Kitchener's views were often ridiculed in the high command, most notably by Sir Henry Wilson, who labeled Lord Kitchener "mad" and "as much an enemy of England as Moltke."[31]

Even when confronted with intelligence about the size of German forces, both British and French generals dismissed the information. On August 11, when Sir John French met with the chief of British intelligence, French's deputy director of operations was dumbstruck at the German numbers being suggested. "He kept on producing fresh batches of Reserve Divisions and Extra-Reserve Divisions," French sputtered, "like a conjurer producing glassfuls of goldfish out of his pocket."[32] France's intelligence officers were relating similar information, yet General Joseph Joffre refused to believe it. Only Kitchener had no trouble envisioning a million Germans sweeping through Belgium and into northern France. When Germany, having declared war on Russia on August 1, and unsuccessfully cajoled and threatened the Belgians to allow their troops free passage through Belgian territory, sent military columns to plow through Belgium two days later, the twentieth century greeted its first mass war.

The German High Command believed Belgium would permit millions of German soldiers to march across their territory without resistance, and were therefore shocked at the tenacity and hatred they encountered once the invasion started. After all, God was on the side of Germany (the German belt buckles said so with *Gott mit uns* or "God is with us"), and Germany needed transit through Belgium to eliminate the threat to its national existence. The natural invasion route in Europe was across the North German Plain, a flat expanse broken only by man-made obstacles and rivers from Flanders to Russia. In German eyes, the Flemish were essentially

German, and German soldiers had come to the aid of Belgium many times in history against the French. A small nation of seven million did not have the right to deny passage to a major power, which would, after all, recompense the Belgians for any and all damage. Going the extra mile, the German High Command considered a neutral's defense of its own territory against German troops passing through illegal. The German military manual, *The Usages of War on Land*, issued in 1902, stated that "if a neutral did not stop one belligerent from marching through, that belligerent's opponent was free to do battle on neutral territory, and a neutral that disregarded its duties had to give satisfaction or compensation."[33]

Since the German General Staff assumed the French would or already had moved into Belgium with the declaration of war by France on Germany, the German Army was free, indeed obligated, to defend itself against the Belgians. In the German view, Belgium had constructed forts on its eastern border facing Germany, but none facing France (at least no major ones), so rather than being neutral, Belgium was actually a belligerent allied with France and England. In the event, it seemed the whole world except for Belgium knew the Germans would attack across Belgium—the French assumed it and the British planned on it.

## "Belgium's Misery"

After briefly assaulting the fortresses around Liège in costly frontal attacks, the Germans hauled up monster cannons, including the Austrian-built Skoda 305s, which, transported in three pieces, could move only twenty miles a day. German iron and steel giant Friedrich Krupp AG had fabricated an even more imposing weapon, the 420, of which only five were in existence when the shooting started. Even slower and more cumbersome than the Skoda guns, the 420s reached the front a week after Germans first entered Belgium; the "overfed slugs" stupefied everyone when they fired their first rounds on August 12. The shells took a full minute to travel to their targets, and the compression and shock of firing was so severe that the guns were triggered from three hundred yards away. Loaders and other members of the 285-man crew remaining close to the gun had ear padding, plugs, eye protection, and lay prone during firing for further safety. Suddenly, Belgian forts that had resisted wave after wave of crack German infantry now surrendered after forty massive explosions.

But the Belgian fortresses bought precious time, adding days to von Moltke's delicate schedule, made flesh by the workaholic general Erich Ludendorff, deputy chief of staff for the German 2nd Army. Described as "friendless and forbidding," Ludendorff had gained a place on the General Staff at age thirty, and directing the bombardment of Liège now reassured everyone that Count von Schlieffen had it right, and that flee or fight, Belgium would be only an annoyance.[34] Part of that confidence emanated from the massive artillery, ponderous though it was. Part of it came from his personal experience. Ludendorff may have been a caricature of the monocled German militarist, but he was also absolutely fearless. Sensing that the bombardment of Liège was taking too long, he found a brigade whose commander had been killed and led it forward into the city. He ordered his adjutant to drive him to the Citadel. Somehow they made it through swarms of Belgian soldiers in the city to the Citadel's gates, which he pounded on with the pommel of his sword. They opened, and Ludendorff found himself facing a mob of Belgian soldiers. He demanded they surrender, and the Citadel fell to the two German officers.[35]

Most of Ludendorff's faith in the Schlieffen Plan, however, derived from the meticulous logistical planning of the German General Staff, all dependent on railroads and essentially stopping at the Belgian border. Germany moved 550 trains a day across the Rhine, including one every ten minutes crossing the Hohenzollern Bridge at Cologne. France's rail network responded, shifting around three million troops in seven thousand trains. Germany's rail mobilization plan dwarfed that of the Russians, who had one fourth as many railroads, and who had deliberately built rail gauges wider than the Germans' so as to impede invasions. But once the battle reached Germany, it meant the Russians would have to stop and switch trains at the border. But the implications of this, while unforeseen, scarcely figured into von Schlieffen's calculations, as he intended to have already forced a French surrender by the time Mother Russia slothfully mobilized, which, according to his timeline, would take forty days.

Von Schlieffen never planned on the near-suicidal Belgian resistance. Nor did any of the German High Command expect efforts by Belgian civilians, few as they were, to slow down, tie up, and harass German columns. Already inflated by the morality and justness of their cause, the German soldiers were shocked and outraged that the Belgians did not welcome them as friends but as invaders. Shortly following the first incidents of sniping, property destruction, and simple insubordination, German commanders began posting stark warnings about brutal punishment for anyone remotely interfering with their "visit." The extreme overreaction by Germans at all levels was rooted in their experience during the Franco-Prussian War, when French *franc-tireur*s (free shooters) or civilian snipers took a heavy toll of German soldiers after the French were defeated. The actions by these guerrillas did not affect the outcome of the war, but substantially raised German casualties and caused the Germans to consider all such citizen actions dishonorable and unlawful.

At first, only suspected guerrillas were arrested or shot; then hostages were taken—the city council, mayor, or other important local persons; then randomly one of every ten men were held and then both men and women were shot in reprisal; then finally substantial groups of civilians were shot and their villages put to the torch. At Namur, 2nd Army commander Colonel General Karl von Bülow took ten hostages per street, all to be shot if any German was fired upon by a local. At nearby Andenne during the Battle of Charleroi, following an incident in which Germans claimed townspeople had shot at them, between one hundred and two hundred civilians were executed.

Dozens of small towns were looted, others burned, including Louvain in late August 1914, with its magnificent library of more than 250,000 volumes and 750 medieval manuscripts. Hugh Gibson, then with the American legation, went with officials from other nations to investigate the reports on August 28, only to find the Germans boasting of their destruction. Troops moved from house to house, stealing valuables and setting fires, as the officer in charge ranted to the international observers, "We shall wipe it out, not one stone will stand on top of another. . . . We will teach them to respect Germany."[36]

Some of the most brutal pillaging occurred at Dinant, two days before Louvain was burned, when troops under General Max von Hausen accused Belgians of "perfidious" activity, including interference with bridge rebuilding, and arrested hundreds of civilians. Forcing them into the town square, the grenadiers ordered the men to one side, women to the other, then firing squads—shooting in opposite directions—mowed down the townspeople. As at Louvain, troops then looted what remained of the town. The resistance by the small Belgian army and the unreasonable German fear of civilian guerrillas helped doom the German right wing attack as the Germans had to siphon off excessive numbers of troops to maintain their lines of communication. Without question, the Germans reacted harshly and, in some instances, hysterically to the reports of franc-tireurs.

German troops and officers claimed to see violent resistance at every turn, ignoring evidence that the resistance either broke out spontaneously or was nonexistent (in some cases nervous German troops fired on other Germans), and in no way was directed by the government. Invoking "international law," the Germans unsuccessfully attempted to claim the moral high ground for their barbarism. Most of the world rejected their rationalizations. "Brave Little Belgium" became an international symbol of courage and hope in British propaganda while Germans were increasingly portrayed in posters, cartoons, and newspapers as "Huns," replete with bearskin capes and blood-drenched fangs.

Although atrocities had been regularly visited on civilian populations throughout history before 1914—and indeed were simply viewed as ordinary side effects of war—Germany had signed the Hague Conventions of 1899 and 1907 that attempted to establish rules of law to govern warfare between civilized nations. It was recognized that rebellions, civil wars, and conflicts with backward countries such as those encountered in colonial conquests were often extremely brutal by necessity and therefore exempt from such rules. America's Civil War demonstrated that guerrilla atrocities were normal for such conflicts; Britain had responded to Boer resistance with civilian "concentration camps" during the Boer War; and *all* the European nations had horrific records of incivility in their colonial conflicts. But 1914 was different—this was a civilized nation, perhaps the most civilized in Europe—systematically inflicting atrocities on a small, helpless country of other Europeans. Historian Jeff Lipkes has effectively proven that the execution of Belgian civilians was part of an intentional policy of brutally subduing the Belgians by the German army and German occupation authorities.[37] Ultimately, however, Progressive governments had not expected this and later refused to learn from the example, creating further treaties to curb excesses in war that were notable mainly for their failure to have any positive effect. While burnings of homes and buildings in the Great War would later be considered almost inconsequential in comparison with those of World War II, the number of civilian deaths raised an immediate outcry because it was so visible to the press and because it was one "civilized" state abusing another. Approximately 5,521 Belgian civilians (and 906 French) were executed by the Germans.[38] But in a larger sense, the "Rape of Belgium" continued throughout the entire war. Belgians were forced to work on German entrenchments, and large numbers were deported to Germany for work in German industries. Food supplies were cut, and all Belgians in German-occupied territory suffered greatly. The Belgian economy was wrecked, all productivity was subordinate to German direction, and Belgium even paid large indemnities to Germany during the war, setting the table for the Allies to demand reparations from Germany in 1919.

Significantly, attempts to criminalize wartime actions and bring Germans accused of atrocities to account through trials after the war largely came to naught. Previous treaties ending wars amnestied those committing possible criminal behavior, and Germany successfully arranged for war crimes trials to be held in Leipzig under German law. Those few individuals who stood trial were either found not guilty or given light sentences. The British lost interest in prosecuting war crimes by 1921 and the French by 1925.[39] Nonetheless, the principles leading to Nuremberg and the four new Geneva Conventions starting in 1949 had been established (more or less) for warfare between "civilized" nations, and the historical significance of Belgium's misery reached far beyond the four years of German occupation in World War I. Neither France nor Britain launched any serious operation to rescue "Brave Little Belgium," since Belgium was of little value to the Allies militarily. After all, the Belgian army consisted of only six divisions—a pair of bloated Prussian corps, or about 117,000 men—ill trained and dispersed through the fortress system. Aside from the forts, there was no Belgian artillery, and the Germans had twice as many machine guns per soldier. According to prewar plans, Britain took up positions near Mons and Dinant to block the German right wheel, assuming defensive positions. Earlier bluster about sending five French infantry divisions was quickly dismissed. Instead, three divisions of French cavalry scouts rode 110 miles in three days, passing gallantly through Belgian villages, their cuirasses shining and their black horse-hair plumes streaming. Sobbing townspeople and bands playing the "Marseillaise" greeted them, assuming the Allies had come to the rescue. But the French brushed within miles of Liège without even dismounting, then turned to explore the Ardennes, their reconnaissance complete.

These realities raised three important points about the new nature of the war. First, heavy automatic firepower brought to an end the era of cavalry—and the end of infantry attacks in line or column as well. The age of massed formations, brightly colored uniforms, and decisive battles had vanished with the saber. Bloch's black vision had become flesh. While hand-to-hand combat still constituted a necessary reality of warfare, the range at which death was dealt had expanded by an order of magnitude or more from just a century earlier.

The second reality of the new war was that the mobility of armies stretched beyond the area where traditional communications technologies were effective—tanks, for example, still relied on flags for orders, and there was insufficient wire communication to allow officers to stay in contact with forward troops. World War I was the only conflict in human history wherein commanders lacked real links to the battlefield. It has been suggested that this accounted for more loss of life than even the presence of automatic weapons. Previous eras had seen units directed by voice, bugle, drum, or flag. While imprecise and unreliable, those forms of communication nevertheless fit the speed of combat. Massed formations of troops firing muskets could discern whether they were advancing or retreating based on the movement of the flag and the call of the bugle. While generals of armies, such as Marshal Ney at Waterloo, Ulysses S. Grant at Shiloh, or Lord Raglan at Balaclava, attempting to see the big picture from an elevated position, could find themselves dangerously misinformed or might dispatch ill-written orders via runner or rider, the battlefield of 1914 had expanded beyond the capabilities of any person to visually comprehend it. That opened the way for radio—except in 1914, radio communication (especially on the field of combat) was ludicrously unreliable, uneven, and cumbersome. A few grasped the importance of electronic communication: when U.S. general John "Black Jack" Pershing arrived in France in 1917, he immediately ordered the Army Signal Corps to string twenty-two thousand miles of telephone lines to his Chaumont headquarters, leasing an additional twelve thousand miles of line from the French. Pershing also requested four hundred American telephone operators fluent in French to facilitate communication and cooperation between the armies.[40] Boasting that the female telephone operators "will do as much to win the war as the men in khaki," Pershing also understood that the preexisting familiarity with telephone technology made training and the facility with phone communication vastly easier. In America, there were 14 telephones per one hundred people as opposed to only 1.5 telephones per hundred persons in France, meaning that frequently American men or women arrived on the scene with telephone skills.[41] However, for most of the war, the men in the trenches were rarely in direct contact with headquarters, and even less so when they left the trenches to attack.

Finally, European powers had been engaged for almost a century fighting natives in the colonies. Having largely ignored the U.S. Civil War with its stunningly high casualties (the Union lost 30 percent of the troops committed at Fredericksburg; Lee lost a similar percentage at Gettysburg) and then downplayed experiences in the Franco-Prussian War or the Boer War, Europeans had disregarded the lessons of almost a thousand years of Western military history. The recurring message was that Western armies and navies, when arrayed against non-Westerners, employed technology and precise drill, backed by a culture of individual rights and private property, to elevate their ability to kill on a massive scale. Those trends, as Victor Davis Hanson has shown, dated well back to the Greeks, resulting in combat success unparalleled in the rest of the world, and with the invention of firearms, especially automatic weapons and long-range cannon, the margin of victory grew even larger. Lost in this narrative, however, was the obvious corollary that when Western armies fought other Western armies, the carnage could be unprecedented, particularly in light of the staggering rise in firepower.

That the French still touted the bayonet charge and relied on *élan*, and that all combatants (save the Americans, when they finally arrived) still fielded significant numbers of cavalry wielding lances, indicated that whatever modern technologies nations employed, the core thinking of their military commanders remained at least a generation behind. Germany's General Staff may have embraced trains and planned loads to the last boxcar, but the presence of brigades of uhlans (German cavalry) reflected the continued overemphasis on nineteenth-century horse-drawn transport and reconnaissance by cavalry. Early fighting in the Ardennes, Lorraine, Alsace, and Mons served as a warning that any Napoleonic-style mass infantry tactics were hopelessly outdated. Nor did cannon fire, for all its thunder and visual pyrotechnics, significantly erode the fighting capability of a dugin enemy. A look at Grant's inability at Vicksburg and Petersburg to reduce Confederate lines to any degree by artillery fire was testimony enough that entrenched infantry could not be significantly affected by bombardment. So preoccupied were the general staffs on each side with their pivots and wheels, each seeking to outflank the other where he was (supposedly) weakest, that neither appreciated the fantastic damage that even half-strength units could inflict from defensive positions.

## Von Schlieffen's "Wheel"

Following the Schlieffen Plan, the German armies swung wide through northern France against the Allied left. At the same time, the French attempted to counterattack through the Ardennes on the German left. Each plan, whatever its original flaws, soon unraveled. The French failed to break through the entrenched positions of the German left, often attacking uphill through dense forests where they were mowed down by machine guns. Von Schlieffen's plan may have been fundamentally sound, but the Russian attack against German territory in East Prussia in August 1914 so panicked the High Command that two corps were hustled out of the German "wheel" and shipped by rail to reinforce Paul von Hindenburg's army, where they would arrive too late to aid in the German victory at Tannenberg. Military historians have long debated whether those troops would have indeed made the critical difference in the West, but that was not Germany's only deviation from von Schlieffen's plan of envelopment. The original plan had placed seven eighths of the German strength in the West in the right wing, but von Moltke became nervous over the gamble. France actually possessed superior numbers on the Western Front, along with a vast network of fortresses along its eastern border with Germany, and von Moltke was concerned about French offensive action.[42] In his Deployment Plan of 1908–09, von Moltke reassigned an entire army corps (about 42,000 men) to defend the Upper Alsace, and in the Deployment Plan of 1913–14, he increased the strength on the southern flank to a full two armies under Prince Rupprecht. He thereby reduced the relative strength of his right wing from seven-to-one in his favor to only three-to-one.[43] That meant, in raw terms, that the German left wing was strengthened by 85 battalions (150,000 men) and the right wing weakened by 96 battalions (more than 170,000 men), dooming the right wing to insufficient strength to accomplish its objectives from the outset. Rupprecht, commander of the German left flank with the 6th and 7th armies, had begged to launch an offensive of his own at the French right, rather than holding his ground as the "anvil" upon which the offensive "hammer" would crush French forces. Von Moltke provided additional strength for this possibility, but Rupprecht still was unable to break through the French fortresses. In one of those key moments in history, his troops had therefore been denied to the critical right wing effort for no purpose.

On the Allied side, France's plan suffered from the additional weakness of depending inordinately on British cooperation. *If* the British did exactly as France wanted, and *if* they held the line (even while French forces were retreating), then General Joseph Joffre's grand scheme might work. When Britain failed to send the planned six divisions (and instead sent four, consisting of 90,000 men total) and failed to hold the Germans at the Belgian border, the magnificent "offensive" of which Joffre dreamed turned to ash.

By late August, both the French and British were on their heels, and both British generals Douglas Haig and John French, being particularly sensitive to Kitchener's admonition not to lose the army, knew they had to avoid massive losses at all costs.

Even after the Germans had pushed within one hundred miles of Paris, Joffre dismissed any thought that his elegant offensive might have been the cause of French collapse. "Poor Joffre," he would moan softly while rubbing

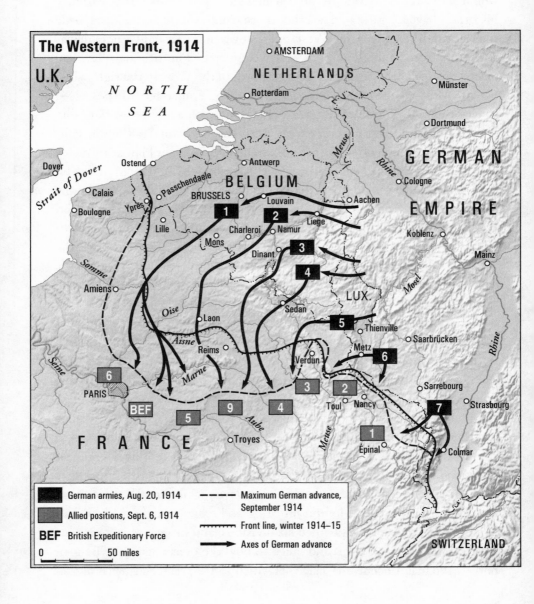

**The Western Front, 1914**

| | German armies, Aug. 20, 1914 |
| | Allied positions, Sept. 6, 1914 |
| **BEF** | British Expeditionary Force |

– – – – Maximum German advance, September 1914

·········· Front line, winter 1914–15

⟶ Axes of German advance

0      50 miles

his head, indicating to his staff that he refused to hear bad news.[44] Irritated by anyone trying to change his mind or contradict him, he was adrift once plans demanded constant modification and alteration. Nevertheless, he was fixed when it came to any notion that France would lose. His tenacious attitude gave the army confidence at its lowest point, and the crises provided by the German advance finally prompted Joffre to sack some of his officers. General Charles Lanrezac, appointed by Joffre to lead the 5th Army, had objected to the French offensive from the beginning. Once matters unfolded badly, he did not hesitate to blame headquarters. But at least he fought. Britain's Sir John French, on the other hand—in the face of orders (albeit gently worded ones) from Kitchener to maintain solidarity with the French line—withdrew under the weight of the German thrust and exposed his ally, and, along with it, the illusion of Anglo-French unified command.

Despite a steady, agonizing retreat from the Belgian border, then Amiens, British propaganda maintained a constant drumbeat of optimistic reports. (The names of the towns being fought over, however, made painfully obvious to the reader that the Allies were moving in the wrong direction.) In particular, the myth of British resistance against the might of the German advance at Mons, where supposedly the bulk of the German forces were concentrated, reached epic levels overnight. News releases claiming Britain had faced the "brunt of the blow" (an oft-used phrase) ignored the fact that British troops faced only three, of thirty, German corps. It soon became commonplace to hear that England had not only saved France, but "saved Europe, saved Western civilization, or, as one British writer unabashedly put it, 'Mons. In that single word will be summed up the Liberation of the World.'"[45] Instead, another single word, "Flanders," would eventually define the British effort on the Western Front, with virtually none of the glory that percolated up in 1914.

Not only did the "myth of Mons" thrill the British citizenry—so too did rumors of a massive Russian relief force sailing to England, then across the channel. Before long, the rumors had Cossacks on the Thames, or landing in Scotland, all but conducting a ceremonial review in front of Buckingham Palace. In reality, the Russians were suffering a dramatic defeat at Tannenberg.

Von Moltke witnessed the final unraveling of von Schlieffen's plan from late August through September 4, when the "wheel" made its final pivot, ignoring Paris and seeking the envelopment of the French army. Already the German army was consuming vast amounts of supplies and the logistic effort was falling behind. The 1st Army alone, under Alexander von Kluck, relied on 84,000 horses that gobbled up two million pounds of fodder per day. As reports of victory poured in to the General Staff, von Moltke's dour mood was, for a change, appropriate. "We have hardly a horse in the army who can go another step," he warned. "We must not deceive ourselves. We have had success but not victory. Victory means annihilation of the enemy's power of resistance."[46] Above all, it was the lack of prisoners that hinted to von Moltke that the French remained a bloodied, but effective, fighting force: "Where are our prisoners?" he exclaimed. (This was the same phenomenon that would cause the German High Command in World War II to conclude the war against the Soviet Union was lost even before the Battle of Stalingrad.) Certainly some beaten French units wanted to surrender: at Champagne, German soldiers observed French troops shoot their own officer because he would not surrender in a hopeless situation. But the bulk of the French forces had withdrawn in orderly fashion with determined resistance, taking their lead from the unimaginative yet inflexible Joffre.

Von Molke also suspected the Schlieffen Plan was played out. Already there had been too many missteps, too many delays: unexpectedly heavy Belgian resistance, the lure of the "double envelopment" with Rupprecht's forces on the French right, the hopelessly inadequate logistics train, then finally, von Kluck's impulsive decision to bring his forces up *alongside* those of General Karl von Bülow—who was thought to be delivering the crushing blow—instead of supporting von Bülow from the northwest to guard the right flank. Between von Kluck's quest for glory and his unfounded certainty that the French army was broken and shattered, Germany's fate was sealed.

German forces reached the Marne on September 4, by which time von Moltke was dispatching warnings to the right wing to swing westward to face an attack from that direction. Paris's military governor, the former colonial soldier General Joseph-Simon Gallieni (who had briefly been Joffre's superior), audaciously organized the Paris defense forces, which included the core French 6th Army under General Michel-Joseph Maunoury, into a critical flanking attack from the west as von Moltke feared. Von Kluck, suddenly under attack on his open flank, began to siphon off troops to block the surge. At the same time, Joffre, despondent that British Field Marshal French was cooperating only reluctantly, personally contacted Kitchener, who in turn promised to keep the British forces on the line. By the time von Kluck, on September 5—often set as the opening day of the First Battle of the Marne—wheeled to engage the 6th Army at the Battle of the Ourcq, Germany's chance of a decisive, quick victory had faded. That evening, von Kluck was persuaded to withdraw north of the Marne River and go on the defensive.

When the Schlieffen-planned breakthrough ground to a halt outside Paris, it had produced 206,000 French military casualties, or one eighth of the entire French army, not including losses of garrison troops and territorials. Those casualty lists were about to grow exponentially. In the four years of unprecedented bloodshed that followed, France would see one man killed for every 28 French men, women, and children; Germany's ratio, of one per 32, was only slightly lower. England lost one man for every 57, and Russia one for every 107. Now, in the first of the twentieth century's million-casualty battles, the French counterattack on the Marne would usher in an entirely new era of combat.

One of the most memorable moments at the Battle of the Marne occurred on September 6 at the Ourcq River, where 600 taxicabs, assisted by a potpourri of trucks, wagons, race cars, buses, and private vehicles of all types, each carrying at least five soldiers, brought 6,000 desperately needed reinforcements to the battlefield. Having dumped their customers in the streets, the cabs arrived at the appointed hour to load soldiers for the sixty-kilometer journey. Some men rode on rooftops; drivers—given only wine for rations—peered through the 4 A.M. darkness as they traveled without headlights. Reinforcing Maunoury's faltering 6th Army, General Louis Franchet d'Espèrey began the Miracle of the Marne in earnest the following day, having replaced Lanrezac after his "failure" at Charleroi (where he failed to dislodge a defending army twice the size of his own), sending his men plowing into the German 2nd Army. Franchet d'Espèrey achieved complete surprise, forcing open a gap between von Kluck on the German right and von Bülow's 2nd Army. When von Bülow "refused" his right flank—pulling it back at a 90-degree angle—it isolated von Kluck.

It was then Germany's turn for a miracle: instead of an aggressive French commander versed in the offensive, the gap between the two German armies loomed before the McClellanesque Sir John French, who moved too slowly to exploit it. On September 7 and 8, the British advanced only twenty-four miles against negligible opposition, falling twelve miles short of entirely severing von Kluck from the other German forces. Nevertheless, the very real possibility existed that, having marched through Belgium to the gates of Paris, the juggernaut of the German offensive was now about to see two entire armies—the 1st and 2nd—encircled. At that critical juncture, the German 1st Army fielded 128 battalions of infantry (224,000 men) engaged against 191 battalions of the French 6th Army and the British Expeditionary Force (or 320,000 men). This left von Bülow with only 134 battalions (235,000) against more than 450,000 French.

After hearing nothing from the 1st or 2nd armies for two days, von Moltke dispatched Lieutenant Colonel Richard Hentsch under oral instructions to communicate with von Kluck and von Bülow as a special emissary from the Army High Command. A gifted General Staff officer, Hentsch assumed he was acting under normal General Staff practices, and believed he had been given full power of authority to act in von Moltke's name and order a retreat if necessary. Once again, the German military structure was placing a low-ranking officer in a position to command the compliance of higher-ranking officers to his will; in this case a lieutenant colonel would determine what two colonel generals should do. Before Hentsch returned, von Moltke lost his nerve and suffered a nervous breakdown. He became lethargic, and when Crown Prince Rupprecht of Bavaria saw him on September 8, a sick, broken man stood before him. By the 14th, von Moltke was no longer able to conduct operations, and the Kaiser ordered him to step down on grounds of "ill health."

Meanwhile, the French saw themselves threatened with encirclement and had already hurled in their reserves. From their side, defeat appeared imminent, but Hentsch became pessimistic while talking with von Bülow and decided the German forces needed to retreat and reposition themselves at the Aisne River. Hentsch blinked: von Bülow ordered a general retreat, and Hentsch informed von Kluck, who believed he was handling the British and nearing a decisive victory over the French 6th Army. Von Kluck acquiesced with a heavy heart and accepted defeat.[47] In the German 5th Infantry Division, the unit that had held up the British Expeditionary Force and the French Cavalry Corps all by itself for five days in the gap between the 1st and 2nd armies, the order to retreat was incomprehensible. The men did not feel defeated, although they had been fighting against nearly ten times their number. With tears rolling down their cheeks, the fighting men plodded northeastward in columns.[48] Von Moltke was replaced by Erich von Falkenhayn, the minister of war who had been sniping at von Moltke behind his back, but already things were out of the hands of such men. Both sides now raced to extend their lines to the English Channel, lest they be flanked: "Division by division, corps by corps, army by army they spread out virtually due northward, meeting, clashing violently, then forced to dig in and lie motionless. . . ."[49] In one such fight, the British Expeditionary Force stopped the Germans at Passchendaele near the Belgian town of Ypres, benefiting from the Belgians' opening their sluice gates and allowing the Yser River to end the German advance. A major German attack resumed on October 22, and on October 29, at the crossroads of Gheluvelt, the Germans launched a powerful thrust by Army Group Fabeck, which contained a new division of young, zealous volunteers. After reaching the town of Gheluvelt—and threatening to puncture the Allied line (orders were even drafted for a general retreat)—the 364 men of the 2nd Worcesters, including cooks and orderlies, counterattacked and despite being outnumbered five to one, regained the town and pushed the Germans out, with heavy losses. Particularly devastated were the fresh volunteers, who were completely outclassed by the veterans of the Boer War, and whose slaughter was eulogized in Germany as the *Kindermord bei Ypern* (the "Massacre of the Innocents" or literally the "murder of the innocents near Ypers"). Britain was also greatly aided by Indian troops. It would not be the last time Dominion troops saved the Allies.

## The Chemists' War

An informal Christmas soldiers' truce occurred in Flanders on December 25, 1914, when British, French, and German troops spontaneously left their lines by the thousands to meet the enemy in no-man's-land, as if they had suddenly had enough. In this unofficial cease-fire, they exchanged tobacco, gloves, watches, cigarettes, chocolate, biscuits, and other items. Each unit thought it was somehow unique, yet this practice occurred up and down the front. The Lancashire Fusiliers traded beef tins to the Germans for helmet badges: the "bargain is complete," recorded the divisional diary, "except for the slight disagreement as to who shall come out of his trench first. . . ."[50] When the German concert singer Walter Kirchhoff made a front-line appearance for the 130th Württembergers, French troops across Flanders quietly climbed to the tops of their parapets, applauding so long at the end that Kirchhoff performed an encore.[51] On Christmas Day, the British 6th Gordons, discovering the Germans had a barber in their ranks, arranged for shaves and haircuts right in the middle of the battlefield. When reports of the spontaneous truce reached the rear, they were dismissed as fantasy, but in some sectors, the truce lasted until New Year's Day. Although General Horace Smith-Dorrien, head of the British II Corps, issued orders forbidding consorting with the enemy, the end of the truce came naturally as the holiday passed. After that time, anyone leaving the lines was warned back by opposing troops, and, shortly thereafter, the shooting started again.

Following a fierce but unresolved French/British offensive at Champagne and Loos in March, the Germans were reinforced and counterattacked in April, when they introduced chlorine gas on the Canadian, Moroccan, and Algerian French colonial troops. Prying open a four-mile hole in Entente lines, the Germans flowed through until units from the Commonwealth of Canada plugged the gap at the Second Battle of Ypres, where casualties exceeded 100,000 on both sides. By late May 1915, the Ypres salient was substantially eliminated, marking a turning point. Along with the elimination of the Ypres salient came a grim understanding of what the Germans were in for—it was a war against an empire that spanned the globe. A writer in *Der Tag* recorded:

> We expected that . . . India would rise [against Britain] when the first shot was fired in Europe, but thousands of Indians came to fight with the British against us. We thought the British Empire would be torn to pieces, but the Colonies appear to be united closer than ever with the Mother Country. We expected a triumphant rebellion in South Africa; it was nothing but a failure. We thought there would be trouble in Ireland, but instead, she sent her best soldiers against us. We anticipated that the "peace at any price" party would be dominant in England, but it melted away in the ardour to fight Germany. We regarded England as degenerate, yet she seems to be our principal enemy.[52]

In fact, Britain had drawn on her empire for 16 percent of all troops in the war—the last time some of the colonies would overwhelmingly support British military aims. Only Australia, New Zealand, Canada, South Africa, and, to a limited extent, India, would send forces to fight in British armies in the Second World War. Great Britain held back over 1,500,000 British soldiers in England during 1918 (to keep Field Marshal Haig from using them up on futile offensives) while continuing to put its Commonwealth troops into battle and calling for the United States to assume an everheavier burden.[53] This did not go unnoticed either by the commander of the American Expeditionary Force or by the Commonwealth nations.

It proved somewhat ironic that soldiers from the colonies would be some of the first victims of a new weapon of war on the Western Front, poison gas. The use of gas helped characterize World War I as "the chemists' war," in that chemistry was critical—whether in the production of gas, ammunition, or medicines. In all its iterations, including tear gas, chlorine gas, and mustard gas, the new weapon struck terror into the hearts of soldiers. Although first used on Russian positions in the East, large-scale introduction of gas on the Western Front occurred in April 1915 north of Ypres against positions held by French colonial forces from Martinique. The fear it involved was not confined to the Allied troops, as German soldiers hesitated to move forward to exploit the gap it made in the Allied line. Defenses and counters to gas were developed rapidly (even horses had gas masks), and after initial horrific encounters with chlorine gas, troops learned to respond with hurried, but effective, donning of gas masks. For the side using gas, the wind was fickle, making gas a potential weapon for the enemy. Though gas remained in use throughout the war, it was not the miracle weapon hoped for by the Germans. On the propaganda front, however, it was the use of poison gas, even more than the Zeppelin bombings and U-boat attacks, that seemed to set Germany apart as particularly barbarous, even though the Allies developed and experimented with poison gas before the war as well and the British used it in September 1915, only five months after the Germans.

Both the Hague Declaration of 1899 and the Hague Convention of 1907 had prohibited the use of poison gas weapons, but Germany's manpower disadvantage led it to repudiate the international agreements. When a nation perceives its survival to be threatened, previous treaties signed by a politician become, in the words of German chancellor Theobald von Bethmann-Hollweg, just a "scrap of paper." Chemist Fritz Haber thought chlorine gas in particular could offset the Allies' superiority in numbers. But it was in fact the French who first used gas (though tear, not chlorine, or "poison," gas) in August 1914. Germans employed T-Stoff tear gas against the Russians in January 1915, with no results, as it froze before it could affect the enemy. In April 1915, however, when chlorine gas was deployed at Ypres, it quickly became known that men who ran suffered more; those who stayed on the parapet, less, as the heavy gas fell quickly. The greenish cloud could be easily spotted, and by July the British had already introduced a "smoke helmet" that was moderately effective.

Of course, the British immediately adopted their own gas shells, which were often as ineffective as the Germans' had been. A French chemist refined phosgene gas, which was colorless, in 1915, providing a more powerful killing agent, in that effects often did not show up for twenty-four hours. Mustard gas, introduced by the Germans in 1917 (also known as "HS" or "Hun Stuff" by the British), had a delayed reaction that was every bit as deadly, causing skin blisters before showing up in the lungs. Gas could be delivered by artillery, and its psychological impact was often greater than its physical harms. Lieutenant Colonel G. W. G. Hughes, of the Medical Corps, wrote, "I shall never forget the sights I saw by Ypres after the first gas attacks. . . . Men [were] lying all along the side of the road . . . exhausted, gasping, frothing yellow mucus from their mouths, their faces blue and distressed."[54] In the end, a British report on chemical warfare in 1919 concluded that "gas is a legitimate weapon in war."[55]

Each new implement—gas, the flamethrower, the U-boat, the airplane—was rolled out with the grand hope that it would overcome the trench, the ideas being that the U-boats would outflank the trench network entirely, while airplanes would punish them from above. None succeeded. Networks of earthen cuts that disfigured northern France and Belgium remained, mocking each army's attempts to go around, over, or through them, in the process absorbing the blood of a generation as new reinforcements arrived daily.

## War on a Global Scale

New technology could change the casualty rolls, but could not end the war. Nor could the insertion of hundreds of thousands of colonial troops—actions that made the war truly global. By 1915, Britain had, including colonials, 750,000 men on the Continent (up from under 100,000 in 1914, when the Germans first attacked). Life in the trenches imposed a surreal existence on all, from clean-shaven recruits to grizzled veterans. Conditions were so horrid and unbearable that troops came to unwritten agreements not to fire at one another during mealtimes. Once constructed, trenches changed warfare entirely, and were ultimately rendered ineffective only by the combination of a technological breakthrough—the tank—and innovative tactics. Neither was ready before 1918, although tanks made their first appearance in September 1916. Thus, short of merely holding their ground, both armies repeatedly attempted costly, nineteenth-century offensives (although marginally modified with drab uniforms for cover, and by the introduction of squad- and platoon-level tactics).

Further, both sides came to believe that all that stood between them and the eternally evasive breakthrough was more artillery, more shells. Since few European powers had sent observers to the American Civil War, none except the British had seen the ineffectiveness of massed artillery in eliminating troops in fixed positions, especially if entrenched. At Chemin des Dames in April 1917, both sides would fire a staggering *eleven million shells* over a thirty-mile front during a ten-day exchange, without a clear advantage to either side.[56] As soon as the shelling stopped, soldiers ran to the parapets, set up their machine guns, and put up a wall of small-caliber fire. Memoir after memoir recorded the suicidal futility of infantry advancing against troops entrenched with machine guns. A German: "When we started firing we just had to load and reload. They went down in their hundreds. You didn't have to aim, we just fired into them."[57] A Frenchman: "The Germans fell like cardboard soldiers."[58] A Brit likened the Germans to targets in a shooting gallery.[59] After only one year of fighting, the carnage was such that most front-line regiments were manned by reserves. Britain's 11th Brigade of the British Expeditionary Force had been almost wiped out, reduced to 18 percent of its officers and 28 percent of its men. The 7th Division, which arrived in France after Ypres, lost 356 of 400 officers and 9,664 of 12,000 men.

Trenches, however, were torture to endure even for the defenders. Rain, mud, and constant drizzle, all exacerbated by the cold French climate, had men shivering twenty-four hours a day and left soldiers miserable even when not being shelled. Sausage turned to ice, potatoes were frozen, and even hand grenades became stuck together in the cold. Vermin of all sorts attacked the soldiers, especially lice and rats (some the size of cats). The rats ate through haversacks and ration bags, springing to life at night, provoking battles that were nearly as fearsome as those against the Germans during the day. Percy Jones of the Queen's Westminster Rifles wrote in his diary, "I am addicted to rat hunting," and his weapons of choice were the spade and the pick handle.[60] On one occasion, Jones and his comrades chased a rat back to the second trench line, where a sentry almost shot them, and a year later, near Ypres, he recorded, "We had a great battle last night [against the rats] and killed nearly a hundred. [We] ran out of ammunition and had to come back for more bricks."[61] Another English soldier described a night in the trenches during the battle of Verdun: "Lights out. Now the rats and the lice are masters of the house. You can hear the rats nibbling, running, jumping, rushing from plank to plank, emitting their little squeals . . . a noisy swarming activity that just won't stop."[62] The only relief to be gained from the rats came from something even worse—gas, which purified the trenches of all vermin for a while.

Whether death and mutilation came by artillery shell, machine gun bullet, gas, or the bayonet, the result was the same. It was even more tragic when the shells were fired by one's own artillery: "friendly" artillery treated all men alike: the French reported 75,000 troops killed by their own artillery, and Major Charles Whittlesey's "Lost Battalion," unable to radio distress signals, was repeatedly subjected to shelling from Allied guns. Regardless of the origin of the ordnance, the casualties piled up, bringing with them the reality, even the inevitability, of dying. A French soldier, a month before being killed, wrote "Death! That word which booms like the echo of sea caverns. . . . Now we die. It is the wet death, the muddy death, death dripping with blood, death by drowning, death by sucking under, death in the slaughterhouse."[63]

## Victory Through Attrition

After the Marne, Ypres, and the Gallipoli debacle—in which British, Australian, New Zealand, and French Senegalese soldiers were sent to seize a point on the Dardanelles defended by entrenched Turks, producing a slaughter—the dominance of the trench was confirmed in blood. At the Battle of Sari Bair near the original Gallipoli landing zones, one New Zealand battalion saw 711 of its 760 men killed or wounded. Trenches snaked across France and Belgium, the Turks held the Dardanelles, the Russians verged on collapse, and the Austrians proved only slightly more capable than the Italians. New commanders now led each army in the West: Sir Douglas Haig for the British and General (later Marshal) Ferdinand Foch for the French Northern Army Group in 1915, General (later Marshal) Philippe Pétain commanding the French Army Group Centre in 1916, and Erich von Falkenhayn, chief of the German General Staff. By 1916, convinced the French were on the verge of collapse and the British exhausted, von Falkenhayn ordered a fresh offensive at Verdun, the linchpin of the Allied line. For the first time, there was no real strategic objective, other than simply killing enemies economically in a war of attrition (von Falkenhayn calculated his forces could exact five enemy dead for every two of their own). A disputed Christmas memo to the Kaiser, appearing only in von Falkenhayn's memoirs, argued that a breakthrough was beyond Germany's means, but was unnecessary at any event.[64] France would either attempt to cling to Verdun or surrender the town and its location as a jumping-off point for Paris, while at the same time forcing the British to mount a counteroffensive in their sector. Either way, the result was the same: a massive German assault could be undertaken with the hope of ending the war.

Beyond that, von Falkenhayn had not selected the salient capriciously. A German railhead was only twelve miles away, while French lines were supplied by only the *Voie Sacrée*, the single road still available to the French to supply Verdun. As with many Great War offensives, the plan looked good on paper. In practice, once the German troops advanced outside of their artillery cover, and into the range of French guns, each additional mile came at fantastic cost. Nor did the French supply train, coming up the "Sacred Road," fail. During a single push into the village of Douaumont, four German regiments were eliminated through a crossfire from each side of the Meuse valley. At the peak of the fighting, 100,000 shells poured into the Verdun salient every hour. After capturing Fort Douaumont and Fort Vaux, the Germans were forced to retreat in October–November 1916 after the French brought up heavy 400 mm railway guns, directed by aircraft spotters. By December, von Falkenhayn's offensive had failed.

The bloodletting eclipsed anything seen up to that time, which, given the casualty lists, says a great deal. France lost half a million men, the Germans 434,000. England, in the Somme counterattack, suffered another 420,000 casualties (including a staggering 58,000 killed or wounded on the first *day*). Von Falkenhayn's promise to "bleed France white" proved only partially true: now, all the combatants were bled white and warfare became a battle of accounting. "Here," wrote Ernst Jünger of the Somme counterattack, "chivalry had disappeared for always. . . . Here the new Europe revealed itself for the first time in combat."[65]

Just as von Falkenhayn believed Germany was close to winning, so too did the British commander, Sir Douglas Haig, think that a summer offensive at Ypres (or Passchendaele) could succeed. Capture of the Messines Ridge in June 1917 suggested that Haig might be correct in his view that the Germans were nearing collapse. Haig dawdled, insisting on waiting until the end of July. Typical heavy shelling to break up the wire tipped off the Germans that an attack was coming, but more important, once the attack was in progress, torrential rainstorms turned the battlefield into a mud pit. Soldiers stumbled into shell craters and drowned, tanks became trapped, and infantry could barely move.

War in the West proved a bloody slugfest, and dragged on seemingly endlessly. The Schlieffen Plan had specifically called for a rapid victory over France in order to deal with the expected larger threat of the Russian armies. But while the Russian forces were large, they also were largely inept. Stretching over one thousand miles from the Baltic Sea to the Black Sea, the eastern theater of war pitted about 1.2 million Russian soldiers at the outset against the German 8th Army (166,000 men) and the Austro-Hungarian Empire's 1 million troops, plus 117,000 Turks on the southern flank. In August 1914, the Germans smashed the Russian 2nd Army at the Battle of Tannenberg, with the Russians suffering more than ten times more casualties and prisoners than the Germans. The German victory more than offset an Austrian loss at the Battle of Galicia in Ukraine, where the Austro-Hungarian Empire lost one third of its forces (including more than 130,000 prisoners). Despite success at Tannenberg, the collapse of the Austrians forced Germany to keep the newly created 9th Army in the eastern theater, denying those troops to the encirclement wheel of the Schlieffen Plan. By 1915, the German/Austrian forces had advanced through Russian Poland and secured the Eastern Front—but at the cost of desperately needed men in the West.

## Mexico's Robin Hood

While Europe convulsed in seas of blood, combat of a different sort became common in America's southern neighbor, Mexico, where multiparty gangs battled constantly. This Mexican interlude would soon play an important part in America's entry into the European conflict. In August 1914, just before World War I broke out, Sonora governor Adolfo de la Huerta had briefly seized power, but the U.S. government under Taft had refused to recognize him. Incoming president Woodrow Wilson promised to continue Taft's policy, announcing, "I will not recognize a government of butchers."[66] Using the chaos in Mexico as an excuse, Wilson landed troops in Veracruz in April 1914 to produce "an orderly and righteous government" (and oust Huerta), and after the Americans seized the city in a sharp fight, Huerta resigned. Wilson then recognized Venustiano Carranza, a former pro-American general every bit a butcher like Huerta, as president, whereupon Francisco "Pancho" Villa, who felt betrayed by the American support of Carranza, led his army of *banditos* on a raid of Columbus, New Mexico, in March 1916.

Alternately described as animalistic, magnetic, shrewd, cruel, catlike, and tough, the stocky Pancho Villa (born José Doroteo Arango Arámbula in 1878) was the embodiment of the macho bandit. A womanizer of epic proportions and an excellent gunfighter, Villa was also so renowned for his horsemanship that he was nicknamed "The Centaur of the North." His mood swings were instantaneous and complete, hurtling from rage to tears in seconds, and (as Hitler later would) he acquired praise and admiration from Americans, including John Reed and William Jennings Bryan, who called him the "Mexican Robin Hood," or "a Sir Galahad." Pro-American until Wilson decided to ally with Carranza, allegedly because Carranza "looked honest" with his long, white beard, Villa himself had once supported Carranza before Carranza decided to ditch his *bandito* element—which included Emiliano Zapata—in an attempt to gain respectability in American eyes.

Villa began with only fourteen loyal followers, but this band soon ballooned into an army. Arrested earlier by Huerta, Villa had escaped from jail by sawing through the bars with a smuggled saw and seemed to live a charmed life. Allied with Carranza, he used the aura of the Constitutional Party to legitimate his expropriation of landowners' money and property. Why he attacked Columbus, even with a force of 400 men, is still under debate. Certainly he knew that a local detachment of the U.S. Army's 13th Regiment was garrisoned nearby when his men arrived at four o'clock in the morning. Villa's bandits burned the town and seized military supplies and food, but not without resistance from Columbus's armed citizens, who fought back with fierce determination. American soldiers suffered 8 dead and 6 wounded, along with 10 civilians killed, but their resistance cost Villa nearly 100 men killed and 30 captured—one fourth of his entire force. It was a disastrous foray which guaranteed further American military action.

Within a week, Wilson ordered General John J. "Black Jack" Pershing to lead a 10,000-man expeditionary force to capture Villa. Pershing's force was filled with oddities and ironies: Custer's old reconstituted 7th Cavalry was present, including Pershing's second in command, George Dodd, a sixty-three-year-old colonel who had fought the Indians with the 7th Cavalry. The 7th had, in fact, regained some of its honor at the Battle of Bear Paw, where Chief Joseph's Nez Perce surrendered in 1877, lost it again in 1890 at Wounded Knee, and regained it for good in the Filipino campaign a decade later. Pershing had also commanded troops in two African-American regiments, the 10th and 24th Infantry, whose glory included the charge up San Juan Hill in 1898 and action in the Philippines. Pershing, an advocate of black rights, felt Wilson's racist hand on his shoulder at all times, and carefully separated the units from white troops as Wilson demanded. For his association with the all-Negro units, Pershing earned the nickname "Black Jack."

Pershing had languished under the Army's slow promotion policies in spite of his obvious talents as a military leader until marrying Helen Frances Warren, daughter of Senator Francis E. Warren of Wyoming in 1905. Pershing was only a captain, but in 1906 he was suddenly promoted from captain to brigadier general, leapfrogging 862 more senior officers. Apparently the fact that Senator Warren was chairman of the Senate Military Affairs Committee (now the Armed Forces Committee) did not hurt Pershing in the least. Although the promotion was heavily criticized as gross favoritism, Pershing had been highly recommended by leading generals in the Army, and enjoyed the support of President Roosevelt since his days alongside him at San Juan Hill. Following another six years in the Philippines, Pershing had been placed in command of the 8th Brigade in San Francisco, and then ordered to El Paso, where he was when Villa attacked Columbus.

Using Curtiss Jenny observation planes and armored cars as scouts, the Americans crossed into Chihuahua, pushed relentlessly by Black Jack. American troopers came close to nabbing Villa in late March, but Mexican guides misled the *yanquis* and delayed their arrival until the *banditos* had fled. In April, Lieutenant George S. Patton's advance units located one of Villa's top officers, Julio Cárdenas, and Patton personally shot him and two of his men. Patton ceremoniously notched his revolvers before tying the bodies to the hoods of the cars so that he could return them to the base for identification. Although a second Villa general was shot later, the Expeditionary Force increasingly bumped into Mexican Federal Army units. Two separate clashes between Pershing's men and the *federales* forced Carranza to warn Pershing off, by which time the American forces had lost precious manpower to liquor and venereal diseases.

Both Wilson and Carranza feared they were stumbling into war, and the Mexican president knew he would lose, while the American president knew a conflict with Mexico might well be a distraction for the larger, almost inevitable, entry into the European conflict. By spring of 1916, the danger from U-boat attacks, tremendous British financial losses, and French casualties made it obvious to Wilson that the United States would be drawn into war. Villa, meanwhile, soon after having his leg operated on without anesthetic, led a new offensive against the Mexican government in Chihuahua City. When that Carranza garrison fell, Villa issued his "Manifesto to the Nation," denouncing the "twin evils" of the "barbarians of the North" and the "most corrupt Government we ever had." Wilson reined in Pershing, infuriating George Patton, who said the president had neither "the soul of a louse nor the mind of a worm or the backbone of a jellyfish."[67]

American troops were finally withdrawn in January 1917, having failed to capture Villa or stop the raids. A bitter Black Jack later said he had been "outwitted and out-bluffed at every turn," and denounced the withdrawal, describing it as "sneaking home under cover, like a whipped cur with its tail between its legs."[68] Villa, on the other hand, had become a hero, in part because he managed his publicity and massaged his image. He permitted legendary writer Ambrose Bierce to tag along with his *banditos*. Bierce was with Villa in Chihuahua in 1913, then mysteriously disappeared in December of that year, writing to his niece just before his death, "Good-bye—if you hear of my being stood up against a Mexican stone wall and shot to rags please know that I think it was a pretty good way to depart this life. . . . To be a Gringo in Mexico—ah, that is euthanasia!"[69]

Another reason for Villa's success was his identification with the peasant classes, building a school and freely redistributing wealth. Not only did most Chihuahuans protect and revere him—he had been Carranza's governor of Chihuahua—but his impressive victory at Tierra Blanca brought him a Hollywood contract with producer D. W. Griffith's production company. Film units tagged along with Villa on his battles, and the Revolution got half the profit from the movies they made. He also robbed trains, forced unwilling hacienda workers into his army, and extracted money at gunpoint from hacienda owners. But he knew how to mug for the camera, and American journalists and movie producers ate it up. The fact that he evaded the mighty gringo army only added to his mystique, as did his spectacular and grisly death. Accepting retirement under a negotiated peace with interim president Adolfo de la Huerta in 1920 after his archenemy Carranza was assassinated, Villa agreed to cease his revolutionary activity and retire on some land and a small stipend provided by the Mexican government. A lifetime of enemies, however, could not be negotiated away. In July 1923, assassins pounded 150 shots into Villa's car, riddling the *bandito* leader with bullets. After his death, Villa's legend grew, with pawn shops claiming to possess his trigger finger, tombstones set up on both sides of the border, a famous statue in Zacatecas, and over two dozen movie depictions by such stars as Yul Brynner, Wallace Beery, Telly Savalas, and Antonio Banderas.

Celebrated in rock songs and horror movies, Villa became in death far more influential than he was in life.

## Neutrality in a Worldwide Conflict

Americans may have had their attention on their southern border, but slowly and steadily, Europe pulled an "isolationist" America into the fray. Ground warfare, with all its massive carnage, was unable to decide anything after two full years, but it was events at sea that eventually brought the United States into the Great War.

At the outbreak of hostilities, the German High Seas Fleet had thirteen of the new dreadnought battleships and three fast battle cruisers, while the British had twenty dreadnoughts and four cruisers. Both sides had built the new submarines, but the Germans—who were slower to adopt U-boats (*Unterseebooten*) than the British—caught up rapidly and unleashed the subs against merchant ships in February 1915. After the Battle of Jutland (May 31–June 1, 1916), the high command of the German Imperial Navy became convinced it had to rely on U-boats to break British sea power. The Battle of Jutland itself involved a total of twenty-eight British battleships of all varieties and another forty-three cruisers of different classes aligned against sixteen German battleships and twenty-two cruisers and pre-dreadnought warships. But the German High Seas Fleet under Vice-Admirals Reinhard Scheer and Franz Hipper sought to run the British through a gauntlet of U-boats before the heavy surface ships clashed. British admirals Sir John Jellicoe and Sir David Beatty were able to unite their forces before the German U-boats were ready, and in the ensuing battle, fourteen British and eleven German ships were lost. Even though the sheer numbers indicated a German victory, the German High Command became convinced the fleet could not survive all-out fleet-to-fleet exchanges, and it remained in harbors for the remainder of the war. (There was a single foray on August 19, 1916, but Scheer abruptly turned his fleet around when he learned the British were waiting.) By ceding the oceans to the Royal Navy, the Germans allowed the concept of "rights of neutrals" to mean whatever the British said it did. After Jutland, all German sea warfare was reduced to actions by U-boats, although the British were forced to maintain a presence in the North Sea in case the High Seas Fleet sortied out again. Reliance on U-boats proved risky in the extreme, because of the possibility of a U-boat commander's accidentally sinking a civilian vessel or an American ship. That, in turn, was certain to provoke American reaction—as it did on May

7, 1915, when a German submarine sank the RMS *Lusitania*, a British lux-
ury liner traveling from New York. The *Lusitania* had changed course off
the Irish coast to avoid U-boats, ironically pulling into the path of U-20, a
German submarine low on fuel with only three torpedoes. No one knows
how many torpedoes Kapitänleutnant Walther Schwieger fired (his log said
one, although some think it was doctored), but however many were fired,
the *Lusitania* went down in eighteen minutes, taking along 1,198 civilians.
Of the 139 Americans aboard, 128 died, leading to howls of protest from the
United States. Britain, of course, fanned the flames of outrage, hoping to
draw the United States into the war.[70]

Germany's U-boat fleet had been forced into "unrestricted submarine
warfare" (firing torpedoes from a submerged position at targets that could
not always be positively identified) by the British use of "Q-boats"—vessels
that looked like freighters, but which concealed guns beneath phony "cargo"
boxes on deck. In reality, the Q-boats were far less effective than they appeared. Some 180 Q-ships were used during the war, but they achieved only
28 U-boat kills. Still, they made U-boats more cautious, and attacking an
unidentified ship was like playing Russian roulette for a U-boat commander.
According to international law, the sub was to surface near the target, signal
a warning, and allow time for evacuation, even if the intended victim broadcast the U-boat's presence to the Royal Navy by radio. German U-boats
faced a dilemma: if the subs "played by the rules," they ran the risk of surfacing in front of a Q-boat and being quickly eliminated or sought out by
British naval units. If they attacked without surfacing and warning their
intended victim, sooner or later passenger ships or neutral vessels would be
sunk. Aware of the danger of angering the United States, Germany began
publishing disclaimers in port city papers in America warning that a state
of war existed between Germany and Britain, and that passengers assumed
the risk by sailing in "war zone" waters. Such disclaimers worked no better
then than legal disclaimers about physical injury or even death at amuse-
ment parks work today. Simply put, Americans blamed the Kaiser for the
*Lusitania*—and all subsequent American deaths through U-boat attacks.

William Jennings Bryan, President Woodrow Wilson's pacifist secretary of state, resigned in 1915 in anticipation that the United States would
declare war on Germany. In fact, Wilson issued a formal protest to Germany only after the *Lusitania* disaster. Convinced that Wilson was a cow-
ard, British soldiers took to calling a shell that did not explode a "Wilson."
Indeed, U.S. response to the *Lusitania* sinking was remarkably tame, given

that Americans had absorbed unfettered British propaganda about Germany. Allied propaganda told of soldiers smashing babies' heads against walls, raping nuns, humiliating the elderly before shooting them, and destroying churches. Some charges were true, if exaggerated: the Germans shelled the Reims cathedral (mistaking German troops already in the city for the enemy); they terror-bombed Paris, hitting the cathedral of Notre-Dame. Yet their rationale differed little from American explanations about the need to raze Monte Cassino in World War II. "Better a thousand church towers fall than that one German soldier should fall as a result of these towers," wrote one German historian in terms echoed by frustrated Americans ninety years later in Iraq, where terrorists routinely carried out operations from mosques.[71]

The Kaiser did not help his cause by celebrating the sinking of one million tons of Allied shipping in October 1916, nor did it endear Americans to Germany when five Allied ships were torpedoed within sight of Nantucket Sound.[72] A passenger liner, the *Marina*, was sunk a few days before the U.S. election in 1916, killing six Americans. Nevertheless, in the United States isolationism still reigned, especially as it seemed Wilson might become the peacemaker that Teddy Roosevelt had played between Russia and Japan in 1905. Perhaps also the Progressive Wilson realized the power that would be unleashed, both abroad and domestically, by the new state he had created. If the American people were led to war, he prophesied in 1916, "they'll forget there was ever such a thing as tolerance. . . . The spirit of ruthless brutality will enter into every fibre of our national life."[73]

Antiwar groups recognized the possibility of the United States' being drawn into the European conflict, and staged marches down Fifth Avenue in New York when the first shots were fired. In 1915, high-profile Americans such as Jane Addams and Henry Ford denounced any suggestion that the United States had an interest in the outcome. Ford even chartered a "Peace Ship" to sail to Stockholm and negotiate a cease-fire. Satirized by the newspapers—one blared a mocking headline, "GREAT WAR ENDS CHRISTMAS DAY: FORD TO STOP IT"—and blasted by Theodore Roosevelt, who said, "Mr. Ford's visit abroad will not be mischievous only because it is ridiculous," Ford bulled ahead.[74] Many American notables who had egged him on and promised to go now backed out: Addams was ill (but feared the scheme would fall into the hands of "fanatical and impecunious reformers"); Thomas Edison, department store magnate John Wanamaker, Helen Keller, and Ida Tarbell all begged off.[75] Others invited by Ford had never indicated they supported his scheme, including William Howard Taft, "Colonel" Edward House (referred to because he was a "Kentucky Colonel," not an officer), and Louis Brandeis. Edison and his wife actually came to the Hoboken docks to see Ford off, whereupon Ford pleaded with the inventor to sail, offering him a million dollars to make the trip.[76] Edison shook his head and left. The *Oscar II* departed from port with 115 pacifists and a gaggle of reporters as a band struck up "I Didn't Raise My Boy to Be a Soldier." Ford confided that he didn't expect to end the war immediately, but to increase psychological pressure on the warring powers—an entirely ineffective strategy. Typical of many "peace" efforts, the group on board the *Oscar II* quickly had sharp disagreements over producing a statement critical of Wilson and calling for universal disarmament. "Pacifist," observed William Bullitt, one of the passengers, "means a person hard to pacify."[77]

In contrast to the press of the late twentieth and early twenty-first century, the reporters of 1915 were cynical and critical of the peace mission, drawing the ire of many of the "delegates." Ford ordered them to ignore the reporters, but one of Ford's companions, Rosika Schwimmer, was accused of tampering with dispatches and listening to journalists' conversations at keyholes. Predictably, American leftists and radicals, including Walter Millis and Upton Sinclair, praised the mission. Ford, meanwhile, became ill on the voyage and after arriving in Christiana, Norway, quietly returned to America, denying from New York that he had abandoned his friends, who plodded on to Sweden, Denmark, and Holland for talks. "The comedy of errors is over," noted the *Tribune* when the gangplank of the returning ship *Rotterdam* was pulled in and the delegates headed home. Ford claimed to have gotten a million dollars' worth of advertising for an investment of $465,000 in peace and participants claimed it had resulted in a conference that offered an alternative to war. In reality, nothing in Europe changed one iota. Trenches still cut across the French and Belgian landscapes, and U-boats still ravaged vessels at sea.

Sentiment in the United States, except for pockets of German support in Milwaukee, St. Louis, and a few other cities, was pro-British from the outset. J. P. Morgan's syndicates kept Britain and France alive financially, despite Wilson's plea that Americans be "impartial in thought as well as action"—a clear impossibility and practically unattainable, given that the United States was trading heavily with Britain and France. Rather than being impartial himself, Wilson refused to recognize the "war zones" published by Germany where neutral vessels were at a high risk of being torpedoed. Wilson restated Americans' right to sail anywhere at any time they wished, and emphasized that any consequences would be the fault of Germany. To a large degree, Wilson actively forced Germany into a box from which there was no good strategy for escape.

It is doubtful that "globalization of the conflict was an inevitable consequence of British involvement," as historian Niall Ferguson has argued. The Germans were already seeking to align Turkey—the mission of the *Goeben*, ordered to Constantinople early on August 4, 1914, would have occurred regardless of British actions (Britain only decided to declare war that night)—nor would the war have ended immediately if the Germans had forced a French surrender.[78] Instead, given Germany's prewar state of mind, it is entirely likely that a much more successful and arrogant Germany would have pressed her advantages even further, and at even greater human cost. At the same time, U.S. trade with Germany immediately evaporated with the British blockade, dropping to a percentage of its prewar levels by 1916, and the British severed Germany's international cables and broke the main German naval codes.

Britain correctly assessed the reality of the Anglo-American relationship, perceiving that it would be easy to draw in the United States by maneuvering the Germans to commit an outrage. While Britain's blockade violated international law (the Declaration of London, 1909, known as the "Declaration Concerning the Laws of Naval War") and subjected neutral ships to harassment and diversion to British ports, this proved far less visually jarring and emotionally charged than the sinking of a passenger liner. Germany's own colonial secretary, Bernhard Dernburg, acknowledged as much before the *Lusitania* was sunk, noting, "The American people cannot visualize the spectacle of a hundred thousand . . . German children starving by slow degrees as a result of the British blockade, but they can visualize the face of a little child drowning amidst the wreckage caused by a German torpedo."[79]

At any rate, trade and capital flows to England accelerated to double the prewar levels by the time America eventually entered the war. With almost three fourths of U.S. overseas trade going to Europe, and the majority of that arriving in Britain, certainly the isolationists' charge that bankers were drawing the United States into the war was not entirely wrong, although certain military realities took precedence over economic interest.[80] Either way, American credit shifted the world's financial center from London to New York, a position that city would not relinquish until, briefly, Tokyo assumed it in the 1980s. When Wilson permitted U.S. bankers to sell bonds for the Entente, J. P. Morgan's son Jack placed $500 million worth of securities with investors through a network of more than two thousand banks despite the vocal opposition of Irish and German groups.[81] Throughout the course of the war, the Morgan banks would handle orders for more than $3 billion from the Allies, and after America joined the war, Morgan loaned the U.S. Coast Guard the *Corsair*, his father's famous yacht where the U.S. Steel agreement with Carnegie had been consummated, for duty as a submarine chaser. While the "merchants of death" theory has been effectively destroyed by scholars, there was little question that America's sympathies—and wallets—rested with Britain and France.[82]

Wilson, however, could not admit that financial considerations played any role in his policy decision. Nor would he admit that it was in American national security interests to ensure that Prussian militarism was not successful on the Continent. Wilson campaigned on the slogan "He kept us out of war," defeating Charles Evans Hughes, a former New York governor, by a mere 3,000 votes in California to win a narrow victory of 277–254 in the electoral college. (Some have attributed Hughes's California defeat to the flub he made during a campaign swing through the state when he stayed in the same Long Beach hotel as Republican governor Hiram Johnson. Unaware that Johnson was in the hotel, Hughes failed to meet with him, leading Johnson to think he had been snubbed.) During the campaign, Hughes had been forthright about his intention to prepare America's military in case war came, which Wilsonian papers played as an attempt to drag the nation into the conflict. Wilson also benefited from a temporary German suspension in U-boat warfare. When the Russian revolution of March 1917 threw out the last nondemocratic Allied power, in Wilson's mind a clear case of "democracy vs. autocracy" emerged. Actual entrance into the war needed only another slight push. Wilson got two.

The first was the Germans' announcement on January 31, 1917, that unrestricted submarine warfare would resume on February 1. Even before the official announcement, German submarines had continued to sink American ships, including the *Housatonic* and the *California*, meaning the United States already had ample grounds for war. Resumption of unfettered U-boat attacks destroyed the façade of civilian government in Germany, and Chancellor Theobald von Bethmann-Hollweg was forced out in July 1917 after his ability to restrain the military ended in January with the announcement of the U-boat offensive.

The second push came when, in anticipation of the renewed U-boat offensive, German foreign secretary Arthur Zimmermann dispatched a telegram on January 16, 1917, to the German ambassador in the United States, Johann von Bernstorff, who forwarded it to the German ambassador in Mexico. It sought to lure Mexico into a military alliance if the United States entered the war and promised to return to Mexico California, Arizona, New Mexico, and Texas, states lost during the Texas Revolution and the Mexican War. The Zimmermann telegram was intercepted and decrypted by the British, who naturally shared it with the United States on March 1. The telegram outraged Americans, whose memories of Pancho Villa's depredations remained fresh. Henry Cabot Lodge observed that it aroused the country more than any other event, and Secretary of State Robert Lansing said it transformed the apathy of the western states into "intense hostility to Germany" and "in one day accomplished a change in sentiment and public opinion that otherwise would have required months to accomplish."[83] This finally prompted Wilson, on April 2, to seek a declaration of war from Congress, which it granted four days later.

## The Progressives' War

American preparations for war commenced, giving Wilson latitude to implement his Progressive vision, only part of which had been enacted before 1917. Wilson and his Progressive allies had no scruples about reinterpreting the Constitution for their own devices, and recognized no limitations on government (particularly executive) authority. "America is not now and cannot in the future be a place for unrestricted individual enterprise," Wilson intoned.[84] Presaging today's advocates of the Constitution as a "living document," Wilson wrote in his book *Congressional Government* that "government is not a machine, but a living thing."[85] Constitutionalism was a phase, but government, Wilson wrote in another work, *The State*, "does now whatever experience permits or the times demand."[86] What he called "living political constitutions" (as opposed to Lincoln's concept of *the Constitution*) "must be Darwinian. . . . it must develop."[87] More important, Americans needed to abandon their "blind devotion" to the Constitution. As Jonah Goldberg has noted, "Wilson was the first president to speak disparagingly of the Constitution," mocking "Fourth of July sentiments."[88] Wilson's disparagement of the Constitution went deeper, to the very root of American exceptionalism and foundational dogma—Wilson had no higher view of liberty, as the concept had "no permanent nature." Liberty had "different meanings in different epochs,"[89] a frightening position for an American president.

Wilson subscribed to the Progressive view of the individual's place in society espoused by Jane Addams: "we must demand that the individual shall be willing to lose the sense of personal achievement, and shall be content to realize his activity *only* in connection to the activity of the many" (emphasis ours).[90] This view was a dangerous and absolute departure from the Lincolnesque view of society as a collection of individuals, each empowered, ambitious, separate, and distinct, with inherent volition and autonomy. For Wilson, society was the primary focus, with individuals as tools to an end. Fellow Progressive and founder of the "Social Gospel" movement to which Wilson allied himself, Walter Rauschenbusch, insisted, "New forms of association must be created. Our disorganized competitive life must pass into an organic cooperative life."[91] For Wilson, "men are as clay in the hands of the consummate leader," who "cares much—everything—for the external uses to which they may be put."[92] As the "consummate leader," Wilson had no regard for the opinions of others. The masses, he said, "must get their ideas very absolutely put, and are much readier to receive a half truth which they can promptly understand than a whole truth which has too many sides to be seen at once."[93]

Wilson's brand of Progressivism borrowed heavily from the Germans he now had to fight. He was particularly enamored with Otto von Bismarck—the "moral force of Cromwell and the political shrewdness of Richelieu; the comprehensive intellect of Burke [and] the diplomatic ability of Talleyrand."[94] Describing Bismarck's welfare state as an "admirable system . . . the most studied and most nearly perfected in the world," Wilson staffed his agencies with economists trained in German universities. A 1906 survey of 116 top economists and social scientists in the United States revealed that half had studied in Germany—Johns Hopkins University was built on the German blueprint—and whether or not they all accepted "top-down socialism" as practiced by Bismarck, many were hostile to capitalism. Richard Ely became the leading light of the Progressive economists. His Wisconsin brand of socialism, Teddy Roosevelt once said, "first introduced me to radicalism in economics and then made me sane in my radicalism."[95] Hitler would later agree with Wilson on the applicability of Bismarck's top-down socialism and the usefulness of war to implement it, noting that war would enable solutions to problems that "could never have been solved in normal times."[96] Like Ely, the atheist John Dewey saw the war as full of "social possibilities."[97] He relished the notion that war would force Americans to "give up much of our economic freedom. . . . We shall have to lay by our good-natured individualism and march in step," killing off "individualism" and elevating "public need over private possessions."[98] Even Jane Addams was "eager to accept whatever progressive social changes came from the quick reorganization demanded by the war."[99]

Having implemented the income tax and centralized banking in the United States under the Federal Reserve system, Wilson's Progressives now mobilized for war. Whether Wilson actively desired war is unclear, as he maintained the conflict would threaten his domestic agenda: "every reform we have won will be lost if we go into this war. [We have the new tariff] and currency and trust legislation. . . . They are not thoroughly set."[100] But he had enthusiastically sent American forces into Mexico. Once the war started, however, Wilson and his Progressive planners recognized an opportunity to remake the United States in the image they desired. Ely, for example, praised the draft, arguing that the "moral effect of taking boys off street corners and out of saloons and drilling them is excellent, and the economic effects beneficial."[101] There were, Wilson noted, "some splendid things that come to a nation through the discipline of war."[102] His predecessor Teddy Roosevelt, also a Progressive, agreed: "The military tent where they all sleep side by side will rank next to the public school among the great agents of democratization."[103]

Most of all, war enabled Wilson to raise taxes, and in fact, a year before the United States entered the war, Congress passed the 1916 Revenue Act, which doubled the bottom tax rate (to a still-low 2 percent) and almost tripled the top rate (from 6 percent to 15 percent). It is important to recall that support for the Sixteenth Amendment had been won only because voters had been promised that: 1) rates would be low, with most people exempt from any taxes at all; 2) the law was extremely simple, essentially consisting of a page or two for most people; and 3) it eliminated all the "backroom politicking" over tariff schedules that resulted in perceived inequities for different groups of people. Now the Revenue Act of 1916 wiped out the first benefit altogether, adding excise taxes and new "excess business profits" taxes. As the U.S. Treasury's own Web page itself notes in retrospect, "Driven by the war and largely funded by the new income tax, by 1917 the Federal budget was almost equal to the total budget for the years between 1791 and 1916."[104] Another Revenue Act was passed in 1917, and where prior to this act, a taxpayer had to have $1.5 million in income to be subject to a

15 percent tax, afterward, anyone making $40,000 was subject to such a rate, while the income earner making $1.5 million was subject to a stunning tax rate of 67 percent. Nor was Wilson's Treasury Department through, raising taxes again in 1918, this time to an astonishing top rate of 77 percent. Significantly, the lowest rate now stood at 6 percent, or the same amount the richest of the rich paid when the income tax amendment was ratified!

J. P. Morgan anticipated that tax rates would rise effortlessly to an oppressive level, pleading for the Treasury to finance the war solely through bonds, but the goal was more than merely funding the military effort. Progressives intended to keep the high tax levels in place after the war—Wilson's designated successor, Dayton, Ohio, newspaperman James M. Cox, made this plain. High income taxes would thereby permit the redistribution of wealth that many of the more honest advocates of the income tax celebrated when they passed the amendment. As a historian of the income tax noted, "Central to the appeal of a highly progressive income tax during the 1890s was the claim that it would both reallocate fiscal burdens according to ability to pay and also help restore a virtuous republic free of concentrations of power."[105] Redistribution of wealth constituted one of the three Progressive planks that the reform of war could provide, heavy regulation of business and massive centralized planning being the other two. War gave the Progressives the excuse they needed to remake the American economy.

## An Industrial Dry Run

As it had in the American Civil War, the U.S. government acquired weapons and supplies from the private sector rather than establishing large numbers of government-owned plants, armories, and factories. During the Civil War, virtually all of the advanced weapons acquired by *both* the Union and Confederate governments came from the labs and workshops of private inventors—Richard Gatling's machine gun, Christian Sharps's breechloader, Ambrose Burnside's carbine, George McClellan's saddle, Christopher Spencer's repeating rifle, John Ericsson's ironclad *Monitor*, Horace Lawson Hunley's submarine, and a host of heavy cannon from Thomas Rodman and Robert Parrott (both were officers, but Parrott resigned his rank to work for a private firm and Rodman worked with a private foundry). Even at the more basic level of supply, John D. Rockefeller and others provided massive amounts of boots, uniforms, buttons, packs, and bayonets, not to mention railroad locomotives and rolling stock. Political scientist Richard

Bensel's contrast of the two governments at war concluded that the Union, in large part, won because it was the freer, more capitalistic economy, and the North could "skim off the top" of its private sector economy without disrupting the wealth-generating mechanisms needed to also provide capital for the war.[106]

Smaller-scale wars, such as the Mexican War and the Spanish-American War, had not demanded as much from the American industrial system, although Samuel Colt, whose bankrupt armory was just being revived when the war with Mexico began, provided thousands of his new pistols, which made a critical difference in at least one battle.[107] At first it appeared that World War I would follow the pattern of the Civil War. Already Ford had introduced a four-wheel trailer designed to be pulled by a Model T, making the use of trucks for transport a reality; by 1917, truck convoys running from Detroit to Baltimore proved the feasibility of long-distance truck transportation.[108]

But World War I was destined to be run differently, following Progressive ideology. Even though production had soared since 1914, bringing the U.S. economy to near full capacity by 1916, Wilson's administration broke with tradition and funded government shipyards and munitions factories. More than five thousand agencies vied with one another for turf, overlapping their mandates, replicating work, and leaving gaps in responsibilities. As a result, the Army spent more than $14 billion in a three-year period due to an inefficient supply system. Ignoring private innovation, government bureaus specified both how to manufacture an item and the performance standards the item would have to meet. Failure to follow the government's direction or meet the government standard *even if the factory followed the government's processes exactly* constituted grounds for product rejection. Such all-encompassing control of industry yielded extremely high prices for government contracts to cover losses created by Uncle Sam himself.

Of most immediate concern, even before the U.S. declaration of war, was shipping, since it was subject to constant U-boat attacks. High risk for transport demanded high rates, in turn prompting Wilson's treasury secretary William Gibbs McAdoo to accuse shippers of an "orgy of speculation" and of charging "absurdly high" rates.[109] In a sharp break from the successful policies of the past, Wilson asked Congress to create the Emergency Fleet Corporation in 1917, giving the U.S. government absolute control over all merchant shipping related to the war. He wisely put steel man Charles Schwab in charge, and Schwab replaced the "cost-plus" system at shipyards with a "fixed price" system (always preferable when the design is known and risks few), but also allowed for bonuses to be paid to companies that exceeded their quotas or beat their timelines. When necessary, Schwab paid bonuses out of his own pocket; he gave pep talks to shipyard workers; and he buttonholed Rear Admiral Frank Fletcher, convincing him to award medals and flags to overachieving plants.[110] Carnegie called it a "record of accomplishment that has never been equaled," but the Emergency Fleet Corporation was an exception.

Schwab, like many of the "Dollar-a-Year" men (so called because the law prohibited the government from accepting free services, thus they were paid a dollar a year), represented the fusion of business and government. As the ranks of businessmen running programs inside the bureaucracy swelled, their opinion about the ills of government softened. Not surprisingly, after World War I, many spoke less harshly about Uncle Sam's interference and more favorably about regulation if there was money to be made in government contracts. At the same time, government agencies observed firsthand how executives planned their operations, leading to the introduction of business models and planning throughout Washington, most notably in the establishment of the Bureau of the Budget (later, the Office of Management and Budget). Created under the Budget and Accounting Act of 1921, the bureau was charged with monitoring government expenditures and planning for new revenues.

But in 1917, the newfound affinity of business for government, and vice versa, failed to introduce massive new efficiencies into the procurement of weapons. After a sputtering start, when some thirty-five committees handled forty basic industries—and the committees were begetting more committees—the Wilson administration sought to streamline procurement through the War Industries Board (WIB) created in July 1917.[111] The WIB continued to flounder until all power was handed to Bernard Baruch as chairman in March 1918. Branded as an "indefatigable worker of industrial miracles," Baruch had lobbied for military preparedness for two years as a partner in the A. A. Houseman & Company brokerage firm.[112] In 1916, he had left Wall Street to serve on the Advisory Commission to the Council of National Defense. His main challenge upon assuming his new position as chairman of the WIB was determining what needed to be produced first. As Baruch explained it, "Should locomotives go to [General] Pershing to carry his army to the front or . . . to Chile to haul nitrates needed to make ammunition. . . ? Should precedents be given to destroyers needed to fight the U-boats or to merchant ships . . . being decimated by the German subs?"[113] Endowed with powers not granted before to a government agency, the WIB under Baruch had the authority to seize and operate plants and to deal with labor management disputes. Baruch chose subtle methods when possible. He cajoled, bribed, and persuaded, playing on business's traditional respect for the federal government, and it worked to a degree: production increased 20 percent, although nowhere close to the levels American production would attain in the next war.

Ultimately, Baruch had more success getting business to work with the bureaucracy than he did getting the bureaucracy to work with the military. Subject to McAdoo and Baruch, American innovators proved far less productive than they had in the Civil War, when they were generally left to their own devices. Aside from a few inventions—the Browning automatic weapon, the Lewis machine gun, or the Holt caterpillar, which became the basis for the British-designed tank—the U.S. military found itself outclassed by both Allied and enemy gear. (Ironically, J. Walter Christie, unable to sell his designs to the U.S. Army, sold them to the Russians, where one became the basis for the famed T-34 tank.) By the end of the war, the United States was still relying substantially on French-made 75 mm guns, although this was partly by design. Both the British and French feared the United States might not be able to gear up in time for war, leading the French especially to promise to make available all necessary hardware (except rifles and ammunition) if the Americans just transported their soldiers "over there." A more important factor, however, was the ulterior motive on the part of both the French and British to use American soldiers as mere replacements in their own divisions, so all the Yankee troops needed were their rifles and ammunition.

In fact, American factories had been filling orders for the Allies for some time, especially for such items as artillery shells, but often on European specifications. Consequently, instead of the 1903 Springfield—the official service rifle, which could not be produced fast enough—the U.S. Army adopted the British Enfield, which already was being produced by the American companies Remington and Winchester. Although a bolt-action rifle, the Enfield was easy to use, reliable, and had a slick mechanism allowing for a high rate of fire. Moreover, it fit perfectly with the American tradition of sharpshooters. As one military historian noted, while doughboys (as the Americans were called) never attained British-level fire discipline, "at least they were well armed."[114] That is, they were "well armed" when they set foot on French soil. Until that time, many of the men had never trained with the Enfield; virtually none had ever fired a machine gun or thrown a grenade, and were put off when the British tried to teach them the "cricket" style of hurling grenades. Doughboys rebelled at what they considered "sissy" styles, and threw grenades like baseballs.

While Baruch tried to streamline the production of war goods, McAdoo centralized control over finances. The son of a Georgia attorney, McAdoo moved with his family to Knoxville at fourteen, when his father became a professor at the University of Tennessee. Practicing law in Tennessee, he nearly went bankrupt investing in the Knoxville streetcar system before moving to New York City. Forming a new law firm with Francis Pemberton— the son of Confederate general John C. Pemberton and cousin of the inventor of Coca-Cola, John S. Pemberton—McAdoo returned to railway projects, seeking to build a tunnel under the Hudson River and running the Hudson and Manhattan Railroad Company. An active Democrat, he had caught Wilson's eye in the 1912 campaign before marrying Eleanor Wilson, the president's daughter. Wilson had already tapped him to head the Treasury Department, and it was McAdoo's order to close down the New York Stock Exchange when the Europeans started to withdraw gold from the United States in 1914 that prevented them from draining American gold supplies. A "dry" when it came to alcohol, a pragmatist when it came to stacking the Treasury with talented businessmen, McAdoo is remembered for his quip, "It is impossible to defeat an ignorant man in an argument." As treasury secretary during the war, McAdoo knew the conflict would be phenomenally expensive—ten times the cost of the Civil War in real dollars, or about $112 billion, in addition to $10 billion in loans to the Entente. Both the machinery of the income tax and the Federal Reserve System permitted the government to raise revenues at unprecedented levels. New war bond campaigns, led by movie stars (including Mary Pickford, Douglas Fairbanks, and Charlie Chaplin), brought in billions. To administer the finances, McAdoo oversaw creation of the War Finance Corporation in 1918, whose chief function was to provide financial support to war-critical industries. Since railroads were also within his expertise, McAdoo was charged by Wilson to take control of the railroads in December 1917, running them through yet another board, the U.S. Railroad Commission, called by one liberal historian the "most drastic mobilization of the war."[115]

## Socialist Criticisms, Progressive Responses

While the Wilson administration's departure from the tradition of relying on the private sector to supply weapons was noteworthy, it paled next to the domestic centralization the Progressives instituted, beginning with the Espionage Act of June 1917. Under this act, use of the mail to oppose the war was punishable by large fines and/or imprisonment. Under the heavy hand of Postmaster General Albert Sidney Burleson, the Post Office targeted the Socialist Party, which had passed a resolution for "vigorous resistance" to the war, and which in the summer saw mailing privileges withdrawn for a dozen Socialist newspapers. All foreign-language editorials referring to the U.S. government, any of the belligerents, or the conduct of the war itself had to be translated into English and submitted in advance to the Post Office.

Prominent Socialists, such as Upton Sinclair, quickly broke with the national convention to declare their support for the war. George Creel's Committee on Public Information, described by author Jonah Goldberg as "the West's first modern ministry for propaganda," enlisted the support of such former civil libertarians as Clarence Darrow, who said, "When I hear a man advising the American people to state the terms of peace . . . I know he is working for Germany."[116] Creel's CPI and the Post Office pressured any group or individual who resisted the censorship of the Sedition Act (banning the "uttering, printing, writing, or publishing of any disloyal, profane, scurrilous, or abusive language about the United States government or the military"). The most notable case involved Max Eastman's radical journal *The Masses*, which was charged with attempting to hamper recruitment by urging men to resist the draft and by opposing the war. Although six editors won hung juries in a New York trial, it hardly constituted a blow for freedom of speech. When three espionage cases came before the United States Supreme Court in 1919, the convictions in each were upheld, with Justice Oliver Wendell Holmes, Jr., declaring that "when a nation is at war many things that might be said in time of peace are such a hindrance to its effort that their utterance will not be endured."[117]

During the war, dozens of journals, newspapers, and magazines were censored or banned from the mails for perceived antiwar messages, stories, or even cartoons. Some of the cases were egregious violations of civil rights, such as the state official in Wisconsin who was sentenced to more than two years in jail for criticizing the Red Cross, and the movie producer who received a ten-year jail sentence for making a film about British troops committing atrocities in the American Revolution.[118] After new sedition amendments were added in May 1918, federal prosecutors were given wide latitude to round up offenders, and prosecutions tended to be highest in the western states, where the socialist International Workers of the World (IWW, or "Wobblies") were active. Lest anyone think Wilson was prepared to return to "normalcy" and suffer criticism, in December 1919 he sought a peacetime version of the Sedition Act to replace the wartime law, but Congress ignored it. After the war, of course, many Progressives would stage a post-hoc criticism of the "excesses," claiming, as Walter Lippmann did, that society had gotten "too big, too complex" for men to understand, hence the rabid racism, Germanophobia, and xenophobia. What was Lippmann's solution? Another agency, an intelligence bureau under the direction of a "special class" of Progressive intellectuals.

While the Progressives tinkered with social engineering and intellectuals attempted to decide which of the two values, pacifism or Progressivism, was more important, there was still a war to be won. American troops arrived in France in large numbers in 1917, where they constituted the first completely unified American draftee army ever put into the field (as Union and Confederate conscripts had fought against each other). As evidenced in previous wars, the volunteer nature of most U.S. military forces led friend and foe alike to underestimate them as fighters. Certainly there was nothing imposing about the draftees and volunteers who showed up in 1917. The 79th Division of the U.S. Army, for example, "included in its roster a murderer, several moonshiners, and bootleggers, a newspaper reporter, a professional baseball player, several lumber-jacks, a couple of 'ham' actors, a couple of high school professors and at least one lunatic."[119] Famous gangsters, such as "Wild Bill" Lovett and "Monk" Eastman, were decorated heroes—Lovett won the Distinguished Service Cross, and Eastman was so chewed up by knife and bullet wounds that he nearly flunked the physical. They arrived with similar tales: "I can hardly remember a single instance of serious discussion of . . . war issues. We men, most of us young, were simply fascinated by the prospect of adventure and heroism," said one. Another noted, "War had been declared and I thought my country needed me," and a recent Italian immigrant was even more succinct: "Ma name Tony Monaco. In dees country seex months. Gimme da gun."[120] A third-generation Frenchman, Jean Pierre Godet, enlisted in November 1917, a day his father marked with a "mixed sense of joy and pain." "I feel," the elder Godet wrote, "a strange contradiction between my love for [my son] and my love for America."[121]

## The Yanks, and Black Jack, Arrive

By October 1917, British and French commanders, their armies already bled white, sought to have Americans fight alongside and within their own units before assuming an independent command. Privately, the British didn't trust the American soldiers to perform, while the French simply needed bodies to plug into the ever-growing number of holes in their ranks. British representatives even argued for doughboys to "be arranged immediately into provisional battalions, and shipped to Europe with little more than the uniforms on their backs," whereupon they would be trained and used as replacements for British divisions.[122] Of course, this meant being trained by British trainers in all things British, but after all, in the British view England had paid to bring American bodies over in British ships, had fed and clothed them, and now deserved to use them in battle.

But the French knew better than to advance this proposal, choosing a more diplomatic approach. In a secret memo to high command, the head of the French military mission, in a moment of perspicacity worthy of de Tocqueville, sized up the Americans as having "a highly developed national pride and a strong spirit of independence." Anticipating the changes afoot in the world, he perceived, "they are all convinced that their country is now predominant [and the United States thinks it is] holding the balance of power, by virtue of its enormous resources in men, money, and supplies." They had decided, he added, "not to submit to any subordination whatsoever," but to demand equal footing," to which "we must resign ourselves." He concluded that the French had to trust the Americans, who were "gifted, in general, with a sound common sense, and a spirit of fairness. . . . Our real and only danger lies in failure to make allowances for the spirit of the American people, and for the idiosyncrasies of the American mentality."[123] Nonetheless, the French also sought to train and use American soldiers for their own purposes, a move strongly and successfully resisted by General Pershing. To put matters to rest, Pershing finally abolished the use of French and British trainers for American soldiers, calling British training "a detriment" and French instructors "useless."[124]

The critical need for American troops in the spring of 1918 was due to the Russian Revolution of 1917, and to Lenin's having signed a peace treaty with Germany. Not only had Germany accomplished all of its war aims in the East (and perhaps more), the Treaty of Brest-Litovsk in March 1918 freed hundreds of thousands of German POWs and troops for service on the Western Front. Fortunately for the Allies, the Germans had occupied so much territory that it required hundreds of thousands of troops to guard and control the new acquisitions. Those forces could have been more effectively employed in the West. Nevertheless, enjoying a numerical superiority not seen since August 1914, the Germans mounted a series of offensives against the British and French using their new "Hutier tactics" of bypassing strong points to achieve breakthroughs in depth, bringing the Allies to the brink of destruction. Pershing allowed a quarter million American troops to assist in the defense, but only in American formations and commanded by American officers. By July, the Germans had suffered one million casualties and the Allies could go on the offensive with the American doughboys.

Pershing had been tasked by Wilson with keeping the American Expeditionary Force a "separate and distinct component" of the Allied forces. This was necessary not only because of the need to preserve American autonomy, but also because Pershing worried that the low morale of the battle-weary British and French would rub off on his untested units. Given little other direction by Wilson, Pershing shaped the American war effort in Europe more than any other single U.S. commander in military history. Pershing's unsuccessful expedition into northern Mexico to track down Pancho Villa had presented him with a lesson in the value and limitations of the new technologies. Airplanes under his command had scouted the vast desert, while automobiles commanded by Patton had pressed Villa. The Mexican campaign had instructed the United States in a much different type of guerrilla warfare from the one the more successful Philippine campaign had offered—indeed, many of the units had just come from the Philippines—and contributed to a larger body of knowledge of what worked, and didn't work, in battling guerrilla forces over large, open areas.

Pershing took a great deal more with him than knowledge and experience from his days in Mexico and Texas. While stationed at Fort Bliss in August 1915, he had received a crushing call from an AP correspondent who thought he was speaking to Pershing's lieutenant: "Lieutenant Collins, I have some more on the Presidio fire." Earlier that morning, a fire had engulfed Pershing's home in San Francisco, killing his wife and three daughters by smoke inhalation—only his son Warren survived. The general sobbed on a friend's shoulder the entire two-day train journey back for the funeral. Among the letters of condolence was one from Pancho Villa.[125]

Like many famous American commanders who were educators or involved in education—William Tecumseh Sherman, Joshua Chamberlain, Robert E. Lee (after the Civil War), and both Stonewall and Andrew Jackson (briefly)—John Pershing had been a schoolteacher for a short time after graduating from high school and before attending West Point.[126] His service in education continued with a posting to West Point as a tactical officer, and to the University of Nebraska as an instructor in military science, where he established the first of the "Pershing Rifles" drill teams. As an officer with the 10th Cavalry "Buffalo Soldiers," Pershing fought as a brevet major at San Juan and Kettle hills alongside Teddy Roosevelt and won what later became the Silver Star. With his unprecedented promotion to brigadier general, solid service in the Philippines, and notoriety from the Villa expedition, Pershing was one of only six people qualified to command the American Expeditionary Force in Europe. Two were due to retire in a year, and two were in ill health, making his only serious rival for the command General Leonard Wood. It turned out to be no contest as Wilson believed Wood harbored ambitions to become president, and while both Wood and Pershing were Republicans, Pershing's presidential aspirations did not come into focus until after the war. Both Pershing and Wood actively campaigned for the command, but Secretary of War Newton D. Baker chose Pershing and Wilson approved. Pershing met with President Wilson only once, and received no instructions as to the course he should pursue. "In the actual conduct of operations I was given entire freedom and in this respect was to enjoy an experience unique in our history," Pershing said later.[127] It is also worth noting that while virtually all national reporters knew of Pershing's departure date and on what ship he sailed, there were no "leaks" of the information, so patriotic were the journalists of the day. No one wanted to give the enemy a chance to sink Pershing's ship.

Ironically, Pershing's training concepts and tactics were decidedly "retro," greatly resembling the failed French notions of *élan*. He emphasized rifle fire accuracy, the use of the bayonet, and above all, the soldier's spirit. Instead of massed formations bedecked in brightly colored uniforms, however, doughboys would fight from a tactical background outlined in the *Infantry Drill Regulations*, which emphasized fast-moving infantry operating in smaller units with khaki or camouflage uniforms. Pershing appreciated the firepower of machine guns, but did not want his men dependent on them, fearing they would slow the advance. But he remained wedded to the frontal assault—to be sure, using broken-field "combined arms" tactics—in which the key was to identify the vulnerable strong points and overcome them using bayonets. The problem in the Meuse-Argonne offensive (September–November 1918), where the United States played a major role, was that lacking their own artillery or tanks, and demonstrably weak in coordinating with what air power there was, the Americans were reliant on the French. Time and again, artillery proved poorly directed; tanks broke down or French crews abandoned them under heavy fire; and Colonel Billy Mitchell's airplanes bombed and strafed behind the lines, not in support of advancing American infantry. The saving grace was that, whenever possible, subordinates were allowed to redefine tactics in light of battlefield circumstances—an American tradition.

Old-fashioned American innovation, adaptation, and, above all, individual autonomy made the Expeditionary Force a much different military unit from the cynical and hardened British and French armies it now joined. The level of preparedness was striking compared with that of the Europeans. Whereas Britain had gone to war with a general staff of 232 and Germany 650, the United States had only 41, and by law no more than half could be in Washington at the same time.[128] By the fall of 1917, a million Americans had arrived in Europe to little fanfare. They were greeted by no bands, no flag-waving civilians—"a funeral," as Captain George C. Marshall put it.[129] Yet the disembarking Americans seemed different, described by one European as "emanating a powerful impression of ruddy, clean-shaven youth, of lithe, athletic bodies with strong, clean limbs—the only really youthful army in the field in 1918."[130]

## Teufel Hunden

At first, however, the results were mixed. Early skirmishes produced easy victories, but the Americans were confronted with the awesome reality of twentieth-century combat when ordered into Belleau Wood to support a French operation. From June 6 to June 26, 1918, American infantry and Marines (who earned the nickname "Devil Dogs," or *Teufel Hunden*, from the enemy in the battle) fought against well-placed German positions arranged in kill zones, finally seizing the Wood, but not before suffering a shocking 5,200 casualties. Pershing's version of *élan* underwent an instant evolution in the hands of sergeants and junior officers, who realized the "reckless courage of the foot soldier with his rifle and bayonet could not overcome machine guns well-protected in rocky nests."[131] Trusting this commonsense, bottom-up refinement of tactics, Pershing told a subordinate

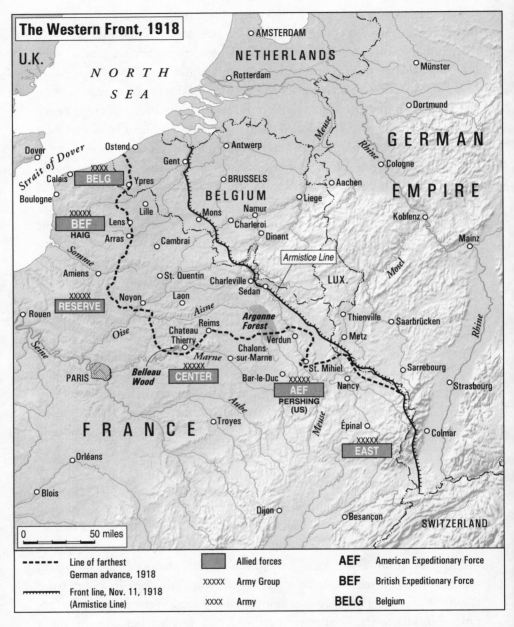

**The Western Front, 1918**

| | | |
|---|---|---|
| — — — | Line of farthest German advance, 1918 | ▮ Allied forces |
| ┄┄┄┄ | Front line, Nov. 11, 1918 (Armistice Line) | |

| XXXXX | Army Group |
| XXXX | Army |

**AEF** American Expeditionary Force
**BEF** British Expeditionary Force
**BELG** Belgium

that Americans had developed "a type of manhood superior in initiative" to the Europeans'.[132] Belleau Wood taught them that neither guts nor initiative alone would defeat the entrenched Germans; but it also showed that Americans could take a shot and persevere. Pershing therefore called Belleau Wood the most important battle for the American military since the Civil War.

Along with the education under fire came the official formation of the American 1st Army in August, consisting of fourteen infantry divisions, supported by French artillery, tanks, and trucks. France's Marshal Foch, who had by then become Supreme Commander of the Allied Armies (Pétain was Commander in Chief of All French Armies), continued to press for dispersing American forces to plug gaps in Franco-British lines, but Pershing angrily refused, telling the marshal, "While our army will fight wherever you decide, it will not fight except as an independent American army."[133] What "Black Jack" lacked in tactical ingenuity, he made up for in his skill in dealing with the French.

Foch relented. In September 1918, the half-million-strong U.S. 1st Army assaulted the St. Mihiel salient, which was only lightly defended by the Germans. Nevertheless, it resulted in a reassuring success, and Pershing boasted, "We gave 'em a damn good licking, didn't we!" But in the Meuse-Argonne offensive of September through November of 1918 they encountered a different German army, one of grizzled veterans instead of aged or very young reserves. Brimming with confidence, the American Expeditionary Force advanced toward its objectives. One survivor later recalled, "We were Power, and nothing could stop us. We were Americans!"[134] Division after division slammed into German artillery, gas, machine guns, and wire, shredded in the process and gaining little ground. Troops advancing from the rear lines were appalled to see up to two hundred ambulances delivering wounded to a single medical station. However wedded Pershing was to the bayonet offensive before the Meuse-Argonne, he reconsidered tactics after five days of heavy losses. Colonel Billy Mitchell, who had promised to clear the skies of German aircraft, similarly reappraised his work when German planes repeatedly filtered through his patrols to attack Americans on the ground. Mitchell refused to criticize the air corps, but he knew it had failed to live up to his promises.

By the end of September, Germany's defensive line had been breached, but with terrific American casualties and phenomenal psychological cost to those who had endured. As a pastor serving with the 80th Division wrote, "We became beasts lusting for blood and flesh. We were no longer normal, but abnormal. . . . Men swore who never swore before, men who taught Sunday School classes back home."[135] By then the American military force was too big for one man to lead while also commanding an army directly. Pershing replaced himself as commander of the 1st Army with General Hunter Liggett—a better tactician—and formed the 2nd Army under General Robert Bullard, thereby limiting his duties to Commander in Chief, American Expeditionary Force. The 1st Army had suffered somewhat under Pershing due to his being heavily involved in AEF matters and not having sufficient time to devote to it. His staff was fragmented, and a higher headquarters was long overdue, but Pershing wished to gain experience in army command. Fulfilling that desire had been a mistake, and now Pershing corrected it.

Pershing's insistence on an independent American command had alienated the British and the French, but in truth, from the outset both allies hoped to use American men piecemeal as replacements for their own losses without permitting a separate American presence. His doggedness in demanding an American Expeditionary Force separate from the British and French no doubt saved thousands of American lives. Americans would have been hurled piecemeal into action as part of British or French commands, negating their own training and unit *élan*. It also ensured that the United States had the most powerful army left in the field—a significant advantage to Wilson at any postwar bargaining table.

In the summer of 1918, eight divisions of American forces had seen their first actions at the Second Battle of the Marne, and then in the Meuse-Argonne offensive in September–November 1918 punched forward through the Argonne and pinched in on both German flanks. The U.S. advance was bloody and hard-fought with horrendous casualties and saw the debut of the famous Browning Automatic Rifle (BAR). And while German resistance didn't show it, the Kaiser's army in the Meuse-Argonne was out of reserves after expending everything it could scrape up to hold back the Americans. It is a wartime myth that the Germans were ready to surrender when the Americans arrived on the scene. In part, postwar French and British writers fed the tale in order to explain the doughboys' success, although progress had come at a fearsome price. Some divisions were at one-quarter strength; others were cobbled together from broken units. On the other hand, as New Left historians began to dominate the academy, they swung in completely the opposite direction, arguing that the Meuse-Argonne offensive was relatively insignificant. All the revisionism aside, the advance clearly demonstrated that the Americans—if not significantly better than the British, French, or German forces—were certainly no worse, and that now there were a lot of them. German hopes for victory all but faded with the offensive, as mutinies and riots spread back home in response to the death and stagnation at the front.

Optimistic stories, spread with the help of reporters, reached eager eyes back in the United States. And no greater heroic exploits could be reported than those of Alvin York. A deeply religious, barely literate Tennessean, whose conversion to pacifism came after a saloon fight that resulted in a friend's death, "Sergeant York" (a corporal when the battle of Meuse-Argonne began) had registered for the draft and answered the question, "Do you claim exemption from the draft (specify grounds)?" with "Yes. Don't Want to Fight."[136] He later denied having ever stated he was a conscientious objector and was drafted in November 1917. A year later his battalion was involved in actions north of Chatel-Chéhéry, France. During the advance on October 8, 1918, York and 16 others had moved behind enemy machine gun positions, capturing a headquarters unit and taking several Germans prisoner, when they themselves came under machine gun fire from a hillside. York happened to be in a perfect shooting position to pick off any machine gunner who raised his head to sight the guns. Or, in York's parlance, he "jes teched him off." He estimated there were 30 Germans with machine guns firing at him, and he responded "as fast as I could. I was sharp shooting. . . . All the time I kept yelling at them to come down."[137] After killing several, York found himself being charged by six Germans across a twenty-five-yard clearing, and he "teched off" the six one at a time with his pistol, killing the last one in line first so as to not alert the men in front. He then returned to sniping the other machine gunners with deadly accuracy. All the while, York was yelling at the Germans to surrender, telling them he did not want to kill them. Finally, the German lieutenant who had already surrendered was so stunned at York's shooting that he crawled up near him and said, "If you won't shoot anymore, I will make them give up." When York and his comrades finally returned to Allied lines, he had 132 prisoners and had killed at least a dozen more.[138] Promoted to sergeant, York was awarded the Medal of Honor and the Distinguished Service Cross, and France bestowed on him the Croix de Guerre and the French Legion of Honor.

Many have heard the exploits of Sergeant York, but few know of the amazing courage of Daniel Richmond Edwards, a machine gunner with the 1st Division, at the Battle of Cantigny in May 1918, and at the Battle of Soissons in July. The details are sketchy, but sufficient to have him nominated for two Medals of Honor. In one episode, according to a somewhat enhanced story by writer Lowell Thomas, an artillery shell exploded near Edwards, leaving him with a shattered right arm. Edwards shot several advancing Germans, and others threw down their weapons. Military rules prohibited more than one Medal of Honor award in a single action, so Edwards received the Distinguished Service Cross and the Medal of Honor consecutively.[139]

## The Final Push

In heavy fighting from October 16 through October 31, the 1st Army finally took the ridgeline over the Aire Valley, breaking the western wing of the German defensive perimeter, the *Kriemhilde Stellung*. Once again, it came at a terrific cost to the American forces, but Germany was out of men, and as one German officer put it, "The Americans are here. We can kill them but we can't stop them."[140] At the same time that the Germans were acknowledging the inevitability of American advances, the British cabinet received a scathing report saying that the "American Army is disorganized, ill-equipped, and ill-trained with very few non-commissioned officers and officers of experience. It has suffered severely through ignorance of modern war and it must take *at least a year* before it becomes a serious fighting force (emphasis in original)."[141]

The British were right about learning how to fight in a modern war. Liggett, addressing his corps commanders, impressed on them the need to change tactics and abandon the clumping up, massed lines, and frontal assaults, all things the British themselves appeared never to learn. The United States needed to keep casualties to a minimum with five thousand miles between the front lines and the replacement centers.[142] With his address, Liggett elucidated the first formal recognition of a deeply embedded American tradition that has now found its way into official doctrine, namely the concept of sanctity of life. In most ways the U.S. military essentially epitomized the "Western way of war" already seen in British and French forces, but with Liggett's declaration, widely referred to as the "casualty issue" after the war, the American military made economy of soldiers' lives an official policy.[143] Civil War–level losses would no longer be tolerated. America's military leaders would look to training and firepower as "equalizers" for countries using the bodies of their young men to achieve victory. In the next war, while the G.I.s' reliance on overwhelming firepower would fail them at times, no one ever regretted sending an artillery shell—instead of a soldier—over a hill.

The American Army underwent another change in the formation of units and loss replacement. In earlier wars, citizen-soldiers were recruited by companies from specific towns or areas, often by a single leader. Counties and states formed the regiments, which were placed in brigades and divisions under a commanding general from the home state. This greatly increased unit cohesion, and in part accounted for the remarkable staying power of veteran regiments in the Civil War. In World War I, the Army experimented with larger units (roughly 20,000 men per division versus 5,000 men during the Civil War). America's Rainbow Division was made up of units from different states, whose object was to spread casualties out more evenly among the United States geographically so as not to risk the destruction of entire towns' male populations. The experiment appeared to work satisfactorily, and henceforth all units other than National Guard units would be filled by draftees from all parts of the nation. Replacements would be distributed almost randomly and sent to combat units direct from distribution centers, and if the unit was actively engaged in combat, the new arrival would be thrown into action with no prior training or association with the others in his unit. Over time, American unit cohesion suffered greatly and casualties increased due to the lack of in-unit training—but towns and counties no longer needed to fear losing all their young men in a single action.

Liggett also insisted that frontal assaults had to be replaced with fire and maneuver and combined arms—not that the Army hadn't already preached this, but with so little training time, no units had successfully coordinated themselves. Billy Mitchell also quietly changed his focus from strafing and bombing rear support and supply areas to hitting the front lines in coordination with advancing infantry. By November 1918 the Americans had as many airplanes as the Germans, although only one in five of them was American-made; in addition, for the first time they had ample artillery ammunition. With battle experience surfaced the autonomy of American fighters who, unlike the British and French soldiers, were allowed to trust their instincts. Squad-level tactics to take out machine guns by flanking developed as veterans discovered what worked.

Consequently, the American advance on November 1, 1918, was a crushing defeat for Germany's defenders; now gains came in miles instead of yards. For the first time, American units saw entire columns retreating, and the doughboys set up their own kill zones to ambush the enemy, crossing the Meuse on November 3–4. In a four-week period, 1.2 million American soldiers and Marines conquered the Meuse-Argonne and drove out the Germans. The American victory, however, had come at a terrible cost—

26,277 dead, 97,786 wounded, accounting for half of all U.S. wartime casualties. American troops had inflicted 100,000 casualties on the Germans and had also taken 26,000 prisoners, but it was far from a draw, as the last of the Kaiser's frontline combat veterans were gone. No one could oppose the Allies now, and General Liggett thought that a few more days of fighting would have "reduced [the German Army] to a mob."[144] British historians later noted that Americans had suffered disproportionate losses compared with the British advance farther north, but the territory over which the Americans fought was far more difficult, and the enemy fought tenaciously, with forty-four divisions thrown into the fight.[145] Therefore it is fair to say that while the Americans certainly did not win the war, they tipped the scales for Allied victory. Arriving in large numbers—untrained or not—the fighting men of the United States snatched the last glimmer of hope from the heart of Imperial Germany.

The farther toward Germany the Allies moved, the more it became apparent to the commanders on the ground that they had limited time to achieve decisive results before the politicians negotiated an unsatisfactory peace. When the Kaiser abdicated on November 10, everyone knew that time was even shorter, and indeed, emissaries were dispatched from Spa immediately to inquire as to terms. Allied military commanders Foch, Pétain, Pershing, and Haig, sensing the end was near, had met on October 25, 1918, at Senlis to discuss what the terms for an armistice or cease-fire should be if there was to be an armistice. Pershing suggested that all U-boats and their bases be surrendered, but British Field Marshal Haig said, "That is none of our affair. It is a matter for the Admiralty to decide."[146] Since the conference was only about an armistice, Pershing said nothing about what he really favored—unconditional surrender. However, after receiving instructions from Secretary of War Newton D. Baker, Jr. that seemed to indicate he was authorized to bring up alternatives to an armistice, Pershing laid out the case for unconditional surrender to the Supreme War Council in a memo on October 30. "It is the experience of history that victorious armies are prone to overestimate the enemy's strength and too eagerly seek an opportunity for peace. . . . I believe the complete victory can only be obtained by continuing the war until we force unconditional surrender from Germany."[147] Pershing's words would ring prophetic over time, in light of Adolf Hitler's convincing "stab-in-the-back" theory of the war's end. Germany, however, also knew that its time was short, and its leaders began discussing the prospect of an armistice after Allied successes in the

Battle of Amiens on August 8, 1918, or what Ludendorff called the "black day of the German Army." Soon, no other choice was possible. Mutinies at home convinced German war leaders that Germany needed to extract itself from the war before it was occupied—and before Pershing's unconditional surrender was imposed on it.

Although the United States had celebrated its heroes in previous wars, after the Great War attitudes changed. Glorifying combat and warriors was not a priority for Progressives—often the returning veterans were simply ignored. Returning troops might receive a parade upon their homecoming, but then they rapidly disappeared into the general population. There they sometimes experienced acceptance, regaining their old jobs or civic positions, but other soldiers returned to find their jobs had been taken and people were uninterested in what had happened in Europe. Unemployment shot up to nearly 9 percent by the end of 1921—almost double what it had been at war's end. Moreover, unlike after the American Civil War, there was no presumption back home that merely fighting in the war qualified a man for positions of political leadership. For the first time in American history a major American war did not generate a president from a top commander: the Revolution produced Washington; War of 1812—William Henry Harrison; Mexican War—Zachary Taylor; Civil War—Ulysses S. Grant; Spanish-American War—Theodore Roosevelt; but Pershing would not make the list. Only once more would the previous pattern emerge—Eisenhower from World War II. The Korean War, Vietnam, and the Middle Eastern wars would not produce presidents, although a number of veterans would be contenders. Times had definitely changed.

That was not to say that World War I didn't yield magnificent heroes with compelling stories such as York and Edwards. Like Iwo Jima flag raiser Ira Hayes, who would never come to terms with his fame, Charles Whittlesey, the unlikely hero of the "Lost Battalion," struggled with the ghosts of the Argonne, finally committing suicide by jumping overboard on a fruit liner headed for Havana, leaving behind eight notes. "I'm a misfit by nature and by training," he wrote, "and there's an end of it."[148]

Most people were not interested in misfits after the war, even those who had recently been heroes. Veterans in American cinema and fiction were invisible—one exception was *The Big Parade* (1925), directed by King Vidor, about a businessman who goes to fight in France and loses a leg. Other movies that depicted war dealt with fliers, including *Wings* (1927), *The Dawn Patrol* (1930), and *Hell's Angels* (1930). York and Whittlesey were celebrities (and Whittlesey played himself in a 1919 film, *The Lost Battalion*), but York's story was not told on film until 1941, when it was as much a World War II propaganda film as it was an homage to the hero.

## Europe's Myths and Malaise

If American veterans were reabsorbed into society with little fanfare, a different mood descended in Europe. England, deeply affected by the body counts of World War I, having lost 750,000 British and 250,000 colonial troops, bought into the myth that "the First World War had been futile; that it had been fought for nothing."[149] France sank to levels of depression and denial about the Western Front (the French even banned the word "Verdun" from schoolbooks temporarily, so great was the slaughter of the Republic's youth). No sooner had the guns fallen silent than eulogies were written and publicized, not merely for the dead but for national self-confidence and moral certitude.

Britain's grief was expressed through the "lost generation" interpretation—the belief that the brightest minds of Oxford and Cambridge had fallen in the trenches (as indeed, thousands had—with more than 37,000 British officers dead on the Western Front). As British historian Paul Johnson pointed out, a bevy of postwar writers and poets, "obsessed with death, futility, and waste," always unheroic and replete with the moral that national goals were meaningless, cultivated the lost generation myth. Well into the 1980s, the BBC's *Blackadder Goes Forth* (1989) continued to portray the British experience in World War I as an "unmitigated disaster." As late as 1996, the most quoted British figures of the First World War were not generals or statesmen, but the "War Poets" such as Rupert Brooke, Wilfred Owen, Ivor Gurney, and Siegfried Sassoon.[150] Many, including Brooke, Owen, Edward Thomas, and Charles Sorley, died before war's end.

In fact, the British casualty numbers were "commensurate with the scale of Britain's role in the fighting and the issues at stake, while the losses assumed by enemies and allies were even greater."[151] Nor was there evidence of any unusual disenchantment or disillusionment with the war effort among British soldiers. Nonetheless, it would not be totally inaccurate to say that France never regained its national strength after losing entire age groups, and Britain national confidence was so severely damaged that it rapidly declined into a "nanny" state after the Second World War completed what the First World War began. Germany, too, was not unaffected, and after the last hurrah of World War II, fell into a pacifism from which it has not yet recovered. All of the warring European nations began to experi-ence declining birth rates; by the end of the twentieth century, many ob-servers openly discussed the end of a Caucasian, Christian Europe in the ensuing century.

The facts of the war did not alter perceptions, and most people felt that Britain's military leadership had been incompetent, if not criminal. After the war, British films, including *The Dawn Patrol* (1938) and *The Life and Death of Colonel Blimp* (1943), depicted officers shipping off untrained pilots on virtual suicide missions. An Italian-born Canadian, Humphrey Cobb, who had served in the Canadian Army in World War I, penned a haunting novel, *Paths of Glory*, which follows a mutiny against a French general who sends his men on a suicidal frontal assault on a German trench in the West-ern Front. (Mutinies in the French Army occurred on a substantial scale after the failed Nivelle Offensive in 1917, so the plot was grounded in real-ity.) When the attack fails, the general attempts to shift blame for the disas-ter by executing three randomly selected soldiers. Despite the injustice, the men were found guilty at trial and executed for the sins of the division. Cobb's book met with minor success until 1957, when director Stanley Ku-brick adapted it to the screen in a powerful drama starring Kirk Douglas.

The carnage on the Western Front was certainly unprecedented, but despite many assumptions, this did not result from the introduction of bet-ter technology and advanced firepower alone. This, of course, had been Ivan Bloch's reasoning for why war would be avoided in the first place, namely that the cost would be too great due to more lethal weapons. Rather, World War I's shocking casualty rolls owed much to the repeated and egre-gious misreading of military history over the previous half century. Euro-peans' horror at the bloodletting now swung them in the opposite direction, as Progressives and Socialists attempted to guarantee that human disagree-ments or misunderstandings would never again have to be settled by vio-lence. As a utopian ideal, it was misguided. As a policy for the postwar world, it was dangerous and self-defeating. Combined with American do-gooder Progressivism, Europe's recoil from national security enforced by sound military practices virtually ensured that World War I would in fact not be the "great" war and that its murderous education would require yet more lessons. One of those lessons was already unfolding in Russia, whose Revolution had taken it out of World War I, but which had only begun to show itself as the natural end point of Progressivism by 1919.

## Progressivism's Red Metamorphosis

An old European saying holds that "Russia is never as strong as she looks, and Russia is never as weak as she looks." Certainly World War I confirmed this—the vast Russian manpower pool that had terrified von Schlieffen and other German planners had proven ineffective and often incompetent. The Czar's government, unable to balance "guns and butter," left itself open to anger and hostility from starving cities, conscripted soldiers, and abandoned families. Although the Czar's secret police, the Okhrana, never came close to approximating the terror inflicted by later Soviet organs such as the NKVD, it nevertheless struck fear in the breast of every Russian and provided ample fodder for the writings of political dissidents.

Bolshevism, a Marxist political subcurrent throughout Europe before the war, concerned almost all European governments, but most possessed sufficiently developed political systems to address social concerns through the existing machinery of the state. Not so with Russia, a truly backward nation by European standards. It had largely missed the Renaissance and to some extent the Enlightenment. Its "educational standards were woeful, legal norms went unheeded, and poverty was awesome."[152] Prewar reforms had alleviated some suffering, but they were too little, too late. Czar Nicholas II, whose wife, Alexandra, had come under the influence of the mystic priest Rasputin, had lost the confidence of the nobility and landlords. Russia's entrance into the war resulted from its solidarity with Serbia, but also involved the misapprehension that Germany certainly would not dare fight on two fronts. Early defeat at Tannenberg meant that Russia had become embroiled in a long and fatal war. Food was drained out of the countryside to support the troops, en route often getting stuck in cities where corrupt officials hoarded or resold it. Land reforms undertaken prior to August 1914 had scarcely made a dent in Russia's inequality, and on the eve of war there were still well over 123 million landless peasants, *bednyaks* (poor peasants) and *batraks* (seasonal workers), along with some 40 million landed peasants, *serednyaks* (middle-income peasants) and *kulaks* (high-income peasants). That left a few million actual "proletariat" in urban factories and a handful of educated elites precariously perched on top.

Any program that offered what would become the Bolshevik slogan, "Bread, peace, land," was certain to gain widespread support. The question was never if there was to be change—only how quickly it would come and whether or not it could be managed. Lenin provided the answer to that question, as well as the catalyst the Bolshevik minority needed to gain the crest of the wave of anger and unrest.

A disagreeable little man with perpetually angry eyes, a peasant cap, and, later, a goatee, Vladimir Ilych Ulyanov took the name "Lenin" from the Lena River in Siberia. The son of an Orthodox Christian mother, a schoolteacher, and a public school bureaucrat father who longed for democracy, Lenin absorbed little from his parents. Indeed, the Ulyanovs raised a viper's nest of radicals: one brother, Aleksandr, plotted to assassinate Czar Alexander III with a bomb and was hanged; a sister, Anna, was exiled to the village of Kokushkino for antigovernment activism. Vladimir himself became radicalized at Kazan State University, but rejected anarchism as he sought direction for his anger. He found it when he was expelled from Kazan State for participating in student protests, then enrolling at the University of St. Petersburg, where he absorbed Marx's teachings. Like Marx, he immersed himself in books, political tracts, and official statistics; like Marx, he never toured a factory—let alone worked in one. From the 1890s to 1924, "there was little change in his basic thinking," and Lenin could "live for years in a locality—be it London, Zurich or Moscow—and fail to draw the conclusions about his surroundings that came easily to others without his hardened prejudices."[153]

Contrary to modern popular perceptions, Lenin was a poor public speaker and a dense writer. Only a few well-informed theoreticians had ever read his works. Punctilious to the point of obsession in his daily regimen, Lenin's pursuit of control in his personal existence may have reflected his inability to control his health. Incapacitated by serious illnesses, including ulcers, migraine headaches, heart attacks, and a recurring affliction called "St. Anthony's fire"—a nervous inflammation characterized by severe and sharp pains in the limbs—Lenin was absent at decisive moments in the rise of communism in Russia due not only to self-imposed exile to escape prosecution and prison but also disease.[154]

Absorbing the inherent violence of Marxism, with its refusal to tolerate any dissent at all, and its atheism (which reinforced the violent tendencies), Lenin was nevertheless unfaithful to the doctrine. He easily adopted bourgeois values, readily admitting that only European civilization mattered. He read the classics, abandoned his wife, and took a sophisticated French mistress. In the process he not only personally embraced bourgeois values but substituted the bourgeoisie as a class for the proletariat as the vehicle of revolutionary upheaval. It was a monumental paradigm shift that laid the groundwork for investing subsequent intelligentsia with the authority to demand social change—something that would have been impossible if Marx's proletariat had remained the dominant revolutionary class. Until Lenin, the appeal of Marxism was that it had represented the physical laborer, the industrial worker, whose difficult life elicited sympathy and admiration from elites (though elites rarely wished to engage in physical work). After Lenin, the rhetoric of the "common man" and the language of the "oppressed masses" was retained by Communists for propaganda purposes, but the educated classes—particularly those with excess time on their hands—became the real agents of the revolution. Their knowledge of human behavior, psychology, sociology, and economics under the canopy of new "scientific" approaches to these subjects had already propelled the Western Progressives to victory. Now, scientific knowledge became one more arrow in the quiver of Bolshevism to slay class enemies. Science was a tool to be used for political ends, not simply a source of human understanding.

As writer and historian Barbara Tuchman observed:

> Revolution appealed more to intellectuals who had no doubt of their capacity to manage society than it did to the working class. . . . Organized Socialism . . . was a movement not of, but on behalf of, the working class. . . . Although it spoke for the worker and made his wants articulate, goals and doctrine were set, and thought, energy and leadership largely supplied by, intellectuals. The working class was both client and ultimately, in its mass strength, the necessary instrument of the overthrow of capitalism. . . . The working class was no more of a piece than any other class. Socialist doctrine, however, required it to be an entity with a working-class mind, working-class voice, working-class will, working-class purpose. In fact, these were not easily ascertainable. The Socialist [and Marxist] idealized them and to be idealized is to be overestimated.[155]

Lenin himself is proof positive of the correctness of Tuchman's analysis. Yet his drastic inversion of Marxist doctrine did not demonstrate the mind of a clear thinker—quite the contrary, his notebooks reeked of contradictions. For a decade Lenin, by adhering to Marxist principles of what "should" happen, had been consistently and stupendously wrong. Virtually every major event took him by surprise, from the aborted 1905 revolt to the arrival of war to the utter failure of an "international" (that is, a global Communist movement) to arise. (In this he would be in the company of Marx, who also seemed perpetually wrong in his predictions.) Lenin was surprised at the ouster of Nicholas, surprised by Aleksandr Kerensky's gullibility in releasing political prisoners, and surprised by the continuation of the war. His inability to predict events correctly, or to apply the lessons either of history or of Marxist theory, was exceeded only by his keen talent for action and manipulation once events erupted.

One final break by Lenin from Marxist theory came in his insistence that "vanguard elites," led by individuals, had to direct the revolution. Marx, on the other hand, had argued that the masses would spontaneously arise. Lenin's theoretical redefinition reinforced his practical efforts to crush all internal opposition by any means necessary. It was only this adoption of violence and the use of any tactic to achieve his ends that differentiated Lenin from the Progressive Wilson and his later followers in the United States who were building an elite-based Progressive/Bolshevist state on behalf of the working class. Wilson and his Progressive successors faced another problem that Lenin didn't—namely that in the United States the middle (bourgeois) class needed first to be reduced to proletarian status before a revolution could succeed.

Lenin's close confidants recognized his oppressive direction early. Leon Trotsky saw the terror coming a decade before it arrived, but the inevitability soon became apparent to all: murder, mass terror, shooting, killing, exterminating, jailing—these all appeared as common terms for use against his "enemies list," the schoolteachers, priests, nuns, Whites, kulaks, wreckers, traitors, or any other label he could affix to those who disagreed with him in any way. Sooner or later, almost every Communist insider of the Revolution ended up on the enemies list. Georgy Plekhanov, a faithful Marx popularizer and cofounder of Communist groups in Switzerland, soon found himself on the opposite side of Lenin, whom he viewed as a dictator. Plekhanov was fortunate enough to die of tuberculosis before Lenin could consign him to a firing squad.

Yet many stuck with him, recognizing in Lenin the single-minded focus on obtaining power that would result in the success of their cause. His opponents saw this obsessive drive in him as well. One labeled him a "political Jesuit," another, the anti-Bolshevik Fyodor Dan, lamented about the absence of a Lenin on his side: "there's no such person [as Lenin] who is so preoccupied twenty-four hours a day with revolution, who thinks no other thoughts except those about revolution and who even dreams in his sleep about revolution."[156]

Lenin's will to power, and the elevation of the individual leader as the embodiment of the revolution, enabled him to accomplish much. With only twenty thousand core followers, he would conquer a nation of 160 million. In his 1902 pamphlet *What Is to Be Done?* he laid out the means by which he would seize power: he would organize and radicalize the elites, who, in turn, would agitate the proletariat into revolution. He said nothing about the peasants—who, in fact, would be the backbone of the revolution while the factory workers resisted.

Lenin had no interest in democracy, or process, or rights. Violence itself constituted the ultimate scoreboard, and he cared nothing for how a program or idea would be received by the people. Not just the masses, but the rulers, too, were insignificant gnats to be swept away—only the Bolshevik state could remain. Having determined that the revolution could come through the elites, he turned on them as soon as the violence started, shifting back to the Marxist claim that the bourgeoisie was now the enemy. Attempting to find consistency in Lenin's words or deeds was thus a fool's errand, especially so when his objective was power. That is why he could just as easily flip-flop on the war (one minute it was despicable, the next it was useful) as he could on prices later when he employed the very mechanisms of the free market he detested. Since the working class was not bolshevized, he easily switched gears to making the peasants the revolutionary arm. Who cared what Marx wrote? What mattered was moving forward to a Bolshevik state, not how one got there. As he told author Maxim Gorky, the party needed to "beat [the people] over the head, beat them mercilessly even though we, as an ideal, are against any coercion of people. [It's] a hellishly difficult necessity."[157] A useful intellectual exercise is to compare the predominance of the term "exterminate" in Lenin's vocabulary with that of "liberty" in the writings of the American Founders: the former never appeared in the works of the Founders, while Lenin never used the latter, even by accident.

The reason Lenin could so easily tack back and forth between invoking references to the "common man" and his own elite-oriented program lay in the concept of the "Soviet man," a new person engineered entirely by the state. Any and all destruction of living, breathing people was sanctioned and even desirable, for the quicker the "old" man was eradicated, the sooner the new Soviet man could emerge. Practically, Lenin's logic led to the Red

Terror. Like Hitler's Germany and the Stalinist successor state, Lenin's revolutionary agenda could not have been implemented without the vicious application of force. Over time, the millions of people killed tended to be forgotten as a statistic, but Lenin had an obsession with murder in the name of politics. "How can you make a revolution without firing squads?" he asked, despite the fact that the Americans had pulled it off quite nicely just a century earlier.[158] "If you can't shoot a . . . saboteur," he asked, "what sort of great revolution is it?"[159] As British historian Paul Johnson has noted:

> [Lenin's] writings abound in military metaphors: states of siege, iron rings, sheets of steel, marching, camps, barricades, forts, offensives, mobile units, guerilla warfare, firing squads. They are dominated by violently activist verbs: flame, leap, ignite, goad, shoot, shake, seize, attack, blaze, repel, weld, compel, purge, exterminate.[160]

To crush the kulaks he urged the Bolsheviks to "Hang (and I mean hang so that the people can see) not less than 100 known bloodsuckers."[161] Lenin issued a similar set of orders in August 1918. One Communist paper boasted that "we will kill our enemies in scores of hundreds. Let them be thousands, let them drown themselves in their own blood."[162]

Before Lenin could "kill" or "drown" anyone, he had to have control of the Russian government. But in February 1917, a series of strikes and demonstrations in Petrograd initiated the first Russian revolution. Troops called out to quell the demonstrations—many of them untrained or unreliable reserves not sent to the front—refused to fire on the crowds. Some mutinied; officers went into hiding; and the Czar's ability to stem the tide of protest vanished. When the Czar traveled to Petrograd to personally intervene, he found military and civilian officials aligned against him, and was persuaded to abdicate. On March 15, he stepped down, and six days later he was placed under house arrest. (In July 1918 the Czar and his entire family would be executed at a holding house in Yekaterinburg.) A provisional government took control, led by the brilliant orator and member of the Socialist Revolutionary Party Aleksandr Kerensky. A member of the Duma's Provisional Committee and vice chairman of the Petrograd Soviet (that is, "workers' council"), Kerensky was appointed minister of war in May 1917, but he could not marginalize or neutralize the Bolsheviks, particularly after Lenin arrived in April. When Kerensky allowed the war to drag on, Lenin had his chance to lead the resistance, not just be its visionary, although the takeover of the Winter Palace was led by Trotsky in October.

The Bolsheviks' hold on power was tenuous. Not only did the monarchists and non-Socialists oppose them, but other groups on the Left struggled to grab power, and Kerensky enjoyed support in the middle of the political mix. These divisions enabled Lenin's bloody words to attain a sort of logical status. After all, it did appear that there were "enemies" on all sides for the Bolsheviks. When fellow revolutionary Isaac Steinberg asked Lenin why he even bothered with fancy names, Steinberg said, "Let's honestly call [the Extraordinary Commission] the Commissariat for Social Annihilation . . ." to which Lenin replied, "Well said! . . . but it can't be stated by us."[163] Consolidating the regime required terror, but it also demanded sensible strategy, which Lenin supplied: control the rail centers at Moscow and Petrograd, and eliminate recalcitrant officials. This was easily handled by the terror squads picking off opponents one at a time, and without a constitutional system of protective law, no institutions existed in Russia to stop it. All that vanished in the Red Terror.

The Communists also benefited from two other factors. First, although badly outnumbered, they were consolidated, whereas their enemies in the civil war that followed were split among three armies that rarely coordinated. The "Whites," the enemy of the "Reds," led by the czarist generals, had allies in the form of the Czech Legion of upwards of 35,000 volunteers who fought on their side. But these ultimately proved unreliable, and all too often the battle was not between the Whites and the Reds but also among a dozen smaller splinter groups that muddled the battle lines. Had the Whites managed to unite, either among themselves or with the other opponents of the Bolsheviks, Lenin's group might have been doomed.

A second factor that worked in the Bolsheviks' favor was the public dissatisfaction with the war. In June, despite a promise to the contrary, Kerensky's Provisional Government ordered new troop deployments to the front. Mutinies followed which Kerensky could not control. Although new demonstrations burst out, Lenin sensed it was still too early (the Bolsheviks controlled only about one in five of the delegates) and he fled to Finland while the uprising withered. Czarist general Lavr Kornilov, claiming the radicals were about to seize the Petrograd government, marched the 3rd Army into the city and asked for reinforcements—in reality plotting a coup. Kerensky relieved him of command, but not before being forced to seek help from the Bolsheviks. They called up the Red Guards, and Bolshevik agents, instead of assisting the troop movements, slowed trains and halted telegraph communications. The coup fizzled, but in the confusion, Kerensky had sent signals that his government was weak and, worse, desperate for help in stopping Kornilov, he had armed his enemies from government weapons stores. War demands also led Kerensky to alienate the peasants when the Provisional Government's March decree requisitioned virtually all available food for the military.

By October, Lenin was convinced the time was ripe, and he returned to snatch power, forming the "Political Bureau" under Kerensky's nose on October 9. In November, Kerensky briefly led aborted attempts to retake the major cities before fleeing to France. Once in control, the Bolsheviks immediately announced a cease-fire with Germany, which provided masses of disgruntled men ready to claim their reward for years of fruitless combat. Entire regiments had returned to the cities by October, becoming prime targets for Bolshevik recruitment. At the same time, the peasantry was drifting into the Bolshevik camp, and the government's war-induced food shortages added to the interruption of the land redistribution program, also necessitated by the war. Once theft by the government seemed legitimized, order broke down everywhere, all to the benefit of the Bolsheviks. Resistance to government food collections grew so marked that five sixths stayed in the hands of the peasants, who hid and hoarded. On October 25, armed Bolsheviks took control at gunpoint, then forced the Congress to rubber-stamp their coup d'état.

No grandiose socialist slogans accompanied the Bolshevik seizure of Russia, no high-minded rhetoric about the good of the masses characterized the takeover. It was a quasi-military operation whose tyrannical nature was, temporarily at least, concealed by Lenin in numerous votes, appointments of "opponents" (such as the Mensheviks and Kadets) to power, and faux exercises of "democracy." Lenin realized that by controlling the head, the body would follow, and therefore made no attempt to interfere with daily life or to publicly restructure the Congress. Instead, enemies would quietly be purged from the party—and killed. But he moved instantly to secure the real levers of power, slamming shut any newspapers that opposed him and running all news through two house organs, *Pravda* ("Truth") or *Izvestia* ("News"). In latter years, a dark Russian proverb surfaced: "There is no Truth in the News, and no News in the Truth." Indeed, the real truth was that Lenin was staffing the government right down to the local level with party faithful, overwhelming the people with lots of show elections.

For a population utterly unfamiliar with voting and unused to genuine democratic power, the result was predictable: Lenin got his men in the right positions.

By this point, Lenin's perpetual illnesses had returned, made worse by a series of heart attacks that increasingly left him incapacitated. Several candidates waited to replace him, including Trotsky, but none more vicious and determined than Joseph Stalin. Born in 1878, Iosif Vissarionovich Dzhugashvili, a Georgian, Stalin was beset by injury as a child, suffering from smallpox, which left him with a pockmarked face; at age twelve he suffered permanent arm damage in a pair of carriage accidents. A seminary student, Stalin was expelled when he failed to pay his tuition, whereupon he landed on the writings of Lenin. He joined the Bolsheviks in 1903, operating chiefly out of the Caucasus, where he raised money through bank robberies and kidnapping. Calling himself Koba Dzhugashvili, he was captured several times by the secret police, but repeatedly escaped, even from Siberian exile. There is strong evidence that he became a police spy or informant for the Okhrana, the Czar's secret police, and later his Okhrana dossier became a subject of much speculation, particularly during the de-Stalinization of the USSR under Nikita Khrushchev. In 1912, Koba was in St. Petersburg when funding was obtained for the newspaper *Pravda* through the Okhrana, and was present when the first issue was created, largely through the efforts of another young Communist, Vyacheslav Skryabin, who took the name Molotov (Russian for "hammer"), although Koba would later attempt to take credit for the newspaper. When Koba was arrested again, he escaped once more and took the name "Stalin," or "man of steel."[164]

Lenin had watched Stalin rise through the ranks, an obedient soldier and reliable leader. He assigned both Stalin and Trotsky to the Politburo, where the two frequently clashed, although Lenin considered Trotsky a better military leader and more inspiring speaker and favored him for his status as a secular Jew. Stalin countered with three of his own supporters, Lev Kamenev, Lazar Kaganovich, and Grigory Zinoviev, and was able to whittle away at Trotsky's support. (Only Kaganovich would later survive Stalin's purges.)

As the first general secretary of the Communist Party of the Soviet Union's Central Committee from 1922, Stalin's alliance with Kamenev, the chairman of the executive committee, Zinoviev, full Politboro member and head of the Comintern, and Kaganovich, who was responsible for all appointments and assignments within the Communist Party bureaucracy, proved invaluable. The Party had made Stalin Lenin's intermediary, but their relationship deteriorated and Lenin grew increasingly distrustful of the Georgian. Lenin's letter naming Trotsky as his successor was discovered by Stalin, who, in his official capacity as "caretaker" of Lenin's health, effectively buried the letter out of sight of the Central Committee, and Trotsky did not learn of the deception. With Lenin's death in 1924, Stalin plotted to excise two of his former allies, Kamenev and Zinoviev, who could become future rivals—as well as Trotsky—and by the end of 1926 had consolidated much of the Party's power in his own hands, helped considerably by Kaganovich, who placed Stalin's adherents in critical positions throughout the Party.

In late 1927, with the collapse of Soviet agriculture, Stalin overturned Lenin's "New Economic Policy" and instituted a dramatic and deadly collectivization process that brought all agriculture under state control.[165] When—as would be expected—production fell, Stalin blamed it on the *kulaks* ("grasping hands"), or small private farmers who owned more than eight acres per male family member and constituted less than 5 percent of the population of the USSR (which at the time included all of modern-day Siberia, Uzbekistan, Turkmenistan, and Kazakhstan, though not yet the Baltic states of Estonia, Latvia, and Lithuania and some of the World War II territories the Soviets would seize). Stalin virtually declared war on the kulaks, and ordered farmers rounded up, shot, deported, and stripped of their land. The kulaks retaliated by refusing to sell their crops or give up their lands, slaughtering their animals rather than taking them to market. By 1930, Stalin, convinced the Ukrainian peasants were hoarding grain, refused to release reserves that might have alleviated the forced famine. Sometimes called the Ukrainian genocide, the imposed famine in the region killed between 10 and 20 million. One study determined that yearly deportations of kulaks and middle-income peasants from 1930 to 1941 reached a peak of 1.8 million in 1931 and fell to 930,000 by 1940. Approximately three million of the deportees died in the gulag, while the remainder of the peasants died of starvation.[166] Later termed the "Harvest of Sorrow," the Communist-induced famine constituted one of the most widespread, systematic mass murders of all time.[167] This reaper's bill came on top of the nine million who died in the Russian Civil War.[168]

Western leftists gushed about Stalin, particularly the *New York Times* correspondent Walter Duranty, who personally witnessed the bodies strewn along the way on his travels in the USSR and mysteriously forgot those scenes in his reporting. Perhaps the most effusive Western supporter of Stalin was George Bernard Shaw: "Jesus Christ has come down to earth," he announced. Stalin had "delivered the goods to an extent that seemed impossible ten years ago."[169] To a Leningrad audience, he rhapsodized, "If the future is . . . as Lenin saw it, then we may all smile and look forward to the future without fear." Of course, that did not apply to the millions of kulaks and "wreckers" who were terrorized on a daily basis. When the Bolsheviks abolished private property in the countryside, it produced the greatest famine in human history, all man-made. Peasants rebelled at the confiscation of their livestock and crops, burning wheat and slaughtering animals by the millions—upwards of two thirds of the sheep and goats, and close to half of all cattle. The seizure of grain left millions starving as they ate "cats, dogs, field mice, birds, tree bark and even horse manure. . . . There were even cases of cannibalism."[170] As starvation and murder winnowed out the peasants, the numbers (completely ignored in the West) grew to mind-boggling proportions. In 1987, Robert Conquest, then slurred as a right-wing ideologue, produced his landmark book, *Harvest of Sorrow*, estimating the "terror-famine," as he called it, to have accounted for 14.5 million deaths.[171] Subsequent work in the post–Cold War former Soviet archives suggests Conquest's figures were too low. Normal population increases would have put Russia's 1937 population at 186 million, when the census counted only 156 million. Where did the 30 million go? Depending on what years are included, the Lenin-Stalin tag-team murder combo accounted for between 20 and 40 million Russians, Ukrainians, and subjugated people dead *before Hitler's war machine ever invaded*.[172]

Russia's descent into a Bolshevik Hades would have worldwide repercussions for decades, rearranging the map of Europe, reordering entire populations, but most important, offering an undeniable example of the total failure of Communist theology. And a theology it had become: communism, often called "godless," had elevated the state itself to the position of a deity. A short string of venomous dictators took turns as high priests, proving in the process how interchangeable they were. Until the curtains to the holy of holies could be pulled back, and the murderous essence of Marxism incarnate exposed, European elites and Progressives would praise the perceived accomplishments of the USSR. Hypnotized by statistics and dizzied by a surface egalitarianism that was already quickly devolving into the most medieval of aristocratic class systems, Europeans of all classes rapidly gravitated to socialism and statism, leaving an isolated America and wounded Britain nearly alone.

# CHAPTER THREE

# Seeking Perfection in the Postwar World

## Time Line

1918: Armistice (November 11); German troops withdraw from France; Kaiser Wilhelm II abdicates; Poland "created" under Józef Piłsudski; Russian Civil War (Reds vs. Whites); Spanish flu pandemic kills 50 million worldwide

1919: Versailles Treaty signed; U.S. Prohibition Amendment ratified; U.S. lands troops in Russia to fight Reds; Polish-Soviet War; Greco-Turkish War; 1st Communist International meets; Eugene Debs imprisoned; Einstein's Theory of Relativity confirmed; American Communist Party founded; Pope Benedict XV agrees to a Catholic political party in Italy; Sun Yat-sen rejuvenates Chung-kuo Kuomintang (Chinese Nationalist Party) in China

1920: 1st peaceful social democratic government formed (Sweden); France prohibits sale of contraceptives; Women's suffrage amendment in United States; Poles defeat Red Army in Poland; Obregón assumes presidency of Mexico, ending revolution; anarchists bomb Wall Street, killing thirty-eight; Warren G. Harding elected U.S. president

1921: German reparations payments begin; end of civil war and famine in Russia leaves 10 million dead; Chinese Communist Party established; first baseball game broadcast; aircraft led by General Billy Mitchell "sink" *Ostfriesland*

1922:    Joseph Stalin becomes general secretary of Soviet Communist Party; Benito Mussolini becomes premier of Italy; British Broadcasting System (later BBC) formed; Ottoman Empire abolished; hyperinflation in Germany begins; USSR formed; unemployment in United States nears 12 percent; Washington Naval Arms Conference

1923:    Stalin assumes control of USSR; Pancho Villa assassinated in Mexico; Beer Hall Putsch by Adolf Hitler in Munich; French and Belgian troops occupy the Ruhr; German hyperinflation reaches 4.2 trillion marks to the dollar; Miguel Primo de Rivera's dictatorship established in Spain; Warren Harding dies and Calvin Coolidge assumes presidency; Andrew Mellon tax cuts enacted

1924:    Hitler imprisoned and writes *Mein Kampf* (published 1925); U.S. Immigration Act of 1924 and Asian Exclusion Act passed; J. Edgar Hoover appointed head of Federal Bureau of Investigation

1925:    Mussolini assumes dictatorship of Italy; *The State of Tennessee v. John Thomas Scopes* (Scopes "Monkey" Trial); Locarno Treaty; Mitchell court-martialed for insubordination

1926:    Józef Piłsudski becomes dictator of Poland; Lithuania overthrows elected government; dictatorship established in Portugal; U.S. unemployment hits all-time low of 1.6 percent

1927:    1st transatlantic phone call placed; League of Nations abolishes slavery; Charles Lindbergh completes first solo transatlantic flight; Stalin begins war on kulaks; Chinese civil war erupts between Nationalists and Communists

1928:    Jinan Incident (China); 1st scheduled television broadcasts; Hoover elected U.S. president; Kellogg-Briand Pact; Hirohito enthroned as Japanese emperor; Italian forces complete Libyan campaign (begun 1922)

1929:    Color television demonstrated; Pope Pius XI ends sixty years of popes' self-imposed imprisonment in Vatican;

Young Plan for reparations in Europe; Smoot-Hawley
Tariff clears final congressional committees; Great Crash
on Wall Street

For a conflict started by staggering misperception and bungling, fought
in squalor, and responsible for the loss of a colossal number of lives, the
end of World War I constituted a great beginning for so many who believed
that the Treaty of Versailles, which officially ended the conflict, represented
a fresh idealism, awash in good intentions and even better plans. For the
first time, politicians—the professional planners—were in charge of organizing the new nation-states and setting their agendas. Surely they could
govern better than the aristocrats or the monarchs who had led them into
the carnage.

At the center of this optimism stood President Woodrow Wilson,
whose record as a wartime administrator had been mixed at best and whose
trail of Progressive programs would later prove disastrous. The pivotal role
he was to play evolved out of European expectations that he would be a
miracle worker, the willingness of the Allies to pragmatically horse-trade
specific material gains for lip service to Wilson's nebulous slogans, and
Wilson's own grand design. Unfortunately, the American president had no
lack of idealism, and even though his actions in Europe in 1919 indeed remade the world, no one could foresee the ruinous consequences that lay
down the line.

## Peace in the Progressive Era

Much has been made of Woodrow Wilson's Fourteen Points, which he first
presented to Congress in January 1918, ten months before the war ended,
and which he insisted should become the basis for ending the war. The
policy as a whole was a culmination of recommendations from "The Inquiry," a 1917 study group run by Colonel Edward House and Sidney Me-
zes, an American philosopher and delegate to Versailles. When Wilson first
presented the Fourteen Points, they included "Open covenants of peace,"
freedom of the seas, equality of trade, reductions in national armaments,
and several specific elements related to evacuation of territories taken by
Germany in the war. Wilson also insisted upon an independent Polish state
and stated the need for what would become the League of Nations—a "general association of nations" to ensure political independence and territorial

integrity. Generally, the Fourteen Points rested on a presumption of democratic government, openness, and benevolent empires that would pave the way for self-government in their colonies. Possibly the most controversial stipulation in the document was that claims on territories, specifically the Balkan states, were to be adjusted based on the interests of the populations. Some historians have criticized this requirement as promoting "national self-determination" (a phrase never used in the document itself), and credit the document with calling for the creation of independent countries such as Czechoslovakia thanks to the stipulation of providing "territorial integrity" to states and their borders.

These ideas were nothing new. In 1914, Lenin had called for "the right of self-determination," and the Soviet constitution (in theory) permitted the secession of its republics. This precedent caused Wilson to expand the concept even further at Versailles by stating that "every people has a right to choose the sovereignty under which they shall live."[1] The establishment of a new Polish state was already in the works; when Russia had left the war with the Treaty of Brest-Litovsk in 1918, the failure to specifically mention Poland in its terms had sparked nationalist riots and ended all Polish support for the Central Powers. Farther south, the Ottoman Empire sat, ready to be carved up, its constituent parts believing the independence of Arab tribes in the Middle East to be promised as part of British strategy that pitted them against the Turks during the war. The sultan, Mehmed V, had presided over the beginning of the partition, then his successor Mehmed VI hung on only until 1922. As a dynasty, the Ottoman Empire—the "Sick Man of Europe"—had outlasted many of the great European monarchies, including the Hapsburgs, Hohenzollerns, and Romanovs—all dispatched in 1918—leaving only a handful of petty kings and emperors orbiting a pair of exhausted democracies. Belgium, the moral winner of the war due to its perceived victim status, had been pillaged and leveled; Italy, humiliated.

At least four of the items in the Fourteen Points referred to "independence of various national groups" or other national boundary "readjustments," all of which found their way into the Treaty of Versailles in more than a dozen article subpoints related to territorial shifts. Meanwhile, the creation of Poland out of Prussia and Russia to serve as a buffer between Germany and Russia was supported by everyone—except, of course, Germany and Russia. It put an independent nation (albeit one with initially little strength and indefensible borders) in a position to threaten both if it suddenly became powerful. This was the "big Poland" concept, and it constituted simply another example of good intentions gone astray. Westerners such as Wilson, Britain's foreign minister A. J. Balfour and her prime minister David Lloyd George, and Prime Minister of France Georges Clemenceau all assumed that a "big Poland" would in fact find favor with the Russians, and hoped they would see it as a further diminution of German power. Quite the contrary: Russia feared a revived Poland—her traditional enemy—every bit as much as a "big Germany." Thus, Poland created a built-in target of expansion for the new Soviet Union, while Poland's small wars against other nearby states of Ukraine, Lithuania, and Czechoslovakia ensured minimal support from those countries later when Poland's own borders were violated.

Yet the whole notion of sovereignty based on "nationality" was troubling every bit as much for the victors as for the vanquished. Britain, after all, ran the largest, most heterogeneous amalgam in the world, though each ethnic group was, for the most part, confined to a specific geographic territory. This contrasted with the Austro-Hungarian Empire, with its Serbs, Romanians, Magyars, Czechs, Slovaks, Croats, Germans, and, of course, Jews and Gypsies, all mixed together despite sharp differences in languages, beliefs, and customs. Now Wilson would split all these apart? Would the peacemakers ignore the fact that Alsace-Lorraine, now "restored" to the French, was predominantly German? It soon became clear that the Allies, anxious to unload custodianship of former Central Power territories, could be influenced by promises of friendship and the wheels that squeaked would be greased quickly and copiously. Thus, Italy received part of Tyrol and Dalmatia; Romania was handed Bukovina; Japan got Shantung. In the Middle East, Britain and France awarded land to different claimants so fast that England actually promised the same small strip of land, what would become Israel, to both the Arabs and the Jews!

These and other mistakes of the Versailles Conference might have been avoided had Wilson not ordered Colonel Edward House to Europe to meet with the Allied Supreme War Council on October 29, 1918, and had House not met secretly with Clemenceau and Lloyd George to modify the Fourteen Points that Germany had already agreed to as a basis for "negotiation." Wilson had no intention of negotiating the Fourteen Points, only implementing them. To do so he needed the British and French, and House knew it, sending Wilson an interpretive "Commentary" in which he outlined the positions the Allies would, and would not, support. Britain opposed "freedom of the seas," while France wanted reparations. Each sought different ways to ensure future German military impotence. In any case, the British and French saw the discussion as one of principles, not particulars, whereas Wilson saw the Fourteen Points as concrete and clearly defined. By their meeting in secret—without the Germans—the ensuing peace would be a dictate, not a negotiated settlement; and by allowing House to horse-trade alone, without any Republican insight or advice, Wilson guaranteed that the final document (or parts of it) would meet with strong opposition at home.

To make matters worse, Wilson viewed the European participants "a cynical and evil crew," bound by idiosyncratic traditions, corruption, and irrelevant public opinion.[2] They responded in kind. Lloyd George was aggravated by Wilson's "little sermonettes." Their impatience with Wilson's Fourteen Points, focused as they were on Wilson's own grandiose, unenforceable, and unattainable plans and ignorant of the clear, material (and attainable) objectives of the Europeans, and the famous riposte that God Himself only had ten, became well known. But the Europeans all, of course, played along as much as possible to attain their own well-defined goals of a demilitarized and de-fanged Germany, territorial acquisition, and the creation of buffer states around Germany regardless of how or whether those new nations reflected "national self-determination." The Allies were trading air for substance, and Wilson enthusiastically participated in the exchanges. But the reality for those millions of Europeans caught on the Versailles chessboard was staggering. At a May 1919 meeting of the Conference, British diplomat Harold Nicolson walked into a study to find Lloyd George, Clemenceau, and Wilson bending over a giant map spread on the carpet:

> They are cutting the Baghdad railway. . . . Clemenceau [with his blue-gloved hands] down upon the map . . . look[s] like a gorilla of yellow ivory. . . . It is appalling that these ignorant and irresponsible men should be cutting Asia Minor to bits as if they were dividing a cake . . . Isn't it terrible, the happiness of millions being discarded in that way?[3]

Before leaving for Versailles, Wilson had privately planned to go over the heads of the European rulers: "I can reach the peoples of Europe," he promised.[4] Wilson's Progressive concepts of democracy had infused him with a sense that intermediary institutions (caucuses, parties, legislatures, and even elections) were irrelevant if, Rousseau-like, the "leader" knew the "will of the people." Hence, he believed he could appeal to the masses over the heads of those empowered by those institutional intermediaries. After all, he had "reached" them merely by arriving, and Wilson's ego did not allow for the possibility that his ideas were not everyone's. Always sure of himself, Wilson told Italian prime minister Vittorio Orlando that (after spending three days in Italy) he understood the Italian people better than Orlando did.[5]

In Wilson's eyes, these European politicians were merely obsolete appendages of failed nationalism. The nation-state itself had to be rendered harmless and nonaggressive, and the transitional organization that would gradually supersede the selfish nationalistic tendencies was another Wilsonian proposal, the League of Nations. It was not only the hope of a new Europe, but a Europe led by America. As *The New York Times* intoned, "the eyes of Europe are turned toward America these anxious days," putting full responsibility for the life of what would become the League of Nations on American shoulders.[6] To Wilson, the League embodied Progressive principles at their best—and the diminution of American exceptionalism. By transferring power from sovereign nations to an international body that could override the concerns of individual states, Wilson and other Progressives thought they could eliminate one of the major causes of wars: patriotism and nationalism, with their petty fights over borders and ideologies. Moreover, the League would epitomize the Progressive views of Walter Lippmann and John Dewey, who believed that all problems could be solved through better communication. Simply providing a forum for nations to express their views, the Progressives believed, would eliminate many conflicts. Walter Lippmann argued that people could be persuaded to accept uncongenial policies by teaching them to recognize Progressive realities and their self-interests. They had to be taught what British and French power meant to the security of America's vital interests.[7] It was all about communications: communicating the "right" ideas and realities to the masses would enlighten them. Encouraged by praise from sources such as *The New York Times*, Wilson's ego was stroked even more and he regressed into ideology and messianic altruism as he arrived in Europe.

Wilson chose to head the peace delegation personally, in spite of Colonel Edward House's fear that it would damage the president's reputation. Needless to say, Wilson never considered delegating such an important and high-profile task as providing the world with peace to a subordinate or a committee. Only one of the five peace commissioners was a Republican, Henry White, who passed along Henry Cabot Lodge's nine-page manifesto making clear that "under no circumstances" should the League of Nations, that glittering jewel of Wilson's Points, be a part of the treaty. The League constituted a fundamental reordering of national security from an alliance system (which had existed from the dawn of time) to "collective security," in which all members would agree to police rogue states.

There had been a forerunner of the League with the Inter-Parliamentary Union (IPU) in 1889, which featured twenty-four countries focused on arbitrating international disputes. The IPU has survived to the present day but developed into a group promoting democracy (as understood by Europeans) and world governance, and since World War II has been proposed to function as the United Nations Parliamentary Assembly by the Socialist and Liberal internationals. But in 1919, Wilson's new League, a central element of the Versailles treaty in the final point, was a different beast: "A general association of nations must be formed under specific covenants for the purpose of affording mutual guarantees of political independence and territorial integrity to great and small states alike." In its final incarnation, the League counted forty-four members who made up the Assembly, which became the institution's driving force. A court of international justice was also envisioned. But of course many of the details would be left to the delegates to craft.

These ideas were heavily influenced by the South African prime minister Jan Christiaan Smuts and his 1918 treatise, *The League of Nations: A Practical Suggestion*, but became identified as Wilson's own. When he arrived in Europe, Wilson ignored White's cautions, as well as those of his secretary of state, Robert Lansing, who thought the League was not necessary to a practical peace settlement. But Wilson had a critical ally in the press, which had taken to Progressivism as the way to get ahead and cement their positions behind the levers of power—a trend that would deepen to the current day. Journalists flattered Wilson, elevating him to almost godlike status—such that French prime minister Georges Clemenceau nicknamed him "Jupiter."

So to Europe Wilson went, arriving in January 1919 to a reception of two million people at the Champs-Élysées, where he was greeted by crowds weeping and carrying flowers. Politicians who had witnessed the coronations of kings stood awestruck at the reception. Captain Harry S. Truman, then in Paris, said, "I don't think I ever saw such an ovation." Wilson received similar welcomes as he stopped in England for preliminary meetings with the British, and later on a five-day trip to Italy, where in each case massive crowds unleashed their adulation. In Italy he was hailed as the "God of Peace," convincing Wilson even more of his messianic mission.[8] The praise continued when he delivered his opening remarks in Paris on January 18, a chilling and snowy day, warmed by Wilson's insistence that this was "the supreme conference in the history of mankind."[9]

Yet even as the American president basked in the glow of his admirers, his counterpart, Prime Minister David Lloyd George, was winning an overwhelming victory in British elections based on his promise to impose a harsh peace on Germany, while in France, Georges Clemenceau, speaking to his Chamber of Deputies, refused to commit himself to untested forms of collective security, instead insisting on traditional balance of power alliances. Thus, the three leaders had vastly different views as to what the postwar world should look like. These were fundamental differences, not mere details. Britain and France came to the table seeking material reductions in Germany's military and tangible limitations to her geographic power—both of which were attainable—while Wilson approached the negotiations from a diplomatic Olympus, seeking eternal solutions to insoluble human realities. Even Italy sought only territorial gains that could be physically measured and militarily protected. When it came to stripping Germany of her overseas possessions—something on which the British insisted—Wilson wanted the territories placed under the administration of the League of Nations, a position that horrified and angered the British, who saw the territories as just compensation for England's wartime losses. France had already submitted a proposed conference organization just two weeks after the Armistice, but Wilson arrived with his own program, which is to say, no program other than the Fourteen Points.

It was a bad combination: a self-appointed messiah in Wilson, varying understandings about the objectives of the meeting on the part of the participants, and an absence of procedures, rules, or processes. And for all the energy the president had poured into the Fourteen Points, it became clear that thirteen of them would be sacrificed to achieve the League of Nations, as Wilson continually vetoed practical measures that might have ensured a more permanent peace. As Colonel House assessed the developments, "the situation could not be worse."[10] The French were more practically focused on stripping Germany of territory taken during the war and, above all, of their economic production capabilities. They took Silesia's coal and, with

Britain, announced an occupation of the Rhineland, with its Krupp ammunitions factories at Essen.

Britain had less interest in what went on with Germany's borders and more with the status of her navy and colonies. The Royal Navy kept up its blockade of Germany, actually maintaining a wartime stance, isolating Germany and exacerbating German food shortages and hardships. Older French diplomats, such as Clemenceau, had seen their country invaded twice, and now warned "in six months, in a year, five years, ten years, when they like, as they like, the Boches will again invade us."[11] The ability of Germany to make war had to be permanently eliminated. Above all, both Britain and France insisted that Germany be assigned sole responsibility for starting the war, thus forestalling any genuine attempt at negotiations and instead arriving only at terms to be delivered to a prostrate foe. It was an unnecessary condition, rubbing salt in the wound, and was made all the more problematic by the fact that some Germans felt they had actually won. Friedrich Ebert, who was named German chancellor just days before the armistice, welcomed returning troops as "unvanquished from the field."[12]

Meanwhile, German officials, who expected genuine peace negotiations, arrived in Paris to find a fait accompli. Despite the perceptions and the publicity of the Fourteen Points, Clemenceau was basically running the conference, doggedly attaining his goals while Wilson pontificated. This was hardly auspicious, as Clemenceau was a former editor of a radical newspaper, *La Justice*, and was not a conciliator. His nickname, *le Tombeur de ministères* ("the destroyer of ministries"), aptly described his disdain for traditionalism. As interior minister he had used the military to crush strikes in May 1906, and he relished his role as the *premier flic de France* ("the first cop of France"). Seeing an opportunity to position himself between the Socialists and the Right, Clemenceau had used his new newspaper, *L'Homme libre* ("the Free Man"), to criticize the government while at the same time supporting the war. When the paper was censored anyway, he changed the title of the publication to "The Man in Chains" (*L'Homme enchaîné*). He had refused the position of justice minister in the new wartime government, preferring, in the words of Lyndon Johnson, to be "outside the tent pissing in," and was rewarded with the prime ministership in 1917, whereupon he took an active role in visiting the trenches and encouraging the troops. His speeches demanded total war, he promised retribution against traitors, and, despite his Progressive/radical views, supposedly championing liberty, he imposed a harsh censorship on the press. But Clemenceau was devoutly condescending toward the United States, as evidenced by his well-known quip, "America is the only nation in history which miraculously has gone directly from barbarism to degeneration without the usual interval of civilization."[13] When Wilson announced his Fourteen Points, Clemenceau saw the opportunity to use them in bargaining for the transfer of Alsace-Lorraine to France, a sticking point since 1871 when the Germans had seized it during the Franco-Prussian War, creating a festering sore of resentment for nearly five decades.

David Lloyd George was less enthusiastic about a Carthaginian peace. The son of a teacher, he was a lifelong champion of Welsh rights, winning a seat in Parliament as a Liberal in 1890. He opposed the Second Boer War, during which he charged British generals with failing to care for their sick and wounded. Brought into the cabinet of Sir Henry Campbell-Bannerman, he became chancellor of the exchequer in 1908, where he attempted to reduce military spending while lobbying for old age pensions and unemployment benefits. Going into the war he had been considered a pacifist, but during the conflict he reversed course and supported military action, becoming minister of munitions in 1915 and secretary of state for war the following year. Even as prime minister, however, Lloyd George faced strong opposition from the Conservatives until the end of the war, when his reputation reached its apex and even his opponents respected him. As one Conservative gushed, "He can be dictator for life."

Having previously insisted that Germany bear the entire brunt of postwar burdens, Lloyd George changed his mind when he arrived at Versailles. Destroying the German economy, he concluded, would achieve nothing, and he attempted to persuade Wilson to ameliorate the terms, fearing both the dominance of a resurgent France and a lingering thirst for revenge on the part of Germany. But his last-minute change of heart had no effect on "Jesus," as he called Wilson. The president and his delegation, shaped in part by an anti-German contingent that included John Foster Dulles, remained wedded to their call for reparations.

Had more Republicans been included in the American peace delegation, some argue, the opinions of its members might have extracted some concessions from Wilson. It is true that many did not trust the British, and also true that most were isolationist and distrusted Wilson's internationalist assumptions. Wilson, however, may well have been impenetrable: he routinely lectured George, Orlando, and Clemenceau in moral terms throughout the conference. At any rate, he surrounded himself with yes-men, including the lone Republican peace commissioner, White, keeping his own counsel. As a result there were no negotiations between equals, only terms of surrender, including a deadline before which Germany had to accept the peace. Count Ulrich von Brockdorff-Rantzau, Germany's representative at the conference, accepted the Treaty, "yielding to overwhelming force," but it was clear to other participants and observers that not only was this a shock to the Germans but it would also likely lead to more problems later on. Wilson's secretary of state, Robert Lansing, surmised as much, watching the German representatives sign "with pallid faces and trembling hands," as if "called upon to sign their own death warrants."[14]

To those outside the "big three" of Britain, France, and the United States, the conference offered an opportunity to address colonialism and to end European imperial domination of their lands. A small army of colonial representatives arrived with their own hopes and frustrations—all of which should have fallen perfectly within Wilson's goal of "national self-determination." Among them: Nguyen Tat Thanh, a busboy at the Ritz Hotel who sought freedom for French Cochin China and later became Ho Chi Minh; Faisal bin Hussein, a Bedouin Hashemite prince who arrived with dreams of Arab unity (under his rule, of course); Edvard Beneš, a foreign minister of the future Czechoslovakia; Chaim Weizmann, who wanted a Jewish national homeland; and a host of others, from Japanese princes to Polish freedom fighters and Balkan revolutionaries. Some had received promises from European statesmen such as Arthur Balfour or from living legends such as British lieutenant colonel Thomas E. Lawrence (Lawrence of Arabia), but all had bought into the premise that they would receive a fair and open hearing from the proceedings. Yet when it came time to address their concerns, the conference all but ignored them; the British and French in particular saw an opportunity to expand their dominance over African and Asian lands at Germany's expense, not diminish it. Versailles's failure to deal with the colonial issue turned what might have been a potentially orderly transition of power in the 1920s into a series of recurring bloodbaths after World War II, when the imperial forces could no longer moderate or co-opt independence movements.

Paris provided the backdrop to the diplomacy. With its Parisian social scene and parties, the conference attracted sophisticates and artists from around the world such as actress Sarah Bernhardt, celebrity designer Elsie de Wolfe, writers Jean Cocteau and Marcel Proust, and China's ambassador to the United States, Wellington Koo, a Columbia University graduate who

"still delighted in singing his college fight songs" to a kaleidoscope of so-
cialites, soldiers, journalists, and hangers-on.[15] Hotels gleefully overcharged
these foreign rubes, particularly the bureaucrats.[16]

Many of the relatively young attendees of the revelries were diplomats,
and they received assignments that were breathtaking in their audacity.
They redrew maps of the Hapsburg Empire and generated policy papers for
the delegations. A secret group of 126 researchers (recruited mostly from
Ivy League schools) churned out more than a thousand reports for the Wilsonian delegation and later subcommittees on ethnicities, tribes, borders,
history, populations, and other relevant topics. They had begun their work
at the New York Public Library even before the conference, and were often
lacking in any expertise whatsoever for their assignments. Members of the
Arab group included a specialist on American Indians and two Persian language instructors, all chaired by a scholar on the Crusades. Ultimately,
some 250 foreign service officers versed in the dialects of Central Europe
would arrive in Paris to determine the fate of Poland, the former provinces
of the Austro-Hungarian Empire, and the Balkans. And, of course, every
delegation had its own bevy of espionage agents gathering information on
every other attendee. The U.S. spies employed a code based on sports and
college slang. "ARCHIE ON THE CARPET 7 P.M. WENT THROUGH THE HOOP AT
7:05" reported one operative assigned to watch a Hapsburg archduke.[17] But
despite the antics of spies and the massive network of private relief workers
delivering food, delegations confronted real, serious work when it came to
restoring peace and confidence in Europe.

## The Failure of Wilson's Vision

In his efforts to reshape Europe at Versailles, Wilson may have been idealistic and unrealistic, but he was not deceitful: he genuinely expected American-style democracy to work in Europe's new states as it had in North
America and in line with the Progressive worldview. But we should recall
that the context of terms used by Wilson—"democracy," "representation,"
"self-determination," and others—all flowed from a heritage in the United
States that went back more than 120 years, enmeshed in and enriched by a
tapestry that took on an entirely different meaning in Europe. When he
spoke of "representative democracy," it was entirely within his understanding of the checks and balances that had served America so well. Indeed, *none*
of the newly created states (and few of the Great Powers) in Europe possessed the four pillars of American exceptionalism or even understood why

they might be necessary. The Dutch and some of the Scandinavian countries were Protestant, had (more or less) free markets and private property, but lacked the tradition of common law. Elsewhere, even Britain had no separation of powers in the American sense (especially after the House of Lords was stripped of its veto power in the early 1900s). In Italy, Pope Benedict XV only allowed Catholics to participate in the political process by voting for the *first* time in 1919—having held out for the re-creation of the Papal States until that time. Poland had no history of independent democratic governance before Versailles and rapidly fell to the dictatorship of Józef Piłsudski; Romania, Greece, and Bulgaria were prewar monarchies; Serbia and other provinces of the Hapsburg Empire became Yugoslavia in a monarchy. Although Hungary had a four-year stretch of independence in the 1800s, it had subordinated itself to Austria in 1867. Hungarian princes traded effective control in their own land for greater standing in the Empire (just as the Scottish lords did with England for generations). Perhaps Czechoslovakia could be counted as a republic, but it possessed other gnawing problems in the form of radical ethnic and cultural diversity that eroded its nationality.

So Wilson indeed meant for Europe to have "national self-determination," civil rights, and so on; but no one in Europe had ever seen the American iteration of such concepts and no one possessed the religious, economic, or legal heritage to adopt them even if they understood what they meant. Of course, the British and the French knew this, which is partly why they supported Wilson, knowing full well the new Europe would not look like America. And Wilson had the endorsement of all the aspiring colonial states that wanted independence (which Britain and France were intent upon squelching). On the mainland, in the newly created states, Britain and France paid lip service to democracy and tolerated it only when it weakened Germany or served their ends in Europe; neither intended to actively apply it to imperial possessions, nor did they intend to enforce democracy in Russia—yet another example of a European power entirely lacking America's exceptional foundations. On the other hand, Versailles scarcely considered any system other than democracy as an acceptable form of government in this new order. A somewhat perverted interpretation of European history arose from this view in which such nondemocratic systems as fascism later were seen as "a form of mass madness over which reason must eventually prevail," and Europe became "a continent led astray by insane dictators [instead of] one which opted to abandon democracy."[18] An old Right—a monarchical conservatism of emperors and dictators—was passé; the Left, its legitimacy compromised by its support of the Great War, was also temporarily impotent. What emerged was a group of new fascists: strong men of Europe, such as Francisco Franco of Spain (named head of state in 1936), or Ioannis Metaxas of Greece, who grabbed power that same year.

As the years between the world wars unfolded, Europe sank into a dark abyss. Versailles provided no mechanisms for encouraging or promoting democracy, let alone enforcing it. Fledgling states, unfamiliar with elections, voting, separation of powers, consent of the governed, private property, individual freedom, and bills of rights—yet steeped in a recent tradition of socialist ideology—did not stand a chance when it came to erecting an edifice that could withstand a crisis. When these states were artificially packed with ethnic subgroups with axes to grind, the result was short-lived experiments in self-rule. Instead, dictatorships of one sort or another rapidly emerged. Greece drifted from constitutional monarchy to dictatorship; Hungary was a monarchy with a regent; Bulgaria, an autocratic monarchy; and Yugoslavia, an unproven experiment melding Serbs, Croats, Bosnians, and Slovenes into a constitutional monarchy. Albania's King Zog I turned his country into a fascist state resembling Mussolini's Italy. Poland yielded democratic rule to the dictator Piłsudski, then to a military junta that overthrew him. Germany embraced full-blown fascism under Hitler, Spain endorsed a slightly softer fascism with Franco, and Portugal adopted the proto-fascist Salazar government. Only a handful of constitutional monarchies—Belgium, Holland, Denmark, Great Britain, and Norway— existed alongside France, Czechoslovakia, and the Communist Soviet dictatorship (which absorbed the Baltic states) in making up the hodgepodge of European states that would drift into World War II.

If democracy was the goal in the post-Versailles era, it was remarkably absent. António Salazar, who ascended to power in Portugal in 1932, would note two years later, "the political systems of the nineteenth century are generally breaking down and the need for adapting institutions . . . is being felt. . . . I am convinced that within twenty years . . . there will be no legislative assemblies left in Europe."[19] Time almost proved Salazar right: by 1941, thanks to Hitler's war machine, England, Sweden, Turkey, and Switzerland had the only reasonably operational republics in Europe (with Sweden and Switzerland existing only through the indulgence of Nazi Germany). Even in France before 1940, some called for the ouster of liberal democracy in favor of the new crypto-fascism parading as nationalism. Writers such as Charles Maurras, prominent in Action Française (and aptly demonstrating that Europeans never seem to have understood the difference between a democracy and a republic) insisted, "There is only one way to improve democracy: destroy it."[20]

How had Woodrow Wilson's quest to remodel the Continent with American-style democracies gone so awry? How had he and other architects of the Versailles Treaty been so tone-deaf to the demands for true popular government—no matter how distasteful that government's policies may have been to the American and British nation builders? The answer lay in part with the nearly universal multiparty system which constituted one of the main impediments to establishing American-style democratic institutions in Europe. America's "winner-take-all/single-member-district" structure, a feature of American exceptionalism and the U.S. constitutional system, never took hold in the European states. A popular joke of the day was that three Englishmen would establish a colony, three Germans would start a war, and three Frenchmen would form five political parties—a commentary that contained a kernel of truth. America's system allowed for broad constituencies to gather under only a few (usually two) parties. This two-party system inexorably pushed both sides to the middle, leading to the pejorative phrase, "There's not a dime's worth of difference between the two parties." But this was the point—the sharp edges were dulled by the need to appeal to 51 percent of the public, and the separation of powers and staggered elections made change slow and difficult. The Europeans, on the other hand, employed proportional representation which increasingly produced parties with a much narrower focus. Politics frequently drifted into legislative paralysis. Few countries could boast a cabinet that lasted as long as two years, and in the post–World War I period, the average lifespan of a cabinet was measured in months: eight in Germany and Austria, five in Italy, and in Spain after 1931, four. More often than not, coalitions of parties were necessary to form a government in almost all of the European nondictatorships, under which each party would receive various government ministries, departments, and functions to administer. Legislatures tended to be unicameral, and the bureaucracies reported to an individual in the cabinet headed by a prime minister, premier, or chancellor elected not by the people but by the members of the majority party in the legislature. That meant that most European leaders lacked separation from their legislatures, and few were subject to checks and balances of the American sort, which often condemned them to unceasing bickering and in-fighting, with an endless procession of ministers resigning and being replaced. After Joseph Paul-Boncour formed his French government in 1932, he declared, "Restoring the authority of the State in a democracy . . . will be . . . the first and most essential element of our intended programme," whereupon his Cabinet shortly disintegrated.[21] America, of course, had already had over a century's worth of experience as a republic with democracy, while most European states were still developing their first constitutions and possessed real fears of tyranny by either a monarch or the masses. Legislative bodies with genuine power were a rarity. Daily activities of the most mundane sort continued to be performed by the bureaucracies: licenses were granted, garbage collected, and paperwork churned out, but important national decisions spiraled into a cycle of emergency decrees as crises developed. In Germany, which had only sixteen such decrees from 1925 to 1931, nearly sixty emergency orders were issued in 1932, almost twice the number of laws enacted by the legislature. It was an emergency decree by Chancellor Franz von Papen that imposed martial law that year, legitimating Hitler's authoritarianism before he ever took office. Constant agitation by the Communists, as well as parties on the Right, made the public yearn for stability and order. This was, for many Europeans, precisely what democracy was failing to deliver on a wide scale.

## The Myth of Collective Security

In the end, Versailles delivered two titanic failures. The first, as we have seen, was the inability to impose or sustain democratic republics amid the national hatreds and ethnic animosities of Europe. But the second, related failure, involved the collapse of collective security in which the world's nations would enthusiastically restrain any aggressor. From 1922 through 1930, a steady succession of agreements, treaties, compacts, and pacts emerged from the Europeans, all with the goal of ensuring permanent peace. Not only did they fail, but the nature in which they did so provided abundant lessons in the folly of believing that nations with no stake in a fight other than the intangible principle of "peace" would willingly send men to die.

Perhaps the most notable of these examples is the 1932 World Disarmament Conference at Geneva organized by the League of Nations. According to a modern definition, this was an effort to "actualize the ideology of disarmament." It had begun as a preparatory commission in 1925 and by

1931 held preliminary meetings under the leadership of former British foreign secretary Arthur Henderson, foundering almost immediately on the question of whether certain weapons were "offensive" or "defensive." Moreover, the conference seemed impotence incarnate when it sat idly through 1935 while Hitler was rearming Germany, the Japanese invaded Manchuria, and the Italians waged aggressive war against Abyssinia. The unwillingness of the Europeans to dispatch troops around the world to fight a growing Japanese empire in the netherworld of China was one thing, but it was entirely another for the League to ignore a weak Italian army, whose assault on the backward Ethiopians could have been scotched in a few weeks by the interposition of the Royal Navy and the French fleet.

Historical timing is always a subject of keen interest: what would have happened if Kennedy's motorcade schedule had been moved up? If an equipment malfunction on an airplane had delayed one of the flights on 9/11? If Archduke Franz Ferdinand had dallied at his speech longer? On a broader scale, historical events take on a determinism that never exists in the moment. Hitler was aided in his rise by economic circumstances in Germany, was given a further boost by American trade laws, and benefited from the fact that up until that point the fascist model had not proven a failure anywhere. No economic dislocation, however, proved potent enough by itself to produce the powerful dictator he became, and nothing contributed more to his success than the unwillingness of Britain and France to enforce the peace they had just won at great cost.

If anything, the two victorious powers cooperated less than ever. Despite the alliances, so easily knotted in 1919, Britain, France, and Poland found the threads unraveling under the strain of divergent and conflicting goals. There were personality issues. Not only did Raymond Poincaré, the French prime minister after the war, and the British foreign secretary, Lord George Curzon, detest each other, but the entire British ruling hierarchy deemed the French paranoid over the prospects of German revival. England wanted Germany to recover economically to become a trading partner once again—their only issue was that Germany should never again threaten the Royal Navy's command of the sea.

There was a recent history between Britain and France as well. France had withdrawn troops from Chanak in 1922, leaving Britain holding a small zone on the Dardanelles. In the humiliating aftermath—following a long harangue by Poincaré to Curzon—Canada refused to back Britain (accelerating her own move to independence) and David Lloyd George's government collapsed. Of course there were temperamental differences between the two nations, with France still clinging to the illusion of European leadership and "great power" status, but beyond that, practical budgetary pressures dictated a sympathetic view to German rehabilitation if a nation needed funds for social projects, as France precisely did.

All along, the issue was not reparations (which, as we have seen, may have been distasteful but actually drew Germany closer to the United States and, hence, stability), but rearmament. Well before Adolf Hitler embarked on a massive remilitarization of Germany, the Weimar Republic was already encouraging weapons makers to set up holding companies abroad, from Rotterdam to Oslo. Substantial work was shipped to the USSR, including the joint manufacture of tanks, the training of crews, military exercises, and the development of planes and pilots. French leaders suspected as much and saw the Rapallo Treaty of 1922, in which both Russia and Germany renounced World War I territorial claims against each other, as a cover for more dangerous secret agreements, which it was. Four months later, on July 29, a confidential addendum was signed that essentially voided the military clauses of Versailles.

That did not mean that France did not bully Weimar when she could. When Germany halted reparations payments in January 1923, the French sent troops (including Africans, whom the Germans particularly detested) to occupy the Ruhr and extract German coal for their own use. Germans needed no further incentive to hate the French, but Poincaré certainly provided it, alienating Britain and the United States in the process. Prior to the war, Germany had lacked self-esteem, or at least saw the rest of Europe as unappreciative of Teutonic contributions to civilization. Now, it was France's turn to feel unappreciated. The stark facts were that since 1870, France's borders had been successfully penetrated twice, and that except for dogged early assistance from England and later reinforcements from America, France would have lost World War I. Britain may have created the melancholy myth of the great "lost generation" taken by war, but in France's case it was true. Britain, on the other hand, jealously guarded and aggressively protected her dominance on the waves.

## Idealism at Sea

Britain never faced a serious threat of invasion during the war, and, after Jutland, the German High Seas Fleet no longer even ventured out to do battle with the Royal Navy. U-boat warfare took a monstrous toll, but submarines could not project power, attack land targets, or put ashore large bodies of men. For that, a surface navy was still needed, replete with big battleships and heavy cruisers. It was natural, then, that postwar Britain concerned itself with future threats from the oceans, where two potential new rivals had emerged since 1910: the United States and Japan. Both the United States and Britain expressed concern about Japanese claims on China, but the sentiment for disarmament in both nations was strong. In the Senate, the arms control lobby headed by William Borah of Idaho, the Great Opposer, led the revolt against the proposed postwar naval buildup. He finagled a six-month freeze on naval construction in 1921, then convinced House members to support a low naval appropriations bill six months later over the objections of President Warren Harding and with uniform disregard for the opinions of professional naval officers. Boxed into a corner, Harding had to call a conference on naval arms limitations in November 1921 involving especially those powers having interests in the Far East. Japan participated out of a desire to obtain recognition of her interests in China but also to achieve a measure of equal standing with the "white nations" and secure a naval treaty with the United States and Britain.

Limitations on battleships and heavy cruisers absorbed much of the delegates' attention. The Washington Naval Treaty (also called the "Five-Power Treaty") resulted in the "5:5:3 ratio"—an agreement on the tonnage of capital ships that the signatories could build: 525,000 tons for the United States and Britain, 315,000 tons for Japan, and 175,000 tons each for France and Italy. No ship could exceed 35,000 tons; no ship could have a gun larger than sixteen inches; but only moderate limitations were put on aircraft carriers as their potential was still largely unrecognized. That the Japanese were unable to achieve a better bargain in the Naval Treaty was in part due to American intelligence having broken the Japanese code outlining their bottom-line negotiating points.

Immediately, the nations involved looked to circumvent the treaty in other ways. In short, they cheated. Japan, for example, got around the restriction that it have only twelve cruisers with eight-inch guns by building the "B" class of cruisers which had armor capable of withstanding heavy shells and whose triple six-inch turrets could be switched out to eight-inch guns in short order.[22] In turn, this forced the United States to build *Brooklyn*-class cruisers and all nations to consider building classes of ships that were not optimal, but which fit within the treaty. Gun size on surface ships might have been limited, but numbers of guns were not, and speed and new armor systems were developed that would not be affected by the treaty. Italy simply lied about its tonnage, and in 1936, Japan withdrew entirely, already in the process of building the battleship *Yamato*, which violated the treaty displacement limits by 95 percent and featured eighteen-inch guns that made a mockery of disarmament terms.[23]

Planned battleship and cruiser hulls were converted into aircraft carriers as naval aviation advanced. In fact, since the upper limit of carriers was 27,000 tons but the upper limit of carriers converted from other ships was 33,000 tons, numerous ships were switched over. By encouraging nations to construct carriers, the Washington Conference pushed all the modern countries away from obsolete battleships, a status as yet unrecognized, and into the deadlier carriers.

Submarines, not covered by the treaty, could be built in unlimited numbers. Germany's U-boats had proven deadly during the First World War. (It was estimated that the Germans had only thirty to fifty operational U-boats at any given time but were able to sink 1.4 million tons of shipping in a single four-month stretch.) England decried the decidedly "un-British" weapon that symbolized "organized barbarism and brutality," but at the Washington meeting could find no allies willing to ban submarines.[24]

The Law of Unintended Consequences applied to the Five-Power Treaty in numerous other ways. Undertaken as an "arms control" agreement, the effect failed to advance the cause of peace. Even though Japan agreed to the naval limitations, the fact that Japanese capital ship levels were below those of the "white" superpowers stuck in their craw. As soon as Japan felt ready, it would abandon the treaty. As the Japanese general staff warned, "failure to obtain [the desired 10:7 ratio of capital ships with the United States] would fatally compromise the naval security of the empire."[25] Already the Japanese government had announced its goal of eight super-dreadnought battleships by 1927, along with eight super-heavy cruisers. This would give Japan twenty-five state-of-the-art capital ships in an era when battleships were still viewed as the ultimate weapon. In 1918, Japan's Admiral Tomosaburo Kato declared that "the last word in naval warfare rests with the big ship and the big gun."[26] This supposed universal truth died hard. Aside from a few squeaky wheel air-power advocates such as Isoroku Yamamoto and Shigeyoshi Inoue, big-ship dogma dominated Japanese naval thinking as late as 1934, when the 64,000-ton *Yamato*, with its eighteen-inch guns, was laid down. Whether this was, as some argued, the result of deeply held Japanese concerns about raw materials scarcity, or whether it was the fruit of a Japanese imperialist vine that was growing daily, will be discussed in the following chapter. Suffice it to say that in 1921–22, Japanese leaders were torn between their desire to exert power in their own backyard and the need to placate the much larger and technologically adept Western republics.

Of course, that was the view from the Japanese side of the Pacific. American planners, analyzing a future war in Japanese waters far from any repair bases, would require a U.S. advantage of close to 66 percent or more; and even at that, there was an excellent opportunity for Japan to concentrate her naval forces to thwart an American attack. As U.S. Navy leaders concluded, "relatively, therefore, the Japanese Navy is very much *stronger* than a mere computation of its ships and men would suggest."[27] That introduced the issue of overseas bases back into the equation, making ships and overseas territories inseparable items in the negotiations.

One result of the Washington Conference—the alienation of Japan and the severing of the Anglo-Japanese understanding in the Pacific—was completely predictable and inevitable. England ultimately had to choose to ally with the United States or Japan, and there was never a choice, although Britain continued to see the Americans as myopic. Austen Chamberlain, representing the typical European view at the time of the conference, described the Americans as living "in a different world [of] insularity, blindness, and selfishness. . . ."[28] But as American bases extended across the Pacific, including Midway, Guam, the Philippines, and Wake Island, England knew that it must take sides. To add urgency, Canadian demands in the Atlantic meant that Britain could not afford even a semihostile major sea power on her flank.

Meanwhile, the Japanese were focused on achieving great power status, a quest that dominated their actions at the conference.[29] Despite the obvious advantages to siding with America, the finality of the Anglo-Japanese divorce shook Arthur Balfour, the foreign secretary, so much that one observer could "see in profile, motionless and sober, the distinguished head of Mr. Balfour. As the last sentence sounded and the Anglo-Japanese Alliance publicly perished, his head fell forward on his chest exactly as if the spinal cord had been severed."[30] Such a perception was remarkable, given that many Americans thought they "had been had" in the negotiations, and that *England* was the winner. In fact, neither Britain, nor America, nor Japan fully appreciated the directions the Washington Conference would take them.

The Washington agreement was followed by a host of binational treaties and pacts, each pledging peace and nonaggression. Germany promised to observe French and Belgian borders and in the Locarno Pact (1925) all relations between the Allied powers in World War I (except the Russians, who had already signed a separate treaty at Brest-Litovsk) and Germany were restored. Weimar Germany was thus admitted back into the family of nations a mere six years after assuming full blame for the worst conflict in human history. In 1928, French foreign minister Aristide Briand, seeking to solidify an American alliance with France, suggested a compact between the two nations. Americans, however, remained wary of future interventions in Europe, and the U.S. secretary of state, Frank Kellogg, turned the proposal into a blanket prohibition of war as "an instrument of national policy." The ensuing Kellogg-Briand Pact enlisted sixty-five nations that signed an agreement outlawing war. It proved utterly irrelevant in stopping the Japanese invasion of Manchuria three years later, or in affecting the Italian invasion of Abyssinia in 1935, or in restraining in any way a single national aggressive move in the 1930s.

In the failure of those treaties and the numerous other compacts entered into during the 1920s, the concept of collective security ignored the most salient point. Collective security *can* work if—but only if—the participants have a direct stake in the outcome. A classic example of this was the American "Wild West," where it was long thought that bank robberies were common. In fact, however, they were extremely rare . . . due to collective security. While every town had a sheriff, it was the *armed citizens* who acted as a collective security force. Any bank robbers had to effect their escape from the middle of a town (the normal location of a bank) through the gunfire of almost every citizen—and depositor—between them and the outskirts of town![31] Such was not the case in post–World War I Europe, where collective security failed because at no time could European nations (or America) see clear interests in fighting wars in remote places that were not their own.

## Command of the Air

In its attempt to limit weapons at sea, the Washington Conference produced one of the more remarkable unintended consequences of the post–World War I era by accelerating the rise of air power as a strategic tool. Naval air power, of course, was relatively new, but the advances in aircraft design were obvious to all. Between 1912 and 1920 alone, average aircraft speeds had increased from 126 mph to 171 mph. Although the controversial Italian general and central director of aviation at the General Air Commissariat, Giulio Douhet, had written his influential *Command of the Air* (1921), for which he was jailed (it constituted a scathing attack on Italian war leadership for failing to properly prepare for war in 1915), only a handful of visionaries truly understood that, when correctly used, aircraft could carry out important tactical and strategic aims. American aviator Colonel Billy Mitchell met with Douhet in 1922 when he visited Europe, thereafter circulating an excerpted translation of Douhet's book. By then, Mitchell had already stunned the Army and Navy brass with his "Project B" bombing demonstration in 1921. Secretary of War Newton Baker and Secretary of the Navy Josephus Daniels had agreed to hold trials to test Mitchell's highly public claims that he could sink ships at sea with land-based bombers.[32] Mitchell was particularly critical of the (in his view) misallocated spending in which a thousand bombers could be built for the cost of a new dreadnought.

Mitchell's claims that land-based bombers could sink capital ships ruffled feathers among the admirals, who could nevertheless not ignore a genuine aerial threat. They agreed to the demonstrations, but a week before the test Mitchell was dismissed from the project, only to be reinstated by the new secretary of war John Weeks, in part because of Mitchell's public support. Assembling a group of Martin, Handley-Page, and Caproni bombers, Mitchell trained the crews in antiship bombing techniques, aided by Alexander de Seversky, a Russian who had attacked German shipping in World War I. In July 1921, Mitchell's planes hit their targets with bombs after two unsuccessful tries, "sinking" the German battleship *Ostfriesland* according to the rules of the experiment. Navy officials insisted the test meant nothing, but Mitchell and an influential young officer named Curtis LeMay, who would perfect long-range bombing during World War II, were convinced otherwise.

Mitchell seemed to tromp into a puddle of controversy with every new step. After a tour of Hawaii and Asia, he returned with a report that anticipated a war with Japan and the attack on Pearl Harbor.[33] Following a demotion to colonel, which was not an entirely unusual postwar rank adjustment, Mitchell found himself in an obscure posting in remote Texas. Some suspected this was due to his criticisms of the Army before the congressional Lampert Committee. His constant lobbying for weather stations at all air bases seemed prescient when the Navy dirigible *Shenandoah* went down in a lightning storm, killing fourteen crewmen. An incensed Mitchell accused the top brass (and President Calvin Coolidge, by inference) of "almost treasonable administration of the national defense."[34] Coolidge could not allow such insubordination to stand unchallenged, and Mitchell was court-martialed, found guilty, and reduced in rank. He resigned rather than accept punishment.

Prescient as Mitchell was, his grating style and outspokenness limited his ability to effect change. That fell to another Billy, Billy Moffett, a South Carolina–born naval officer who fought in the Battle of Manila Bay, then won a Medal of Honor at Veracruz in 1914. Moffett himself did not fly, yet was instrumental in founding the Navy's Bureau of Aeronautics in 1921, often conflicting with Mitchell in his desire to develop a separate naval air arm. Together, the two Billys brought American military aviation into the forefront of weapons design and war planning. Neither lived to see the application of American air power in World War II, Moffett dying in a blimp crash in 1933, Mitchell succumbing three years later to multiple illnesses. One of the high ironies of World War II occurred as the United States languished at its lowest point following the attack at Pearl Harbor and the invasion of the Philippines, when a single morale-lifting counterstrike changed the war's momentum. Lieutenant Colonel Jimmy Doolittle's crews flew B-25 bombers from an aircraft carrier to Japan in broad daylight, dropped their lethal loads, and galvanized patriotic enthusiasm. The nickname of the B-25? The "Mitchell."

The most famous aviator of the age, however, was not Billy Mitchell or Giulio Douhet, but a lanky engineering school dropout and the son of a Minnesota congressman, Charles Lindbergh. Enrolling in flying school just as Moffett was getting the Bureau of Naval Aeronautics off the ground, Lindbergh became a "barnstormer" who flew professionally (despite lacking a pilot's license) across the American Midwest. During the interwar years, American influence in Europe grew robustly, with no greater symbol than Lindbergh's successful solo transatlantic flight in 1927. Responding to a reward of $25,000 offered by hotel owner Raymond Orteig to the first man to complete a nonstop flight from New York to Paris, the former mail pilot left the dirt runway of Roosevelt Field on Long Island on May 20 with "four sandwiches, two canteens of water and 451 gallons of gas."[35] Just over thirty-three hours later, after a journey of 3,500 miles, he set down at Le Bourget Field to be mobbed by 100,000 people. For his courage and historic achievement, Lindbergh was the "new Christ," a term only a few years earlier applied to Wilson. As a European writer observed:

> Parisians craved to see him. They wanted to acclaim him, touch him, hoist him on their shoulders, worship him. They trampled the iron gates and barbed-wire fences of the airport; they trampled each other. . . . He was feted like no one else in previous history, not kings or queens, statesmen or churchmen. . . . [Now he was] a modern Icarus who, unlike his mythical forebear, had dispelled tragedy.[36]

Awarded the Legion of Honor in France, Lindbergh returned home to the acclaim of four million Americans lining the streets of New York before he embarked on a nationwide tour sponsored by the Guggenheim fund. In March 1929, just before leaving office, President Calvin Coolidge presented Lindbergh, a reserve military officer, with the Medal of Honor. Lindbergh remained in the reserves until 1941 when he resigned as a colonel in the Army Air Corps after President Franklin Roosevelt publicly questioned his loyalty to the United States because of his noninterventionist activities with the America First Committee.

Lindbergh represented the first true American international celebrity—the American that foreigners wanted to be. By the 1920s, there was already more to America, though, than a flash-in-the-pan celebrity aviator. Lindbergh seemed the quintessential American who ignored the odds and overcame the impossible. Increasingly Europeans identified with, and wanted to emulate, average Americans. Americanophilia was largely a factor of the growing American cultural influence through movies, which still celebrated rugged individualism, entrepreneurship, self-deprecation and humility, and above all, material accomplishment. Adolf Hitler's untitled "second book" admitted as much. "The European today," he wrote, "dreams of a standard of living, which he derives as much from Europe's possibilities as from the real conditions of America."[37] In 1930, Sinclair Lewis won the Nobel Prize for literature, becoming the first American to do so, and forced Europeans to acknowledge a distinctly American form of writing. Lewis, in books such as *Babbitt*, presented "crusading social criticism" with "cheerfulness and alacrity" as opposed to the "weightily serious" realism of the Europeans.[38] Now, after only a decade since an American planted the U.S. flag at the North Pole and only a few years after the Americans opened the Panama

Canal, at a time when American architecture and engineering had gained equal status with that of Europe, Lindbergh's flight offered one more example of the growing reality of the influence of the United States across the spectrum.

Lindbergh's accomplishment also forced Europeans to realize that America was a serious competitor, not just culturally, but technologically as well. Even though the French and British rapidly caught up with the United States, then surpassed American airplane designs during World War I, the first transatlantic solo flight seemed to underscore their second-class status in aviation, which had first become apparent with the Wright brothers. When the Wright brothers staged their first demonstration flights in France, distraught French aviators were embarrassed. "We are beaten—we just don't exist," said one. "We are like children compared to the Wrights," mourned another.[39]

But the Lone Eagle's flight marked another achievement for America by underscoring its rugged individualism and lack of dependence on government. After a brief fling with government-subsidized aircraft under Samuel Langley, whose $50,000 in aid from Uncle Sam did him little good in his competition with the unsubsidized Wrights, the United States embarked on what would become a long-standing policy of using the mails to encourage private builders and airlines to make their own choices. Cornelius Vanderbilt had repeatedly overcome hefty congressional subsidies to competitors in the 1840s and 1850s to provide superior service in packet steamers to California and across the Atlantic, driving the government-subsidized firms into oblivion. Now, in the 1920s, the U.S. Postal Service used the lucrative mail contracts to keep the infant American airlines in business.[40] Unfortunately, no government assistance comes without a price. In the case of the American airlines, the Post Office dictated schedules and even engine designs for the planes. Ultimately, however, the flexibility of the system proved far more beneficial than direct government control or ownership, leaving the Americans when war arrived in 1941 with a dozen major aircraft manufacturers, each with different areas of expertise and experience.

## Life Unworthy of Life

As the 1920s commenced and soldiers returned to civilian roles throughout Europe and America, unemployment surged. Noncombatant workers had taken many of the jobs, leaving returning soldiers without work. Production of farm goods—which met the wartime demands of armies—now became overproduction as fighters became farmers. With the subsequent fall in agricultural prices, farmers became bankrupt farmers. Recovering from wartime devastation and retooling from weapons manufacturing took time and money, and thousands of disaffected veterans, unemployed unionists, and displaced, homeless civilians fell in the gap. Many were impatient for postwar policies to provide relief; many looked to politicians who promised faster solutions.

In Italy, Benito Mussolini introduced a seemingly new political philosophy that many, mostly Europeans, found appealing in an ideology called "fascism," for the Roman *fasces* or bundle of sticks. Mussolini essentially slapped a national label on widely accepted European socialism. All fascist movements were, at their core, socialist, and Mussolini, the son of a blacksmith and newspaper editor from Naples, perceived that a glaring weakness of Marxist doctrines was the absence of national unity that ethnically cohesive populations craved. He shrewdly glimpsed that in the wake of the Great War, while complaints about excess nationalism abounded, no one wanted to entirely abandon the premise of national identity. Then, to adapt socialism to the twentieth century, Mussolini wedded it to big business through corporatism, permitting companies to manufacture and distribute products, but only after government had answered the fundamental economic questions of what was to be made and who would receive it. Corporate leaders retained their perks, companies made "profits," but these were little more than crumbs dribbled out to party supporters. The only difference between "pure" socialism and fascism lay in the single layer of companies that carried out the wishes of the regime. The companies became closely aligned with the government, often in what would later be termed "public-private partnerships." Others would call these alliances "crony capitalism," but in any case the national government selected compliant corporations, regulated their industries, and insured their profitability through government loans, subsidies, and contracts.

Although scholars differ over a comprehensive definition of fascism, a usable description would be a system wherein the government controls the production and distribution of goods and services through regulation, financial support, and the management of public money to benefit the state and its citizens as a whole. Fascism is centered on a state, nation, or group of nations, with top-down control of the citizenry, determining laws and managing education, employment, health, and social welfare. Often fascism includes a certain racial or religious component, but not always.

Once economic, and to an extent, social control was ceded to the state without intermediary institutions, such as legitimate courts, bills of rights, or the church, anything became acceptable in the "public interest." Particularly when it came to the newly unfolding field of public health, fascist states could easily meld nationalism into ethnic purification. After all, what was a German? Who was an Italian? Now the state decided. Ultimately, such definitions almost invariably involved calculations of who was of greater value to society, and from there, it was a short step to adopting eugenics in the name of improving public health. It also entailed a certain sterile judgment that appealed to statisticians, sociologists, and economists. (German economists and the statisticians at the German Institute of Business-Cycle Research, whose chief, Ernest Wagemann, advocated Keynesian-style reflation, were particularly attracted to Nazism.)[41] Characteristic of these trends was *Permission for the Destruction of Life Unworthy of Life* (1920) by Karl Binding and Alfred Hoche, which calculated the cost of one "idiot" to GNP.[42] Hoche went so far as to argue that some were "mentally dead," including the "incurably stupid," that is, people lacking imagination or self-consciousness.

American and English Progressives found these elements of fascism appealing, and were drawn to their own variants of selective breeding, eugenics, race purification, or other such programs to ensure that only the "right" people (that is, those like them) survived. Keynes was at the forefront of the English eugenics movement, along with H. G. Wells, George Bernard Shaw, the Webbs, Huxleys, and Havelock Ellis. British Socialist economist Sidney Webb insisted the "wrong" people were out-breeding the "right" ones, a trend putting Britain at risk of "national deterioration" or of falling into the hands of the "Irish and the Jews."[43] H. G. Wells would regulate the right of an individual to bring a child into the world based on what he called "a certain minimum of personal efficiency," namely whether the parents were worthy, based on "a certain minimum of physical development," and free of disease.[44] For society to attain Wells's perfection, "swarms of black and brown, and dirty-white and yellow people" would have to go: the "sterilisation of failures [sic]" was the only hope for improvement of "human stock."[45]

In America, similar ideas were embraced by the likes of Margaret Sanger, Charles B. Davenport, and Madison Grant, whose book *The Passing of the Great Race* (1916) propounded a Nordic approach to history, in which Aryan races were the most evolved, and embraced eugenics wholeheartedly.

A "rigid system of selection," Grant argued, would eliminate the "weak or unfit." (Hitler wrote Grant, saying, "The book is my Bible.") Woodrow Wilson himself had written of "progressive races" versus "stagnant nationalities," Progressive code words for racial superiority. While governor of New Jersey, his Board of Examiners of the Feebleminded had established criteria for the state to decide when "procreation was inadvisable" for those living in poverty, for criminals, or for mental defectives. Herbert Croly, a leading intellectual, lobbied for enforcing celibacy on lunatics and criminals; one of Teddy Roosevelt's advisers, Charles Van Hise, took it even further, declaring, "He who thinks not of himself primarily, but of his race, and of its future, is the new patriot."[46]

One of the leading American race-suicide theorists, sociologist E. A. Ross, having already authored a book called *Social Control* (1901), in 1914 described immigrants as "hirsute, low-browed, big-faced persons of obviously low mentality . . . ox-like men [who] are the descendants of those who always stayed behind."[47] Sentiments such as these lay behind the sterilization laws for "confirmed criminals, idiots, imbeciles, and rapists" passed by thirty states, Canada, and many countries in Europe from 1907 to 1937. This was not far from the Nazi racial program against Jews, Gypsies, and Slavs, nor from the Third Reich's program of sterilization of all undesirables: both invested doctors and medical science with a new and powerful authority as experts who could give the final word on mental capacities and inherited, unchangeable characteristics.[48]

American Progressives copied the Europeans and the British by implementing racial control through economics and public health. Margaret Sanger and others specifically targeted Negroes and mental defectives for extinction through their programs. Other early American Progressives, including Jane Addams and Theodore Roosevelt, as well as labor leader Samuel Gompers, had first invoked racial quotas to combat what they viewed as unfair competition in the labor market in the late 1800s. As Ross explained when advocating the minimum wage, "The Coolie cannot outdo the American, but he can underlive him."[49] A minimum wage was also advocated by many in the American Economic Association who thought they could exclude an "unemployable class," in the words of Sidney Webb, from the workforce using a higher wage, thereby putting them on the path to extinction. "Of all the ways of dealing with these unfortunate parasites," Webb contended, "the most ruinous . . . is to allow them unrestrainedly to compete as wage earners."[50] The subject of inferior breeding also loomed large in the writings of many Progressives, including Princeton economist Royal Meeker, who favored a minimum wage that would lock out undesirable workers. "Better the state should support the inefficient wholly and prevent the multiplication of the breed than subsidize incompetence and unthrift, enabling them to bring forth more of their kind."[51] John R. Commons, the dean of American labor economists, likewise feared immigrants' competition: "competition has no respect for the superior races," he intoned, and the race with the "lowest necessities" displaces the others. Ironically, Commons identified Jews as the source of unfair low-wage competition (the "Jewish sweat-shop is the tragic penalty paid by that ambitious race").[52]

American Progressives called for the limitation of the reproduction of "undesirables" as an effort to protect the public health. Edward Larson's extensive 1996 study of Progressive eugenics in the South revealed how pervasive the sentiment was even in the medical community for controlling what were viewed as undesirable populations. One Alabama doctor at the turn of the century advised his colleagues, "People who have [dysgenic] hereditary traits ought not to be allowed to get married, and men who persist in [degenerate behavior] ought to be confined in reformatory institutions, or have their testicles removed. . . ."[53] Another Georgia pediatrician recommended, "Sterilize all individuals who are not physically, mentally or emotionally capable of reproducing normal offspring."[54] These views were not confined to rural areas or the "backward" South. Chicago surgeon A. J. Ochsner advised that sterilization "could reasonably be suggested for chronic inebriates, imbeciles, perverts and paupers."[55] North Dakota and Nebraska established central registries for mental defectives and would not allow them to get marriage certificates unless one of the partners was sterilized.

California had one of the most advanced sterilization programs, performing procedures on 2,500 patients in state institutions by 1920, and ultimately more than 20,000 by the 1930s. Originally passed in 1909, the first sterilization law focused on the mentally retarded and convicted sex offenders. A second law, passed in 1913, repealed the first and broadened the range of people to be considered for sterilization, including anyone "afflicted with hereditary insanity or incurable chronic mania or dementia," as well as those included in the 1909 categories.[56] The state's general superintendent of the Commission on Lunacy, F. W. Hatch, sought to expand the program even more, calling for the sterilization of "confirmed criminals, habitual drunkards, and drug habituates, epileptics, sexual and moral perverts."[57]

Hatch was supported by such academic leaders as Stanford's president David Starr Jordan and philanthropist E. S. Gosney, who founded the Human Betterment Foundation, a California organization which distributed information about compulsory sterilization "for the protection and betterment of the human family in body, mind, character, and citizenship."[58] Hatch also had the backing of the California State Board of Charities and Corrections, which noted that for the benefit of society, children of the insane were better off "not to be born."[59] In the Deep South, only one top mental health official publicly opposed eugenics, while the proceedings of the southern states' medical associations revealed a deep commitment to hereditary causes of criminal behavior, epilepsy, and mental disease. Thomas Haines, of the National Committee for Mental Hygiene, stated that "the way to prevent much of the crime, immorality and degeneracy of the community today is to *prevent this class of persons from propagating* (emphasis in original)."[60]

Throughout the West, pressure to limit the number of social undesirables grew out of the burgeoning public health movement, which propagated the idea that such individuals contributed to the spread of disease. Reflecting this development, Germany's social hygiene movement came to dominate its state welfare system in the 1920s under its umbrella of benign-sounding goals, such as protecting the health of mothers and children and combating psychiatric disorders.

But beneath the noble goals of improving national public health lay a darker mission. In America, this would take the form of the Tuskegee syphilis experiments beginning in 1932; in Germany, it manifested itself in the quest to attain German racial purity even before Hitler and the Nazis were in power.[61] Venereal disease and tuberculosis were the two most common targets of public health officials in both countries since these were usually associated with "lower classes," poverty, and overcrowding. In Germany, these were largely dealt with through emergency legislation until a permanent anti-VD law was passed in 1927, which, among other things, abolished compulsory medical exams for prostitutes but required medical treatment for anyone infected with a sexually transmitted disease. A "healthy lifestyle" became a state concern in Weimar Germany, especially when tied to the post–World War I epidemic of venereal disease. This provided a convenient target and enabled a further extension of German state power, as "voluntary welfare services that had proliferated during the war were institutionalized as professional careers in social work."[62] Demonstrating a pattern common to all welfare state bureaucracies, the German system first and foremost benefited not the clients but the welfare workers themselves, with social control transcending the rights of individuals and "defin[ing] new spheres for the exercising of coercion."[63] Thus, Weimar produced one of those historical ironies in which the "concerned" social hygienists and health experts were often easily converted to eugenicists under the Nazis.

But sterilization as a means of enhancing social health saw its largest growth in the United States, where eugenics talk was disguised in the titles of nonthreatening, even benign-sounding institutional names: the American Conference for the Prevention of Infant Mortality, or the National Mental Hygiene Committee. Others, such as the American Eugenics Society, made their purposes more obvious. Founded in 1922 by Madison Grant, with the support of Alexander Graham Bell, biologist Charles Davenport, economist Irving Fisher, and Luther Burbank, the Society promoted sterilization of unsuitable groups (the mentally retarded and the "feeble minded," a flexible definition that could include almost anyone at a given time). Establishing state chapters, the American Eugenics Society saw its greatest successes in California, where the record of cleansing undesirables was exceeded only by Germany. Biologist Paul Popenoe, who published with E. S. Gosney a favorable report on the California sterilization program, was widely cited by the Nazi government in Germany.[64] By 1920, some fifteen states mandated that rapists and imbeciles face compulsory sterilization. Another sixteen states passed sterilization measures in the 1920s, particularly after the *Buck v. Bell* Supreme Court case upheld a Virginia state law that required compulsory sterilization of the retarded "for the protection and health of the state." Sterilization operations shot up tenfold.

Race was also an issue. Sacramento banker Charles M. Goethe, founder of the Northern California Eugenics Society and the Human Betterment Foundation, campaigned against blacks and Mexicans as "low-powered" and "socially unfit."[65] The Tuskegee syphilis experiments were directed only at blacks, for example. This clear racial component to eugenics was nothing new: the Immigration Restriction League (founded in 1894) had been at work for almost thirty years seeking to bar other racial groups from entering the United States due to the view that they were "inferior races," and as Larson points out, the same criteria were enthusiastically applied to blacks in the deep South.[66]

Eugenics found powerful supporters—if a somewhat lukewarm public reception—among elite biologists and sociologists, not to mention government professionals. It appealed to the current of scientific rationalism, which held that science could solve every problem. Legislators were attracted to the ideas because they offered low-cost and clear-cut answers to social ills. The Kansas Free Fair in 1929 included exhibits and charts outlining genetic inheritance of "pure" and "abnormal" parents; the Sesquicentennial Exposition in Philadelphia featured a booth sponsored by the American Eugenics Society that had a counter-board with flashing lights revealing how many tax dollars were spent every fifteen seconds on people with "bad heredity," that every forty-eight seconds a "mental deficient" was born, and that only once every seven and a half minutes was born a "high grade person . . . who will have the ability to do creative work and be fit for leadership."[67]

## Race, Eugenics, and Margaret Sanger

Support for the eugenics movement was generally restricted to leftist intellectuals in the United States and remained weak among average Americans, except when it came to immigrants. In one of the great ironies of history, Asian immigration was restricted in an effort to limit the number of "feebleminded" in the population through the Chinese Exclusion Acts of 1882 and 1902, and continued by the "Gentleman's Agreement" of 1907–8. Yet over a century later, California would exclude Asian college applicants on the grounds that they were, in essence, *too* smart and outperformed whites, blacks, and Hispanics. During immigration debates, genetic racial differences became a recurring theme, with witnesses emphasizing the genetic weaknesses of eastern and southern European races. Even then, attracting the middle class with genetics arguments proved more difficult than the threat of lower wages.

The most fertile ground was plowed among the intellectuals and radicals, particularly feminist Margaret Sanger, a New Yorker who blamed her mother's death on excessive childbirth and became the guiding light for and founder of Planned Parenthood. Sanger's theories of racial culling and procreation reached a large audience through her newspaper, *The Woman Rebel*, where she pounded the institution of marriage, labeled Italians and Jews unfit to breed, and suggested certain political figures be assassinated.[68] While the presumption that she favored abortion is a mistake (she labeled it "barbaric," and said it resulted in "the killing of babies," an "outrageous slaughter"), she certainly approved of her friend Lothrop Stoddard's recommendation to "isolate bacterial invasions" of people by "limiting the area and amount of their food supply, so we can compel an inferior race to remain in its native habitat."[69] Upon reading this, Sanger promptly put Stoddard on the board of directors of the American Birth Control League, which she had founded in 1921 and presided over until 1928.

Sanger's pornographic writings violated the 1873 Comstock Law (which made it illegal to send lewd or obscene materials through the mail), leading to her indictment in 1913. She promptly fled to England, where she engaged in multiple affairs while simultaneously absorbing Malthusian overpopulation nostrums. By that time, it was clear that "lower" groups would not buy her recommendation that they limit their birthrates to ensure that "higher" races remain in positions of power, so she adopted the language of liberation. Charity was too successful: "The dangers inherent in the very idea of humanitarianism and altruism . . . have today produced their full harvest of human waste."[70] Benevolence perpetuated "defectives, delinquents, and dependents," while birth control offered a means to weed out "the unfit," aiming toward the "creation of a superman."[71] Her *Birth Control Review* (1917) endorsed eugenics through its articles, including "Some Moral Aspects of Eugenics," "The Eugenic Conscience," "Birth Control and Positive Eugenics," and "Birth Control: the True Eugenics," all of which made the critical link between birth control and selective race breeding. Sanger's journal contained a favorable review of Stoddard's book *The Rising Tide of Color Against White World Supremacy* (1923).

Sanger's view of blacks was more guarded but still unabashedly racist. As the keynote speaker to a Ku Klux Klan rally in 1926, she wrote in her autobiography that she had "accomplished her purpose." What that purpose was was unclear, but she added, "A dozen invitations to speak to similar groups were proffered," so clearly the Klan agreed with what she had to say. Perhaps it was something close to her statement that black children were "destined to be a burden to themselves, to their family, and ultimately to the nation."[72] Sanger was sensitive enough to the criticism that her policies were designed to target blacks that in 1939 she wrote a letter to Clarence Gamble in which she argued for hiring "three or four colored ministers, preferably with social-service backgrounds," to promote birth control in black communities, or as she called it, "The Negro Project." Suitable ministers were, in fact, found, including Adam Clayton Powell Sr. Using an organization called the Birth Control Federation, Sanger embarked on whittling down the black population. The "mass of significant Negroes still breed carelessly and disastrously, with the result that the increase among

Negroes . . . is [in] that portion of the population least intelligent and fit," the Federation's report noted. But that sounded shockingly like eugenics, and Sanger added, "We don't want the word to go out that we want to exterminate the Negro population."[73] To aid in covering its origins and basic thrust, Sanger's Planned Parenthood gave its Margaret Sanger Award to Dr. Martin Luther King, Jr. in 1966, surely one of history's most calculated attempts to mislead the public. Later Sanger's disciples supported (and continue to support) government-funded abortion, since it provided a ready solution for lowering the black population, while demonizing white Christians who consider all life precious.

Twenty-eight states did have miscegenation laws on the books, and briefly in 1912 a movement to amend the Constitution to prohibit interracial marriage appeared, then faded. However strong racial eugenics were beneath the surface, they were not institutionalized in America the way they were in Europe, which was only a few years away from Adolf Hitler arguing that the Spartans' "abandonment of sick, frail, deformed children—in other words, their destruction—demonstrated greater human dignity and was in reality a thousand times more humane than the pathetic insanity of our time, which attempts to preserve the lives of the sickest subjects. . . ."[74]

Instead, a watered-down "Social Darwinism" gained popularity, beginning in the 1870s in America and attaining international prominence with the formation of the Monist League in Germany in 1904. Ironically, the term "Social Darwinism" was always reserved for the "Right," due to its origin and writings by William Graham Sumner, but it was actually a creature of the liberal/left/Progressive wings of the American political system insofar as it was implemented and used to control, manipulate, and abuse the lower classes. Far from being "Darwinian," business leaders (demonized as "Robber Barons") were usually influenced by Christianity and its practices of charity. Carnegie, though not a practicing Christian, argued in his "Gospel of Wealth" that the duty of the rich was to make money so they could give it away to the poor. Virtually all of them believed that capitalism lifted all boats, and this belief dwelled constantly on how their product could help the common man, usually through lower prices. John D. Rockefeller stressed providing kerosene to the average worker ("We are refining oil for the poor man and he must have it cheap and good") while Samuel Insull went broke and nearly to jail trying to drive down the cost of electricity for the "common man."[75] "Here is an industry," said Insull, "which supplies convenience and comforts to the day laborer, which kings could not command but a century ago."[76]

Nothing in Insull's or Rockefeller's views contains a hint about leaving the poor to die—quite the contrary, the captains of industry only got rich by providing the poor with more goods and services at lower prices. Often, however, the offspring of the "Captains of Industry" bought into eugenics. Mary Harriman, daughter of railroad tycoon E. H. Harriman, brought Charles Davenport together with her mother, successfully persuading her to fund the Eugenics Record Office at Cold Spring Harbor, New York. Where Harriman had toiled to help common men and immigrants, his wife and daughter now sought to eliminate them through genetic sifting.[77] When the Record Office was up and running, Davenport giddily wrote Mrs. Harriman with a macabre prophecy: the fire "you have kindled. . . . [is] going to be a purifying *conflagration* some day!"[78]

That "some day," of course, was only twenty years away when the Holocaust began, and Davenport had spoken in metaphorical terms and would have recoiled at the work of the Third Reich with its gas chambers and ovens. Although most businessmen felt no animosity toward the lower classes, a strain of anti-Semitism crept in by the early 1900s, much of it associated with concerns over the power of large Jewish banking houses in New York City. Henry Ford was among the most notable of the Jew-hating American businessmen, with his views made well known through the *Dearborn Independent*, a Detroit newspaper he financed. The *Independent* ran a series of anti-Semitic articles highlighted by "The International Jew: The World's Foremost Problem" (1920). Hitler supposedly came to admire Ford, reportedly having a picture of the American on his wall. At the same time, however, Ford personally was never accused of discrimination against Jewish workers, and Ford Motor Company was one of few major companies that hired African-American workers during the twenties.

There had been an undercurrent of fear about the power of Jews in the banking system prior to the creation of the Federal Reserve, with the term "New York Money Power" code lingo for "Jewish Money Power" throughout the 1890s. It was all vague, of course, and common to almost all nations. French poet Charles Maurras decried the Versailles Treaty as a combination of "Anglo-Saxon finance and Judeo-German finance . . . our *Demos* flanked by its two friends, the German and the Jew."[79] Simultaneously, the Germans worried about the influence of American Jewish financiers, and the French fretted about the power of German Jewish financiers.

## Social Engineering in Europe

American eugenicists, while influential in science, academia, and leftist society, never went to the extremes with their eugenic views that Europeans did. The British government touted a study in the 1930s called *Heredity and the Social Problem Group*, where it was claimed that the poor were a distinct biological group. But neither the American nor British anti-Semites ever achieved the critical mass they did elsewhere in Europe, where health advocates, sexual reformers, ardent nationalists, pacifists, and leftists all warmly embraced eugenics. Even large numbers of Jewish scientists (supposedly the "secular" Jews) accepted principles of eugenics, as did "many eugenic radicals," including Julius Schwalbe, Eduard David and Victor Adler (the leader of the Austrian Socialists), Max Hirsch, Martin Hahn, Arthur Crzellitzer, and Julius Tandler.[80] This would prove a fatal attraction: even the delegate from the Jewish Welfare Organization did not oppose sterilization measures at the 1932 conference on sterilization in Prussia. Many of the Jewish eugenicists eventually paid for their folly with their lives. Crzellitzer, for one, died in a concentration camp.

Anti-Semitism has, of course, existed for centuries, but it was the rise of the centralized state, and its machinery of "public health," that transformed European anti-Semitism into organized murder.[81] In the nineteenth century, as long as cities and towns were geographically isolated, and the mandates of court and king difficult to enact, Jews as individuals or as groups retained some protection. Pogroms in Russia, riots in Poland, discrimination in France and Germany were all real, often deadly, always unjust, but they never achieved the horror of Hitler's attempt at total eradication because government lacked both the administrative apparatus and the technological machinery to pull it off. For more than a century, Jews had practiced two forms of survival: assimilation and isolation. Assimilationists were Jews who considered themselves more Polish, more German, more French than Jewish. High rates of intermarriage and industriousness in business had incorporated Jews into the fabric of many European societies. By the 1920s, for example, one third of all German Jewish marriages and one fifth of all Hungarian Jewish marriages were to Gentiles. In fact, many states removed barriers to Gentile-Jewish marriage: Germany was the last major country outside of Russia and Hungary to maintain such laws, and it removed them in 1875.

On the other hand, isolationists—usually Orthodox Jews—stood out through their dress and behavior, and in times of persecution became easy targets. In the long run, neither strategy proved effective, either in diminishing suspicion in native lands or commanding respect for adherence to the faith.

Europe in particular had seen an uptick in anti-Semitic books, novels, articles, "scientific" papers, and political discussions as the nineteenth century wore on. And increasingly, the language of the eugenicists bubbled up, as in a Reichstag debate in 1895, where one deputy referred to Jews as "cholera bacilli," and called for their extermination. A few years later—long before Hitler would do so—the German Social Reform Party announced its goal of a "final solution" to the "Jewish question," with the "annihilation" of the race as the ultimate objective.[82] The use of the term "bacilli" is as instructive as it is common. Paul de Lagarde (1887) referred to the Jews as "bearers of decay," and "trichinae and bacilli." It was not enough to categorize Jews as a subpopulation of France, Germany, Poland, or Russia, but rather it was necessary to portray their very existence as a disease—something that must be eradicated. Hence, it would not only be Hitler calling for the "purification of the blood," but also ordinary people during World War II who insisted on "No extermination of the German People and of Germany [by the Allies] but the complete extermination of the Jews."[83]

Historian Niall Ferguson has identified four factors that contributed to anti-Semitism, particularly in Russia: Jews were a substantially urbanized group (Kiev's Jewish population had grown by 500 percent over a ten-year period in the late 1800s); the Jewish population on the whole was wealthier than the native population, making them an easy target for class envy; involvement in revolutionary movements by Jews was extraordinarily high (although accounting for only 1.8 percent of the Russian population in 1939, they made up 11 percent of the Bolsheviks, 23 percent of the Mensheviks in 1907, and constituted the majority of Lenin's Central Committee in 1918); and the modern Sangerite version of racial anti-Semitism had started to take root by 1900.[84] The 1903 *Protocols of the Elders of Zion*, published in the Russian newspaper *The Banner*, exemplified the high pitch of anti-Semitism that rose in Europe. The "Protocols" were reproductions of an early fictitious French work by Maurice Joly about Napoléon III whose fictional plotters to overthrow the emperor were Jesuits. Over time, the ideas were blended with the work of Hermann Goedsche, who introduced a "Jewish conspiracy" in his novel *To Sedan* (1868). Although the definitive author of the *Protocols* remains unknown, many suspect that Pyotr Rachkovsky, the head of the Russian secret police office in Paris, acquired the novel, gave it a Russian twist, and published it as evidence of an anti-czarist plot. The *Protocols* outlined a world takeover by Jews that would include destruction of the Christian religion by materialism, fomenting international unrest and war, undoing the Western educational systems, and controlling international finances. Copies of the *Protocols* were disseminated throughout the Russian army as "The Root of Our Misfortunes." Collectively, their urbanization, wealth, radicalization, and characterization as a conspiratorial group of questionable genetic breeding produced a perfect storm of Jew hatred that bred pogroms in early twentieth-century Russia, while festering in Poland and Germany as well.

The relative political power Jews and other minorities held became even more contentious as Europe faced a decline in births. Even before the Great War, Giuseppe Sergi, an Italian eugenicist, prophesied that Europe's "superior races" were in decline; another Italian noted that "The present fall in the European birth rate is an evil against which it is necessary to react in the name of Western civilization." In the midst of World War I, British books such as *Cradles or Coffins? Our Greatest National Need* saw great circulation.[85] After the war, the pro-natal pressures escalated. France lost one tenth of its male population, and Germany had to deal with a half million wartime widows, making the conflict the "greatest sexual catastrophe ever suffered by civilized man."[86] Of those who returned, thousands were "destroyed men," incapable of normal sexual or social relations, leading to the rise of a generation of fatherless boys who turned to the streets. Divorce rates rose, and both the Left and Right looked upon the developments with horror. The French government issued a gold medal for productive mothers who bore ten children; Belgium had a "League of Large Families"; British papers warned of declining birth rates; and Hungarians faced a "battle without hope . . . [against] folk-death."[87] Mussolini decried the decline of the Italian family—the population grew by only 1 percent in the interwar period—warning that his country would become a colony to other nations.[88] Another Italian claimed "most biologists, economists and politicians fully endorse the view that numbers are the strength of the Nation."[89] "The attention of many European governments," he noted, "has been called to the decreasing birth rate of the white races during the last decades."[90]

There was more to these movements than nationalism, however: a strong element of race permeated all of the early eugenics/birth-rate debates. In 1928, the *Eugenical News* announced a contest with a $5,000 prize for the best paper researching demographics of the "Nordic peoples." A paper called "Comparative Birth-Rate Movements Among European Nations" won the first place prize and again emphasized the falling European birth and marriage rates.[91] In many respects, the apex of Caucasian power, certainly that of Europe, was realized in 1940 and has declined ever since to the point that by 2010, whites made up only 16 percent of the earth's population, while Asians and south Asians reached 46 percent. European colonies began to disappear at a remarkable rate, and it was only the Cold War between the two polyglot superpowers, the United States and USSR, that obscured the decline in Caucasian hegemony.

In an effort to bolster the birth rate, abortion was outlawed in France in 1920; Britain followed in 1929. Fascist Italy saw Mussolini admonish its female citizens, "Go back home and tell the women I need births, many births."[92] Even in Soviet Russia the concern with birth rates led to yet another of Marx's predictions being ditched in favor of a new Soviet commitment to the traditional family.[93] In Weimar Germany, the Reichstag outlawed contraception, noting, "The general welfare of the state has to have precedence over women's feelings."[94]

Germany, in particular, appreciated its delicate situation, sandwiched as it was between the vast USSR and France, prompting German demographers to sound the clarion call about dwindling populations and diminishing family size, as well as family destruction. One of the leading criticisms of the Versailles Treaty was that it stripped Germany of 10 percent of its population due to the creation of Poland and Czechoslovakia. Bavarian statistician Friedrich Burgdörfer warned of another dangerous trend, an aging population. The Weimar Republic had become so concerned with a potentially smaller population that the constitution offered housing and economic incentives for the "child rich" (defined as families with more than four children), and organizations such as the Local League for the Child Rich of Frankfurt sprang up.[95] Across Europe, however, the population bust troubled observers, irrespective of ideology. The 1937 Irish constitution stated that the "family was the natural, primary, and fundamental unit of society," and "Red Vienna," arguably the most socialist city outside of the USSR (with the exception of Hamburg), saw its Marxist council members developing a "social contract" with families that included financial assistance for baby clothing.[96] The city built sixty thousand new family residences in fifteen years—a state-financed 1930s version of Levittown. France, Spain, and Italy even banned the advertising and sale of contraceptives.

Declining birth rates and population issues took on greater significance not only because of the military value of a large population, but also because the new Progressive social-welfare approach to children permeating the United States and Europe turned what were once units of production into units of consumption. Well-meaning legislation forced children out of the workplace and into schools, while at the same time moralists demanded that parents properly house, clothe, and feed families, placing new (and, once the Depression started, often unbearable) burdens on families in industrialized nations. British busybodies visited housing run by the London metropolitan government to report on cleanliness and to encourage tenants to shape their family behavior in line with government wishes.[97]

## Medicine, Eugenics, and Social Engineering

Concerns about population and social hygiene allowed eugenicists to worm their way into various health and welfare groups, where they insisted on a heavier state investment in public health programs. Sweden, Denmark, Finland, and one Swiss canton all had eugenic sterilization measures for the retarded or feeble-minded. Supporters of state sterilization in England included Lord Horder, the physician to King George VI, and in America, H. L. Mencken. Ireland and Italy both established incentives to keep people from moving to the cities without work; Britain tried the opposite approach, establishing lures for people to move back to the country. It was widely accepted among the elites that overcrowding led to poor hygiene, which in turn produced mental deficiency. The new fascination with sterilization as a means of "improving national health" occurred while a sexual revolution of sorts was simultaneously taking place, pitting pro-contraception/abortion groups against the "big family" advocates.[98] Overcrowding in cities was therefore only part of the tension in the war over natal policies that included a new abortion offensive.

For example, by the late 1920s in Germany the sexual reformers appeared to be gaining the upper hand, and it is estimated there were over 800,000 abortions in 1930 alone.[99] As early as 1920, lawyer Karl Binding and psychiatrist Alfred Hoche called for the "destruction of life that is no longer worth living."[100] Hoche even cited a "national duty" for doctors to prevent the nation's collapse by eliminating a half million "idiots" and "valueless" lives. (Hitler would use similar language at the Nuremberg rally in 1929, saying the nation's welfare policies were breeding the weak and that Germany needed to rid itself of "burdensome lives.") These ideas were not isolated, even in the 1920s. Quite the contrary, another lawyer published a draft law for killing the mentally ill, and a popular novelist argued for murdering crippled children at birth. During the decade, thousands of forced sterilizations took place in Weimar, but in Austria, England, and Denmark, sterilization legislation was also proposed.

While sterilization and euthanasia were never supported by most Europeans, even most Germans—indeed, many of the advocates of sterilization and eugenics writers provoked powerful reactions—the apparatus of the state using the cover of public hygiene and general welfare made substantial inroads across Europe and throughout America. A Soviet Eugenics Office was created in 1921; the United States had its Eugenic Record Office; the British Social Hygiene Council wanted to institutionalize all mentally ill and offer sex education in schools; France created a Superior Council for Social Hygiene. Voluntary sterilization laws were passed in Sweden, Switzerland, Denmark, Norway, Finland, and Estonia. Britain's Wood Report on Mental Deficiency identified those with mental disorders as a "social problem group" of four million, for which British eugenicists championed forced sterilization as the answer. Even more astounding was an event that occurred in 1936 when King George V, extremely ill and completely bedridden, was euthanized by his private doctor with the family's blessing with a mixture of cocaine and morphine as a way to circumvent the problem of having a nonfunctioning monarch. When even kings were susceptible to the law, what chance had commoners?

Race, disease, and social control all could be enforced through marriage laws, which usually required a tuberculosis and venereal disease test. In Germany, the Reich Health Council concluded that education alone was insufficient, and that mandatory medical exams would be necessary, supervised by specialized "Marriage Examiners." Sweden's marriage law had been extended in its scope to include a requirement for disease testing in 1919. Weimar Germany rejected mandatory exams, but taxation and financial assistance to families deemed fit were considered a means of racial purification and social cleansing. Alarmed by the success of the sexual reformers and the sudden rise in abortions "of choice" and unrelated to eugenic causes (but also out of a need to replace the massive population losses of the war), the medical establishment and the government sought to rejuvenate births within traditional families. Copying the United States, an official German "Mother's Day" was proposed in 1922. (After World War II, foreign women desiring to marry American servicemen were obliged to undergo thorough medical examinations to determine their fitness and gain the approval of military commanders.) Almost all states adopted the requirement for blood tests to obtain a marriage license in the 1930s, and by 2010 eight states still required them. Various explanations have been offered to explain such requirements, but they all developed out of the eugenics movement to control breeding.

The early battlefield for the sexual reformers and the large family forces were the marriage clinics (first established by the Weimar Republic in 1924), which tried to encourage the destruction of "unfit" babies. Soon, Berlin and all other major cities had marriage advice clinics, which, combined with new benefits for maternity leave and prenatal care, attracted the support of the eugenicists. These clinics marked a critical transition point from which population planning, once the domain of a few educated professionals, became a state-supported policy.[101] By virtue of their presence at the municipal level, and their aura of medical authority—sanctioned by studies from the Kaiser Wilhelm Institute—the clinics became the precursors to the Nazis' own racial and welfare clinics.

A second battlefield involved biological concepts of "blood," which drew on wartime research in heredity. By the late 1920s, German anthropologists were convinced that different races were defined by blood groups. The Rockefeller Foundation provided funds for much of this research, particularly that of Eugen Fischer, whose work would later become a point of embarrassment for the Foundation after it was used to support Nazi theories. Fischer was not alone, and indeed labored within a milieu of several competitors, including anthropologist Otto Reche, as well as colleagues such as Munich's Ernst Rüdin and Erwin Baur, a German who coined the phrase "Nordic Ideal."[102] Baur coauthored with Fischer a text on eugenics that Hitler studied while in jail, and which was later cited as a primary source for the Nazi racial laws. Fischer, Rüdin, and others conducted a massive 1932 survey that collected material on a quarter million people, focusing on genetically inherited talent and degeneracy. The survey enlisted medical professionals, schoolteachers, doctors, welfare administrators, and even priests in reporting abnormalities or criminal tendencies, rewarding them with money for their cooperation. By 1934, Germany, Poland, and Austria had more than forty university institutes dedicated to studying eugenics.[103] In less than a decade, those who had seen themselves as virtuous saviors of public health discovered they had been perilously co-opted, to the point that some technocrats could no longer back out (and to the point where many others did not want to relinquish their power). Reinterpreting medical and social welfare in terms of biological costs and benefits allowed the state to intervene in every fabric of society.

Under a thorough reformulation of concepts of racial hygiene, health professionals were mobilized to identify the problems of the underclasses, in the process using science to tag and police undesirable groups. Weimar's eugenics movement found itself melded into Nazism with surprising ease, co-opting the doctors and scientists. As Paul Weindling, the historian of the German eugenics movement, observed, a Faustian pact was signed between the scientists and the Nazis. The more "scientific their outlook, the more politically naive they were. The more scientists tried to maintain authority and status, the more concessions had to be made to Nazism."[104]

By 1933, compulsory sterilization was formalized with the Law for the Prevention of Hereditarily Diseased Progeny, which over the next twelve years would sterilize a third of a million people on the basis of schizophrenia, deafness, epilepsy, and a host of other disabilities. (Two years later, castration for homosexuals was added under the legislation.) This law not only cemented the relationship between the state's authority and the machinery of the medical profession, but enjoyed a massive publicity campaign about heredity and race. Doctors set up more than 250 tribunals to administer the sterilization drive, sucking in many of the eugenicists of the 1920s who had championed public health measures, all wrapped in yet more surveys and studies. Subsumed under the Reich Office for Family Research, which issued official certificates of Aryan ancestry, the Nazi Party had essentially corralled all authority over race by 1934. Within five years, compulsory registration and identification cards were instituted—all carefully sorted to determine who was permitted to settle in occupied territories (when Germany obtained them). The reaction of the American Eugenics Society was to praise Hitler's courage and statesmanship by tackling such an important issue.[105] Supporters of the California eugenics law, including the head of Riverside's Bureau of Welfare and Relief, cited sterilization as a weapon to halt the "menace to the race at large."[106] Sacramento banker Charles Goethe, a leading supporter of eugenics in the state, noted in 1936 that the United States and Germany were the leaders in eugenics ("two stupendous forward movements") but that despite having a quarter-century head start, California was passed quickly by the Germans. That same year, Paul Popenoe, a partner with Gosney in the Human Betterment Foundation, actively corresponded with Nazi officials so as to make certain that "conditions in Germany are not misunderstood or misrepresented."[107] California eugenicists knew that the Nazis were targeting the Jews in particular and still approved of Germany's approach to "race hygiene," and, given the law's passage, few can doubt the politicians' support of the programs.

## Underclass and Empire

Long before the Third Reich would employ eugenics for its own purposes, the new thinking about race and population control throughout Europe was already intertwined with the issue of the colonies. Race and citizenship, population and childbirth policies all became different facets of the same dilemma—whether to liberate people of other ethnicities or incorporate them into the motherland and "civilize" them. The surprising loyalty of the colonies to Britain and France during the Great War only complicated matters. India and the African territories had sent waves of troops, most of whom were mistreated and poorly used at the fronts. France especially came to view the colonies as a source of manpower, and hence emancipation or liberation was unthinkable. Algeria and French-occupied Arab lands, especially, received massive investment after the war due to the ease of extracting profits from countries just across the Mediterranean. French-controlled North Africa and the Middle East received four times as much investment as other French provinces in Africa.[108] In theory, French citizenship eventually awaited Algerians. Realistically, France never intended to grant equal status to Arab Africans, and when the first test came in 1936, under a Popular Front bill to grant citizenship to a handful of Muslim veterans, it was scuttled in Parliament by the deputies of French settlers in Algeria.

In the colonies themselves, a ruling class emerged among the Europeans. France's resident-general of Morocco, Marshal Hubert Lyautey, who had served there since 1912, however, despised the Algerian French colonists. Many who settled in Algeria and Morocco ended up in administration, where their numbers exceeded those of British officials in India. England's colonial administrators, in comparison, came from a particular social class that stood apart from the French or Belgians. Its landed groups dominated the army, the bureaucracy, and the judicial system, and its young men were all trained at elite schools in public leadership, steeped in heroism, sacrifice, and disdain for physical comforts on behalf of the empire. Rudyard Kipling's line about sending "forth the best ye breed" typified the British colonial administrators: they were prepared educationally and psychologically for foreign service. But the extensive demands of foreign service also opened the doors for people from other classes to advance through assignments overseas. At the same time, a small but growing chorus urged Britain to divest itself of foreign territories. These voices included John Ruskin, a professor of fine arts at Oxford, Arnold Toynbee, Arthur Glazebrook, and Albert (Lord) Grey, heads of what was known as the "Little Englanders." Most of those in government or with influence, however, shared the imperialistic views of Cecil Rhodes. An undergraduate when Ruskin delivered his inaugural address (Rhodes copied it longhand and kept it for more than two decades), Rhodes advanced through the ranks to become prime minister of Cape Colony in 1890. He controlled the South African diamond mines and made a fortune from them.[109]

Rhodes and Alfred (Lord) Milner, however, were also responsible for a program of "equal rights for all civilized men south of the Zambezi," thereby introducing a degree of fair treatment of natives. While he brooked no tolerance for Zulu practices such as those that required a young male to kill someone or steal cattle to be eligible for marriage, he urged Zulus to direct their energies to working in the mines, convincing them that it was onerous and difficult (which it was) and itself constituted a display of heroism (it did). After five years, the Zulu miners returned with enough money to buy cattle for marriage eligibility.

Politicians such as Rhodes set England on a course to gradually prepare native populations for freedom, and, as Lionel Curtis, secretary to Lord Milner, put it, "the peoples of India and Egypt . . . must be gradually schooled on management of their national affairs. . . . I regard this challenge to the long unquestioned claim of the white man to dominate the world as inevitable and wholesome."[110] Curtis became one of the leading voices for "Imperial Federalism," or a commonwealth system of independent former colonies still tied to England.

Lord Milner and Secretary of State for India Edwin S. Montagu took a similar view. As early as 1917, Milner argued that the goal of the British government was to increase "association of Indians in every branch of the administration and [to ensure] the gradual development of self-governing institutions . . . with a view to . . . responsible government in India," a code phrase everyone understood as "independence."[111] England established a Dominion Department to govern the colonies, complete with conferences every four years to monitor progress. Even Canada received a high degree of autonomy with the Statute of Westminster in 1931, which established nearly complete legislative independence from Parliament (although full independence did not come until well after World War II).

In most African colonies, of course, movements toward dominion status produced radical disparities between the masses of blacks and the handful of whites. Kenya had over two million blacks and only three thousand whites in 1910, most of whom were government employees. The British hoped that as natives learned English and acquired an education, they would leaven their home countries and lift others up. Instead, educated natives used their skills as a passport to escape to England or the United States.

Dislocations produced by Versailles established numerous protectorates and mandates throughout Africa and the Middle East, mostly to the benefit of England and France, and often blindsided the hopeful colonials who had arrived at the peace conference in 1919 expecting to receive a path to independence. One of the most profound pieces of mismanagement involved the dissection of the Ottoman Empire. At the peak of its power, the Ottoman Empire was larger than any contemporary European state in area and population, stretching from Morocco to the Persian Gulf, from the Balkans as far north as Poland and to the northern shore of the Black Sea. These vast provinces were administered by twenty-one governments overseeing seventy *vilayets* (subprovinces), each under a pasha. The Turkish state was strictly Islamic in religious practices, secular in orientation and government processes, and impervious to genuine reform.[112] One group longing to escape from under the Turkish thumb, the Arabs, constituted a disparate band of tribes whose animosity to one another strongly resembled that of the Plains Indians in America. During World War I, the British had established an Arab Bureau, which promised important and self-promoting Arabs, such as the Saudi-born Faisal bin Hussein, assistance and recognition once the fighting ended. Facilitated by an unorthodox and uncontrollable British colonel fluent in Arabic, T. E. Lawrence, the Arab Bureau gave birth to a group called the "Intrusives," whose objective was to "shape the Arab world to fit the needs of the Empire."[113]

Lawrence's reputation first rose after he rescued a British force that had marched from India only to be ambushed outside of Baghdad. Functioning inside Arabia (later Saudi Arabia, Palestine, and Syria), Lawrence concluded that an Arab revolt could be led only by one of Hussein's sons, Emir Faisal, with his army of some four thousand irregulars. In a well-known transformation, permanently glamorized in David Lean's 1962 film, *Lawrence of*

*Arabia*, the British colonel "went native," donning robes, the kaffiyeh (headdress), and sporting a gold, curved dagger. Despite Lawrence's cash disbursements to Faisal, a rival in Riyadh named Ibn Saud mounted his own program with the British to head postwar Arabia. Harry St. John Bridger Philby, the British emissary to the region, backed Saud so much that he converted to Islam. Thus Lawrence and the Hashemite tribe under Hussein bin Ali were pitted against Saud and the Wahhabis supported by Philby, in the process fanning their tribal hatreds. To make matters worse, Britain and France had, in the 1916 Sykes-Picot Agreement, already sliced up the Middle East even before the Ottoman Empire had fallen. This arrangement contradicted the Balfour Declaration of 1917 (which established a national homeland for the Jews in the region) by recognizing an Arab state in the place. It also promised Russia control of Constantinople and the Turkish Straits. Nevertheless, across the Atlantic, Wilson's own report writers were producing a "Report on the Proposals for an Independent Arab State" that suggested Arabia be united with a caliphate located in Mecca. When the Versailles Conference actually started, however, Ibn Saud was in Riyadh while Faisal and Lawrence were lobbying in France for Hashemite dominance. For a moment it appeared they might successfully coax the Allies into forming a united Arabian state, but the French held firm in their determination to have a chunk of the Ottoman Empire (Syria), and Wilson was beaten down through the need to repeatedly concede points in return for support for his League of Nations.

Saud's forces attacked Hussein's troops while the dignitaries met in Versailles, and Lawrence hustled back to negotiate a cease-fire before the House of Saud took over everything. Faisal established a freely constituted government in Damascus—in French territory—but the French crushed his troops and forced him into exile. In 1921, the British colonial secretary, Winston Churchill, installed Faisal as the king of Mesopotamia (now Iraq), a British protectorate, after a rebellion against direct British rule there had been put down at great cost. Ibn Saud eventually controlled all of the largely desert wasteland later known as Saudi Arabia, and the region probably would have remained insignificant internationally for centuries had it not possessed vast resources in oil. Following centuries of precedence in which successful revolutions afterward eliminate their more radical adherents, in 1929 Saud destroyed the followers who had brought him to power, the troublesome Ikhwan brotherhood, when they attempted to extend the borders of his Wahhabist realm.

## Britain, Balfour, and Israel

Of course, one other issue complicated all the other tribal and national struggles already laid upon the table: the national Jewish homeland promised by British foreign secretary Arthur Balfour to Chaim Weizmann, president of the World Zionist Organization. Weizmann became a convert to Zionism in 1896 when he met Theodor Herzl, author of *Der Judenstaat* ("The Jewish State"). Weizmann thereafter dedicated himself to its creation. A chemist who had sold his discoveries to I. G. Farben, Weizmann moved to England where he met Balfour in 1906, the year Balfour won his seat in Parliament. Spurred by C. P. Scott, the editor of the influential *Manchester Guardian*, Weizmann and Balfour developed a compelling argument that Britain should encourage the formation of a Jewish state, and in the process provide a regional protector for the Suez Canal and an outpost for British power in the Middle East. Weizmann labored to line up a coalition inside Parliament for his cause.

In 1918 the British government sent a Zionist Commission to Palestine to lay the groundwork that would implement the Balfour Declaration. Dodging German U-boats in the Mediterranean, the Commission, including Weizmann, set up shop in Tel Aviv. Weizmann immediately met General Edmund Allenby, but overall found the officer corps unfriendly to his cause. Many had arrived with copies of the fraudulent *Protocols of the Elders of Zion*. Despite their opposition, Weizmann won over the general. Other unfriendly encounters occurred with the former Jerusalem official Musa Kazim al-Husayni, who carried a copy of the *Protocols* with him, as well as the grand mufti of Jerusalem, Kamel Bey al-Husseini, a rabid anti-Semite and future acolyte of Adolf Hitler. Weizmann's meeting with Faisal in the Sinai went somewhat better, with the Jewish leader shepherded about by Lawrence of Arabia. Both Lawrence and the Arabs thought the Zionists could be instrumental in advancing Arab objectives with Britain at a future peace conference.

However, the problem all along was that the Balfour Declaration—whatever intention Britain had of living up to it—constituted only a single statement by one government. Weizmann and his allies, therefore, drafted a plan for a Jewish state in Palestine under British authority. Then on January 3, 1919, Weizmann and Faisal signed a bilateral agreement acknowledging the creation of independent Jewish and Arab states. Perhaps at that time, more than any other, the reality of "Middle East peace" was closest:

both men agreed their people had suffered under colonialism and promised to work together.

Fittingly, even as those with the most to lose—the Arabs and Jews—moved toward harmony, the French destroyed the moment. Sylvain Lévi, a Jewish French confidant of the Jewish Baron Edmond de Rothschild who had a personal grudge against Weizmann, spoke. He shattered the case laid before the delegates by warning that newly arriving Jews would disrupt the region, and alluded to the "Bolshevik" influences of the Russian Jews. Perhaps when contrasted against the pro-Zionist arguments it wasn't much, but given that many of the delegations were wary of *any* potential dislocations or upheaval that might cause future problems in the Middle East, the discussion of the Jewish state became a nonstarter.

Quickly, the Versailles delegates dropped the Palestine issue and moved on to the disposition of Germany, leaving the Palestinian porcupine for England to hold. Still full of hope, Weizmann sailed to Palestine, where hostile British officers almost prevented him from landing. Then the Zionists discovered that the British government would give them no land at all and that they had to raise funds to buy every tract. "We found we had to cover the soil of Palestine with Jewish gold," Weizmann dourly noted.[114] Over time, Jews would continue to trickle into Palestine, until in July 1937 Britain announced yet another special commission under Lord William Peel, who reported that "Arab nationalism is as intense a force as Jewish [nationalism]. . . . The gulf between the races is thus already wide and will continue to widen if the present Mandate is maintained." There is "no common ground" between the Jews and the Arabs, he continued: "Their national aspirations are incompatible."[115]

## Frameworks for De-colonialism

Unlike the Americans, who had established a logical, sensible policy for admitting new peoples into the Union as full citizens (i.e., Hawaii) or setting them on a genuine road to independence (as seen in the Philippines), the Europeans lacked any such framework, let alone an effective one, in spite of their centuries-old experience with colonies.

Thus the ironic phenomenon unfolded in which colonial states demanded democratic rights they had never understood or practiced (or, often, even seen up close) from nations that were only in the infancy of learning how to operate democratic institutions themselves. Germany and Russia still had functioning kings as late as 1917 in Russia's case, 1918 in

Germany's, and Belgium still had one. France had experienced a shocking turnover rate in the type of government (empire, monarchy, republic) it enjoyed, careening from Napoléon to Louis XVIII to Louis Philippe to Napoléon III to the Third Republic in less than a century. Only England and Holland had long histories of peaceful, nonrevolutionary self-government. Nevertheless, it was to the democratically dysfunctional European nations that the colonies looked for role models.

After the Treaty of Versailles, the French colony of Cameroon requested "the right to choose the [European governing power that supervised it]" and demanded civil rights, security for chiefs, and an end to land expropriations. South Africans insisted on universal suffrage in 1921, and the African National Congress (ANC) in 1923 issued a "declaration, statement or Bill of Rights" that endowed the Bantu and non-African coloreds with "liberty of the subject, justice and equality for all classes in the eyes of the law." It also called for "democratic principles" of equality of treatment and citizenship in the land, "irrespective of race, class, creed or origin."[116] These were admirable sentiments, almost never seen in action in the mother countries, and certainly glassy-eyed romantic notions given the absolute absence of the recognition that tribes still dominated most of the African colonies.

Europeans ignored such appeals. Instead, they displayed their possessions proudly at international gatherings. From May to November 1934, the Colonial Exhibition in Paris attracted eight million visitors. It was elaborately staged to celebrate France's colonies, including African and Tunisian pavilions with natives dressed in traditional garb. A previous counterdemonstration, the anticolonial exhibition in 1931, had drawn only four thousand.[117] Soviet attempts to agitate within the colonies mostly floundered. Two Soviet Africanists working at the Russian African bureau collaborated with nationalist Albert Nzula of the Orange Free State to publish *The Working Class Movement and Forced Labor in Negro Africa* (1922). The book was astounding given that the Soviets were "busy turning the Ukrainian farm belt into something resembling Leopold II's Congo Free State."[118] It had little impact, and Nzula later died in Russia due to overdrinking, passing out, and lying in the freezing Moscow streets for hours as people walked by.[119]

Despite the illusion of a commonwealth of cheerful brown, black, and yellow people pulling together for the mother country, the reality was quite different. The Great War had produced ever new and more severe problems for the European colonial empires, not the least of which was their eventual disposition. A few had already seen the future: Frederick Lugard's book *The Dual Mandate in British Tropical Africa* (1922) argued that "the civilized nations have at last recognized that while on the one hand the abounding wealth of the tropical regions of the earth must be developed and used for the benefit of mankind, on the other hand an obligation rests on the controlling power not only to safeguard the material rights of the natives, but to promote their moral and material educational progress."[120] But there is no indication that policymakers gave it much more consideration than they had Nzula's tract.

Britain held out the possibility of national independence for its colonies, and in India's case, virtually promised it. Critics maintained that even in the case of India, the British weren't serious; apologists that independence was only a matter of when, not if. Not so: while going through the motions of independence, Britain circled, constantly searching for the perfect time and ideal process, neither of which could ever appear in the real world.

Other European countries wandered aimlessly with their colonial policies. France was in the process of absorbing large numbers of foreigners from its colonies, giving citizenship to some 2.3 million between 1889 and 1940, while allowing another 2.6 million foreign noncitizens to remain in the country. This was in keeping with European notions that people from the empires could be assimilated on a slow basis into the homeland. On the other hand, many French politicians had no intention of granting millions of Algerian Muslims citizenship. In 1920, the resident-general of Morocco, Marshal Hubert Lyautey, called for a "radical change of course" for Algeria and its Muslim population, and the governor-general of Algeria, Jean-Baptiste Abel, warned that if France refused to admit Algerians into their national structure, "beware lest they do not soon create one for themselves."[121] Rather than Algerians becoming French, settlers (known as *colons*) populated Algeria and exploited the locals. Lyautey likened *colons* to Germans in their racism.[122]

The vast pool of native manpower enticed French officials, who not only looked back at the staggering losses from the war, but also looked forward at the potentially higher German birth rates. Only through empire could France generate the numbers needed to offset potential European threats—armies that would never materialize, but which remained tantalizingly near in 1939, when the minister for the colonies promised to raise two million native troops for the defense of France. Then there was the ever-present need for raw materials. This, too, preoccupied the French at Versailles, where the Mosul oil fields were part of a "Greater Syria" France coveted. Instead, Lawrence of Arabia had put the Arabs in physical (if not political) control of Damascus, leaving only Lebanon for *la Mère-patrie*. Instead of oil, France obtained a beautiful port plus the headaches of keeping the Lebanese Christians—Lebanon was formed to provide a state in which Lebanese Maronite Christians would predominate—and the local Arabs separate, foreshadowing the no-win "peacekeeper" role the United Nations would adopt unsuccessfully in future decades. French colonies in Africa gobbled up capital, and the French share of investment going to territories rose to almost half of all French investment, mostly in Algeria. A more neglected colony was French Indo-China, which, like Morocco, was overpopulated with European bureaucrats—more than in all of British India.

For most Europeans, the colonies were a net drain, and had been since the 1700s, at least insofar as the spotty data reveals. One study of British investment in their empire concluded that colonial finance played only a minor role in capital markets, returns on investment were low relative to domestic investment, and imperialism was a net cost to the taxpayers.[123] With few exceptions, African and Asian territories were money losers. Rubber, tin, and diamonds paid off, but capital poured into independent states in Latin America seldom produced a return, and in any event, merely getting products to market demanded expensive and permanent construction and maintenance of railroads, port and harbor facilities, communications, hospitals, and schools. In India, from 1891 to 1938 the British laid forty thousand miles of railroad track, doubled the number of irrigation facilities, and created a postal and telegraph system. France built the Congo-Ocean Railway from Point-Noire to Brazzaville, but at horrific cost. One estimate put the number of native workers who died on the project at sixteen thousand, and the construction led to the revolt of the Gbaya people near French Cameroon in 1928 and the subsequent Kongo-Wara War. European railroads in Africa reduced transport costs by 90 percent, but still profits were elusive. Not surprisingly, then, foreign investment abroad shrank for every leading colonial power between 1914 and 1930.[124]

Whatever gains that were realized came from work gangs and forced labor, supplied in part through imperial justice meted out to noncitizens. Under such a system, there was no motivation for natives to invest in their

colonized homeland themselves. South of the Sahara, for example, the opportunity for French citizenship was even more remote than in Algeria. By
1936, only two thousand nonwhites held French citizenship in lower Africa,
leading to the steady flight of blacks to neighboring British provinces where
infrastructure was better and there was greater opportunity for employment.

Colonial economic structures thus produced uneven growth at best,
leading critics to maintain that "forced development" did not work, regardless of benevolent intentions. Statistics tended to indicate that top-down
development failed. Excluding the years of the Great War, from 1870 to
1946, India's GNP grew at only .5 percent per year or less. Ghana grew at
1.3 percent from 1870 to 1913. Overall, African growth during the imperial
years was .6 percent from 1870 to 1913 and .9 percent from 1913 to 1950.
But these numbers failed to tell the whole story, and the dark fact may well
be that Africa's growth rate *only* managed to achieve such pathetically weak
rates *because of* European investment and interference. At any rate, it seemed
to matter little what policy was overlaid on top of the territories. Free trade
models, instituted by the British and Dutch, seemed no better than protec-
tionist frameworks erected by France, Spain, Italy, and, for some time, the
United States.

Whatever the purpose of the initial investment, colonial powers usually discovered it was no inexpensive matter (a lesson the Americans had
learned in the Canal Zone). Once built, factories and plantations could rely
on native labor, but seldom did they profit from the "networking" benefits
of highly skilled employees who made incremental improvements in the
production process. High-skill jobs were therefore imported from the colonial power and retained at home. To a large degree, advanced economies
tended to invest in one another—Isaac Singer built his grand sewing machine factory in Scotland, where it employed fourteen thousand—rather
than in the undeveloped backwaters of Africa and Asia. Natives who lacked
skills made poor wage workers, and attempts to bring vast numbers of
them into the wage economy proved fruitless. According to economist
E. J. Berg, less than 5 percent of sub-Saharan Africans worked for wages at
any time during the year as late as 1950, producing demands to import
Pakistani and Indian laborers, who added yet another ethnic tension to the
mix.[125] In the Boer republics during the late nineteenth century more than
ninety thousand workers were recruited from England to provide skilled
and semiskilled labor—a move that ultimately cost the Boers their nations.

English workers claimed they were discriminated against by not being allowed to vote; England took the side of their countrymen, and after two costly wars, England brought the Boers to heel and combined the Cape Colony, Natal, Transvaal, and Orange Free State into the Union of South Africa, a British dominion. There was a lesson here, but one missed by Western politicians.

Another lesson that Progressive politicians refused to learn was that colonies needed first to develop at least some of the underpinnings to American exceptionalism in order to avoid tyrannies and establish democratic republics. Since Europeans themselves did not have checks and balances in their political systems, they were not inserted into colonial governments. Private property became something maintained by force rather than law, and combines of government and private corporations established crony capitalism in which influence in government was vastly more important than ideas, hard work, and business efficiency. Common law was missing altogether; indeed, all laws were promulgated by high officials, often located outside the colony; religion was normally autocratically administered; and a form of serfdom throughout the native population was institutionalized. Given these deficiencies in colonial social and political structures, democracy did and would remain a pipe dream, understood only in propaganda slogans, for many long years to come.

## "Democratizing" Asia

If Americans had a higher opinion of their "yellow brothers" in Asia than they did of their "brown brothers" in Latin America, they never made it known. Modernization in Asian political systems and economic structures proceeded at almost as slow a pace as it did in South America. During their periods of industrialization, neither Japan nor China elicited much interest or direct investment from the Americans or Europeans, save for the establishment of some trading posts and the carving out of "spheres of influence." European military presence in both nations was minimal and the commercial presence scarcely larger, but the stark contrast of such advanced foreigners motivated both Japan and China to modernize.

Earlier reforms in Japan had led to the Meiji Constitution of 1868, wherein the shogunates were ended and an oligarchy of four western clans operating under the Emperor Meiji (Mutsuhito) moved to rapidly industrialize Japan. By 1905, following the slogan "Enrich the country, strengthen the military," Meiji leaders imposed conscription, enacted land reforms, and privatized shipbuilding, ironworks, and textile mills. Japan urbanized rapidly, and silk and coal production soared.[126]

Emperor Taisho (Prince Yoshihito prior to becoming emperor in 1912), an unbalanced semirecluse who was not a part of the governing process and whose edicts required ministers' signatures, had little actual power. Nor did the Diet (parliament), which could pass budgets and little else. Power resided in the *zaibatsu*, huge financial and industrial conglomerates that controlled Japan's economy and much of its daily life. Initially the "Big Four" of Mitsubishi, Mitsui, Sumitomo, and Yasuda formed the main power base in the Meiji period, but these were later joined by Fujita, Furukawa, Nissan, Nakajima, and Kawasaki, among others. These vertical monopolies could and did form alliances with the Japanese military for imperial expansion, and their very structures fostered autocratic governance.

Taisho demonstrated all the oddball characteristics of a grown child. When inspecting his troops on parade—that is, when he didn't fall off his horse—he alternated between slapping the soldiers or embracing them. Once, addressing the Diet, he rolled up his written speech and made it into a telescope, peering through it at the dumbfounded members. At the same time, however, he was the "Divine Emperor," the living god on earth, which meant he was the final source of law. His dynasty survived a wave of Christian missionaries who failed to convert—or even significantly alter—the Japanese. Under Taisho, Japan borrowed heavily, almost obsessively, from China and the West, including Confucian literature, Sung art, poetic verse, Taoist sayings, technology, railroads, dress, and even business and administrative models from the American managerial revolution.

If the Meiji leaders could have frozen the frame in 1911, they would have, embracing Western technology and select concepts, while rejecting the deep conversion to Western values—including freedom of speech, constitutional limitations, a growing respect for women, and above all the de-deification of the emperor. It was no surprise that after World War II General Douglas MacArthur insisted on giving women the vote as a means to introduce a greater feminine influence into Japanese politics. But as much as the Japanese in the Meiji and Taisho periods flirted with Western concepts, none of those ideas truly penetrated the moral fiber of the nation. Instead, aware that *some* internal faith and religious adherence undergirded Western success, between 1912 and 1930, Japan melded Shintoism, an animistic religion of study that incorporated ancestor worship with natural deities from the earth, waves, skies, and other forces (*Shinto* means "Way of the Gods"), with a new state-encouraged warrior ethos called *Bushido* or "Way of the Warrior-Knight." Bushido called for supreme loyalty to the emperor combined with Japanese-style chivalry that blended martial arts, frugality, and honor—if necessary, to death. Shinto had been established as a state religion in the late 1800s, then entrenched as a social code as early as the 1920s. Fortified and reinforced by military victories, it was then finally elevated in 1941 into a full political religion replete with national religious ceremonies. In both Nazi Germany and Imperial Japan, therefore, the state co-opted or perverted the mitigating hand of religion in such a way as to make it a servant of its policies.

Westerners mistook universal male suffrage and the trappings of democracy in Japan for genuine processes and indicators of liberty, but in reality power was concentrated in a few hands. Over a period of thirty-three years of cabinet governance, eighteen cabinets held office with only nine different premiers, only two of whom were not of the Choshu or Satsuma clans, and five of whom were military men.[127] Meanwhile, the emperor's favorites controlled the bureaucracy, thus neutering the Diet, and bribes, force, and tricks were used to obtain favorable votes.

World War I opened new doors to Japan. Deprived of European suppliers, and operating outside the Europeans' restraints, the Japanese dramatically increased exports, foreign trade, and manufacturing, acquiring new Asian markets, all enhanced by the presence of a rich stratum of skilled tradesmen who could apply iron-making and shipbuilding technology. Industrial development, however, can carry one only so far, and in a Japan lacking common law—indeed, lacking any fixed legal code, save that of the Divine Emperor—business could grow only so much.

Beginning about 1840, China sought to modernize to save itself from Western invasion and interference in internal matters that were epitomized by the Opium Wars and Britain's involvement in the Taiping Rebellion. Under the Qing Dynasty, Western-style factories were built under the principle of *Yang Wu*, or "self-strengthening." This modernization only went so far, and China remained behind Japan, seeing her navy crushed by the Japanese in 1894–94 in the Chinese North Sea. In fact, these setbacks only reemphasized one of the tenets of the "Western Way of War," which is all things being equal, the freer nation tends to win military conflicts due to its superior productivity and motivated forces. China reacted with the Xinhai Revolution under Sun Yat-sen in 1911, resulting in the nation's first elected parliament. For the next twenty years, the "Golden Age" unfolded until Japan ended the era with its invasion in 1937.[128] However, this era was hardly golden and was punctuated by civil war, incessant strife, and continual economic disruption.

Sun Yat-sen, the respected "Father of Modern China," stood the best chance of pointing China on the road to Western-style progress and republicanism. Born to a poor Cantonese family, he had emigrated with a brother to Hawaii, where he received an education. After the failed 1895 revolt, Sun hopped from the United States to England, then to Japan, attempting to raise funds for a revolutionary effort. He returned to China in 1911 to develop the Kuomintang, a political party dedicated to republicanism and land reform. That year, delegates from sixteen provisional assemblies established the Republic of China and elected Sun the "provisional president." But his self-imposed exile had left him with a meager power base, and as soon as he assumed office, Sun sent a telegram to General Yuan Shikai, whose Beiyang army was one of the most formidable. Acknowledging his own lack of any military forces, Sun announced to Yuan that the presidency "is actually waiting for you, and my offer will eventually be made clear to the world. I hope that you will soon decide to accept this offer."[129] In truth, Sun was a missionary, not a militarist; and Yuan proved a tyrant, not a democrat. He assumed power with Sun's endorsement in January 1912 and during the subsequent elections, the leader of the majority party was assassinated, then Yuan outlawed the party itself.[130] Disbanding the newly created parliament, Yuan established himself as president for life and intended to name himself emperor before he died in 1916. Rival groups battled for leadership in China, with Sun operating out of Canton, but his lack of military training and his discomfort with military leadership soon forced him to flee from his own generals.[131]

It was inevitable that Japan and China—Asia's two rising powerhouses—would clash. Japan's Twenty-one Demands, which were imposed on China in 1915 ostensibly to protect Japan's sphere of influence (but suspected in China of being a conspiratorial agreement between then-president Yuan and the Japanese for Japan's support of the Yuan government), led to a change in world opinion about Japan as a quaint, amusing sideshow of a nation. Following the Sino-Japanese War of 1895 and the Russo-Japanese War, which ended in 1905, Japan stood astride large regions in northern China and Manchuria. Sun Yat-sen maintained that the Twenty-one Demands existed only because of General Yuan's maneuvering to gain the emperorship. After joining World War I on the Allied side, Japan increased

her demands to include German territories in China. Among the most ob-
noxious of these additional demands were those known as "Group 5," which
included putting Japanese advisers in the Chinese central government and
police forces. Japan withdrew those forces in short order, but the entire
process alienated the United States (which still stood behind the Open
Door policy negotiated in 1898–99 by John Hay) and irritated the British.
In no mood for confrontations in Asia, the United States sought a compromise, and the Lansing-Ishii Agreement (1917) resulted, in which Japan
promised to uphold the Open Door. Everything was finalized by the Versailles conference two years later.

Neither Britain nor America could fully trust Japan after that point—
although oddly, Winston Churchill, who astutely saw the dangers of an
expansionist Nazi Germany, never discerned that Japan posed a similar
threat on the other side of the world. At the same time, neither Britain nor
the United States could actually do much on the mainland in Asia due to
their lack of an army presence. Spared regular interaction with European
powers, Japanese nationalism increased, as did antipathy for the "white nations."

What one witnessed in Africa and Asia was the dysfunctional "land
feedback loop" present in much of Europe and often repeated in less advanced countries. Scarce land meant low wages, as there was no agricultural
alternative available to workers to substitute for low-wage jobs, and low
wages led capitalists to substitute labor for machinery, a trait displayed by
China during much of its Mao and early post-Mao period. The substitution
of labor for machines, in turn, required little in the way of skills, and without skills, workers could not successfully demand higher wages. This was
the opposite of what had traditionally taken place in America, where available frontier land always allowed workers to quit their job and start a farm,
which forced industrialists to substitute capital for labor, then to hire highly
skilled employees to work the machines and pay them well.

## Policies for Colonial Success . . . and Failure

Colonial powers, whether in Asia or Africa, had no intention of introducing
private land ownership for their subjects. With land in private hands, imperialism was doomed for two reasons. In economic terms, a colony would
eventually have no use for the imperial power if it had its own thriving industrial base—America was the key case in point. But unlike Asia and Africa, in America the British had extended land ownership to immigrants

due to the need for labor. Instead of providing more laborers, however, English policies created more landowners—and more wealth. English Americans by 1770 *already* had incomes rising as fast as their colonial masters "across the pond," and *already* had higher per capita incomes than the Turks, Russians, or Mexicans of the 1990s.[132] Even more astounding, compared with India or parts of Africa, the British made few investments in the American colonies: analysis by numerous economic historians found that the system of bounties and duties enacted by the British left the Americans with a net loss of about $1 million in 1770, or $.40 per person per year (about 1 percent of income).[133] Put another way, Americans had caught up to the British despite carrying the dead weight of the Navigation Acts and managed to exceed modern (supposedly advanced) nations, all because British America had, more or less, a free market in land.

Of course, it wasn't just the availability of land that made this possible. Access to property required that open land not merely exist, but be on the market. England, with its enclosure laws, possessed vacant land, yet it was unavailable for use. Moreover, a free process demanded a system of assigning reliable title deeds quickly and fairly. By the late twentieth century, it was nearly impossible to impose a system of titles and deeds on native populations. One of the first economists to discern the need to create a market in land that operated within a functioning and just framework of legal titles and deeds was the Peruvian Hernando de Soto. His phenomenally influential book, *The Mystery of Capital*, published in 2000, revealed that wealth without an institutional framework to guarantee legal title would fail just as surely in a free market as it would in a collectivist economy.[134] Others, however, found that tribal customs occasionally made it difficult or even impossible to determine who owned the land to begin with.[135] More recent analysis has shown that legal title alone is not sufficient, but it was at least a central component, and one sadly lacking in European-controlled Africa and Asia.[136] By contrast to what had taken place in the American colonies, in 1931, the 1.8 million colonial Europeans owned more than ten times as much land as the native population, which was six times larger; in Rhodesia, the imbalance was over two-to-one in favor of whites; and in Kenya, virtually the entire country was either in private white ownership or government "reserves," which the Africans had no hope of obtaining.

Americans had faced a similar predicament with the Indians. After being treated as friendly foreigners living in autonomous nations inside American borders, followed by autonomous tribes to be protected, subservient pawns to be moved at will, and semiautonomous tribes without American citizenship rights, the Indians finally became semiautonomous tribes (actually "wards of the State") with full American citizenship. When worldviews of property rights conflict (white/Indian, or free soil/slavery), one or the other must triumph in order to maintain a unified state. Ultimately, the American Indians ceased to be a "problem" (as defined by achieving a somewhat tolerable unemployment rate, lowering the alcoholism rate, and seeing the tribes become prosperous without government transfers) only when the Indians finally, and by then, enthusiastically, fully entered the market economy of casinos. To an extent, they still relied on government favors, wherein casinos were not allowed on state lands, but at the very least by the twenty-first century the once unimaginable sight of "Help Wanted" signs on Indian reservations indicated the market had finally penetrated Indian lands.

The American Indian policy could never have served as a model for European colonies in Africa or Asia. By the late 1800s, Indians in America constituted a few red dots in a sea of white. Europeans in Africa and Asia, however, were outnumbered by natives by several orders of magnitude. In addition, in America the Indians were eventually granted full citizenship rights, but full citizenship for native peoples under their European colonial masters was never considered a part of the European concept of "equality." Americans' adherence to the Declaration's "all men are created equal" principle eventually resulted in American realities living up to her ideals. In fact, outside of some extraction industries and trading ports, the Europeans did not think much about their territories at all. This was evident in the ratio of Europeans to natives within the colonial populations. Britain had 1,315 officials in Nigeria for 20 million subjects; the Belgians, 2,384 in the Congo for 9.4 million; and France, just over 4,400 to govern 18.2 million in Equatorial and West Africa.[137] Government in the colonial possessions was administered through the elevation of locals, often creating tribal chiefs where none existed previously. Germany, for example, invented the position of chief in Tanganyika, eventually producing a revolt against the newly appointed elders. Usually, however, the Europeans found an appropriate leader—occasionally a despot—handing over to him duties such as tax collection or labor recruitment, producing no small amount of graft on the part of the intermediary and festering envy on the part of the inhabitants. Europeans also struggled merely to define their possessions legally. Were they "colonies"? "Protectorates"? "Mandates"? "Trustees"? None of the colonial powers agreed on the proper designations, and there was no consistency of approach in managing them.

For the British and French, cultural representations of their possessions included brightly colored maps and postage stamps, exotic exhibitions, stuffed wild game vividly displayed in the mother country, and, of course, outrageous uniforms for native armies and for European forces stationed abroad. For more recent would-be colonialists, including tyrants in Africa, the Middle East, and North Korea, displays of power were often accompanied by lavish parties, wicked punishments for the smallest violations, and regular demonstrations of military might. Most crucially, the aspiring nations looked to Britain and America as their role models—that is, the success of the Anglo-American democracies was the expected outcome of an orderly transition to self-rule. Some, mostly those colonies that had been governed by France, expected more of a French model, but the outcome in any case was expected to be the same: a stable nation with functioning democratic institutions. Unfortunately, virtually no attention was paid by either the imperial powers or the colonies to the centuries of incubation that republican concepts had undergone in the West. Worse, *no one* at any time examined the strictly exceptional American characteristics, the four pillars of American exceptionalism, particularly the sanctity of private property and common law, that had permitted a multiethnic population to congeal around civic republicanism.

A few native leaders, without entirely appreciating the causes of the disconnect, started to realize the grim reality that the colonial powers had no intention of granting either full citizenship rights within the empires or independence from them. At the same time, the Europeans increasingly recognized that maintaining vast expanses of foreign lands and controlling masses of native people took a financial and spiritual toll on the mother countries. Britain, for example, understood that the empire had left it more exposed than ever, with more land to protect and more sea lanes to police. No institution felt this exposure more than the Royal Navy. Having already declined by the early 1900s to near-parity with the U.S. Navy, the British Admiralty could no longer consider a "two-war" scenario, which would require fighting in separate oceans. In the Pacific alone, Britain could not equal either the Japanese or Americans. Then to simultaneously protect the Middle East, Singapore and Hong Kong, and the African possessions, *and* maintain a cordon sanitaire ("safe zone") around the British Isles? Impossible. Moreover, offensive ground action of any sort would require heavy naval escorts, further drawing down British sea power. In 1922, Andrew Bonar Law of the Conservative Party warned, "We cannot alone act as the policeman of the world."[138] Four years later, the Foreign Office echoed the former prime minister, saying, "whatever else may be the outcome of a disturbance of the peace, we shall be the losers."[139] The Chiefs of Staff warned that British naval weakness in the Pacific would be extreme in case of war, possibly exposing Australia and New Zealand to invasion.[140]

Not just in Britain, but throughout the West, budgets and security were unavoidably and dangerously intertwined. Domestic tranquillity depended on low taxes and the newly emerging social welfare supports. Allocating large sums for armies and navies in a time of peace and prosperity proved nearly impossible for democracies. In a time of economic distress, it was out of the question. Coming full circle then, the Versailles security agreements ultimately depended not only on keeping Britain and France—as victors— prosperous, but also on simultaneously keeping Germany prostrate and economically feeble. However, Britain especially found that it was advantageous to get the Germans back on their feet sooner rather than later to relieve the burden of feeding them (and to accelerate reparations payments). Europe's colonial tensions, then—supervising the colonies, policing them, and benefiting from them financially—were intertwined with and shaped by the post-Versailles realities on the European mainland.

## The Reparations Triangle: Germany, the Allies, and America

Virtually every aspect of the Versailles Treaty produced unintended consequences. By forcing the Germans to build 100,000 railroad cars and locomotives to replace those French units destroyed by war, France's own railroad factories took a severe hit. Britain's demand that Germany replace shipping sunk by U-boats had the same effect on the British shipbuilding industry. America's recession led it to attempt to get Allied loans paid back, which further burdened the German economy because Britain and France would only pay the United States out of German reparations. Everything that appeared free came at a spectacular cost to the victors, and at times, to Germany as well. Reparations payments were originally to be made in gold. After Germany's gold reserves dwindled, payments were made in paper money, becoming a source of finagling and trickery when the German government inflated the mark. Many of the reparations were made through bonds, which reduced Germany's real liability to less than half the stated amount. Some historians, such as Sally Marks, question whether in fact the connection between the inflation and the level of reparations payments existed.[141] At the very least, American investment in the German industrial economy helped offset some of the dislocations. "In the end," Marks argues, there was a net cash flow into Germany and "the victors paid the bills."[142]

Of course, the French didn't spend marks, but converted them, shipping the paper money back to Germany where it sparked inflation that rose at meteoric rates. Already the price levels in Germany were five times what they were before the Armistice, but under the flagging economy and demands for reparations, the wholesale price index reached 14.3 percent by 1921, and leaped to almost 37 percent a year later. Confidence in money completely vanished with the assassination of foreign minister and former industrialist Walther Rathenau, an event which produced so much uncertainty that people rushed to convert cash into commodities. Families that had no musicians purchased pianos, and desperate people bought staples, hats, sweaters, soap, and shoes in bulk to guard against price increases.

The impact of the German hyperinflation, which began to bleed into the currencies of other countries, affected all of Europe by wiping out the savings of the growing middle class. As a result, the resentment of average people turned not against authoritarian governments but against constitutions and parliaments put in place after the war. Only the United States avoided this inflation and the systematic deflationary pressure of the Fed in the 1920s and the soaring productivity caused, in part, by the Harding-Coolidge tax cuts and the reduction of the national debt from 1921 to 1926. But with Germany reeling, it was time for the political teeter-totter to swing. The French, concerned about getting their payments, sent an army into the Ruhr, further humiliating Germany and destroying public confidence in the Weimar Republic. A few industrial conglomerates, including Krupp, Thyssen, and Farben, welcomed the inflation because it made German goods cheaper for export, but everyday transactions took on a surreal character. In one astounding example, a student at Freiburg University who purchased a cup of coffee for a menu price of 5,000 marks ordered a second, but by the time the bill came, it had gone up to 7,000 per cup.[143] Prices, even by previous standards of ridiculously high inflation, skyrocketed: by July 1923, 300 paper mills were working nonstop and 150 printing companies had 2,000 presses running constantly just to print money. Debtors who had once celebrated inflation found themselves as broke as ever. On a single day,

October 25, 1923, the Reichsbank printed 120,000 trillion marks, but the day's demand for money was one million trillion. Housewives burned cash in stoves for heat and wallpapered apartments with it. By 1923 a million marks would not purchase a postage stamp.

Other countries have since experienced worse hyperinflation (Hungary in 1945–46 and Yugoslavia in 1992–94), but the impact in Germany with its fledgling Weimar Republic perched uncertainly on an electorate unfamiliar with self-rule portended drastic political change. In the short term, a new government introduced the Rentenmark in 1923, which was carefully limited in its circulation and maintained its value until a new Reichsmark pegged to gold was introduced in August 1924. The Dawes Committee, headed by Chicagoan Charles G. Dawes, convened in 1924 to save Germany from collapse and ensure continued reparation payments. One of the key participants, General Electric's Owen Young, helped negotiate the final arrangement that allowed the Germans to reduce their overall debt while at the same time borrowing from the United States to make some of the payments.[144] For the second time in history America saved Europe, but by no means would this be the last.

The upshot of these disruptions was a new geopolitical/financial strategy that sought to align Weimar Germany with the United States as a counterbalance to France and Britain. Carefully exploiting the U.S. reparations agent, Wall Street banker Parker Gilbert, German chancellor Gustav Stresemann and the president of the Reichsbank (Germany's national bank), Hjalmar Schacht, embarked on a policy of soliciting heavy loans from the United States to repay the British and French—who had to then repay their war debts back to the Americans. This "Atlanticist" strategy seemed viable, but it ran completely counter to the other current gaining momentum in Germany, the National Socialist (Nazi) Party, which interpreted the rising power of the United States as a threat to Germany's very survival. Adolf Hitler viewed America as under control of the Jews, and just another nation in the international Jewish/capitalist/Bolshevik conspiracy. We shall return to Hitler's seemingly contradictory conflation of capitalism and communism under the same Jewish rubric later, but for now it is important to realize that not only did Hitler believe it, but he also sold the notion to millions of Germans. Only a German-dominated Europe could "stand up to North America," he warned in his "Second Book" (written in 1928, but not published). "It is the task of the national socialist movement to strengthen and prepare its fatherland for this mission."[145] Versailles, he ranted, was concocted by the "crook" Wilson and his "staff of 117 Jewish bankers and financiers."[146]

What stands out is that as early as the *1920s*, Hitler focused on the United States as the ultimate enemy while Britain, France, and Russia were all minor players to be swept aside. To the bitter end, Hitler clung to his perverted fantasy that a Judaic America defeated him. In 1945, he told his private secretary Martin Bormann, "An unfortunate historical accident fated it that my seizure of power should coincide with the moment at which the chosen one of world Jewry, Roosevelt, should have taken the helm in the White House. . . . Everything is ruined by the Jew, who has settled upon the United States as his most powerful bastion."[147]

As the historian of Third Reich economics Adam Tooze explained, there were alternatives to the nationalist/anti-Semitic Hitlerian view, but the competing Stresemann/Schacht model ran aground on the Young Plan. When the United States discovered Germany lacked the gold reserves to comply with the Dawes Plan, Owen Young introduced new measures to reduce German reparations further. As a corollary, however, the United States demanded further German austerity measures, which provoked dissatisfaction among Germans affected negatively by those policies. Insisting that their economy required restoration of industrial areas given away at Versailles, German leaders sought to attach territorial revisions to reparations payments, hoping they could regain some of their lost land after a certain amount of payments were made. German demands antagonized many active and potential American supporters and contributed to the collapse of talk about a German-American alliance. America complicated matters with the Smoot-Hawley Tariff, the single largest tax increase in American history, which imposed slightly to extremely higher accelerated tariffs on virtually all imported goods (some industrial raw materials saw their tariff rates leap by almost 30 percent). The effect on Germany (and all European nations) was to throttle trade at the very moment it needed to export more to acquire gold to make the reparations payments American politicians required. At the same time, increasingly interventionist fiscal policies the Allies pressed on Germany sought to restrict German spending. In the short term, Chancellor Stresemann's successor, nationalist Heinrich Brüning, responded by deflating the currency, sparking a wave of bankruptcies that nearly took down Weimar's premier steel firm, Krupp-Thyssen. All these contradictory and destructive policies coincided with the American stock market crash (which some claimed was brought on by the pending Smoot-Hawley Tariff) and subsequent depression that destroyed the international order upon which the postwar structure was built.[148]

What aligned the sunlight of liberty behind the dark moon of totalitarianism was, simply, money. The Great Depression, already under way in Europe, simultaneously sounded the death knell of "corporate welfare" in American industry, destroyed the welfare state security of interwar Europe, and gave the final impetus to the eugenicists' demands for the sterilization of the unfit and unproductive.

## "Abstract Lumps"

Reparations comprised only one dysfunction of the postwar era. Another came in the arbitrary and sizable population shifts forced by the Versailles Treaty. Versailles's formation of a half dozen new countries combined with the propensity of the Great War's winners to impose on their new creations expectations that they themselves had never met only added to the sense of collapse that ended the twenties. In the wake of Versailles, Europeans drafted a bevy of grandiose-sounding treaties and issued statements of rights that "took international law into uncharted waters."[149] Again, these largely resulted from an imprecise and inaccurate understanding of the principles employed by the diplomats at Versailles, and some of this could be laid at Wilson's feet. Robert Lansing had written of Wilson's "self-determination of peoples" speech in 1916 that the president was "a phrase-maker par excellence." He "admires trite sayings and revels in formulating them ... [but] he apparently never thought out in advance where they would lead or how they would be interpreted by others."[150] Later, Lansing had recorded in his diary: "The phrase [national self-determination] is simply loaded with dynamite. It will raise hopes which can never be realized.... What misery it will cause! Think of [Woodrow Wilson's] feelings ... when he counts the dead who died because he coined a phrase."[151] Fellow Progressive Walter Lippmann, in 1915, had observed a complete lack of understanding of these matters in Wilson and his advisers: "We are feeding on maps, talking of populations as if they were abstract lumps.... When you consider what a mystery the East Side of New York is to the West Side, the business of arranging the world to the satisfaction of the people in it may be seen in something like its true proportions."[152] These warnings went unheeded at Versailles, and now, as the twenties unfolded, the structures of government in the newly created states and the international system that had emerged began to crumble under the weight of ethnic hatreds, economic malaise, and ongoing European power grabs.

For example, Versailles set up an international system that "prized the homogeneity of populations under the state . . . rather than the acceptance of multi-ethnicity as the preeminent form of society under dynastic rule"[153] (this was somewhat at odds with America's later mantra on the benefits of "diversity"). Czechoslovakia, for example, contained a large population of ethnic Germans, as did Poland. But other people born in newly created Poland or Hungary were moved to their "rightful" nations. In short, the Versailles Treaty *demanded* forced deportations and massive mandatory relocations of populations to comply with the map drawing that established the new states. This fact was missed by many observers, who thought the intention was always to integrate and assimilate minorities. A Brazilian delegate to Geneva in 1925, for example, insisted that the goal of the League's treaties was to end a situation where minorities saw themselves as "constantly alien" and to bring them into "complete national unity."[154]

Of course, already the French were finding this untenable, deporting thousands of Algerian workers as "unassimilable" in 1919, and Portugal had concluded that large parts of its colonial population could never be made Portuguese. Yet even as the League of Nations and the Hilton Young Commission wrestled with the question of whether Africans and other colonial territories could ever adopt representative government in 1929, the League's own mandate system established at Versailles gave France and Britain governance authority over large parts of the Middle East and Africa. Even more stunning, the League's wizards required former German colonies to arrange their affairs along democratic principles. Intuitively, the idealistic magi of postwar Europe anticipated the very problems that France, Belgium, Germany, Sweden, and the Netherlands would experience with Muslim immigrants in the 1990s, but assumed that assimilation was not possible.

Until 1815, treaties contained protection for minorities, but the idea that religious or ethnic subgroups could serve as a central organizational force of any government was new. For example, no one thought in terms of a "Sunni state" or a "Bantu nation." Even the Austro-Hungarian Empire acknowledged that it was itself a marriage of expedience between two substantially different peoples. Especially after the nations evolved into their more bureaucratic, centralized form in the late nineteenth century, less attention than ever was paid to the concerns of religious or ethnic groups within the larger state. Likewise none of the European leadership ever expected religious minorities to convert to the more dominant religion, and more important, that they would ever govern. With the London Protocol of 1830, new definitions of nationality were employed in which the Greek state became the representative of the Greek people; and both the Berlin Congress of 1878 and the Berlin West Africa Conference of 1884–85 continued this new application of definitions by permitting minorities to be "protected, deported, or civilized," depending on the situation.[155] Likewise, under the Berlin treaty, East Europeans were to be civilized; Armenians and Jews in the Ottoman Empire would both be deported (although many were killed); and generally populations were either to be removed or protected. In Muslim states under Sharia law, non-Muslims became *dhimmis* or protected minorities, but in actuality they became fourth-class citizens with few rights. Regardless of the situation, ethnic and religious groups first had to be "defined and labeled as either minorities or majorities."[156]

Wilson's Commission of Inquiry of 1917 employed the language of minorities and majorities, insisting on the need to protect "minorities or weak [that is, colonized] peoples" and covered a diverse geographical area that included Anatolia, the Balkans, Africa, the Pacific Islands, and Russia.[157] Five years later, under the Rapallo Treaty (1922), half a million Slavs were stuck inside what was now Italy, but more often, rather than borders changing, entire groups of people were moved under the new terms of "population exchange" and "population unmixing" then in vogue. (The term "ethnic cleansing" would come much later.) Finally, in what was perhaps the last World War I treaty, the Lausanne Treaty of 1923 put flesh on the theories by fixing the boundaries of Turkey after a population swap of a million Greek Christians from Anatolia to Greece and 350,000 Muslims from Greece to Turkey. One student of the treaties concluded, "the Lausanne exchange was no violation; it was an intrinsic element of the principles enumerated at Paris."[158] To protect people, the state had to remove them, and so much the better if they were moved to the state of their natural ethnicity—regardless of where they had lived their entire lives. Thus Sudeten Germans were to be uprooted, Poles living in Germany shipped to the newly created nation of Poland, Magyars forced out of Austria, and so on.

Ultimately the Jews would suffer the worst from this reshuffling because they had no clearly defined place of residence. But they were not the only minority to exist amid other nationalities in the postwar era. No group paid a higher price for its minority status in the short run than did the Armenians under the Ottoman Empire. Rakish, with a resemblance to Errol

Flynn, the Ottoman leader Mustafa Kemal Atatürk (1881–1938) embodied the "good" Muslim from the European point of view (or, what in the twenty-first century would be called a "moderate" Muslim). The future Turkish leader had organized the resistance against the Allied occupying forces in 1919, led calls for a Turkish parliament in 1920, then ascended to the presidency of Turkey in 1923 as that state became the world's first Islamic republic. He sought a complete Western-style makeover. Suits replaced robes, secularism replaced clerical rule, Ankara replaced Constantinople as the capital. When it came to the Armenians, however, Atatürk looked much like his predecessors. He brooked little political resistance, and certainly did not tolerate the vibrant Christian Armenian community. This minority, comprising Catholic, Protestant, and Orthodox Christians, had survived the Romans, Greeks, and Persians, and even maintained its Christian identity under Muslim rule. But its existence under the Muslim *dhimmi* system was oppressive in the extreme. As a British visitor reported in the 1890s:

> Turkish rule . . . meant unutterable contempt. . . . The Armenians (and Greeks) were dogs and pigs . . . to be spat upon, if their shadow darkened a Turk, to be outraged, to be the mats on which he wiped the mud from his feet. Conceive the inevitable result of centuries of slavery, of subjection to insult and scorn, centuries in which nothing belonged to the Armenian, neither his property, his house, his life, his person, nor his family, was sacred or safe from violence— capricious, unprovoked violence—to resist which . . . meant death.[159]

In 1909, Armenians were wrongly implicated in a countercoup led by Sultan Abdul Hamid II against the "Young Turks," where Abdul Hamid allied himself against the secularist Young Turks and with the Islamicist factions. In part, he mobilized support by claiming the Armenians had backed the secular government. Troops called into the Adana province to keep order instead went on a rampage against Armenians. After the war, Atatürk focused his attention on eliminating the Armenians, undertaking a systematic slaughter within eyesight of Western naval forces in Constantinople's harbor.[160] Britain and France were outraged at the six thousand Belgians who died under German occupation during the war, but 1.5 million Armenians who were exterminated by massacre, starvation, or exhaustion by the Turks failed to raise an eyebrow.

Scholars remain divided about whether the Turkish government had a systematic program to exterminate Armenians, and debate continues about whether the slaughters constituted "genocide."[161] But the fate of the Armenians again displayed the unwillingness of Europeans to enforce Versailles's ideals of national self-determination and the near-impossibility of doing so if they tried. Combined with the Wilsonians' redrawing of national boundary lines, European nations were condemned to house large numbers of nonnatives: Romania had a minority population of 18 percent, Serbia, 16 percent, and Greece, 10 percent. Eastern Germany was home to three million Poles and hundreds of thousands of other non-Germans. Their fates rested in the same hands that created the very definitions of national identity endangering them—hands that would soon wash themselves clean of any responsibility.

Worse, during the war many of the minorities were viewed as traitors or security risks because governments were unsure if their loyalty was to their nation of residence or to their place of ethnic origin. Once World War I ended, they were easy targets during periods of economic hardship. At a time in the Third Republic when France was perhaps the most open to immigrants and foreigners, the columns of Charles Maurras, in the newspaper *Action Française*, crafted a French version of nationalism that blamed "aliens" for the nation's economic troubles when French jobs went to immigrants. Some states, such as Romania, dealt with minorities by elevating the power of the state above all. The government, noted the Romanian minister of education, must "mold the souls of all its citizens."[162] Even the Church's knee had to bow to the state, as community increasingly came to be defined as *national*, even as national came to be defined as ethnically "French," "German," or another designated majority.

Resettlement ripped groups apart and placed them amid ancestral enemies. Some states engaged in massive relocations of populations across one another's borders, adding to the hundreds of thousands of refugees from the war. To complicate matters, Europe could no longer ship people to America, Australia, or Latin America. Meanwhile, changes in citizenship regulations left even more people without a nationality. Citizenship based on the legal principle of jus sanguinis (by blood—a child's citizenship was determined by the parent's citizenship, normally the father, rather than place of birth) was almost universally adopted, leaving only the United States and a handful of other nations granting citizenship by birthplace (by 2011, the United States would be the only such country). The head of the

International Red Cross lamented that almost a million Europeans were "unprotected by any legal organization recognized by international law," which while true ignored the fact that the Versailles Treaty had guaranteed such an outcome by redrawing the map of Europe.[163] The League of Nations' flimsy system of minority guarantees was egregiously flawed, seeking to force-feed a national sense of identity within states from an outside body, while concurrently blessing the deportation of vast populations under the guise of protecting their "human rights."

## Banditos and Bayonets

While Europe sank further under the weight of unobtainable dreams, the Americas went their own way. The United States applied a realistic, though occasionally harsh, policy of intervention as necessary, in the Caribbean and Philippines, where American troops came under sharp criticism for the "practically indiscriminate killing of natives."[164] Responding to these unfounded accusations, Marine generals Smedley Butler and John Lejeune both insisted that any civilians killed by American troops constituted exceptions, not the rule, but the issue became politicized when Warren Harding, the presidential candidate in 1920, insisted he would not permit U.S. authorities to draft a constitution and "jam it down [the] throats [of Caribbean neighbors] at the point of bayonets."[165] Once in office Harding continued the Haitian occupation with substantially beneficial results to Haitians. The Haitian government was relatively uncorrupt; officials carefully screened all would-be investors to protect their citizens (to the point that they may have actually retarded growth somewhat); and despite press censorship, there was more free speech and criticism of the United States permitted than would have been under most dictators. By 1929, though, when new riots broke out over student vouchers, the United States was tumbling into the Great Depression, and neither President Herbert Hoover nor President-elect Franklin Roosevelt had any interest in the Haitian distraction. Troops were finally withdrawn in 1934 by FDR, having constructed a thousand miles of roads, 210 major bridges, nine airfields, eighty-two miles of irrigation canals, nearly a dozen hospitals and more than one hundred clinics, and a thousand miles of phone lines. Much of this fell into disrepair or complete collapse after the bulk of the American troops left, once again underscoring the problems in attempting to build nations when effective social, economic, and political institutions were absent.

Well into the 1920s, American administrations found compelling reasons to dispatch Marines or other troops to warm tropical locales. American Marines kept a small 100-man legation force in Nicaragua after 1909, and in 1916, the little-known Bryan-Chamorro Treaty gave the United States exclusive rights to build a canal and naval bases there, all as part of an effort to protect the Wall Street banking community's loans and a trans-Isthmian railroad. President Calvin Coolidge, isolationist to his core, ordered the troops out as soon as the debts were paid back to the New York banks, and in 1925, the Marines came home. Immediately, a free election tossed out General Emiliano Chamorro, the president of Nicaragua since 1917, but he led a coup to regain his power in 1926. This time, Coolidge would not support him, and when revolution spread throughout Nicaragua, the Marines came in again (and remained there until 1933) over objections from isolationists like Idaho senator William Borah, who denounced the operation as part of Wall Street's "mahogany and oil" policy.[166]

As in Mexico, relations with Nicaragua produced numerous low-level conflicts in the early twentieth century, including battles between Marines and guerrillas in 1921–22, when American forces were sent in to ensure the repayment of loans to U.S. banks. Smedley Butler, who found himself heading many Caribbean and Latin American expeditionary forces, was later quoted endlessly by the Left when he described himself as a "high-class muscleman for Big Business, for Wall Street and the bankers."[167] Butler may have had an ax to grind after being passed over as commandant of the Marine Corps, but he accurately described the U.S. military's role as a collection agency for American investment interests (though European militaries were just as guilty of such an offense). On the other hand, who else does one send when a foreign power steals one's property?

Whatever the degree of American investment in Latin American countries, it was never the prime factor in those states' failure to exploit their natural resources or to develop an industrial infrastructure. Those advocating the "dependency theory" of undeveloped nations, which claims that their lack of progress stems from their dependence on colonial or capitalist states and that they are constrained from establishing their own markets, sources of capital, and infrastructure by the imperialist and developed nations, have held sway in academic debate for much of the twentieth century. But such academicians have ignored the central and critical fact that those states were missing all four of America's pillars of exceptionalism, and were unable to make substantial progress on their own without first developing the necessary legal and societal framework. In short, the "dependency theory" is dead wrong. One must look elsewhere to explain why Latin and Central America, independent since early in the nineteenth century, have been unable to develop their own markets, capital, and infrastructure for the better part of two hundred years ago.

In fact, domestic upheaval usually accounted for the most important obstacle to development even with direct American investment and building of institutions. Mexico, for example, beset by revolution after revolution that produced a merry-go-round of leaders between 1910 and 1916, saw its textile output fall during the war by 38 percent, despite a captive world market. Indeed, one of the striking features about Latin America during the first part of the twentieth century is how it had monopolies on many products, yet could not take advantage of its good fortune. By 1938, Argentina, Bolivia, Brazil, Chile, Cuba, Honduras, and Mexico all controlled more than one fifth of the world's exports in at least one commodity, with little to show for it. Brazil accounted for 60 percent of the world's coffee as early as 1913, yet its currency value fell, its internal taxes rose, and even though it was thought of as an "advanced" Latin American country, its value-added per person (that is, the difference between the production cost and the sale price of a good) stood at $16 compared with Argentina's $84.[168] Brazil's productivity was "dismal" in the period 1913 to 1940, and real agricultural wages fell in Mexico. These realities have caused recent scholars to admit that the so-called dependency theory—which argues that virtually all of the Third World's economic backwardness stemmed from "colonialism" or "imperialism"—has been "unable to offer much guidance as to why some Latin American countries performed so much better than others."[169] Even in cattle raising, where the Latin American countries should have had an edge, their efforts at cattle breeding were poor, producing low-quality herds and blemished hides. Nor was poor productivity linked in some way to concentration of farmland in few hands as larger estates proved no more, or less, flexible or productive than smaller farms.[170]

What did hold Latin America back were the missing four pillars and a disconnect in moving cottage industries toward large-scale mechanization, partly due to the absence of finance. Successful companies relied on family networks: Di Tellas in Argentina, the Prados in Brazil, the Gómez family in Mexico, and the Edwards family in Chile. Thus, dependence on foreign investment had little to do with a state's undeveloped condition. While foreign investment could occasionally be dominant and result in abuses of power, direct foreign investment "played only a minor role in most countries" during this period and was confined to international trade sectors.[171] The primary problems were local—the inability to establish private ownership of property for collateral and corrupt top-down legal structures requiring bribes to function.

Latin American banking rules favored exports, not long-term industrial loans, and immigrants in Latin America—especially Italians—put their money into banks and exports rather than local development. In exports, South and Central American firms found themselves intensely susceptible to tariff barriers. After passage of the Smoot-Hawley Tariff only Venezuela, with its oil, and Honduras (where, following major strikes, the fruit dealers led by President Vicente Mejía Colindres struck a deal by securing a loan from the U.S. fruit companies to ensure local wages were paid) avoided a collapse. Argentina's debt—which previously had been mitigated by exports—rose sharply from 1929 to 1932, and even Mexico, which at first seemed impervious to the Great Depression, watched its economy collapse in 1938. With the nationalization of the oil companies, Mexico sealed its fate as a Third World country, seeing its exports fall 60 percent by World War II.[172]

Along with the American government, various churches and social organizations marched south. The YMCA moved into Latin America with educational and sports programs, especially in Cuba, Peru, and Mexico, and boasted that it was "Americanizing the Mexican youth."[173] The Rockefeller Foundation joined in, spreading the "Social Gospel," and virtually wiping out yellow fever in Veracruz and the Yucatán in the 1920s, upgrading local medical schools and clinics in the process. Author Jack London, visiting Veracruz, Mexico, in 1914, reported that Americans had purged the streets of "riff-raff" and "able bodied loafers."[174]

No doubt existed among American missionary groups or, in general, politicians that the "brown brothers" would gain from American involvement. Missionary societies contributed "to the diffusion of a new faith whose cultural matrix can be found in the *American way of life* (emphasis in original)."[175] Improving Latin societies to a great degree meant Americanizing them—teaching them English, Protestant Christianity, American-style work regimens, respect for the law, and democratic processes. Unfortunately, this did not establish property rights or streamline the titling process, nor change the civil law legal structure. Over the next decade, an American invasion of the Caribbean, Mexico, and Latin America would sweep the hemisphere. Phelps-Dodge and Standard Oil in Mexico,

International Petroleum Corporation (IPC) in Peru, and United Fruit in Honduras, Guatemala, and Nicaragua (which saw banana exports increase by 300 percent between 1914 and 1920) boosted local economies. Companies offered English training, self-help classes, and tried to impose traditional (legal) marriages to replace local common-law marriages. Alcohol was banned in company towns, sports and films were provided, and safety training was introduced to reduce accidents. United Fruit alone established a medical department to fight malaria and created clinics and hospitals at its plantations. American companies advertised freely in Latin America. One manager said, "I have seen the insides of huts completely covered with American magazine pages."[176] Coca-Cola launched sales drives in the Caribbean after World War I, then moved into Mexico and Guatemala; Ford opened an assembly plant in Argentina. All this was good, but none of it changed the basic institutions of Latin American countries to improve their ability to govern themselves.

Neither American goodwill, missionaries, investment capital, nor soldiers seemed to stabilize Latin American countries. By 1931, almost every Latin American government had defaulted on its loans, and military dictators toppled civilian governments throughout the southern hemisphere, imposing heavy regulation and taxes on foreign investors. President Lázaro Cárdenas in Mexico nationalized American and British oil companies (1938). Peruvian workers went on strike at U.S.-owned mines, and Secretary of State Henry Stimson told the Peruvian government the United States would not help resolve the debts if they did not end the strikes. Bolivia nationalized Standard Oil properties in 1937. Eventually President Franklin Roosevelt negotiated a tiny return from Mexico for the nationalization of American companies' investments in oil production, but they had already lost millions. If the peasants viewed the *americanos* as banditos, they only succeeded in replacing them with their own, far more ruthless, thieves.

## Selling the American Way

Whether in Latin America or Europe, "Americanism" spread steadily, mostly through cultural elements such as music and movies but also through the YMCA and private business organizations such as Rotary International. It was no coincidence that Rotary International met for the first time in Europe in 1930, the same year Sinclair Lewis won the Nobel Prize, indicating that in business as well as literature, Americans had arrived. The American-born Rotary Clubs introduced to the Continent a "service ethic" that balanced an intimate fellowship of members with an outward worldwide movement. Critics saw Rotary in light of an "ever-equivocal relationship [of] capitalist exchange between the commercial impulse that could make society whole and the cut-throat competition that could tear it apart."[177] In Tocquevillian fashion, Rotary Clubs promoted a democracy of recognition,

> based on the effusive ritual that both fascinated and appalled up-per-class Europeans, combined of hearty handshakes, jocular talk, first-name intimacy, and loud chorus singing. Individualistic, yet tamed by small courtesies, this sociability encouraged a mutable new social self, conformist yet enterprising, withholding judgments or expressing them in circumlocutory conventions, yet confident enough to recognize and be recognized by others in distant worlds.[178]

Rotary constituted just one of the many influences of American culture and business (some would term it cultural imperialism), and at the time few thought anything about the notion of spreading American products, cinema, music, or business practices abroad. If anything, the entrepreneurs of the day thought it would introduce the Europeans to new horizons. From 1929 to 1932, for example, auto industrialist Henry Ford and the International Labor Organization undertook a European-based multicountry study on the standard of living and wage levels that introduced to the Continent the concept of the "American standard of living." Despite a new commercial and industrial culture, the study revealed that European consumption of autos, household appliances, dining sets, and so on had failed to produce a rising standard of living as had occurred in the United States. On a number of fronts, the Europeans lagged behind Americans: in business practices, for example, National Cash Register had introduced its mechanical cash registers to Europe in the 1880s, yet as late as the 1920s, Germany, the most mechanized country in Europe, had cash registers in only half its stores, and only one fourth kept regular accounts.[179]

Somewhat more successful in penetrating European practices were the "five and dime" stores, such as F. W. Woolworth. Called *prix unique* in France and *Einheitpreisgeschaft* in Germany, Woolworth was joined by Thomas Lipton in Britain, Dock Remois and Felix Potin in France, Delhaize Le Lion in Belgium, and Latscha in Germany. Woolworth opened its first German store in 1927, and by 1932 had eighty-two locations in that country, including fourteen in Berlin. By the 1930s, more than twelve thousand chain stores had opened across Europe, many of them outside traditional city centers.

The chain stores sold more than consumer products; they sold Americanism, the product of the four pillars of American exceptionalism but not the four pillars themselves. American names became the generic identifiers for all similar products: sewing machines were Singers, vacuum cleaners were Hoovers, razors were Gillettes, cameras were Kodaks. Cigarettes, especially, were advertised in ways that made all cigarettes into "Lucky Strikes" or "Chesterfields," and European tobacco companies strove to achieve "an American cigarette."

A Veblenesque approach to conspicuous consumption fails to take into account a cultural context—that without a grounding in Western civilization, history, and culture, the acquisition of "stuff" becomes irrelevant. How does one enjoy opera without an understanding of the Italian language and culture or the story being told? How does one enjoy visits to ancient ruins without an appreciation of the history represented there? The Europeans in the 1920s found this out. As cultural historian Victoria de Grazia pointed out, "Newcomers similarly wanted access to libraries, hotels, spas, and the seaside, not to mention the first-class compartments of trains, the box seats at the opera, and the motor roads transited by the wealthy in their touring cars. But once the newcomers had access to them, these goods and services could not yield the same satisfaction."[180]

Hence, although Europeans gradually "Americanized" many aspects of their lives, particularly the way they shopped, the entertainments they pursued, and the corporate/business organizations they imposed, the process did not seep down into the European soul, or affect the deep class divisions present (which the United States had largely avoided). Or, to put it another way, Americans changed European consumption habits without imbuing them with the cultural underpinnings necessary to make society work in a representative democracy. Moreover, the American tradition of widespread property ownership and broad freedoms had led U.S. businesses to increasingly treat consumers as quasi-partners in the production process. Consumer choices—and increasingly direct marketing responses from consumers in the form of surveys—shaped the American products themselves.

Such widespread consumer interaction simply did not exist elsewhere, particularly where governments were dictatorial and production and societies were controlled by elites. For American companies, educated consumers were active partners in the production process, experimenting with new products and purchasing arrangements, unshackled by medieval patterns of trade and shopping. With the introduction of chain stores in Europe, for example, lower prices came unevenly, forcing average European consumers to practice purchasing skills, introducing an "American" value system dominated by cost as contrasted with a traditional village system in which the buyer acted on a familiarity with, and trust in, the merchant. This freed consumers from relying on shopkeepers as arbiters of value and social taste, empowering them to discriminate. Newly empowered consumers too often chose on the basis of cost alone, complained the critics, becoming the forerunners to the Walmart shoppers of the late twentieth century. Their lack of taste horrified elites then just as much as it does in the twenty-first century.

Another reason elites were threatened by this new consumer power was that they were no longer in control of the market for goods. Designers ultimately could inspire and suggest, but consumers remained the final arbiters, and by the late twentieth century, astute capitalists had virtually enlisted consumers into their development and engineering teams through hypersensitive attention paid to sales feedback.

Determining what consumers wanted in the 1920s was an art that was coming of age in the form of the advertising industry. Large advertising firms, such as New York's J. Walter Thompson, which pioneered the first ads aimed exclusively at women, originated modern magazine advertising in the late 1800s that by the 1920s had spread into the *Saturday Evening Post*, *Good Housekeeping*, *Ladies' Home Journal*, and *Life*. By the 1920s, the company was a powerhouse, unveiling the first celebrity endorsement ads for Lux soap and then, thanks to the dynamic husband-wife team of Stanley and Helen Resor, drafting the first "sex appeal" ads.[181] The firm had become the world's largest advertiser in 1916, whereupon Thompson was sold to a group that included the Resors. Helen Resor's ads for Woodbury Facial Soap remain classic advertising well into the twenty-first century, featuring a man in a tuxedo and a woman in an evening gown embracing, highlighted with the slogan "A Skin You Love to Touch." Stanley, meanwhile, engineered the first "blind" taste tests of products. Only a few powerful firms, such as Batton, Barton, Durstein, and Osborn (BBD&O) or Lord & Thomas in Chicago, offered first-class competition to J. Walter Thompson. With its chief ad man, Albert Lasker, Lord & Thomas hired unusual characters, such as the tunnel-visioned super-salesman of cigarettes, George Washington Hill, himself a relentless chain smoker placed in charge of the Lucky Strike account. Lasker once soberly commented about Hill, "I would not call him a rounded man. The only purpose in life to him was to wake up, to eat, and sleep so that he'd have strength to sell more Lucky Strikes."[182] Hill and Lasker recruited actress Helen Hayes to direct ads at females, coming up with the catchy phrase "Reach for a Lucky instead of a sweet." This precipitated a mini-war with the candy industry, and exposed large numbers of women to tobacco for the first time.

Of all the American advertising giants, perhaps the most famous was Bruce Barton of the powerhouse BBD&O firm. A devout Christian, Barton had used his writing talents in World War I for the Salvation Army, the YMCA, and the United War Work Campaign. Believing that each new generation would forget the experientially based knowledge of the old, he reasoned that products had to constantly be reinvented and repackaged. Even as he observed, "We are creating, creating, creating all the time," Barton reserved time for a book project, which he completed in 1925 under the title *The Man Nobody Knows*.[183] In it, he presented Jesus Christ as a CEO, possessing exceptional management skills and recruiting abilities. The Lord was, according to Barton, the top advertising man in history! The book went on to sell a quarter of a million copies in one year, and Barton continued to champion a certain morality in advertising throughout his career. He profoundly disagreed with the emerging trend in advertising to use sex appeal or subliminal messages and deeply respected the consumer's sense of value and dignity. In the medieval understanding of caveat emptor, Barton thought that properly informed buyers would make proper choices.

By the 1920s, the Europeans had only started to appreciate the power of American-style advertising, with its lavish decoration, densely packed informative text, and photography. Until then, most European ads were blunt instruments, designed "to deliver as hard as possible a blow between the eyes through the medium of printer's ink."[184] Roger-Louis Dupuy, a French advertiser who sought to maintain European taste and resist the American onslaught, rejected the idea that advertising had to tell a story or exaggerate any benefits. "No need to construct a scenario," he said. The "object, the object alone, the object-king, just solicit it, [and] it will tell its own story."[185] Advertisers developed "a colloquial language," said Canadian sociologist William Leiss, which, "though it mimicked the popular, was by virtue of what it included and left out distinctly of corporate and commercial origin."[186]

Yet tension arose when advertisers tried to figure out what they were actually selling: a product, or a lifestyle. Elites, for example, "believe[d] in representation . . . more than the things represented," said French sociologist Pierre Bourdieu.[187] The calm reassurance of traditional images and moral maxims characterized most ads. Typically, European advertisers distinguished their work according to sex, seeking to "Seduce the Ladies," "Instruct the Gents."[188] For this, the European agencies relied heavily on American input from J. Walter Thompson, with American themes therefore showing up in increasingly strong doses. A dilemma soon emerged: to sell "Americanism," Madison Avenue had to emphasize American *exceptionalism*, which was precisely what made "Americanism" appealing in the first place. Yet how could advertisers do that without subtly reminding Europeans that they were not Americans—even if they bought American goods and enjoyed American entertainment? At some point, the process demanded that Europeans be reminded of their flaws or inadequacies. It proved a thin and eventually impossible tightrope to walk. Europeans preferred to have America remade in Europe's image, whatever its flaws, and surprisingly, they were able to find many American Progressives who perpetually saw things European as superior and therefore helped them.

Like advertising, American film also penetrated European culture and would continue to do so, accounting for between 80 and 90 percent of Europe's film receipts by 2000, when American film exports to Europe in dollar value exceeded European exports to America by 1500 to 1.[189] Using direct-sales offices and employing "block booking," which required the retailers to take all the releases of the distributor, not just the titles that were best suited to their markets, U.S. motion picture companies created an American movie culture in Europe. This often entailed sales campaigns directed against local censorship boards, religious groups, and local governments. Hollywood, through the Motion Picture Producers and Distributors of America, pressured studios to conform to its censorship guidelines and production codes and make films that spoke to universal themes of family, God, patriotism, and fair play, while avoiding sexual situations or other (then taboo) vices.[190] Thus Hollywood at the same time minimized its own dominance abroad while dictating taste. At the same time, American movies sold conformity, "puritanical moralism," and traditional values, while concurrently attacking them through the popular slapstick humor of Buster Keaton and Charlie Chaplin. One European culture critic marveled, "You have to hand it to the Americans. . . . [T]hey subject the world to an often unbearable discipline [then introduce rebellion which] dismantles this self-imposed order."[191]

Briefly, European cinema believed it could compete with Hollywood. In 1926 Vladimir Wengeroff of Westi Films insisted "if cinema is 20% art and 80% industry, we—Europe—have that 20%. That's our strength and that's how we will win. The Americans do not understand that."[192] In reality, Europe couldn't begin to compete, if for no other reason than the comparatively small size of its market. The United States had 18,000 movie houses by 1930, compared with 2,400 in France and 3,000 in Britain, and the Americans were uniquely prepared for the conversion to sound. Above all, American cinema "won" because it presented what foreigners wanted to see: American prosperity and culture, or, in a word, American exceptionalism—even if they didn't understand where it came from. America's films trumpeted an American attitude differing from that of the Europeans'. As merger manager and economist Paul Mazur recorded in his book *American Prosperity* (1928), "Europe tightened its belt to the last notch, whereas the United States let its out to the first. The goal should be to feed the man to fill out the belt, not to yank it tight to fit a shrinking waistline."[193]

American movies featured a background of prosperity and abundance compared with Europe, even in scenes depicting "average" circumstances: saloons with walls of liquor, gangsters in nice cars, or Edith Head's amazing outfits. Fifty years later, Jack Valenti, president of the Motion Picture Association of America, noted that America had succeeded in dominating foreign film markets "not because of armies, bayonets, or nuclear bombs, but because what we are exhibiting on foreign screens is what the people of those countries want to see."[194]

Over the next twenty years, as Europeans grappled with renewed nationalism and questioned the desirability of American influence, American filmmakers found it more difficult to penetrate increasingly closed markets, especially in Germany. At the same time, however, new markets for selling American exceptionalism opened in Latin America, especially after 1933, when Franklin Roosevelt enlisted the film industry in his "Good Neighbor Policy" toward South America. Nelson Rockefeller, in the Office of Coordinator of Inter-American Affairs (OCIAA), worked with Hollywood to make certain films that went "down South" were inoffensive. Scenes were removed from *Down Argentine Way* and OCIAA urged scenes removed from *Juarez*. By the time World War II arrived, pro–Latin American films appeared regularly, including *Simon Bolivar, They Met in Argentina, The*

*Road to Rio*, and one of the most popular, Walt Disney's animated *Saludos Amigos* (1943).[195] In *That Night in Rio* (1941), Don Ameche "warbled a tune called 'Chica Chica Boom Chic'" which said "My friends, I extend felicitations to our South American relations. . . . One hundred and thirty million people send regards to you. . . ."[196] Carmen Miranda and Lupe Vélez, the "Mexican Spitfire," both were popular starlets, and despite the howls of guerrillas such as Augusto Sandino, who referred to "drug-dependent Yankees," "cowards and criminals," "blond beasts," and "blond pirates," Latinos enjoyed American films and admired Yankee prosperity.[197] Once again, the United States had applied the same subconscious strategy used in Europe since 1920: expose everyone to the essence of American exceptionalism. And it worked wonders, even if it didn't export the pillars of American exceptionalism to struggling foreign nations.

## From Boom to Gloom

Above all, film—like every other aspect of American growth—prospered because of the growing access to capital and the willingness of people and companies to assume debt. Companies such as Singer Sewing Machines had offered terms to buyers as early as 1856; Cyrus McCormick conceived of an ingenious credit plan to allow groups of farmers to collectively purchase his expensive reapers in the late nineteenth century; and the per capita debt level of Americans rose every year after 1896. But it positively exploded in the 1920s, when it doubled. It is a critical misreading of history, however, to fall into the trap of explaining the "Roaring Twenties" as pure speculation. The willingness to take on more debt can be either a sign of economic desperation or, in this case, of growing faith in the economy. People borrowed in the 1920s because they had every expectation they not only would, but could pay back their loans. During the Depression, Keynes came up with the speculation explanation later popularized for lay readers by John Kenneth Galbraith in his book *The Great Crash* (1954). According to this theory, average people got sucked into a speculative fever in the stock market, driving up prices beyond all appropriate real values. Further, Keynes would argue in his 1936 *General Theory of Employment, Interest, and Money* that the stock market bubble constituted a great "sump" of wealth that short-circuited consumer spending, thus bringing about the crash in manufacturing.

Both theoretical and empirical evidence, while not totally conclusive, strongly suggests Keynes and Galbraith were dead wrong. First, money—

even invested in stocks—doesn't lie dormant. It demands to be used, and finds its way back into new plants, employment, or other investment opportunities, as evidenced by the phenomenally low unemployment levels in the 1920s. There is simply no such thing as a "sump" of wealth, for by definition it would start losing value and no longer be wealth at all: it's only useful when applied to projects that replace its value. Second, studies of the 1920s stock market have consistently produced no evidence (based on a variety of economic tests) of a "bubble." In fact, stocks correlated with the real values of the companies they represented and/or *reasonable* expectations of future earnings based on past earnings of those firms. If anything, stocks in the 1920s have to be viewed as undervalued, given that from 1923 to 1929, dividends per share on average rose 61 percent. Moreover, stock prices were rising *faster* in France and Germany.[198] Nevertheless, the myth of the "speculative boom" in stocks and its "causal" relationship to the Great Depression remains all too commonly held, and is consistently promoted by many leftist academics and the American media.

Liberals have attempted to blame the Great Crash on the economic and tax policies of the 1920s, often singling out the presidency of Warren Harding for special criticism. The publisher of the *Marion* (Ohio) *Daily Star*, Harding was a senator who promised a "return to normalcy" in his 1920 presidential race. This meant more than just a return to peace but rather a return to low tax rates and prewar isolationism. With the election news carried for the first time by radio (KDKA in Pittsburgh), Harding crushed Democrat James Cox, who, like Harding, was also a newspaper publisher, taking 60 percent of the popular vote.

Immediately Harding showed that he had little in common with Woodrow Wilson. His cabinet was made up of "a cross-section of successful America: a car manufacturer, two bankers, a hotel director, a farm-journal editor, an international lawyer, a rancher, an engineer, and only two professional politicians."[199] When millionaire Andrew Mellon traveled to Marion to meet with the president elect, Harding offered Mellon the position of secretary of the treasury, but Mellon said he didn't want the job. Harding reportedly replied, "I know, and that's why I want you." He ordered Socialist Eugene V. Debs released from jail, where Wilson had stuck him for opposing the draft; and he created the Bureau of Veterans' Affairs to handle the men returning from the Great War. Harding was the first president to call for the outlawing of lynching, and was the first to entertain questions from reporters at press conferences.

Tasked by Harding to study wartime government revenues, Mellon discovered that the more the Wilson administration raised tax rates, the less revenue (proportionally) it received. While Mellon had no disagreement with the proposition that the rich should "pay their fair share," he found it unsupportable for government to maintain a punitive system that provided less funding simply to "soak the rich." Mellon drafted a plan to drastically cut tax rates across the board, though even after his substantial cuts, both the top and the lowest brackets of taxpayers still paid much higher rates than they had before the war. Mellon's approach worked: federal revenues rose, while Harding's budget cuts threw the government into a surplus for eight straight years. More important, Mellon's adoption of what would fifty years later be called the "Laffer Curve," in which tax rates on the rich were lowered to extract higher overall tax levels *and actual revenue* from the rich, proved prescient. The very top tier saw its share of taxes paid skyrocket by over 130 percent, while the two lowest tax brackets saw their share of total taxes paid fall dramatically.[200]

As the wealthy classes poured their money into investments—particularly the wave of new technologies that had matured and been adopted by the public in the previous twenty years, including autos, radios, electrical generators, and telephones—production boomed and employment soared. At one point in 1926, the annual U.S. unemployment rate reached a staggeringly low 1.6 percent. (Economists argue that 4 percent constitutes "full employment" because some people will always be leaving existing jobs to look for others.) Essentially, Harding and Mellon, through tax cuts, had achieved the Communist dream of full employment. The courts assisted the boom by ruling against unions in three cases from 1915 to 1922, and in 1919 strikes by the unions flopped stupendously. Everywhere the success of capitalism was evident: as early as 1927, some 4.7 million American workers were already covered by group health insurance; literacy soared as more books were sold than ever before (especially classics, such as Dickens, Tennyson, and Longfellow); and education spending rose by 400 percent from 1910 to 1930.[201]

Harding's death in 1923 left Calvin Coolidge (literally born on the Fourth of July) as president, but Coolidge persevered with the Mellon cuts and prosperity perked along. More so than even Harding, Coolidge kept his hands off business (famously quoted out of context as saying "The business of America is business").[202] His only soft spot came in his willingness to back farm parity programs, certainly an understandable political move given the carnage in the American agricultural heartland in the decade. Coolidge presided over five years of peace and prosperity, but didn't have the heart to serve longer after his son died of a freak ailment—a blister on his foot that became infected. Some suggest Coolidge also saw the storm clouds of the recession coming and wanted out. Either way, he certainly never trusted his successor, the "Boy Wonder" as the press called Herbert Hoover. "That man has offered me unsolicited advice for six years," Coolidge said, "all of it bad."[203] To his credit, Coolidge hadn't listened. Now, the United States—and, as the mantle of leadership fell on America, the world—would be subjected to Hoover's Progressive principles and policies. Coolidge had some premonitions that a downturn was coming, but his experience was rooted in the short recession of 1920, corrected by Harding's "hands off" policy. Any difficulties, he thought, would be brief and relatively minor. In his final address to Congress, Coolidge observed that "no Congress of the United States ever assembled . . . has met with a more pleasing prospect [and] the country can regard the present with satisfaction and anticipate the future with optimism."[204]

A decade's worth of rearranging populations, imposing ill-thought-out democratic structures, and irrepressible economic meddling had brought Europe into depression and growing civil unrest. All the treaties, compacts, and agreements had produced little more than a tissue-thin paper wall against aggression. None of the postwar structures set in place at Versailles—in Europe or around the world—had contributed to peace, stability, or prosperity. And all it would take to collapse the entire shaky edifice would be a handful of dictators with a will to power. Until that day, America was in the hands of Progressives, first Hoover and then FDR, and the world would never be the same.

CHAPTER FOUR

# The Totalitarian Moment

## Time Line

1930: London Naval Treaty signed; Smoot-Hawley Tariff becomes law; Nazis win 18.3 percent of the vote in Germany

1931: Japan occupies Manchuria; Mao Zedong establishes Chinese Soviet Republic; Empire State Building completed

1932: Battle of Shanghai (Japan vs. China); Dow Jones reaches lowest level in Great Depression (July); Franklin Roosevelt elected president

1933: Hitler named chancellor of Germany (January), becomes dictator (March); New Deal begins in United States; "Bank Holiday" in United States; private ownership of gold prohibited in United States; Vatican signs accord with Adolf Hitler; Albert Einstein immigrates to United States; Prohibition repealed; USSR famine kills millions; France has five governments in one year

1934: Hitler purges SA; Austrian chancellor Engelbert Dollfuss assassinated; Hitler named Fuehrer; Great Purge in USSR

1935: Hitler announces German rearmament; Social Security Act passed (U.S.)

1936:    Germany reoccupies Rhineland; Italy annexes Ethiopia; Spanish Civil War begins; Rome-Berlin Axis announced

1937:    Japan invades China; U.S. gunboat *Panay* sunk by Japanese in China; "Rape of Nanking" in China

1938:    German *Anschluss* with Austria; Munich Agreement; Germany occupies Czechoslovakian Sudetenland; United States loans $25 million to China

1939:    Spanish Civil War ends; Franco becomes dictator of Spain; Germany occupies remainder of Czechoslovakia; Italy invades Albania; German-Soviet Non-Aggression Pact signed; Germany invades Poland (September); World War II begins in Europe

Optimism about a new postwar peace and prosperity, which swept Europe after Versailles and was captured in the wild receptions for Wilson and Lindbergh, began to fade not long after the diplomats packed up their attaché cases. Despite a raft of agreements, pacts, and promises adopted in the ensuing decade, European states were already growing concerned about the new aggression by Benito Mussolini in Italy and the internal strife in Germany. Already, many of the newly formed states, including the German Weimar Republic, created in the mold of European-style democracy with its thick social safety net, pensions, and welfare programs, were unraveling. At Versailles, Wilson and others had failed to appreciate the profound nature of the missing elements in the new nations—namely common law, free-market capitalism, and an American understanding of property rights in a Europe steeped in radical socialism and unionism.

Economic decline only accelerated the already inevitable fraying of these societies, and nations sought new ways to bolster their own positions by taxing their neighbors through tariffs or manipulating their money supply to gain an advantage. Added to those pressures, veterans returning home from war, particularly in Britain, France, and Germany, found themselves trying to reenter industries and agricultural systems that, for all intents and purposes, already stood at full employment in 1919. Almost all industries and farms were at or near capacity in their productivity when the

war ended, meaning that when millions of new workers entered the workforce, a massive labor and product surplus ensued—especially thanks to
wartime spending (with funds coerced from taxpayers that would be impossible to acquire during peacetime). In Britain, plans to increase productivity
by replacing inefficient plants had been put on hold for the better part of
five years during the war, while in America, wartime controls and the heavy
hand of the Sherman Antitrust Act and Clayton Act, which significantly
restricted business combinations and corporate flexibility, stymied real
growth. Wartime taxes had also skyrocketed in the United States, making
a slowdown inevitable. This postwar chaos was only exacerbated by the
dislocations of the Versailles Treaty itself. Compounded by political forces,
particularly the rise of fascism and the continuing infestation of socialism,
communism, and anarchical agitators, the world was ripe for a disaster.

America could have served as both a lender of last resort and a consumer of last resort if the boom of the Roaring Twenties had lasted. But the
downturn in production in late 1928 cascaded into a stock market panic,
caused in part by the Federal Reserve's contractionist monetary policies
and by remaining too long on the gold standard. Although Federal Reserve
blunders might have brought down the economy by themselves, Congress
added insult to injury with the Smoot-Hawley Tariff, passed in 1930.
Smoot-Hawley's duties—averaging a 5 percent increase on most goods but
soaring as high as over 30 percent on many raw materials—massively increased the price for American goods. Over time, this blunder would account for a loss of 5 percent of GNP, or an amount larger than the economic
impact of 9/11 and Hurricane Katrina combined.[1] Work began on the tariff
in 1929, clearing the House in May of the same year. Smoot-Hawley hadn't
even officially passed before businessmen began reacting, as they recognized higher prices would cause sales to plummet. While the Senate debated the bill in October, the markets plunged. Although it is impossible to
quantify the exact cause and effect, and while certainly correlation does not
equal causation, it is clear that the impending price hikes spurred some
companies and investors to sell off stock holdings to get liquid. At the same
time, an anticipated sales slump caused employers to start contracting operations to protect themselves. And, to add a poison cherry on top of the
destructive concoction, the tariff would severely stifle foreign exports to
America and negatively affect other countries' balance of payments, meaning that other nations would respond instantly with new tariff barriers to
protect themselves. International commerce was heading for hard times.

President Herbert Hoover's "big government" solutions made matters even worse, as he panicked at the prospect of deficits. A mining engineer by trade, Hoover had gained a glowing reputation as chairman of the Commission for Relief in Belgium in 1914, and after the United States joined the war he used the American Relief Administration to organize food shipments to starving Europeans. Harding named him secretary of commerce in 1921, and he soon began a hustle-bustle of high-profile activity that made him more recognizable than the president himself. Hoover instituted and oversaw manufacturing statistics, set up subdepartments charged with regulating air travel, and quietly grabbed powers from other departments that, under the low-key Harding administration, chose not to use them. He turned Commerce into a pro-business organization under the term "associationalism," instituted the "Own Your Own Home" campaign, and promoted Hollywood movies overseas. His enthusiasm for business concealed a darker affinity for big-government activism.

Coolidge, attuned to Hoover's Progressivism, was not fooled. He disliked and distrusted him, reversing the press's term and derisively referring to him as "Wonder Boy." Once the Depression came two years into Hoover's presidency, he showed his full colors, ignoring Secretary Mellon's advice to keep the government's hands off the economy. Hoover's labor policies kept wages high at a time when they needed to fall.[2] The recession, according to economics professor Lee Ohanian, was "three times worse—at a minimum—than it otherwise would have been, because of Hoover."[3] To add further barriers to recovery, Hoover hiked taxes, imposing a tax on every personal and business check written, which further slowed commerce. The Reconstruction Finance Corporation (RFC), created in 1932 to support struggling banks, had the opposite effect of inducing panic when news of financial institutions' and other firms' receiving assistance was published (as required by law). Teetering banks tipped over the edge once depositors saw them listed as "troubled" and withdrew their cash. Then, as the coup de grâce, between 1929 and 1933, the Federal Reserve turned the crisis into a depression by failing to support the banking system with adequate cash injections as per its charter.[4]

## Decline, Famine, Murder

America's economic decline strongly affected Europe. Combined, the world's largest economies (including the United States, Britain, and western Europe) fell by about one fifth between 1929 and 1932. Because the

United States was so much larger in its GDP, the magnitude of its drop-off seemed even bigger. Yet even during the absolute worst crisis of capitalism in history, the unemployment rate peaked at 25 percent, meaning that fully three quarters of the working population still had jobs. Whereas the pain was real and deep for some sectors, the realities of depression in the United States were not nearly as harmful as the realities of "recovery" in the Soviet Union. There, communism's murderous policies resulted in one citizen killed for every twenty tons of steel produced.[5] Other Soviet "successes" included the Volga–White Sea Canal and Ural River projects, which consumed (literally) thousands of slave-labor victims.

Nowhere was the Soviet interpretation of "fixing the economy" more on display than in the agriculture sector. Stalin forced private farmers into collectivization, requiring them to give up private land to the government, with the intent of increasing production—but also of imposing his will on the recalcitrant kulaks (literally, the "grasping hands"), private farmers who owned more than eight acres of land.[6]

In 1929 Stalin boasted, "In some three years' time, our country will have become one of the richest granaries, if not the richest, in the whole world."[7] Instead, food production fell by one third compared with precollectivization levels. There were droughts and bad weather in 1931 and 1932 to be sure, but most of the farmers simply resisted by producing less, hiding stores, and killing livestock when their crops were confiscated by the government to be shipped elsewhere. The government retaliated by crushing the kulaks as a class, with Stalin decreeing they "must be smashed in open battle." At least two million kulaks were deported to gulags, forced labor camps throughout the Soviet Union, but those were the "official," untrustworthy numbers, heavily doctored by Party officials. Writer Aleksandr Solzhenitsyn estimated the number at 60 million—probably an exaggeration. Either way, the murderous Soviet regime arrested and executed kulaks with horrifying efficiency, and Stalin grew even more heavy-handed, decreeing that withholding so much as one ear of wheat from the state was punishable by ten years in prison or death.

Although collectivism began on a reduced scale in 1927 and accelerated in 1929, when the Central Committee instituted its winter 1929 collectivization offensive, only about 1 percent of Russian farmland was collectivized. By 1931 the collectivization blitz was in full swing. A famine, due to depletion of food supplies, officially started in 1932, and the effects, forced or not, were devastating. Vasily Grossman, a Soviet writer who toured the rural villages, reported: "People had swollen faces and legs and stomachs . . . and now they ate anything at all. They caught mice, rats, sparrows, ants, earthworms. They ground up bones into flour, and did the same thing with leather and shoe soles; they cut up old skins and furs to make noodles of a kind and they cooked glue."[8] When British journalist Malcolm Muggeridge visited Ukraine in 1933 without the permission of the Soviet authorities, he wrote that Communist Party officials "had gone over the country like a swarm of locusts and taken away everything edible; they had shot and exiled thousands of peasants, sometimes whole villages; they had reduced some of the most fertile land in the world to a melancholy desert."[9] One villager reported, "The people daily died in dozens. The bodies of the dead lay in all the villages, along the roads and in the fields. Special brigades were formed in the villages to bury the dead but they were too weak to collect all the corpses and these were devoured by dogs. . . . The gravedigger of today might be a corpse tomorrow."[10] To Stalin, this was not starvation of the kulak class. It was "building socialism."

Stalin and his cronies were meticulous in concealing the famine from outsiders. Screened and herded to carefully controlled sites, foreign delegations to the USSR were often prevented from seeing poverty and starvation. Sir John Maynard, a member of Parliament, went through Ukraine and reported that he "did not witness those phenomena [of starving people, or of] crowds of beggars and emaciated children [at] the river ports and railway stations, which are normally associated with serious famine," leading him to conclude that Russia's famine was "in no way comparable to the great famines [of other times]."[11]

Many Western writers, sympathetic to communism and eager to tout the success of the Soviet model, utterly ignored the devastation and human suffering. Walter Duranty of *The New York Times*, a notorious Communist sympathizer who led the *Times*'s charge in supporting Stalin, traveled through the USSR, where he wrote a column in March 1933 entitled "Russians Hungry, But Not Starving."[12] Literary figures such as George Bernard Shaw used their considerable clout with liberal elites in the United States to gain widespread approval of Soviet collectivism. Shaw, a lifelong member of the British Fabian Society, a pro-Communist group, spoke of the gulag in 1931 as a benign collective whose large population did not want to leave. Denouncing all reports of starvation, he sympathetically described the unfortunate commissar who shot disobedient workers. Shaw advocated killing those who could not justify their existence through their labor and later defended Stalin's purges during the Great Terror. American journalist Lincoln Steffens also defended Stalinist tactics, stating during the height of the starvation earlier during the Russian Civil War, "I have been over into the future, and it works." At least, it worked for those who did the shooting.

Most Western media refused to acknowledge the reality of starvation, even when the Italian consul in Kiev reported a "growing commerce in human meat," and state authorities put up posters saying "EATING DEAD CHILDREN IS BARBARISM."[13] Stalin maintained the mirage of plenty, increasing grain exports to pretend no problem existed and refusing aid offered by foreign governments.[14] A senior Ukrainian Communist official grimly concluded, "a ruthless struggle is going on between the peasantry and our regime. It's a struggle to the death. . . . but the collective farm system is here to stay. We've won the war."[15]

Only twenty Americans and Europeans visited the USSR during the famine years and provided estimates of the famine deaths, ranging from 1 million (Ralph Barnes) to 5 million (Archbishop of Canterbury) to 10 million (Richard Sallet), with the average estimate placed at 5.5 million. These estimates were universally and grossly low. Robert Conquest, author of *The Harvest of Sorrow*, estimated that 10 to 12 million died, but the actual number easily could have eclipsed 20 million, since the Soviet population in 1939 was lower than expected by a stunning 30 million. In any case, Stalin had become the greatest domestic mass murderer in history, not to be eclipsed until Mao Zedong later in the century.

The death toll from the famine was catastrophic, and by 1934, Stalin realized he was losing the "war" by failing to increase production, even after exterminating most of the kulaks. That year, driven by the realities of a stagnant economy, he reduced state confiscations and allowed households to keep small plots on which they could grow food for themselves. This concession to microcapitalism echoed Lenin's admission that prices worked and effectively ended the forced hunger. It was those small plots, not the collective farms, that sustained the Soviet Union throughout the next fifty years. A grim Soviet-era joke ran: "How do you deal with mice in the Kremlin? Put up a sign saying 'collective farm.' Half will starve, and the other half will run away.' "[16]

## American Farms Fail and Take the Banks with Them

Certainly the United States and Europe experienced none of the mass murder employed by Stalin, but both struggled desperately with extensive, widespread industrial unemployment and hardships in the agricultural sector, especially in the United States. While it is a gross exaggeration to say that farm lobbies in America triggered the Great Depression and in Germany brought down the Weimar Republic (thus paving the way for Hitler), in each case the inordinate political influence of agricultural interests produced policies that threw the world into mayhem, whether in the form of higher agricultural tariffs in Germany's case, or "price parity" programs and the confiscation of privately owned gold in the United States. Since the postwar price plunge, American farmers had been decimated as practically the only sector of the economy to experience hardships in the Roaring Twenties. At the end of the war, massive amounts of new farming took place in Canada, Australia, and the United States: Canadian wheat acreage increased from just under 10 million in 1909 to 22.1 million in 1921–25, while U.S. farming increased by 18 million acres in that period.[17] Then, as overproduction naturally followed, the farmers paid dearly. Between 1926 and 1930, farm foreclosure rates per thousand owner-operated farms (politically designated as "family farms" to allow politicians to posture in defense of America's families and the nation's root culture) hit shocking levels: 70 percent in South Dakota, 58 percent in North Dakota, 50 percent in Oklahoma, and 42 percent in Arizona and Colorado.[18]

From the presidencies of Calvin Coolidge through Dwight Eisenhower, Congress was powerless to resist pressures for "parity" (that is, guaranteeing American farmers prices for their products so their income's purchasing power was what it had been during 1910–14, when farm and urban incomes were allegedly more or less equivalent) or other legislative tricks that could supposedly boost farm income and rescue the agricultural sector. McNary-Haugenism, a plan devised in 1924 by Republicans Charles McNary and Gilbert Haugen and supported by Agriculture Secretary Henry Wallace, would have created a federal agency to purchase farm surpluses and sell them overseas. Coolidge wisely vetoed the act four times, but farm lobbyists found sufficient support within the government to insert dozens of agriculture clauses in the far more destructive Smoot-Hawley Tariff of 1930.

Later, under Roosevelt's New Deal policies, farm subsides became permanently enshrined in the system of federal giveaways under various schemes such as guaranteeing 90 percent of parity, requiring and limiting federal planting allocations (such as with peanuts or tobacco), thereby criminalizing the growing of food without owning an allocation or permit from the federal government, and the "Soil Bank" (which paid farmers to move agricultural land out of cultivation to reduce production). Most of those programs continue today, and some became the basis for nonagricultural policy meddling, such as ethanol subsidies touted as energy conservation measures.

Bleeding from the agricultural wound soon spread into the banking system, a development that went almost entirely unnoticed by all but the unfortunate depositors of small-town banks who suddenly found them closed. Most financial institutions west of the Mississippi were local, often capitalized with as little as $5,000, serving only small farm or mining communities.[19] Some 80 percent of Kansas's banks chartered between 1920 and 1929 had less than $25,000 capital. Bankers usually came from the ranks of general store owners or merchants, who had previously provided credit at their businesses and operated with an on-site safe for cash, before finally constructing a formal banking building. State regulations were lax and state bank examiners often came through only once a year to hastily examine the books, although bankers and customers tended to police themselves with some success. Not only was the banker himself usually well known in the town (and his finances generally a matter of public knowledge), but the building was a solid asset, and the loans were to neighbors who could be carried for a few months if necessary. There was enough competition to keep the banks efficient, but not so much as to force them to operate on razor-thin margins. Hence, the only real danger was one that threatened all of the bank's assets simultaneously, such as a drought or disease (pinkeye among cattle, for example), or a drastic plunge in international prices. Unfortunately, that was precisely what occurred.

Western and southern banks in particular were ravaged during the 1920s by these factors, especially the weather. The upper tier of the West, for example, was hit in the mid-1920s with severely cold weather. Ranchers lost entire herds, and bankers found their books frozen shut.[20] In sixteen western states, the total number of banks fell from 8,092 in 1920 to 4,036 in 1932, and Montana alone saw 214 banks fail between 1920 and 1926, bankrupted by 11,000 vacated farms and stricken by the highest levels of bankruptcies in the nation.[21] Arizona lost 38 of its 86 banks from 1920 to 1929.[22] Something as seemingly unimportant as a boxing match involving Jack Dempsey, labeled a sure thing by local investors, took down a Great Falls, Montana, bank when overflow crowds turned into mobs and, Woodstock-style, took over the seating without paying.[23]

Southern states likewise saw a drastic contraction in the farm sector. In

1920, South Carolina's farms had a value of $813 per farm, yet only two years later, value had fallen 54 percent (even though total acreage fell only by 8 percent).[24] The South was afflicted by a different malady, a massive infestation of the boll weevil that ended Sea Island cotton production among other widespread damage. Linked to farm failure, the number of banks in South Carolina dropped steadily—26 closed in 1927, 17 in 1928, 15 in 1929, along with 30 mergers and consolidations. From 1920 to 1936, South Carolina lost almost 8 percent of its banking institutions.[25]

Despite the various reasons, the result was the same and almost every southern and western state saw its local banks drift into insolvency. Even the South's strong branch banking system, which diversified risk away from a bad economy in a single town or strip of towns, was helpless when the main crops of an entire state were pummeled. Who was at fault? Greedy bankers? Lax regulators? Droughts and insects? In fact, most bank failures of the 1920s were due in large part to insurance schemes developed by the states—anticipating the FDIC under Franklin Roosevelt—which ostensibly provided an umbrella of security for the financial institutions. States with compulsory deposit insurance, in fact, proved the most susceptible to banking weakness, precisely because owners and bank managers did not feel the need to diversify their loan portfolios or develop branch banking, a much safer alternative which was often prohibited anyway by states to force banks to be more local in orientation.[26]

By 1930, the closure of thousands of smaller banks, which scarcely drew the attention of a low-level vice president in New York, was eating away at the money supply. A slow, steady decline relative to goods, services, and productivity ensued. Free-market critics (and even a few otherwise erstwhile supporters, such as British historian Paul Johnson) have looked at the boom on Wall Street and projected that onto the American monetary base. In fact, manufacturing and productivity outpaced money growth throughout the twenties, creating the deflationary paradigm of "too many goods chasing too few dollars." From 1921 to 1929, nominal GNP grew by more than 6 percent a year, consistently faster than the money supply.[27] Instead of lubricating the entrepreneurial growth with money, the Fed was restrictive at best, and deflationary at worst.

Another factor in the mix was the gold standard. All developed nations in the 1920s played by the rules of the gold standard, whereby trade balances were settled by transfers of gold (usually these were just accounting gymnastics, but occasionally actual bullion was moved). According to the great economist Milton Friedman, the process worked when a nation whose exports fell below the imports of another nation's goods had to make up the difference in gold, whereupon the nation with the trade deficit would see its gold reserves fall. That, in turn, would lead to more restrictive credit in that nation, followed by fewer loans to businesses, and eventually, more unemployment. On the other end of the equation, the nation receiving the gold expanded its money supply based on the new reserves, loaned more to businesses, and saw unemployment fall. However, once the economy heated up, prices would rise in the nation receiving gold while the trade-deficit nation would see prices fall—and thus the teeter-totter of prices would cause consumers to change their habits, and the process would slowly reverse. The key was the response of the governments, which had to allow domestic unemployment to rise (with a negative trade imbalance) or prices to rise (with an inflow of gold). However, governments proved unwilling (or incapable) to let business cycles adjust themselves without interfering.

Under the American system of fractional reserve banking, wherein a bank's capitalization was but a small fraction of its assets and offsetting liabilities, the physical money actually in circulation was leveraged through lending out the remainder of the funds. Each little western bank that failed "destroyed" money through a reversal of the money multiplier, in which a dollar deposited yielded several times its amount in dollars "created" through new loans. Now, dollars being withdrawn or walled up inside closed institutions were lost, along with all the "other" dollars they would have "created." When a bank actually failed, not only did the bank lose its capital and the depositors their money, but all the loans that would have normally been supported by those funds also disappeared.

Following the lead of the most famous (but not always right) economic voice of the age, John Maynard Keynes, virtually every major banker, chancellor of the exchequer, finance minister, and treasury secretary in the West was an interventionist (that is, one who actively sought to affect financial markets by injecting or removing cash through government operations). Certainly the central bankers favored activist monetary policy: that, after all, was the message delivered by America's leading banker, J. P. Morgan, Sr., almost two decades before, when he explained after the Panic of 1907 that he and his syndicates could no longer be counted on to rescue the country's banking system. Certainly, the American Bankers Association had approved such a position with its support of the Federal Reserve Act, but beyond that, a broad international network of leading financial lights agreed with the proposition that government (or, in the case of the Fed, a private corporation not subject to government oversights but which shared profits with the government) had to stabilize the economy through monetary and fiscal policy. Émile Moreau, governor of the Bank of France, British economist A. J. Balfour, Kuhn Loeb partner Otto Kahn, Hjalmar Schacht of the Reichsbank, the Bank of England's Montagu Norman, Paul Warburg of Kuhn Loeb and the Warburg banking interests in Hamburg, Lionel Rothschild, the managing partner of N M Rothschild & Sons, and, of course, the governor of the New York Federal Reserve Bank, Benjamin Strong, were all disciples of the stabilization school.

Where the stabilization model went awry was that for the whole to be healthy, at any given time one of the parts might be sick; for the teeter-totter to be up, one end had to be down. Yet no democratic government would long permit its economy to stay sick, and with Keynesian rationale, it would devalue its currency, inflate, impose tariffs, or in some way seek to raise its end of the teeter-totter. Gresham's law ("Bad money drives out good") would arrive with deadly punctuality, as the bad money of the "cheaters" would drive out the gold reserves of the faithful nations, and the pressure would mount until the entire system collapsed. So long as one or two dominant powers, such as Britain and the United States, could withstand the currency manipulations of smaller economies, the system still worked. By the 1920s, however, the combined weight of many developed nations simultaneously seeking to buffer their own recessionary cycles proved the undoing of the entire network. And that was precisely why the heavy hand of the fascist states seemed so appealing: they did not have democratic constituencies to worry about.

## Raw Deal

Herbert Hoover's interventionist Progressive policies—including the RFC, increased taxation, and the Smoot-Hawley Tariff—fell far from reaching their desired goal of reassuring the markets, spooking them even further. Hoover had ignored Mellon's advice to "liquidate everything" (allowing prices for labor and goods to fall to their natural levels and purge the rotten businesses from the economy). An inveterate planner with disproportionate faith in the ability of government to find solutions, Hoover never considered keeping his hands off the levers. Like other Progressive administrators, he believed in a static view of an economy, in which changes in taxation or regulations did not drive individuals' future actions. For example, in the static model, if federal revenues fall, a tax hike would correct it and balance the budget. But in the dynamic world of market economics, tax hikes reverberate through all sorts of individual decisions—people's attitudes toward future investment or consumption. John Maynard Keynes made the same miscalculations in his analyses. Tax hikes could cause federal revenues to *fall* further as people stopped investing (and thus creating more jobs) out of fear of higher taxes. Likewise, Hoover's RFC fiasco had proven a textbook case of unintended consequences of a government bailout, causing more bank failures, not fewer. When U.S. unemployment reached nearly 25 percent in 1932, Herbert Hoover was finished as president. Still, the Left saw his policies as inadequate from their perspective: he hadn't spent enough money, hadn't implemented a full-scale socialist change. It is doubtful with the impact of the Smoot-Hawley Tariff and the Federal Reserve's tightfistedness that Hoover could have avoided a severe recession. But by straddling the fence, Hoover ensured a crushing defeat.

He would have lost to almost any Democrat, but his opponent in 1932 was not just "any Democrat." Franklin D. Roosevelt was a New York elitist politician, clever and well groomed in the art of dispensing favors from his brief career as state senator and governor. Supported throughout life by his mother, FDR briefly worked in a Wall Street legal firm and had never experienced work in the private sector outside the law. But his impeccable social credentials gave him ready entry to the world of politics. No intellectual, Roosevelt was famously described by Justice Oliver Wendell Holmes as having "a second-rate intellect and a first-rate temperament." He had a reputation for adopting any process that worked—and which advanced his career. While assistant secretary of the Navy, he embraced the time-motion studies of Frederick Winslow Taylor to the cheers of Navy brass and the dismay of the unions. Roosevelt had just enough association with the military to be credited with some familiarity with defense issues, serving as assistant secretary of the Navy from 1913 to 1920 (and developing a particular fondness for the Navy over the Army, particularly for the submarine). Although he resigned to run for vice president in 1920, FDR was already tainted by the Navy's Newport sex scandal, in which a homosexual ring operated at the Newport Naval Training Station Hospital was infiltrated by federal agents. As assistant secretary, Roosevelt had approved the investigations and the detainment of many sailors without trial, as well as the requirement that undercover agents engage in illicit sexual acts against their will. For that, he became the target of outraged letters by local ministers in Rhode Island and Maine, and was subsequently denounced in the Senate Committee on Naval Affairs. Roosevelt dodged the accusations, using the Navy as a shield and admonishing the committee for using the branch as a political football. The episode overshadowed his strenuous opposition to President Woodrow Wilson's demobilization of the Navy at the end of the war.[28]

In 1921, Roosevelt contracted polio. His rehabilitation took five years, essentially removing him from politics and leaving him unbloodied during the victorious Republican years of the twenties. Learning to stand with leg braces, FDR downplayed his handicap and won the New York governor's race in 1929. From there he staged his run on the U.S. presidency.[29]

The 1932 election saw Roosevelt forge a broad coalition with, among others, the wealthy Joseph P. Kennedy, newspaper publisher William Randolph Hearst, and Texas political star John Nance Garner. But his success surpassed his alliances, or the fact that he came from a populous state: FDR projected a contagious optimism, convincing Americans that recovery was just around the corner. His jaunty style, clenched-teeth smile sporting his cigarette holder, and aristocratic speech patterns seemed just the right blend of class, confidence, and hope. Those qualities all concealed the fact that the new president had no comprehensive plan or well-conceived strategy. Indeed, his cabinet and advisers were torn between budget balancers and big spenders, although they almost all embraced high taxes and wealth redistribution as a means of social equality.

Nevertheless, Roosevelt pretended to have a thoroughgoing strategy, dubbing his recovery plan for the United States the "New Deal." But it never had a single guiding purpose or any cohesion except to pump up spending and spark the demand necessary for businesses to again invest. Keynes quantified and legitimized this approach in his 1936 book, *The General Theory of Employment, Interest and Money*, but FDR's advisers had already internalized many of his earlier writings and all of them accepted the premise that consumer spending through government "pump priming" could rescue the economy. By tying their explanations of the cause of the malady to the stock market crash (a false assertion) and then tying the crash to speculation (also false), the New Dealers laid the fault of the Great Depression on the taxation and investment policies of the Harding-Coolidge administrations. What Roosevelt actually did—with an assist from Hoover and the Smoot-Hawley Tariff—was turn a cyclical recession into something much worse.

A thorough review of New Deal policies is not needed here, having been dealt with by *A Patriot's History of the United States*, Burton Folsom's *New Deal or Raw Deal?*, and Amity Shlaes's *The Forgotten Man*.[30] Briefly, many programs to one degree or another targeted spending. The CCC (Civilian Conservation Corps) put men to work in the West and in forests, planting trees and fighting soil erosion; the PWA (Public Works Administration) and WPA (Works Progress Administration) "created" jobs (temporarily and usually just before elections) building bridges, laying sidewalks, constructing airplane hangars, even fabricating opera houses; and the minimum wage law raised wages for those lucky enough to keep their jobs after other workers were fired due to the measure. Those programs not directly focused on moving money into the market through spending attempted to provide cash another way, through higher prices mandated by government. Such reasoning stood behind the minimum wage law, as well as the National Industrial Recovery Act (1933), which permitted cartels and monopolistic pricing. Administered by the National Recovery Administration (NRA), the National Industrial Recovery Act in two years established more than 750 industry codes that set prices and wages, and generated 3,000 administrative orders, which amounted to more than 10,000 pages of regulation. Certainly some of the work under normal economic conditions might have been justified, even laudable: NRA-funded activities included construction of the aircraft carriers USS *Yorktown* and *Enterprise*, the Boulder, Bonneville, and Grand Coulee dams, and the highway that connected Key West, Florida, with the mainland. But the dark side was that government sought to control almost all aspects of economic life, especially prices. Seamstresses were dictated to by Washington as to what they could charge to sew on a button; butchers were mandated as to what they could charge to slaughter a hog. Eventually the entire unsustainable structure and constitutionality of the NIRA was brought down by a chicken.

The socialistic National Recovery Administration, a new, Roosevelt-era creation with far more powers than Hoover's RFC, regulated the sale of almost all products, including chickens. Under the New Deal, a "poultry code" governed the sale of chickens from such establishments as kosher slaughterhouses in New York, where in 1934 the four Schechter brothers (Joseph, Martin, Alex, and Aaron) ran a company that sold chickens, some of which had been purchased from out of state for resale in New York City. The government descended on the Schechter Poultry Corporation and issued sixty indictments against it for permitting the sale of allegedly unhealthy chickens, leading Hugh Johnson, one of the NIRA's authors, to call it the "sick chicken case." The issue in *Schechter Poultry Corp. v. United States* involved quite literally whether a person had a right to choose his own bird for dinner, and it came before the U.S. Supreme Court in 1935. Chief Justice Charles Evans Hughes, writing the opinion for a unanimous Court, found the NIRA as a whole unconstitutional and stated that it violated fair competition. "Extraordinary conditions may call for extraordinary remedies," he wrote. "But the argument necessarily stops short of an attempt to justify action which lies outside the sphere of constitutional authority. Extraordinary conditions do not create or enlarge constitutional power."[31]

Aside from the Glass-Steagall Act (1933) which, working from the erroneous argument that the combination of "investment banking" and "commercial banking" had spurred the stock market boom, separated investment from commercial banking, and the Social Security Act (1935), most of the New Deal legislation both failed to achieve its initial objectives and, more important, prolonged the Depression. Then there was the confiscation of bullion gold, a scheme cooked up by FDR and Treasury Secretary Henry Morgenthau to eliminate hoarding and induce spending. It robbed people of their assets, but didn't stimulate spending. Worst of all, it remained on the books and prohibited American citizens from owning bullion gold until 1973, long after the Depression was over. Farmers, paid *not* to plant on some of their land under the Agricultural Adjustment Act, continued to plant almost as much on the remainder of their land and pocketed the taxpayers' money. Farm prices remained as low as ever. Government make-work projects merely sucked tax dollars, desperately needed in the private sector, out of the economy. FDR generated revenue by raising taxes, ultimately to a high of 88 percent plus a special tax of 5 percent on all incomes over $624.00, further drawing down investment dollars.[32] Perhaps the worst legislation, the minimum wage law, has been directly linked to the severe employment downturn and persistent unemployment throughout the remainder of the decade. One 1984 study by economic historian Stephen DeCanio found that virtually all unemployment after implementation of the initial minimum wage law in 1934 could be directly tied to the higher wages foisted on employers. Expectations by business owners about their future prospects plummeted when they saw labor was going to cost them at least 25 percent more under the new bill, and all hiring in the private sector stopped.[33]

Another business historian, Burton Folsom, writing from the vantage point of 2009, has produced an even more damning criticism of the New

Deal, arguing that Roosevelt spent as much time trying to reward friends and punish enemies with his policies as he did trying to put people to work. Opponents of Roosevelt were subjected to Internal Revenue Service audits and harassing visits from regulators, while political pals received timely government expenditures in their districts.[34] All these activities were designed to get more Democrats elected, with the endgame being to so solidify the Democratic Party with federal giveaways and assistance that it could effectively bribe the electorate in the future. To a large degree it worked, with groups such as the American Association of Retired Persons (AARP) later becoming a full-time shill for the Democratic Party and its support of the bankrupt Social Security system. Tearing the Constitution to shreds, FDR's New Deal cronies hounded, cajoled, threatened, taxed, arrested, and jailed many who refused to toe his increasingly socialist line.

Any fantasy that Roosevelt "saved capitalism" deserves a hasty discard into the dustbin of false ideas. Unemployment had climbed back up to 19 percent in 1938, down only slightly from the Hoover peaks in 1932. But that came after billions of government dollars had been spent to no effect, other than getting Roosevelt reelected. Folsom has shown that "fixing the economy" was never the primary objective of FDR's policies: staying in office was, and he dished out federal funds strategically to ensure a wide base of support. Ancillary legislation, such as Glass-Steagall, creation of the Federal Deposit Insurance Corporation, the Agricultural Adjustment Act, and Social Security were all policy time bombs waiting to explode in the future. Within the next sixty years, every one of those programs would create its own special problem that required yet another solution.

## Fascist Miracles

Unable to shake off their economic distress with quasi-socialist policies, the Americans, British, and French gazed with some admiration at the recoveries they thought were taking place in Italy and Germany. Between 1929 and 1938, Italian manufacturing doubled, a growth rate that exceeded those of all the Western democracies. Overlooked was the fact that even with such "growth," Italy claimed only 10 percent of the American share of world manufacturing (2.9 percent to America's 28.7 percent), and that unemployment under Mussolini increased ninefold over the 1920s; Italians still spent half their income on food; and national income declined.[35] Yet much of this remained hidden to outside observers, partly because of a willing suspension of disbelief and partly because of Il Duce's propaganda machine working in tandem with his police state. State-controlled or -influenced newspapers touted the fascist miracle and the commonly used phrase of the day (which, in fact, was not true) was that "Mussolini made the trains run on time." But in a fascist state, perception was reality.

Likewise, Germany's perceived economic strength came from a combination of forced work, favorable trade with southeastern Europe and Yugoslavia, and, as with Mussolini, relentless propaganda. In the first place, as historian Adam Tooze points out, the German economy had already started to recover in 1932—before the Nazis took power. A German business research institute concluded that the contraction had nearly ended in late 1932, and the *Economist*'s Berlin office saw a "glimmer of economic light" for Germany.[36] German unemployment fell from six million in January 1933 to just under three million two years later, and national income rose sharply during that time. But by 1936 military spending exceeded 10 percent of GDP, higher than any other European country, and the balance of payments went negative in 1933—the same year Hitler announced a suspension of all debt repayments. GDP did rise, from 3.2 percent in 1933 to 6.1 percent in 1935, but the military share of GDP growth skyrocketed tenfold during that period, while the share of GDP growth due to civilian or private investment plummeted. All this was quite temporary and unsustainable, even for an iron-fisted government. Nevertheless, it was common for outsiders to assume the situation in the Axis powers was better than their own (the grass is always greener on the other side of the fence), and many in America admired Mussolini and Hitler for their economic "miracles."

The French also were envious of German economic health as they battled domestic labor problems, including a 1938 strike at the Renault plant that Prime Minister Édouard Daladier successfully put down. Capital steadily seeped out of France throughout the late 1930s, making its finances precarious as Hitler began his mischief in Czechoslovakia and Poland. Of course, neither Germany nor Italy enjoyed the kind of economic strength that Americans and French ascribed to them. German exports of chemicals and electronics, with an established postwar presence in Hungary and the Balkans, had collapsed due to inflation in the 1920s, and the German capital there was quickly replaced by investments from the British and French. German industry also faced new competition from the ubiquitous Americans, whose General Electric competed in these regions with I. G. Farben and Siemens. Germans saw such industrial encroachments as threats to national security; Foreign Minister Gustav Stresemann said without I. G.

Farben and coal, there was no foreign policy, and the Austro-German customs union of 1931 was largely aimed at excluding French and British goods
from their countries and breaking the western powers' growing grip on
Czechoslovakia and the Danube region.

The Germans had less success in prying Yugoslavia and its raw materials out of the hands of western Europeans. While Hitler could strong-arm
Hungary, Romania, and Bulgaria into favorable trade agreements, the
western powers were able to enter into clever trade negotiations with the
Yugoslavs by playing on Serbian fears of German Balkan hegemony. As a
result, Yugoslavia exported almost all of its copper, magnesium, bauxite,
and lead to Britain and France, firmly excluding German firms as trading
partners. Given the dire raw materials deficiency in Germany, British intelligence pulled out all the stops and carefully cultivated the trade relationship with Yugoslavia.

Germany followed a two-pronged economic strategy of seeking regional trade dominance and getting the Allies to lift their demand for reparations. The latter finally occurred at the Lausanne Conference in 1932 in
which Germany, Britain, and France agreed to end the burdens of Versailles as it was becoming evident that the worldwide depression was making further reparations impossible. Under Lausanne, a one-year moratorium
on payments became permanent, with the understanding that Germany
would negotiate with the United States for further assistance in meeting
outstanding debts. But the Americans rejected the plan in 1932, and the
prior Young Plan (1929) had expired, making the debt relief permanent.
Once relieved of its reparation obligations, however, Germany saw little
incentive for close relations with the United States, and the potential for
American influence on German domestic politics vanished. It would be too
strong to say that the end of reparations enabled the rise of Hitler, but it
certainly minimized the advantages of German-American friendship.

Debates over the scale, schedule, and even justice of the reparations
payments emanating from Versailles continue to bubble to this day. John
Maynard Keynes had argued in 1919 that the burdens on Germany were
too high, and later felt they provoked German dissatisfaction sufficiently to
enable the rise of Hitler.[37] More recently, however, historians such as Sally
Marks, Niall Ferguson, Stephen Schuker, and Gerhard Weinberg have all
noted that the Germans had plenty of ability to pay, but not the political
will; that the Allies failed to enforce the payments by seizing and holding
Germany territory until the debts were paid; and that American loans more

than offset the burden on Germany.[38] All in all, the preponderance of evidence shows that Germany indeed had the wherewithal to pay, and that it chose every alternative—inflation, loans, delay, shifting the burdens from taxpayers—to avoid meeting its reparations requirements.

The United States was hardly left as a winner in this exchange: without German money flowing in, France, Belgium, Poland, and other countries defaulted on their own debts the same year.[39] Reparations battles and continuing economic crises in Germany also coincided with another fateful shift when the German farm lobby, representing some 13 million farmers, between 1925 and 1933 began to demand relief. This culminated in their calls for trade terms similar to those given American farmers under Smoot-Hawley. Consequently, instead of "big business" bringing down Weimar and assuring Hitler's ascension, the farmers, pandered to by most major politicians, played the critical role. When Chancellor Heinrich Brüning refused to adopt quotas similar to the Americans, the farmers' support for the Republic ended and they shifted their allegiance to the Nazis.

Brüning also made an enemy of the paramilitary organization known as the SA (*Sturmabteilung*, or "storm detachment"), a Nazi thug group that increasingly seemed on the verge of launching a coup. General Kurt von Schleicher, a major influence in the formation of German cabinets from 1930 to 1932, had grown close to the Nazis. Convinced only a "strong man" could lead Germany and serve as a counterweight to the Social Democrats, he hoped to end the Weimar Republic.[40] Following a secret meeting with Hitler, von Schleicher intrigued against Chancellor Brüning and convinced President Paul von Hindenburg to fire him. Von Hindenburg appointed ex-Chancellor Franz von Papen as Brüning's successor, and he served briefly from June to November 1932. For his part in ousting Brüning (and as part of the overall agreement with Hitler), von Schleicher was named minister of defense. In June 1932, the von Papen government dissolved the Reichstag and two weeks later lifted the ban on the SA and SS (*Schutzstaffel*, or "protective squad," originally Hitler's bodyguard, but by 1926 his elite paramilitary organization charged with handling internal Party situations as well as other duties that might be required).

Von Papen recognized the need to accommodate the National Socialists now that they were the largest party in the Reichstag, so he, Hjalmar Schacht, and a few others put together a plan to co-opt the Nazis. They would convince von Hindenburg that they could handle Hitler by allowing him to assume the chancellorship, while von Papen would assume the positions of vice chancellor and Prussian prime minister. In that way, Hitler would have an official position in government (thereby recognizing the Nazis' strength in the Reichstag) while the real power would remain—they thought—with von Hindenburg, von Papen, and the majority of ministers who were not Nazis and could unite against Hitler if he got out of line. This was the first of numerous blunders in which powerful politicians, holding positions superior to Hitler, grossly misjudged him and expressed their confidence in their ability to "control" him. When the aged von Hindenburg administered the oath of office to Hitler in January 1933 surrounded by von Papen's conservatives, von Papen remarked, "All that has happened, is that we have given [Hitler] a job."[41] In reality, von Papen had thrown a cobra into the crib of German government.

The "miracle" recovery had already started under von Papen and von Schleicher, mostly due to Hjalmar Schacht, president of the Reichsbank from 1923 to 1930, and the Cologne banker Baron Kurt von Schröder. They had overseen the end of reparations and established the trade policies placing Romania and Hungary in the German orbit. Schacht devised a new foreign exchange system that helped control German imports and address the imbalance of trade. The rebound, which continued after Hitler assumed the chancellorship, thereby benefiting the Nazis, was in no way attributable to Nazi economic policies except those intrinsic to rearmament (that is, through large government weapons purchases). Nor did rearmament begin strictly with Hitler: during the time Gustav Stresemann was foreign minister (1923–29) the General Staff, led by Generals Hans von Seeckt, Kurt von Schleicher, Wilhelm Heye, Werner von Blomberg, and Kurt von Hammerstein-Equord, had already been modestly and secretly building up German forces, aided significantly by the Soviet Union. When the Paris Convention of 1926 ended the international community's supervision of the German aircraft industry, Germany's air force already consisted of two fighter squadrons, one bomber squadron, and one auxiliary bomber squadron, operating within the framework of Lufthansa, the civilian air transport company.[42] Exploiting that crack, Germany pried open the door further, and by the time of the World Disarmament Conference in 1933, the German delegation felt emboldened enough to walk out after being denied the opportunity to maintain armed forces similar to those of the other major states. By then the *Truppenamt*, which in 1935 became the General Staff, had on paper fleshed out a mobilization strength of twenty-one divisions, 300,000 men in an army equipped with heavy weapons and an air force. In August 1933, the army took delivery of its first tanks, and a tank battalion came into existence in 1934.[43] Between the arms industry, the reinstatement of military conscription in 1935, and the "Battle for Work" (announced in 1933, consisting of Reich support for local subsidized work projects), unemployment fell from eight million in 1933 to under half that a year later, and by 1936 there was virtually full employment.

But the bulk of this came from military-related spending and putting young Germans into the armed forces. Germany reintroduced a draft in 1935, bringing the Reich as close to full employment as it would get short of actual war. By July 1938, the Labor Ministry of the Reich proudly reported only 292,000 unemployed in all of Germany, a scant 1 percent of the workforce. Of these, many were seasonal actors, musicians, and artists who one Reich official suggested should be subjected to "radical occupational redirection."[44] As Adam Tooze observed, "Make-work schemes at their peak [only] directly accounted for 30 percent of the reduction in registered unemployment. Even when they were at their most extensive, they accounted for a minority of jobs created."[45] Germans may have been back on the job, but their standard of living barely improved. Hitler attempted to raise German living standards with higher tariff rates on Germany's neighbors, all imposed by intimidation. Per-capita GDP indeed rose, outstripping England, but the benefits were unequally distributed. Labor's share of the national income fell, despite the rise in employment.[46] Indeed, mortality rates and the measures of the general health and diet of average Germans declined during the 1930s.[47] German industrial production related to the military grew, but starting in July 1934, nonmilitary production (such as textiles) collapsed and the consumer goods sector remained mired in depression.

## Hitler's Rise

Economic stagnation and unemployment provided a fertile field for Hitler's ascension, with the water and nutrients provided by resentments of Versailles. To that mix, Hitler added a unique element, Jew hatred. Born on April 20, 1889, in Austria of Catholic parents, Adolf Hitler attended Catholic school in Lambach, Upper Austria, where the family moved in 1897, and where he was traumatized by his mother's death from breast cancer a decade later. Modern historians often note that his mother's doctor was Jewish, as if this episode were the root of Hitler's anti-Semitism. But surviving letters, in which Hitler praised the doctor's efforts, seem to refute that interpretation.[48]

After living in Vienna in poverty, due to his failure (twice) to gain acceptance to the Vienna Academy of Fine Arts, Hitler obtained his portion of his father Alois's small estate in 1913 and moved to Munich.[49] He admired all things German: he sang "Deutschland über Alles," the German anthem, rather than the Austrian anthem, used German greetings, and tore up his school certificate from Austria. The one Austrian he did admire, however, was Lanz von Liebenfels, a former monk who published the magazine *Ostara, Briefbucherei der Blonden and Mannesrechtler* ("Ostara, Newsletter of the Blond and Masculists"), which promulgated Aryan supremacy and anti-Semitism. In addition to *Ostara*, Hitler explored occult writings and German nationalist works. During World War I, he served as a runner in a Bavarian infantry regiment and received the Iron Cross, Second Class, for heroism. He was wounded in 1916 during the Battle of the Somme when a shell exploded in his dugout, and after a temporary return to duty, he was temporarily blinded in a mustard gas attack and again hospitalized. Stuck behind the lines when the Armistice came, Hitler incorporated the "stab-in-the-back" theory into his anti-Semitism and German nationalism to explain why the "undefeated" German army nevertheless had to accept a Carthaginian peace.

Still in the army after Versailles, he was assigned as an intelligence agent to infiltrate a radical party, the German Workers Party (*Deutsche Arbeiterpartei*, or DAP). Instead of becoming an informant, he became an acolyte. His actual rise to power can thus be traced to September 1919 when he first attended a meeting of the DAP. Seven months later he was discharged from the army and began a career as a full-time politician. An emotional, dramatic speaker who practiced constantly in front of a mirror, Hitler never used notes. His passion attracted crowds, especially at the beer halls he frequented, and he became identified with the Nazi movement even before emerging as its leader in 1921, weathering a mutiny from other DAP members. His message appealed to the unemployed, but also attracted large numbers of those terrified by the rising Bolshevik threat from Russia as well as from domestic Communist parties. He courted business as well, understanding their fears of collectivism, and added "National Socialist" to the party name to broaden its appeal.

Sensing Weimar Germany was ripe for toppling in 1923, he led a failed and comedic attempt to seize control of Bavaria. He and his Nazis interrupted a large public meeting in a Munich beer hall and captured the local officials. This "Beer Hall Putsch" rapidly unraveled when the prisoners es-

caped, whereupon Hitler's group, led by Colonel General Erich Ludendorff, marched on the Bavarian Defense Ministry in a desperate attempt to
regain the upper hand. There they were met by rifle fire from police. Fourteen Nazis were killed, a number wounded (including Herman Göring),
and most of the others, including Hitler, scattered. Two days later, police
arrested Hitler and after trying him for high treason, shipped him off to
Landsberg prison for a five-year term. Already a celebrity prisoner, Hitler
spent most of the eight months he served "receiving a constant stream of
visitors, including admiring women and cringing politicians."[50] He was allowed unsupervised visitors, and more than thirty people celebrated his
thirty-fifth birthday with him in his suitelike cell. Papers from Landsberg
prison reveal three to four hundred signature cards from well-wishers,
leading the owner of a Bavarian auction house that later acquired the papers
to describe Hitler's prison stint as "more like a holiday."[51] Any time he
wasn't chatting with admirers, Hitler used to dictate his manifesto, *Mein
Kampf*, to his deputy Rudolf Hess. This long-winded, often rambling, always overblown book occasionally provided an insightful glimpse of Hitler's plan for European domination. At first few read it, although by 1934 he
had sold a quarter million copies. In 1926, however, few people took his
radical ideas seriously.

As he outlined in *Mein Kampf*, Hitler now realized that Germany
could not be seized in a violent revolution, but was entirely vulnerable to
a democratic takeover. Indeed, Weimar's experience with hyperinflation
fit perfectly with Hitler's tendency to blame everything on Jews and bankers. Obsessed with a Malthusian view of population and convinced Germany's land could not support its population, Hitler looked to Poland (in
his view, as in Stalin's, an entirely illegitimate postwar creation) and, ultimately, Ukraine as places where Germans could obtain "living space"
(*Lebensraum*). This principle served as the staple of his speeches as a politician, then as Fuehrer, but beneath the surface loomed a titanic land-envy
of both the Soviet Union and the United States. "Only an adequately
large space on this earth assures a nation of freedom of existence," he
wrote, and "if we speak of soil in Europe today, we can primarily have in
mind only Russia and her vassal border states."[52] Any future German foreign policy must be "an eastern policy in the sense of acquiring the necessary soil for our German people." It should also "destroy" the "French
efforts toward hegemony in Europe."[53] He then combined Russia's deterioration with "Jewish Bolshevism," thereby making the destruction of

France, Russia, and the Jews synonymous. Anyone paying even the slightest attention to Hitler's language could not doubt his intentions, but many dismissed him as just another perpetually lying politician. Post hoc, most of the appeasers adopted this view, claiming they interpreted Hitler's bombast as mere political puffery—stump speeches and exaggerations for internal consumption.

Lost in modern discussions of fascism and communism is the stark similarity between Hitler and Karl Marx. Hitler's ideas, for example, strongly internalized the Nazi Party Program of 1920, which incorporated all ten points of Marx's *Communist Manifesto*, then enhanced it with several Jew-specific clauses. Hitler himself incorporated Marxist language throughout his speeches and writings. "History . . . represents the progression of a people's struggle for survival," Hitler wrote in his "Second Book," with almost no variation from Marx's "All history is the history of class struggle."[54] Nazi economic theory, such as it existed at all, was a mix of German nationalism combined with socialism. Hitler flatly stated in his "Second Book," "I am a socialist."[55] "People who love to speak of socialism," he insisted, "do not understand that the most socialistic organization of all was the German people's army."[56]

One key element of difference between Hitlerian fascism and communism lay in the former's use of race as the aspect of human struggle and the latter's reliance on class. Hitler's broad discussions of geopolitics and conflict always returned to what he saw as three intertwined realities: the death of the Jew, the life of Germany, and the expansion of the Reich's borders. Germany's survival demanded space and foreign powers, especially Russia (with the Jewish Bolsheviks), and Britain and the United States (whose banks were under Semitic control) would resist the acquisition of that space. In Hitler's view, success depended on removing the Jews from power, but he was not only interested in displacing them. Rather, he advocated their extermination—killing them as the Germans moved in to repopulate their newly won territories with a superior race and spread German blood.

Hitler's anti-Semitism has been the subject of innumerable academic works. Ron Rosenbaum's *Explaining Hitler* analyzed the arguments of more than a dozen historians, theologians, and philosophers, none of whom agreed on the essential origins or character of Hitler's Jew-hatred.[57] Statements by Hitler have been interpreted so flexibly as to render them all little more than literary linguine. However, if one takes them at face value and appreciates the heavy spiritual context within which they were written, they take on new clarity:

- "The mightiest counterpart to the Aryan is . . . the Jew."
- "Since the Jew . . . was never in possession of a culture of his own, the foundations of his intellectual work were always provided by others."
- "If the Jews were alone in this world, they would stifle in filth and offal; they would try to get ahead of one another in hate-filled struggle and exterminate one another."
- "The Jew is led by nothing but the naked egoism of the individual."
- "Thus, the Jew lacks those qualities which distinguish the races that are creative and hence culturally blessed."
- "The Jew cannot possess a religious institution, if for no other reason because he lacks idealism in any form."
- "On this first and greatest lie, that the Jews are not a race but a religion, more and more lies are based."
- "Race . . . does not lie in the language, but *exclusively in the blood*." (emphasis ours)
- "The Jewish influence on economic affairs grows with terrifying speed through the stock exchange."
- "The Jew by means of the trade union . . . shatters the national economy."
- "With satanic joy in his face, the black-haired Jewish youth lurks in wait for the unsuspecting [German] girl whom he defiles with his blood, thus stealing her from her people. With every means he tries to destroy the racial foundations of the people he has set out to subjugate."[58]

And on and on. As Professor Robert Loewenberg once observed, "Hitler's choice to eradicate the Jews *and Judaism* instead of Armenians or Biafrans is what makes for the Holocaust's particularity" (emphasis ours).[59] Understanding Hitler in this way makes it literally impossible to refer to a "Palestinian holocaust," for example. Repeatedly, Hitler invoked spiritually charged pseudo-Christian terms to describe the war against the Jews, referring to "eternal Germanity," effecting a "reconciliation of mankind," emphasizing the "purity of the blood."[60] The fight had to be one to the death, for the Jew intended the "enslavement, and with it the destruction, of all non-Jewish peoples."[61] Connecting Jewishness to trade-unionism and Bolshevism enabled Hitler to demonize the Soviet Union; linking Jewishness to bankers and financiers permitted him to do the same with the United States and Britain. But these connections only constituted necessary tactics to achieve the final goal, the "extermination" (*Ausrottung*) of the Jews as a "race," and this objective was only the first step in replacing Christianity with Nazism. The Nuremberg trials revealed the extent of the Nazis' war on Christianity, noting that "Christian churches were systematically cut off from effective communication with the people. They were confined as far as possible to the performance of narrowly religious functions, and even within this sphere were subjected to as many hindrances as the Nazis dared to impose . . . [including through] illegal and terroristic means."[62] Both the German Evangelical Church and the Norwegian National Church (after the Nazi invasion) were seized by the Nazi government. All other churches were directly controlled through Nazi administration of their finances and through a series of laws that drastically reduced their powers across a broad spectrum of issues. But whether the Jews were (at first) specifically singled out as the end product of Nazi terror, or whether they were the first step toward a National Socialist religion mattered little in practical terms as the decade unfolded and Jews were rounded up, renamed, and eventually gassed.

All the elements worked together—anti-Bolshevism, anti-Semitism (as Hitler claimed the socialist movement was "Jewish"); *Lebensraum* to free the land from the Bolsheviks and Jews; German national fanaticism and liberation from control of the Allies and their (Jewish) financiers; and continued purification of German blood. The latter involved the dual removal of the Jews from German society and concentration of "racial" Germans inside "Greater Germany" (in other words, the concept of *Anschluss* or in *Mein Kampf*, "One blood demands one Reich").[63] Each part fed the other. Each demonic seed grew in perfect harmony, shaded and watered by the rest.

When Hitler was appointed chancellor, only a few Germans and even fewer non-Germans knew what he was up to, but large numbers (perhaps just shy of a majority) agreed with his nationalist impulses and his explanations of why Germany languished. Most thought reparations constituted not only an undue burden on the Weimar Republic, but also an immoral and unjust one. Quickly forgotten were the images of mutinies during the Great War and the public outcry over casualty lists, and in their place came a new wave of resentment and revenge. Betrayal, whether by Wilson promising "peace talks" that quickly became a surrender, or by the French, who hungrily grabbed Alsace-Lorraine and occupied the Ruhr, increasingly became a common explanation for German humiliation.

Each new government intervention or subsidy involving business brought more vigorous regulation and enforcement by Hitler's government. On Hitler's order, the Nazis also embarked on bloody internal purges, starting with the murder of Vice-Chancellor von Papen's secretary and the arrest of his staff in June 1934 during Operation Hummingbird, better known as the "Night of the Long Knives." Von Papen himself barely escaped assassination, but other high-profile former leaders did not. Conservative anti-Nazi former chancellor Kurt von Schleicher and his wife were killed, as was Gregor Strasser, who conceived the Nazi "Battle for Work," the Bavarian officials who had suppressed the Beer Hall Putsch, and some eighty others; then the following month, in Austria, self-identified Nazis shot Austrian chancellor Engelbert Dollfuss.

Large numbers of Austrian Germans longed for a deeper relationship between the two nations, and the Nazis in particular stressed the concept of a "greater Germany" that would incorporate Austria. An Austrian version of National Socialists, founded in 1926, had splintered and failed to gain the widespread acceptance that its German cousin had. A decade later, the Austrian National Socialists attracted only 3.6 percent of the vote. Dollfuss, whose Christian Social Party had governed since 1932, banned the Austrian Nazis in 1933. His successor, Chancellor Kurt Schuschnigg, faced rising domestic violence and hoped closer relations with Germany would ameliorate it. But he also genuinely felt an intense connection to Germany, and in the 1936 "July Agreement," he released all imprisoned Nazis and allowed Nazi newspapers to reopen. From then on, many Austrians believed it only a matter of time before a complete reunification with Germany occurred.

Whether in Austria or Germany, it was tempting for ordinary people to ignore the violence of the Nazis in the early part of the 1930s. The threat of Bolshevism was real; the Communist street gangs were every bit as dangerous as the Nazis, and to some people, the Nazis merely constituted a home-grown defense mechanism. Many Germans, especially, hoped there was some justification in the name of national security and that genuine conspiracies were at work. After all, Europeans were accustomed to carrying a set of documents with them everywhere and registering and deregistering with police when changing residences, but Nazi Germany increased civil-

ian control substantially. Life under Nazi rule became regimented and restricted. Attempts to regulate prices involved the *Reichsnährstand* ("Reich
Food Production," or RNS) in the most mundane of grocery shopping and
meal preparation, and, just like in the Soviet Union, the growing and consumption of food became political acts. To Hitler, farming regulations were
critical if he was going to realize his vision of *Lebensraum*. Where Stalin
conducted nothing less than a war on his peasants, Hitler envisioned the
farmers as the heroic class of Germans who would lead to a "new Germany"
of vastly expanded borders. But his goal presented a paradox: to acquire
lands for the *Volk* involved war; but to fight the war, Germany needed far
more resources than it had—including agricultural resources and land. Resources demanded war, while war demanded new resources, meaning the
"means and ends could no longer be separated [and] War now had to be
contemplated . . . as the logical consequences of preparations being made."[64]

## Origins of the Nazi War Machine

Although the military had played only a peripheral role in the rise of Nazism up to the point Hitler became Fuehrer (leader), and while the Wehrmacht (literally "defense force," but generally applied to the German army
in particular) viewed Hitler with contempt, seeing him as an amateur, Germany quickly personified the perfect embodiment of a "military-industrial
complex," in which the need for military supplies drove the conquest of
territory. Hitler had already insisted that a nation could "become" itself
only through aggressive foreign policy and expansion; therefore it followed
that "the first task of German foreign policy is the creation of conditions
that will enable the reestablishment of a German army."[65] As the new chancellor, Hitler announced that he would spare no expense in making "the
German people capable of bearing arms."[66] Hence from 1933 to 1935, German military spending as a share of national income increased tenfold.[67]
Germany continued to press for more American loans, rightly angering
Roosevelt and his secretary of state Cordell Hull, both of whom viewed the
appeals as a façade for financing further military expansion. Meanwhile,
the Nazis actually provided less funding for such civilian-sector needs as
housing than the Weimar Republic had, and housing finance fell by four
fifths under Hitler.

Rearmament was only half the game. Hitler was busy rallying the Germans against the artificial borders created at Versailles. He also invoked an
approach adopted by Lenin, namely the presumption that no nation's bor-

ders could be considered fixed. "The German borders of 1914," he wrote, were borders that "represented something just as unfinished as people's borders always are. The division of territory on the earth is always the momentary result of a struggle and evolution that is in no way finished."[68] Support for Germany to expand her borders was found in unlikely places, in particular the British Embassy, where Ambassador Nevile Henderson said he realized that "a nation of 75 million must be allowed to expand economically somewhere."[69]

Hitler's rearmament relied heavily on existing companies and their ideas and engineering, sometimes meeting specifications developed by military personnel, but more often promoting their own designs and acquiring military approval. As a result, many of the German weapons were first-class, but the process played havoc with planning. The development of war matériel for the German air force or Luftwaffe ("air weapon") in particular lacked direction as Hitler lurched from one concept and idea to the next. Probably the best two examples of this lack of planning to meet Hitler's stated goals were the failure to put a long-range heavy bomber into production—only prototypes were ever produced—and the sidelining of jet fighter development and production when jets could have entered the war in 1942. German engineering was often spectacular, but German industry tinkered its way to defeat. The United States completed a design of a weapon and mass-produced it, whereas the Germans constantly improved their weapons, greatly lowering production rates and creating a nightmare in the field with each variation having different and noninterchangeable parts with other models. Consequently, the Germans never had enough of any particular weapon and were repeatedly overwhelmed by American and Soviet numbers.

While Hitler's interference did saddle the development of some strategic Luftwaffe planes and weaponry, his support nonetheless made them the most aggressive arm when it came to mobilizing for war. Ratcheted up on Christmas Day, 1936, by Herman Göring, after years of preliminary development, the Luftwaffe reestablished its power quickly, making a mockery of Versailles's ban on German military aviation. For the next four years, the Luftwaffe enjoyed unrestricted budgets, consuming much of the Four Year Plan introduced in October 1936 that sucked up a quarter of all investment in the German economy. Among other goals, it placed the German economy on a timetable to be fit for war in four years; have the German army operational within the same time span; and to reject devaluation of the money. But of all the armed forces, the Luftwaffe was to receive special attention when it came to resources, and this objective immediately clashed with daunting shortages of rubber, iron ore, steel, and particularly oil, which were obtained only in Romania, Czechoslovakia, and Russia. Without "entry into foreign states or the attack and seizure of foreign property," Hitler noted in May 1939, "the solution to [the problem of raw materials] is not possible."[70] None of these ideas were new. Prior to World War I Germans had lusted for French ores, sought iron in Sweden and Austria, and looked toward the east to supply all foodstuffs at some future point. What had changed was Hitler's willingness to risk national existence to achieve a high standard of living (which up to that point had been necessary to mobilize civilian support for military expansion), and his unwillingness to tamper with that standard of living until well into World War II. Relentlessly, then, Germany's insufficiency in raw materials gnawed at it, driving it toward martial conclusions. Having decided that the free market would not produce the desired outcome, Hitler set himself on a course of deceit and violence—but then again, many argue that was his intended path from the beginning.

Hindsight seems to make clear Hitler's intentions. It is worth considering, though, that most of his actions were to be expected, not only in Europe, but in the United States as well. Hitler put his young men into his army, Roosevelt and Stalin theirs into massive civilian work camps—the incentives differed, but the programs themselves, and their intention of full employment, looked remarkably similar. Did French socialism differ significantly? Were not leaders everywhere threatening, bullying, and cajoling private industry with little complaint from the putative watchdog press? Through the prism of nearly universal and outrageous soft socialism of New Deal America and western European governments and the hard communism of Stalin, Hitler's policies appeared, indeed, less radical than those of the Soviets. If Western intellectuals had praised Stalin and brushed off his murder and thuggery, why would they have raised any eyebrows to Hitler?

At any rate, Hitler seemed uncaring about the Western press. He marched ahead with his agenda. Whatever could not be obtained through diplomacy, trickery, and bluster would necessitate war with France and Britain, and to that end Hitler had already foolishly ordered an increase in naval construction, swelling spending on the Kriegsmarine (German Navy) to challenge Britain by 1939. A wary Britain and France responded to this buildup, France doubling her military budget in 1938 and Britain launching a new aircraft production program that would add twelve thousand combat planes to the RAF by 1940. From 1933 to 1939 the "democracies" outspent Germany, Japan, and Italy by 1.5 to 1.[71] And whereas Britain and America could continue to ramp up their naval spending dramatically, such a level of expenditures on ships was unsustainable for Germany. Even later, after the 1939 "Pact of Steel" between Germany and Italy potentially supplemented the Nazi fleet with numerous warships from the Italian fleet, Germany never came close to challenging Britain or America in the Atlantic. In the end, monies poured into shipbuilding, except for the invasion of Norway and submarines, were thrown away.

In May 1938 Hitler ordered the economy to shift into wartime production as its primary objective. Civilian needs would take a backseat to the military, the exception being the *Volkswagen*, Hitler's pet project to rival the productive genius of Henry Ford. A marketing plan was developed that allowed customers to set up a no-interest-paying bank account (the interest went to the bank), and when they had a balance of 750 Reichsmarks, they could order a Volkswagen. The goal was to achieve a price of 990 Reichsmarks per auto, but to meet that target, the Porsche factory had to produce 450,000 cars per year, or more than twice the entire German auto industry at the time. In the event, all the cars produced went to Reich officials until the factory was converted into military production. Except for military and governmental traffic the *Autobahns* saw little use, and Hitler's "people's car" never came close to reality.[72] In contrast, with no government support at all, Henry Ford had succeeded in producing a car for the average American, while the Volkswagen, funded and marketed heavily by the government, never sold a single car to a civilian until long after the war.

Mobilization brought new financial pressures on the Third Reich, and escalating taxes had to be avoided to retain the support of the German middle class and industrialists. Citizens wishing to leave Germany had already been subjected to a "flight tax" in 1931, which by 1938—as Jews grew more desperate to leave—became a major source of revenue. Jews were fortunate to escape with 8 percent of their assets intact, and from 1938 to 1940 brought in almost 850 million Reichsmarks to the Nazi government, or about 5 percent of the Reich's total income. Heightened persecution of Jews also brought unforeseen economic dislocations. *Kristallnacht*, a night of attacks against Jews and their property in November 1938 after a Jew assassinated a Nazi official in France, for example, cost the government three million Reichsmarks for clean-up expenses, and Jews had to rebuild their houses at their own cost and pay an "atonement fee" that amounted to a billion Reichsmarks.

News of Nazi violence against Jews began to reach other nations on a regular basis, permanently turning some in the upper echelon of the British government against Germany, such as Britain's formerly appeasement-oriented foreign secretary, Lord Halifax. It generated a storm of protest in the United States, leading Roosevelt to recall the American ambassador from Germany, but otherwise taking no punitive action. Of course, this only served to reinforce in Hitler's mind the fact that "international Jewry" was headquartered in the United States and to harden his long-term expectation of an inevitable war with America.

Eventually, after the invasion of Poland in September 1939, Hitler drafted a memo to the commander-in-chief of the German army, General Walther von Brauchitsch, and his chief of staff, Franz Halder, providing his strategic assessment of a western war, which he insisted needed to begin immediately because of the expected intervention of the United States. "Because of its neutrality laws, America is *not yet* dangerous to us," he wrote a few weeks later. While the "reinforcement of our enemies by America is *not yet* significant," he noted, it soon would be, and although at that time the situation was "propitious, in six months, however, it may not be."[73] Fritz Todt, the Reich minister for armaments and munitions, told General Georg Thomas, head of the Wehrmacht's Defense Economy and Armaments Office, that the "Fuehrer has again emphasized energetically that everything is to be done so that the war [against England and France] can be ended in 1940 with a great military victory. From 1941 onwards, time works against us (USA-potential)."[74] Even after the Battle of Britain in the fall of 1940—with a massive invasion of the USSR looming before them in May of the next year—Luftwaffe leadership focused as much on "the industrial prerequisites for the coming war with Britain and America as on the imminent invasion of the Soviet Union."[75] As early as July 1940 after the fall of France, Hitler instructed the high command to "consider seriously the Russian and *American* question (emphasis ours)," indicating that one full year before invading Russia, Hitler was already planning for a war against both the USSR and the United States.[76]

Some German opponents of Hitler based their positions on the fear that America would quickly enter a European war. General Ludwig Beck, chief of the German General Staff from 1935 to 1938, opposed a war from the beginning and enlisted Graf Schwerin von Krosigk, the finance minister of the Reich, to prepare such a memo for Hitler in June 1938. Krosigk warned of the "soon-expected active participation of the United States of America in the war," calling it the British "trump card."[77] Thus, at an early stage, the stars were aligning in Germany for an eventual conflict with the United States. America's alliance with Britain, combined with (from Hitler's perspective) the manipulation of Roosevelt's government by a Jewish cabal and the realities of Allied rearmament, all meant that for Germany, the sooner war came, the better. If Germany acted quickly enough, Britain and possibly the Bolshevik Soviet Union could be knocked out before American power might be brought to bear.

## Diplomatic Failure of Will

America's absence left the economically distressed, wobbling, and weak-willed European democracies to deal with the aggressive dictator. None of the Western allies wanted the burden of military expenditures added on top of existing public works and socialist outlays. Diplomatic gymnastics were employed to concoct alliances that would substitute fantasies of mutual support for genuine martial power: France and the Italians discussed military cooperation if Hitler invaded Austria, and the "Little Entente" of Yugoslavia, Romania, and Czechoslovakia, backed by France, seemed to offer hope of uniting to stop Hitler in the East. Each of these alliances collapsed under clever negotiating by German diplomats or as a result of economic pressures brought by the Third Reich. Indeed, it did not take long for Mussolini to abandon France and throw in with Hitler.

When local Nazis killed Austrian chancellor Engelbert Dollfuss in his office, reaction by the democracies was swift in condemning the assassination and threatening action, and Mussolini actually moved four divisions to the Austrian border to support the Austrian army in the event of an invasion from Germany. Though not yet ready to provoke armed confrontation, Hitler publicly announced the following March that the German army had already expanded to more than double the size permitted by the Versailles Treaty, and soon cast aside all secrecy surrounding the Luftwaffe. Hitler also admitted Germany's treaty-busting naval expansion. Shocked emissaries from France, Italy, and Britain quickly met at Stresa, Italy, in April 1935 to present a united front and denounce Germany's military buildup. Like League protests, the Stresa Front lacked any teeth whatsoever, pledged no specifics, and was washed away by Hitler's May 1935 speech proclaiming that Germany "wants peace and desires peace." Western papers, such as the London *Times*, accepted Hitler's words at face value, saying they showed his "sincerity and peaceful intentions."[78] Britain foolishly leaped into negotiations to "limit" the German fleet through the Anglo-German Naval Agreement, which "held" the Nazis to 35 percent of the Royal Navy's power—a ceiling that the Germans would never reach. The agreement represented a diplomatic coup for Hitler that scrapped the last remnants of Versailles between Britain and Germany, and created a wedge between Britain, Italy, and Japan.

At every critical point, comprehensive resistance to Hitler foundered on confusion about his character and goals. There was the parade of British elites who trekked into Germany as apologists for Hitler's positions, foremost among them David Lloyd George and Neville Chamberlain. To them, Hitler seemed rational and sane, just another politician doing his best for his people. British ambassador Nevile Henderson even proposed giving Germany certain African territories that belonged to Belgium and Portugal, though he was careful to exclude British territories in Africa from discussions.[79] His 1939 book, *Failure of a Mission*, offers an interesting study in delusion. "For two years I hoped against hope that the Nazi revolution, having run its course, would revert to a normal and civilized conduct of internal and international life," he stated. "Even today I do not regret having tried to believe in Germany's honor and good sense."[80] The Western press was generally helpful to the Nazis, and sympathizers such as Geoffrey Dawson, editor of the *Times* of London, wrote a correspondent in Germany in 1937, "I do my utmost, night after night, to keep out of the paper anything that might hurt [German] sensibilities."[81]

Of course, German colonies in Africa—should they have actually been transferred—would have left Hitler with the ever-present problem of supply lines being subject to interdiction by the British Royal Navy. A more rational sphere of influence—because it did not involve confronting the Royal Navy, but was well within range of the Luftwaffe—was eastern Europe and the Balkans, and leaders in those states knew it. If they didn't, British diplomats were quick to remind them: in 1938, Romania's King Carol II was bluntly informed that German economic dominance of the region was "inevitable" and was a "German monopoly field."[82] Talk of that kind unnerved Mussolini, who scrambled all the more frantically to form a "Third Europe" coalition of Yugoslavia, Hungary, Poland, Romania, and Italy.

## The Dictator's Ball

Italy had remained quite independent from German ambitions throughout most of the 1930s, finally throwing in with Hitler in the May 1939 "Pact of Steel." The traditional view that Hitler and Mussolini were bosom buddies was accurate only after the Munich Agreement of September 1938, where the Western allies handed over the Czech Sudetenland to Germany without a fight. Mussolini, always alert to who was gaining and losing power, sized up the allies as weak. Until that time, however, the Italians flitted incessantly on the fringes of various alliances with Britain, France, Czechoslovakia, and other states.

What instigated the separation of Italy from the Western democracies was not Hitler's shrewd diplomacy, but Mussolini's land grab in Abyssinia (Ethiopia) in October 1935. Dating back to the humiliation of Italian forces by natives at Adowa in 1896, a succession of Italian governments had claimed Abyssinia as Italian territory, and as a "big power," the Italians felt they possessed the same right to colonies in Africa as the British and French. In December 1934, shooting broke out in southeast Ethiopia between Ethiopian troops and Italian forces from nearby Italian Somaliland, in what became known as the Wal Wal Incident. Italy invaded, presenting the League of Nations a chance to redeem itself from its earlier failure in 1932 to stop the Japanese in Manchuria. Stanley Baldwin, the British prime minister, bravely promised to save Abyssinia through "peace by collective security," which meant little more than economic sanctions. The League imposed sanctions on Italy on October 19, convincing Mussolini (correctly) that different rules were being applied to him from those that governed imperialism by England and France. It further convinced him (also correctly) that a permanent alliance with the Western powers would never involve Italy as a full and equal partner, and he began to shift his stance toward Germany.

The Abyssinian/Ethiopian conflict demonstrated every pitiful frailty of the League of Nations. Committing itself to protecting backward nations such as Abyssinia, a quasi-state which still permitted slavery and could not police its own borders, the League saw legitimacy and equality where none existed. No one wished to send troops to aid the Ethiopians, and indeed the British would not even close the Suez Canal or impose a naval blockade against the transport of Italian forces. Even the United States refused to impose a specific sanction on oil sales, and when Addis Ababa fell

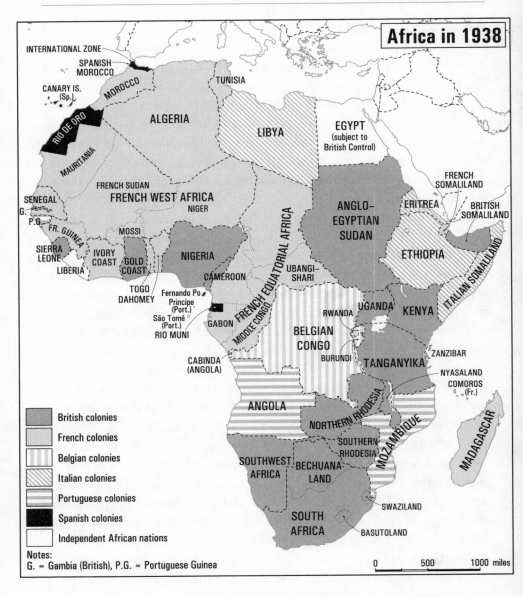

**Africa in 1938**

INTERNATIONAL ZONE

SPANISH MOROCCO

CANARY IS. (Sp.)

RIO DE ORO

MOROCCO

TUNISIA

ALGERIA

LIBYA

EGYPT (subject to British Control)

MAURITANIA

FRENCH SUDAN

FRENCH WEST AFRICA

NIGER

SENEGAL

G.

P.G.

FR. GUINEA

MOSSI

SIERRA LEONE

IVORY COAST

GOLD COAST

LIBERIA

NIGERIA

CAMEROON

TOGO

DAHOMEY

Fernando Po Principe (Port.)

São Tomé (Port.)

RIO MUNI

GABON

FRENCH EQUATORIAL AFRICA

UBANGI-SHARI

MIDDLE CONGO

CABINDA (ANGOLA)

BELGIAN CONGO

RWANDA

BURUNDI

ANGOLA

NORTHERN RHODESIA

SOUTHERN RHODESIA

SOUTHWEST AFRICA

BECHUANA-LAND

SOUTH AFRICA

BASUTOLAND

SWAZILAND

ANGLO-EGYPTIAN SUDAN

FRENCH SOMALILAND

ERITREA

BRITISH SOMALILAND

ETHIOPIA

ITALIAN SOMALILAND

UGANDA

KENYA

TANGANYIKA

ZANZIBAR

NYASALAND

COMOROS (Fr.)

MOZAMBIQUE

MADAGASCAR

British colonies

French colonies

Belgian colonies

Italian colonies

Portuguese colonies

Spanish colonies

Independent African nations

Notes:
G. = Gambia (British), P.G. = Portuguese Guinea

0    500    1000 miles

on May 5, 1936, all sanctions were lifted. A new British-French overture—the Hoare-Laval Pact of December 1935—offered Mussolini whatever territory the Italians already held in Abyssinia. Word leaked to an outraged public, and both Pierre Laval, the French prime minister, and Samuel Hoare, the British foreign secretary, resigned. It was classic appeasement. The Abyssinian episode brought out in sharp relief the weaknesses of the League, the dominance of realpolitik and self-interest (as opposed to upholding the principles of the League) in both Britain and France, and—to Mussolini—the untrustworthiness of Western allies. Ethiopia, however, was instructive in demonstrating what the totalitarians had in mind for their new subjects should they win. Mussolini told his top general there to gas, shoot, or otherwise exterminate anyone who resisted.

Mussolini's ruthlessness never came close to matching that of the Nazis, in large part because of the Italian military's incompetence but more frequently because of his interference with military planning. Despite a victory at Adowa on October 6, 1935, the Italians' advance slowed. Under international pressure, Mussolini demanded a quicker pace, leading General Rodolfo Graziani to douse the Ethiopians with gas sprayed from aircraft, further increasing calls from abroad to end the conflict. By the spring of 1936, the Italians held Addis Ababa and declared victory, but it had taken a modern nation armed with machine guns, artillery, airplanes, and poison gas a year to subdue the poorly armed Ethiopians, many of them possessing no weapons other than spears or bows.

The prowess of the Italian military had hardly improved by 1939 when Mussolini invaded Albania. Filippo Anfuso, the assistant to Foreign Minister Galeazzo Ciano, observed that if the Albanians "had possessed a well-armed fire brigade they could have driven us back into the Adriatic."[83] But both the German and Italian dictators understood the Ethiopian lesson with great clarity: the unwillingness of the League or the democracies to resist at all illuminated the "green light for further acts of aggression."[84]

Certainly not everyone in the West was oblivious to the impression of weakness created by the Ethiopian war. In England, British foreign secretary Anthony Eden predicted in June 1936 that Hitler would use Ethiopia to fracture the Treaty of Versailles (as if it were not already defunct). Some feared the affair would push Mussolini into Hitler's arms, which it certainly did. Prior to Ethiopia Il Duce had maintained a skeptical view of Hitler: "He's a nut," he told his confidants after their initial meeting in June 1934.[85] Hitler now saw an opportunity, and sent top officials, including Göring and Himmler, to Rome to woo Il Duce. Mussolini stated in January 1936 that his nation and Germany shared a common fate, and during the year Mussolini placed Italy alongside Germany politically.[86] Given what Britain had to lose if she alienated the Italians—namely vessels available for home defense since the Royal Navy would have to assign more ships, men, and supplies to the Mediterranean—it was, as historian Correlli Barnett noted, "highly dangerous nonsense to provoke Italy."[87] Nevertheless, by 1937, British war planners were forced by Mussolini's belligerence to treat Italy as an unfriendly power.

One of the indicators the British had already lost Mussolini was the issue of his own "Manifesto of Race" in July 1936, in which the Italian fascists joined the Nazis in the persecution of Jews (although Mussolini also specifically targeted Africans). The Manifesto (which did not go into effect until July 1938) reflected less Mussolini's own anti-Semitism than it did his desire to cozy up to Hitler. Indeed, briefly Il Duce tried to convince Hitler that racism was unproductive, but introduced the Manifesto as "evidence of his good faith. . . . calculated to solidify the Italo-German Alliance [sic]."[88] Despite the Manifesto, Italian fascism never absorbed the same racial anti-Semitism the German variant had. Few publications appeared, and even fewer Italian fascist leaders believed in the premise of race traits—even for Italians. But the Manifesto drew the dictatorships together, and in October 1936, Mussolini spoke of a "Rome-Berlin Axis" intended to be only the rump of a much larger alliance network. Visiting Berlin in September 1937, Mussolini was enthralled by the man he once labeled a "nut," and der Fuehrer reciprocated the praise by labeling Il Duce "the leading statesman in the world."[89] Joining the Anti-Comintern Pact in November 1937 (which a year earlier had bound Japan and Germany to cooperate in opposing the spread of communism), Mussolini sealed his fate by becoming not only a German ally, but, in the minds of the democratic West, just another miniature Hitler.

## Nazi Aggression, Democratic Reaction

While the Western powers were frenetically absorbed with Ethiopia in early 1936, scurrying to meetings, issuing sanctions, and generally being wholly distracted, Hitler sent German troops into the demilitarized Rhineland in violation of the Versailles Treaty. Once again, Britain and France issued protests, but did nothing, despite the fact that along with other continental powers, they could call on a "collective security" force of 140 fully operational divisions to the Germans' five ill-equipped and dispersed divisions. Many in both countries believed that Hitler was only going into his own "backyard," that in recovering German territory Hitler had a just case, and therefore the invasion of the Rhineland did not pose an adequate reason for standing up to the Fuehrer. A willingness to excuse current misbehavior on the basis of the Versailles Treaty's wrongs was widespread and deep. Such thinking opened the door to further violations so long as they were "justified"—and Hitler, if anything, could always produce a justification.

Instead of deploying forces against the Germans, France hunkered down, ratifying its previously negotiated treaty of mutual assistance with the USSR. Britain accelerated its arms program—although an April 1934 report had already erroneously noted it would take five years from that point to catch up to the Germans. Further, concerns remained that Britain could be sucked into a conflict through the back door: Anthony Eden, then lord privy seal, cautioned "great care must be taken that [we in Britain] did not put ourselves in a position where the French were able to bring [us] into action automatically as [if] it were pressing a lever."[90]

Part of the wishful fog of thinking that kept the British from reciprocating military mobilization derived from the "ten year rule," a budgetary guideline that assumed Great Britain would not have to go to war in the next decade. Originally promulgated in 1919, the "ten year rule" had been blithely updated each year until 1932. Churchill had even argued in 1928 for making the rule perpetual, to automatically update itself each year (he would later disavow making the proposal). But even after Britain abandoned the rule in March 1932, it lived on in spirit. Coupled with the effects of the Depression, Britain minimized its defense expenditures until the German rearmament program was well advanced in the late 1930s. Later, British politicians would excuse the appeasement at Munich by alleging that Britain needed time to "close the gap" with Germany, while in fact it was their own policies that had opened the gap in the first place. It would not be the last time a Western democracy locked itself into bad policies based on wrong assumptions, then clung to them for dear life rather than admit its error.

Then there was the very structure of British government, which enabled it to ignore common sense when it came to Hitler. Under this government framework, the Commons and the cabinet were controlled by the same party, while the monarchy, the House of Lords, and the civil service supposedly (but ineffectually) acted as checks on their power. Until the 1930s, Conservative governments often controlled all five of those parts, while Labour could count on holding, at the most, two. Parliament, despite the name "House of Commons," was reserved for the wealthy and, especially, the educated: over 40 percent of the Conservative members went to Eton College or Harrow School, the two premier private schools in the country. Labour, on the other hand, was entirely in the grip of the unions.

Of a total membership in 1936 of 2.4 million, the Labour Party counted 2 million union members, and seventeen of the twenty-five executive committee members were union appointees. In short, there were few in British government who could genuinely speak to the concerns of average people, and certainly not the nonunion middle class who would experience the bulk of wartime hardships if Hitler's aggression was not stopped early.

Studying the reactions in Britain and France, both Hitler and Mussolini discovered the key to getting their way: quick, unapologetic military action that produced the desired result before the waffling democracies could react. The Spanish Civil War (1936–39) gave them the opportunity to test their weapons and tactics. When the young Spanish Republican government drifted into chaos and anarchy in 1936, generals led by Francisco Franco attempted to seize power and were opposed for the next three years by the Communist-supported Popular Front. Although Franco was no fascist in the mold of Mussolini—and certainly not an ideologue like Hitler—the two fascist dictators supported him out of their loathing for communism. Both Italy and Germany volunteered arms support to Francisco Franco's coalition of Carlists (Royalists), conservative Catholics, Nationalists, and the Falange (fascists) against the Popular Front, whose members were predominantly radical Socialists and Communists.

## Spain's *Noche Triste*

Francisco Franco, who emerged from the Spanish Civil War as Spain's strongman of the era, is often unfairly lumped in with Hitler and Mussolini as a fascist from the beginning. While some of his policies had a fascist tinge, and he certainly enjoyed the support of the Germans and Italians, Franco was first and foremost a general, a junta leader possessing exceptional timing and survival skills. Spain's road to dictatorship, though, did not begin with Franco but with the government of Miguel Primo de Rivera from 1923 to 1930. When Primo de Rivera stepped down in January 1930, two months before he died, Spain's political situation fell into chaos. King Alfonso XIII abdicated in 1931, and a Spanish republic under Premier Niceto Alcalá-Zamora was established with the usual multiple parties unable to work with one another.

Spain had civil rather than common law, with no articles resembling an American-style bill of rights and little understanding of democratic forms of government. It had endured authoritarian regimes for hundreds of years, almost all of that time under a monarch, or, briefly, an Islamic caliphate that governed part of Spain. Adding to the chaos after Alfonso's abdication, the Republican government ominously formed a new special police called the Guardia de Asalto (Assault Guards), which functioned separately from the traditional police, the Guardia Civil (Civil Police), left over from the monarchy.

The new government consisted of radical republicans and anticlericals, including the minister of war, Manuel Azaña; Socialists, represented by Francisco Largo Caballero, secretary-general of the Spanish Socialist Workers Party (PSOE), and Indalecio Prieto, leader of the middle-class Socialists; and some Catholics who nevertheless hoped a Spanish republic could work.[91] This was not the view of more traditional Catholics, such as Cardinal Pedro Segura y Sáenz, archbishop of Toledo and primate of the Spanish Church, who openly attacked the new republic in a pastoral letter as too tolerant of Protestants, before being exiled in 1931. Meanwhile, the anarchists in Catalonia, the semiautonomous northeastern region whose capital was Barcelona, had increased their numbers to over a million and a half out of a total population of about twenty-five million in all of Spain. About half of the Catalonian population was anarchist, and some fifty thousand were members of a secret society unwilling to compromise with any other political faction.[92]

Spanish anarchists were unique among the factions, a group brought into being by a reaction against the Catholic Church, Spain's general poverty, and some abuses of Christian teachings. They viewed the Catholic Church as largely responsible for Spain's poverty, repeatedly contrasting the Church's wealth with the people's poverty. As a result, anarchists developed a new variation of Catholicism with a commandment to end hereditary wealth and bring down the rich. This belief produced an exceptionally violent strain of anticlericalism. Under the cover of the revolution, anarchists killed 88 percent of the diocesan clergy in Barbastio (Aragon), most of whom were poor themselves and scarcely lived above the level of the peasants they served.[93] Anarchist communities excised all forms of wealth from their societies, eschewing communism, capitalism, and the Catholic Church.

In the fall of 1931, a constitution for the republic was drawn up, and as usual then in Europe, leftists overrode the concerns of the conservatives to make it a document that expressed their political agenda with no compromises. Following the principles of the French Revolution a century and a half earlier, the constitution stated: "Spain is a democratic republic of workers of all classes, organized in a regime of liberty and justice."[94] Renouncing war, obliterating titles of nobility, and invoking breath-taking anticlericalism, the new constitution effectively banned Jesuits and religious education, placing all religions under the control and sanction of the state. Prime Minister Alcalá-Zamora assumed the office of president—a position previously held by the king. Following an attempted coup by Carlists (a party dedicated to restoring the Spanish monarchy) in 1932, the government began to disintegrate as violence escalated both inside and outside the government. Asalto guards executed a number of anarchists under the authorization of the *Ley de Fugas* (that is, while trying to escape) and new elections were ordered.

An election the following year saw Alcalá-Zamora's Radical Republican Party form a new government, even though CEDA (Confederación Española de Derechas Autónomas, or Spanish Confederation of the Autonomous Right), consisting of five major parties and several tiny ones under Gil Robles, won a plurality. Both Right and Left fragmented, witnessing a rise of the Falange fascist party and the resurgence of disciplined Communists. By 1936, the elections and their runoff, which ended with the Popular Front, consisting of five major parties and several smaller ones, coming out ahead with only 4.1 million votes (out of 8.6 million cast), illustrated the weakness of a democratic system lacking a history of individual liberty and even a skeletal grounding in common law. Alcalá-Zamora was replaced by Manuel Azaña—his prime minister and a non-Socialist anticlericalist who largely failed to carry out any land reform, thereby simultaneously alienating both the Left and the conservatives. CEDA deputies were denied their seats and infiltrated by the growing Spanish Communist Party, while the Popular Front split internally between Largo Caballero and Prieto. Street gangs, anarchists, and anticlericals lined up behind the Communists, provoking a reaction by the Falange. Largo Caballero, who had restrained himself, working nonviolently for years to improve the material circumstances of workers, found himself pulled further left by the Socialist press and street mobs.[95] Gil Robles, the fat, nearly bald bankerlike politician who led CEDA, warned that the new Popular Front was thumbing its nose at half the country. His pleas went unheeded. But the leftist parties were split as well, as Prieto and Largo Caballero were unwilling to be in the same room with each other. Radicals wanted strikes, peasant uprisings on farms, armies of militant youths in the streets—all of which terrified the law-abiding, everyday Spaniard, and most of which was inspired and influenced by Communist malefactors. Violence spread; the army was dispatched on leave; and strikers and peasants occupied factories and farms, all under the approving eye of the Asaltos. Fire-eating Communists such as "La Pasionaria" (Dolores Ibárruri) goaded strikers and gangs to kill Catholic priests and sack churches. La Pasionaria, a dramatic sight with her silver-streaked black hair wrapped tightly in a bun and always in her signature black dress and brightly colored scarf, carried her fanaticism into legislative debates, openly threatening other members of the Cortes.[96]

At that moment, General Francisco Franco took center stage. A supporter of the Republic, he came to see the demonic spread of communism as consuming Spain. Short, pudgy, and introverted, Franco tackled tasks with a plodding diligence and command of detail that had gained him the respect of his military superiors over the years. For four years he led the Spanish Foreign Legion; his reckless courage while heading an attack against rebellious Moroccan tribes earned him the nickname "Ace of the Legion" and convinced his Moorish troops he was *baraka*—protected by the divine. Franco had remained aloof from the violence and the 1932 abortive coup, and as late as February 1936 thought military intervention would be unnecessary. On July 17, four days after José Calvo Sotelo, a leader in the National Front (rightist) Party, was murdered at the order of La Pasionaria, the Communists threatened to seize control of the parliament. Franco reluctantly participated in a rebellion led by Spanish officers headed by General José Sanjurjo. Sanjurjo was Spain's most prestigious general—"the Lion of the Rif"—and at sixty-four years old he commanded great respect throughout the military. But he was in exile in Portugal, separated from the officers and troops in Spanish Morocco, preparing for a flight on July 20 to Burgos and a heroic march on Madrid. Unfortunately, his plane crashed on takeoff from Lisbon, and the leader of Catholic, conservative, nationalist Spain was dead.

Meanwhile, Franco had taken control of the Canary Islands where he had been placed in command in February 1936, remaining safely out of the line of fire much as Napoléon had in Egypt more than a century before. He returned to Spanish Morocco through Casablanca, arriving after the country had been secured by Nationalist rebels and taking command of the army. From the outset, he expected a long war with the big cities supporting the Popular Front government, and recognized that for the rebellion to succeed, he had to lead it. His expectation of a long war was correct—fighting lasted into 1939, and cost Spain nearly 400,000 killed in action, with another 100,000 executed by the Republicans including 13 Catholic bishops, 5,235 priests, and 2,669 nuns.[97] Possibly up to 500,000 more were executed by Nationalists, and tens of thousands of murders, executions, and acts of terror were carried out by rival factions on the Republican side against one another—losses that severely weakened the Republican efforts.[98] Another more scholarly estimate leaves the Republican numbers as above, lowers the number of Nationalist executions to 40,000, but adds deaths by malnutrition, disease, and starvation as being not less than 200,000.[99] Regardless of the actual number of deaths on both sides, it is difficult to underestimate the total suffering by the Spanish people during the war and afterward.

Initially, the Republican Army in 1936 consisted of undisciplined militia, made less reliable by anarchist volunteers, who at the outset were unsure they could support a Popular Front Army. The anarchists were led by a woman, Federica Montseny, the first female minister in a Western government, who had made her name campaigning for abortion on demand in Catholic Spain. To fuse together the anarchists and other forces, the Republicans abolished party affiliation of units and instituted a draft. Communists quickly rose above other factions in quality of fighting forces because of their ruthlessness and discipline.[100] What saved the Nationalists was the ineffectiveness of the Republicans, who never overcame their factionalism. Troops failed to trust units around them, and every setback was seen as treachery from competitors. Murder and betrayal within the officer corps posed further problems.

Despite Spain's relatively small size, its Civil War stood third in line behind the Taiping Rebellion in China and the Russian Civil War in brutality and hardship on the native civilian population. One of the most outstanding features of this conflict was that the rebels were fully mixed in with loyalists (Republicans) at the start of the conflict, and a great many people, both military and civilian, lost their lives simply by being in the wrong place (the minority) when war broke out. There was little opportunity for a conservative Catholic to flee his home and seek safety in a Nationalist-held area at the outset; conversely, if an individual was a known Republican in an area where Nationalist troops were able to establish themselves, arrest and probable death was almost certain to follow. Catholic priests, monks, and nuns were hounded and killed in the most unspeakable fashion, and on the second day of the uprising, sixty churches were burned to the ground in Madrid alone. The Civil Guard almost invariably supported the Nationalists, while the Asaltos allied with the Republic, but groups of either caught unawares were slaughtered by their opponents without mercy.

As battle lines ebbed and flowed, no one could establish order throughout much of Spain. Mob rule often reigned as wealthy landowners, businessmen, and professionals fled for their lives. An exceptionally high number of Nationalist officers, particularly generals and colonels, died one way or another. General Sanjurjo became the first; soon the war also claimed notables such as Generals Emilio Mola, Manuel Goded, Álvaro Fernández Burriel, Joaquín Fanjul, and Miguel García de la Herrán. In Catalonia the anarchists seized power; their administration in Barcelona was chaotic and incompetent beyond belief and marked the only time in Western history when anarchists controlled a substantial governmental entity. It produced a dismal failure. Skill in bombing a police station or stock exchange did not translate into administrative aptitude.

No one remained safe from the chaos and murder. Spanish philosopher Miguel de Unamuno, watching Falangists march past his university building in Salamanca in 1936, observed:

> The truth is that we are on the verge of an international war on our national territory. What a sad thing it would be if, in place of a barbaric Bolshevik regime, anti-social and inhuman, another regime would appear which was just as barbaric, anti-social, and inhuman. Neither one nor the other [Fascism or Communism], for, at the bottom, they are one and the same.[101]

Because Franco emerged as the last dictator standing, it is easy to ignore his competitors or dismiss the level of opposition he overcame. In fact, although he was widely respected by the Spanish Foreign Legion and throughout Spanish Morocco, he stood fourth in line among the leaders of the Nationalist revolt, after General Emilio Mola, who commanded the rebellion within Spain from his headquarters at Burgos; General Sanjurjo; and Manuel Goded. However, Sanjurjo was killed taking off from Portugal, and Goded, the former chief of the General Staff, was captured at the rebellion's onset and later executed for his attempted revolt in Barcelona. Mola's situation rapidly became desperate although he seized the mountain passes leading to Madrid from Navarre in the north. His Carlist volunteers ran out of ammunition, and he was forced to send them a message: "Not one shot more. I have only twenty-six thousand cartridges for the whole northern army."[102] His forces had few tanks, and the few planes fit to fly were still under Republican control. Franco, isolated in Morocco and without transportation to send supplies to Spain, could not help him. Republican forces moved on Seville and the army garrison at Cádiz, and Republican warships controlled the Strait of Gibraltar. Disaster and failure threatened, but Franco rapidly found the solution to his problem—the Germans.

In June, Johannes Bernhardt, an agent of a German export firm in Morocco, had offered to furnish transport planes on credit to assist the revolt. Sanjurjo had rejected the proposal, but Bernhardt had flown back to Berlin, obtained Göring's assistance, and returned with a letter of greeting to Franco from Hitler. A Lufthansa plane was detached from service and ordered to stand by in Morocco for Franco's use. On July 21, facing utter ruin, Franco sent two of his staff officers to Berlin with bank drafts on London banks. Hitler immediately sent thirty transport planes to Spanish Morocco, and Franco enthusiastically radioed Mola to hang on, reinforced the small detachment holding Seville, drove the Republicans out of Cádiz, and sent arms and ammunition to Mola.

Suddenly sensing in Franco they had found a horse they could back, others provided support. Italy sent troops and assistance, Portugal sent supplies. This allowed Franco's Moroccan army to head north to attack Madrid. Mola readily placed himself under Franco's authority, not least because Franco controlled the foreign cash and matériel, and on September 30, Franco was named "Chief of the Government of the Spanish State" and assumed all the powers of the new state, in reality holding dictatorial power. He also brought with him the well-trained Foreign Legion and his Moorish soldiers of the African Army, who tipped the balance in favor of Nationalist troops every time they were employed—and came to be the target of Republican propaganda.

The actual fighting was always brutal and ugly, with heavy casualties on both sides. But when Britain and France signed a Non-Intervention Agreement in August 1936, a Nationalist victory was essentially secured. Although Communist propaganda of "republicans" and "loyalists" fighting against "Fascists" convinced many in Britain, France, and the United States that the angels were on the Republican side, reality was substantially different. Franco's regime became a typical and somewhat benign dictatorship of the type so often formed in Europe. Responding to the propaganda, however, a unit of volunteers called the Abraham Lincoln Brigade was formed in the United States to fight with the Communists. Certainly the name would have been an affront to Lincoln, for neither side stood for individual liberty. The Soviet Union sent planes, pilots, tanks, troops, and supplies for the Republican side, taking as a fee for its efforts the entire Spanish gold reserve, which they had been storing for "safekeeping" since 1936 (nicknamed the "Moscow gold"). Soviet aid and the arrival of the International Brigades probably saved Madrid from the Nationalists in 1936, and certainly gave the Republicans a new lease on life. Germany contributed supplies to Franco and, most famously, the Condor Legion that performed well against the Soviet aircraft, and tank units under Wilhelm von Thoma, who would later command the Afrika Korps. The Condor Legion undertook the first terror bombing of an urban area, the town of Guernica, which foreshadowed the use of air power to a high degree in World War II. But Italy, not Germany, provided the most foreign manpower, 50,000 troops, while France later allowed Soviet and Comintern aid to flow across its borders in 1938. Nevertheless, Germany provided the decisive edge twice: in the opening days by providing transport for Franco's army and supplies to reach mainland Spain, and later in 1938, by sending aid (in return for iron ore mining rights) that allowed Franco to decisively defeat Republican armies in the Catalan campaign and drive the northern Republican forces into internment in France. In short, foreign intervention was critical at a number of points in the war, and to the benefit of both sides.

Hitler's actions in the Spanish Civil War suggest he may have actively sought to prolong it to distract the West from Germany's military preparations and other diplomatic efforts. For example, German officers misdirected the attacks at the battle for Madrid, and from that point forward until the Catalan campaign at the end of 1938, German aid came primarily to keep the Nationalists from being defeated, not to help them win when they were on the offensive. It would later appear that Franco was aware of this policy, and he paid Hitler back by not allowing the Nazis to move through Spain to attack Gibraltar after 1939 or significantly assisting Germany on the Eastern Front.

On March 31, 1939, the Nationalists finally took the remaining Republican cities of Almería, Murcia, and Cartagena, and the following day, the United States recognized Franco's government, leaving the Soviet Union as the only major power not to recognize the Nationalist regime. By summer, all foreign troops had been sent home. In Germany, these returning veterans would figure prominently in World War II, whereas most Soviet returnees were shot or demoted in Stalin's purges because they had been contaminated by their association with the West. Khrushchev publicly regretted their deaths in his speech denouncing Stalin in 1956.[103]

## The Serpent Unwinding

While the rest of Europe was concentrated on Spain's ongoing civil war, Germany marched from the easy *Anschluss* with Austria in March 1938 to demands for the Sudetenland (Southland) in the newly created state of Czechoslovakia. About 3,200,000 ethnic Germans lived in Czechoslovakia, along with 7,450,000 Czechs, 2,300,000 Slovaks, 720,000 Hungarians, 560,000 Ukrainians, and 100,000 Poles in a pot that refused to melt. A majority of the Sudetenland population was ethnically German, so Hitler focused on this German-speaking population, regurgitating Wilson's "self-determination" phrase to argue in favor of taking the territory. Again, he was aided and abetted by the democracies. Chamberlain told his cabinet that if Hitler sought a popular vote there, "it would be difficult for the democratic countries to go to war," despite the fact that Britain and France had already moved millions of people after World War I without a single ballot cast.[104]

Through it all, many in the British government—particularly Chamberlain—fretted endlessly about treating Hitler as a legitimate and reasonable head of state, convinced that the right concoction of rewards and reason would bring him into the family of nations. Indeed, they continued to appease Hitler *despite* the lack of credible evidence that Germany could fight, let alone win, a war. Just before the democracies buckled to Hitler's demands, the Czechs were getting the Sudetenland under control and away from Nazi agitators and had mobilized their army to handle any German attack.

Significantly, the Czech army in April 1938 was larger and better equipped than the Wehrmacht, comprising forty-six divisions, of which twenty-five were field divisions, twenty-one infantry, and four mechanized cavalry, the remainder being static and service troops manning the excellent Czech fortifications facing Germany. German forces that occupied Austria during the *Anschluss* in March had embarrassed themselves; many tanks and motor transport vehicles had broken down and troop mobilization was poor, leaving the Czechs unimpressed. In April the General Staff could count on only twenty-four infantry, one tank, one cavalry, and one mountain division. Although the balance of power was changing rapidly, by

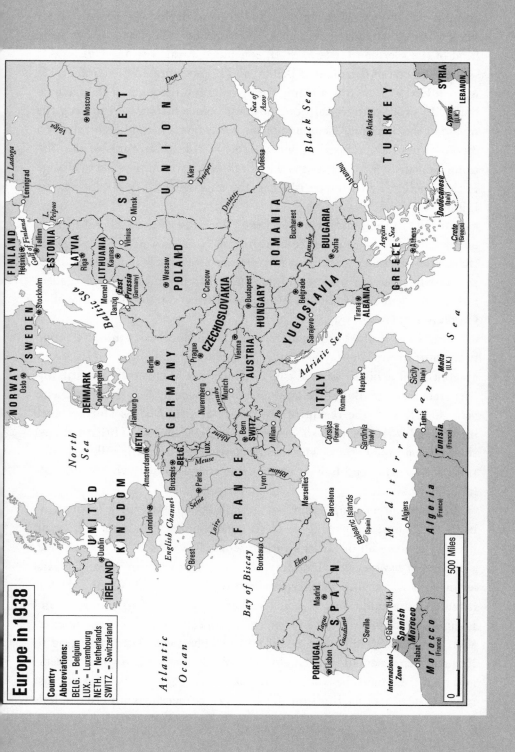

# Europe in 1938

**Country Abbreviations:**
BELG. = Belgium
LUX. = Luxembourg
NETH. = Netherlands
SWITZ. = Switzerland

*Atlantic Ocean*

*North Sea*

NORWAY
Oslo ✪

SWEDEN
Stockholm ✪

FINLAND
Helsinki ✪
*Gulf of Finland*
*L. Ladoga*
Leningrad ○

*Baltic Sea*

ESTONIA
Tallinn ○
*L. Peipus*

LATVIA
Riga ✪

LITHUANIA
Kaunas ✪
Vilnius ○
Memel ○
Danzig ○
*East Prussia (Germany)*

DENMARK
Copenhagen ✪

UNITED KINGDOM
London ✪

IRELAND
Dublin ✪

*English Channel*

NETH.
Amsterdam ○

BELG.
Brussels ✪

LUX.

GERMANY
Berlin ✪
Hamburg ○
Nuremberg ○
Munich ○
*Rhine*
*Meuse*
*Danube*

*Bay of Biscay*

FRANCE
Paris ✪
Brest ○
Bordeaux ○
Lyon ○
Marseilles ○
*Seine*
*Loire*
*Rhône*

SWITZ.
Bern ✪

POLAND
Warsaw ✪
Cracow ○

CZECHOSLOVAKIA
Prague ○

AUSTRIA
Vienna ○

HUNGARY
Budapest ✪

SOVIET UNION
Moscow ✪
Minsk ○
Kiev ○
Odessa ○
*Don*
*Volga*
*Dnieper*
*Dniestr*

*Sea of Azov*

*Black Sea*

ROMANIA
Bucharest ✪
*Danube*

BULGARIA
Sofia ○

YUGOSLAVIA
Belgrade ✪
Sarajevo ○

ALBANIA
Tirana ✪

ITALY
Rome ✪
Naples ○
Milano ○
*Po*

*Adriatic Sea*

*Corsica (France)*

*Sardinia (Italy)*

*Sicily (Italy)*

*Malta (U.K.)*

*Tunis*

*Tunisia (France)*

*Algeria (France)*
Algiers ○

*Mediterranean Sea*

GREECE
Athens ✪

*Aegean Sea*

*Crete (Greece)*

*Dodecanese (Italy)*

TURKEY
Ankara ✪
Istanbul ○

*Cyprus (U.K.)*

SYRIA

LEBANON

SPAIN
Madrid ✪
Barcelona ○
Seville ○

*Balearic Islands (Spain)*

*Ebro*
*Tagus*
*Guadiana*

PORTUGAL
Lisbon ✪

Gibraltar (U.K.)

*Spanish Morocco (France)*
International Zone

*Morocco (France)*
Rabat ○

0        500 Miles

autumn the best the Wehrmacht could hope to deploy was fifty-five divisions of varied strength, equipment, and training.[105] General Ludwig Beck, head of the German General Staff, concluded a war with Czechoslovakia spelled the end of Germany if Britain and France entered the conflict. He warned Hitler and wrote a memo for distribution throughout the General Staff: "In order to safeguard our position before history and to keep the repute of the Supreme Command of the Army unstained, I hereby place on record that I have refused to approve any warlike adventures of the National Socialists."[106] Beck resigned when he saw it was impossible to change Hitler's policy, and later perished in the abortive July 1944 plot against Hitler.

In spite of their advantages and the reluctance of the General Staff to countenance war to achieve Hitler's aims, the Czechs watched helplessly as their most defensible territory was bargained away in a September 15, 1938, preliminary meeting between Hitler and Chamberlain at Berchtesgaden. Czech president Edvard Beneš, left without British support, knew that all of Czechoslovakia was now on the menu.

Hitler had drafted orders to "smash Czechoslovakia by military action in the near future" in May, setting deployment for September.[107] His generals continued to object strenuously, convinced the Wehrmacht was still unprepared for war. But their attempts to dissuade Hitler were met with ridicule. Pleas by the regent of Hungary, Admiral Miklós Horthy, were interrupted by Hitler with shouts of "Nonsense! Shut up!" Hitler canceled the invasion only because Mussolini, likewise assessing the military positions of Germany and Italy as unfavorable compared with those of the allies, implored him to wait.

In a second meeting with Chamberlain at Bad Godesberg on September 22, Hitler raised the ante, and a stunned Chamberlain, after presenting his plan to meet all of Hitler's earlier demands, was told *"Es tut mir Leid, aber das geht nicht mehr"* ("I'm sorry, but that won't work anymore").[108] Hitler made new demands for German troops to immediately occupy the Sudetenland, for additional Czech territory to be ceded to Hungary and Poland, and for Czechs forced from their property to receive no compensation, demands Chamberlain could not possibly meet. After returning to England depressed and distraught, Chamberlain consulted with his cabinet, then announced he would go to Munich on September 29 for one last round of negotiations, this time in a four-power meeting with French, Italian, and German leaders to avoid war. Secretly, the British had already dispatched a mission to Prague to convince the Czechs to give up.

France, however, still seemed ready (though not eager) to fight. In September 1938, French premier Édouard Daladier told Chamberlain he would attack if German forces crossed into Czechoslovakia proper. He was dissuaded by Chamberlain, his own foreign minister Georges Bonnet, and the hundred centrist deputies who visited him and unanimously instructed him to avoid war. Bonnet was an appeaser of the highest level ("rodently for peace," as U.S. ambassador to Russia William Bullitt described him), and no doubt manipulated information to bring yet additional pressure on Daladier to capitulate. It worked: by the time of the Munich Conference, according to Hermann Göring, "Neither Chamberlain nor Daladier were in the least bit interested in sacrificing or risking anything to save Czechoslovakia. . . . We got everything we wanted, just like that [snapping his fingers]."[109]

Before going to Munich, Chamberlain gave a radio broadcast on September 27, in which he lamented Britain's being involved in a "quarrel in a far-away country between people of whom we know nothing."[110] On the contrary, it seems everyone by then knew a great deal about the Germans. The infamous Munich Conference of September 1938, conducted without Czechoslovakia being present, followed and actually *increased* German territory over what Hitler had demanded a week earlier, stripping Czechoslovakia of 70 percent of its electricity-generating plants, most of its chemical works, and its border defenses. Hungary and Poland also acquired the Czechoslovakian territory they wanted. Chamberlain, returning to Britain, stated, "I believe it is peace for our time," while Daladier—seeing the crowd at the Paris airport—was afraid to land as he expected he would be lynched. According to Jean-Paul Sartre, when Daladier saw the people were cheering him, he turned to his aide and said, "Ah, the fools."

Chamberlain's appeasement has been the subject of great historical debate. Critics blame him for failing to stop Germany soon enough, while defenders argue he bought precious time. In any case, the public remained behind him upon his return, with 51 percent of those polled saying they were satisfied with the result.[111] (More ominously, though, a whopping 86 percent of the British population did not think Hitler's territorial demands in Europe were satiated.[112]) A heated debate had occurred within British military and diplomatic circles for years regarding the advisability of allowing Hitler to move eastward. The British ambassador to Germany, Nevile

Henderson, viewed German hegemony east of the Rhine as an unpalatable fact. Others insisted German expansion eastward would weaken Russia to Britain's benefit, but military expert and London *Times* correspondent B. H. Liddell Hart warned that "in the long run, this would be like feeding the tiger" and that Britain, not Russia, remained the "ultimate obstacle to Germany's ambition as in the past."[113] Of course, all that was contained in *Mein Kampf* if anyone cared to read it. When Lord Halifax, in a 1938 memo, asked, "Are we prepared to stand by and allow these vast districts to pass completely under German domination?" Chamberlain scathingly dismissed the question, arguing it was impossible for Britain to do anything about it.

In fact, Chamberlain had bungled the entire run-up to war, not just the last months. Of course, the best chance for Britain to stop Hitler easily and probably bloodlessly had come and gone under Stanley Baldwin's government when Germany marched into the Rhineland in 1936. Since then, however, Chamberlain had consistently failed to appreciate Hitler's appeal to Germans of all types, and the absence of "moderate" elements inside the country who could (and would) oppose Hitler. Perhaps his worst mistake was assuming that Britain and France benefited from delaying the conflict. In terms of financing, that was certainly false. Britain's gold reserves dwindled from 1936 to 1939 due to the high cost of imports, while Germany was still constrained by shortages of raw materials and food that would later become available from Czechoslovakia, Poland, and the United States. Almost one third of German phosphate during this time came from the United States, as did one fourth of its copper, two thirds of its uranium, half of all iron and scrap metal, not to mention $206 million in direct investment.[114]

The advent of war would have almost certainly shrunk these imports to nothing, either by the direct decision of American suppliers or by the British blockade, which in 1938 would have faced even less German resistance than in 1940. Overall, the German economy, while at nearly full employment, nevertheless flirted with bankruptcy as a result of its trade deficiencies. Hitler virtually admitted as much in his widely misinterpreted January 30, 1939, speech, in which he reiterated his support for the Anti-Comintern Pact and emphasized Germany's determination to resist democratic influences from the outside. But he threw in just enough sops to peace that the allies were reassured of the unlikelihood of war. Yet every new concession by the democracies brought not gratitude and stability, but new demands and scorn. Lord Halifax dourly noted in June 1939 that "we were living in what was virtually a state of concealed war."[115] Even more stunning was the shift in military power brought about by waiting: England had 71 *fewer* combat aircraft in September 1939 than it had in January of that year, while Germany had added 800 more planes.[116]

To add insult to injury, handing over Czechoslovakia to the Nazis proved foolish even in purely military terms. Germany was able to add more than 460 new thirty-eight-ton tanks to its arsenal, along with close to 1,500 aircraft and a million rifles, not to mention the massive Skoda arms works. (By comparison, the Nazi panzer units had only 300 Panzer III and IV tanks—the most advanced in their armored units—in early 1940, meaning that the Czech additions essentially doubled Germany's tank forces.) Acquisitions such as these inflated foreign and uninformed estimates of German military power: Charles Lindbergh returned from a trip to Germany and announced the Nazis had 8,000 military aircraft and could manufacture 1,500 a month. In fact, the Germans had 1,500 (plus the Czech planes) and could make another 280 per month. But Lindbergh's overblown tales spread panic in Paris and London, and introduced something close to a state of hysteria among some in Britain.[117] The point was that accurate information was hard to come by, and overinflation of Germany's warmaking capacity could prove as dangerous as underestimating the enemy.

One problem with calls for rearmament by realists such as Winston Churchill was that Hitler was not uniformly feared or hated in England. The Church of England was openly pro-appeasement, portraying the Germans as victims of the Treaty of Versailles. Large newspapers were similarly aligned. London's oldest newspaper, the *Observer*, and its sister paper, the *Guardian*, under the control of William Waldorf Astor, echoed these sentiments. Astor and the "Cliveden set" of upper-class conservatives saw Hitler as a useful buffer against Soviet expansion, and at any rate expected the French military to fold under pressure from Germany. Intellectuals such as Edward Hallett Carr enthusiastically defended appeasement. Treasury official Edward Hale called the "Nazi struggle . . . primarily one of self-respect, a natural reaction against the ostracism that followed the war . . . [and] Hitler's desire for friendship with England is perfectly genuine and still widely shared. . . ."[118]

Perhaps Hitler's greatest admirer across the channel was King Edward VIII, who abdicated his throne in 1936 to marry an American divorcée, Wallis Simpson. Edward's abdication made his reign of less than a year the shortest of any monarch not to have died or been assassinated on the throne, and he was the only British monarch who voluntarily stepped down. But the embarrassment for England was only beginning: Edward visited Hitler at Obersalzberg after the abdication, delivering the Nazi salute for photographers and providing the Nazis with stellar publicity. Albert Speer later quoted Hitler as saying, "I am certain through him permanent friendly relations could have been achieved. If he had stayed, everything would have been different. His abdication was a severe loss for us."[119] Some speculated that had Hitler ever conquered England, he would have attempted to reinstate Edward. At the beginning of the war, Edward was stationed in France as a major-general in the British Military Mission, where allegations arose that he leaked war plans for Belgium's defense. Holed up in Lisbon, Edward gave an interview viewed by Churchill as "defeatist," whereupon he was instructed to return to Britain or face court martial, and he complied. Shipped to the Bahamas as governor ("a third-class British colony," as he described it), he still was viewed with sufficient suspicion that Franklin Roosevelt placed him under surveillance.[120] One investigator in the 1980s claimed an MI5 agent was secretly sent to Germany after the surrender to retrieve correspondence between Edward and Hitler that might prove embarrassing.[121]

Certainly Britain was not alone in refusing to stand up to Hitler, and one of the greatest tragedies of World War II is that at any point prior to the acquisition of Czechoslovakia, Germany was vastly outnumbered by potential allied armies. When the Germans marched into the Rhineland, her neighbors could put more than ten times as much military force immediately into the field. Certainly the League of Nations did nothing to blunt Hitler's violation of the Versailles Treaty. The German chancellor had no intention of keeping the Anglo-German Naval Agreement of 1935, and privately announced he would break it at the first opportunity.

Hitler also sought to favorably shape American popular opinion. Initially, Roosevelt was praised by the German press—one paper called him a man of "irreproachable, extremely responsible character and immovable will."[122] After a year in office, Hitler sent FDR a letter congratulating his "heroic efforts" for the American people and vowing to do the same for Germans. In a letter to William Dodd, the U.S. ambassador, Hitler said that his nation and the United States were both demanding the same "virtue of duty, readiness for sacrifice, and discipline" of their people.[123] Mussolini likewise wrote glowingly of the New Deal, labeling it a spiritual renewal of a "sole will [who] silences dissenting voices." However, when

Americans recoiled at the notion that the New Deal was fascism, although the NIRA certainly would have done either Mussolini or Hitler proud, Mussolini quickly squelched such talk from his press office. Nevertheless, years later Roosevelt still spoke of how he was "deeply impressed" with what the Italian dictator had accomplished.[124]

Only a few clamored for military preparedness on either side of the Atlantic, one of whom was wealthy Wall Street financier Bernard Baruch. Having urged Woodrow Wilson to prepare for World War I, in 1935, Baruch looked with concern on developments in Europe. America's duty, he told *The New York Times*, was to "think peace, talk peace, and act peace," but if war came, the United States needed to be prepared to fight. With some prescience, he predicted, "if the nation has to go to war it will be ready to go in and sock them in the eye and win."[125] Even Norman Angell, who had prophesied the dawning of a new era of peace prior to World War I, first called for the League of Nations to resist aggression, then eventually joined Churchill in criticizing Chamberlain's appeasement. Angell joined a few other English dignitaries to welcome exiled Ethiopian emperor Haile Selassie to London in 1936 when the prime minister, Stanley Baldwin, exited a gathering for tea to avoid greeting him. Worse than that, King Edward VIII would not receive Selassie at Buckingham Palace.[126]

Had no further aggression by Hitler or Mussolini ever occurred, by the end of the 1930s the totalitarian moment had nevertheless arrived. The number of so-called democracies in the world had shrunk dramatically, from a high point in 1922 when 37 percent of the world's nations were democracies (more or less), to 1939 when only 14 percent remained free. But even this measure was misleading, as many of the existing democracies lacked anything close to the degree of liberty found in America. In France, for example, powerful antiparliamentary forces marshaled to push the nation toward the fascists. The 1934 Stavisky Crisis, triggered by the embezzlement and pilferage of Alexandre Stavisky, a Russian swindler known as the "Handsome Sasha," and his cronies who sold bonds from pawnshops, helped destabilize the French government through Sasha's connections to important officials. Subsequent public outcry, along with an organized campaign by the right, forced the government of Camille Chautemps out and let the radical Socialist Édouard Daladier in. Constant demonstrations from January to February 1934 culminated with riots and several French right-wing groups, including the Ligue des Patriotes, the Action Française (founded by Maurras), and the Jeunesses Patriotes (the "Patriot Youth"), among others, descended on the Place de la Concorde in front of the National Assembly on February 6, commencing an hours-long battle with police that resulted in sixteen deaths. Inside the Assembly, fistfights broke out between left-wing and right-wing deputies, leading to Daladier's resignation and sparking counterriots by Communists. The French radical Right lost all faith in parliamentary democracy and the Third Republic, and looked for new opportunities to establish a fascist or national-socialist alternative. "Rather Hitler than the Republic" became the accepted sentiment.[127]

Only in Britain was there steadfast resistance against more government control. But in all the Nazi client states, any semblance of genuine democracies had vanished. In addition, Franco held Spain, Mussolini Italy, Stalin Russia. The question was not democracy or totalitarianism in Europe, but whose variant of totalitarianism, the Fascists' or the Communists'? Even in Asia, the choices were between the theocratic autocracy of Imperial Japan or the dictatorships vying for power in China, one under the quasi-socialist Kuomintang government of Chiang Kai-shek and the other under Communists led by Mao Zedong. By 1939, freedom was a rare flower, blooming only in a handful of carefully cultivated fields.

## The End of the Fascist Façade

Hitler planned to invade Poland in the spring of 1939, even as he occupied the remainder of Czechoslovakia (an event Chamberlain described as the latest in "a series of unpleasant surprises"). Additionally in March, the Memel district of Lithuania, formerly German territory before Versailles, was returned through a treaty forced on Lithuania by Germany. Shortly thereafter, der Fuehrer spoke to his generals, noting that with few exceptions, "German unification" had been achieved, and promised next to secure food supplies. There was no question of "sparing Poland," and while the goal was to isolate Poland from the West, if Britain and France fought for Poland, it would be "better to attack the West and finish off Poland at the same time."[128] He doubted whether the West would interfere, however: "I experienced those poor worms Daladier and Chamberlain in Munich. They will be too cowardly to attack." Comparing himself to Genghis Khan, Hitler instructed the generals to use "quickness and . . . brutality."[129] Yet the West hesitated to support Poland too overtly, wary of feeding Hitler's paranoia of encirclement, leading one British writer to urge that policy makers keep references to British support of Poland out of the German press if at all possible. Meanwhile, Hitler's new demands for the return of

Danzig and the Polish Corridor separating East Prussia from Pomerania received a warm reception in Germany.

Less enthusiastic was German popular opinion for a coming war. Czechoslovakia had been a low-hanging fruit, yet even then (unlike with the Sudetenland) the Nazis were not greeted by cheers, flowers, or elation in Prague.[130] Hitler's Reichstag speech of September 1, 1939, justifying the coming invasion of Poland, excited few Czechs, even Czech Nazis. George Kennan, at the American Embassy, found the streets of Prague deserted, defying even the efforts of professional Nazi Party agitators to whip up public support through demonstrations. At the same time, opinion in Great Britain moved firmly against appeasement. Poland would therefore finally align Britain and France in an active alliance over territory neither could hope to defend, having already ceded the best defensive ground in Europe to Germany with the Sudetenland. Nonetheless, British attitudes swung toward a determination to resist the Nazis.

Poland had been on the carving block since April 1939, when Germany renounced its 1934 nonaggression pact with Poland and made Polish territory a way-station on the drive to destroy the USSR. Hitler could not imagine the British coming to the aid of Poland after sacrificing Czechoslovakia, and he had ordered the German High Seas Fleet to move into full-scale production of battleships, cruisers, and submarines based on a long-range plan for war with England after Jewish Bolshevism had been eradicated. Nonetheless, the stubborn British gave Poland a territorial guarantee in August 1939, complicating Hitler's schemes. As an Anglo-French mission left for Moscow to discuss alliances with Stalin, Hitler was forced to abruptly modify his plans.

Stalin despised the Nazis and feared a German invasion as much as Hitler hated Bolshevism and wished to avoid a two-front war. This focus on a common desire for harmonious relations (temporarily) between their two nations produced a terrifying international alignment of totalitarian gangsters. Moreover, there was a precedent indicating coming events—Mussolini had aligned with Germany in May 1939 with the "Pact of Steel," and promptly plunged into Albania two weeks later. Now the Nazis wooed Stalin, sending Joachim von Ribbentrop to meet with the Soviet dictator, not least to forestall any possible rapprochement between Britain and the Soviet Union. Ribbentrop's reply indicated that the Soviets, too, wanted an arrangement. A division of Poland seemed just the sweetener for the deal.

Addressing the German High Command on August 22, Hitler announced he would "provide the propagandistic pretext for launching the war, no matter whether it is credible," and directed his generals to "Close your hearts to pity. Proceed brutally."[131] The next night, in the Kremlin, Ribbentrop sealed the agreement with Stalin, receiving the dictator's toasts to Hitler, looking much like Chicago mobsters from a decade earlier as they divided up territory between phony handshakes and sloppy kisses. The nonaggression pact virtually ensured that Poland would vanish as a state. Wisely, the Soviets waited until September 17 to seize their part of Poland, allowing Germany to attack first on September 1 and Britain and France to declare war on Germany as the sole aggressor. Stalin was correct that neither Britain nor France would desire war with the Soviet Union in addition to Germany and would overlook the Soviet role in dismembering Poland. In fact, they would turn a blind eye to anything else Stalin would do while at war with Germany, and the pact allowed Stalin to crush the Baltic states and move with impunity against Finland and parts of Romania. Stalin reveled in the deal as he now had free rein, and declared war on Finland in November. Germany, described as a "partner" by Stalin, suddenly benefited from an ironic and ridiculous overnight shift in worldwide Communist propaganda. Whereas only a week earlier Communist publications in England and America had denounced fascism, now Hitler was a friend; war was to be resisted and peace sought.[132]

As long as the pact lasted, Stalin guaranteed Hitler raw materials, including copper, zinc, tin, and food. Both dictators slobbered over each other with grandiose statements, Stalin becoming an originator of "Slavonic-Muscovite nationalism" and creator of "Slavonic fascism." The Soviet premier described Hitler as much like himself, weeding out "extremists."[133]

## Samurai and Supermen

Germany's obsessive march to war in Europe would have occurred without any similar actions in the Far East by Japan during the 1930s. Indeed, except for the Anti-Comintern Pact of 1936—which jointly pledged Japan and Germany to resist the Communist International, or Comintern— Japan and Germany had few initial mutual goals. But as European colonial possessions in the Far East became vulnerable after 1940, the Empire of Japan and Nazi Germany found their interests aligning. Germany's Molotov-Ribbentrop Pact of 1939 constituted the sole hiccup in the relationship: it seemed to violate the anti-Communist understanding with Japan. Under this pledge, Germany and Russia agreed to a nonaggression pact that permitted the Soviets to invade Poland from the east without fear of German retaliation as the Nazis moved into Poland from the west. Hitler personally saw the German-Soviet agreement as a mere truce to be broken at a time of his choosing, and he assumed Stalin did as well.

Japan remained to be drawn into Germany's alliances, in spite of Hitler's agreement with Stalin, for two reasons: to act as a diversion to keep the United States occupied in the Far East, and as a possible partner in the eventual war against the Soviet Union, whenever Hitler decided to take that plunge or if Stalin attacked Germany first. Not wanting to unduly alarm Stalin and provoke an untimely conflict while Britain and France remained undefeated, Hitler put off Japan for a year.

It was not until September 25, 1940, that Foreign Minister Joachim von Ribbentrop informed Vyacheslav Molotov, the Soviet foreign minister, that Germany and Italy had signed a military alliance with Japan. He attempted to reassure Molotov that this was not directed at the USSR. Quite the contrary, Ribbentrop said it was designed to warn off elements in the United States who might be considering entering the European conflict. The resulting alliance, signed in Berlin as the Tripartite Pact, formally established Germany, Italy, and Japan as the Axis Powers.

By that time, however, Japan had come to resemble Germany a great deal, and its own path of destruction through the 1930s seemed to lead inevitably toward just such an alliance. For this reason it is useful to review the decade for Japan as it unfolded half a world away from the coming blitz-kriegs in Poland and France.

Even in its doctrines of racial superiority and imperial expansionism, the underlying philosophies of the Empire of Japan started to resemble the Nazi program in almost every facet. Where the Nazis had their doctrines of Aryan supermen, Japan would belatedly produce in 1943 its own view of racial domination as elucidated in "An Investigation of Global Policy with the Yamato Race as Nucleus" that plotted to populate Asian soil with "Japanese blood."[134] In contrast, Chinese were described as "bacteria infesting world civilization," and "Nanking vermin."[135] Just as the Third Reich had its grandiose scheme for resettling Poland and Russia with Aryans, so too the Japanese envisioned an ambitious global policy that, in its final stage, would incorporate not only China and Southeast Asia and India, but also Turkey, Iran, Iraq, and Afghanistan.[136] By 1942, a geographer working for the imperial government categorized Europe and Africa as part of Asia and proposed renaming America "Eastern Asia" and Australia "Southern Asia."

The world's oceans would be renamed the "Great Sea of Japan." A book of the same year, *The Establishment of the Greater East Asian Order*, claimed that "Asia was on the verge of overturning European control everywhere."[137] Another document, the "Investigation of Global Policy," envisioned 12 million Japanese settlers living in these new lands, including 2 million in Australia and New Zealand. The Japanese language would become the official language of all, and a colonial-style industrial relationship would be imposed in the "southern areas." While many of these planning documents appeared after Japanese military successes early in the 1940s, they all reflected intrinsic and well-established Japanese attitudes throughout the previous decade.

Unlike the Nazis' race policies, the Japanese did not envision extermination of their "parasitic" enemy, but rather the subjugation and quasi-assimilation of these peoples into Japan's empire. All Asians in Japan's "Greater East Asia Co-Prosperity Sphere," introduced in 1943, would be required to learn Japanese; and Japanese settlers had to be wary of racial "pollution." There was to be no intermingling with the Han (Chinese), and personal relationships with people in "child countries" occupied by the Empire would not be permitted. A contemporary and accurate model was available in Korea, which Japan had annexed in 1910 (although the Korean emperor never signed the document). As early as 1939, the Korean language was banned from schools and all Koreans were required to attend Shinto services. Korean laborers were shipped to Japan, just as Poles, Czechs, and Jews of all nationalities were shipped to Germany to work for the Nazis. Without a doubt, the policies of militant Japan were as racist as those of Nazi Germany. While fascism and Bushido could provide a vision of the future in which Japan and Nazi Germany could coexist in principle, the racial demands of each doctrine promised a future conflict even if wars with the Americans, British, and Soviets had not intervened first. It is significant, therefore, that the totalitarians' mind-set was quite uniform. In each case, the violence with which their ideas were implemented spawned substantial resistance within conquered territories, while simultaneously producing a number of toadies who sought self-preservation or some level of power within the system. This helps explain how 136 million Germans and Japanese could dominate seven times their number of subjugated peoples. Contrary to the history of the British Empire, however—where the actual military presence was minuscule and the level of violence relatively minor—

the Axis nations employed both a large martial footprint and brutal, murderous tactics to ensure compliance.

Just as Hitler perceived America to be the most significant long-term threat to Germany, so too did the Japanese. As early as 1907, Japan identified the United States as the "sole imaginary enemy" in its "National Defense Policy."[138] American bases in the Philippines, in particular, galled the Japanese, posing in their view a threatening naval presence in Japanese waters. Of the many naval lessons of World War I, Imperial Japanese Navy authorities took from the Battle of Jutland the maxim that a 40 percent advantage in ships and firepower was necessary to achieve victory at sea. Attaining this ratio—or, at least, preventing the United States from reaching it—demanded that Japan have a 70 percent superiority ratio over the United States in the Pacific.[139]

A thirst for resources led Japan into its decade-long entrapment in China, an adventure that finally produced war with the United States. Some of its aggression derived, as Hitler's did, from the perception of Western weakness. Britain's signature of the London Naval Treaty in 1930, which limited the size of certain classes of warships (at a fixed disadvantage for Japan), symbolized the end of the Royal Navy as the premier force of its kind in the world. The treaty also insulted Japan by imposing lower limits than on the "white" nations, contributing to Japan's decision to ignore the treaty and eventually leave the League of Nations. There seemed to be little danger, since Singapore's defenses had been neglected as numerous British leaders called for reductions in the naval budget and overseas expenditures, citing pledges by Japanese leaders to resolve disputes peacefully.

Although the Soviet Union threatened to halt Japanese expansion on the Asian continent, the Japanese increasingly viewed the United States and Britain as the primary enemies. Smoot-Hawley Tariff increases convinced the Japanese they could not trust the United States as an economic partner, since after the act went into effect, silk prices plummeted by half and prices of imported food threatened the nation's ability to feed its population. Most *zaibatsu* heads (the leaders of Japanese industrial and banking conglomerates) and other officials in Japan had already determined that only through imperialism could Japan solve its problems of overpopulation and underproduction. Kingoro Hashimoto, a soldier in the Japanese Imperial Army and a politician, wrote in *Addresses to Young Men* in 1939 that expansion of territory constituted the only one of the three options open to Japan for growth, with the other two (emigration and free trade) closed off.[140] Like most predator states, however, Japan responded to domestic hardship by increasing spending on the military, ramping up the defense budget to nearly half of the government's total expenditures.

To portray Japan's aggression in the 1930s, however, as solely or even substantially a reaction to American and/or British policies misinterprets the reality and rationale of Japanese imperialism. Some historians have seen a cold, logical quest for raw materials and a response to economic deficiency.[141] And while one could contort the facts to play the resource card, it simply would not win the hand. Japan, pure and simple, fomented what John David Lewis called a "social pathology" and what Kazuko Tsurumi labeled a "socialization for death."[142] The belief in Japanese superiority permeated the educational system, the compromised Shinto religion, and every aspect of Japanese life. Bushido warriors were lionized as the embodiment of the new military ethic. Racial dominance of Japanese was preached at every opportunity, and reinforced in all literature. Concepts of "saving face" and family honor in service to the emperor were enshrined as sacred behavior.

Assassination was so commonplace as to become just another aspect of Japanese protest. Enshrined and venerated as *gekokujo* (insubordination), young officers and patriots could and did honorably call senior officials and officers to account for their perceived deviations from *kokutai* (national policy) through outright political murder. Of course, the lives of the perpetrators were forfeit, and that was expected to occur through ritual suicide (*seppuku*). From 1912 to 1945, six prime ministers and a dozen cabinet ministers were killed. By 1930, the army had also forced out two civilian prime ministers. After Prime Minister Osachi Hamaguchi received a mandate to reduce the armed forces, he was assassinated; then his successor had to resign before being gunned down as well. The plotters of the assassination of the last prime minister, Ki Inukai, intended to shoot him with the visiting American superstar actor Charlie Chaplin, who escaped death only when the ringleaders learned that Chaplin's reception plans had changed. When asked during trial what the significance was in killing Chaplin, one of the conspirators said the actor was "the darling of the capitalist class. . . . killing him would cause a war with America. . . ."[143] Invoking *kokutai*, killers and mutineers could threaten *any* politician with death. Japan therefore drifted into a shadow fascism wholly unrecognizable from British or American representative constitutional government.

Japanese society had became increasingly militarized after the Meiji

Restoration, with the army as the instrument of the emperor's divine will and officers expected to fulfill that will with their lives. The connection between the army and the cult of assassination cannot be overemphasized: when Prime Minister Hamaguchi's murderers came to trial, the court received a petition for clemency signed by thirty thousand holders of the Order of the Golden Kite, Japan's highest military decoration.[144] Perhaps the most influential figure of the day, War Minister General Sadao Araki, was described as "a ferocious bushido ideologue . . . who ran a Hitler-style youth movement."[145] Araki had led a group of officers in "the imperial way," or *Kodo*. An ardent expansionist whose musings encapsulated the Japanese sense of victimhood and grievance, he cited European incursions into China as having no justification.

In stark contrast to purported Japanese racial superiority was the island's perpetual shortage of raw materials so desperately needed for the industrial age. Japan was entirely devoid of oil, had few iron deposits, and needed growing imports of rubber, tin, and other resources—all of which reinforced Japan's key weaknesses. Manchuria offered a solution to many of those deficiencies, particularly iron. As Czechoslovakia had constituted low-hanging fruit to Hitler, Manchuria dangled as a resource-rich plum to be plucked by the Japanese militarists. In 1931, a group of Japanese army officers constructed a plot to blow up a Japanese-owned railway outside Mukden, South Manchuria, and blame it on Chinese dissidents to provide an excuse for the Japanese Kwantung Army to invade North Manchuria. When War Minister Jiro Minami sent a representative to curb *gekokujo* in the Kwantung Army, the officers quickly put their plan into motion and detonated their explosives. They followed that up by using artillery against the Chinese garrison in Mukden. The Japanese then attacked and took Mukden, killing 500 Chinese soldiers in the process. In the aftermath of the "Chinese provocation," the Japanese established a puppet state called Manchukuo in 1932.[146] No military leaders were reprimanded for acting without authority, for to do so would have run against the grain of Japanese society as a whole.

Japan's postwar intellectual heritage had come in large part from the ideas of Ikki Kita, who in 1919 wrote *A Reconstruction Program for Japan* that blended socialism, Japanese imperialism, and Shintoism into a single code. Kita's *Reconstruction Program* justified coups d'état as a means of changing governments, a rejection of parliamentary democracy, support of a dictatorship under the emperor as the representative of the nation, and the prohibition of all political criticism.[147] Kita himself would later be arrested and executed for complicity in the 1936 plot to decapitate the Japanese civilian government.[148]

Beneath the cover of the Shinto religion—itself nonaggressive, but within Bushido, a militarized system as all-influencing as Nazism or communism—Japan turned into a total authoritarian state by the early 1930s. Christian missionaries had made only minor inroads in Japanese society, while attempts to inculcate Western-style individual rights and the respect for the rule of law proved even less sturdy, withering under calls for a totalitarian state. All around them, the Japanese saw powerful dictators rewarded and the response of the pacifistic democracies ignored. Less than a month after Hitler repudiated the Versailles Treaty, mobs carried books of Japan's leading apologist for Western constitutions, Tatsu-kichi Minobe, to a public book burning on top of the Tokyo Military Club.[149] Minobe was derided as "theoretically a materialistic individualist and morally an anarchist."[150] A subsequent statement of "the Japanese mind" issued by the Ministry of Justice held that "there has been no conception of the individual as opposed to the state. . . ." Individuals, noted the ministry, "participate in the highest and greatest value when they serve the state. . . ."[151] In effect, Japanese individuals had become interchangeable parts serving the Japanese state. Neither Stalin nor Hitler could have wished for more.

Prince Chichibu, Emperor Hirohito's brother, had urged him to move toward direct rule—in line with the officers' desire to return to a military shogunate—and many historians pinpoint this movement, called the "Showa Restoration," as the moment their ideas for a radical syndicate-like state coalesced. Unlike the old shogunate, organized around individual warlords, the new Japanese shogunate would place power in the hands of institutions such as the army and navy, with the emperor's role greatly reduced. These sentiments came to a head in the February 26, 1936, incident in which more than 1,400 Imperial Japanese troops killed several leading politicians and occupied the center of Tokyo in the name of purging corruption from political life. They succeeded in killing the finance minister, the inspector-general of military education, and the lord keeper of the privy seal, and by mistake killed the prime minister's brother instead of the prime minister himself. Surrounded by the regular (loyal) army, many of the ringleaders committed suicide; the rest were arrested and nearly two dozen sentenced to death. Several others received indefinite prison sentences.[152] The court trying the assassins saw letters of civilian support for the defendants pour in—many signed in blood—"the Gallup poll of public opinion in Japan," as the contemporary British editor Hugh Byas observed.[153] Byas, who attended the trial, noted that one of the defendants, Lieutenant Colonel Sabura Aizawa, opened his defense with a declaration that most Japanese believed: "The Emperor is the incarnation of the great god who made the universe. The Emperor is absolute . . . ."[154]

In the Bushido system, soldiers' obedience was regularly tied to death for the emperor. In 1941, an army private, Taro Tanaka, published an article explaining what was expected of those who put on a uniform. "No longer is [the soldier's] ego his own; it is the Emperor's." The ideal death, he wrote, was to turn one's face toward the Imperial Palace and shout "Long live the Emperor!"[155] But Japanese citizens were also trained to routinely submit themselves to the state. A July 1941 handbook for imperial subjects denounced "individualism, liberalism, utilitarianism, and imperialism," having just a few years earlier declared the emperor a "deity incarnate."[156] Yet the "deity incarnate" had no inclination to get measured for a coffin like so many of his prime ministers, and allowed himself to be substantially marginalized in matters of policy.

Whether any of this emperor worship or submission to an authoritarian, top-down political structure could have been prevented by better diplomatic efforts on the part of Britain or the United States remains a matter of highest speculation. Paul Johnson's contention that Britain's interests aligned with Japan's, and therefore Britain had an incentive to encourage "constitutional propriety and the rule of law," runs shallow.[157] Britain only had an interest in its Far Eastern colonies, not in adopting Japan as an Asian foster child. Instead of viewing itself as one of many important and rising second-tier powers (as illustrated in the Washington Conference and the Nine Power Treaty), Japan typically took offense, especially at America, which alone had resisted some of the colonial land grabs by Europeans in China. Then there was the immigration issue, where both the United States and Australia enacted new restrictions on Japanese immigration in the early 1920s. Like a child unable to retaliate against his parents, the Japanese lashed out against the dog, in this case, the colossal, lumbering, and incapable giant, China. Many Japanese saw China as theirs by divine right: banker Hirozo Mori wrote, "Expansion towards the continent is the destiny of the Japanese people, decreed by Heaven . . . ."[158] A more modern authority on Japan, Kurt Singer, explained that Imperial Japan sensed the weakness of the Chinese giant. The Japanese, he noted, seemed to "smell [the] decay . . . they can smell decomposition . . . ."[159]

As war clouds in the Pacific gathered, access to raw materials took on greater urgency. A survey by the New York Trust Company in 1940 found that nine of the fourteen strategic raw materials consumed by the United States existed in large volume only in southeast Asia.[160] As early as 1937, U.S. secretary of state Cordell Hull informed rubber industry leaders that they needed to start building up their inventories due to a possible war with Japan, and the following year, Senator David Walsh of Massachusetts warned that even to keep trade routes open required raw materials to build battleships. "So," he concluded, "in very many respects we are in exactly the same situation as Great Britain."[161] The same could be said for Germany, of course, and was. Economic analyst Eliot Janeway wrote in 1939, "it is on the economic front that Japan's drive threatens us most dangerously: the American economy, and with it American defense, cannot be operated without rubber and tin, which at present cannot be obtained in adequate quantity except from British and Dutch colonies in southeastern Asia."[162] The following year, America's chief Far Eastern expert in the State Department, Stanley Hornbeck, said, "the United States finds itself so vitally and overwhelmingly dependent on Southeastern Asia that our entire foreign policy must be adjusted to that fact. . . ."[163] Even after a concerted attempt at stockpiling, American reserves of tin in December 1941 were adequate for only thirteen months' worth of consumption.[164] But the Dutch oil in the East Indies lay as a glittering black solution to Japan's needs.

## The Samurai and the Dragon

Japan had begun its aggression in China with the Mukden Incident (September 1931–February 1932), then attacked the Great Wall region in 1933. A major invasion, sparking the Second Sino-Japanese War, was triggered by the clash at the Marco Polo Bridge between Japanese troops and Chinese forces on July 7–8, 1937. An unrelenting march south ensued, constituting a continuation of Japanese aggression that the world had refused to confront in Manchuria or even in the League of Nations. Japan then moved rapidly to consolidate her position in Southeast Asia with daring new demands on the Vichy French government (after the fall of France) for military bases in Indochina, particularly the naval base at Cam Ranh Bay. That alone posed a threat to Indonesia and to American supplies of tin, rubber, and other materials. More to the point, American policy makers, including

Hull, feared that Indochina was a precursor to further southern moves, especially after an intercepted dispatch from Japan stated flatly, "After the occupation of French Indochina, next on our schedule is the sending of an ultimatum to the Netherlands Indies. In the seizing of Singapore the Navy will play the principal part. . . . [W]e will once and for all crush Anglo-American military power and the ability to assist in any schemes against us."[165] These attitudes, in fact, were common throughout the Japanese military. Chief of staff from 1923 to 1926 and later vice-minister of war General Shinji Hata, like many Japanese officers, had studied in Germany. He viewed the United States as the inevitable enemy: "America will always obstruct Japan . . . Against what power America's armaments are directed is only too plain."[166]

An already-convinced Roosevelt did not need Hata's words to realize the Empire of Japan had no intentions of stopping short of Indonesian oil fields—and perhaps not even then. He froze all Japanese assets in the United States and all trade licenses with Japan on July 25, 1941, effectively shutting off the oil spigots, and the British Commonwealth followed suit. This move did not end all oil shipments to Japan, however. Exports could still be approved on an ad hoc basis by the State and Treasury departments, and American oil companies continued to deliver prepaid shipments for several months. But the writing was on the wall. While it certainly *could* have—as postwar Japanese apologists insisted—"pushed Japan to war," the fact is that it certainly didn't have to. Quite the opposite; a reasonable, truly liberal and democratic government would have stepped back, reined in the warlords, purged the militarists, and regained control of its country. But Japan was not democratic. It was totalitarian, and chose to do none of those things. The "we caused it" mentality, typical of many post-9/11 Westerners, simply ignores the reality that the "other side" has choices—*moral* choices—and continually decided against doing the right thing, even when confronted with a war it could not win. Indeed, Roosevelt had to explain to Americans why he curtailed domestic consumption while continuing to ship oil to the Japanese, noting that it was done in the hope of dissuading Japan from its continued aggression toward Indonesia. Put another way, when Japan moved into Indochina, it signaled to the Roosevelt administration the failure of America's appeasement policy.

The exact timing of Roosevelt's move is thought by many historians to reflect FDR's concern that the Soviet Union, which had been invaded by Germany only three days earlier, would collapse under the Nazi onslaught and leave Britain and the United States to face Germany and possibly Japan alone. Lend-Lease had started only three months earlier, conscription only nine months earlier, and the United States was woefully unprepared for war. Even so, there was no time to waste—the United States needed to get into the war sooner rather than later. World War I had shown that it took the nation over a year to mobilize, and FDR needed to get the American public on board. China, Russia, and Britain needed help to defend themselves, and the only way to invigorate the country into becoming prepared was to ratchet up war fever. Rather quickly, FDR began to maneuver the American public into war.

One card remained in play to slow down Japan—China. Roosevelt held out hope that China might siphon off so many men and so much fuel that little would remain for the East Indies or Malaya adventures. The MAGIC code-breaking intercepts revealed this to be another failed hope. From July to December 1941, Japan's inactivity masked a consolidation of troops in Indochina and preparations for war against the United States. The Japanese deflected Hull's objections to their presence in Indochina as necessitated by food demands and rice supplies. Japanese diplomats staged an effective choreography of delay, pointing to the need to reconcile the "China Incident" (as they termed it) before they could remove troops from Indochina. Generalissimo Chiang Kai-shek, leader of the Chinese Kuomintang Army, realized his leverage in such a situation. Cleverly using his lobbyists in Washington to obtain ever-increasing levels of aid, he steadfastly refused any demands that he liberalize or moderate his policies. It would be a marriage repeated when the Kennedy administration hitched its star to South Vietnam's Ngo Dinh Diem in 1961, with the "bride" too vital to lose and too powerful to control. Whether Hull and Roosevelt "kept Japan talking" while rearming the United States, or whether FDR had in fact followed systematic appeasement, even if in line with American public opinion—neither policy worked. U.S. preparations needed until the spring of 1942 to reach a reasonable level of military efficiency, but the speed of the German drive into Russia and the fear that Moscow was about to fall called for the earliest possible entry into the war. In November Secretary Hull took a hard line in his negotiations with Japan (surprising the Japanese), and the fat was in the fire.

On December 7, 1941, America was scarcely better prepared for war than it had been in July, particularly in the Philippines, where most analysts thought the brunt of the Japanese offensive would come. Reinforcements had only included the 4th Marine Regiment of 750 men which was removed from China, the 200th Coast Artillery Regiment of 1,700 men, and a pair of tank battalions, with a total of 108 tanks and 838 men, and an ordnance company. The token air force in the Philippines in July was strengthened with 81 fighters and 35 bombers, but by December 8, only 54 of the fighters were operational. A bombardment group's ground crew and aviators had arrived, but their planes hadn't. The total American force in the Philippines at the start of the war was close to 20,000, the majority of which were service troops—an anemic force to defend the whole of the Philippines.[167]

Japanese ambassador Kichisaburo Nomura's peace offensive of November to Hull reinforced this false dichotomy, insisting that "a cessation of aid to CHIANG . . . is a most essential condition" for further negotiations.[168] Nomura had merely followed the successful negotiating ploys of his counterpart in Germany, Joachim von Ribbentrop: stall and delay official action until the desired result is achieved.[169] Nomura continued to emphasize China, the United States, and Southeast Asia. By late November 1941, Roosevelt had a modus vivendi based on four points—partial renewal of U.S. economic relations with Japan, a cessation of all new Japanese troop deployments in southeast Asia, a promise by Japan not to honor the Tripartite Pact if the United States entered the war in Europe, and the United States' providing a mediator between Japan and China. A further stipulation promised an end to the embargo on the condition of full Japanese withdrawal from Indochina. Naturally, the Chinese expressed concerns.

Shortly after Roosevelt originated the modus vivendi, he was informed of new Japanese troop movements southward from Shanghai, and also that Moscow was expected to fall. Time had run out, and the United States would have to go to war with what it had. Instead of delivering the softer modus vivendi, on November 26 Hull handed Nomura a tougher ten-point plan developed by the State Department. (Later, he admitted he knew this would be rejected, and introduced it only for the historical record.)[170] All that remained was to determine where Japan would strike, and all indicators were in the south and southeast, toward the Dutch. Thus the Japanese fleet, known to be at large, was widely considered to be on its way to Thailand or Singapore. It is important to note, in light of later "Roosevelt knew" charges, that analysts thought this fleet, dispatched from Shanghai, was already on its way south-to-southeast and that the other Japanese fleet was in harbor in Japan. Roosevelt then took a most controversial step of personally ordering Admiral Harold Stark to deploy small vessels to form a "defensive information patrol" around the Philippines and off the Indochina coast. Stark knew immediately that stationing such small ships in harm's way to perform a task that aircraft could do routinely had only one purpose, to provoke an incident that Roosevelt could take to the Congress for a declaration of war.[171] One ship, the *Lanikai*, actually set sail but was recalled.

Between the absence of long-range reconnaissance in Hawaii in the summer of 1941 and General Walter Short's reversal of the alert codes (moving 3 as the highest level to lowest, and vice versa—and *not* informing Washington), Pearl Harbor was even more of a sitting duck than the one the Japanese expected to find on December 7, 1941. Japan's sneak attack turned what would have been a debilitating strike into a full-blown, humiliating, bloody disaster, but one that would rouse the American colossus from its slumber.

The bombs that fell on Pearl Harbor on December 7 ended the hope among many Americans that the United States, somehow, could avoid the world conflagration. Hitler's declaration of war on the United States on December 11 extinguished the last embers of optimism that America could contain its fight to Asia. That a rearmed and more powerful U.S. military would have affected many calculations made from 1932 to 1941 by the Axis seems unlikely given the widespread isolationist sentiment in the United States. But it is certain that a better-prepared America would have shortened the war. In one of the ironies of history, for all his strengths, Calvin Coolidge had allowed the Japanese war machine to gain its footing while at the same time permitting the American military to atrophy; and for all his egregious faults, Franklin Roosevelt would over the next four years work tirelessly to rein in the Japanese and rebuild the U.S. armed forces.

# CHAPTER FIVE

# The Hounds Unleashed

## Time Line

1940: Russia annexes part of Finland; Katyn Massacre in Russia of Polish POWs; German occupation of Denmark, invasion of Norway, conquest of Holland, Belgium, and France; Vichy government established; Dunkirk evacuation; USSR occupies Latvia, Lithuania, and Estonia; Battle of Britain; Italy attacks Greece; Britain and Italy clash in North Africa; American rearmament begins; United States initiates draft; Destroyers-for-bases deal between United States and Great Britain; Roosevelt gives "Arsenal of Democracy" speech; Japan occupies part of Indochina

1941: Lend-Lease begins; Erwin Rommel and Afrika Korps go to North Africa; Germany attacks Yugoslavia, Greece, Crete; Germany attacks Russia; Rommel defeats British in North Africa, besieges Tobruk; Battle of Moscow; Japan attacks Pearl Harbor, Philippines, Southeast Asia

1942: Japan conquers Philippines, Singapore, Indonesia, and Burma, and occupies Thailand; Doolittle Raid; Battle of Midway; Battle of Guadalcanal; Battle of Stalingrad; Battle of El Alamein; Operation Torch (Allied invasion of North Africa); Germany occupies remainder of France

1943:    Americans advance in Solomon Islands, New Guinea;
         North Africa falls to United States, Britain; Battle of
         Kursk; Allied victory in Sicily; Italy invaded; Tarawa in-
         vaded

Has any conflict in history so severely reoriented all of the civilizations on the planet as the Second World War? Not only did many consider it unfathomable that a war of such epic proportions could follow just twenty years after another devastating conflict had torn the world asunder, but the reasons why this happened are still pondered by historians. Nonetheless, many of the outcomes of World War II are irrefutable and their effects last to this day. Fascism in the Hitlerian model as an ideology was permanently crushed; Japan as an expansionist military power was vanquished; Britain and France lost massive imperial holdings; untold numbers of African, Asian, and Middle Eastern states were born into chaos and bloodshed; and in the end only the United States and the USSR remained standing as genuine superpowers.

Yet it is the First World War that history labels "the Great War," while (to Americans at least) World War II was "the Good War." These descriptors in part reflect the fact that, however noble its causes, the Second World War left Europe in second-tier status. Much of its power loss emanated from the separation of the world into two armed camps headed by superpowers, the United States and the Soviet Union, and Europe's impending loss of its empires as a result of wartime destabilization and liberation. This hardly explains Europe's characterization of the conflict. For Americans, who saw themselves as "rescuing" both Europe and Asia (or, at least, parts of it) from tyranny, the fight had brought out the finest in American ideals. Europeans, on the other hand, emerged from the war with well-deserved guilty consciences: the Germans for allowing the Nazis to seize power; the French for their dismal military performance followed by the Vichy regime's cowardly subservience to Hitler; and the British for their consistently bad assessments of military capabilities of friend and foe alike. Piled on top of the guilt was the gnawing reality that Britain and Continental Europe owed their survival to either the crude Americans (with their money and manpower) or the brutal Soviets and their unrelenting, high-cost offensives. Although the British Empire could point to a handful of successes in North Africa (Medenine, El Alamein) and India (Imphal), the bulk of the war effort after 1942 was carried by Yanks and Reds.

## Expansion and Extermination

Japan's incursion into China and Germany's march eastward were both driven by a near-psychotic fear of running out of raw materials, most notably oil, in the run-up to war. Illustrating this perceived urgency, a 1939 telegram from the German Foreign Office to its Yugoslavian minister begged for new supplies with the words "Copper is a life and death matter. . . . A life and death matter!" but the phrase could have applied to oil, iron, or any of a dozen other raw materials.[1] As early as 1935, Hjalmar Schacht, president of the Reichsbank and German economic minister, insisted, "Germany must have access to more raw materials and have it soon. . . . Nothing can stop [the deterioration of Germany's standard of living] except much freer world trade, especially the acquisition by Germany of foodstuffs and raw materials."[2] Of course, Schacht did not mean free trade—in which Germany would have been the loser—but a managed trade in which Britain, France, and the United States would permit Germany to acquire more colonies. In the mid-1930s, Hitler had extracted favorable trade terms with Franco's Spain, at one point even acquiring the lion's share of Spanish iron ore, but, unable to provide credit, Germany lost that advantage to the British in 1939.

Thanks again to Smoot-Hawley, Germany and other exporting nations like England saw access to American markets shut during the 1930s. Only through "harsh and discriminatory curtailment" of American imports could Germany pry open the U.S. market again, but this strategy risked much greater retribution by America.

Meanwhile, on the other side of the world, trade had drawn the United States ever closer to Japan and China. In the 1920s, American trade in China was about $22 million, eclipsing Sino-Japanese trade, while Asian markets accounted for over half of the raw materials imported into the United States. Britain compensated for losses incurred thanks to Smoot-Hawley by increasing imports from her empire, while France likewise extracted trade from her colonies. But Germany possessed no such alternative. She could bully the Balkan states, but only after achieving a position of military superiority. Both America and Britain were hurt in trade on the Continent as the doors closed, but Germany and Japan were hurt far worse by their inability to trade with these giant economic blocs.

Increasingly, Hitler's obsession with raw materials and *Lebensraum* marched Germany toward war. "The final solution," he argued, "lies in the expansion of living space with respect to the raw material and food supply of our people."[3] This dovetailed perfectly with the position—accepted across almost all strata of German society, not just among the Nazis—that Poland's existence was illegitimate and unacceptable. Poland had not existed for 124 years, from 1795 to 1919, when it was carved out at Versailles from German and Russian territory. As early as 1922, General Hans von Seeckt, who had concealed the banned German General Staff under a new organization called the Truppenamt ("troop office"), was a radical anti-Pole. Seeckt worked without the knowledge of the Weimar government to negotiate with the Soviets to partition Poland in the future.[4] As head of the army, he saw Poland as the linchpin of the Versailles agreement and as "France's advance post of power."[5] "Poland's existence," he insisted, "is intolerable, and incompatible with Germany's vital interests."[6] Nine years later, he repeated the sentiment, saying "Poland should be regarded as a principal and unconditional enemy."[7] Count Ulrich von Brockdorff-Rantzau, later the ambassador to Moscow, echoed Seeckt's comments: "Poland has to be finished off." Germany had attempted economically to do just that. From 1924 to 1930, Polish exports to Germany declined from 34.5 percent to 27 percent, but the Poles proved resilient and adapted their trade policies. Poland, like Germany, suffered from shortages of raw materials and began to look hungrily at the coal-producing state of German Silesia as a potential zone of annexation. Any thoughts of expansion, however, were hampered by Poland's unsecurable borders, particularly with respect to their corridor through German territory to the Baltic Sea. The Locarno Pact (1925), which guaranteed French borders, said nothing about Poland's borders, becoming a source of anxiety for the new Polish government and a window of opportunity for Germany.

Within hours after the August 31, 1939, Gleiwitz incident—a phony attack staged by Germans posing as Poles on a German radio station at Gleiwitz, Upper Silesia—Hitler launched *Fall Weiss* ("Plan White"), the invasion of Poland. Wehrmacht forces crashed in on the north, south, and west of Poland. According to Allied defense plans, Poland should have been able to defend itself for two to three months, and the Poles estimated they could hold out at least twice that long. But that was against one enemy. As the Poles retreated to more defensible positions, expecting support from Britain and France (and indeed both declared war on Germany on September 3), they were smashed from the east by the Red Army on September 17. Britain and France did not declare war on Russia, and Polish forces were quickly crushed between two superior armies. On the first day of fighting, the Luftwaffe destroyed most of the Polish air force on the ground, and drove the remainder from the skies. Only 98 Polish planes survived and fled to friendly Romania. Polish mounted infantry proved no match for the panzers (tanks, which at the time were small and lightly gunned—but still superior to infantry without heavy weapons). By September 13, the Germans had eliminated most resistance in the west, and two weeks later Soviet armies mopped up the remaining eastern forces. On September 28, the Polish government collapsed (though it never officially surrendered), and administration of the former Second Polish Republic was divided up between the USSR and Nazi Germany. Throughout it all, the British and French, in what was deemed the "Phony War," offered little assistance to Poland. Instead, they hunkered down to wait for the invasion of France they expected to come next.

## Myths of the Nazi War Machine

In retrospect—especially after the fall of France in 1940—the German blitzkrieg took on an aura of inevitability that in fact was not warranted. Hitler had ramped up his arms program dramatically in the late 1930s, but it still had fallen far short of what was necessary to carry on aggressive warfare. Once the initial stimulus of employment through conscription washed through, the Nazi economic "miracle" stalled. Production fell short of the demands of all military branches, even the vaunted Luftwaffe. Only thirty U-boats, including coastal units, were operational and on station when war broke out in September 1939, dropping to twenty-two in February 1941. The rate of delivery of new boats during the first half of 1940 was only two per month, increasing only to six per month during the second half.[8] War arrived far too quickly for the German Navy, or Kriegsmarine, and the "Z" naval expansion plan of 1939, calling for ten battleships, four aircraft carriers, and effective striking abilities in the Atlantic Ocean by 1946, was scrapped the instant the shooting started.

The Luftwaffe was little better off, in spite of Herman Göring's holding the position of "minister without portfolio" since 1933. As such, Göring headed both the Luftwaffe and, after 1936, directed the Four-Year Plan, allowing him to give special consideration to his air force's matériel needs. Yet at the time of the remilitarization of the Rhineland in March 1936, not a single German fighter plane was truly operational—some planes had no ammunition and those that did lacked synchronization gears to fire through propellers.[9] Bad luck followed the Luftwaffe; General Walther Wever, Germany's main proponent of strategic bombers and the man responsible for the Luftwaffe's rapid buildup under Göring, was killed in an airplane crash in 1936. His successor Ernst Udet, the highest-scoring ace to survive World War I, hated paperwork, and as chief of the Technical Office, began sixteen aircraft production programs, all of which failed. Greatly depressed and holding himself responsible for the Luftwaffe's lack of development, he committed suicide in 1941. After the fall of France, the Luftwaffe was dropped to fifth in the priority list in armament planning, and would decline steadily as a functional force in comparison to the Allies.

Shortages took their toll across service lines. Production of machine guns was curtailed in 1939, as was production of tanks. The Luftwaffe saw its aircraft goals cut by over two thousand in 1940. At various times, German industry suffered from severe shortages in steel and nonferrous metals (particularly copper); production of all mortar shells stopped in the spring of 1939; and output of heavy artillery was cut almost in half, to 460 guns per year. Even Hitler's pet ammunition production project had fallen woefully short of its quotas to the point that the General Staff calculated that the army's ammunition was sufficient for only two weeks' worth of fighting. Many of the deficiencies arose because the eternal meddler, Hitler, kept changing priorities to pet projects. The ammunition crisis of World War I was seared in the memory of the former infantry corporal, and he increasingly micromanaged production planning. One month after the invasion of Poland, Hitler's *Führerforderung* (Leader's Challenge) gave priority to ammunition, raising production of some types of howitzer shells eightfold, and most ammunition production was to be increased by an average of 500 percent.[10] Such reallocations came at the expense of other weapons programs, including tank development. Many higher-ranking German officers privately referred to the army as a *Schaufensterarmee* (store window or display army), one that looked good from the outside, but lacked substance. Critical equipment was in short supply—machine guns, artillery, transport, tanks, proper clothing—everything needed to keep a modern army in the field. The German economy was simply not large enough to outfit an army going from 150,000 men with no heavy equipment to two million completely mechanized troops in five years.

All these problems could have been solved with time, but Hitler did not give his military that precious commodity. It didn't help that Germans tended to be engineering perfectionists. For example, many parts for a Tiger I tank developed in 1942 could not be used on a Tiger II produced two years later. As a result of excellent engineering, the German Panther and Tiger tanks were the best in the world for their time, far superior to the American Shermans and in armor and firepower the equivalent or superior of the Russian T-34. The problem was, the Americans built 60,000 Shermans, the Soviets 40,000 T-34s (and later, fielded the new IS-2, specifically designed to defeat German Tigers and Panthers), while the Germans produced only 6,132 Panthers and 1,840 Tigers.

Two viselike realities ensnared Hitler as he prepared for war, both of his own making. Each new burst of armaments further solidified western opposition against him, thereby further confirming in his mind that Germany needed to rearm. German freedom—German *survival*—demanded that he arm his military to the hilt, yet it was increasingly clear that the Reich could not outproduce even Britain and France, let alone the United States. Just prior to the Battle of Britain, in June 1940, the United States agreed to deliver 10,800 aircraft over the next year and a half, complementing Britain's existing fleet of 15,000, in contrast to total 1940 German production of 7,829 aircraft.[11] Between 1940 and the end of 1941, America shipped more than 7,000 aircraft to Britain while ramping up to an astounding production total of almost 85,000 airplanes by 1943. Indeed, the United States had mobilized its air industry immediately after the fall of France, not after Pearl Harbor, providing the foundations for the Allies' winged victory.

## The American Shadow

Temporarily forgotten in the conquest of Europe was Hitler's long-range concern about a war with the United States. The notion that the United States would have avoided the war in Europe if not for some nefarious scheme by FDR to manipulate Japan into attacking and drawing America in via the "back door to war" completely ignores the entire dynamic of why Hitler engaged in the moves he did. Since 1928, his writing was quietly obsessive about American power. In his "Second Book," Hitler warned that the reason "the American Union is able to rise to such a threatening height is not based on [its millions of people] but on the fact that [it possessed millions of] square kilometers of the most fertile and richest soil . . . inhabited by [millions of] people of the highest racial quality."[12] Despite his misreading of the racial component of the United States, he swerved into a telling truth, that the "individual quality of these people [gives them] a cohesive, inclusive commitment to fight the struggle for survival."[13] Indeed, the "significance of the *menacing American hegemonic position* appears to be determined primarily by the quality of the American people," he observed (emphasis ours).[14] He fumed that "whatever the Germans in North America achieve specifically, it will not be credited to the German people, but is forfeited to the body of culture of the American union." Germans abroad, he claimed, were "only the cultural fertilizer for other peoples."[15]

Hitler's early views of the United States were in large part shaped by German writer Karl May's stories of the American frontier and Indians; his limited reading on American immigration history; the conspicuous numbers of American-made autos in the Weimar Republic; and finally, the 1940 American movie *The Grapes of Wrath*.[16] He watched the film many times and "assumed that it represented the whole United States for all time."[17] Hitler himself never visited the United States, and rarely talked to anyone who had. In any event, he remained torn between the notion that the United States had risen to its position of international power due to Nordic influences on the one hand, and on the other that its "mongrelization" through immigration and black slavery had made it corrupt and weak. The latter view was apparent in his comments about the American Civil War. He observed, "the Southern States were conquered against all historical logic," and when "the principle of slavery and inequality were destroyed in the war, [it also destroyed] the embryo of a future truly great America."[18]

It was this image of a weakened United States that finally won out in Hitler's mind. After Pearl Harbor, he said, "I'll never believe that an American can fight like a hero," and added, "I don't see much future for the Americans." America "is a decayed country."[19] Once lashed to this mast, Hitler had to reverse his views of American industrial potential, which he had previously admired. Once war was declared, he thereupon considered U.S. economic power a figment of Franklin Roosevelt's imagination. His assessments were reinforced when Rommel easily defeated the American 2nd Corps at Kasserine Pass, Tunisia. Only later in the war, after he was delivered many stinging lessons by American forces, did Hitler occasionally return to his 1928 views of American productive might.

Taken in this light, Germany's entanglement in Russia was entirely predicated on the premise that Germany was already confronting an Anglo-American alliance, and that Hitler was de facto at war with the United

States before Pearl Harbor. The sheer disparity in industry and resources alone meant that for Germany to succeed, Hitler had to capture the Russian oil fields as well as Romania's.

## The World by a Thread

After the fall of Poland, Britain and France did little to attack Germany, although they made plans to support Finland in its defense against the Soviet Union. By doing so, Britain and France could kill two birds with one stone—repel the Soviet invasion of Finland that started on November 30, 1939, and shut off the supply of raw materials from Sweden to Germany. Working leisurely, by late January of 1940 Britain had put together a plan for three simultaneous operations, one in northern Norway, another in southern Norway, and a third in southern Sweden. Britain would command a joint force of 100,000 British and 50,000 French and Polish troops, backed by the Royal Navy. The departure date was set for March 13,[20] but at the last moment, the Finns capitulated to the Soviets, and the plan was scrapped.

Meanwhile, Norway had come to Hitler's attention. There had been absolutely no German plans to invade Norway at the outbreak of war, but with obvious British activity to aid the Finns, Hitler convened a staff on February 5, 1940, to plan a way to secure the iron ore route that ran through the Norwegian port of Narvik. The operation was given the code name *Weserübung* (Weser [a river in northern Germany] practice). Then came the incident on February 14 involving the German tanker *Altmark*, which was carrying 300 British seamen who had been taken prisoner by the German pocket battleship *Graf Spee* in December 1939. The *Altmark* entered Norwegian waters, and the Norwegian government permitted it to proceed to Germany. In spite of Norwegian protests and protection of the *Altmark* by Norwegian torpedo boats, Royal Navy warships entered the fiord where the *Altmark* lay at anchor, sent a party aboard, and secured the British prisoners. Norway's unwillingness or inability to defend its sovereignty and neutrality against British intruders incensed Hitler. He demanded the Wehrmacht's planning for the invasion of Norway be accelerated.

Chief of Staff Alfred Jodl recommended General Nikolaus von Falkenhorst to command the effort. Hitler interviewed von Falkenhorst, telling him to take a couple of hours and come back with ideas on how to take Norway. Von Falkenhorst immediately went to a bookstore, purchased a Baedeker's travel book on the country (he had never been there), made some sketches, wrote down ideas, and returned to present them. Hitler approved von Falkenhorst's plans and ordered him to build a staff and make preparations immediately. Von Falkenhorst's scheme soon expanded to include both Norway and Denmark, both operations to occur simultaneously. Help and intelligence were obtained from Vidkun Quisling, a pro-Nazi Norwegian defense minister, and the invasion took place on April 9.

It was a high-risk operation, and the Norwegian part dangerously exposed the Kriegsmarine to destruction by the much more powerful Royal Navy. Germany's shipbuilding program, as we have seen, had already been squelched (except for U-boats) and the Kriegsmarine lacked aircraft carriers to provide air cover. Admiral Erich Raeder feared the loss of much of his surface fleet to the British (there was no Norwegian navy of any substance) and specified that German vessels had to return immediately to German ports as soon as all troops and supplies were disembarked. The Germans encountered a brief delay near Oslo when the *Blücher* was sunk, which provided enough time for the Norwegian government, including the king, parliament, and treasury, to escape to Britain, forming a government-in-exile. Ironically, the *Blücher*—Germany's newest heavy cruiser—was sunk by shells from 1905 Krupp guns located in a fort built during the Crimean War, and torpedoes manufactured by an Austrian firm at the turn of the century.[21]

Quisling took to the airwaves on April 9 to proclaim himself the new prime minister, and Norway soon surrendered, even though only 10,000 German troops were in the first wave (ultimately reinforced to about 25,000). Oslo was captured so effortlessly that a German military brass band led the Nazis into the city. Upon removal of the German heavy surface forces to safety, the Royal Navy cornered ten German destroyers in Narvik Fjord and sank them all, thereby reducing Germany's destroyer fleet by half. Two German light cruisers were sunk near Bergen and Kristiansand, and twenty-seven other vessels, including transports and supply ships, were lost through the middle of June. It was a catastrophe for the Kriegsmarine and one from which the surface fleet never recovered. The German Naval High Command commented in its war diary that *Weserübung* "broke all the rules in the book of naval warfare," but it was also the first time in history when an army, air force, and navy had operated intimately together with interlinked tasks and objectives (today called "combined arms").[22] Once again the German military had broken new ground, showing the rest of the world how to conduct military operations, but at a high cost. Quite possibly, however, it was all unnecessary. German general Walter Warlimont and others have maintained that even if the Allies had established themselves in Norway, the country could have been taken more easily after the fall of France given the proximity to Germany, the presence of Nazi traitors, and Britain's lack of long-range bomber power.[23] Once the invasion of France started, the point was moot: the Allies decided they needed to concentrate their forces in France, and more than 25,000 British, French, and Norwegian forces, along with King Haakon VII, were evacuated in late May. Including Denmark—which surrendered after two weeks in April 1940 at a loss to the Nazis of 16 soldiers—Hitler had bagged two more countries at a total cost of fewer than 4,000 men and about 100 aircraft and looked more unstoppable than ever.[24]

In addition to a steady supply of valuable iron for Germany, Norway also contained a minor prize, the Vemork hydroelectric plant, which could produce heavy water (deuterium oxide) as a by-product of fertilizer production. The deuterium was seen by German scientists as a key component of plutonium production for their nuclear energy program. Prior to the German invasion, the French removed all stocks of heavy water from the facility, but the Allies worried the Germans would produce more. From 1940 to 1944, a number of sabotage operations were mounted that included Norwegian resistance and Allied bombing, one raid finally putting the plant permanently out of commission. Subsequent research has shown that German scientists created far too little heavy water to start a nuclear reactor, but at the time, Allied intelligence had to presume the Nazis could develop such capabilities. (As late as 1944, Allied assassination teams still scoured France for Werner Heisenberg, originator of the Heisenberg Uncertainty Principle and head of the German atomic bomb effort, unaware that Hitler had scrapped all atomic bomb plans a year earlier.)[25]

## France's Epic Failure

Whether in Paris, London, or Washington, military and civilian leadership thought matters on the Western Front would unfold much as they had in 1914. But a great deal had changed in the interim, some of it ironic and even amusing. Tales of horrors in the Great War, for example, drove many men to search for "safer" areas of service in World War II—artillery, or logistics. One British unit still retained the name "Hussars," which fooled many recruits into thinking it was a horse cavalry regiment instead of the frontline combat force it had become.[26] Soldiers' fear of recreating the trench scene of 1915–18, while understandable, created its own self-fulfilling morale

problems under German attacks, most notably the shocking disintegration
of French ground forces. In truth, the western democracies proved totally
inept and irresolute: the Dutch surrendered in four days after 3,000 battle
deaths, the Belgians in seventeen after losing 6,000, the French after 80,000
died in only forty-three days, and British forces were chased from the continent in twenty-three days except for 136,000 troops trapped in northwestern France and evacuated from French harbors as shipping became available.
German military superiority was stunning beyond comprehension, proving
to many that the West was beyond recovery.

Upon reflection, France's total collapse was entirely predictable, and
not merely because the Maginot Line was a monument to military stupid-
ity. As ineffective as they sometimes were, tanks in World War I had proven
the obsolescence of fixed defenses, yet the Maginot Line—an unbroken
string of defenses stretching from Switzerland to Luxembourg, replete with
barbed wire, concrete pillboxes, long-range artillery, and underground
tunnels to rapidly move troops to threatened positions—was merely an updated version of the trench. French strategy assumed that it could thwart
any direct assault, and therefore would force the invaders to enter Belgium
as they had in 1914. France and Britain would then move three French
armies and the British Expeditionary Force (BEF) to the Dyle River and
other defensive positions, hoping to halt the expected German attack before it penetrated French territory. But just as the Belgians refused German
passage in 1914, now the Belgian government refused France entry into its
country to take up positions until after hostilities commenced. By putting
the Allies in a reactive mode from the outset, Belgian policy gave the Germans a decided advantage. In addition, France originally planned to build a
Maginot-type static defense line one hundred miles long in Belgium (which
never materialized), but rapid movement to that line would have to be attempted under wartime conditions with relatively little transport available.
This was not a plan for victory; it was an exercise in attrition like World
War I. Even then the disposition of troops, irrespective of the strategic
plan, was badly flawed. Holland had to defend itself with its eight divisions;
north of Dinant, the Allies would field Belgium's twelve fully equipped divisions of 204,000 men (plus ten divisions with minimal equipment), the
BEF's nine divisions (237,000 men), and twenty-six French divisions for one
hundred miles. Meanwhile, France retained sixty divisions (approximately
1.6 million men) at the Maginot Line. Unfortunately, this setup left a gap
of ninety-five miles in the Ardennes Forest, supposedly impenetrable for a

modern army, with only sixteen reserve divisions stationed there to defend the area.

It must be noted that the mobilized French Army in 1940 numbered 2,776,000 men, and her Army of the Interior, 2,224,000.[27] Although British, French, Dutch, and Belgian forces enjoyed a substantial numerical superiority in ground troops over the Germans on the eve of battle, they were dispersed, uncoordinated, and lacked joint training. The Germans placed fewer than 2.5 million men on the Western Front, while the Allied total was more than 3.5 million. The French even had more and better tanks than the Germans, including 405 medium Char-Bs, the best tank on the battlefield, but rendered relatively harmless through poor tactics.

While the Allies enjoyed superior forces in the field, the Germans possessed forward-looking military strategists and tacticians. Lieutenant General Erich von Manstein, chief of staff to General Gerd von Rundstedt, commander of Army Group A, which would bear the brunt of the fighting, had introduced a plan that departed radically from the old Schlieffen wheel, still the basic plan of the German High Command. Where Schlieffen pivoted south to pin French forces against German units on the border with his "swinging door," von Manstein, with support from panzer general Heinz Guderian, commander of the elite armored 19th Army Corps, devised a rapid stab through the Ardennes toward the English Channel to isolate the Allied northern armies. When two German officers fell into Belgian hands on January 10 carrying the First Air Fleet's Operation Order of *Fall Gelb* ("case yellow"), which contained details of an army-strength attack into Belgium west of Maastricht and airborne assaults between the Meuse and Sambre rivers on January 14, the Belgians opened their borders to French troops, and the French battle plan was exposed. Von Manstein himself was removed from his position, probably due to his opposition to the current version of *Fall Gelb*, and made commander of an infantry corps then forming in Silesia (thereby sent into obscurity). Politicking through Hitler's adjutant, Rudolf Schmundt, von Manstein obtained an audience with Hitler on February 17 where he was able to present his plan. Hitler was immediately persuaded, and, after following the plan, the Germans were able to cut off the British and French as they rushed pell-mell northeast into Belgium to meet the originally planned German attack. France was doomed.[28]

Major operations began on May 10, 1940, through the Netherlands, where a botched attempt to parachute forces into the Hague cost the Luftwaffe Transportgruppen almost 50 percent of their strength and half of the paratroopers involved in the operation. The bombing of Rotterdam occurred four days later, a tragedy of errors wherein attempts to cancel the German bombing of a Dutch force already negotiating its surrender resulted in bombing the city through an obscuring cloud of smoke and haze. More than eight hundred Dutch citizens died, the legend that no city was safe from German terror bombing was born, and the Dutch were finished.

At the same time, Germany established bridgeheads into Belgium behind unprecedented tactical bombing by the Luftwaffe and then, farther south, punched through the Ardennes against little resistance. The famed *Blitzkrieg* ("lightning war") did not come about by design. Quite the opposite, it was forced on the Germans as an "inspired, high-risk improvisation, a 'quick military fix' to the strategic dilemmas, which Hitler and the German military leadership had *failed* to resolve up to February 1940."[29] Germany could win only wars of fire and maneuver, not wars of attrition. In fact, throughout the assault on Belgium and France, panzer columns including 1,200 tanks and nearly 550 other armored vehicles stretched one hundred miles long and would have been astonishingly vulnerable to Allied air attacks had any been launched. Physical demands on the tankers and drivers were so great that thousands of doses of "tank chocolate," a variant of amphetamines, were handed out. Nor had weapons planning provided the Nazis with superior tanks. Quite the contrary, German panzers were lightly armed and the French had far more powerful tanks. Germany was, in fact, still relying heavily on *Americans* for her armor: as late as 1939, Adam Opel's company—taken over by General Motors in 1929—and Ford were Germany's largest producers of tanks, and, of course, German armor benefited greatly from the acquisition of several hundred Czech tanks.[30]

Two of the French army's weakest divisions were posted in the critical Sedan hinge, in the Ardennes where the Maginot Line was replaced by the Belgian border. The 71st Infantry had only two regular army officers, and while regular divisions fought bravely in spots, reservists were hopelessly outclassed by the Germans, especially once panzers smashed holes in the French lines. Methodical trench-warfare tactics were of little use in a moving battle of improvisation and chaos for which the French were entirely unprepared. Armored units bypassed numerous pillboxes, panicking French units who heard rumors that Germans were already behind them. However, the popular image of Germans always advancing behind armored spearheads is incorrect. Breaching the Meuse at Sedan, for example, required German infantry to cross the river in rubber rafts, taking the high ground beyond so *pioneers* (engineers) could build bridges for armor. In those cases, superior German leadership and cohesiveness at the small-unit level carried the day.

French officers were no better than their men in adapting to the fast-moving fog of war. General Erwin Rommel's 7th Panzer Division, which breached the defenses of the French 9th Army at Dinant in twenty-four hours, captured 10,000 French in two days and was struck by how quickly they capitulated. In one case, hundreds of French officers marched to detention for miles without a guard. A German reporter asked how it was possible that "these French soldiers, with their officers, so completely downcast, so completely demoralized, would allow themselves to go more or less voluntarily into imprisonment."[31] Even some of the colonial troops, particularly the Moroccans, held out longer than veteran French units.

Guderian, meanwhile, had turned his panzer divisions northwest in an advance toward the English Channel at Abbeville on the Somme. With their tanks possessing superior radio communication, the Germans—with their smaller guns and lighter armor—were faster and more nimble. At one point Rommel charged through the French 5th Motorized Division, which had lined its tanks up in an overnight bivouac right in his path. Only three of the French tanks escaped. All this should have added up to an astounding victory, and it did, but the rapidity of the movements was unnerving to the Fuehrer. As was evident in Poland, Norway, and now in France, Hitler tended to lose his nerve in a crisis, this time raging that the advance was too fast, and, as General Franz Halder noted, he "keeps worrying about the south flank . . . and screams that we are on the way to ruin."[32] Hitler should have been more trusting (a trait invariably absent in dictators), for at the time Hitler's generals were still willing to use their own initiative under the long-established German command principle of subordinate independence, and they ignored his attempts to retard their advance.[33]

Even as Hitler stormed about the "ruin" that his generals might cause, French prime minister Paul Reynaud, a bantam little man with unceasing energy, telephoned the new British prime minister Winston Churchill, who had replaced Neville Chamberlain when the first German tanks rolled into Belgium. Reynaud somberly informed Churchill, "We have been defeated. We are beaten; we have lost the battle."[34] Cut off from the French interior and driven against the coast at Dunkirk, more than 338,000 men were evacuated on 861 ships to England from May 27 to June 4; the bulk of them British but also nearly 140,000 French, plus Poles, Belgians, and a few Dutch troops. One fourth of the vessels were sunk in the "miracle at Dunkirk," the largest and most successful military evacuation by sea in history. Churchill, however, glumly noted, "Wars are not won by great evacuations."

Top French officers soon issued searing indictments of their nation's troops, including General Maurice Gamelin, who complained, "The French soldier, yesterday's citizen, did not believe in the war. . . . Too many failures to do their duty in battle have occurred. . . . The rupture of our [force] dispositions has too often been the result of an every-man-for-himself attitude at key points."[35] Intended for the eyes of Édouard Daladier, France's minister for national defense, Gamelin's assessment arrived after Daladier had already been relieved of that position by Paul Reynaud. Gamelin himself was soon given the hook, only nine days after the German attack commenced. The embodiment of a senior officer corps desperate to dodge blame for the fiasco, Gamelin was sixty-seven years old, small and heavy-set, and famous for his bland imperturbability. His replacement, General Maxime Weygand, had never held a field command and was even older (seventy-three). After the surrender in June, France's generals blamed one another for the rout. Despite their failures as military leaders, however, the "defeated generals and untried admirals were . . . among the biggest political winners in 1940; they became members of France's new ruling class."[36]

Churchill flew to Paris on May 16, while the French government was already frantically burning its archives and preparing to evacuate. He met with Reynaud, Daladier, and Gamelin, all standing around a table as if it were a coffin, shrouded in utter dejection. They stared grimly at a map showing the Germans pouring through at Sedan. An optimistic Churchill asked, "Where is the strategic reserve?" and, again in French, "*Où est la masse de manoeuvre?*" General Gamelin turned, shrugged and said, "*Aucune*" ("There is none").[37] Undeterred, Churchill asked where and when Gamelin proposed to counterattack the bulge, only to have Gamelin soberly state, "Inferiority of numbers, inferiority of equipment, inferiority of method."[38] He was correct only on the last count, and might have added, "inferiority of leadership, inferiority of will."

When Churchill again visited France on June 11–12, his fourth visit since Hitler's invasion of Poland, he met first with Weygand, Reynaud, and others at the French General Headquarters. Weygand, reputed to be the illegitimate son of Empress Carlota of Mexico (the daughter of Belgian King Leopold) and General Alfred van der Smissen, was a monarchical Catholic possessed of an intense dislike of parliamentary governments. He asked Churchill to send all available air power from Britain, but the prime minister refused: he needed the Royal Air Force for the defense of England, he announced. Furthermore, Churchill told all present that Britain planned to fight on—alone, if necessary. The French simply didn't believe him.[39] World War I Marshal Henri Philippe Pétain, who would soon surrender and head what would become the Vichy government, "was mockingly incredulous" at Churchill's intention to go it alone. Paris would not even attempt to mount a resistance.[40] The best Churchill could do was secure a promise from Admiral Jean François Darlan that the Germans would never get the French Navy.

Churchill returned the following day to meet with French officials at Tours, where the government was then located. Reynaud asked that France be released from her obligation to fight on so French honor could be upheld. Churchill would not agree and stated, "At all events England would fight on. She had not and would not alter her resolve: no terms, no surrender . . . death or victory."[41] Reynaud, unmoved, said, "We cannot count on American help. There is no light at the end of the tunnel. . . . We have no choice."[42] Three days later, he resigned and went into hiding with his mistress; soon thereafter he plowed his car into a tree, killing his mistress and injuring himself. While recuperating before being arrested, Reynaud confided to the American ambassador, "I have lost my country, my honor and my love."

When Churchill returned to England, he delivered one of the most powerful and memorable speeches in history to the House of Commons on June 18:

> . . . the Battle of France is over. I expect that the Battle of Britain is about to begin. Upon this battle depends the survival of Christian civilisation. . . . The whole fury and might of the enemy must very soon be turned on us. Hitler knows that he will have to break us in this island or lose the war. If we can stand up to him, all Europe may be free and the life of the world will move forward into broad, sunlit uplands. But if we fail, then the whole world, including the United States . . . will sink into the abyss of a new Dark Age, made more sinister, and perhaps more protracted, by the lights of per-

verted science. Let us therefore brace ourselves to our duties, and so bear ourselves that, if the British Empire and its Commonwealth last for a thousand years, men will say, "This was their finest hour."[43]

A month and two days after the panzers rolled into Belgium, France declared Paris an open city. To defend it, as General Weygand later wrote, "would have condemned the city to irreparable loss of human lives and of national treasures."[44] On June 22, France signed the Second Armistice at Compiègne, in the same railroad car in which Germany had signed the 1918 armistice, and established German and Italian zones of occupation. The National Assembly voted on July 10 to give eighty-four-year-old Marshal Philippe Pétain the position of prime minister of the Third Republic and grant him extraordinary powers that allowed him to govern in line with German wishes. Pétain's collaborationist government, located at Vichy in the south of France, did something no other conquered or puppet government in all of Europe did—it voluntarily rounded up Jews and shipped them to Germany.

Hitler had everything he wanted: a neutralized French navy and complete control of France without the necessity of stationing additional troops in the South. But the British still held concerns that Darlan or the Vichy government would be unable to maintain the neutrality of French sea power, such as it was. Churchill ordered the Royal Navy to attack the French at Mers-el-Kebir, Algeria. The fleet there was put out of action on July 3 by British warplanes from the carrier *Ark Royal* and broadsides from the battleships *Valiant* and *Resolution* and battle cruiser *Hood*. Nearly 1,300 French seamen were killed on two older French battleships (one sunk, one run aground) and the newer battlewagon *Dunqerque* (beached). Eschewing halfway measures, the British bottled up another French battleship and four cruisers at Alexandria and damaged the battleship *Richelieu* at Dakar. Nonetheless, the French remained true to Darlan's promise and scuttled their remaining fleet at Toulon when the Germans occupied Vichy France in November 1942.

## Operation Sea Lion

From Wehrmacht records it would seem that Operation Sea Lion (the invasion of Great Britain) was never a serious effort, unless, of course, the island was made ready to fall through Luftwaffe attacks. Germany severely lacked landing ships capable of making the operation a reality, and was, in any case, more concerned with the Soviets. On July 13, 1940, Hitler decided to disband seventeen divisions and release the manpower back into his starving industrial base. But seventeen days later, he reversed his decision and ordered planning to begin for a campaign against the USSR.[45] Nevertheless, Hitler knew, if the Luftwaffe could prevail in Britain, the removal of British support of the USSR would aid his efforts in Russia. He therefore permitted the night campaign against England's armaments industry and urban centers to go forward, but with the proviso that it would be discontinued unless a complete success, and in any case, before losses in the campaign would affect the Luftwaffe's employment against the USSR.[46]

Churchill knew the Nazis wanted England defeated and occupied. To stave off an invasion, however, the British needed only a draw in the air battle. Their naval strength required Germany to have absolute air superiority, or crossing the Channel would be impossible. Nearly a century later, the "Battle of Britain" remains clouded in its specifics, such as when the first German attacks occurred. Bombs fell on July 31 in Cornwall, Devon, and elsewhere, but Britain adopted the arbitrary dates of July 10 to October 31 to define the conflict. What is less in dispute is the difficulty Germany had in winning. Both sides had approximately the same number of fighters available (1,032 for the British to 1,011 for the Germans; and each side had fewer trained pilots ready than planes); but England had vastly superior production. The Ministry of Aircraft Production under Lord Beaverbrook from June to October 1940 produced 5,185 fighters—almost double the German total during the entire year.[47] Thanks to better radar and the Ultra decryptions of the German Enigma machine, the Royal Air Force had infinitely better intelligence about Luftwaffe plans, and was able to intercept German bomber formations at precisely the right place and minimize their fuel consumption. Other factors also ensured Germany's defeat in the Battle of Britain, not the least of which was—again—poor prewar weapons planning that left the Luftwaffe with only twin-engined Ju-88 and He-111 bombers when they needed longer-range four-engine aircraft. (Probably the most disappointing airplane produced by the Germans and used in the skies over England was the Messerschmitt 110, a two-engine heavy fighter: its handling proved no match for the superior Supermarine Spitfire or even the less agile Hawker Hurricane, and the model was withdrawn after heavy losses.)

England not only won the Battle of Britain, but in the process elevated the stature of both Churchill, through his inspiring speeches, and the royal family, who braved the onslaught in the bomb shelters with everyone else.

Indeed, King George VI went on meat rations like an average London clerk, picked up a shovel and helped dig people out of the rubble, and personified leadership. At the end of the war, when public opinion polls found that virtually every institution in British life had seen its popularity fall, the monarchy had actually gained ground. But it was Winston Churchill, not King George, who became the face of British resistance to the world.

Churchill knew war personally. A former cavalry officer in the British Army, he had seen action in India against Pashtun tribesmen and later rode with the 21st Lancers at Omdurman. After these adventures, Churchill returned to England in 1899 to unsuccessfully run for office in the House of Commons.[48] When the Boer War broke out, he became a correspondent for the *Morning Post;* while part of a scouting expedition he was captured and imprisoned as a POW. Escaping from the Boer prison camp, Churchill traveled nearly three hundred miles to the Portuguese-held Lourenço Marques, then promptly joined General Redvers Buller's forces at the siege of Ladysmith. After these adventures Churchill returned to England, again running (this time successfully) for the House of Commons as a Conservative. In 1904 he crossed the aisle to sit as a member of the Liberal Party, where he campaigned for free trade. The following year, he was appointed under-secretary of state for the colonies, mainly focusing on South Africa. After several years in Parliament, he was named first lord of the Admiralty, where he was serving as war erupted in Europe in 1914.

At the Admiralty, Churchill backed the development of the tank (accounting for the tank's nautical terminology—hatches, decks, ports, and so on). Arguing for a landing at Gallipoli in 1915, Churchill displayed for the first time his obsession with the so-called "soft underbelly of Europe," and subsequently lost credibility and support when the invasion proved a bloody disaster. Resigning from his cabinet post under fire in 1915, he exercised his privilege as a reserve major in the Queen's Own Oxfordshire Hussars in November to go on active duty with his regiment in France, where he was soon promoted to lieutenant colonel and given a battalion in the 6th Royal Scots Fusiliers. After his battalion was combined with another due to heavy losses, he returned to Parliament in May 1916. Continuing to be tapped for important positions, he served as minister of munitions, secretary of state for war, and secretary of state for air. His next controversy came in 1918, when seeing the threat posed by a Communist Russia, he lobbied for landing British troops at Archangel to secure the delivery of supplies to the Whites, another venture that proved a failure.

Rejoining the Conservative Party, he became secretary of state for the colonies in 1921, and in 1924, he was appointed chancellor of the exchequer in the Stanley Baldwin government, which presided over a period of unemployment. When the Conservatives lost in the 1929 election, Churchill turned to writing and speaking, particularly on the topic of Indian independence. He thought Mahatma Gandhi a fraud, and expressed his willingness to allow Gandhi to starve himself to death if he so chose. Like many, he hoped Hitler might become a reasonable leader and bring Germany "to the forefront of the European family circle."[49] The degree to which he formed a consistent opposition to Hitler at an early date is questionable, but certainly he was among the first to appreciate the threat Nazi Germany posed, and for several years immediately before war broke out, rowed against the tide of appeasement and pacifism.

Portly, chomping his cigars in public and painting portraits in private, Churchill could agitate and irritate with the best of them.[50] Against the "heroic defender of the realm" persona that Churchill would, in part, help create through his own writings, several realities emerged to tarnish the portrait. He never saw any state except Germany as a threat, thus downplaying and even ignoring the rise of imperialistic Japan. Combined with his unwillingness to entertain independence for India, Churchill not only weakened the British position in the Far East, but made the American row tougher to hoe. As late as 1928 he favored the "ten-year rule" for British rearmament (then in its last year of implementation), voted and spoke against increasing defense expenditures until 1935, and proved all too willing to leap into bed with any government for a cabinet position, undermining the picture of a lonely British Paul Revere riding through the streets, shouting his alarms about the Nazis.

On the other side of the scales, he never hesitated in tying the Nazis' policies to the ultimate destruction of the Jews. More important perhaps, as a multiwar combat veteran he never shied away from advocating military force in an era of pacifism and international cowardice. As early as 1934, his speeches thundered on the floor of Commons, detailing ultimately accurate predictions of future air attacks on England, the "flying peril," as he called it. The following year, he abandoned all restraint in his attacks on the government, although the Hoare-Laval Pact (which turned parts of Abyssinia into an Italian zone), which discredited Stanley Baldwin and was repudiated, left Churchill divided. Britain, he said privately, was not strong enough to be "law-giver and the spokesman of the world."[51] "Smash[ing] up Italy," he thought, would "cost us dear," and probably drive Italy into Hitler's arms. When it came to the French standing strong during the Rhineland crisis, however, he had no compunction about criticizing French weakness as leading to more Nazi aggression.[52] It didn't hurt that Churchill was one of the best orators in England, and a convincing one, too. He was also a prolific writer, churning out more than 530,000 words of his four-volume *History of the English-Speaking Peoples* by the time Germany invaded Poland. This comprehensive history was not completed and published until 1956 due to delays encountered while Churchill assembled his later, more pressing project, a six-volume history of the Second World War.

Then there was Churchill's sense of political theater, something all great leaders have possessed. Following the Czech crisis, the House took up debate over the Munich agreement, where Churchill spoke on the third day of debate—when the entire House was present and the press in rapt attention. Churchill proved remarkably prescient, warning that the Czech state's future could be measured only in months, and indicted Britain for allowing the "whole equilibrium of Europe" to be turned upside down. What awaited England, he predicted, was "a bitter cup" unless "by a supreme recovery of moral health and martial vigor, we rise again and take our stand for freedom."[53]

Thus, by the time Chamberlain resigned in May 1940 after the invasion of France, and Lord Halifax turned down the king's offer to become prime minister, Winston Churchill stepped squarely onto the stage at the precise time when history had written the role which he had prepared for and aspired to his entire life. It unfurled like a flag with his May 13 "blood, toil, tears, and sweat" speech to Parliament as he became the new prime minister:

> You ask, what is our policy? I will say: It is to wage war, by sea, land and air, with all our might and with all the strength that God can give us; to wage war against a monstrous tyranny, never surpassed in the dark, lamentable catalogue of human crime. That is our policy. You ask, what is our aim? I can answer in one word: It is victory, victory at all costs, victory in spite of all terror, victory, however long and hard the road may be, for without victory, there is no survival.[54]

And he knew whatever followed, America must be secured as an ally or England could not survive, even after the defeat of the Luftwaffe in the skies over Britain.

## Securing the Grand Alliance

In the months immediately before and after the Battle of Britain, the Axis powers seemed to advance on every front. U-boats prowled the Atlantic, sinking thousands of tons of vital shipping. Italy besieged Malta, invaded British Somaliland, and pushed into Egypt in September 1940. At the end of that month, Japan, Italy, and Germany united in the Tripartite Pact, formally establishing the "Axis." The pact committed the participants to go to war with any country except the USSR that engaged in hostilities against any member of the alliance. As Britain's isolation and desperation increased, Roosevelt instructed Secretary of State Cordell Hull to agree to the fore-runner of Lend-Lease, called the "Destroyers for Bases" agreement, in which the United States acquired ninety-nine-year leases for nine naval or air bases in the Caribbean and Newfoundland in exchange for fifty "flush deck" destroyers. Britain immediately pressed those ships into service against U-boats, and in the short run it greatly helped Britain with her shipping problem. The following March, Congress passed Lend-Lease, which allowed the United States to ship $50 billion worth of supplies to England at no charge. If matériel was damaged, or ships sunk, the adminis-tration charged a fraction of what they were worth.[55]

These efforts to aid Great Britain masked myriad other ways in which the United States was already being drawn into the war. Roosevelt an-nounced a security zone in which the Americans would provide air and sea cover for British convoys across nearly half the Atlantic. Sinkings of indi-vidual American ships, such as the *Robin Moor*, a freighter sunk by a U-boat off the coast of Africa in May 1941 (after the crew and passengers were per-mitted to abandon ship), increased tensions and anti-German hostility. The sinking of the *Robin Moor* had relied in part on information from the infa-mous Duquesne spy ring, a coven of thirty-three German espionage agents with key jobs in the U.S. government. Eventually the ring was broken with the help of FBI double agent William Sebold, who had penetrated it over a sixteen-month period from 1940 to mid-1941; the FBI arrested the spies and all were convicted on charges of espionage. It remained the largest success-ful prosecution of spies in American history, and elevated FBI director J. Edgar Hoover to a powerful force in the federal government. What the FBI did not know—and indeed no one discovered until long after the war—was that the British had a "ring" of their own in the form of agents in major U.S. opinion polling organizations, such as Gallup. Those agents rigged polls to reflect stronger interventionist sentiments in the United States than actually existed.[56] But neither the Nazi provocations nor manipulations by MI5 could sway the overwhelmingly isolationist sentiment of the American public. Technically, the United States had to insist it was a neutral nation, even though FDR searched for new ways to support England.

Meanwhile, the United States rapidly built up its military might far beyond the quiet naval expansion Roosevelt had promoted since 1933 to meet Japanese threats in the Pacific. At that time the entire navy consisted of 372 ships, some 150,000 tons short of its treaty allowance, but the Vinson-Trammell Expansion Program of 1933 had authorized the addition of 1 aircraft carrier, 12 cruisers, 65 destroyers, 30 submarines, and 1,184 planes to be put into service by 1942. FDR obtained further authorization for 2 more carriers and 6 cruisers in 1936; in 1937 2 battleships were authorized; and in 1938 an additional 2 carriers, 2 battleships, 8 destroyers, 4 submarines, and nine auxiliary vessels were added, along with an increase in naval aviation to 3,000 planes.

But the real push for American military preparedness began in 1940 after the fall of France. In June, Congress voted twice to increase tonnages in literally all classes of ships. The acts provided for an increase in the Navy by 1,492,000 tons, and the total increase was planned as 7 battleships, 22 carriers, 35 cruisers, 115 destroyers, 50 submarines, 75,000 tons for auxiliary vessels, and a naval aviation strength of 4,500 planes. Clearly, the United States had grown concerned about its maritime strength. Its building program in aircraft carriers would give it a planned two-to-one advantage over the Imperial Japanese Navy in carriers by 1944 (although in reality from 1941 to 1945, America outbuilt the Japanese *seventeen-to-one* in major fleet carriers).

The U.S. Army, however, was a much different matter. In June of 1940, the American Army's authorized strength of 227,000 men was less than that of Romania.[57] Even worse, the Army was nowhere near its authorized strength and most tactical units existed largely on paper. The regular Army consisted of eight under-strength infantry divisions, one cavalry division, and one mechanized cavalry brigade.[58] In short, the fighting strength of the U.S. Army was smaller than that of the Dutch, who had held out only four days against the Germans. Although in theory this force was supplemented by eighteen untrained divisions of the National Guard, those units were poorly equipped with obsolete equipment. Many West Point graduates had left the service, but a hidden strength was present in that most serving officers knew one another's capabilities and were a tight, effective core. When it came time to promote officers into positions of high command, relatively few selections would prove totally unsuitable.

After the fall of France, the Army undertook a frantic expansion. Numbers increased through the Selective Training and Service Act (draft), passed in September, and 16 million men were classified. Roosevelt federalized the National Guard in September, and by July 1941, the Army's strength had been brought to over 1.2 million men on paper, many of whom, however, remained little more than uniformed untrained mobs. This force suffered in leadership and quality as many of the best potential draftees opted to volunteer for the Navy, Marines, or Army Air Corps. Additionally, many of the National Guard officers were overage or physically unfit, and in their untrained state, leaders had to be trained alongside their men. No one knew exactly how many men would be needed, or whether the United States would go it alone: General Albert Wedemeyer postulated an army of 215 divisions in the fall 1941 Victory Program, assuming the USSR would shortly capitulate and the United States and Britain would be isolated. When the USSR survived the winter of 1941, General George Marshall and Secretary of War Henry Stimson decided that 89 divisions would be sufficient, although Japanese capabilities did not figure significantly into their calculations. These numbers are significant, even astonishing, given that the Soviets would routinely hurl 200 divisions into offensives against the Nazis, but U.S. military leaders determined that firepower, not manpower, would provide the critical edge.

Although the German army had undergone a similar rapid expansion in 1937–39, it possessed cultural advantages the United States did not have. Membership in the Hitler Youth, mandatory since 1936, prepared boys for military service, and German army units were formed by locality to enhance unit cohesion. The United States adopted a policy of thoroughly mixing hometowns and states in units to lessen the effects on a locality if the unit suffered severely in battle—as had occurred so often in the Civil War—but this greatly reduced unit cohesion without extensive training. In fact, unit cohesion was largely ignored in U.S. planning, for as soon as trainees became proficient in their duties and required skills, the best men were siphoned off to form cadres for new units. Worse, the Army's Specialist Training Program (ASTP) allowed 150,000 of the brightest (or most well-connected) men to continue college after induction (Robert F. Kennedy was one).

In addition, the ultimate capping of the army's size at 89 large divisions handicapped the maintenance of morale and effectiveness in the field. Divisions could not be rotated out of battle for rebuilding and training with replacements as in the German system, and the American replacement system resulted in excessively high casualties and reduced unit cohesion. Replacements received less training than original unit members, and when immediately assigned to a unit in combat, frequently became casualties before they could reach any state of effectiveness—sometimes they died before fellow squad members even learned their names. What the 89-division cap did do was ensure that the massive American industrial capacity would outperform all other combatants by leaps and bounds because it kept so many men in the workforce. Nonetheless, America's huge industrial and military potential went almost unnoticed by European states facing a rampaging Nazi Germany.

Having already seized Poland, Denmark, Norway, Belgium, Holland, France (and her North African territory), and Albania, and forced Spain, Sweden, and Switzerland into neutrality, the Axis powers became the beneficiaries of a bandwagon effect. Other nations—Hungary, Slovakia, and Romania—seeing the writing on the wall, joined the Tripartite Pact. Just as the Luftwaffe engaged the RAF in the skies over England, Italy pushed into Greece, sensing an easy conquest. That was an error which infuriated Hitler, who viewed the Mediterranean as an uninteresting sideshow. Greece fought off Mussolini's troops, and the Italians were pushed back to their Albanian bases, holding on by the skin of their teeth. So far-reaching was this debacle that the official German history of World War II titled its chapter on this action "Mussolini's Surprise Attack on Greece and the Beginning of the End of Italy's Role as a Great Power."[59] British and Australian troops hurled the Italians back out of Egypt and East Africa, then went on the offensive against them in Libya. These efforts were substantially due to Churchill's decision—against the advice of his war cabinet and the military—to reinforce Egypt with nearly half of Britain's available tanks even though they required a journey around the Cape of Good Hope. In addition, a carrier-based air attack by the British against the Italian naval base at Taranto dealt heavy damage to the Italian fleet—a success the Japanese would study in preparation for their Pearl Harbor operation. At the Battle of Cape Matapan, off Greece, three Italian heavy cruisers were sunk and another battleship wrecked, forcing Italy's navy essentially out of the war.[60]

With no domestic raw materials, little martial ardor, and a tiny industrial base, Italy was more a liability than an asset to Hitler. He was forced to send forces to Libya in February 1941 to prevent Mussolini's total defeat and expulsion from North Africa, involving Germany in a debilitating and long, seesaw campaign in North Africa. He picked up Bulgaria as yet another ally in April, but not one that would provide troops or take an active part in his campaign against Russia. Meanwhile the situation in Albania deteriorated, and Mussolini begged him for another intervention to save his ally. With British advisers in Greece aiding the Greek army against Mussolini and British agents active in Yugoslavia, Hitler's southern flank was in disarray. On December 13, 1940 Hitler gave orders to plan Operation Marita (the invasion of Greece) to secure his southern flank and drive the British from the Balkans.

The necessity to clear the Balkans of unfriendly forces became urgent on March 27, 1941, when the Yugoslav government was overthrown in a coup, replacing a German-friendly regent Prince Paul with a hostile King Peter II and taking Yugoslavia out of the Tripartite Pact they had joined two days earlier. Hitler immediately ordered Yugoslavia to be conquered at the earliest possible date. Although some historians have held that Hitler's actions against Yugoslavia and Greece significantly delayed his timetable in Russia, thereby losing weeks of campaign time, others argue persuasively that Hitler's stage-wise postponement of his attack on the Soviet Union from May 16 to June 22 was primarily because of inclement weather.[61] In any case, Hitler attacked Yugoslavia and Greece on April 6, easily brushing aside Yugoslav defenders of their country and ending organized resistance in a week of fighting. Greece was more difficult with over 420,000 troops in the field, but they were no match for the heavy weapons, armor, and close-in fighter-bomber support of the Germans. Greece's only hope lay in the British forces that had been concentrating there since mid-March, numbering more than 62,000 veterans from the British Desert Army in Libya and including the British 1st Armored Brigade, a New Zealand division, an Australian division, and seven squadrons from the RAF. Superior combined arms assaults by the Germans carried even the best defensive positions, including Thermopylae, forcing the British Commonwealth forces to the Peloponnesus, then from Greece altogether. By April 29 it was all over, the Greek armies had surrendered, and the British were on their way to Crete or back to Egypt.

On May 20 the Germans assaulted Crete from the air, initially taking heavy casualties in their paratroop and glider forces. Nonetheless, the paratroopers hung on grimly, slowly clearing British positions singly and in small groups. The issue was in doubt until the second day, when the Germans began flying in reinforcements directly into Maleme airfield, which was not yet under full German control. In spite of horrendous casualties, they secured the airfield by nightfall, and a foothold on the island had been won. By June, when the British evacuation was completed, only 52 percent of the Commonwealth forces had been rescued. A myth arose about Crete to justify the Commonwealth losses: that the Germans suffered so heavily in airborne troops they never again carried out an airborne assault; however, over two years later Germany successfully employed parachute forces in the Aegean Sea's Dodecanese Islands in a campaign wresting them from British control.

As the battle for Crete unfolded, the German battleship *Bismarck* was sunk in the North Atlantic and the Axis suffered a setback in the Middle East when a pro-Nazi coup in Iraq was scotched by British troops. Shortly thereafter, the Free French helped the British invade Syria and Lebanon, solidifying some of the region for the British. But a defeat in North Africa would render those minor victories irrelevant, and the longer-term threat, no matter how remote in hindsight, was that somehow the Japanese would subdue India and join with the Germans near Iraq or Iran. Soon the German general Erwin Rommel, the "Desert Fox," would chase the British out of most of Libya, making even the most outlandish scenario seem possible.

## Fatal Misjudgment

Just as Nazi Germany and fascist Italy seemed unstoppable in Europe, Japan had continued its expansion from Manchuria southward into Longzhou, China, nearly closing off avenues for allied support of Chiang Kai-shek. The Yunnan–Vietnam Railway still allowed supplies to come from Haiphong, Indochina, to Kunming, China, and Japan took steps to seal off this lifeline. After repeated requests to the Vichy government to close the railway in French Indochina, Japan threatened invasion and Vichy gave the Japanese basing rights inside Indochina. Japanese forces quickly exceeded the parameters of the agreement. French troops fought back, but were overwhelmed and by the end of September 1940, northern Indochina was in Japanese hands.

Franklin Roosevelt, looking at the ominous developments in Europe, recognized that it would not take much for the United States to be isolated facing both Nazi Germany and Japan alone. Britain was barely holding its own behind the moat of the English Channel, while the USSR was still allied with Germany (though acting like a neutral). Communists in the United States were singing Germany's praises because of the German-Soviet Non-Aggression Pact, and the leftists in Roosevelt's administration only tepidly supported American rearmament.

All that changed overnight on June 22, 1941, when Hitler launched Operation Barbarossa against the Soviet Union. True to his words in *Mein Kampf*, he sought to crush Bolshevism once and for all. A few overtures to bring the USSR into the Axis had taken place in November 1940, but contrary to some recent claims by historians, those were short-term expedients at best. Hitler had no intention of permanently allying with Bolsheviks and Jews, as he characterized the Soviet Union.[62] Behind the scenes, Hitler had told his generals a full year earlier that the defeat of France "finally freed his hands for his important real task: the showdown with Bolshevism."[63]

Hitler's invasion of the Soviet Union came as no surprise to anyone except Stalin, who had deluded himself into thinking the Germans wouldn't attack until 1942 at the earliest. He had given Hitler no reason to invade; the Soviet Union had been furnishing Germany with raw materials and food religiously since the partition of Poland, and had stood aside when Hitler gobbled up the remainder of eastern Europe, the Balkans and Greece. Although he said on May 5, 1941, that "war with Germany is inevitable," Stalin continued Soviet economic aid to the Nazis unabated.[64]

Nor was evidence of Hitler's intentions lacking. For months British intelligence had been picking up key data that Germany was preparing for an invasion and warned Stalin repeatedly.[65] He blew off these warnings as British provocations, suspecting the West was trying to start a war of mutual annihilation between his country and Germany. Repeated Luftwaffe incursions into Soviet air space were forgiven with mild protests, and the Wehrmacht's explanations for its troop concentrations in Poland were accepted at face value. Even more evidence came from the "Red Orchestra" ring of Soviet spies in Berlin; Rudolf Roessler, code-named "Lucy" in Switzerland; and German deserters, one of whom accurately furnished Barbarossa's exact attack date and time—but Stalin discounted them all. Even more astounding, Stalin refused to accept information from his own commanders that panzers had crossed into Soviet territory and were under fire.

According to Hitler's early writing in *Mein Kampf*, the destruction of the Soviet Union was a critical element in Germany's plans for a "Thousand Year Reich." Others saw the situation differently based on their per-

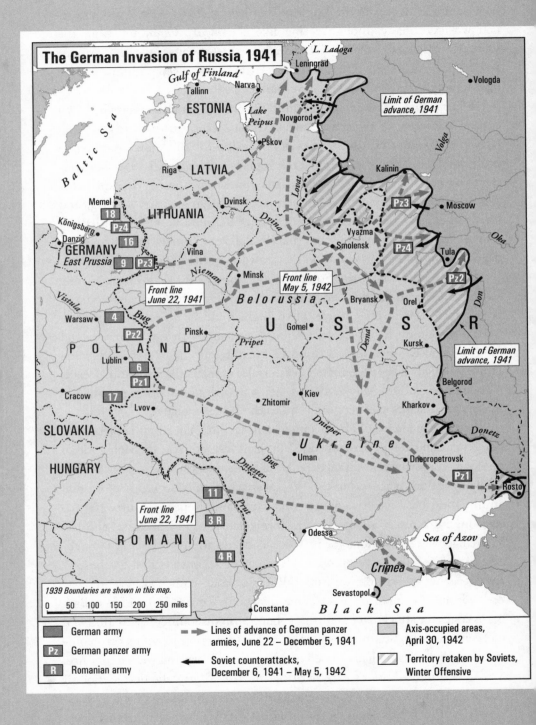

# The German Invasion of Russia, 1941

*L. Ladoga*

*Vologda*

Leningrad

*Gulf of Finland*  Narva

Tallinn

ESTONIA  *Lake Peipus*

Novgorod

**Limit of German advance, 1941**

*Volga*

Pskov

Riga  LATVIA

Kalinin

*Dvina*

**Pz3**  Moscow

Memel  **18**

Dvinsk

LITHUANIA

*Oka*

Königsberg  **Pz4**

Vyazma

Danzig  **16**

*Dvina*

Smolensk  **Pz4**

Tula

GERMANY

*East Prussia*  **9**  **Pz3**

Vilna

*Nieman*  Minsk

**Pz2**

*Vistula*  **4**  *Bug*

**Front line June 22, 1941**

*B e l o r u s s i a*

**Front line May 5, 1942**

Bryansk

Orel

*Don*

Warsaw

Pinsk

*Pripet*

Gomel  U  S  S  R

Lublin  **6**

**Pz1**

P  O  L  A  N  D

Kursk

**Limit of German advance, 1941**

Cracow  **17**

Lvov

Zhitomir

Kiev

Belgorod

Kharkov

SLOVAKIA

*Dnieper*

Donetz

HUNGARY

*Dniester*  *Bug*

Uman  *U k r a i n e*

Dnepropetrovsk

**11**

*Prut*

**Pz1**

Rosto

**Front line June 22, 1941**

**3 R**

R  O  M  A  N  I  A

**4 R**

Odessa

*Sea of Azov*

*Crimea*

Sevastopol

*1939 Boundaries are shown in this map.*

0  50  100  150  200  250 miles

Constanta

*B l a c k  S e a*

| ■ | German army |  | ⇢ | Lines of advance of German panzer armies, June 22 – December 5, 1941 | | Axis-occupied areas, April 30, 1942 |
| **Pz** | German panzer army |  | ← | Soviet counterattacks, December 6, 1941 – May 5, 1942 | | Territory retaken by Soviets, Winter Offensive |
| **R** | Romanian army |  |  |  |  |  |

sonal perspectives. Albert Speer, later Hitler's minister of armaments and war production, felt oil was "a prime motive" behind the invasion, and it was certainly the target in 1942 for Case Blue, the summer offensive aimed at Stalingrad and the Baku oilfields. Hitler's generals repeatedly warned against invading the Soviet Union, but almost exclusively from an economic perspective since Hitler regularly dismissed their advice on military matters. Consistently lucky through his unbroken string of victories, Hitler had become "Gröfaz" (Gröösster Feldherr aller Zeiten—greatest military commander of all time). He told General Georg Thomas—who had prepared reports detailing the potential disastrous economic consequences of an invasion—to change his tune. Thomas's obedient new report envisioned an utterly depopulated Russia, the urban residents starved to death and rural dwellers forced eastward to create vast swatches of agricultural lands for exploitation by Germany.

Barbarossa featured a three-pronged pitchfork of invasion routes, and Hitler intended that Leningrad would fall first, followed by Moscow. Despite the enslavement and extermination planned for Russians, Hitler expected they would willingly help overthrow Stalin's regime ("We have only to kick in the door and the whole rotten structure will come crashing down"). He was correct to an extent, and many Soviet inhabitants initially welcomed the Germans, particularly in the Baltic states recently absorbed by Stalin, Ukraine, White Russia, and among the Cossacks, Tatars, and other ethnic groups in the Crimea and southern Russia. Hitler's policies were self-defeating, however; they called for brutal treatment of civilians and confiscation of their supplies except in the Baltic states, and although Soviet Hilfswillige (willing helpers) became a large part of the Wehrmacht's strength on the Eastern Front, Soviet guerrillas or partisans more than made up for the anti-Soviet helpers.

Seeking to avoid Napoléon's fate and destruction at Russian hands, the Wehrmacht sent Army Group North after Leningrad, Army Group South through Ukraine toward Kiev, and Army Group Center through Smolensk to Moscow. But the Germans had no appreciation for the immensity of the Russian landmass, nor its bottomless pool of manpower reserves. Even as they invaded with 166 divisions (out of 210 divisions in the entire Wehrmacht), the Germans faced 316 total Soviet combat divisions (with about 190 in the immediate western districts). Making this more deceptive was the new Soviet doctrine of defense-in-depth, where echelons were staggered three to four hundred miles apart. And while the Germans could count 3.9 million men in their invasion force, these forces included numerous lesser-trained, -equipped, and -motivated allied units supplied by Finland, Hungary, Romania, Slovakia, Croatia, Italy, and even one from Spain (later Latvian, Estonian, Lithuanian, Cossack, and Russian anti-Soviet units were added). Approximately 90 percent of Germany's mobile forces were dedicated to the Eastern Front, 3.05 million men and 3,350 of its 5,200 tanks.[66] These were opposed by 23,700 Russian tanks.[67] While the Soviet T-34, unknown to German intelligence in June 1941, was superior to any German tank at the time, the Russians had not solved the problems of tank unit command or control in battle. Whereas German commanders stayed in constant communication with their units through a unique throat radio microphone, eliminating exterior noise, Russian tankers still relied on pennants and hand signals—often useless on dusty battlefields or in storms.

In addition, Soviet military forces had just begun to recover from Stalin's Great Purge of 1937–38, in which 3 of 5 Soviet marshals, 13 of 15 army commanders, 50 of 57 corps commanders, and 154 out of 186 division commanders were executed. On the other hand, Stalin knew that the post-Purge leadership was intimidated and ideologically pure, and would suicidally throw itself at the enemy should he order it.[68]

The German army, however, had its own problems, starting with the panzer divisions, whose tanks were woefully undergunned. Then there was the army's transport—still horse-drawn as of 1941. Only in Hitler's imagination was the army mechanized. The German industrial base was much too small to support a war machine like the one Hitler demanded on an across-the-board basis. It could, for short bursts, produce large numbers of specific items, but had no chance to compete with another controlled economy such as Russia's, which dwarfed the Nazis' in raw materials and manpower. Moreover, the sheer lack of manpower for such breathtaking offensives doomed the Germans in a war of attrition. In Russia, Germany needed to win quickly, especially before winter arrived, or the numbers would simply catch up with them.

Consequently, the inadequate manpower and mechanization soon became obvious. Horse-drawn infantry units could not keep up with the armored spearheads that ranged far in advance, sending back hundreds of thousands of prisoners, unarmed, but often with negligible supervision and guards. With no provisions for such volumes of prisoners, many starved, but many escaped to join partisan bands. And even when the infantry caught up and helped to form stop lines in encirclement battles, hundreds of thousands of Red Army soldiers slipped through the thin lines. Supply vehicles and tankers returning from the front for supplies and fuel in rear areas had to pass through unsecured zones, where these thin-skinned vehicles and their escorts were often destroyed by roving Soviets. And then snow fell early in Moscow, on October 7, and the long Russian winter began for the unprepared German soldiers. Guderian sent an inquiry for immediate winter clothing, receiving the reply that it would be issued in "due course." He never received any.

Yet the Wehrmacht's weaknesses initially were masked by the staggering number of enemy POWs, aircraft destroyed, and territory gained. In the early stages, Germany encountered unimaginable success, matched (or surpassed) only by the Japanese onslaught in the Pacific. The Luftwaffe claimed to have destroyed 1,489 Soviet aircraft (later the figures proved that in fact more than 2,000 were destroyed) against the loss of only 35 German planes.[69] Then British and American Lend-Lease aid poured in, constituting a critical resource. From 1941 to 1942, for example, the best-performing Soviet fighter, the British Hawker Hurricane, was not even the best fighter in the RAF (that was the Spitfire). More Hurricanes saw service in the Red Air Force than any other plane, including Russian-made aircraft.[70] As Alexander Hill noted, "even aid that might seem like a drop in the bucket in the larger context of Soviet production for the war played a crucial role in filling gaps at important moments during this period."[71] With only 670 tanks (out of a total of 1,731) available to defend Moscow in 1941–42 (having lost 10,000 tanks in the first month alone!), the arrival of even 466 subpar British tanks by the end of the year proved dramatic for the Red Army.[72] Soviet factories fell behind production schedules, turning out only 3,200 medium and heavy tanks in the last six months of 1941. Even the final volume of the official Soviet history of the "Great Patriotic War," published in 1965, admitted that Allied support "was not inconsequential, especially the supply to troops and the rear of automotive transport, fuels and lubricants," but tanks, aircraft, and artillery pieces were small in number and outdated.[73]

The Soviet invasion of Finland had led the Roosevelt administration to exclude Russia from aid, but after the German invasion of the USSR, Roosevelt revisited the ban, and permitted exports through Britain. For a nation supposedly self-sufficient, requests coming from the USSR were odd and inflated: 3,000 fighter aircraft, 3,000 bombers, sonar, antiaircraft guns, aluminum, and rubber. Stalin's "commanding heights" apparently were not as high as he wished. After the September/October conference in Moscow, attended by Averell Harriman, FDR's special envoy to Europe and coordinator of the Lend-Lease Program, for the United States, and Lord Beaverbrook for Britain, the Western nations committed to providing 1.5 million tons of supplies to the USSR within six months. Promises of future raw material deliveries from the Soviets were accepted as payment.

More important, the United States and Britain had tacitly committed to delivering supplies and equipment through northern Russian ports, thereby adding American and British naval protection to the aid. This in turn permitted Soviet factories to shift their efforts from submarine production to tanks. Americans and British naval units provided convoy protection, minesweepers, fueling, and other naval support the USSR was incapable of offering. When the war began in June, the Soviets had only two minesweepers in the entire Northern Flotilla. American and British ships exponentially increased the minesweeping capability in a few months, in no small part due to British-supplied ASDIC (sonar), the first many Soviet officers had ever seen. U.S.-supplied Airacobras proved one of the USSR's best fighters and were easily the most successful of the Lend-Lease planes sent to Russia.

Most tanks shipped by the British and Americans in late 1941 and early 1942 were vastly inferior to Russian models, but they saw action nonetheless, both at Moscow and as late as Kursk, in 1943, when 20 percent of Soviet armor still consisted of Lend-Lease tanks.[74] Where the Wehrmacht remained an army reliant on horse transportation, however, American jeeps, Studebakers (350,000 of them), and Dodge trucks turned the Red Army into a modern, mobile force. Indeed, "Studebaker" and "Villies" (Willys) became familiar words to Russians who survived the Great Patriotic War.[75]

Armor got the glory, of course—especially on the Eastern Front—but in myriad other ways, America and Britain fortified the Soviet military, delivering more than 23,000 field telephones in 1942; more than 250,000 miles of cable, critical metal-cutting machinery, presses, compressors, and heavy machine tools; and setting up the Soviets with gun-laying radars they did not possess. Some forty imported machine tools to a single aviation factory in July of 1942, for example, allowed the plant to reach full capacity in a mere two months. These tools, like the airplanes and tanks, arrived at a key juncture in the fight when Soviet production was struggling. Military experts estimate that between 50 percent and 60 percent of all Soviet military supplies came from the United States or Britain; the amount supplied by America alone was equal to between 4 and 8 percent of Soviet GDP.

Nevertheless, Soviet wartime production, especially for a nation in the throes of economic collapse and facing utter annihilation, proved remarkable. Stalin moved every factory he could eastward, well beyond the capability of the Luftwaffe to touch them. More important than the contributions of Soviet manufacturing in the war, however, was the sheer size and, before long, professionalism of the Red Army. Stalin hoarded his reserves, at one time holding a full four armies back. While conscripts were dumped into battles such as Stalingrad without rifles, by 1943 most Soviet units were not only equipped and trained, but well equipped and trained. Backed by massed artillery unseen even by American ground forces, Red infantry repeatedly overwhelmed the Germans. Panzer production could not begin to keep up with the armor pouring out of Russian factories (and supplemented by Lend-Lease trucks and tanks).

Whatever the strength of American and British support for the Soviets, Hitler's own policies managed to produce vast numbers of new enemies when different policies might have delivered armies of allies. The invasion of Russia triggered an ideological struggle between the Nazis' incompatible goals of exterminating Jews and enslaving Slav *Untermenschen* (subhumans) and the enlistment of Russians and minorities anxious to throw off the Communist yoke. The plan to feed the Wehrmacht from Russian sources— and have excess food shipped back to Germany—admitted "there can be no doubt that many millions of people will die of starvation [in Russia]."[76] Soviet civilians were therefore caught in a vise between starvation from Stalin's policies and starvation from the Nazis' stripping their land. Torn between a foreign dictator and a domestic one, many Russians opted for the devil they knew. Hitler was determined to make the war against the Russians a war of extermination against Bolshevism, and to that end all political officers, commissars, or other Communist Party officials were to be shot on sight.[77] This policy ensured that Communists would fight fanatically to the death and force as many other Soviet soldiers as possible to do likewise.

## The Decisive Turn: Moscow, 1941

From the very beginning of Operation Barbarossa, Commander-in-Chief Hitler began wavering on his original battle plan. His armored forces proved too weak to maintain the momentum of an attack on all fronts, and when an encirclement of huge numbers of Soviet troops beckoned in

Ukraine, he overruled Guderian and diverted armor from the Moscow attack, sending it south to the east of Kiev. The resulting battle was one of true annihilation; the Soviet forces in the western Ukraine were destroyed, and more than 450,000 (possibly as many as 600,000) prisoners were taken. As a result of this deviation, however, General Franz Halder, head of the Army General Staff, and General Kurt Zeitzler, commander-in-chief of the Army, became convinced even before the Kiev battle had ended that the war would extend into 1942.[78]

Halder, of course, was right. The plan for a quick war had failed. Nevertheless, and still believing in victory, Guderian and the other commanders regrouped as fast as they could and resumed their push on Moscow, but with greatly reduced strength, having by then suffered a 53 percent loss in armor and a 22 percent loss in mechanized transport. Army Group North's panzer army was brought by rail to strengthen the attack on Moscow, thus ending all hopes of capturing Leningrad in 1941, but it too had been in constant combat since the campaign began and was seriously depleted.

Then the Germans needed to face the "Napoléon problem" of resupply in Russia. For its attack on Moscow, Army Group Center required twenty-seven trainloads of supplies per day in September but received only twenty-two; in October it required twenty-nine and received only twenty; and in November, only three trainloads per day reached it.[79] Nonetheless, good leadership overcame those difficulties, and the resilient Germans created twin envelopments that bagged another 675,000 men in battles around Bryansk and Vyazma. Soviet forces defending Moscow were in great peril, but the German armored formations were critically worn down.

The first failure in Barbarossa came when Army Group North, still with armor, failed to seize Leningrad. Then, Army Group Center frittered away its resources on the Kiev encirclement, which regardless of its success, prevented Moscow from being taken before winter. Once snow was on the ground and the temperature dropped to 10 degrees below zero, it was too late. Despite throwing all they could at Moscow, the Germans were stopped as much by weather as by dogged Soviet defenses, built in desperation by some 150,000 Moscow inhabitants urged by Stalin to protect "Mother Russia." Both sides counted divisional tank strength in dozens, and the Germans could not prevail in a strictly infantry battle. Weapons and vehicles froze, troops became rapidly exhausted in the extreme cold, and the supply system ground to a halt. The temperature dropped to 30 and 40 below zero, and a frantic call finally went out to the German civilian population to donate winter clothing. Even then the supply system couldn't get the clothing to frontline units, and the *Winterhilfe* (winter help), as it was called, supplied with great fervor by German civilians, went for naught. Troops retreated to village huts, ceding the countryside to the Russians in their thick, warm boots and quilted uniforms. A German soldier, Siegfried Knappe, recorded his tribulations that winter:

> We arranged a schedule that rotated the men in and out of the available huts during the night. . . . we had only the same field uniforms we had worn during the summer, plus a light overcoat. . . . The cold numbed and deadened the human body from the feet up until the whole body was an aching mass of misery. Each man fought the cold alone, pitting his determination and will against the bitter weather. We reduced sentry duty to [15 minutes]. On December 5, the temperature plummeted to 30 degrees below zero . . . the flesh on our faces and ears would freeze . . . and we tried to wrap anything around our heads to prevent frostbite. Our fingers froze even in gloves and stuffed into our overcoat pockets . . . we could not have fired our rifles . . . the cold was beyond human endurance. . . .[80]

Moreover, the drain of casualties during the first four months had exceeded what Colonel-General Halder had estimated, and replacements were not available for the decimated panzer and motorized divisions. Offensive warfare became impossible when shelter meant survival and even short periods outside meant frostbite or death by freezing. On top of that, Marshal Georgy Zhukov threw three new armies at the exhausted and frozen Germans on December 5, and catastrophe loomed.

Although Stalin is often hailed as the savior of Moscow, it was Zhukov who was his instrument. Forty-five years old during the battle for Moscow, the stout Georgy Konstantinovich Zhukov was born in a one-room cabin in Kaluga Province near Moscow. His father, a shoemaker, typified the plight of the lower class Russian and was arrested by the Czar's Okhrana for supporting the 1905 revolution. Zhukov received no education until he was ten years old, when he was apprenticed to his uncle, a furrier in Moscow. There he learned to read and worked until drafted into the Czar's army in July 1915. The cavalry agreed with him, and he became a noncommissioned officer (NCO), winning two St. George crosses for his bravery and exploits in

the First World War. In many ways, Zhukov was the ideal NCO. He felt the
training was exemplary, and although discipline was brutal, individuals like
him became the backbone of the Army.[81]

As an enlisted soldier he developed those traits that characterized him
later: he was proud, demanding, and tenacious. Coupling his personality
with his physical appearance, that of a relatively short NFL offensive line-
man who has been in many scrapes, he became an intimidating force in the
Red Army. When his squadron was taken over by Bolsheviks in February
1917, Zhukov was elected chairman of the soldiers' committee. The following year he joined the 4th Moscow Cavalry Regiment of the Red Army, and
while fighting against Admiral Aleksandr Kolchak and the White armies in
1919, Zhukov was allowed to join the Communist Party. In 1920 he became
a sergeant-major and a platoon leader and was soon promoted to squadron
commander. In the demobilization of the Red Army that reduced its
strength from 5.5 million men to 562,000, Zhukov's squadron was retained,
with him as its commander. Thereafter he rose steadily through the ranks.
In 1938 he was appointed to command the 1st Soviet Mongolian Army
Group, then promoted to chief of staff after a highly successful war game,
whereupon he was sent to Leningrad after the Nazi invasion to prevent it
from being taken. Within a month, the German advance was brought to a
halt. Stalin tapped him again to defend Moscow, and in October he took
charge of its defenses. By December 4, Zhukov's men halted the German
advance after a twenty-day battle that cost Hitler 155,000 men and almost
all remaining tanks in Army Group Center.

Then came Zhukov's famous counterattack. Stalin released three
armies for the Moscow sector and the Germans were overrun, abandoning
large amounts of equipment. Hitler ordered "fanatic resistance," sacked his
best panzer generals, Guderian and Erich Hoepner (plus all three army
group commanders), and named himself commander-in-chief of the army.
Zhukov wasn't finished: in January and February he plunged ten more
armies into the battle, along with additional armor. With the entire front
collapsing and the Soviets advancing as much as sixty-five miles, Hitler issued his famous "Not one step backwards" order on January 2, 1942 (he
would issue the same order again at El Alamein some nine months later):
"The present situation demands that we cling to every town and village,
retreating not a step, fighting to the last cartridge, to the last grenade."[82]
Against all odds, the Germans held, suffering another half million casualties in the winter battle. It would not be until von Manstein's counterstroke

at Kharkov in the late winter of 1943 that the Germans would win a winter battle, and that would be their only one. In Zhukov's counteroffensive, Stalin's contributions yielded poor results, showing he often was little better than Hitler at military meddling. He ordered a general offensive, which failed (leaving the historical Soviet records deafeningly silent about the battles within the offensive, most likely because they showed Stalin's decision was incorrect).[83]

Two other great command personalities were involved in the defense of Moscow: Marshal Ivan Stepanovich Konev, commanding the Kalinin Front that conducted the most successful counterattack, and Marshal Konstantin K. Rokossovsky, a Polish-born general commanding the 16th Army directly in front of Moscow. Konev, a year younger than Zhukov and born in a peasant village, joined the Communist Party and served during the Russian Civil War. Konev was sent to Mongolia to dislodge the Japanese from the Nomonhan area; upon failing, he was replaced by Zhukov. Zhukov's subsequent success earned him Konev's everlasting hatred, a feeling that became mutual. Stalin observed this, using the rivalry to his advantage and to keep the more successful Zhukov in line.

Marshal Rokossovsky, born in 1896, the same year as Zhukov, had been orphaned at age fourteen when he enlisted in the Russian army. Like the others, he joined the Communist Party, then rose steadily in the Red Army during the Russian civil war. Arrested during the Great Purge, he endured extensive interrogations by the NKVD, lost many of his teeth and all of his fingernails, yet survived. Restored to command in 1940, Rokossovsky displayed substantial initiative and independence, participating in the defense of Moscow. Zhukov then transferred him to the Don Front in 1942, where he orchestrated the decisive breakthrough that doomed the German 6th Army at Stalingrad.

## The Awakened Giant

When France fell in 1940, FDR concluded that Britain stood alone and would have to be saved. Although the United States remained at peace, it was already producing as much military equipment as any of the major combatants engaged in the war, and it was understood that any excess would be sold—or given—to Britain. Churchill explained to Roosevelt that Britain would pay what it could, then, "when we can pay no more you will give us the stuff all the same."[84] He was right. England's special relationship with the United States became stronger than ever. French diplomat Charles

Maurice de Talleyrand had once observed, "Every Englishman who ever goes there [America] is home. . . . ; no Frenchman ever is."[85] Long before Churchill assumed office—in 1939 before the invasion of Poland—Prime Minister Neville Chamberlain had informed Roosevelt that the British Empire could not afford to keep a major fleet in the Far East, and requested the United States take over patrol duties of the Pacific. Unbeknownst to the American public, or even anyone in the U.S. Navy, Roosevelt agreed to do it. Britain transferred all but two battleships and their auxiliaries to the Atlantic, leaving one carrier in the Indian Ocean. America was left as the protector of the helpless east of India.

Without the backdrop of the European war, Japan's actions seemed to be little more than aggression from another regional power. But when it looked as though the Soviet Union might fall or Germany would take Egypt, an awesome threat loomed. If the Japanese seized Malaya, Burma, and the Dutch East Indies, the Axis powers would command most of the world's natural resources and become superpowers threatening the United States. Before Pearl Harbor, American attention in the Far East, while focused on China in its diplomacy, was geared strategically to supporting the British base at Singapore and American outposts in the Philippines. Since the 1920s, America's War Plan Orange, which outlined strategies to be used in the event of war with Japan, assumed the Philippines would be the key to victory. But the series of plans (which morphed through five variations over time) never solved the problem of how to actually defend them. Manila would have to be held long enough for the U.S. Navy to arrive and secure the sea lanes, but the Navy never possessed the capability (even on paper) to relieve the islands in time. As early as the 1920s, FDR, then assistant secretary of the navy, thought it "more than probable" the Philippines would fall and called it "dangerous in the extreme" to count on acquiring another base in the Far East to replace them. He thought once the Philippines fell, the American public would demand action to guarantee a base there.[86]

Two events made the American entry into war nearly inevitable. First, in September 1940, after the Vichy French government signed its armistice with Germany, Japan knew that France could not—and Nazi Germany would not—protect the French possession of Indochina, and Japan was able to convince the Vichy regime to give it the right to station troops in Indochina. Then came Russia's threatened collapse in 1941—and the prospect of Britain going it alone against the Axis. Those events convinced FDR that if war was coming against Japan, better sooner than later. He had increased trade sanctions against Japan in the spring and summer of 1941 and declared an oil embargo immediately after the Germans invaded Russia. Sales of scrap iron, airplanes, machine parts, and aviation gasoline were also all halted.[87] All new oil exports to Japan ended in July, but by then the Japanese had already accepted the "southern strategy" of getting their oil from the Dutch East Indies by conquest. Acquiring this "Southern Resource Area," as the Japanese called it, would necessarily involve war with Britain and the United States. Admiral Isoroku Yamamoto, who commanded Japan's Combined Fleet, gained permission to plan and train for an attack on the American fleet at Pearl Harbor in the spring of 1941 (although final permission from the emperor was not secured until November).[88] Japan's strides toward war took a leap in October; following the U.S. rejection of a Japanese plea for a summit, Prime Minister Fumimaro Konoe resigned and General Hideki Tojo, the war minister and a strong proponent of war with America, was appointed in his place. Emperor Hirohito, anxious to reach a diplomatic solution, instructed Tojo to "go back to blank paper" for a new overture to the United States. The State Department contrasted Tojo's new attempts at negotiations with Japan's apparent relentless march toward Singapore, and blasted an alert out to all American Pacific bases: "BEST INTELLIGENCE SUGGESTS JAPAN MIGHT ATTACK RUSSIA OR BRITISH AND DUTCH COLONIES IN THE EAST INDIES."[89]

Following the U-boat attacks in the Atlantic on the American destroyers *Kearny* and *Reuben James*—the latter sunk—America drifted very close to war despite a strong sentiment within the United States to avoid any foreign conflicts. Roosevelt's generals had already identified Germany as the most serious threat but the Navy needed time to prepare for Japan if war came in the East as per War Plan Orange.[90] However, through MAGIC, an American code-breaking project involving the Army's Signals Intelligence Section and the Navy's Communication Special Unit, the United States was reading the Japanese diplomatic code. With such superior intelligence, it was assumed the Japanese could be managed. FDR now learned that Ambassador Nomura had until November 15 to secure a settlement with the Americans, but received no indication of what the deadline portended. Ambassador Joseph Grew repeatedly warned that the Japanese were in a "*Hara-kiri*" mentality—indicating they would risk national suicide to attain their aims—but a Japanese former consul, Saburo Kurusu, was dispatched to Washington to present a two-part initiative for peace. This included a modus vivendi in which Japan would agree to halt all military operations in return for a million gallons of aviation fuel. Kurusu's back-door overture was dead on arrival. Kichisaburo Nomura arrived with the formal modus vivendi on November 10, and Secretary of State Cordell Hull rejected it four days later. Less than a week after that, the Pearl Harbor strike force (*kido butai*) sailed for its organizational and supply rendezvous in the Kurile Islands. Tojo told the Imperial Conference that "Matters have reached the point where Japan must begin war with the United States," and Operation Z (the Pearl Harbor attack) received final approval.

The Army welcomed such news. In the *Confidential War Diaries* compiled by the War Plans Section, an entry on November 29 recorded: "America as yet making absolutely no preparations for war. We are truly on the verge of achieving a blitzkrieg against the US that will outdo even the German blitzkrieg against the Soviet Union."[91]

Great controversy has surrounded the actual attack on Pearl Harbor—and America's shocking unpreparedness. Charges that "FDR knew" resurface decade after decade. Several facts are indisputable. First, the United States, through MAGIC's decryption of both the "Purple" diplomatic codes and the Japanese naval code (JN-25b), simultaneously offered both clarity and confusion. The Japanese fleet (or fleets) were all on the move, but no one knew where. American fleet intelligence at Pearl Harbor, headed by Captain Edwin T. Layton, still thought the Combined Fleet was in the Inland Sea on December 2. When asked by Admiral Husband Kimmel, head of naval operations in Hawaii, if the Japanese "could be rounding Diamond Head and you wouldn't know about it," Layton replied, "I would hope they could be sighted before that."[92] The following day, Naval Intelligence in Washington learned that Japanese embassies had been ordered to destroy their codes, cipher machines, and sensitive documents—an unmistakable sign that war was imminent. Meanwhile, the carrier *Lexington* left Hawaii for Midway on December 5 to deliver Marine aircraft. The other two carriers based at Pearl Harbor, the *Enterprise* and *Saratoga*, were also not in port, the *Enterprise* having left on November 28 for Wake Island, and the *Saratoga* was in Puget Sound undergoing repairs. On December 2 Yamamoto received the order, "Climb Mount Nitaka"—code words to attack the American base.[93] Although Japanese plans called for the destruction of the Navy yard and oil storage facilities, the grand design anticipated the war would be decided long before those facilities came into play. Critically, the Japanese failed to understand that if the oil storage facilities were destroyed, the U.S. Pacific Fleet would be compelled to retire to San Diego.

Yamamoto also intended to have a declaration of war precede the attack by thirty minutes. A draft memorandum surfaced in 1999, dated December 3, 1941, that showed a "vigorous debate" took place within the Japanese government over whether to inform the United States of the termination of negotiations, with the conclusion being to maintain a strong façade of negotiations. A December 7 diary entry noted "our deceptive diplomacy is steadily proceeding toward success."[94] Tokyo transmitted the "14-part message" to the Japanese Embassy in Washington—which was broken long before the diplomats actually delivered it—but it did not officially declare war. A declaration of war was printed in Japanese newspapers on the evening of December 8, but American officials did not see these until after the attack. Although the message was not officially delivered to Hull until after the attack started, notification a half hour before hostilities would have made little difference in Pearl Harbor's readiness. In the end, the Japanese succeeded in a determined, complete surprise attack.[95]

In less than an hour, Japan had sunk or disabled virtually all of the battleships in Pearl Harbor, destroyed most of the aircraft on Oahu, and damaged or sunk dozens of other vessels. All but two of the battleships, the USS *Arizona* (later declared a national memorial and never raised) and the *Oklahoma*, saw action in the Pacific after substantial repairs. Admiral Chuichi Nagumo, who had directed the attack from his carriers, withdrew before launching a third strike on the oil facilities as per the original plan, and later suffered appropriate criticism for failing to use initiative to finish off the base. Nevertheless, the damage was profound, the shock, unmatched in American history (save, perhaps, Lincoln's assassination), and the emotional response by Americans to a "sneak attack," unprecedented. Roosevelt went to Congress the next day, calling December 7 a "date which will live in infamy," and was given a war resolution against Japan. No event in American history, including the destruction of the battleship *Maine* or the siege of the Alamo, had filled Americans with the sense of righteous outrage they felt after Pearl Harbor. In the coming years, Japan would pay a heavy price for her "sneak attack."

# CHAPTER SIX

# Canopy of Freedom

## Time Line

1942:   Japan conquers Philippines, Singapore, Indonesia, and Burma, and occupies Thailand; Doolittle Raid, Battle of Midway, Battle of Guadalcanal; Battle of Stalingrad; Battle of El Alamein; Operation Torch (Allied invasion of North Africa); Germany occupies remainder of France

1943:   Americans advance in Solomons, New Guinea; North Africa falls to United States, Britain; Battle of Kursk; Allied victory in Sicily; Italy invaded; Tarawa invaded

1944:   United States captures Marianas, invades Philippines; Red Army destroys German Army Group Center, advances to near Warsaw; Romania surrenders; Greece liberated; Rome taken; D-Day (June 6); Paris liberated; Battle of Leyte Gulf; Battle of the Bulge (December)

1945:   Iwo Jima captured; Berlin falls, Germany surrenders; atomic bomb tested; Battle of Okinawa; atomic bombs dropped; Japan surrenders

## Roar of the Awakened Giant

Admiral Yamamoto never said the apocryphal words attributed to him in the film *Tora! Tora! Tora!* ("I fear we have awakened a sleeping giant and filled him with a terrible resolve"), but he certainly believed it. Having lived in the United States from 1919 to 1921, then again as a naval attaché in

1926, he had seen America up close and knew the war would be decided by the end of 1942 for Japan—that either the Americans would quit and negotiate a settlement, or the Japanese Empire would be crushed. He believed this because the U.S. industrial potential dwarfed anything his own country could muster. Even Yamamoto, however, most likely underestimated the power of the American war machine when it got fully geared up.

The statistics of production for a war-engaged United States were nothing short of staggering. Ford alone outproduced all of Italy in total wartime goods during the war. Henry Kaiser's shipbuilders, who constructed a "Liberty Ship" from scratch in 1942 in a mind-boggling *four and a half days*, turned out 1,400 warships and thousands of transport vessels. A single ammunition maker promised a billion bullets for defense. General Motors had 120 different wartime plants, with its subsidiaries such as Pontiac retooled to fabricate torpedoes, and Oldsmobile, 155 mm howitzers. American factories turned out 95,000 tanks, almost 300,000 aircraft, built 31 fleet and light aircraft carriers from scratch in six years (while the Japanese built only one new fleet carrier), and armed and equipped more than 16.5 million men in the armed forces, while still dedicating its best resources to build the atomic bomb.

Production did not occur by happenstance, or even because the United States simply possessed such capabilities. The United States, with a population of 150 million, put about 14 percent of its population into uniform, while the Germans drew out approximately 24 percent for military service. Germany exceeded total military personnel during the war (about 19.4 million men under arms, as opposed to the American total), but were only able to maintain a much smaller productive capacity by making extensive use of slave labor from occupied countries. The ceiling on what America chose to put in the field reflected the importance placed on keeping those forces supremely well supplied.[1]

Much has been said about how World War II introduced women into the American labor force, and "Rosie the Riveter" has become an iconic figure of the time. Actually, 25.2 percent of the labor force was already female in 1940, and it rose only to a high of 29.2 percent in 1944 before falling back to 27.8 percent in 1946.[2] The general upward trend continued, however, reaching 29.6 percent in 1950 and by 1990 was in the mid-40-percent range. A major cultural change, however, involved the introduction of women into heavy manufacturing jobs like steel production where they hadn't been before, but overall, the statistics do not show a huge influx of women into the workforce to replace men entering the armed forces. The massive increase in American production was due to its capitalist system, not to the first-time employment of women.

From the strategic level down, then, American performance was a testament to free enterprise, despite the fact that the customer was the government. FDR's administration had harassed, investigated, and taxed entrepreneurs such as Henry J. Kaiser to the hilt during the New Deal, but when he was needed for the war effort, Kaiser found Roosevelt enthusiastic about dropping all restrictions, including price. Just build ships, Kaiser and others were told. The message was clear: whereas the New Deal had been an interesting experiment in social engineering, this was serious. This was war.

Liberal historians have often attempted to minimize the miracle of American capitalist production. Shortly after the war, John Morton Blum claimed government "supplied [Kaiser's] capital, furnished his market, and guaranteed his solvency on the cost-plus formula—and so spared him the need for cost efficiency. . . ."[3] There are three serious flaws with such arguments. First, if government control was good, why did the more heavily government-controlled industries of the Axis powers fail to match American productivity—or, for that matter, even British productivity? Second, Kaiser, Andrew Jackson Higgins, and most of the other American production kings *did* achieve cost efficiency even though it was not required. Third, and perhaps most important, the old Hollywood maxim about films—you can have it good, cheap, or fast: pick two—applied to wartime industry. America needed weapons good and fast. Cost was no object, for if we failed at this, future debt would be irrelevant. Needless to say, the national debt soared.

In keeping with the failure to properly appreciate the role of the businessman in the American industrial tsunami, many skeptics point to the careers of people such as Howard Hughes and Preston Tucker. After the war, both Hughes and Tucker were hounded and persecuted by the government—Hughes for his monster wooden airplane, the "Spruce Goose" (the Hercules), and Tucker for his ultra-advanced "Tucker Torpedo" automobile. Neither of the machines proved cost-effective or practical; and both men faced trials or public hearings during which their visions were attacked. Hughes was charged with "war profiteering," Tucker with mail fraud. Whereas during the war Tucker had made ball turrets for bombers, which earned him partial redemption in the eyes of the jury, Hughes had produced, as his only other wartime airplane, the twin-engine wooden XF-11 experimental spy plane that had malfunctioned with Hughes at the controls, plummeting to earth and crashing near the ninth hole of the Los Angeles Country Club. However, failure with the XF-11 had in a certain sense been as valuable as some of the most successful inventions of the war for discovering what "didn't work."

It was precisely individuals such as Hughes who gave the United States its critical—and unmatched—edge. For every Hughes whose idea did not pan out, there was a Kaiser or a Higgins. One could find this in a flexible system that encouraged risk, sparking inventors and innovators into new designs and concepts, so that the best weapons and processes could emerge. Nor was someone like Howard Hughes a mere war profiteer; a millionaire with an obsession for flying, Hughes had a deeply held faith in the performance and possibilities of wooden aircraft. Only in America could someone like Hughes have emerged, simultaneously vilified and admired. Born in 1905 in Texas to the inventor of the two-cone roller bit, which permitted drilling for oil in previously inaccessible spots, Howard inherited his father's Hughes Tool Company. Contrary to popular belief, he did not squander the company's money, nor was he entirely distant from the business, frequently making important design suggestions.

In creating Hughes Aircraft in Glendale, California, Hughes personalized aviation and set air speed records on both closed courses and nonstop transcontinental flights. Hughes's love of aviation, for which he won numerous flying awards, and its glamour dovetailed with his entrance into filmmaking, where he made the classic flying movie *Hell's Angels* (1930) after already turning out three Academy Award–nominated pictures. In 1928, Hughes won an Oscar for best director for his work on *Two Arabian Knights*. Personally involved in his film ventures, Hughes romanced many of the actresses he worked with. Throughout his dalliances, he never lost sight of the serious side of flying, and even insisted on piloting experimental aircraft himself, ultimately flying the XF-11 in 1946, when he crashed and sustained severe injuries.[4]

Capitalism is a continual churning in which the market sorts out the good from the bad. Wartime innovation was no different: in a climate where as many ideas as possible were needed under all manners of risk, the American system surpassed all others. Hughes, along with hundreds of others, typified a willingness to entertain new ideas, from any source at any level. When Andrew Jackson Higgins, later called by Dwight D. Eisenhower "the man who won the war" because of his landing boats, fulfilled an order for the Marines of a light, fast, wooden landing craft, General Victor "Brute" Krulak noticed that the design could be greatly improved by adding a "spoonbill" or "tongue" that dropped down at the front, allowing troops to run directly onto the beach.[5] Higgins, casting aside his ego and resentment of an officer telling him what to do, instantly improved the design. Higgins typified the American entrepreneur. A boat builder born in landlocked Nebraska, who had made his fortune by providing rum-runner boats during Prohibition, he spent the post-Prohibition years designing and racing some of the fastest craft in the world, including the famous *Dixie Greyhound.*[6] His landing craft made possible all the invasions, which would have been infinitely more difficult and costly in human life without his contributions.

While the Left routinely touts the battlefield performance of the Russian T-34 tank as evidence of the superiority of a state-controlled system (forgetting that it was a chassis based on American Walter Christie's design, lacked radio controls, and, after 1941, greatly outnumbered opposing German armor), the United States produced weapons and machinery of war the likes of which no other country even attempted. Germany had no need for ocean-going assault boats and landing craft, nor did the USSR. Who else produced carriers to match or even challenge the United States after 1942? (The Soviets built *none.*) All the cargo ships built during the war by the rest of the world combined did not rise to a small fraction of U.S. output, and Kaiser's yards alone exceeded the total industrial output of the vast majority of nations. Germany had some superior weapons (never enough, however), but the United States had more, and without the hundreds of thousands of trucks and the many million tons of supplies sent by the United States to the Soviet Union, Russia's defeat of Germany was nowhere near assured. On the contrary, it would have, without question, taken much longer and been far costlier. The B-29 had no equal, and the P-47 and P-51 were the best piston-driven fighters anywhere. Only the jet-propelled Me-262 could compete with the P-51 because of its speed, but the German plane crashed in accidents as often as it shot down an American fighter. No other country possessed a night fighter like the Black Widow, no one else possessed caterpillar tractors and bulldozers capable of turning jungle into an airstrip in twenty-four hours, and on and on.

American production brought about a shift in world naval power, too, as Britain's previously uncontested position now yielded to the rising American presence. Before 1940, the Royal Navy had 5 fleet carriers to America's 7, and each had 15 battleships, although the Americans had nearly double the number of submarines as England. When the Japanese surrendered in September 1945, the British still had not added a single fleet carrier to the Royal Navy, while the United States had built 12 more fleet carriers and 71 escort carriers to *one newly built* escort added to the British fleet. The postwar United States Navy counted 1,166 warships, even after suffering losses during combat—but that did not count the amphibious vessels, supply ships, auxiliaries such as tankers, all of which added more than *five thousand more* ships to the American numbers. The Royal Navy, which prior to 1940 had ruled the seas, was now in a very distant second place, and no other country, Allied or Axis, could make a claim to having any significant fleet for third.

Germany's weakness at sea, including the romantic but ultimately strategically meaningless missions of the *Graf Spee* and the *Bismarck*, concealed British decline, which was only made apparent in December 1944 when the Royal Navy cobbled together its most powerful task force of the entire war under Admiral Bruce Fraser. With four of Britain's five fleet carriers, two newer battleships, five cruisers, plus destroyers and support vessels, Task Force 57 sailed for the Pacific to join the U.S. Navy for action against Japan. Upon Fraser's arrival, though, he discovered his "large" force nearly lost in the seemingly limitless numbers of American ships, and he further learned how far behind the British were when it came to replenishment at sea, a necessity for maintaining operational tempo in the vast Pacific. Embarrassingly, Fraser's task force needed substantial training to function in the new style of sea battles fought by the United States and Japan. Not until March 1945 was Task Force 57 ready for action on a par with the Americans, and ultimately its most important action for England was to break off from fighting Japanese and take possession of Hong Kong before the Americans could contest its recovery for the British Empire.

In the air, it was only a slightly different story. Here, too, America's military production was astonishing and fit perfectly with the capabilities of the British at the time. Having suffered through the "Blitz," England had only one means to strike back directly at Germany, namely through the air. Commander in chief of Britain's Bomber Command, Sir Charles Portal, who assumed the post in 1940, was a devout advocate of Giulio Douhet's concept of a total air war on the enemy. "Any distinction," Douhet had written after World War I, "between belligerents and non-belligerents is no longer admissible . . . because when nations are at war, everyone takes part in it; the soldier carrying his gun, the women loading shells in a factory, the farmer growing wheat, the scientist in his laboratory."[7] It was Portal who crafted an air strategy of "area bombing" targeting German morale. In September 1941, Portal told Churchill,

> [the] attack on morale is not a matter of pure killing, although the fear of death is unquestionably an important factor. It is rather the general dislocation of industrial and social life arising from the damage to the industrial plant, dwelling houses, shops, utility and transport services. . . . [Therefore] the morale of the country as a whole will crack provided a high enough proportion of town dwellers is affected by the general dislocation produced by the bombing.[8]

Portal predicted such a campaign would require four thousand heavy bombers, at a time when Britain had only five hundred available for service on any given day. Area bombing received approval as a strategic plan among the British war councils because they could do nothing else. Lacking the numbers of land troops to invade Europe—even if they had control of the skies, which they did not—Britain could either play defense for years, or use her bombers. American-style precision bombing was out of the question, and British attacks in 1940 were so imprecise that German analysts, seeing bomb craters strewn over hundreds of miles, could not discern the actual intended target. Churchill tepidly endorsed civilian bombing in October 1941, warning that even if "all the towns in Germany were rendered uninhabitable," military control might not weaken, especially given the dispersion of the Nazi empire throughout Europe.[9]

When Americans arrived in England in 1942, Britain's air chief marshal Sir Arthur "Bomber" Harris, now in charge of the bombing campaign, failed to persuade Generals Henry H. "Hap" Arnold and Ira Eaker of the benefits of nighttime area bombing, nor could the Americans convince the British that daylight precision bombing was possible. The American strategy was based on a theory developed at the Air Corps Tactical School in Montgomery, Alabama, which postulated the existence of a vulnerable "industrial web." According to this theory, precise and relentless attacks on steel, ball bearings, electricity, and other interconnected industrial choke points in this "web" could collapse an enemy's economy. Ultimately, Eaker's offhand comment, "We'll bomb them by day. You bomb them by night," became official policy emanating from the two sides' irreconcilable differences.[10] The British night bombing concerned the Germans far less than the daylight precision bombing by the Americans. Even the British finally admitted as much in an intelligence briefing, saying, "There can be no doubt that Germany regards defence of the Reich against daylight air attack as of such supreme importance that adequate support for military operations in Russia and the Mediterranean has been rendered impossible."[11]

Despite terrific casualties—some nights, 30 percent of the British bombers would either not return or return with heavy damage—the air war in the West increased in scale and devastation. Using ingenious "bouncing bombs," the Royal Air Force breached the Ruhr dams (at the high cost of fifty-six air crews), but the key Sorpe Dam was not destroyed. As part of the Ruhr air offensive, other targets were attacked but the overall assault lacked coordination and, above all, repetition. Albert Speer later claimed the war could have been decided in 1943 with a more sustained effort in the Ruhr. Meanwhile, between March and July 1943, Essen, Duisburg, Bochum, Krefeld, Düsseldorf, Dortmund, Barmen-Wuppertal, Mülheim, Elberfeld-Wuppertal, Gelsenkirchen, and Cologne were flattened by more than a thousand bombers escorted by an equal number of fighters, thoroughly disrupting and devastating the Reich's wartime economy. Speer contributed to the ease of Allied destruction by concentrating German production into larger factories more easily targeted (in contrast to the Japanese, who dispersed their inferior production facilities in the face of sustained bombing). Speer met with Hitler three days after Hamburg was reduced to ashes in July 1943 (where 42,000 people perished in firestorms) and stated flatly that armaments production was collapsing. He told Hitler if six more German cities were devastated in the manner Hamburg was, war production would halt. Hitler replied, "You'll sort it out." After the Ruhr bombings, party members stopped wearing their badges in public and people no longer gave the Nazi salute.[12] Aerial destruction forced reallocation of resources, as the Germans needed trainloads of quicklime for disposal of thousands of corpses and had to send armies of repair and debris-clearing teams into urban areas so trucks and trains could again move.

Amazingly, Speer did "sort it out," and was able to raise German war production in spite of Allied bombing, reaching its peak in late summer and fall of 1944, a year that accounted for nearly 38 percent of all German war production from 1939 to 1945. Factories were moved underground, and railroads were maintained in a high state of efficiency through herculean efforts by the populace. It was only after the loss of Romania and its critical oil supplies in August 1944 that German production flagged.

One reason the bombing did not significantly retard, let alone end, German wartime production was that the Nazi armaments industry was fed by sucking in millions of foreign slaves as factory workers. The high irony of Speer's armaments "miracle" was that he had succeeded in reversing Lebensraum by colonizing Germany with millions of foreign workers—seven million by 1944. Locomotive production, considered one of Speer's great accomplishments, rested on a 90 percent increase in the workforce in 1942, most of it from Nazi-occupied territories. Conquest supplied the muscle power that fed armament production, which in turn would have fueled more conquest, but now staved off economic collapse. One aberration in the feedback loop was the disposition of Jews. Dead Jews weren't workers—quite the contrary, exterminating Jews absorbed precious resources in the form of trains, guards, camps, even quicklime needed to dispose of corpses.

Enslavement of large labor pools worked in the totalitarian states, but in the free nations other measures were needed. In Britain, especially, liberals used the necessities of war to lay the foundations for a postwar welfare state. William Beveridge, who delivered a 1942 paper called "Social Insurance and Allied Services," saw his wartime work as "a contribution to a better world after the war."[13] Keynes, of course, had already drafted an unpublished declaration of war aims that emphasized the need for social security after the war. Only Friedrich Hayek, an Austrian economist at Oxford, ran counter to this. His 1944 book, *The Road to Serfdom*, insisted that socialism was incompatible with human freedom, and those who argued that economic planning could coexist with personal liberties were delusional. Planning would always, he observed, rest on the "naked rule of force."[14] Even though Hayek and Keynes shared an aircraft watchtower at Cambridge University during the war, Keynes's ideas were in vogue while Hayek's free-market ideas were less popular. This trend reflected a deeper, depressing view of the nature of existence itself. Albert Camus in 1944 wrote, "I continue to believe that this world has no ultimate meaning."[15] This philosophy (or, more appropriately, nonphilosophy) undergirded the effort to use the war to advance postwar socialism under a variety of definitions. Jacques Maritain, writing in 1943, reasoned, "It is not a question of finding a new name for democracy, rather of discovering *its true essence* . . . [and] it is a question of passing from bourgeois democracy . . . to an integrally human democracy, from abortive democracy to real democracy."[16] William Temple, the Archbishop of Canterbury who attempted mightily to marry socialism with Christian faith, echoed Maritain, advocating a "'Democracy of the Person' as opposed to an egotistical 'Democracy of Individuals.'"[17] That these individuals utterly lacked an understanding of the American representative democracy goes without saying.

Whereas the First World War was popularly seen in Europe as the end of monarchies and unfettered capitalism, its replacement by social democracy had spawned communism and fascism, or socialism controlled by nationalists. Deep in World War II, this view even affected leftist academics in the United States who turned further left, following the European elites by blaming the war on capitalism, seeing Nazism as National-Capitalist, not National-Socialist. Ford, General Motors, ESSO (Exxon), and IBM were castigated for enabling Hitler's ascent to power, whereas delusional socialism, unable to satisfy the needs of people through state planning, was overlooked.

Even worse, Christianity was seen by many to contribute to Nazism. Pope Pius XII was especially criticized due to his 1933 Concordat with the Nazis (signed by him when he was Vatican secretary of state), for continuing to support the Third Reich as Europe's bulwark against Bolshevism almost until the end of World War II, and for fracturing Italy into equal parts of communism and Catholicism after the war; and Protestant German clerics were taken to task for not standing up to Hitler. Those who did went to concentration camps and were executed (the most famous being Dietrich Bonhoeffer, who joined in a plot to assassinate Hitler), but to someone safe from combat or the horrors of fascism back in the United States, that was no excuse. As a result of the hammering by the Left, Christianity's credibility was damaged. Faith was replaced by skepticism and atheism. Temple's contributions marked the beginning of that decline in Britain, and the country wouldn't wait for the war to be over to reject Churchill for a socialistic government.

Hence, at the very time that European intellectuals and policy makers abandoned, at least in their limited concept, liberty, democracy, free markets, and even Christianity, for socialism and state control of individuals, the United States had turned to freer industrial production to save the West and the world. And by the end of 1942, the Americans had shifted from defense to offense.

## Remember Pearl Harbor, Remember Bataan!

The transition came only after the Imperial Japanese Navy went on a rampage throughout the Pacific such as the world had never seen. Even before Pearl Harbor, Japanese forces had landed on the Malay Peninsula and begun their march to Singapore, while pounding the city with bombs. Wake Island, the Philippines, Hong Kong, and Guam were soon assaulted and conquered, and the Japanese racked up an unbroken string of successes. Isolated Wake fell after repelling one Japanese assault in a heroic but futile defense, Guam's tiny force didn't last a day, and Hong Kong's 14,000 British, Canadian, and Indian troops resisted for seventeen days, but the outcome and fate of Westerners in the colony was sealed from the start. One day after Pearl Harbor, Japanese aircraft caught the British battleship *Prince of Wales* and battle cruiser *Repulse* in the Gulf of Siam and quickly dispatched them to the bottom. Singapore fell to General Tomoyuki Yamashita's bicycle-riding troops in seventy days, and the bastion Churchill had called "impregnable" became a glittering Japanese prize, wiping 85,000 British Commonwealth troops off the British order of battle along the way. Held up only in the Philippines, the Japanese raced into the Dutch East Indies, annihilating the mixed American, British, and Dutch naval forces in their path, and capturing the vital oil fields for their war machine. The run of successes made the Japanese appear invincible, particularly when the task force that struck Pearl Harbor raided Ceylon, destroying the British presence in the Indian Ocean, sinking an aircraft carrier, three cruisers, three destroyers, and various miscellaneous vessels.

The Philippines were the only sticking point, but they too were doomed. Lieutenant General Masaharu Homma directed the invasion against the islands, defended by 151,000 troops, mostly untrained and lacking arms and equipment, although 12,000 were Philippine Scouts, taken in and made a part of the American Army. The Scouts would soon prove their effectiveness on Bataan, the peninsula on Luzon where the allied forces concentrated for defense. American forces were under the leadership of General Douglas MacArthur, who, retired from the army, had served as an adviser to the Filipino armed forces. He had been reinstated and named commander in July 1941 when FDR federalized the Philippine Army. At that time, the Filipino forces consisted of about 10,000 U.S. troops and the Philippine Scouts. MacArthur, controversial and flamboyant, brilliant and mistake-prone, had a penchant for self-promotion. Even the issue of his popularity with his men remains one of historical uncertainty. He seemed both to exhibit recklessness—he had exposed himself to German fire in World War I and would gain a reputation for showing up to inspect positions under fire in World War II—and, at the same time, earned the nickname "Dugout Doug" for his unwillingness to visit troops on Bataan. His stay on Corregidor, the rock island off Bataan where the U.S.-Filipino troops made their last stand, and his subsequent evacuation—ordered by Roosevelt personally—went down poorly among those men who remained to enter captivity.[18]

In his headquarters in Manila, he received the news of the attack on Pearl Harbor at 3:00 A.M., which called for him to enact the Rainbow 5 war plan and attack Japanese bases on Formosa (Taiwan). But his failure to act aggressively (weather reports said Formosa was experiencing heavy fog) and confusion among recently arrived personnel caused squadrons of aircraft in the Philippines to be on the ground just as the Imperial Japanese forces struck first. Only three American fighters got off the runways.

American and Filipino troops were quickly driven off the beaches, then withdrew in confusion, ultimately evacuating to the Bataan Peninsula, which protruded between Subic Bay and Manila Bay. Initially, MacArthur had 43,000 troops on the Peninsula to supply by barge from Manila, although before long another 80,000 troops and refugees arrived. Food and medical supplies were rapidly exhausted, leaving the survivors to face grim conditions. On January 23, having consolidated their forces, the Japanese assaulted Bataan, and as the position weakened, Franklin Roosevelt ordered MacArthur to personally evacuate to Australia as Supreme Allied Commander South West Pacific Area. Upon arriving safely in Australia after a hazardous journey by PT boat and a B-17 bomber, MacArthur issued his famous "I shall return" statement, making the Philippines' liberation his personal mission. Out of food, medicine, and ammunition, the U.S.-Filipino troops on Bataan surrendered on April 10, leaving 11,000 men, many of them wounded, on Corregidor to carry on the fight.

What followed was the infamous Bataan Death March, in which 75,000 U.S. and Filipino POWs were marched sixty miles to a railhead for transport to Camp O'Donnell. The Allied forces, already starving and exhausted, with many wounded, were denied food and water in the blazing heat and humidity. Thousands dropped out, and Japanese guards shot or bayoneted them while those continuing on were beaten unmercifully with bamboo sticks and rifle butts. So-called cleanup crews killed anyone missed by the

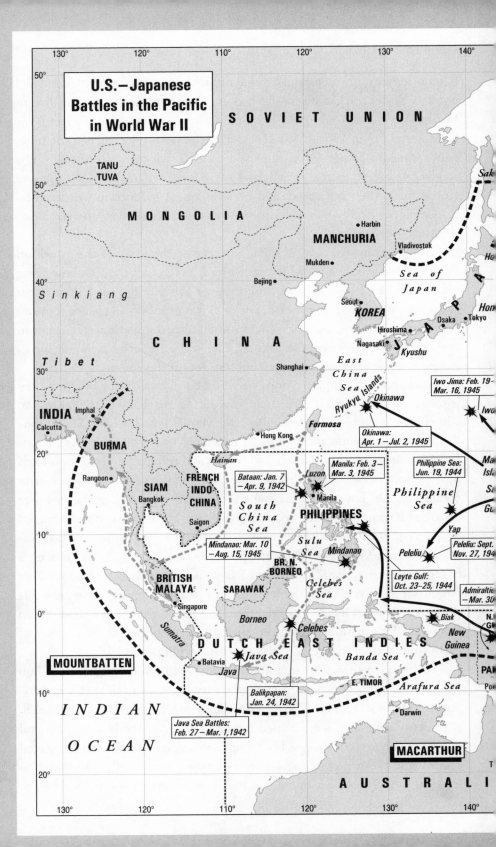

## U.S.–Japanese Battles in the Pacific in World War II

SOVIET UNION

TANU TUVA

MONGOLIA

MANCHURIA
• Harbin
• Vladivostok
• Mukden

*Sinkiang*

CHINA

• Bejing

*Sea of Japan*

Seoul •
**KOREA**

*Tibet*

• Shanghai

Hiroshima •
Nagasaki •
Osaka • Tokyo •
**JAPAN**
*Kyushu*

*East China Sea*

**INDIA**
Calcutta •
Imphal •

**BURMA**

Rangoon •

Ryukyu Islands  Okinawa

*Iwo Jima: Feb. 19– Mar. 16, 1945*

*Iwo*

*Okinawa: Apr. 1–Jul. 2, 1945*

Formosa

• Hong Kong

Hainan

**FRENCH INDO CHINA**

**SIAM**
Bangkok •

Saigon •

*South China Sea*

*Bataan: Jan. 7 –Apr. 9, 1942*

Luzon
• Manila

*Manila: Feb. 3– Mar. 3, 1945*

**PHILIPPINES**

*Philippine Sea: Jun. 19, 1944*

*Philippine Sea*

Yap

*Mi Isl*

*Sa Gu*

*Mindanao: Mar. 10 –Aug. 15, 1945*

*Sulu Sea*  Mindanao

Peleliu

*Peleliu: Sept. Nov. 27, 194*

**BRITISH MALAYA**

**BR. N. BORNEO**

**SARAWAK**

*Celebes Sea*

Singapore •

*Sumatra*

Borneo

Celebes

*Leyte Gulf: Oct. 23–25, 1944*

*Admiraltie –Mar. 30*

Biak •

**N.**
**G**

New Guinea

**PA**

**MOUNTBATTEN**

• Batavia
*Java*

*Java Sea*

**DUTCH EAST INDIES**

*Banda Sea*

Por •

*INDIAN*

*OCEAN*

*Balikpapan: Jan. 24, 1942*

E. TIMOR  *Arafura Sea*

• Darwin

*Java Sea Battles: Feb. 27 – Mar. 1, 1942*

**MACARTHUR**

T

AUSTRALI

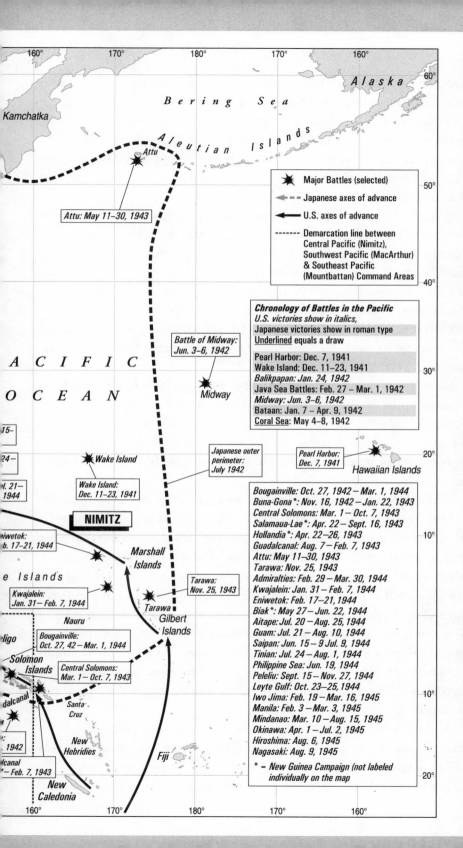

**Major Battles (selected)**

◄ ◄ ◄ Japanese axes of advance

◄──── U.S. axes of advance

------- Demarcation line between
Central Pacific (Nimitz),
Southwest Pacific (MacArthur)
& Southeast Pacific
(Mountbattan) Command Areas

**Chronology of Battles in the Pacific**
*U.S. victories show in italics,*
Japanese victories show in roman type
<u>Underlined</u> equals a draw

Pearl Harbor: Dec. 7, 1941
Wake Island: Dec. 11–23, 1941
*Balikpapan: Jan. 24, 1942*
Java Sea Battles: Feb. 27 – Mar. 1, 1942
*Midway: Jun. 3–6, 1942*
Bataan: Jan. 7 – Apr. 9, 1942
<u>Coral Sea</u>: May 4–8, 1942

*Bougainville: Oct. 27, 1942 – Mar. 1, 1944*
*Buna-Gona\*: Nov. 16, 1942 – Jan. 22, 1943*
*Central Solomons: Mar. 1 – Oct. 7, 1943*
*Salamaua-Lae\*: Apr. 22 – Sept. 16, 1943*
*Hollandia\*: Apr. 22–26, 1943*
*Guadalcanal: Aug. 7 – Feb. 7, 1943*
*Attu: May 11–30, 1943*
*Tarawa: Nov. 25, 1943*
*Admiralties: Feb. 29 – Mar. 30, 1944*
*Kwajalein: Jan. 31 – Feb. 7, 1944*
*Eniwetok: Feb. 17–21, 1944*
*Biak\*: May 27 – Jun. 22, 1944*
*Aitape: Jul. 20 – Aug. 25, 1944*
*Guam: Jul. 21 – Aug. 10, 1944*
*Saipan: Jun. 15 – 9 Jul. 9, 1944*
*Tinian: Jul. 24 – Aug. 1, 1944*
*Philippine Sea: Jun. 19, 1944*
*Peleliu: Sept. 15 – Nov. 27, 1944*
*Leyte Gulf: Oct. 23–25, 1944*
*Iwo Jima: Feb. 19 – Mar. 16, 1945*
*Manila: Feb. 3 – Mar. 3, 1945*
*Mindanao: Mar. 10 – Aug. 15, 1945*
*Okinawa: Apr. 1 – Jul. 2, 1945*
*Hiroshima: Aug. 6, 1945*
*Nagasaki: Aug. 9, 1945*

\* = New Guinea Campaign (not labeled
individually on the map


Alaska

Bering Sea

Kamchatka

Aleutian Islands

Attu

Attu: May 11–30, 1943

PACIFIC OCEAN

Battle of Midway:
Jun. 3–6, 1942

Midway

Wake Island

Wake Island:
Dec. 11–23, 1941

NIMITZ

niwetok:
b. 17–21, 1944

Kwajalein:
Jan. 31 – Feb. 7, 1944

e Islands

Marshall
Islands

Japanese outer
perimeter:
July 1942

Pearl Harbor:
Dec. 7, 1941

Hawaiian Islands

Tarawa:
Nov. 25, 1943

Tarawa
Gilbert
Islands

Nauru

ligo

Bougainville:
Oct. 27, 42 – Mar. 1, 1944

Solomon
Islands

Central Solomons:
Mar. 1 – Oct. 7, 1943

dalcanal

Santa
Cruz

New
Hebridies

Fiji

1942

lcanal
– Feb. 7, 1943

New
Caledonia

guards, and by the time the POWs reached their destination, between 5,000 to 10,000 Filipinos and 650 Americans had died.[19]

Corregidor finally fell in May, and concerned about saving lives, the American commander, General Jonathan Wainwright, extended the terms of his capitulation to all American forces in the Philippines. Many Americans and Filipinos repudiated the surrender and took to the hills to fight on as guerrillas.

Meanwhile, the British badly bungled the campaign in Burma and were driven out to take refuge in India. Only the terrain, heat, humidity, impenetrable jungle, and lack of supply lines kept the Japanese from following. Losing Burma was serious for another reason, however, in that the Burma Road that supplied Chiang's Nationalist Chinese forces was cut, and the Chinese were already frayed by having to deal with the Communists and various free-agent warlords. Although Chiang ostensibly had 1.2 million men in his forces, only half that number were directly controlled by his generals.

Allied forces elsewhere fared no better. In Papua New Guinea the Japanese secured the excellent harbor at Rabaul, and pushed eastward into the Solomon Islands. By May the Japanese Navy was ready to send an invasion force to secure Port Moresby, on the south coast of New Guinea, as a stepping-stone to attack Australia. The situation in the South Pacific looked dire.

While the arithmetic of war output and personnel overwhelmingly favored the Americans and British in the Pacific, that was not obvious in early 1942. Quite the contrary, Japan's onslaught had gained unprecedented areas of territory and people—more than any other empire in human history in so short a time. Despite Franklin Roosevelt's boast in April 1942 that "for every advance that the Japanese have made . . . they have had to pay a very heavy toll in warships, in transports, in planes and in men," the price Japan paid was minimal and, at times, nonexistent.[20] They had lost virtually no important ships prior to May 1942. In fact, it was a strategically meaningless air raid by Colonel Jimmy Doolittle on the Japanese home islands that revived American morale, and, in a sense, turned the entire Pacific war in a new direction.

Doolittle's raid was the brainchild of Navy captain Francis Low, who was on the staff of the antisubmarine warfare division.[21] Twin-engine B-25 Mitchell bombers were to take off from the deck of an aircraft carrier, fly over Tokyo and other targets, then continue on to safe havens inside China.

Removing all nonessential weight and expanding the planes' fuel capacity, the crews trained on specially marked landing fields, then the aircraft were flown to Alameda Naval Air Station and loaded aboard the *Hornet*. On April 18, 1942, seven hundred miles from Japan, the *Hornet* was spotted by a Japanese picket boat and Doolittle's raiders were forced to take off well ahead of schedule and with two hundred extra miles to fly. All the planes were lost, but some flyers, including Doolittle, were rescued by Chinese who took them safely out of Japanese-held territory. Others were captured, subjected to show trials in Japan, and executed. Regardless of this heavy price for what was virtually a stunt, the Doolittle raid electrified the American public and terrified the Japanese, who concentrated on defending their home islands. Indeed, Doolittle's men practically forced Admiral Yamamoto into his attempted invasion of Midway, which would prove Japan's undoing.

The story of the Battle of Midway is well known to many Americans as one of the greatest victories in American history. Courage and luck probably played equal parts, helped by excellent intelligence work in Hawaii and sound decision making by Navy commanders.

A preliminary battle was fought in May 1942 in the Coral Sea which pitted Rear Admiral Frank Jack Fletcher's two American carriers against two of the Japanese fleet carriers that had been at Pearl Harbor and a light carrier. In the first naval engagement strictly between carriers and in which no surface vessel saw an opposing vessel, Fletcher lost the *Lexington*, the Navy's largest carrier, while sinking the Japanese light carrier, damaging one of the fleet carriers, and downing a hundred planes. Whether it was labeled an American defeat or draw, its most important impact was that the heavy loss in aircrews forced both large Japanese carriers to miss the upcoming Midway campaign.

Admiral Yamamoto led a massive strike force, spearheaded by four fleet carriers under Vice Admiral Nagumo—the overseer of the Pearl Harbor attack—to seize Midway atoll (and its airstrip) and to simultaneously lure out the remaining American carriers (the Japanese thought there were only two left, thinking both of Fletcher's vessels had been lost at Coral Sea). Vice Admiral William "Bull" Halsey, who normally would have commanded the American force, was in the hospital, afflicted with a nasty skin rash. In typical American style, a subordinate, Rear Admiral Raymond Spruance, stepped into the breach to command Halsey's task force of two carriers. Fletcher's last carrier, the *Yorktown*, had been damaged at Coral Sea, but superlative repair work by 1,500 workmen at Pearl Harbor—some ferried by plane to the carrier while it was still en route—allowed him to catch up with Spruance and take command. Armed with intelligence that confirmed Midway was indeed Nagumo's target, the Americans positioned themselves northeast of the atoll, and despite numerous Japanese reconnaissance flights—one of which flew directly over the U.S. force—remained undetected. Nagumo's planes failed to knock out the landing strip on Midway, requiring a second strike, but just as Nagumo ordered the planes to rearm with bombs for attacking a land target, spotters saw American torpedo planes coming in. During the brief, deadly fight that followed, the U.S. forces scored no hits and lost most of their planes, but in the process, Nagumo's fighters had to land and refuel. At that precise moment, with all the carrier decks full of planes, fuel, and bombs—and no air cover to speak of—two squadrons of dive bombers appeared in the skies over the Imperial Fleet. Three carriers were set ablaze immediately by American bombs. Nagumo sent his remaining squadrons of dive-bombers and torpedo planes to the last known location of the *Yorktown*, which took crippling injuries, forcing the *Yorktown*'s returning planes to land on Spruance's *Enterprise*. Fletcher delegated tactical command to Spruance, who launched a retaliatory strike with a cobbled-together force of *Enterprise* and *Yorktown* dive-bombers that destroyed the last Japanese carrier. Midway was saved, and the pride of the Japanese strike force was scuttled. Hard fighting was ahead, but after Midway, the negotiated peace leaving Japan as the master of Asia and the Pacific was a pipe dream.

Guadalcanal followed as the United States was able to seize the initiative. The islands of Guadalcanal, Tulagi, and Florida, part of the Solomons group, had fallen into Japanese hands and constituted a dagger aimed at the supply lines of Australia. In August 1942, Allied forces led by the American 1st Marine Division under Major General Alexander Vandegrift landed to scatter the few Japanese defenders and Korean laborers. Over the next five months, heavy Japanese reinforcements staged suicidal attacks on land and seven major naval assaults to reclaim the island. Fighting in extreme tropical weather and often in knee-deep mud, the Marines held on grimly. At one point, on Edson's Ridge, 830 Marine Raiders defeated 3,000 Japanese supported by artillery in heavy fighting.[22] As Henderson Field on Guadalcanal became operational and was able to mount serious air attacks in conjunction with naval forces, the Japanese were forced to reinforce their troops at night through the infamous "Tokyo Express" of destroyers dashing down the "Slot" (New Georgia Sound) to the northwestern tip of Guadalcanal. By December the decimated 1st Marines had been withdrawn and replaced by two Army divisions, the 25th and the Americal, the 2nd Marine Division, and various other smaller units. The issue was no longer in doubt: Japan had to withdraw in an operation completed early in February 1943.

After Guadalcanal, the United States went permanently on the offensive. MacArthur attacked in New Guinea, and American submarines began to whittle down the Japanese merchant marine. Although both sides lost twenty-four warships in the Solomons battles, Japan could not afford to break even, especially considering the massive naval construction program started by FDR in 1940, which bore fruit in 1943. The Japanese army attempted to defend its acquisitions, spreading large numbers of troops throughout the Pacific, but MacArthur's "Island Hopping" campaign cut off those forces from supplies; then, often in grueling tunnel-to-tunnel combat, eliminated the suicidal troops who still remained. Slowly, Americans came to understand that this was no traditional Western enemy who surrendered when doomed: the Japanese were Bushido warriors who fought to the last.

## Germany's Russian Quagmire

As the United States focused its attention on the Pacific, in Europe the Eastern Front took center stage. The Wehrmacht once again reminded the Allies that it was the world's most efficient army, and rapidly recovered from its horrendous losses during the winter. After the spring rainy period called *rasputitsa* when the roads became bottomless mud bogs that were impossible to traverse, Germany planned Case Blue—a strategic offensive aimed at the rich oil fields of the Caucasus Mountains in southern Russia. The German offensives during the spring had been resounding but worrisome successes: in Operation Fredericus, Kharkov was saved from a Soviet attack, virtually annihilating Soviet marshal Semyon Timoshenko's three armies and capturing 240,000 prisoners and 1,249 tanks.[23] The southern flank was secured by the capture of the Crimea by von Manstein, netting another quarter million prisoners.[24] Ostensibly those were successes, but they took longer than planned, and resulted in fewer prisoners than expected. The Soviet Army in 1942 was a different army from that of 1941—mass assaults were not as common as individual units became more capable, and surrenders were much fewer.[25]

Some in the German High Command, particularly the chief of staff,

Colonel-General Franz Halder, already thought Case Blue constituted the last throw of the dice. With the Wehrmacht unable to replace its losses during the winter—as the Soviets had, with their seemingly endless pool of men—unless a decisive summer campaign could be mounted, the end for Germany was inevitable. Victory in Russia needed to occur in 1942, in order to confront the Americans who could be expected to attack in late 1942 or 1943. Even more critically and urgently, Germany needed to secure the coal and industrial area of the Don basin and seize the Caucasus oil fields to mechanize its army.

Army Group Center had barely survived the winter of 1941–42, and on the entire Eastern Front through March 1942, the German Army had suffered losses of 1.1 million men, or 35 percent of its force. General Staff estimates put the army at 625,000 fewer men on the Eastern Front than it had at the start of Barbarossa.[26] German infantry divisions fell to one half and even one third their normal strength, and Hitler (at Speer's urging) refused to release German males from industrial production. In addition, more than 180,000 horses had died during the winter, and only 20,000 replacements had been received.

Nonetheless, on April 5, Hitler issued ambitious new orders for a summer offensive: destroy the remainder of the Soviet military forces and control the principal war-making industrial facilities and resources. Army Group North was to capture Leningrad and link up with the Finns, Army Group Center was to remain stationary, and Army Group South was to break through, seize the oil-producing area in the Caucasus, and reach the Caspian Sea, a goal that suggested the Nazis potentially aimed to reach Persia.

Indeed, it is critical to understand the genuine apprehension that consumed all Allied leaders in mid-1942. Japan had yet to lose a major battle prior to Midway and seemed unstoppable; there were even fears of a Japanese landing in Santa Barbara, California. FBI reports showed that Japanese spies in Hawaii and California were active, and those memos—unavailable until recently and virtually uncited by historians—constitute evidence that explains in large part Roosevelt's internment orders for Japanese-Americans.[27] In Russia, the Soviet winter offensive might have been nothing more than a temporary setback for the Nazis and their losses made good by reinforcements. Who was to say that the astounding success of the Germans in the fall of 1941 could not be repeated? Who knew if the next wave of Soviet soldiers would fare any better than the first? And what if, by some stretch of the imagination, Germany held the Caucasus and Japan marched westward through Burma and reached Persia to link *all* the Axis powers in one massive alliance that controlled much of the earth's oil?

In hindsight it is easy to dismiss such fears as vast overreactions, but in the context of 1941 and early 1942, the Allies had yet to stop either the Nazis or the Japanese on any kind of permanent basis. One could later see the

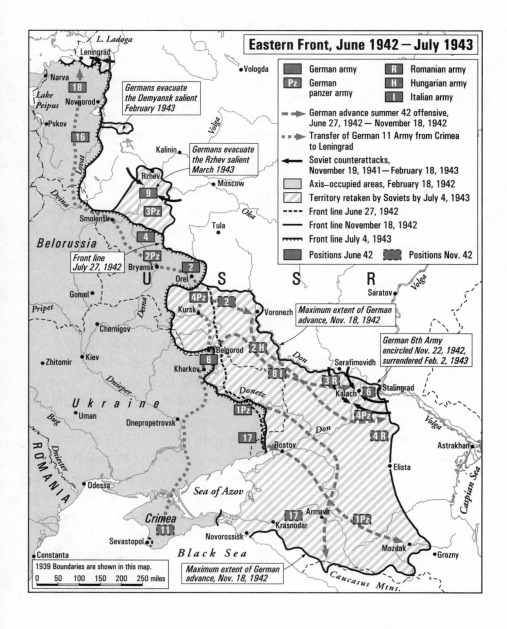

astounding weaknesses of the Wehrmacht, the Luftwaffe, and Japan's continued abyss in China—yet these weaknesses had existed in 1939, and look at what Axis power had accomplished. What the Battle of Britain, Doolittle's raid, and the defense of Moscow did, more than anything, was restore confidence that in fact the Allies were *not* facing supermen, either Aryan or Nipponese, and that reasoned, ordered, and steady counteroffensives could prevail.

Inside Hitler's headquarters, however, the thirst for raw materials—particularly oil—reached desperate levels. Hitler's gaze was transfixed on oil—Germany's future lifeblood, and, as he saw it, the driving force in technology for the next few centuries.[28] Here, Hitler proved unusually prescient—Japan went to war over oil, and oil would become arguably the dominant economic resource for the next hundred years. In May of 1942 at the Wolf's Lair (Hitler's Eastern Front headquarters near Rastenburg, East Prussia), Field Marshal Wilhelm Keitel told General Georg Thomas, "The operations of 1942 must get us that oil [in the Caucasus]. If we're not successful, we will not be able to mount any operations in the next year."[29] Hitler went further. Speaking to his assembled generals in Poltava a few days later, he said, "If I can't acquire the oil from Maikop and Grozny, then I must liquidate [put an end to] this war."[30] He announced that the destruction of Soviet forces in front of the Don was merely a preparation for capturing the Caucasus oil fields and crossing the Caucasus Mountains.

Halder, who personally opposed the strategy, nevertheless continued to support Hitler's plans. During the spring of 1942, however, he decided an operation across the Caucasus was no longer possible (mostly due to German transportation problems), and in June assessed a coordinated attack from Russia and North Africa against the Middle East as equally impossible. He became increasingly pessimistic about the Russian operation ("criminal madness," he labeled it), estimating Case Blue would take 700,000 to 800,000 Soviet prisoners, but not destroy the Red Army's ability to continue the fight. German intelligence on the Eastern Front noted that even if the new offensive achieved complete success, the Red Army would lose forty divisions but replace them with one hundred new divisions by winter. Halder concluded the war was no longer winnable, especially after he looked at POW totals that reflected an insufficient number of surrendering enemy soldiers. If the army succeeded in capturing the oil fields by some extraordinary feat of arms, the Russians surely would have destroyed them, and even if not, there was no possibility, either by land or across the

Black Sea, of transporting the oil back to Germany. No German Rocke-feller existed to lay miles of oil pipeline per day, let alone defend it.

It made no difference, as Hitler couldn't keep his eye on the ball. Against Halder's advice, in July he transferred Field Marshal von Manstein and five divisions of his army that had conquered the Crimea to Leningrad to help capture that city—using troops that could have helped take the Caucasus. Then he decided to attack Stalingrad and the Caucasus simulta-neously, a move for which Halder knew the German forces were inadequate. A frustrated Halder ineffectually opposed Hitler almost daily, particularly with respect to the capabilities of the Red Army. When Hitler remarked that in spite of constant victories, the great destruction of the Red Army eluded him, Halder informed him that Stalin avoided decisive engagements deliberately. Hitler responded, "Nonsense, he's fleeing, he's finished, he's at his end from the blows we've given him in the last several months."[31] Hal-der's diary recorded, "The continual underestimation of enemy possibilities is taking grotesque forms; it's becoming dangerous."[32] Hitler "retired" Hal-der in September, and the general was fortunate not to be shot. History would record Stalingrad as the war's "turning point" (although some histo-rians point to Kursk in the summer of 1943, where German armor was de-cisively defeated), but actually the improved Soviet efficiency in battle during the summer of 1942 shut the door on any ultimate German victory.

## Death in the Desert

Although the Italian-German campaign in North Africa was seen by Hitler to be a secondary and relatively unimportant theater, it wasn't for Mussolini and Italy. Libya, most of which Italy had incorporated into its national ter-ritory, possessed 1,100 miles of Mediterranean coastline. Although the provinces of Tripolitania and Cyrenaica were considered strategic by Italy, the area was a drag on the Italian economy, exporting less than $6 million in goods to Italy in 1938 while importing more than $46 million in subsi-dized goods and services by the Italian government. After acquiring Libya in 1912 from the Ottomans, Italy had made some efforts to colonize it: by 1939, out of a population of 900,000, 150,000 were Italians. Libyan oil re-serves would have been a major consideration for Italy had anyone known about them, but oil was not discovered in Libya until 1959.

Every bit as acquisition-minded as Hitler, Mussolini sought an Italian empire, making a stab at adding Egypt in 1940. After his army had ad-vanced sixty-five miles into Egypt, it halted and dug in. Strategically, the

86,000 British troops in the entire Middle East were being threatened by not only Marshal Rodolfo Graziani's 250,000-man Libyan army, but also the 350,000-man Italian Army in Ethiopia and East Africa. The Western Desert Force defending Egypt comprised two divisions: the 4th Indian Infantry and the British 7th Armored, plus a heterogeneous force called the Selby Group. Thirty-six thousand men under General Richard O'Connor, a bold and uncharacteristically aggressive British officer, would attack an army of more than 200,000. Bantam-weight, shy, and soft-spoken, O'Connor struck with great audacity on December 7, and after three days, the only Italians left in Egypt were prisoners. By early in January, the British had captured the bulk of Graziani's army. O'Connor's men had advanced six hundred miles, taking more than 130,000 prisoners.

At that point, Winston Churchill intervened—Greece needed reinforcements—and halted O'Connor. Many of those troops never returned, as the Germans handed the British successive defeats in Greece and Crete. Meanwhile, Hitler reinforced Axis forces in Libya, dispatching General Erwin Rommel and the Afrika Korps. In April Rommel drove the British out of Libya entirely, except for Australians holding the fortress of Tobruk. Early in the campaign a German scouting party captured a British staff car containing O'Connor and two other British generals, and the resulting loss of its command structure threw the British army into disarray. One indicator of O'Connor's value came when the overall commander of British forces in the Middle East, Sir Archibald Wavell, offered to exchange O'Connor for any six Italian generals of choice; there were no takers.

Rommel, who would be made the youngest field marshal in the German Army after his successes in 1942, was a Swabian, the son of a schoolmaster. A short, solidly built, wiry man, Rommel had blue eyes, unbounded energy, and a quick mind. Myths surround him: contrary to legend, he was never a Nazi Party member, never a member of the Freikorps, never a policeman, and never a storm trooper.[33] His family was solid middle-class with no military tradition, but when his father forbade him from seeking employment at the Friedrichshafen Zeppelin plant, he joined the army as an officer cadet. From this background of moderate means and no connections, essentially ineligible to join the General Staff, under normal circumstances he could have expected to retire as a major at best.

During World War I Rommel fought on the Western Front, where he won an Iron Cross 2nd Class, and later the Iron Cross 1st Class. Promoted to lieutenant, he was sent to Romania, then in 1917 to Italy, where with only

5 men, he captured 43 officers and 1,500 men, and was awarded the coveted Pour le Mérite (the Blue Max), Germany's highest decoration. Between the wars he advanced steadily until his manual, *Infanterie Greift An* ("Infantry Attacks"), attracted the attention of higher-ranking officers and Hitler himself. After he commanded Hitler's escort battalion, he emerged as a favorite. His performance as commander of the 7th Panzer Division in France brought him acclaim as a master of panzer tactics. Promoted to lieutenant general, he assumed command of the German troops in Libya. Later, he would oppose the Allied landings on D-Day, join the July 20, 1944, plot against Hitler, and pay with his life.

Rommel's primary problem lay not in his British enemies, but in obtaining support from the German High Command. There was a nagging and unending issue of insufficient supplies, for which transport to Libya was an Italian responsibility. His was an unimportant theater to High Command, and not without reason. Unless Hitler could convince Turkey to enter the war on the Axis side, he possessed no way to transport Middle Eastern oil to Germany. Already, the Royal Navy, supported by the U.S. Navy and merchant marine, had kept Malta open despite increasing raids and Gibraltar had never been captured. Nor could Rommel guess that the British were reading his communications. Penetration of communications with the Italian High Command via Enigma machines gave the British notice of all sailings of supply ships, and the Desert Fox was often fortunate to receive any supplies at all. Air raids from Malta constituted a sharp thorn he could not overcome.

Failing in the siege of Tobruk in 1941 and exhausting his forces in the subsequent fights, Rommel fell back to his starting point at El Agheila in January 1942. Resupplied and reinforced, he bounced back in May 1942, heavily defeated the British in the Battle of Gazala and took Tobruk in a walk, capturing more than 32,000 prisoners. Driving into Egypt, he was forced to halt at El Alamein. Rommel had outrun his supply line and was henceforth unable to meet the British on reasonably equal terms. His immediate superior, Field Marshal Albert Kesselring, had advised him to go no farther east than Tobruk, but the pressure from Hitler to seize the Suez Canal grew too great.[34] A glance at the vast discrepancy in supplies explains the hopelessness of Rommel's efforts: in August 1942, the Afrika Korps received 13,000 tons of supplies; the British 8th Army, 500,000 tons. General Bernard Montgomery assumed command of the British 8th Army in August and transformed the atmosphere in his army from defeatist to optimistic.

Aloof and arrogant, Montgomery was a caricature of the snooty, elitist British officer, but a man who occasionally fought well. His tank superiority over Rommel topped ten to one by the time he went on the offensive (not counting the useless Italian models) and his manpower advantage, two to one. Down to only thirty operational tanks and in defiance of Hitler's order, Rommel asked to be allowed to retreat to a defensible position where he could be supplied, but Hitler forbade a withdrawal. Suffering from jaundice and unable to lead from the front as was his custom, Rommel retreated, and in September, returned to Germany for medical treatment.

While the Axis was advancing on all fronts, Britain and the United States were hammering out a strategy to eventually win the war. FDR and Churchill agreed to a policy of "Europe First," meaning that the bulk of their efforts would be directed against Germany before turning to Japan. In practice, this was ameliorated by American public opinion and its anger against the Japanese, and by Admiral Ernest King, chief of naval operations, who made sure most naval forces were diverted to the Pacific. He would later be criticized for the excessive losses among the American merchant marine in the Atlantic, but his primary concern was the regular Navy. As a result, it was more dangerous to be in the merchant marine during World War II than in the U.S. Navy.

U.S. generals, led by General Marshall and his protégé, Dwight D. Eisenhower, favored an early invasion of continental Europe across the English Channel. The British Imperial Staff, headed by Field Marshal Alan Brooke, considered the Americans to be rank amateurs, echoing the sentiments of British commanders in North Africa who referred to them as "our Italians."[35] Dwight David Eisenhower possessed no combat experience, and had been elevated from an obscure lieutenant colonel to commanding general in only sixteen months. The British were intransigent, holding that a cross-Channel invasion would not be feasible until 1944, if then. Churchill favored a Mediterranean strategy that would reestablish British hegemony in the area, and American proposals of Roundup, the cross-Channel invasion, and Sledgehammer, a contingency plan to help the Soviets if they neared collapse by making a landing in the French Pas-de-Calais region, were discarded. Instead, Operation Torch, an invasion of French North Africa, was proposed and agreed to on July 22. Accordingly, planning began on Torch, and Eisenhower was placed in command, much to the consternation of the French generals Charles de Gaulle and Henri Giraud, both of whom expected to lead the North African invasion.

In November 1942 British and American forces finally went on the ground offensive on the Western Front with Torch, a three-pronged amphibious assault that seized key ports and airfields from Algeria to Morocco. General George Patton commanded the Western Task Force of 35,000 troops, landing near Casablanca, Rabat, and Safi, northwest of Marrakech. The Center Task Force, with 18,000 men, under General Lloyd R. Fredendall, landed at Oran, and the Eastern Task Force, headed by British lieutenant general Kenneth Anderson, moved ashore at Algiers. The strategy at Casablanca called for the Allies to withhold a bombardment, under the hope that French troops would not fight back, but after French batteries opened up, Allied warships returned fire. A few French warships sallied forth and were destroyed. Oran likewise surrendered after a brief battle, as did Algiers. Hoping to solidify authority in the region with minimal effort, Eisenhower, with the initial and unenthusiastic backing of Roosevelt and Churchill, offered Vichy French admiral Jean Darlan control of French North Africa if he would join the Allies, meaning that Vichy France technically would remain in power. But Darlan was murdered by a member of the French Resistance on December 24, by which time Hitler and Mussolini had occupied Vichy France and reinforced Axis units in North Africa.

Convinced they could no longer trust France's commitments, the Germans initiated Operation Lila on November 27 to seize the French fleet at Toulon, whereupon units from the 7th Panzer Division rolled into the city and toward the docks. The French transmitted orders to scuttle the fleet, and just as the German tanks reached the piers, ship after ship exploded. More than seventy-five vessels, including three battleships and seven cruisers, were destroyed. Some cruisers were restored by the Italians later, and General De Gaulle was outraged that the Vichy admirals had not sailed the fleet to Algiers. Nonetheless, the event rendered France a complete nonplayer in future naval considerations.

Germany established a holding force in Tunisia, awaiting Rommel's westward retreat from Libya. Montgomery, in what would become a nagging point of criticism, pursued slowly (some would say, glacially), allowing Rommel to turn on the Americans. Reinforced Afrika Korps units attacked in February 1943, striking General Fredendall's forces at Kasserine Pass, a disastrous encounter that showed the Americans' lack of combat experience, poor leadership, lack of coordination, and inadequate training: some of the G.I.s had never fired live ammunition. Even before Kasserine, Alan Brooke, a constantly pessimistic artilleryman whose main claim to military expertise was his troop handling during the British withdrawal from the Continent in 1940, had lobbied through Churchill to relieve Eisenhower of operational command. As Brooke said in his diary, "Eisenhower . . . had neither the tactical nor strategic experience required." In installing General Sir Harold Alexander as Eisenhower's deputy and placing operations in his hands, Brooke said, "We were pushing Eisenhower up into the strato-sphere . . . where he would be free to devote his time to the political and inter-allied problems, whilst we inserted . . . our own commanders to deal with the military situations . . ."[36]

Kasserine, with 1,000 dead and a total of 6,500 casualties, marked one of the most embarrassing military defeats in American history, ranking with the Bladensburg Races in 1814 and the Little Bighorn in infamy. Fredendall, who had remained safe in a concrete bunker far behind the lines, was sacked, replaced by Patton. But Patton would not face Rommel, who had returned to Germany to plead with Hitler for a withdrawal from Tunisia, a maneuver that resulted in his removal from command. Without their daring leader and experiencing increasing shortages of supply, the Germans who remained were doomed. A combined British-American offensive from March to May forced the Axis troops into a pocket. After the British took Tunis and the Americans took Bizerte, all the remaining Axis forces—nearly a quarter of a million Germans and Italians—went into the bag.

Part of the Axis failure in North Africa stemmed from an inability to eliminate the island base of Malta, which came under repeated attacks by German air. The island sat astride Axis supply lines, its aircraft roaming far out to sink and harass shipping. Just as Doolittle's men sent a message from their carriers in the Pacific, so too little Malta signaled defiance. Germany made an all-out effort in February 1942 to wipe out the island's defenses, and in a six-month period, more than six thousand tons of bombs rained down on the island. In June 1942, German attacks had become so devastating, sinking thirty-seven supply ships, that the fate of the bastion rested on a single ship and its cargo, the world's fastest tanker, the SS *Ohio*. Through the efforts of two Americans, Frederick Larsen and Francis Dales, who manned guns to keep the Luftwaffe attackers at bay, the *Ohio* limped into Malta with decks awash to deliver tons of precious oil that kept the aircraft, generators, and antiaircraft operations alive.[37]

## G.I.s, Joes, or Jive?

Subsequent criticism by historians of the American military capabilities during the war remained muted at the time, thanks to heavy, and arguably much-needed, censorship of the press under the Roosevelt and Churchill administrations. But the U.S. Army's performance at Kasserine and later battles ignited much discussion after the war over the effectiveness of American troops, especially as contrasted with that of German units. S.L.A. Marshall concluded that 25 percent of American infantrymen failed to fire their weapons in combat. Other writers such as Martin van Creveld presented a devastating attack on the American replacement system in which new recruits were constantly fed into units individually rather than withdrawing units from battle and allowing time for veterans and replacements to regain unit cohesion. Such a process, it was argued, lowered unit cohesion and effectiveness, leaving replacements as outsiders who died like flies before their comrades even learned their names. However, some authors have risen to the American G.I.'s defense, one of the most recent being Peter R. Mansoor, who cited the fact that historians sometimes compared American line troops with SS panzer divisions—the elite of the German army in 1943 and afterward—and when U.S. Rangers, for instance, were measured against those SS units, their performance was roughly equivalent.[38] There are many factors making a one-to-one analysis difficult, such as that American infantry divisions were fully mechanized, enjoyed air supremacy and excellent supply, while the German *Landsers* (G.I.s) possessed no such benefits.

Without question, the German Army had the advantage of having the years from 1934 to 1940 to train and build its force, whereas the Americans had only four years, from 1940 to 1944. Certainly the paramilitary training German youth received before being conscripted played a part in accelerating their effectiveness, although Boy Scout training and the familiarity with firearms by rural American youth tended to balance this out. In Germany, monoethnic and monocultural units were formed from localities and kept together as much as possible to foster unit cohesion. A much different polyglot American Army contained multicultural and multiethnic units, purposely formed by assigning individuals from all parts of the country and all walks of life as if they were interchangeable parts. With extensive training, mixing such diverse groups could work, but during the replacement process, American forces suffered from the addition of soldiers who were expected to fight as a team yet didn't know one another. Whereas American divisions received a constant stream of new, but entirely inexperienced, troops, German divisions fought themselves out, then were rotated to the rear for reorganization, filling out with replacements and training to meld them back into a cohesive unit. At any rate, the American Army performed creditably, and combat units tended to learn rapidly from their mistakes. What differences there were, if any, between the American G.I. and German *Landser* were a result of their respective armies' organization, training, and policies, in particular in leadership training (German leadership training to accomplish the mission went all the way down to corporal), replacements, and rotations.

A radical difference in soldiers' mentality and attitude could also be detected among the Americans, especially as contrasted with Russians and British. The G.I., as one analyst noted, "regarded himself as only a temporary soldier," retaining a level of autonomous identity unique among the armies.[39] During the American Revolution, Baron von Steuben, training George Washington's soldiers, had already come to the conclusion that American fighters had to understand their orders, not just obey them: "You say to your [French or Austrian] soldier, 'Do this' and he doeth it; but I am obliged to say, 'This is the reason why you ought to do that,' and he does it."[40] Having evolved from a militia tradition where units elected their own officers and thought independently, Americans represented the epitome of the Western Way of War for better or worse on the battlefield.

Whether the upper echelons of the Army learned, or whether it was small unit improvisation that led to American victories, is hard to tell. Critics maintain that American military planning was poor, there was little understanding of the combined arms doctrine, and no one made allowances for high casualties.[41] But in this war, no army did, least of all the Russians, who hurled an astonishing 600 divisions (with a total of 34 million men serving) at the Germans. This was more than five times what the Nazis had (117 divisions) when they invaded Russia in June 1941, not counting satellite forces. During the five years the Soviets were at war, they put over 20 percent of their population in uniform, compared with 24 percent for Germany and only 11 percent for the United States. The Soviets lost more than 8.7 million men from 1941 to 1943 alone, and losses topped 13 million over the course of the war. This constituted a jaw-dropping 37 percent military death rate, exceeding Germany's 35 percent rate, and dwarfing the U.S. military death rate of 2.5 percent. Simply put, the American approach was to employ firepower whenever possible to minimize casualties, and the Soviets appeared not to care.

What U.S. experience showed was that the high levels of individuality and exceptional battlefield autonomy possessed by G.I.s made improvisation not only possible, but routine. Consider the hedgerows in Normandy, which tanks could not climb over without exposing their vulnerable underbellies, and enemy troops could lurk on the hidden back side to threaten infantry. A sergeant, Curtis Culin of the 102nd Cavalry Recon Squadron, welded steel teeth to his unit's tank. The teeth dug into the embankment and created a gap in the hedgerow without exposing either the tank or the men, an innovation soon widely used and known as the "Rhinoceros" attachment.[42] It was not a naval board or even an admiral, but a machinist on the USS *Yorktown*, Oscar W. Myers, who determined that the USS *Lexington* was sunk at the Battle of Coral Sea in large part due to gasoline fires on deck caused by poor fuel control. On the spot, Myers invented a system of draining the carrier's fuel pipes after use and filling them with inert $CO_2$ gas. After Captain Elliott Buckmaster approved of the project, the *Yorktown* was outfitted with the new system, which likely saved the ship from a calamitous fire after a direct bomb hit during the Battle of Midway.[43]

## Death from the Skies

America's insistence that her troops be more than just cannon fodder and that every precaution be taken to reduce casualties played out in the bombing campaign that unfolded over Europe. Where the British pursued the phantom goal of breaking German morale, thereby reducing industrial output, the Americans homed in on destroying the Luftwaffe and German industry and transportation facilities supplying its frontline troops. If that required destroying industries and cities in the process, *c'est la vie*. This long-term strategy was elaborated on at an April 1942 meeting, where General Ira Eaker informed Allied leadership, "The prime purpose of our operations over here . . . is to make the Luftwaffe come up and fight. If you will support the bomber offensive, I guarantee the Luftwaffe will not prevent the cross-channel invasion."[44] The thousand-plane raids of early summer 1943 were just a warm-up. In August, General Curtis LeMay led a massive series of attacks on the Schweinfurt ball-bearing plants, meeting unprecedented resistance in which the Luftwaffe unleashed relentless, head-on attacks. One bomb group leader noted that B-17s were falling from the sky so fast it "became useless to report them."[45] By the time they reached the first ball-bearing factories, 8th Air Force had lost 32 of the 330 bombers that began the mission, and lost still more on the way home. The final casualty rate was 20 percent, but the blow delivered to the Nazis was even more crushing, reducing ball-bearings production by almost 40 percent. The Americans begged the British to follow up, but the British Air Staff found excuse after excuse not to attack, and once again, Speer observed, "we barely escaped a further catastrophe."[46] For all the widespread damage caused by British night bombing, the Germans had come up with an effective defense created by General Josef Kammhuber's *Nachtjagd-Division*, or night-hunting force. Kammhuber had coordinated flak, searchlights, and well-spaced fighter forces. Using searchlights to "time" the airspeed of a bomber, nearby fighters had three minutes to find it in the light and kill it or search for another target. The bombers entered a chain of searchlights some eighteen miles deep, divided into quadrants of sixty-inch searchlights, then ran a gauntlet of night fighters. The Hamburg raid had been particularly effective due to a new radar-thwarting tactic of dropping tin foil strips known as "Window," which filled German radar screens with snow. But the Germans countered Window fairly quickly, and it proved less useful from that time forward.

Bombing, particularly the Americans' daylight raids, consumed the most attention of German defense planners. Despite the crushing defeat at Stalingrad and the growing superiority of the Red Air Force, Hitler kept moving planes west to counter the bombers, and Joseph Goebbels admitted in his diary that the bombing kept him from ever sleeping.[47] The RAF estimated that of 2,750 fighters in the Luftwaffe, 1,900 were deployed on the Western Front, almost four times what was sent to Russia! One assessment of the pivotal battle of Kursk, while the Germans still had a chance to slow the Red Army, concluded that a 30 percent increase in German tactical air forces, which comprised the Nazis' entire antibombing effort in the West, would have swung the fight.[48]

In fact, General Carl Spaatz *wanted* the Luftwaffe in front of him, where he could destroy it. During the "Big Week" in February 1944, 1,000 U.S. bombers and 900 fighter escorts with long-range drop tanks (a seemingly simple idea that proved dauntingly complex, requiring 150 separate valves and pressure pumps) headed for Germany. This time, Spaatz had issued new directives to his fighter jockeys. "Seek and destroy" the German pilots, he told them, freeing the fighters from bomber escort to achieve "nothing less than annihilation of the Luftwaffe. The strategy [was] to bait them. . . .

Send in the bombers—the bait—to destroy the aircraft factories and then massacre the planes and pilots that came up to defend them."[49] The bombers, of course, were far more than merely "bait," smashing the Ju-88 and Me 109 factories, destroying the Reich's ability to put up new aircraft. The raids exceeded Spaatz's expectations. On the first day, Germany lost 150 fighters, and over the next five days, and from then on, between 40 and 50 fighters per raid. Brunswick's air production, Daimler-Benz's engine and vehicle manufacturing in Stuttgart, and Regensburg's Messerschmitt factories were all flattened, and the British joined in, pounding Leipzig, Berlin, Aachen, Munich, and a half dozen other cities. Augsburg was nearly eradicated. Attempting to defend Berlin, the Luftwaffe lined up its fighters 50 abreast and flew head-on into the bombers as P-51s shot down between 70 and 170 planes—they fell so fast no accurate count could be made.

Speer recorded later that February–March of 1944 marked the virtual end of German air power, as approximately 60 percent of German aircraft in the West were shot down in a two-month period. By May, new attacks on oil-producing facilities meant "the end of German war production," and by July, the attack on the synthetic oil plant at Merseburg left it entirely unusable.[50] Whereas in May, the Reich still had 180,000 tons of aviation fuel available, a month later it had only 10,000 tons, leading Speer to inform Hitler that the loss of aviation petrol neared 90 percent. The economic miracle had come crashing down, and the steady increase in Nazi production since 1942 abruptly sputtered. A collapsing economy dovetailed with an increasing level of pessimism and defeatism among the civilian sector, to which the Reich courts responded by issuing death sentences for negative talk and sabotage to the tune of one hundred per week by 1943. Two Deutsche Bank managers were arrested and executed in the fall of 1943 for "defeatist" comments, as was a board member of the electricity company RWE.

Even though Nazi industry continued to produce, turning out 2,900 fighters alone in the months from February to September 1944, such industrial productivity was irrelevant when the Luftwaffe's entire complement of fighter pilots was either killed or seriously wounded over a five-month span in 1944.[51] Throwing inexperienced pilots up in more advanced planes amounted to sending children onto the Los Angeles freeways in Ferraris. Ironically, the success of bombing on several levels intersected with the Nazi acceleration of the Holocaust, most notably in forcing the Reich to rely ever more heavily on slave labor.

Between the bombing campaign and the millions of new subjects in the conquered lands who consumed resources, Germany was caught in a vise. At first the subjugated lands had provided a windfall of food and ores. Goebbels called German extraction "digesting" the occupied territories. After 1942, in fact, food rations were increased thanks to the doubling of deliveries from conquered territories—not only wheat, but potatoes and meat.[52] Much of the food never got into Germany at all, however: the Wehrmacht consumed over half of the rye and potato imports and two thirds of the oats. Matters were made worse by the RAF's attacks on the Dortmund-Ems canal, the bomber offensive's attack on the Hamm marshaling yards, and the blockage of the Rhine in October when the Cologne-Mülheim bridge was destroyed. Without coal or iron ore, steel production shriveled. Coal shortages plagued the Reich after late 1944; by that time, the arms industry had ground to a halt. Late in 1944 while Americans were churning out a Sherman tank every forty-five minutes, Germany could put a total of only one hundred Tiger I tanks in operation on the entire Eastern Front. All "King Tigers" (Tiger IIs) were being reserved for the Battle of the Bulge.

## Solutions, Final and Otherwise

Shortages in the Reich always posed a conundrum for Nazi leadership, for Germany badly needed laborers—every Jew killed was one who could not work. "The hard truth," Heinrich Himmler said, was that "this people must disappear from the face of the earth."[53] But a harder truth was that every German man in a factory was one less in the field. The first group to benefit from this problem was the Soviet prisoners captured early in the war; the initial policy was to starve them, but by November 1941, Hitler reversed himself and decided to use them in Germany as workers, even though a malnutrition policy continued. The Reich had been consuming fuel and wasting manpower to move hundreds of thousands of Russians to Germany, but then left them to die, serving no useful purpose. Even as workers, allowing them to die was counterproductive: industrial workers needed training, also an investment of time and expertise—a loss of capital with every death.

Throughout 1942 slaves continued to arrive—an astonishing reverse Lebensraum. Prisoners were concentrated in labor and prison camps throughout virtually every industrial city in Germany, most of them without housing, often utterly disorganized, presenting, according to one hardbitten Nazi, "a picture of desolation and immiseration."[54] Nor was this new:

forced labor had built the Nazi military machine sent to Russia after the invasion of France. By 1941 alone, Germany had more than a million foreign prisoner-workers (mostly French) and a million more "civilian" workers from Poland and other occupied countries, all of whom made up over 8 percent of the workforce. A million more soon arrived from Poland after Russia was invaded, including large proportions of teenagers, followed by almost two million more throughout 1942. Gauleiter Fritz Sauckel, who headed the labor mobilization agency (GBA), delivered 34,000 new workers per week for seventy-eight consecutive weeks.[55] At its peak, the foreign labor force constituted one fifth of Germany's labor: Munich alone had more than 16,000 slave laborers for its BMW plant, and some labor populations actually grew in size as the Wehrmacht was chased out of Russia, evacuating some 400,000 people back to work camps. Until that time, German factories littered conquered lands—prior to the withdrawal, Ju-87 Stukas were 80 percent constructed in Russia.

Even with the Russians and Poles, however, the manpower crisis continued as Hitler's Holocaust exterminated Jewish workers. Millions were gone by 1942 alone, eliminating almost 2.4 million potential workers, and another 1.1 million died in "work" camps, along with 175,000 Soviets. Auschwitz was only one of many concentration camps to farm out its inmates for industrial work with I. G. Farben; Sachsenhausen provided labor for Daimler-Benz; and so on, to the tune of 500,000 workers. Many of them were driven by "performance feeding," whereby underperforming workers had their rations deducted and the difference given to better workers. Friction resurfaced between the SS and administrators of industrial programs, with the former interested in decreasing the inmate population and the latter seeking to stabilize it. After the winter of 1942, steps were taken to increase food rations and provide basic medical care. The primacy of food for slave labor—Jews especially—produced something of an irony, as Hitler had begun his "Second Book" with an extensive discussion of food, calling "the struggle for daily bread . . . the top of all vital necessities."[56]

Productivity statistics from slave workers remain murky, but even after allowing for the additional costs of guards and an overall productivity level only 40 percent that of a free German laborer, prisoner labor still constituted a net gain for the Nazis. Not all forced laborers were equally productive, and French prisoners seemed less efficient than German Jews or other German prisoners, while Poles and Soviets badly underperformed western Europeans. In short, Nazi Germany's experience with slave labor scarcely differed from that of the American Confederacy—and these were generally industrial workers already capable of performing mechanized tasks. And, as always, better-fed workers tended to be more efficient.

Here was the internal contradiction of the "Hunger Plan"—the program of systematic starvation of Jews and other foreign prisoners: performance at even low levels demanded a certain caloric intake. Food set aside for workers was food not going to the Wehrmacht, yet without workers, the army had no guns, tanks, or ammunition. Ultimately, the Nazis reverted back to the racial genocide decided upon earlier, creating a "perverse functional connection between the extermination of the Jewish population . . . and the improvement in food rations that was necessary to sustain the labor force working in the mines and factories of the Reich."[57] The Jews would be excluded from food supplies, regardless of the industrial cost. In the short run, the mass murder of Jews freed up substantial food stores for the military. Exclusion of Poles from rations soon followed in March 1943 when they lost their bread allotments. After that (with a few exceptions), it was only a matter of time before even the most productive Jews and Poles became useless.

Concomitant to the extermination program, Nazi doctors struggled with the dual challenges of keeping their own soldiers protected from typhus and other easily transmitted diseases (which required protection for all populations, including Jews and Russians) while at the same time advancing the mission of murder.[58] One solution was to combine "disinfecting" with the extermination process, and to burn bodies after killing them. Already the terminology of Jews as "lice" was in vogue; hence it was a short step to move from disinfecting in the literal sense to the Nazi application of racial purification through gas and fire. Again, however, battles within Nazi ideology had to be fought over even something as inhumane and twisted as the cremation of bodies killed for racial cleansing. In 1932, the Nazi Party condemned cremation as left-wing and materialist, but a concerted effort to embed the process into Nazi policy succeeded, and within a year, cremation was not only acceptable, but also (like everything in a totalitarian society) written into law. Inside the Nazi health establishment (itself an oxymoron), the new German mythos portrayed cremation as "a heroic Nordic rite for the master race," certainly not a fitting end to "lice," although it did become the preferred method for ridding camps of their Jewish prisoners.[59]

Following the *Einsatzgruppen* (SS death squads) program of exterminating Soviet Bolsheviks, Nazi leadership had to finally come to grips with the herculean task of murdering entire populations. Large-scale executions began in Poland in October 1939, but were still oriented toward eliminating Polish leadership, not exterminating Jews.[60] Bullets and fire were too time-consuming and costly, and early experiments with mobile gas vans likewise proved ineffective. Heinrich Himmler, the "architect of genocide," insisted on "a more clinical approach from his SS general(s) and troops."[61] With the Holocaust's institutional underpinnings already in place under the delousing programs necessary for evacuated peoples in the East and for forced labor sent to Germany, it was then only a small step to apply the delousing infrastructure—which already included both chemical "showers" and cremation facilities for bodies—to Judeocide. As Himmler put it,

> Anti-Semitism is exactly the same as delousing. Getting rid of lice is not a question of ideology: it is a matter of cleanliness. In just the same way, anti-Semitism for us had not been a question of ideology but a matter of cleanliness which now will soon have been dealt with. We shall soon be deloused.[62]

The concentration of Jews in the Warsaw ghetto, justified as a sanitary precaution, in fact magnified the spread of disease. Warsaw alone had twenty delousing stations capable of servicing seven thousand prisoners a day, which were later easily converted into gassing centers. Nazi propaganda increasingly linked Jews and disease, portraying Jews as inherent typhus carriers—a point that worked in the inmates' favor at Auschwitz, where indications of typhus tended to ward off SS guards, providing precious extra days or weeks of life.[63] Within ghettos and most camps, however, preventing typhus became a symbol of resistance, an act in defiance of the program of mass murder. At any rate, mass delousing became a near impossibility as the Wehrmacht absorbed millions of Russian prisoners and still more civilians from captured lands.

Chelmno became the first fixed killing installation, commencing operations on the same day Japanese bombs fell on Pearl Harbor. There and at Belzec by August 1942, the killing chambers were first disguised as disinfectant showers, invoking antityphus measures. Sobibor and Treblinka had already installed their own gas chambers, complete with signs saying "FOR DISINFECTION." Auschwitz soon followed the others, gassing Poles and Russians for several months before being converted to a Jewish extermination center. Crematoria technology had been modified to mass-process bodies, with new designs such as that at Birkenau consisting of a two-floor arrangement: gas chambers underground and crematoria above, with bodies carried up via elevators. Rudolf Hess boasted, "Now we had the gas and we had the procedure."[64] Not quite: what Hess still lacked was complete authority from Hitler over Jews, which was given to Himmler in January 1942 at the Wannsee Conference. There, in a posh, elegant villa, "in a cultivated suburb, in one of Europe's most sophisticated capitals," fifteen well-educated and supposedly civilized bureaucrats decorously and methodically (and certainly enthusiastically) agreed to the systematic execution of nine million people.[65] That the originators of this carnage had such high levels of education typified the entire German extermination experience—a point that should concern politicians espousing education as a means of producing civil and tolerant bureaucrats. Of twenty-five *Einsatzgruppen* leaders, fifteen possessed the equivalents of Ph.D.s in jurisprudence or philosophy. And most of the Wannsee conferees were young—half were under forty—giving the lie to the premise that the youth are necessarily pure and gentle.[66]

Wannsee marked the last step in the Nazi murder march that had begun in many ways two decades earlier through the systematic destruction of Jewish civil rights. Hitler and his henchmen briefly dabbled in an expulsion policy, discussing relocation of Jews to Madagascar. This transitioned to a policy of relocation inside the German empire with the opening of Polish lands, then Russia (where Hitler intended to create a "Garden of Eden"), then, following setbacks in Russia, vanished in a sea of impracticality and irrelevance. A temporary measure fell to Reinhard Heydrich, Himmler's subordinate, following the conquest of Poland in 1939. Heydrich established enclosed ghettos in which Jews were to be confined in Polish cities. Lodz, the first ghetto within the German empire, set the standard by which others would be created and governed.[67] Heydrich preferred concentrating Jews in major cities alongside rail routes so "future measures can be accomplished more easily," a phrase that indicated ghettoization was not, in fact, the end point.[68] Adolf Eichmann, a major organizer of the Holocaust, at his interrogation in 1961, said the expression for removal of the Jews commonly used—*Die Endlösung* ("the final solution")—during 1941 referred to "physical extermination," meaning the principle of mass executions was on the table much earlier than Wannsee. In July 1941, in fact, Hitler had already decided to permanently eradicate the Jews, leaving the details to Heydrich, Himmler, and Eichmann to perfect methods of killing.[69] By that point, concentration camps already existed for prisoners and condemned workers, and the practice of allocating half rations to the ghettos meant that slowly the death rate was producing the intended result through starvation.

Thus the tension between wartime production and Jewish extermination increased. With each new country that fell into Hitler's grasp, a network of identification and deportation of Jews followed, although German Jews were not entirely shipped east until 1943. Reich officials such as Joseph Goebbels were shocked to learn from Eichmann in March 1941 that "the Jews . . . cannot be evacuated from Berlin because 30,000 of them are working in armaments factories."[70] Only in April 1941 did Hitler mandate that no Jews could remain in Germany for any reason, and six months later Heydrich ordered there could be "no emigration by Jews to overseas."[71] All that remained was to determine the definitive methodology accomplishing the final solution and what processes would be required. The Wannsee Conference stipulated that all previous plans had been "interim solutions" providing "practical experience" in dealing with Jews. Wannsee definitively established when and how to kill, although the conflict between needing laborers and the imperative to exterminate Jewry continued until almost the end of the war.[72] Himmler, who had been appointed as Reich commissioner for consolidation of German nationhood in 1939, had already ordered a "racial cleanup" in the East, and in 1941 he led a genocide conference aimed at the decimation of Russian Slavic populations, then put at 30 million.[73] But once the decision was made to trap all Jews in Europe, no outcome other than death was possible, except through an Allied victory.

How the Holocaust escaped Allied knowledge for so long—if it did at all—was explained in part by the fact that until Wannsee, the façade of delousing had permitted the Germans to conceal exterminations. Nonetheless, the Vatican learned about extermination of Jews in Poland as early as February of 1942, according to later military tribunals.[74] Representatives of the Jewish Agency sent a letter to the apostolic nuncio in Berne on March 17, 1942, outlining in detail Nazi crimes against Jews in Eastern Europe.[75] At the same time as Wannsee, the Vatican lobbied South American nations at the Rio de Janeiro Conference to continue their neutrality rather than declaring war on Germany as desired by the United States.[76]

During the Warsaw Uprising of 1944, RAF squadrons flew support missions passing over Auschwitz on a daily basis yet failed to take notice of what was happening there. Facilities were soundproofed and camouflaged, but word leaked out nonetheless. A British consular official in Switzerland, relying on Czech underground information, transmitted the ghastly plan in July 1942, and FDR learned about the genocide that year. When it finally became possible to bomb the rail lines in 1944, Churchill met with Chaim Weizmann, head of the World Zionist Organization, and agreed that something should be done. Shortly thereafter, the Jewish Agency sent a note to Roosevelt urging action against Auschwitz itself. It didn't take long for the British Air Ministry to reject the notion, or for John J. McCloy, the U.S. assistant secretary of war, to similarly dismiss attacks as impractical and a diversion of resources. Years later, McCloy would claim that FDR likewise opposed the idea, but Roosevelt allowed no notes to be taken during his conferences or meetings and there is no supporting evidence that this was the case.

To what extent the average soldiers of the Wehrmacht willingly joined in the brutalization of Jews and occupied peoples is a legitimate question, and new studies have heaped guilt on the entire German army. As of 1995, a slight majority of Germans believed the Wehrmacht had committed war crimes, but two thirds of those above the age of sixty-five rejected the proposition.[77] Nevertheless, scholars today debate only the motivations of troops in engaging in extraordinarily cruel behavior, especially to Jews and Russians, not the fact that such monstrous behavior occurred. Nor is there much debate about the fact that intelligent and educated men carried out systematized murder. Nazis with Ph.D.s led the "Extraordinary Pacification Programme" and shot 3,500 Polish intellectuals outside of Warsaw. Overall, the attitude of the German population ranged from passive indifference to objective complicity to energetic enthusiasm. Ian Kershaw summarized the Holocaust and its relationship to ordinary Germans by noting that the most important success of Nazi propaganda was to depersonalize the Jews, and that

> the "Jewish Question" was of no more than minimal interest to the vast majority of Germans during the war years. . . . Popular opinion, largely indifferent and infused with a latent anti-Jewish feeling further bolstered by propaganda provided the climate within which spiraling Nazi aggression towards Jews could take place unchallenged. But it did not provoke the radicalization in the first place.[78]

The "road to Auschwitz," he wrote, "was built by hatred, but paved with indifference."[79]

## Deadly Seas and Sands

The ethnic cleansing perpetrated by the Japanese came in a slightly different form, and with smaller total numbers, largely because Japan had not racialized its murder system to one particular group: all foreigners were *gaijin* ("barbarians") and subject to death if necessary. More important, the Japanese had failed to gain control over China's population the way the Nazis had in Europe. Examples of extermination abound, including the "Rape of Nanking" and the murder of 250,000 Chinese peasants in reprisal for helping conceal Doolittle airmen after the raid. Nor could Japanese civilians claim to have no knowledge of these atrocities: Japanese newspapers widely publicized killing contests near Nanking, making heroes out of two sub-lieutenants who raced to see which one could behead a hundred captives first. The contest was ruled a tie when both murderers exceeded a hundred victims. Perhaps worst of all was the mass distribution of opium by Japanese to Chinese; some 20 million Chinese became addicted to the narcotic and were summarily eliminated from providing effective resistance to Japanese authority. However, pockets of resistance dotted China, and the jungles of Southeast Asia facilitated guerrilla warfare such as the Germans found only in the Balkan Mountains. That Japan saw China swallow massive amounts of men and supplies—more than half of the Japanese army was in China—demands a new interpretation of the "ineffectiveness" of Chiang Kai-shek's resistance.

Japanese soldiers had been inundated with propaganda about the brutality of the Americans, which, when coupled with Bushido, explains why surrender was considered dishonorable to oneself and one's family. With the invasion of the Philippines in late 1944, widespread use of leaflets encouraging the Japanese to surrender helped increase the ratio of Japanese prisoners-to-killed from one in one hundred to one in seven by 1945. But already Americans had become convinced that the defeated foe must be impressed with the reality of who actually won. Some G.I.s in Europe, for example, wanted all Germans to feel the full effects of the terrors of war. One 101st Airborne soldier wrote, "Unless we take the horror of battle to Germany itself, unless we fight in their villages, blowing up their houses . . . unless we litter their streets with horribly rotten German corpses as was done in France, the German will prepare for war, unmindful of its horrors."[80] Most, however, surprised their officers by continuing to see the enemy as "men just like us."[81] Throughout the conflict, the War Department worried that soldiers who "lack vindictiveness are probably standing on the shaky ground of too much identification of the enemy as a human being. . . . These men need to be convinced that America's very survival depends upon killing the enemy with cold, impersonal determination."[82] These admissions were fully in keeping with the broad outlines of the "Western way of war" in that more than other societies, the West (and in particular, America) had a deep reverence for the sanctity of life that was breached only occasionally—and with extensive groundwork—by societies such as Nazi Germany and Imperial Japan. Ostensibly, both the Germans and Japanese were "Westernized," and supposedly were just soldiers like Americans. This similarity, however, was superficial at best, for the ideologies that lay behind those enemy forces proved themselves radically different from those of the United States and Britain. American commanders applied American law to limit brutality and crime against civilians by military personnel, but even when such actions occurred, crime by American soldiers was minuscule compared with the other warring nations, and only 140 U.S. soldiers were executed for murder and rape.[83]

American soldiers, sailors, and Marines found themselves struggling for their lives on previously unknown or unimportant beaches or desolate tracts of ocean. Pacific islands that few Americans had even heard of before December 7, 1941, became the topics of household conversations, and Guadalcanal probably was the single most discussed battle on the home front in 1942. In jungle fighting there, repeated *banzai* attacks without regard to losses were turned back with difficulty: the Japanese seemed to seek death, and the Marines obliged them whenever possible. Both Marines and the U.S. Army remembered combat there for its ferocity, horror, even occasional surrealistic quality. Frank Mathias, an Army saxophonist, recalled huddling in the rain-soaked foxholes at night hearing the Japanese, just a dozen yards away, shout obscenities to the Americans in the few phrases of English they knew: "Babe Ruth eat $@&!" Obligingly, the Americans yelled back, "Tojo eats @$#!" But when the attacks came, there was no mercy, and certainly no humor.[84]

When the Imperial Navy conducted its evacuation of troops from Guadalcanal, only one third remained.[85] Equally important, Japan lost six hundred planes, and in the vast majority of cases, the pilots and aircrews were lost with the aircraft. Aircraft were replaceable, but the crews were not, a factor all the more significant in Japan's case because of their practice of training only a small number of pilots to be a truly elite and highly capable weapon. After Guadalcanal, neither the Japanese Army pilots nor their naval aviation counterparts exhibited the high degree of competence they had displayed in the first nine months of the war. The individual Japanese soldier was courageous to the point of self-sacrificing, but the material power of the United States coupled with the bravery of its soldiers could not be overcome.

Erecting a defense perimeter from Burma to the Aleutian Islands (after occupying two American islands, Attu and Kiska), Japan spread its forces throughout the Pacific. Japanese war planners expected the U.S. forces to break on this perimeter like waves on the beach—doing damage, but then receding. This played into the long-term strategy by the imperial planners, which recognized they could not achieve genuine victory, but could raise the stakes so high that a favorable negotiated peace could be obtained. It would be the code of Bushido that would be decisive. They expected the "soft" Americans to shy away from the heavy casualties fighting Japanese soldiers would entail, and seek to end the war since the Western Pacific was not a strategic area for the United States (as seen through Japanese eyes). But American military leadership, General Douglas MacArthur in Australia and Admiral Chester Nimitz in Hawaii, developed a strategy of "island hopping," picking various islands of strategic value to assault because they had or could have airstrips, and leaving the garrisons on the others to starve from neglect. MacArthur originated the strategy, but both South Pacific and Central Pacific commands employed it with great effectiveness. It minimized casualties and sidelined large numbers of Japanese troops on islands not sufficiently important to attack, and beyond the Imperial Navy's ability to keep supplied.

Although FDR and Churchill had agreed on a "Europe first" strategy, the first ground victories for American forces took place in the Pacific as the Rising Sun began its long descent into darkness. MacArthur began his "Return to the Philippines" campaign within four months of landing in Australia by strengthening the defenses of Port Moresby, on the south side of New Guinea, facing the continent. Australia was nearly defenseless, and most of the nation's troops were in North Africa fighting Rommel or defending India. While MacArthur hounded Army chief of staff George C. Marshall for more men, Australian prime minister John Curtin pleaded with Churchill for the return of the "Diggers" from North Africa to defend their homeland. Two Australian divisions were hurriedly retrieved from North Africa in March and April, over the objection of Churchill, who insisted there were "no signs of such mass invasion [by the Japanese]."[86] Mac-Arthur went about scraping up what troops he could find, and in September the Japanese were halted by Australian troops as they approached Port Moresby from Buna following the Kakoda Trail. An Allied counterattack back over the Owen Stanley Mountains forced the Japanese back to the north side of New Guinea. In an extraordinarily difficult campaign, MacArthur's forces secured Buna in February of 1943, giving the Japanese another defeat to report to their emperor.

Douglas MacArthur, born in 1880, was born to military greatness. His father, Arthur MacArthur, had won the Medal of Honor when he was just a scrawny, nineteen-year-old adjutant of the 24th Wisconsin Regiment by leading the successful charge up Missionary Ridge above Chattanooga during the Civil War.[87] Raised as an army brat, Douglas spent his childhood on a series of Army posts in the West, learning to ride and shoot at a young age. His domineering and controlling mother moved to a nearby hotel when young MacArthur attended West Point, specifically to keep an eye on him. Displaying an exemplary record of scholarship, MacArthur graduated first in his class in 1903, then received a posting to the Philippines where he killed two guerrillas who attempted to ambush his working party.

MacArthur was tall with a commanding presence, and he learned to carefully cultivate an image of superiority in all things. He rose rapidly through the ranks, and as a staff officer on the expedition to Veracruz in 1914, he distinguished himself through his initiative, finding needed locomotives in a neighboring town, and shooting five Mexican horsemen while receiving four bullet holes in his clothes. Like George Washington, he seemed impervious to enemy fire, a trait always appreciated by his troops, who took his invincibility for their own. MacArthur was recommended for a Medal of Honor for his exploit, but since the reconnaissance had been unauthorized, the approval board declined to endorse the citation. In World War I, as chief of staff of the Rainbow Division, he won the French Croix de Guerre for taking part in a French raid on German positions. Promoted to brigadier general, he developed an unforgettable persona in appearance, removing the ring that stiffened his cap, sporting a corncob pipe, jauntily carrying a riding crop (an affectation that many officers would later copy with a "swagger stick"), and wearing a bright sweater, which only reinforced the image of his disdain for enemy fire. This showmanship would pay dividends, and the general's flamboyance was not lost on George S. Patton, who would similarly polish his public persona. Yet despite MacArthur's air of invincibility, he was wounded three times and was awarded seven Silver Stars, two Distinguished Service Crosses, two Croix de Guerres, and the Distinguished Service Medal. Again he was recommended for a Medal of Honor, but received a Distinguished Service Cross instead. By the end of the war he was a major general and in command of the 42nd (Rainbow) Division.

After the war MacArthur married—much to his mother's disapproval—and was shipped off to the Philippines again, where he might have languished in that backwater. Instead, although his marriage fell apart (while he was in Manila a reporter showed him an AP wire that his wife had divorced him in Reno), MacArthur was appointed Army chief of staff. In this capacity, he received a great deal of criticism for ordering the dispersal of the "Bonus Army" of veterans that descended on Washington in 1932 to demand immediate payment of their military service certificates (or bonuses). Almost unnoticed at the time was the participation of Major Dwight D. Eisenhower and Major George S. Patton in the same action. MacArthur unequivocally stated—even later when he wrote his memoirs—that the riots were caused by Communist agitators. Nevertheless, his role in the Bonus Army attack permanently marred his reputation.

During the Roosevelt administration, MacArthur's constant drumbeating for a stronger military made him unpopular in a White House focused on domestic issues. A convenient solution was found by appointing him military adviser to the Philippines while simultaneously installing him as field marshal of the Philippine Army. MacArthur threw himself into creating a legitimate army there, but lack of money and resources seriously hampered his efforts. His doting mother accompanied him this time to the Philippines, as did Major Dwight Eisenhower.

In July of 1941 when the Soviet Army was reeling from the German onslaught and FDR imposed his oil embargo on Japan, MacArthur was recalled to duty as commanding general, U.S. Army Forces in the Far East. The sins of unpreparedness in the United States were visited upon him, and MacArthur and his men in the Philippines paid the price, made all the more surreal when FDR ordered him to Australia and (finally) awarded him a Medal of Honor. An embarrassed MacArthur made a solemn promise to the people of the Philippines: "I shall return." Not "we shall return" or "the United States shall return"—it was a personal pledge made by the man biographer William Manchester called an "American Caesar."[88]

Admiral Chester Nimitz, similar to MacArthur in his tall and distinguished bearing, had none of "Caesar's" showmanship and unbounded ambition. (Actually most top American commanders were exceedingly tall: Nimitz, Spruance, MacArthur, Eisenhower, Patton, Omar Bradley, Mark Clark, King, and many others, leading one historian to comment that in the United States height was considered integral to leadership.) When Nimitz told his wife after Pearl Harbor he had been named to replace Admiral Husband E. Kimmel as commander in chief of the Pacific Fleet, she reminded him that that was what he always wanted—command of the fleet. "Darling," he replied, "the fleet's at the bottom of the sea."[89] Fifty-six years old when he was tapped to replace Kimmel, Nimitz looked ten years older due to his already silver hair. Born in Fredericksburg, Texas, Nimitz was raised by his grandfather, a former seaman in the German merchant marine. Staying close to his German heritage, Nimitz grew up bilingual. He wanted to attend West Point, but the local congressman, James Slayden, had no appointments available so he asked young Nimitz if he would take an examination for the U.S. Naval Academy. Nimitz, eager to better himself and recognizing this as an opportunity, took the examination and won the appointment, although he had never heard of the Naval Academy before.

With his natural self-discipline and hard work coupled with a likable personality matched only by Eisenhower's, Nimitz rose steadily in the Navy. Although he preferred sea duty and disliked service in Washington, he understood that power was gained in the capital through connections and social graces. In 1939, he received a plum assignment as chief of the Bureau of Navigation, a misnomer for what later became the Bureau of Personnel. In that position he controlled personnel assignments, and would be automatically considered for the next top post of his choosing, which came on December 16, 1941. Admiral Kimmel's name was irrevocably associated with the Pearl Harbor disaster, and Secretary of the Navy Frank Knox suggested Nimitz to Roosevelt, in part because the Texan could get along well with Admiral Ernest J. King, the irascible chief of naval operations. Roosevelt agreed. "Tell Nimitz," he said, "to get the hell out to Pearl and stay there till the war is won." Indeed, Nimitz hopped a Navy plane and, despite no rest and motion sickness, commanded the pilot to give him an aerial tour of Pearl. What he saw shocked him: even though the attack had taken place more than two weeks earlier, wreckage was still strewn everywhere. Nimitz addressed the officers, refused to assign blame, and coolly informed them that while it would be a long haul, the United States Navy would soon exact vengeance.

Working for Admiral King was no picnic. He was known and feared for his harshness, and inspired respect but not affection. Best known for his activities in seducing other officers' wives, King proved a stern taskmaster who made no mistakes and brooked no treason among his subordinates with contrary opinions. Yet with a single exception, Nimitz was able to handle this difficult personality effectively. That exception came when King and Commander John Redman, head of King's Navy code-breaking operation in Washington, initially believed the Japanese were going to strike the West Coast—later they altered their prediction to the Aleutians, then Samoa—instead of Midway in June of 1942.[90] Nimitz sided against King with Commander Joseph J. Rochefort, the brilliant head of Hawaii's Combat Intelligence Office, who had broken the Japanese naval code, JN-25b, and sent his carriers to ambush the Japanese task force at Midway. Rochefort had engineered the most extraordinary intelligence achievement of the war, and had been able to brief Nimitz on the complete Japanese plan and predict *exactly* where Frank Jack Fletcher's task forces would find the Japanese carriers. In spite of the victory, or because of it, King, urged on by Commander Redman and his brother, Rear Admiral Joseph Redman, chief of naval communications, arranged for Rochefort to be transferred into oblivion for being right.[91] King's and Redman's payback constituted a waste of Rochefort's exceptional talent and almost certainly extended the war and cost American lives; Washington never again was able to read JN-25 except for low-value, repetitive traffic. It took Admiral Edwin T. Layton's 1985 book *And I Was There* to win a greatly deserved posthumous Distinguished Service Medal for Rochefort. Nimitz, unable or unwilling to protect Rochefort, thereby put the only major blot on his record. Otherwise, Nimitz's skill in balancing such wildly different, yet effective, personalities as Vice Admiral William ("Bull") Halsey and Vice Admiral Raymond Spruance testified to the loyalty of his subordinates and Nimitz's willingness to allow them wide discretion.

## Red Storms in the East

While the United States clawed back into the Pacific war, the USSR moved from defense to offense against the Nazis. If Moscow in 1941–42 had not been the turning point, certainly the destruction of the German 6th Army at Stalingrad was. There, bled white against Soviet defenses kept strong by constant infusions of new manpower to replace the fallen, the Germans nevertheless appeared poised for victory. By November, 90 percent of Stalingrad lay in Hitler's control. Notable among the defenders was Front Commissar Nikita Khrushchev, the round and ruthless protégé of Lazar Kaganovich, the only Jew among the "Old Bolsheviks" to survive Stalin's purges.

On July 28, 1942, Stalin issued his famous People's Commissariat of Defense Order 227, "Not a step back."[92] His armies in the field took his words seriously, for failure to do so meant execution or service until killed in a penal battalion. While consuming German attention and assault forces in Stalingrad, the Soviets had marshaled new armies for counterattacks, which commenced in November as the weather again turned cold: one (Operation Mars) would encircle the German forces of Army Group Center, and another (Operation Uranus) swept against the northward-facing Italian, Hungarian, and Romanian positions along the Don River, all the while attacking northwestward from south of Stalingrad on the Volga to encircle the 6th Army in Stalingrad.

Operation Mars was a failure, and has been almost totally ignored by historians in the West as well as in the Soviet Union. Zhukov was the architect of both Mars and Uranus, yet the Soviets have trumpeted one while not mentioning the other. In Mars, Zhukov attacked both sides of the Rzhev salient in late November of 1942 with seven armies comprising 817,000 men and more than 2,000 tanks. At the end of the month-long battle, the Soviets had lost 1,600 to 1,800 tanks and 335,000 men, and the battle lines had not appreciably changed.[93] For modern readers, its significance is lost, but this meaningless battle demonstrated the terrific losses the USSR was willing to sustain: in this single engagement, the Soviet Union suffered 85 percent of the battle deaths the U.S. Army recorded in Europe during the entire war.

Operation Uranus, on the other hand, met with great success, easily overrunning the Romanians, Hungarians, and Italians. Within a few days, the Soviets had encircled the German 6th Army. Hitler peremptorily ordered the 6th Army commander, General Friedrich Paulus, into the pocket with his army, where 205,000 German soldiers and almost 52,000 Russian volunteers were trapped.[94] Hitler quickly recalled von Manstein from Leningrad and made him commander of Army Group Don, which included the 6th Army. But instead of ordering 6th Army to immediately organize a breakout to the West, Hitler chose to supply the encircled troops by air while von Manstein organized a relief force to break the encirclement. Hitler wanted to hold Stalingrad at all costs, and that rapidly became a fatal error.

Von Manstein cobbled together a relief force that attacked the Soviet ring from the southwest on December 12, coming within thirty miles of 6th Army, but Paulus didn't cooperate. Since Hitler had not authorized a withdrawal, the timid Paulus was unprepared to break out, would not go against Hitler's wishes, and secretly feared any such attempt would end in disaster.[95] The moment passed; von Manstein had to rush his men back to fight the Soviets at Rostov, and Paulus was left to his fate with his troops. On February 2, 1943, more than 95,000 Germans surrendered, of whom only 5,000 ever saw their homeland again.

Von Manstein still had a few rabbits to pull out of his hat. The overwhelming Soviet forces were slowed but not stopped when the Germans abandoned Kharkov against Hitler's express order. Suspecting the Soviets were overextended, von Manstein launched a major counterattack using newly formed SS panzer units, advancing northward behind Soviet positions, cutting the enemy off, and retaking Kharkov. The shocking Soviet defeat surprised and greatly angered Stalin. Somehow von Manstein had been able to pull off the single German winter victory of the war, stabilize the line in Ukraine, and set the stage for a decisive battle after the spring muddy period.

But Kharkov would be the last major victory enjoyed by the Germans in the Soviet Union. Despite the Red Army's enormous losses in offensives, the Soviet superiority in weapons, manpower, and supply had become impossible to overcome. By the end of 1942 the Red Army had 2.7 times the number of tanks, most of them now T-34s, twice as many guns, and 1.8 times the number of combat aircraft as it had at the end of 1941.[96] Stalin had moved 1,300 factories east out of the battle zone and they were now in full production. The manpower disparity between the Soviet and German forces remained as large as ever, and the Germans were able to maintain their Eastern Front army at an operative level only by replacing 2.1 million German factory workers with foreign labor.

## Snapping the Axis

After Kharkov, the war turned permanently against the Nazis. Soviet forces had taken Kursk in February 1943 and created a large salient in German lines north of Kharkov that begged to be pinched off. In the summer, the Germans took their last chance to reverse the war in the East, and the largest tank battle in human history resulted. Armed with 2,928 tanks—many of them new Tiger and Panther models—the Nazis sought to cut off the salient and encircle a large part of the Red Army. But the Russians had dug in while the Germans waited for the new equipment to arrive, erecting a series of defensive networks known as "defense in depth," whereby minefields, artillery zones, and antitank emplacements stretched more than two hundred miles deep. Even worse for the Germans, the Russians outnumbered them in tanks and men almost two to one. Only in aircraft were the two sides even close in numbers. After the Nazis fought through two defensive belts, they were exhausted and faced at least five more rings. Typical of the losses suffered throughout the army in the battle, one German armored unit began the attack with 118 tanks and when it retreated had only 20. In retrospect, the Luftwaffe might have provided the critical difference—but one third of its planes were busy with American and British bombers in the west.

Just two months before Kursk, in "Black May," the German Navy had lost 25 percent of its operational submarines while sinking only fifty-eight merchant ships. But July was the critical month in a number of ways. Hamburg went up in a massive Allied firebombing, and Sicily was invaded in July. (It fell to the Americans and British in August.) Coming on top of Kursk, these body blows rattled Hitler—and his Italian allies, who sought a way out of the war. Italy concluded an armistice with the Allies on September 3. Hitler would not tolerate a defection so close to the Fatherland and rushed German troops in to defend the Italian peninsula, some of them pulled out of Kursk while the outcome was still in doubt (at least in the eyes of the German generals there). But the temporary plug in the dike in Italy paled in comparison to the leaks springing everywhere else in German territory. Kiev fell to the Red Army in October, and as 1944 dawned, Nazi forces had been pushed back to the prewar Ukrainian border.

The Japanese had not fared any better. In March 1943 the Battle of Bismarck Sea resulted in the loss of all eight Japanese transports and four of their escorting destroyers by U.S. ships and planes under the command of Lieutenant General George Kenney in the Americans' first application of game theory to military decision making. (Kenney constructed a matrix to predict the likeliest routes that Lieutenant General Hitoshi Imamura would use to reinforce his forces, weighing the different routes with the expected payoffs.) Then Admiral Yamamoto was killed while flying on an inspection tour in the Solomon Islands in April—an operation involving four P-38 Lightnings specifically authorized by Roosevelt to assassinate the admiral. Japan lost the Aleutian island of Attu and evacuated Kiska Island in the summer. The Allies, everywhere, were on the march.

Many of these operations were difficult, and few came without savage fighting. At Tarawa in November 1943, for example, Marines had to cross more than one hundred yards of underwater coral atoll on foot, under extreme fire, as the boats were unable to land them on the beach. Meanwhile, Army troops eliminated the last remaining Japanese stronghold on New Georgia while MacArthur's forces advanced up the northern New Guinea coast. Bougainville in the Solomons was assaulted, and a critical airfield constructed. And to close out 1943, the 1st Marine Division went ashore at Cape Gloucester on New Britain. All of these operations were fiercely opposed, but the Japanese could no longer stop the United States from seizing whatever island it wished. Only in Burma against the British and in China were the Japanese able to make advances, and in the greater scheme of the war, the Burmese front was now meaningless.

In the West, Roosevelt and Churchill met at the Casablanca Conference in January 1943 to work out future strategy and policies for the war. Seeking to avoid any repetition of the "stab in the back" theory developed when the Allies failed to invade Germany in World War I, Roosevelt and Churchill agreed the Axis powers had to surrender unconditionally. The Battle of the Atlantic received top priority (to supply England), and assistance to Russia received second place. Third was to continue operations in the Mediterranean, with the conquest of Sicily. Operations in the Pacific were to continue, Burma was to be reconquered (and restored to the British Empire) and the Burma Road reopened. Going along with British planning, the two heads of state put off a cross-Channel invasion of Europe until 1944, with a British general, Frederick Morgan, as chief of staff to plan the operation. This decision outraged Stalin and convinced him the Americans and British were allowing the Nazis and his Red Army to fight each other to exhaustion. Stalin had not attended the meetings, claiming that military operations kept him in Moscow, but actually he was terrified of flying and he did not trust leaving Soviet territory, lest he be overthrown.

Casablanca saw the British gain significant advantages. Marshall and King headed the American contingent, which arrived with a skeletal staff, apparently expecting a polite, high-level discussion of strategy in which each American service, Army, Army Air Corps, and Navy, could offer its different point of view. The British, however, brought an overwhelming staff of "experts," a general disdain for the Americans as military amateurs, and firm goals in mind. They sent a 6,000-ton liner to Casablanca before the conference to serve as a floating headquarters and communications resource, complete with technical details that would cover any proposed operation.[97] Marshall and King, outmaneuvered at every turn, agreed to strategy that greatly strengthened the British in the Mediterranean and their empire. U.S. general Albert Wedemeyer put it differently: "We came, we listened, and we were conquered."[98] Nor did the British stop there. Churchill placed Harold Macmillan in Eisenhower's headquarters to represent Britain's political interests and to act as a spy. FDR agreed to Macmillan's presence, and there was nothing Eisenhower could do. The infuriated King left the conference and advocated that the United States relegate Europe to second priority behind Japan. It was a Pyrrhic victory for the overreaching British, who would face ever-increasing American resentment and reluctance to give in to British points of view, as well as the willingness of FDR to side with Stalin against Churchill.

FDR pleaded constantly for a meeting of the "Big Three," which Stalin finally agreed could take place in Tehran, Iran, a location the Soviets could secure. This constituted the only time in his life that Stalin flew in an airplane.[99] To work up a united front beforehand, the British and Americans met in Cairo (the Cairo Conference), but FDR was in poor health and in no mood for sub rosa dealings with Churchill. As a result Stalin dominated the Tehran meeting (November 28–December 1, 1943), bullying FDR, who continued to think he could talk to Stalin alone and establish a working relationship built on mutual trust. Instead, the Soviet dictator obtained everything he wanted in return for apparently agreeing to his western Allies' war policies. Postwar Poland's borders were fixed on the Curzon Line in the East, and the Oder and Neisse rivers in the West, effectively moving the Soviet border substantially westward. Eastern Europe was acknowledged to be in the Soviet "sphere of interest," meaning Stalin not only could reannex the Baltic states but would also obtain control over the postwar governments of Poland, Czechoslovakia, Hungary, Bulgaria, and Romania. Certainly throughout the negotiations Stalin knew his ace in the hole, his agents well placed in Roosevelt's administration, could get whatever he wanted. Through Harry Hopkins, Roosevelt's personal adviser, Harry Dexter White, the assistant secretary of the Treasury, and Vice President Henry Wallace, the KGB exercised astounding influence. What else did Roosevelt have to bargain with? Russian Lend-Lease supplies had already been guaranteed for another year on October 19 when the third London Protocol was signed. The United States had agreed to send 5.1 million tons of Lend-Lease supplies and material to the Soviet Union through the Persian Gulf

and Vladivostok. For the second time the United States had been outmaneuvered and outnegotiated. Yalta and Potsdam in 1945 would complete the
unbroken series of American conference defeats.

Always mistrustful, Stalin never ceased to look for hidden motives in
British and American actions, and when the Casablanca Conference confirmed that Britain and the United States would fritter away a year in the
Mediterranean, Stalin used what he claimed was Western perfidy to build
resentment in the Soviet Union against the democracies. But he scarcely
would have needed it, and in a closed shop such as he ran, no other opinions
were possible. Stalin's ideas were everyone's ideas, to the extent anyone
wanted to stay alive.

Churchill had endeavored to keep Stalin supplied no matter what. After
the destruction of convoy PQ-17 to Murmansk in June of 1942, Churchill
had escorted the next convoy, PQ-18, with no less than seventy-seven warships for forty merchantmen, a commitment the Royal Navy could not
maintain.[100] He therefore wanted to skip PQ-19, scheduled for departure on
October 2. Roosevelt begged Churchill to honor their pledges to Stalin, but
the best Churchill would commit was to allow eight merchantmen to leave
in several groups. Only five arrived safely in the USSR. At the same time
Britain and the United States proposed a plan to Stalin to help secure the
Russian oil fields in the event the Red Army collapsed. Stalin concluded
that if the Western allies had no supplies for his troops in the thick of the
fight for Stalingrad and the Caucasus—but could spare forces to secure
Soviet oil—that said much about their priorities. Nevertheless, seldom if
ever in human history had essentially free peoples done so much to support
and strengthen a barbaric, despotic regime, even if out of self-interest.

After capturing Sicily in 1943 and knocking Italy out of the war, Allied
troops appeared close to securing Italy in 1944, despite a stubborn defense
in front of Monte Cassino. As the Americans had in the Pacific, the Allies
attempted an end-run around the Germans' positions in the Cassino line
with an amphibious assault at Anzio. After surprising the Germans and
capturing a beachhead, the Allied forces moved slowly, allowing German
reinforcements to seal off the invasion force. Elsewhere, Axis forces were
defeated consistently. The Soviet offensive during the winter of 1943–44 in
Ukraine pushed the Germans back, and north of Kiev two German corps
comprising nine divisions were trapped by Marshal Konev's forces in the
Cherkassy (Korsun) pocket due to Hitler's refusal to abandon part of the
Dnieper line. Those formations fought for their lives, and after five

weeks of battle in a pocket "wandering" westward, 40,000 out of the trapped 65,000 escaped to fight another day.[101] Germans considered this a victory of sorts because, unlike at Stalingrad, strenuous efforts made by von Manstein to rescue the encircled troops were generally successful. Merely the fact that the men understood they would no longer be abandoned (at least by von Manstein) served as a morale booster. Hitler didn't see it that way, sacking von Manstein for losing so much territory, although prior to departing he also saved the encircled 1st Panzer Army north of the Dniester.

In February, Nimitz's Central Pacific forces assaulted the Marshall Islands, taking Kwajalein and Eniwetok. Japan's huge naval base in the Carolines at Truk, long a thorn in the side of the Americans, was bombed, and the Japanese abandoned the Central Pacific to concentrate on a defense of the Marianas (Guam, Tinian, and Saipan). Everywhere except in Italy and the China-Burma-India Theater, Allied forces advanced steadily during the first half of 1944, but then Polish troops finally took Monte Cassino and the Germans were driven north of Rome, the city falling on June 4. But that momentous news was driven off the wires by the events of June 6—the long-awaited cross-Channel invasion.

## Closing in Europe While Advancing in the Pacific

Heading the effort was the Allied Supreme Commander, European Theater, Dwight D. Eisenhower. At fifty-three years old, he had been a general officer for less than three years. Like Nimitz, Ike was born a Texan, but grew up in modest circumstances in Abilene, Kansas. His mother was a Mennonite, then became a Jehovah's Witness, although Eisenhower himself never was. Later he joined the Presbyterian Church, and although he remained largely unattached to any "sect or organization," as he put it, he called himself "one of the most deeply religious men I know."[102] He graduated from West Point in 1915, then served out World War I in training camps in the United States. Universally liked by other officers and superiors, Ike languished as a major from 1922 to 1936, during which time he held a series of interesting positions, including working on MacArthur's staff in the Philippines where he demonstrated his fine talent for writing. Contrary to popular lore that MacArthur and Eisenhower did not like each other, there had to be some reason for Eisenhower to have remained at MacArthur's side for seven years. MacArthur once turned in a fitness report on Eisenhower that said, "This is the best officer in the Army. When the next war comes, he should go right to the top."[103]

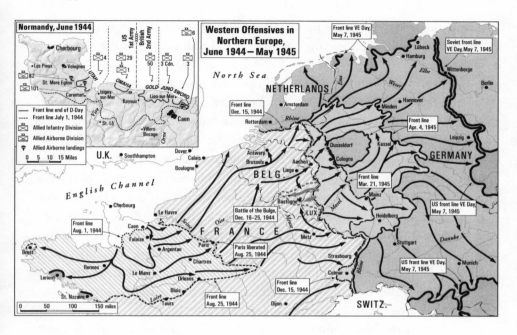

From lieutenant colonel (1941) to major general (March 1942), and to Commander, European Theater, on June 15, 1942, Ike jumped over some forty officers senior to him and received extraordinarily fast promotion. General George C. Marshall's secretary, Colonel Walter Bedell Smith, telephoned Ike on December 12, 1941 (he was stationed at the time at Fort Sam Houston), and told him to come to Washington as Marshall wanted his assessment of the Philippines. When Eisenhower arrived on the 15th, Marshall reviewed MacArthur's force levels and asked Ike, "What should be our general line of action?"[104] Eisenhower requested a few hours to compose an answer, and when he returned, recommended using Australia as the United States' main base to reinforce and supply the Philippines. He frankly admitted that major reinforcements could not reach the Philippines while the garrison there still held out if the Japanese committed major forces to the battle, but that everything possible needed to be done. "The people in China, of the Philippines, or the Dutch East Indies will be watching us. They may excuse failure, but they will not excuse abandonment."[105] Marshall was so impressed that he immediately placed Eisenhower in charge of the Philippines and Far Eastern Section of the War Plans Division. Marshall then turned his cold eyes on Eisenhower and said, "Eisenhower, the Department is filled with able men who analyze their problems well but feel compelled always to bring them to me for final solution. I must have assistants who will solve their own problems and tell me later what they have done."[106]

Eisenhower soon found his main problems were twofold: his old boss MacArthur and Admiral King, chief of naval operations. To Eisenhower, MacArthur was panicking, and King was a bully. He once groused, "One thing that might help win this war is to get someone to shoot King."[107] Nonetheless, Ike was able to win the cooperation of both, and that paid big dividends. Just when it looked like he would end his career in Washington as a staff officer, Eisenhower lost his temper with Marshall, only to find a week later that Marshall had recommended him for promotion, telling President Roosevelt that Ike was his operations officer. After Marshall decided the Philippines were beyond help, he had Ike work up a plan for a cross-Channel invasion of France (code name: Roundup), but by March it was obvious the British were dragging their feet. Eisenhower was dispatched to England to unfreeze the bottlenecks.

There, Eisenhower almost immediately ran afoul of the British, most particularly General Alan Brooke, chief of the Imperial General Staff, and Lieutenant General Bernard Law Montgomery, Brooke's arrogant protégé. When Eisenhower lit a cigarette while Montgomery was speaking, the British general announced sternly, "I don't permit smoking in my office."[108] It was not an auspicious start. Neither Brooke nor Montgomery had any use for Americans, Marshall and Eisenhower in particular. Brooke's prejudice bordered on hate, and he described Marshall as "overfilled with his own importance." The fact that Ike had no combat experience weighed heavily, but to the British it was merely par for the course, and to be expected from colonial amateurs. Eisenhower's continual promotions must have shocked them, all the more so when Marshall appointed him Supreme Commander of all the Allied Forces in Europe.

On June 22, 1943, Eisenhower's "blackest day in history," Churchill obtained Roosevelt's agreement to cancel the cross-Channel operation. Certainly the insufficient number of Higgins boats contributed to the strategy, but to Ike, it seemed his ally gave him more trouble than the Germans. Indeed, Eisenhower's genius and skill lay in his uncanny ability to hold his American officers in check (they endured slights and disrespect seemingly daily from their British counterparts). Not that his own subordinates were perfect. Few vexed Ike as much as his talented three-star general, George Patton, who had directed a brilliant end-run around Sicily while Montgomery was bottled up on the coast. But during the campaign, Patton had visited an Army hospital in August 1943 where, amid all those with horrifying physical injuries, he found a soldier, Private Charles H. Kuhl, suffering from what is commonly known as "battle fatigue" or "shell shock," a condition that includes symptoms like nightmares, excessive startle reactions, depression, severe anxiety, and shaking. At the time, however, it was not well accepted as a legitimate problem by frontline officers, who thought men who claimed to suffer from it were malingerers. Patton slapped Kuhl with his gloves, and threatened to have him sent back to the front. Ten days later, Patton reprised the incident almost identically with a second soldier, Private Paul G. Bennett, at another hospital. (At least one of Patton's biographers suspects Patton himself was suffering from combat fatigue at the time.)[109] The press, which on the whole preferred the less aggressive Omar Bradley ("a soldier's soldier," went the typical report), tended to let the incident slide, but muckraker and Patton enemy Drew Pearson howled for the general's scalp. Eisenhower, of course, hadn't the slightest intention of losing his best field commander and normally would have shown little concern for the wishes of the press, but temporarily removed him to get Patton out of the cross-hairs of Pearson and his congressional buddies looking for publicity. Hollywood later inflated and sensationalized Ike's required apology from Patton, which occurred on a private basis to Kuhl and Bennett. If anything, the Supreme Commander protected Patton from himself until he could be unleashed. In particular, the competition between Patton and Montgomery—Patton was clearly the superior general, but Montgomery with Brooke behind him won all the key commands and decisions—gradually wore Ike down, especially when he had to sideline old "Blood and Guts."

With regard to the Supreme Allied Commander position, Brooke had expected it to go to him, notwithstanding the fact that Britain was clearly the junior partner with respect to troop strength and resources. A Peter Sellers look-alike without the actor's humor or charisma, Brooke could not understand Churchill's agreement on the selection of Eisenhower, and his relations with Americans became worse than ever.[110] Brooke considered himself a military expert who had indeed inaugurated the French concept of a "creeping barrage" into the British Army during World War I—a tactic that epitomized his approach to battle, cautious and scientific. As low of an opinion as he held of the Americans, he held a disproportionately high view of the Germans. And, of course, he disapproved of the American high command, whom he held in contempt. In dealing with the American chiefs of staff, he said, "all matters have to be carefully and slowly explained and re-explained before they can be absorbed."[111]

In London as Supreme Commander, Eisenhower rejected the palatial accommodations provided by the British, complete with liveried footmen, and he soon moved to more modest quarters. With little ground action taking place in western Europe other than the stalemate in Italy, reporters focused on Ike, his grin, his enthusiasm, and his upbringing, if not in poverty, then at least in very economically deprived circumstances. This appealed to the British public, if not the British aristocracy or, especially, the tradition- and perquisite-oriented British military.

The other main protagonist with whom Ike dealt, Field Marshal Bernard Montgomery, was a small, wiry man who affected a flair by wearing nonregulation sweaters and hats. Jaunty Monty, as he was known, carefully built a MacArthur-like reputation as England's foremost and most successful general, although prior to El Alamein, his main claim to fame was in handling the retreat of his unit to Dunkirk in 1940. He enjoyed the full backing of Brooke, another general who made his reputation during the defeat in France, and had become the master of the "set-piece" battle, one in which he was given overwhelming force by the Americans. Methodical, and without flexibility, Montgomery typified the British officer who always considered himself a good commander. Monty's penchant for thorough planning and plodding execution had been learned during the World War I battles of the Somme and Passchendaele as a staff officer. A bully in his childhood, he even set a fellow student's shirt on fire while at Sandhurst. Montgomery was disliked by many officers for his arrogance and dictatorial style of command.[112]

These traits made him almost universally loathed by American officers, particularly when his treatment of them mirrored how the Germans treated the Italians. Montgomery would stumble badly in Normandy and then excuse himself by saying his actions were not meant to succeed in anything other than holding the Germans. He neglected to clear the approach to Antwerp and thus delayed the opening of the port for a critical two months. In addition, he failed again in Holland with Operation Market Garden (a massive airborne-armor operation to secure a bridgehead into Germany at Arnhem that failed to secure the final, critical bridge); inaccurately claimed credit for holding the Germans in the Battle of the Bulge; was the last to cross the Rhine; and needed to be continually prodded by Eisenhower to occupy the portion of North Germany assigned to him. Montgomery became a cross for Eisenhower to bear, one that he carried in good humor until the field marshal became nearly intolerable in January of 1945.

When the Allies began D-Day on June 6, 1944, Eisenhower was again in overall command while General Alexander ruled in the Mediterranean, but the ground commander for the Normandy battle was Montgomery. D-Day's history, particularly from the viewpoint of some of the participants, has been exquisitely documented. Rugged fighting occurred everywhere—the paratroops who dropped in the night of June 5 experienced dramatic stories of survival and success, including a horrific drop into St.-Mère-Église on top of a supply company guarding French civilians putting out a fire—but the invasion itself went largely as planned except for Omaha Beach. There, American troops—at least those who made it ashore—found themselves on a narrow sliver of beach—with the Germans entrenched above them. Many officers went down quickly, leaving their troops in the hands of lieutenants and sergeants, whose heroic leadership somehow got the men off the beach. Once Omaha cracked, however, nothing could hold the Allies back.

Yet prior to the invasion, England was drenched in storms that most commanders, Allied and German, thought would prohibit an Allied landing at that time. However, Ike had committed the invasion force to sail largely on the word of a single weather officer on June 5, who discerned a break coming in twenty-four hours. This required a supreme act of faith on Eisenhower's part: the rains poured, and the winds howled. Waves in the Channel would swamp many landing craft if the storm front persisted. Ike was assured that it would let up, and he ordered the paratroops into the skies while the rain still fell. If the officer had erred, most of the 101st and 82nd Airborne, plus numerous British and Polish paratroop units, would have fallen permanently into enemy hands. As the task force pushed off, Eisenhower drafted two notes for the press: in case of defeat, Ike assumed full responsibility, but if successful, he only gave credit to others. The "success" press release immediately became history. But Ike found the "failure" note tucked inside his wallet a month later, which he gave to his naval aide, Captain Harry Butcher. It read, "Our landings in the Cherbourg-Havre area have failed to gain a satisfactory foothold and I have withdrawn the troops. . . . The troops, the air and the Navy did all that bravery and devotion to duty could do. If any blame or fault attaches to the attempt it is mine alone."[113]

Once a beachhead was established, the Allies prepared for a breakout. Even then, Montgomery lagged again. While the Americans took the Cotentin Peninsula and prepared to break out from their lodgment, Montgomery mounted no fewer than eight operations, six to capture Caen at extraordinarily high cost, and two to link up with American forces racing across France and seal off the Falaise pocket. Nonetheless, the Battle of Normandy, and the encirclement of the German 7th Army after the American breakout, resulted in another half million German soldiers taken out of the fight.[114] At the same time as Normandy the Soviets completed their destruction of Army Group Center. Attacking on a front of 350 miles, in three weeks they had moved forward 250 miles, killed or captured 300,000 Germans, and caused the German High Command to write off twenty-eight divisions and their troops from the German order of battle. Later in the summer combat in Romania saw another eighteen divisions and six corps headquarters eliminated.[115] Romania made peace with the Soviet Union and declared war on Germany.

Overconfident Allied journalists boasted that the troops would be home for Christmas, but the war was not yet over, and reporters failed to notice that the British Army was shrinking swiftly due to England's inability to provide replacements. As in Germany, units were being consolidated to retain a formation's fighting strength. And this was not only a problem for the British; Eisenhower was having trouble maintaining a sufficient flow of replacements as few new troops were being sent from the States. Merely supplying the Allied forces from French ports was taxing in the extreme. The enormous logistics "tail" of the American Army seemed to be a ravenous monster, at one point supplied by the famous "Red Ball Express" of trucks until even that grew so long as to become unworkable. As historian John Keegan pointed out, "Of the 11 million men in the United States Army . . . less than 2 million belonged to the [89] combat divisions of the land forces, and of those 2 million less than 700,000 represented tank crews or infantrymen."[116]

With eastern Europe and the Balkans rapidly being occupied by Soviet troops, Churchill and his foreign secretary Anthony Eden flew to Moscow in October to hold talks with Stalin. At stake was hegemony in Europe and the continuance of the British Empire (in part), and the matter needed to be resolved. They did not bother to involve the Americans. In Moscow, spheres of influence were created, and the percentage of influence in countries was split between the Soviet Union and Britain. Churchill wrote proposed percentages on a half sheet of paper and pushed it to Stalin, who quickly placed a blue tick on it. Churchill then said, "Might it not be thought rather cynical if it seemed we had disposed of these issues, so fateful to millions of people, in such an offhand manner? Let us burn the paper." Stalin replied, "No, you keep it."[117] Greece was 90–10 in favor of Britain, Romania 90–10 in favor of the USSR, Bulgaria 75–25 USSR, Yugoslavia and Hungary 50–50. With respect to Poland, Czechoslovakia, and Hungary, only a delusional mind could fail to comprehend that these states were going to end up, sooner or later, with Communist governments under the heel of a Soviet boot. Churchill sought to sugarcoat the prospects for those countries in messages to Roosevelt, without mentioning what he had agreed to, but Stalin insisted that his puppet Lublin group would control a postwar government in Poland.

Euphoria over the pending victory in Europe obscured MacArthur's advances in the Pacific. Finally, however, he prepared for an invasion of the Philippines in October of 1944. The Marianas were captured in the Central Pacific, and the Battle of the Philippine Sea had effectively eliminated the Imperial Navy's carrier-based aviation capability. At the "Marianas Turkey Shoot," as the battle was known, more than three hundred Japanese planes were shot down, many operated by pilots fresh out of training. American forces began landing on Leyte Island in the Philippines on October 20, and MacArthur's promise was fulfilled. He strode ashore, amid combat photographers filming him reenacting the arrival, replete with sunglasses and corncob pipe.

But the Japanese Navy struck back. In the Battle of Leyte Gulf, a series of disjointed battles which resulted in the destruction of the Japanese Navy as a threat to future U.S. naval operations, the last hope of Japan to protect itself from an invasion of its home islands disappeared. Like the Germans in Ukraine, the Japanese had alienated the Filipinos to the extreme.

Perhaps no better indication of the follies of a modern occupying force applying draconian repression policies exists than the success story of Wendell W. Fertig in the Philippines. In 1941, Fertig, a middle-aged mining engineer who failed to graduate after five years at the Colorado School of Mines in the 1920s, had nonetheless become a mining engineer and consultant. But he had managed to complete the ROTC course while in college, becoming an officer in the Army Reserve, U.S. Corps of Engineers, and attaining the rank of lieutenant colonel in 1941. Having lived in the Philippines since 1936, Fertig sent his wife and daughters back to the States when war broke out, whereupon he supervised construction projects on Luzon and Bataan. On his way to Mindanao, his Navy aircraft crashed during landing, cutting Fertig off from the main U.S. command when the Japanese forces slashed in behind him. When he heard the Americans had surrendered, Fertig refused to join the POWs and instead built the largest guerrilla organization ever commanded by an American, reaching over 35,000 men, Americans and Filipinos, tying down up to 60,000 Japanese until finally reinforced by MacArthur's troops in March of 1945.

Respected and feared by the Japanese as "Chief in the Philippines," Fertig was denigrated and dismissed as competition for the affections of Filipinos by General MacArthur. The tall, lanky, red-haired Fertig became widely loved and respected throughout Mindanao: he was considered a hero, and a Filipino. (When he returned to Mindanao in 1958, he was greeted by thousands of cheering Filipinos and a banner that read "WELCOME THE PATRIOT WHO LESSENED HUMAN SUFFERING ON MINDANAO.")[118]

Yet in Europe and Asia the anticipation of a quick resolution in both theaters turned dark rapidly. Hitler, despite the astounding collapse on the Eastern Front, continued to obsess about America and the Western Front, hoarding his finest new tanks and moving fresh divisions into hidden reserve positions to launch a counteroffensive in December. With Allied aircraft denied the skies by poor weather and American lines in particular overstretched and thin, the Germans smashed through the American lines in the Ardennes and threatened to march to the coast. Eisenhower rushed the 101st Airborne to the defense of Bastogne, where it became encircled and a potential disaster loomed. As the northern American flank stiffened, Patton swiftly struck the southern in an awe-inspiring 90-degree turn, moving northward to attack with two full divisions on the third day after the German offensive began, and following with another division and a combat command a day later. While General Courtney Hodges and Patton did all the work, and Ike handled the planning, as usual Montgomery boasted to the press that his efforts had saved the day.

Then Monty went one step further: he sent Eisenhower what amounted to an ultimatum that "[o]ne commander must have powers to direct and control the operations! You cannot possibly do it yourself, and so you would have to nominate someone else." Of course, the "someone else" was Monty.[119] Eisenhower fumed. Either Montgomery or he would have to go. Ike drafted a message to be sent to the Combined Chiefs of Staff through General Marshall to choose between himself and Montgomery. Allied unity was threatened to the core by one egomaniacal individual, and Hitler's ill-fated offensive on the battlefield came close to succeeding at the strategic level in breaking the Allies apart. Montgomery, alerted by his chief of staff that his job was in peril, quickly wrote a pacifying note to Eisenhower: "Whatever your decision may be you can rely on me one hundred per cent to make it work, and I know Brad [Omar Bradley] will do the same. Very distressed that my letter may have upset you."[120]

Of course, Eisenhower got nearly as much static from his own subordinates, particularly Patton (whose performance, nevertheless, earned him the right to carp). Patton begged for more gas and supplies to launch a single-column advance into Germany, and especially (in his view) to beat the Russians to Berlin. Already sensing the postwar strategic implications, Patton hated Communists as much as he did Nazis, fearing Soviet control of much of Germany would prove a disaster—and he was right. Of course, Patton was spared Ike's strategic alliance concerns, and the single-thrust approach was fraught with dangers of being cut off and surrounded, as exemplified by the Ardennes offensive. That failed to stop Patton's incessant calls for more gas, or his unending complaining to his friend (and now superior) General Omar Bradley. Still, true to his word, Patton's forces crossed the Rhine without stopping and he ceremoniously urinated in that symbolic river before heading toward Berlin.

Before the fall of Berlin, Roosevelt died on April 12, 1945, at Warm Springs, Georgia. His death momentarily convinced Hitler the Allies might fracture, but der Fuehrer's fantasies disappeared as Harry Truman—a much less malleable and progressive leader than his predecessor—assumed the presidency. While Roosevelt was mourned, his death was not unexpected by those who knew him closely. He had been in poor health for some time. But it had little effect on the men at the front, especially as they stood on the threshold of victory in Europe.

By agreement, the Russians got to take Berlin, which fell on May 2. Hitler, who had been in his Berlin bunker since January 16, and nearly mad, had taken to moving phantom units around on maps and haranguing his remaining subordinates hourly. The failed July 1944 "Wolf's Lair" assassination plot ("Valkyrie"), orchestrated by top Wehrmacht officers, including Generals Henning von Tresckow and Friedrich Olbricht, and Colonel Claus von Stauffenberg, had left him more paranoid than ever. As the Soviets closed in, on April 29 he married Eva Braun, then after midnight, on April 30, gave her poison. He chomped down on poison while simultaneously shooting himself to ensure he did not fall into the hands of the Red Army. On May 8, General Alfred Jodl, chief of the operations staff of the high command, offered the unconditional surrender of all German forces to the Allies.

Little was left of the once-dominant Nazi Germany that had devastated Europe. Out of 84 million ethnic Germans, 7 to 9 million were dead, 4 to 6 million were prisoners, and another 3 million would disappear in the convulsions still taking place as national boundaries were realigned. But other nations paid an even higher price, particularly the USSR, which lost nearly 27 million people; while another 3 to 4 million were in the gulag or would shortly disappear as Soviet prisoners. Other countries in Europe suffered greatly as well: Poland (5.7 million dead), Yugoslavia (1 million), the Baltic States (931,000), Romania (833,000), Greece (800,000), Hungary (580,000), France (568,000), Italy (457,000), Czechoslovakia (345,000), and Holland (301,000). Great Britain lost a comparatively low 451,000, while the United States, in both Europe and the Pacific, suffered 419,000 deaths. Vast numbers of young men had been drawn into wars—with much of the combat in Russia—that had no ideological meaning to them, no higher purpose. Hungarians, Romanians, and even Belgians froze to death or were gunned down in unnamed hamlets in the Soviet Union merely because their nations had fallen into Hitler's grasp. When combined with the six million Jews and four million others that the Nazis deliberately exterminated, the horrific cost of appeasement from 1935 to 1939 stood out as starkly as a gravestone with the inscription "Do Not Repeat!"

Tragic as the physical loss was, the division of Europe, which came at the Yalta Conference in February of 1945 between FDR, Churchill, and Stalin, and cemented the principles discussed at Tehran, proved nearly as destructive to the human soul over the next forty years. As always, the Soviets would fail to meet their obligations under the agreement or keep their promises, especially free elections in Poland. This was true for both the public components and their private pledges, withheld from the British and American public until the 1950s for political reasons. Potentially the provisions of Yalta were worse than those of Versailles in that Europe was left in two armed camps, one of which, the Soviet Union, had dedicated itself to the destruction of the other. Versailles, at least, left the European countries more or less disarmed with no dominant continental power.

## Divine Wind and Atomic Fury

Japan, though badly mauled and incapable of further offensive operations, nevertheless remained unbowed and unrepentant in the Pacific. On February 19, 1945, Marines assaulted Iwo Jima in what became the bloodiest engagement in Corps history. Dug-in Japanese pummeled Leathernecks on the beaches and shelled them from the 546-foot-tall Mount Suribachi, which seemed impervious to naval gunfire or bombing by air. Nearly every inch of the island had to be taken by hand-to-hand combat: flamethrowers and grenades were commonly used to eliminate Japanese pillboxes and tunnels, and the enemy refused to surrender. Out of the 20,000 Japanese troops who held Iwo Jima, scarcely 1,000 gave up. Perhaps the greatest image of victory in World War II came when Marines and a Navy corpsman raised Old Glory on top of Suribachi. The famous scene, of course, was the second such flag-raising: the first flag had been requested as a souvenir—a request that outraged the battalion commander, Lieutenant Colonel Chandler Johnson, who said it belonged to the unit. Thereupon, Johnson ordered Lieutenant Ted Tuttle to find a replacement, shouting as Tuttle hustled off, "And make it a bigger one."[121] Tuttle returned with the flag from a tank landing ship and got it to the command post, where Johnson gave it to Rene Gagnon (one of the six men who raised the flag). Gagnon and forty other Marines headed back to the summit, where Joe Rosenthal, a photographer for the Associated Press, had replaced the man who photographed the first flag, Staff Sergeant Louis Lowery. Rosenthal, who put down his camera to help pile rocks, nearly missed the shot, but as the Marines lifted Old Glory, he snapped the photo. Three of the Marines were killed within days (Michael Strank, Franklin Sousley, and Harlon Block), and for years Block was misidentified as Sergeant Hank Hansen (who had raised the first flag). Gagnon and Ira Hayes drifted into alcoholism and "survivor's guilt," with Hayes—a Pima Indian—dying of alcohol poisoning in 1955. John Bradley, who died in 1994, never spoke of his experience, and it was only through the efforts of his son, James, that the details were uncovered and published as *Flags of Our Fathers* (2000). Rosenthal's photo won the Pulitzer Prize, and in 1954 Navy petty officer Felix de Weldon completed the sculpture of the event that stands as the Marine Corps War Memorial in Arlington Cemetery.

As the final step before assaulting the home islands, Okinawa was attacked in April. By then, the U.S. ground forces totaled 548,000 men, the largest amphibious operation carried out in the Pacific. Okinawa proved a tough nut to crack as the Japanese employed suicidal kamikaze attacks on American ships with the objective being to exchange a single Japanese pilot for 1,500 American sailors. As on Pelelieu and Iwo Jima, the Japanese forces made the Americans pay for every inch they gained in the hope of raising the U.S. casualty level to beyond what the American public would accept. As General Mitsuru Ushijima wrote to his troops, "One Plane for One Warship."[122] In fact, the suicide attacks convinced the Americans more than ever that they needed to employ firepower first and advance with human forces later. A member of the 1st Marine Division, E. B. Sledge, recalled, "The mud was knee-deep in some places. . . . For several feet around every corpse, maggots crawled about in the muck . . . There wasn't a tree or bush left. All was open country. Shells had torn up the turf so completely that ground cover was nonexistent."[123] Japanese generals committed suicide rather than suffer capture.

The Japanese suicide attacks sealed the fate of Japan itself by ensuring that if the opportunity arose, the United States would use any means other than human assault to take the home islands, including—once the new secret weapon became available—the atomic bomb.

Suicide tactics caused a great deal of concern to Army and Navy planners working on the invasion of Japan. After witnessing similar tactics at Guadalcanal and Leyte Gulf, American officers anticipated extensive use of kamikazes and human bombs of all types when they invaded Kyushu and Honsu. In 1941, General Hideki Tojo had issued a military order—"Do not stay alive in dishonor"—instituting a principle similar to the one that would send generations of Islamic suicide bombers to their graves over ensuing decades. Against the United States in World War II, this dictum resulted in a mere 7 percent of all Japanese soldiers surrendering. (After Okinawa was "taken," American teams spread out back over the previously "conquered" territory killing nearly 9,000 *more* snipers and holdouts!) Based entirely on what the Japanese saw as American weakness in its affinity for life, the Empire successfully struck at American morale on June 5, 1945, with large-scale attacks on the battleship *Mississippi* and the cruiser *Louisville*. Overall, the Okinawa kamikaze campaign sank twelve major ships and damaged four fleet carriers, three light carriers, ten battleships, five cruisers, and more than sixty destroyers, making it the most deadly campaign in the history of the U.S. Navy. Worse, the Japanese high command exaggerated the losses, reinforcing its view that the war could indeed turn on suicide bombing. To a large degree, the safety of the American naval presence in Japanese waters depended on neutralizing this tactic, and planners hoped that few aircraft remained in Japan's arsenal for homeland defense. Indeed, as military historian Victor Davis Hanson has argued, the Okinawa invasion made the use of the atomic bombs all the more certain, as the United States would seek to avoid a repetition of Okinawa's fanatical defense writ large all over the Japanese home islands. Kamikazes, paradoxically, provoked the loosening of America's self-imposed restraint. In subsequent conflicts in the Middle East, jihadists would attempt (unsuccessfully) to use this very tactic to perpetuate a religious war between the West and all Muslims. Most, fortunately, would not buy into the propaganda as far as the Japanese had in 1945.

Harry S. Truman, Roosevelt's successor, seemed utterly determined to see the war through to unconditional surrender. Reports of the kamikaze attacks and the horrible toll of taking Okinawa that summer had convinced Truman that nothing less than victory over Japan was acceptable. He was prepared to order the full invasion of the Japanese home islands, even after numerous briefings indicating that the casualties would be high. Public pressure was already beginning to chafe at the terrible losses in the Pacific, and troops who had fought for three hard years in Europe balked at being sent to the Far East. If anything, American intelligence consistently underestimated the cost of taking the Japanese islands had an invasion been required. After the war it was found that Japan had mobilized more than 17 million men, women, and children to repel an invasion, and more than seven thousand planes had been held back for use against the invading fleet. Although the military had estimated upward of a million casualties, the actuality of Japanese preparations probably meant this estimate was low by as much as a factor of five. The so-called casualty myth would be raised by postwar leftist historians to claim that the atomic bombs were employed only to cow the Soviets through "atomic diplomacy." But even Japanese historians, such as Sadao Asada, and American scholars, such as Richard Frank, have concluded that an invasion would have been horrifically bloody and that if anything, the Americans had seriously underestimated the costs—both to their own forces and to Japanese civilians.[124]

Three events, taken together, rendered all invasion planning unnecessary. First, the United States had developed the atomic bomb, tested it in July, and Truman gave approval for the Army Air Corps to drop the only two in existence on Japanese cities of strategic importance. On August 6, the first bomb was dropped on Hiroshima, flattening the city and causing 66,000 to 87,000 deaths. With the military in firm control of the Japanese government, the use of the bomb and the heavy casualties incurred did not seem to alter the government's steadfast refusal to consider surrender. Indeed, the Japanese war leadership summoned its top nuclear scientist to determine if developing their own bomb was possible. At the same time, Japan protested the weapon (through the Swiss embassy) to the international community as a "disregard of international law by the American government," and referred to the "new land-mine used against Hiroshima."[125]

Second, on August 8, the USSR declared war on Japan, and immediately broke through the Kwantung Army's defenses. According to many recent revisionist historians, the Soviet declaration of war constituted a blow every bit as staggering as the first atomic bomb. Yet still Japan did not surrender.

Third, the second bomb was dropped on Nagasaki on August 9. In truth, the United States had a limited number of bombs—two more were scheduled to be dropped on August 13 and 16, and only two more would be ready by December, then there would be a long lull before any more radioactive material could be extracted. Aware of this, Truman sought to make it appear that the United States made the terrible new weapons as easily as it had turned out Liberty Ships or Sherman tanks, and he alluded to exterminating the Japanese people if surrender was not forthcoming. The conventional B-29 raids also continued, with Tokyo experiencing a full day's worth of bombing on August 13.

Even after these three events, the following day the Japanese government announced it would only accept surrender terms with the understanding that they did not contain any demand that would lessen the prerogatives of the emperor. Admiral Kantaro Suzuki, then prime minister, had to plead with the emperor, contrary to tradition, to intervene directly, which he did ("I was given the opportunity to express my own free will for the first time without violating anyone else's authority," he recalled).[126] A revolt broke out by diehards unwilling to admit defeat, but they failed to prevent the emperor's speech on August 15 calling on the Japanese people to "endure the unendurable" being broadcast over the radio.[127] After that speech reached the public, many of the military leadership committed suicide, including the war minister. Surviving Japanese officials flew to Manila on August 19 to meet with MacArthur to arrange details. American occupation forces began to land on August 28, and MacArthur arrived two days later. On September 2, at the formal surrender ceremony aboard the battleship *Missouri*, the Americans put every ship possible in view and flew seemingly endless flights of aircraft overhead. "We wanted them to know who won the war," said one participant. MacArthur reinforced the point on September 27 when he met Emperor Hirohito—a man he wanted on his side—and yet wore only khakis instead of his ceremonial dress uniform.

Horror at the use of atomic bombs had tarnished the image of the United States in the minds of some, and even British historian Paul Johnson, who otherwise heaped praise on the Americans, likened the bombing (all civilian bombing, not just the use of atomic weapons) as the equivalent of terror. In fact, bombing of cities constituted a continuation of Clausewitz's "total war" doctrine in place in every advanced nation since Napoléon's time, and in the modern world, where civilians mass-produced weapons and the military used roads and railroads to move the machinery of war, it was not only inconceivable but impossible not to view civilians as part of the total war effort. Although British "area bombing" failed to achieve its reductions in industrial output, prior to 1942 all indicators pointed to it as effective in reducing the enemy's ability to fight, if only by siphoning military resources from the Eastern Front. Atomic bombs were orders of magnitude bigger, but only in effect, not in concept. History had seen countless states and empires entirely eradicate enemies, to the point of leveling the cities that once existed.

Nor did America or the West engage in the kinds of genocide or human rights abuses as a matter of policy that were characteristic of Nazi Germany, Imperial Japan, or Communist Russia. Nowhere in the Western powers' areas of occupation did concentration camps exist for the purpose of exterminating the enemy. Leftist historians point to the American internment camps for Japanese as similar. In fact, they were different in intent, operation, and, of course, result. Japanese-Americans' life in the camps was no picnic. They lost property in the relocation. But they were not put into forced labor as were Stalin's victims (even average Russians who merely disagreed with him), deliberately starved like the subjects in the Nazi camps, or experimented upon, as were the hapless Chinese tortured by the Japanese. Nowhere in the West did democratic institutions cease to function, even under the more repressive of FDR's war orders; nowhere did free elections stop. Attempts to compare wartime actions in free societies to those of Communists and Nazis constitute nothing more than moral relativism at its worst, usually undertaken with the intent of minimizing or ridiculing American exceptionalism.

Nor did America severely restrict American liberty at home under the guise of expediency or necessity to achieve wartime efficiency. Libertarians point to conscription, but the Selective Service Act was voted in by a representative democratic assembly of two houses of lawmakers. There was also rationing, but the government attempted to minimize its impact on the civilian population as much as possible by limiting the number of goods rationed to only the most critical for the war. As a result, the average daily caloric intake in the United States did not decline under rationing, and no one starved.

Charity still reigned as a Christian principle, and the civilian population was not made to suffer purposefully to provide war materials or support. Actions in the United States were mostly voluntary, with ordinary citizens willingly purchasing war bonds to help defeat totalitarian aggressors. Wartime executions did not increase, either, and where the Nazis executed more than 30,000 of their own soldiers for various offenses, the United States executed just one in a military context, for the crime of desertion.[128] Even as occupiers in Japan, American forces were instructed by General MacArthur not to eat scarce Japanese food. There is simply no moral equivalent in the way the United States prosecuted the war, either domestically or in battle in foreign countries, with the normal and widespread actions by the Communist or fascist powers. To say otherwise is simply mendacious.

Internment of ethnic Japanese, both American citizens and aliens, during World War II has been held by those who would find fault in everything America does as evidence of institutionalized racism and inherent inequalities in the American republic. But such criticisms overlook the evidence in FBI files of actions supporting Japan by ethnic Japanese in the United States before internment, and that the internment was eminently successful in controlling an actual and potential fifth column. Similar internments of Italians and Germans, although in much lesser numbers, are rarely mentioned. And, of course, the Italians and Germans did not attack the United States at Pearl Harbor, and by so doing incur America's wrath. Japan imprisoned Americans under exceedingly harsh conditions during World War II, and one wonders if Japanese leaders gave any thought at all to what might befall ethnic Japanese in the United States during the war due to their actions.

As to the charge that Japan was forced into war and Pearl Harbor by the actions of Franklin Roosevelt, this hypothesis fails on all accounts. Even accepting the premise that FDR's economic pressure triggered Japanese adventurism that bordered on national suicide, Japan had other options. In a very real sense, the potential for a Soviet and British collapse may have dictated FDR's timing. Ultimately, however, the trade embargo with Japan came as a response to Japan's domination of China. Japan had been acquiring Chinese territory and killing its citizens for ten years, and the alternative to a conflict with the United States was to withdraw from China. Instead, Japan forced a war on America to achieve the same aim.

And finally, there is the leftist argument that the United States proved its moral bankruptcy at Hiroshima and Nagasaki. This involves a "what if" theory, unprovable and untestable, against the reasonable belief in 1945 that an invasion of Japan's four main islands was necessary to force a surrender. History cannot tell us how many Japanese would have died in that campaign, let alone the numbers of Americans and other casualties. Estimates run from a ridiculous and self-serving several hundred thousand, to as many as ten million or more. Against those numbers, Hiroshima and Nagasaki's losses seem light. But again, Japan had alternatives to continuing the fight. Okinawa proved Japan could win only by causing the American public to lose heart by inflicting unacceptable casualties on Americans, themselves, and other nations. Even then, when surrender was an option to spare everyone further losses to no purpose, Japan chose to continue to fight. Only after the bombs demonstrated that Japan might be the *only* country to face enormous, even catastrophic, losses did Japan capitulate.

America's moral power was also clouded by the wartime alliance with Stalin's hideous gulag-ridden Soviet Union, which had sided with Hitler at the outset, invaded Finland, crushed Estonia, Latvia, and Lithuania, shipped off thousands of repatriated prisoners to new concentration camps, murdered 14,000 Polish officers, spied energetically on its allies, and perpetuated as many atrocities as it later prosecuted as part of the victorious war crimes tribunals. Barbarities on the part of the Americans absolutely occurred, and enthusiastic researchers can find examples of a G.I. who shot a surrendering German or a Marine who sent a skull home.[129] More often than not, however, such excesses were provoked by the behavior of the Axis themselves: the Japanese, in particular, simply refused to surrender, occasionally turning themselves into human bombs, and word of the execution of Doolittle raiders had already reached American ears. The Japanese had ordered the flyboys to write their final letters home before tying them to crosses and shooting three of them (others were given temporary reprieves).[130] For the "Aryan Supermen" whom Hitler had convinced were destined to rule the world or the *Yamato-damashii* who were descendants of the gods and for whom all others were subhumans, atrocities by definition could not be extraordinary at all. It was par for the course, tasks that had to be performed to attain a position of international dominance. One wonders what new or different barbarities a clash between the Nazis and Knights of Bushido would have produced. Americans, however, were ordinary men pulled into dirty, violent, and bloody circumstances, and to concoct a moral equivalence between these competing societies is as dangerously misleading and false as it is stupid. As it had been expressed in 1776, American actions came at the end of a "train of abuses," many of them disgusting in the extreme, and the remarkable fact of the Second World War was that the United States and her Western allies did not deal *more* harshly with the vanquished. And when it was over, the United States had protected much of the world with an umbrella of freedom heretofore unseen in the annals of human conduct.

As a hard peace settled across the world, the United States entered an

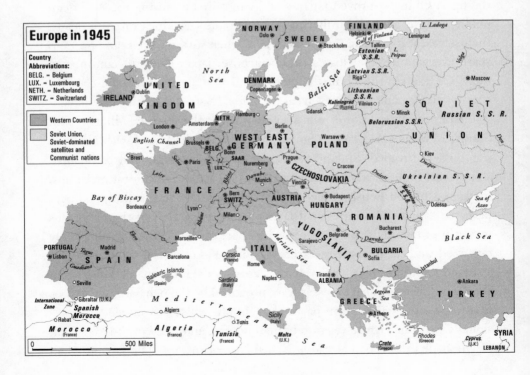

era of growth and prosperity created by the golden accident of the global conflagration. In one of the rare times in history, a major nation was at the same time the world's top producer and consumer. Over the next quarter century, America would dominate world trade and production as no country—or empire—ever had. Europeans, ravaged by bombs and bullets, would recover rapidly, but even at that they remained heavily dependent on American goods, and goodness, to survive. And to do so, they would embrace a soft state socialism that set them on a path to long-term bankruptcy and social collapse. Stalin's Soviet Union would recover as well, but through a much different dynamic, its influence succeeding through a grip of iron, imposed from Moscow, reinforced by Lenin and Marx from the grave.

Those exceptional American characteristics that had brought freedom to much of the world and which would soon extend an unparalleled prosperity to all non-Communist nations came with a structural kryptonite, in that the postwar systems all depended on the simultaneous moral and fiscal integrity of the United States yet also required lavish lending, heavy military commitments, and an American unwillingness to dominate the free world the way previous victors had. That postwar world asked of the United States that it share its resources unreservedly, restrain itself economically, and rebuild its former allies and enemies enthusiastically. More challenging still, the postwar society would demand freedom, not just for suppressed peoples within and without America's borders, but liberation from the very structures and moral restraints that had produced the triumphs in the first place. A legitimate and long-overdue revolution in civil rights for minorities within America's borders and an end to colonialism abroad would be accompanied by social upheavals that contained the seeds of decay for Western society. Wealth and leisure provided by America's influences soon would erode the institutions and disciplines needed to maintain, let alone expand, wealth and leisure for others.

Behind these demands and the theories under which the United States attempted to meet them was the astounding ignorance throughout the world and even among America's elites of what had made America great and why and how it had achieved the dominant place it occupied. Foreigners seemed pathologically incapable of understanding American exceptionalism, the four pillars that produced it, and why their adoption was necessary to replicate the American miracle. Their difficulties in this regard were also excusable—they did not understand American society, and most frequently possessed *none* of the four pillars in their own countries. Yet they still attempted to apply such words as "liberty," "democracy," "republicanism," and "freedom" to their own political structures and societies, and reproduced them by rote in constitutions. More reprehensible was the "nation building" that would be attempted by American elites through the imposition of American political and economic structures without first establishing a foundation grounded by the four pillars. Indeed, whole books have been written on the "myth" of American exceptionalism, usually making it one of the least understood phenomena in the United States.[131] A great amount of work clearly lay ahead at home and abroad to foster the understanding of what would produce human dignity and prosperity, using the American way or any other.

This would be the challenge of the next seventy-five years: to provide an umbrella of liberty and perpetuate American exceptionalism while allowing in just enough rain of difficulty and disappointment to remind Americans—and the world—that the era with which we all had been blessed was itself no golden accident.

# ACKNOWLEDGMENTS

When Michael Allen and I began work on *A Patriot's History of the United States* in the 1990s, we never contemplated the kind of success it has enjoyed. It has become better, printing by printing and edition by edition, thanks to the comments and, yes, corrections by our readers. This is exactly the kind of participatory technology/business that futurists have been predicting for a decade. One of those who appreciated *Patriot's History* in its original form—but not without criticisms and corrections—was my coauthor on this book, Dave Dougherty. He has since become a friend, business associate, confidant, and writer on other projects. And the collaboration all began when I responded to his Amazon.com book review of *Patriot's History*. Welcome to the future!

Michael Allen has continued to be a source of inspiration, ideas, and suggestions on all the books, even those that do not bear his name. Thanks, Mike! David Limbaugh read early drafts of this book and encouraged me to see it through. As one can probably tell, I owe a great deal to the inspiration of Paul Johnson, who, as a nonhistorian, has written better history than many of the faculties at some of the best schools in America. Thanks to Philip Schwartzberg, who did a wonderful job on our maps and illustrations.

The late Ed Knappmann was our agent on *A Patriot's History of the United States* and all books leading up to, and including, this one. He is missed: a rare, up-front guy who never sold you a rainbow and never took no for a (permanent) answer. Since Ed's death, Roger Williams has stepped in admirably and in every way possible maintained Ed's high standards. We are in capable hands with Roger.

Although she hasn't worked on my books for five years, I still feel like Bernadette Malone Serton has been a voice of inspiration. Her replacement at Sentinel, Brooke Carey, and her associate, Natalie Horbachevsky... well, to say they've done a magnificent job on an immense manuscript is an understatement. They deserve much of the credit for the finished product. Thanks also to the entire publicity and publishing staff at Sentinel, and to Adrian Zackheim, who, as always, has run point on my projects.

The success of the (now-trademarked) Patriot's History series—it now includes a reader, a children's book, and a television series in preproduction—owes a massive debt of gratitude to Rush Limbaugh, who interviewed me for his *Limbaugh Letter* in 2004 when *A Patriot's History of the United States* first appeared, and to Glenn Beck, who in 2010 launched a one-man publicity campaign that drove the book to number one on the *New York Times* list. But while I can't name them all, the hundreds, perhaps thousands, of homeschoolers who have used our books have played a critical role in shifting the marketplace for conservative (i.e., honest) history.

Research and production of this volume was greatly assisted by my son, Adam Schweikart—who could be a great historian if he chose—by my friend Brian Bennett, by my brother-in-law Chris Castelitz, by Amanda Cruse, and by Cynthia King at the University of Dayton. UD has been extremely generous in providing everything from funding to release time, most of that due to the efforts of Dean Paul Benson and history department Chairman Julius Amin.

Finally, my wife, Dee, steadfastly allows me isolation time to write, although strangely our intermittent shopping trips also permitted me extensive periods of reading, something that isn't as easy to find as one might think.

—Larry Schweikart

Although it is not customary to laud one's coauthor, I am indebted above measure to Larry Schweikart, not only for his work on this volume but also for his friendship and guidance. Although our relationship began in a most unorthodox fashion as he states, it has developed into close collaboration with daily phone calls and e-mails being the norm. I can't imagine a better partner or having a more fulfilling working relationship.

My interest in history began at the age of ten, when my brother Ralph gave me a book of biographies of famous persons to read. It stated that Alexander the Great had set civilization back one thousand years while Karl Marx was a great economic and political thinker. Even then, in 1950, I recognized spurious propaganda when I read it and began regularly checking books out of the Denver Public Library to read further. The next Christmas my parents gave me *Life's Picture History of World War II*, followed in 1953 with Douglas Southall Freeman's three-volume work, *Lee's Lieutenants*, and Walter Goerlitz's *History of the German General Staff* in 1954. That was supplemented by *Statesmen of the Lost Cause* from J. Howard Marshall, Jr.'s later wife, Bettye Bohanon. In short, I was hooked on history at an early age and never took a college history course. Many of my parents' friends and acquaintances took part in stimulating further reading on my part, and their names are too numerous to mention.

In El Paso, where I lived for more than twenty years and was a professor of business–computer science, a close friend, Gary Thompson, guided me through dark times and encouraged me to produce several novels, which I made no serious effort to publish. More recently another friend has loomed large, Shirley Wunderlich. Following the death of her husband in January 2011, she has spent many hours reading my work and offering suggestions and corrections. She deserves my special thanks and appreciation.

For the past ten years the continual requests for historical and political tracts from conservatives here in northern Arkansas have proven especially stimulating. The bedrock people who are the backbone of our country but scorned by our elites have an abiding thirst for historical knowledge and are the pond in which I swim. Hardly a day goes by in which I am not asked some serious historical question or to provide background for some current political issue.

Last, one rarely learns anything from someone whose opinion is the same as his own, and I am privileged to live in a rural environment where the meaning of life is not a question for sociologists, but is found in the Bible. After cutting fifty bull calves and turning them into steers, one gains a different perspective on life.

—Dave Dougherty

# NOTES

## Introduction

1. Leonard Huxley, ed., *Scott's Last Expedition: Vols. I and II* (London: Smith, Elder & Co, 1913), 1:595.

2. Alex Cairncross and Barry Eichengreen, *Sterling in Decline* (Oxford: Basil Blackwell Pub. Ltd, 1983).

3. Barack Obama News Conference, April 4, 2009, http://www.presidency .ucsb.edu/ws/index.php?pid=85959&st=american+exceptionalism&st1= #axzz1Tn2f9R8i.

4. Guillaume Thomas François Raynal, *Histoire Philosophique et Politique des Établissements et du Commerce des Européens dans les deux Indes*, 4 vols. (Amsterdam, 1770), quoted in Thomas Jefferson, *Notes on the State of Virginia*, David Walstreicher, ed. (New York: Bedford, St. Martin's, 2002 ), 125.

5. Personal interviews by David Dougherty, 1963–65. See also R. A. C. Parker, *Chamberlain and Appeasement* (New York: St. Martin's Press, 1993), 44, to see Neville Chamberlain's opinion of the United States: "We have the misfortune to be dealing with a nation of cads." Parker also states, referring to 1935: "Enlightened, progressively minded British citizens felt a sense of duty to the world. This went . . . with a long-established sense of British power and influence. . . . It still seemed natural to believe that London could and should organize the world" (ibid., 25).

6. Donald Smythe, *Pershing, General of the Armies* (Bloomington: Indiana University Press, 1986), 267.

7. Niall Ferguson, *The War of the World: Twentieth-Century Conflict and the Descent of the West* (New York: Penguin, 2006), xli.

8. Paul Johnson, *Modern Times: A History of the World from the Twenties to the Nineties*, rev. ed. (New York: HarperCollins, 1991), 160.

## Chapter 1: American Emergence Amid European Self-Absorption

1.    Ronald Spector, *Admiral of the New Empire: the Life and Career of George Dewey* (Baton Rouge: Louisiana State University Press, 1974).

2.    John Barrett, *Admiral George Dewey* (New York: Harper & Brothers, 1899), 14–15.

3.    David M. Potter, *The Impending Crisis, 1848–1861*, completed and edited by Don E. Fehrenbacher (New York: Harper Colophon, 1976), 198.

4.    "De Lome Letter," http://en.wikisource.org/wiki/De_L%C3%B4me_ Letter.

5.    Henry J. Hendrix, *Theodore Roosevelt's Naval Diplomacy: The United States Navy and the Birth of the American Century* (Annapolis, MD: Naval Institute Press, 2009); William Henry Harbaugh, *Power and Responsibility: The Life and Times of Theodore Roosevelt* (New York: Farrar, Straus and Cudahy, 1961), 95; William R. Braisted, *The United States Navy in the Pacific, 1897–1909* (Austin: University of Texas Press, 1958). According to Braisted, Roosevelt "was perhaps more responsible than any other individual . . . for the shaping of the Navy into an effective instrument of war and diplomacy."

6.    "Report of the Secretary of the Navy, 1898," http://www.history.navy .mil/wars/spanam/sn98-13.htm.

7.    Halford J. Mackinder, "The Geographical Pivot of History," *The Geographical Journal*, 23, April 1904, 421–37.

8.    Peter Krass, *Carnegie* (New York: John Wiley & Sons, 2002), 259; Robert Seager, "Ten Years Before Mahan: The Unofficial Case for the New Navy, 1880–1890," *Mississippi Valley Historical Review*, 60, December 1953, 491–512.

9.    See Burton Folsom, Jr., *The Myth of the Robber Barons: A New Look at the Rise of Big Business in America* (Herndon, VA: Young America's Foundation, 1991), 75.

10.   Barrett, *Admiral George Dewey*, 59, 66.

11.   Sylvia L. Hilton and Steve J. S. Ickringill, eds., *European Perceptions of the Spanish-American War of 1898* (Bern, Switzerland: Peter Lang, 1999), 12; J. Fred Rippy, "The European Powers and the Spanish-American War," *James Sprunt Historical Studies*, 19, 1927, 22–52.

12.   Hilton and Ickringill, *European Perceptions of the Spanish-American War*, 16.

13.   Lester B. Shippee, "Germany and the Spanish-American War," *American Historical Review*, 30, July 1925, 754–77; Terrell D. Gottschall, "Germany and the Spanish-American War: A Case Study of Navalism and Imperialism," Ph.D. dissertation, Washington State University, 1981.

14.   Louis M. Sears, "French Opinion of the Spanish American War," *Hispanic American Historical Review*, 7, 1927, 25–44; James Louis Whitehead,

"French Reaction to American Imperialism, 1895–1908," Ph.D. dissertation, University of Pennsylvania, 1943; John L. Offner, "The United States and France: Ending the Spanish-American War," *Diplomatic History*, 7, Winter 1983, 1–21.

15.  Leonid A. Shur, "Russian Volunteers in the Cuban War of National Liberation, 1895–1898," in R. H. Bartley, ed., *Soviet Historians on Latin America: Recent Scholarly Contributions* (Madison: University of Wisconsin Press, 1978), 221–33.

16.  J. H. McMinn, "The Attitude of the English Press toward the U.S. During the Spanish-American War," Ph.D. dissertation, Ohio State University, 1939; Robert G. Neale, "Anglo-American Relations During the Spanish American War: Some Problems," *Historical Studies: Australia and New Zealand*, 6, 1953, 72–84, and his *Great Britain and Untied States Expansion, 1898–1900* (Lansing: Michigan State University Press, 1966); Geoffrey Seed, "British Reactions to American Imperialism Reflected in Journals of Opinion, 1898–1900," *Political Science Quarterly*, 73, 1958, 254–72, and his "British Views of American Policy in the Philippines Reflected in Journals of Opinion," *Journal of American Studies*, 2, 1968, 49–64.

17.  Nico A. Bootsma, "Reactions to the Spanish-American War in the Netherlands," in Hilton and Ickringill, *European Perceptions of the Spanish-American War*, 35–52.

18.  Bootsma, "Reactions to the Spanish-American War in the Netherlands," 50.

19.  Francisco Diaz Diaz, "The Spanish American War—One Spaniard's View," http://www.spanamwar.com/Spanishview.htm.

20.  Sylvia L. Hilton, "The United States Through Spanish Republican Eyes in the Colonial Crisis of 1895–1898," in Hilton and Ickringill, *European Perceptions of the Spanish-American War*, 53–70 (quotation on 56). Hilton claims the Republican criticism of the war was in reality directed at the Spanish government. But even if one accepts her view that the Republicans' ultimate object of vituperation was Spanish government incompetence, leading to a catastrophe, that hardly elevated their view of the United States. Tortuously, Hilton argued, the Spanish Republicans saw the vindication of *republicanism* in their view that, in a contest between a Republican Spain and a republican United States, Spain would triumph.

21.  Larry Schweikart, *America's Victories: Why the U.S. Wins Wars and Will Win the War on Terror* (New York: Sentinel, 2007), 70–71.

22.  Mark W. Kwasny, *Washington's Partisan War, 1775–1783* (Kent, OH: Kent State University Press, 1996), 3.

23.  Edward M. Coffman, *The Old Army: A Portrait of the American Army in Peacetime, 1784–1898* (New York: Oxford, 1986), 166.

24.  Justin H. Smith, *The War with Mexico*, 2 vols. (New York: Macmillan, 1919), 1:105–6.

25. Ibid., 1:105; London *Times*, July 5, 1845.

26. Markus M. Hugo, "'Uncle Sam I Cannot Stand, for Spain I Have No Sympathy': An Analysis of Discourse About the Spanish-American War in Imperial Germany, 1898–1899," in Hilton and Ickringill, *European Perceptions of the Spanish-American War*, 71–93.

27. Ibid., 87.

28. Nicole Slupetzky, "Austria and the Spanish-American War," in ibid., 181–94 (quotation on 183–84).

29. Hilton, "United States Through Spanish Republican Eyes," 64.

30. Ibid.

31. Ibid., 67.

32. Slupetzky, "Austria and the Spanish American War," 184.

33. Hilton, "United States Through Spanish Republican Eyes," 64.

34. Ibid., 65.

35. Slupetzky, "Austria and the Spanish-American War," 183.

36. J. B. Atkins, *The War in Cuba, The Reminiscences of an Englishman with the United States Army* (London: Smith, Elder & Co., 1899), 24–26; Joseph Smith, "British War Correspondents and the Spanish-American War, April–July 1898," in Hilton and Ickringill, *European Perceptions of the Spanish-American War*, 195–209 (quotation on 198).

37. Smith, "British War Correspondents," 198.

38. George Lynch, *Impressions of a War Correspondent* (London: George Newnes, 1903), 100; *Daily Mail*, May 2, 1898.

39. C. E. Hands, "Uncle Sam's New Bike," *Daily Mail*, June 25, 1898.

40. C. E. Hands, "Seeing the Battle," *Daily Mail*, August 4, 1898.

41. Douglas McPherson, *Daily Graphic*, August 18, 1898.

42. Niall Ferguson, *Colossus: The Rise and Fall of the American Empire* (London: Allan Lane, 2004), 41.

43. Hilton, "United States Through Spanish Republican Eyes," 69.

44. Slupetzky, "Austria and the Spanish-American War," 193.

45. Ibid., 69.

46. Hugo, "'Uncle Sam I Cannot Stand, for Spain I Have No Sympathy,'" 90. Ludmila N. Popkova, "Russian Press Coverage of American Intervention in the Spanish-American War," in Hilton and Ickringill, *European Perceptions of the Spanish-American War*, 111–32 (quotation on 126).

47. Daniela Rossini, "The American Peril: Italian Catholics and the Spanish-American War, 1898," in Hilton and Ickringill, *European Perceptions of the Spanish-American War*, 167–79 (quotation on 179).

48. Hugo, "'Uncle Sam I Cannot Stand, for Spain I Have No Sympathy,'" 89.

49. Thomas F. O'Brien, *Making the Americas: The United States and Latin*

*America from the Age of Revolutions to the Era of Globalization* (Albuquerque: University of New Mexico Press, 2007), 71.

50.   See also Jack C. Lane, *Armed Progressive* (Lincoln, NB: University of Nebraska Press, 2009), 71, 86–113.

51.   Max Boot, *The Savage Wars of Peace: Small Wars and the Rise of American Power* (New York: Basic Books, 2003), 132.

52.   O'Brien, *Making the Americas*, 72.

53.   Brian McAllister Linn, *The Philippine War 1899–1902* (Lawrence: University Press of Kansas, 2000), 3.

54.   Ibid., 6.

55.   Graham Cosmas, *An Army for Empire: The United States Army and the Spanish-American War* (Columbia: University of Missouri Press, 1971), 121.

56.   Ibid., 102.

57.   Richard Stewart, ed., *American Military History, vol. 1: The United States Army and the Forging of a Nation, 1775–1917* (Washington, DC: Center of Military History, United States Army, 2005), 355.

58.   Timothy K. Deady, "Lessons from a Successful Counterinsurgency: the Philippines, 1899–1902," *Parameters*, Spring 2005, 53–68 (quotation on 55).

59.   Ibid..

60.   Boot, *Savage Wars of Peace*, 137.

61.   Ibid., 136; Dana G. Munro, *Intervention and Dollar Diplomacy in the Caribbean, 1900–1921* (Princeton, NJ: Princeton University Press, 1964), 65–77; David Healy, *Drive to Hegemony: The United States and the Caribbean, 1898–1917* (Madison: University of Wisconsin Press, 1988), 100–106; Lester D. Langley, *The United States and the Caribbean in the Twentieth Century*, 4th ed. (Athens: University of Georgia Press, 1989), 22–27; Donald Yerxa, *Admirals and Empire: The United States Navy and the Caribbean, 1898–1945* (Columbia: University of South Carolina Press, 1991), 16–20.

62.   Smedley Butler, *War Is a Racket* (Los Angeles: Feral House, 2003); Anne Cipriano Venzon, "General Smedley Darlington Butler: The Letters of a Leatherneck, 1898–1918," editor's thesis, Princeton University, 1982.

63.   Francis Reginald Wingate, *Mahdiism and the Egyptian Sudan*, 2nd ed. (London: Frank Cass, 1968).

64.   Jonathan Derrick, *Africa's Agitators: Militant Anti-Colonialism in Africa and the West, 1918–1939* (New York: Columbia University Press, 2008).

65.   Ibid., 13.

66.   Ibid.

67.   Ibid., 175.

68. Daniel Gazda, *Mahdi Uprising, 1881–1899* (Warsaw, Poland: Balonna, S Cl., 2004).

69. Lance E. Davis and Robert A. Huttenback, *Mammon and the Pursuit of Empire: The Economics of British Imperialism* (Cambridge, UK: Cambridge University Press, 1988).

70. Niall Ferguson, *The War of the World: Twentieth-Century Conflict and the Descent of the West* (New York: Penguin, 2006), 9.

71. Richard Franklin Bensel, *The Political Economy of American Industrialization, 1977–1900* (New York: Cambridge, 2000), xvii.

72. Ibid., xx.

73. Waverly Root and Richard de Rochemont, *Eating in America: A History* (New York: Ecco Press, 1995), 134–35.

74. Larry Schweikart and Michael Allen, *A Patriot's History of the United States from Columbus's Great Discovery to the War on Terror* (New York: Sentinel, 2006).

75. Michael D. Bordo and Hugh Rockoff, "The Gold Standard as a 'Good Housekeeping Seal of Approval,'" *Journal of Economic History*, 56, June 1996, 389–428; Donald N. McCloskey and J. Richard Zecher, "How the Gold Standard Worked, 1880–1913," in Barry Eichengreen, ed., *The Gold Standard in Theory and History* (New York: Methuen, 1985), 66–72.

76. *Commercial and Financial Chronicle*, June 13, 1896.

77. Bensel, *Political Economy of American Industrialization*, 26.

78. *Appleton's Annual Cyclopedia of 1892* (New York: D. Appleton, 1893), 616–17.

79. Larry Schweikart and Lynne Pierson Doti, *Banking in the American West from the Gold Rush to Deregulation* (Norman: University of Oklahoma Press, 1991).

80. Lance E. Davis and Robert J. Cull, *International Capital Markets and American Economic Growth* (New York: Cambridge University Press, 1994).

81. Alfred D. Chandler, Jr., *Visible Hand: The Managerial Revolution in American Business* (Cambridge, MA: Belknap, 1977); and for a few examples of specific roads, see Stewart Holbrook, *James J. Hill: A Great Life in Brief* (New York: Alfred A. Knopf, 1955); Albro Martin, *James J. Hill and the Opening of the Northwest* (New York: Oxford University Press, 1976); James Marshall, *Santa Fe: The Railroad That Built an Empire* (New York: Random House, 1945); Larry Schweikart, *The Entrepreneurial Adventure: A History of Business in the United States* (Fort Worth, TX: Harcourt, 2000), chapter 5.

82. Robert H. Bork, *The Antitrust Paradox: A Policy at War with Itself* (New York: Basic Books, 1978); Harold Demsetz, "Barriers to Entry," *American Economic Review*, 72, March 1982, 47–57; Dominick T. Armentano, *Antitrust and Monopoly* (New York: Holmes & Meier, 1982); and James

Langerfeld and David Scheffman, "Evolution or Revolution: What Is the Future of Antitrust?" *Antitrust Bulletin*, 31, Summer 1986, 287–99.

83. David McCullough, *The Path Between the Seas: The Creation of the Panama Canal, 1870–1914* (New York: Simon and Schuster, 1977), 248.

84. Ibid., 249.

85. Edmund Morris, *The Rise of Theodore Roosevelt* (New York: Random House, 1979), xxiv.

86. Theodore Roosevelt, "Citizenship in a Republic," Speech at the Sorbonne, Paris, April 23, 1910, http://www.theodoreroosevelt.org/life/quotes.htm.

87. Daniel J. Kevles, *In the Name of Eugenics: Genetics and the Uses of Human Heredity* (Cambridge, MA: Harvard University Press, 1997), 9.

88. W. Elliott Brownlee, *Federal Taxation in America: A Short History*, new edition (Washington, DC: Woodrow Wilson Center, 2004), 55.

89. Ibid., 57.

90. Bensel, *Political Economy of American Industrialization*, passim.

91. O'Brien, *Making the Americas*, 85.

92. McCullough, *Path Between the Seas*, 53.

93. Ibid., 58.

94. Ibid., 53, 85.

95. Ibid., 85.

96. Ibid., 146.

97. Stephen Kinzer, *Overthrow: America's Century of Regime Change from Hawaii to Iraq* (New York: Henry Holt and Company, 2006), 58–59.

98. McCullough, *Path Between the Seas*, 378.

99. Ibid., 408.

100. Ibid., 462.

101. Ibid., 422–23.

102. Ibid., 467.

103. Ibid., 510.

104. F. R. Sedwick, *The Russo-Japanese War* (New York: Macmillan Company, 1909); Ian Nish, *The Origins of the Russo-Japanese War* (New York: Longman, 1985).

105. Geoffrey Regan, "The Battle of Tsushima 1905," in *The Guinness Book of Decisive Battles* (London: Guinness Publishing, 1992), 176–77.

106. Oron J. Hale, *The Great Illusion, 1900–1914* (New York: Harper, 1971), 263.

107. Larry Schweikart, "Polar Revisionism and the Peary Claim: The Diary of Robert E. Peary," *The Historian*, 48, May 1986, 341–58. In 1986, Larry Schweikart was one of the first historians to examine the Peary Diary,

and concluded that it was, in fact, genuine; that it was written on the trail—not afterward as some alleged—and that, combined with the experiences of other explorers, it was consistent with Peary's claim that he attained the North Pole. To this day, the Cook family has sought to tarnish Peary's image, while the Scandinavian exploration community, naturally, has sought to reject it in order to bolster the claims of the great Roald Amundsen as the first man to reach *both* poles and live. Sadly and ironically, I was in the National Archives to examine the diary of one great explorer on January 28, 1986, when another group of explorers, the crew of the Space Shuttle *Challenger*, died in a horrific explosion.

108.  Larry Schweikart, "Evaluating Polar Revisionists: An Examination of Peary's 1909 Polar Claim," *Historicus*, 2, Fall/Winter 1980, 88–126. This is a student journal from Arizona State University, and research for this paper formed the bulk of my later work, cited above in "Polar Revisionism and the Peary Claim."

109.  Schweikart, "Polar Revisionism and the Peary Claim," 343–44.

110.  Susan Solomon, *The Coldest March: Scott's Fatal Antarctic Expedition* (London: Yale University Press, 2001), supports Scott's explanation by citing weather statistics showing that, in fact, the weather was extremely and uncharacteristically horrid. See also Robert Falcon Scott, *Scott's Last Expedition*, *Vols. I and II*, ed. Leonard Huxley (London: Smith, Elder & Co., 1913), with volume 1 being Scott's diary. Roland Huntford, *The Last Place on Earth* (London: Pan Books, 1985), is highly critical of Scott; David Crane, *Scott of the Antarctic: A Life of Courage, and Tragedy in the Extreme South* (London: HarperCollins, 2005), more favorable.

111.  Calvin S. Hall, *A Primer of Freudian Psychology* (Cleveland, OH: World Publishing Co., 1954) 13.

112.  Ibid., 15.

113.  Ira Progoff, *Jung's Psychology and Its Social Meaning*, 2nd ed. (New York: The Julian Press, 1953), 39.

114.  Frank Lloyd Wright, *An Autobiography* (New York: Duell, Sloan and Pearce, 1943); Merle Secrest, *Frank Lloyd Wright: A Biography* (New York: Knopf, 1992).

115.  Earl Nisbet, *Taliesin Reflections: My Years Before, During, and After Living with Frank Lloyd Wright* (Petaluma, CA: Meridian Press, 2006); Patrick Meehan, ed., *Truth Against the World: Frank Lloyd Wright Speaks for an Organic Architecture* (New York: John Wiley, 1987).

116.  Franklin Toker, *Fallingwater Rising: Frank Lloyd Wright, E. J. Kaufmann, and America's Most Extraordinary House* (New York: Knopf, 2003); William Allin Storrer, *The Architecture of Frank Lloyd Wright: A Complete Catalog*, 3rd ed. (Chicago: University of Chicago Press, 2007).

117.  A New York sheet-metal magnate, Joe Massaro, bought the house in 1991 and began a renovation project based entirely on Wright's original designs that was completed in 2007. See David Coleman, "Loving

Frank," *New York Home Design*, September 10, 2007, http://architecture lab.net/2007/09/15/loving-frank/.

118. Gijs Van Hensbergen, *Gaudí: A Biography* (New York: Perennial, 2001), 14.

119. Van Hensbergen, *Gaudí*, 138.

120. Rainer Zervst. *Antoni Gaudí: A Life Devoted to Architecture* (Cologne: Benedikt Taschen Verlag, 1988), 162; Cesar Martinell, *Antoni Gaudí: His Life, His Theories, His Work* (Cambridge, MA: MIT Press, 1975).

121. Van Hensbergen, *Gaudí*, xxxiii.

122. George Orwell, *Homage to Catalonia* (London: Secker and Warburg, 1938), quoted in Van Hensbergen, *Gaudí*, xxxiii.

123. Iain Boyd Whyte, ed., *Crystal Chain Letters: Architectural Fantasies by Bruno Taut and His Circle* (Cambridge, MA: MIT Press, 1985).

124. Modris Eksteins, *Rites of Spring: The Great War and the Birth of the Modern Age* (Boston: Houghton Mifflin, 1989), 39; Igor Stravinsky and Robert Craft, *Memories and Commentaries* (Garden City, NY: Doubleday, 1960), 29; Vera Stravinsky and Robert Craft, *Stravinsky in Pictures and Documents* (New York: Simon and Schuster, 1978), 76–105.

125. Eksteins, *Rites of Spring*, 39.

126. Oron J. Hale, *The Great Illusion, 1900–1914* (New York: Harper, 1971), 163.

127. Barbara Tuchman, *The Guns of August* (New York: Bantam, 1979), 25.

128. Martin Gilbert, *A History of the Twentieth Century, Vol. One: 1900–1933* (New York: Avon, 1997), 51.

129. Ibid., 52.

130. Carroll Quigley, *Tragedy & Hope: A History of the World in Our Time* (New York: Macmillan, 1966), 61.

131. Ibid., 135.

132. Ferguson, *War of the World*, 4.

133. Quigley, *Tragedy & Hope*, 103.

## Chapter 2: Cataclysm

1. Niall Ferguson, *The War of the World: Twentieth-Century Conflict and the Descent of the West* (New York: Penguin, 2006), 93.

2. William L. Shirer, *20th Century Journey* (New York: Simon and Schuster, 1976), 216; Harold Rosenberg, *The Tradition of the New* (New York: Horizon, 1959), 209; Modris Eksteins, *Rites of Spring: The Great War and the Birth of the Modern Age* (Boston: Houghton Mifflin, 1989), 44.

3. Eksteins, *Rites of Spring*, 44.

4. Ibid., 48.

5.   Ibid., 91.

6.   Ibid.

7.   Ibid., 193.

8.   Ibid., 91–92.

9.   Ibid., 93.

10.  Friedrich von Bernhardi, *Germany in the Next War*, trans. Allen H. Powles (Honolulu: University Press of the Pacific, 2001), 17–18.

11.  Paul Johnson, *Modern Times: A History of the World from the Twenties to the Nineties*, rev. ed. (New York: HarperCollins, 1991), 19.

12.  Oron J. Hale, *The Great Illusion, 1900–1914* (New York: Harper, 1971), 242.

13.  Barbara Tuchman, *The Guns of August* (New York: Bantam, 1979), 21.

14.  Ferguson, *War of the World*, 102.

15.  Ludwig Thoma, quoted in Eksteins, *Rites of Spring*, 92.

16.  Eksteins, *Rites of Spring*, 93.

17.  Ralph Freedman, *Hermann Hesse: Pilgrim of Crisis* (New York: Pantheon, 1978), 168.

18.  Emile Ludwig, "Der moralische Gewinn" ("The Moral Victory"), *Berliner Tageblatt*, August 5, 1914, 392, and his novel *Juli 14* (Berlin: E. Rowohit, 1929), 1–120.

19.  Eksteins, *Rites of Spring*, 93.

20.  Ibid.

21.  Erich Kahler, *The Germans* (Princeton, NJ: Princeton University Press, 1974), 272.

22.  Eksteins, *Rites of Spring*, 119.

23.  Tuchman, *Guns of August*, 105.

24.  Barbara W. Tuchman, *The Proud Tower* (New York: The Macmillan Company, 1966), 462.

25.  Tuchman, *Guns of August*, 140.

26.  Ibid., 55.

27.  Robert Blake, ed., *The Private Papers of Douglas Haig, 1914–1919* (London: Eyre & Spottiswoode, 1952), 84, citing Haig's diary entry of January 22, 1915.

28.  Tuchman, *Guns of August*, 38.

29.  Ibid., 222.

30.  Ibid., 223.

31.  Ibid., 229.

32.  Ibid., 231.

33. German Ministry of War, *The Usages of War on Land*, translated by J. H. Morgan (New York: 1915), 196–97, as referenced in Larry Zuckerman, *The Rape of Belgium* (New York: New York University Press, 2004), 41.

34. Tuchman, *Guns of August*, 193.

35. Holger H. Herwig, *The Marne, 1914* (New York: Random House, 2009), 113.

36. Tuchman, *Guns of August*, 359.

37. Jeff Lipkes, *Rehearsals: The German Army in Belgium, August 1914* (Leuven, Belgium: Leuven University Press, 2007).

38. John Horne and Alan Kramer, *German Atrocities, 1914: A History of Denial* (New York: Yale University Press, 2001), 74.

39. Horne and Kramer, *German Atrocities*, 371.

40. Larry Schweikart, *America's Victories: Why the U.S. Wins Wars and Will Win the War on Terror* (New York: Sentinel, 2007), 184.

41. John S. D. Eisenhower, *Yanks: The Epic Story of the American Army in World War I* (New York: Free Press, 2001), 59–60; James Dunnigan and Albert Nofi, *Dirty Little Secrets of World War II: Military Information No One Told You About the Greatest, Most Terrible War in History* (New York: Quill, 1994), 26.

42. Herwig, *The Marne*, 37.

43. Ibid.

44. Tuchman, *Guns of August*, 359.

45. Ibid., 432.

46. Ibid., 467.

47. Walter Goerlitz, *History of the German General Staff* (New York: Praeger, 1953), 161–62.

48. Herwig, *The Marne*, 302.

49. Cyril Falls, *The Great War, 1914–1918* (New York: Perigee, 1959), 72.

50. Eksteins, *Rites of Spring*, 106.

51. Wilhelm, Crown Prince of Germany, *My War Experiences*, in Eksteins, *Rites of Spring*, 110.

52. Martin Gilbert, *A History of the Twentieth Century, Volume One: 1900–1933* (New York: Avon, 1997), 405.

53. Smyth, *Pershing*, 77, 113.

54. Eksteins, *Rites of Spring*, 162.

55. "Report of the Committee on Chemical Warfare Organisation," in Eksteins, *Rites of Spring*, 164.

56. Carroll Quigley, *Tragedy & Hope: A History of the World in Our Time* (New York: Macmillan, 1966), 228.

57.  John Ellis, *Eye-Deep in Hell* (New York: Pantheon, 1976), 94.

58.  Eksteins, *Rites of Spring*, 146.

59.  Herbert Read, "In Retreat: A Journal of the Retreat of the Fifth Army from St. Quintin, March 1918," in *The Contrary Experience: Autobiographies* (London: Faber and Faber, 1983), 248.

60.  Eksteins, *Rites of Spring*, 149.

61.  Ibid.,

62.  Ibid.

63.  Louis Mairet, quoted in ibid., 153.

64.  "Planning Total War? Falkenhayn and the Battle of Verdun, 1916," in Roger Chickering and Stig Foerster, eds., *Great War, Total War: Combat and Mobilization on the Western Front, 1914–1918* (New York: Cambridge, 2000)

65.  Eksteins, *Rites of Spring*, 144.

66.  Peter H. Smith, *Talons of the Eagle: Dynamics of U.S.-Latin American Relations* (New York: Oxford, 1996), 55.

67.  Max Boot, *The Savage Wars of Peace: Small Wars and the Rise of American Power* (New York: Basic Books, 2002), 201–2.

68.  Ibid., 204.

69.  Richard O'Connor, *Ambrose Bierce: A Biography* (Boston: Little, Brown & Co., 1967), 299.

70.  Controversy persisted for years about whether the *Lusitania* was carrying explosives not considered small arms. The second explosion has been substantially confirmed by numerous studies as either coal dust or as the torpedo causing a boiler to blow up. Kent J. Layton, *Lusitania: An Illustrated Biography* (London: Amberley Books, 2010); Keith Allen, "*Lusitania* Controversy," http://www.gwpda.org/naval/lusika05.htm; and most recently, Robert Ballard and Spencer Dunmore, "Exploring the LUSITANIA," whose underwater investigations showed that the magazine spaces were undamaged, leading to the conclusion that coal dust or a nonweapons explosion caused the second gash in the vessel. See Robert D. Ballard and Spencer Dunmore, *Exploring the Lusitania* (New York: Warner Books, 1995).

71.  Eksteins, *Rites of Spring*, 144.

72.  Larry Schweikart and Michael Allen, *A Patriot's History of the United States from Columbus's Great Discovery to the War on Terror* (New York: Sentinel, 2006), 512.

73.  Foster Rhea Dulles, *The United States Since 1865* (Ann Arbor: University of Michigan Press), 263.

74.  Allan Nevins and Frank Ernest Hill, "Henry Ford and His Peace Ship," *American Heritage Magazine*, 9, February 1958, http://www.american heritage.com/articles/magazine/ah/1958/2/1958_2_65.shtml.

75. Barbara S. Kraft, *The Peace Ship: Henry Ford's Pacifist Adventure in the First World War* (New York: Macmillan, 1978), 75.

76. Dr. Moses Stearns of Philadelphia was invited, then uninvited, as he was a mayoral candidate and Ford didn't want any politicians on the voyage. Stearns threatened to sue for public embarrassment (Kraft, *Peace Ship*, 79).

77. Nevins and Hill, "Henry Ford and His Peace Ship."

78. Ferguson, *War of the World*, 109.

79. Robert K. Massie, *Castles of Steel: Britain, Germany and the Winning of the Great War at Sea* (New York: Random House, 2003), 530.

80. W. Elliot Brownlee, *Dynamics of Ascent: A History of the American Economy*, 2nd ed. (New York: Alfred A. Knopf, 1979), 369.

81. Larry Schweikart, *The Entrepreneurial Adventure: A History of Business in the United States* (Fort Worth, TX: Harcourt, 2000), 286.

82. Anne Trotter, "Development of the Merchants-of-Death Theory, in Benjamin Franklin Cooling, ed., *War, Business, and American Society: Historical Perspectives on the Military-Industrial Complex* (Port Washington, NY: Kennikat Press, 1977), 93–104.

83. Barbara W. Tuchman, *The Zimmermann Telegram*, new ed. (New York: The Macmillan Company, 1966), 199.

84. Ronald J. Pestritto, *Woodrow Wilson and the Roots of Modern Liberalism* (Lanham, MD: Rowman and Littlefield, 2005), 255.

85. Woodrow Wilson, *Constitutional Government in the United States* (New York: Columbia, 1908), 56.

86. Wilson quoted in Jonah Goldberg, *Liberal Fascism: The Secret History of the American Left from Mussolini to the Politics of Meaning* (New York: Doubleday, 2007), 86; Wilson, *Constitutional Government in the United States*.

87. Goldberg, *Liberal Fascism*, 88.

88. Ibid., 86, 88.

89. Pestritto, *Woodrow Wilson and the Roots of Modern Liberalism*, 255.

90. Goldberg, *Liberal Fascism*, 87.

91. Ibid., 87.

92. Woodrow Wilson, *Leaders of Men*, T. H. Vail Motter, ed. (Princeton, NJ: Princeton University Press, 1952), 20–26.

93. Ibid., 25.

94. Woodrow Wilson, *The Papers of Woodrow Wilson* (New York: Harper, 1927), 1:6–10.

95. Murray N. Rothbard, "World War I as Fulfillment: Power and the Intellectuals," *Journal of Libertarian Studies*, 9, Spring 1989, 81–125 (quotation on 103), and his "Richard T. Ely: Paladin of the Welfare-Warfare State," *Independent Review*, 6, Spring 2002, 585–89.

96. Goldberg, *Liberal Fascism*, 107.

97.   David M. Kennedy, *Over Here: The First World War and American Society* (Oxford: Oxford University Press, 1980), 50.

98.   Michael McGerr, *A Fierce Discontent: The Rise and Fall of the Progressive Movement in America, 1870–1920* (New York: Free Press, 2003), 282.

99.   Ibid., 282–83.

100.  Kennedy, *Over Here*, 11.

101.  Goldberg, *Liberal Fascism*, 107.

102.  "Gov. Wilson Stirs Spanish Veterans," *New York Times*, September 11, 1912.

103.  Kennedy, *Over Here*, 17.

104.  www.policyalmanac.org/economic/archive/tax_history.shtml.

105.  W. Elliot Brownlee, *Federal Taxation in America: A Short History*, new ed. (Cambridge: Woodrow Wilson Center Press, 1996), 44.

106.  Richard H. Bensel, *Yankee Leviathan: Origins of Central State Authority in America, 1859–1877* (Cambridge, UK: Cambridge University Press, 1990).

107.  Harold Evans with Gail Buckland and David Lefer, *They Made America: From the Steam Engine to the Search Engine: Two Centuries of Innovators* (New York: Little, Brown and Company, 2004), 58–69.

108.  Keith L. Bryant, Jr., and Henry C. Dethloff, *A History of American Business*, 2nd ed. (Englewood Cliffs, NJ: Prentice-Hall, 1990), 143.

109.  William Gibbs McAdoo, *Crowded Years* (Boston: Houghton Mifflin, 1931), 296–97, 304–9.

110.  Robert Hessen, *Steel Titan: The Life of Charles M. Schwab* (New York: Oxford University Press, 1975), 236–44.

111.  Stanley L. Gaskins, "Bernard Baruch, Exponent of Preparedness," master's thesis, University of Cincinnati, 1950, 28.

112.  Ibid., 31.

113.  Bernard Baruch, *Baruch: the Public Years*, quoted in Sidney Ratner, James H. Soltow, and Richard Sylla, *The Evolution of the American Economy: Growth, Welfare, and Decision Making* (New York: MacMillan, 1993), 411.

114.  Edward G. Lengel, *To Conquer Hell: The Meuse-Argonne, 1918* (New York: Henry Holt, 2008), 34.

115.  Kennedy, *Over Here*, 253.

116.  Goldberg, *Liberal Fascism*, 111.

117.  *Schenck v. United States*, 249 U.S. 47 (1919).

118.  Goldberg, *Liberal Fascism*, 114.

119.  Arthur H. Joel, *Under the Lorraine Cross: An Account of the Experiences of Infantrymen Who Fought with the Lorraine Cross Division in France during the World War* (privately printed, 1921), 8.

120. Lengel, *To Conquer Hell*, 33–35.

121. Larry Schweikart and Michael Allen, *A Patriot's History of the United States* (New York: Sentinel, 2007), 517.

122. Lengel, *To Conquer Hell*, 25.

123. Ibid., 25.

124. Donald Smythe, *Pershing: General of the Armies* (Bloomington: Indiana University Press, 1986), 170.

125. Ibid., 12–13.

126. Schweikart, *America's Victories*, 112.

127. John J. Pershing, *My Experiences in the World War*, 2 vols. (New York: Frederick A. Stokes, 1931), 1:37.

128. Smythe, *Pershing*, 10.

129. Lengel, *To Conquer Hell*, 43.

130. James H. Hallas, *Doughboy War: The American Expeditionary Force in World War I* (Boulder, CO: Lynne Rienner, 2000), 195.

131. Lengel, *To Conquer Hell*, 45.

132. Smythe, *Pershing*, 186–87.

133. Ibid., 175–76; Frank E. Vandiver, *The Life and Times of John J. Pershing*, 2 vols. (College Station: Texas A & M University Press, 1977), 2:937–39.

134. Ray N. Johnson, *Heaven, Hell, or Hoboken* (Cleveland: O. S. Hubbell Printing, 1919), 94.

135. Lengel, *To Conquer Hell*, 68–69.

136. Christopher Capozzola, *Uncle Sam Wants You: World War I and the Making of the Modern American Citizen* (New York: Oxford University Press, 2008), 67–69.

137. Sergeant York Patriotic Foundation, "Sgt. Alvin C. York's Diary: October 8, 1918."

138. Ibid, 280–82.

139. There is much humbug about Edwards's life, due in part to the sensationalized biography cowritten by Lowell Thomas (*This Side of Hell: Dan Edwards, Adventurer* [New York: Tribune Books, 1932]) and to an imposter who toured the country giving talks as Edwards. Other sources include "Legionnaire Has 70 Decorations to Pay for Arm, Leg," *Dallas Morning News*, October 8, 1929, and "Fifteen War Heroes Get Medals Here," *New York Times*, April 6, 1923. For a review of some of the claims and counterclaims, see "Daniel Edwards," http://www.cemetery.state.tx.us/pub/user_form.asp?step=1&pers_id=1124.

140. Lengel, *To Conquer Hell*, 381.

141. Kennedy, *Over Here*, 200.

142. Lengel, *To Conquer Hell*, 385.

143. Evan Andrew Huelfer, *The "Casualty Issue" in American Military Practice: The Impact of World War I* (Westport, CT: Praeger, 2003), passim.

144. Lengel, *To Conquer Hell*, 419.

145. Paul F. Braim, *The Test of Battle: The American Expeditionary Forces in the Meuse-Argonne Campaign* (Newark, DE: University of Delaware Press, 1987), 145.

146. Smythe, *Pershing*, 220.

147. *United States Army in the World War, 1917–1919*, 17 vols. (Washington, DC: Center for Military History, 1988–92), 10:19–30.

148. Lengel, *To Conquer Hell*, 434.

149. Sheffield, "Shadow of the Somme," 30.

150. G. D. Sheffield, "Oh! What a Futile War: Representations on the Western Front in Modern British Media and Popular Culture," in Ian Stewart and Susan L. Carruthers, eds., *War, Culture and the Media* (Trowbridge, Wilts, 1996), 54–74 (quotation on 63). The most famous war poem, "In Flanders Field," was written by Canadian John McCrae.

151. Sheffield, "Influence of the First World War," 30; Sheffield, "Oh! What a Futile War," 54.

152. Robert Service, *Lenin: A Biography* (London: Pan Books, 2002), 2.

153. Ibid., 8.

154. Ibid., 8–10.

155. Tuchman, *Proud Tower*, 413.

156. Paul Johnson, *Modern Times: A History of the World from the Twenties to the Nineties* (New York: HarperCollins, 1991), 53; Service, *Lenin*, 243.

157. Service, *Lenin*, 273.

158. Ferguson, *War of the World*, 150.

159. Ibid., 151.

160. Johnson, *Modern Times*, 55.

161. Ferguson, *War of the World*, 150.

162. Service, *Lenin*, 273; Ferguson, *War of the World*, 151.

163. Service, *Lenin*, 322.

164. Ibid.

165. Johnson, *Modern Times*, 62.

166. Ferguson, *War of the World*, 151.

167. H. Montgomery Hyde, *Stalin: the History of a Dictator* (New York: Popular Library, 1971), 105.

168. Allan Bullock, *Hitler and Stalin: Parallel Lives* (London: HarperCollins, 1991), 269; Robert Service, *Stalin: A Biography* (Cambridge, MA: Belknap Press, 2005), passim.

169. Lynne Viola, V. P. Danilov, N. A. Ivnitskii, and Denis Kozlov, *The War*

*Against the Peasantry, 1927–1930* (New Haven, CT: Yale University Press, 2005); "Kyiv Court Accuses Stalin Leadership of Organizing Famine," http://www.kyivpost.com/news/city/detail/56954/; "Findings of the Commission on the Ukraine Famine," http://www.faminegenocide.com/resources/findings.html.

170. Quigley, *Tragedy & Hope*, 401.

171. Robert Conquest, *The Harvest of Sorrow: Soviet Collectivization and the Terror-Famine* (New York: Oxford University Press, 1986).

172. Ibid., 54, 127.

## Chapter 3: Seeking Perfection in the Postwar World

1. Niall Ferguson, *The War of the World: Twentieth-Century Conflict and the Descent of the West* (New York: Penguin, 2006), 160.

2. Alexander L. George and Juliette L. George, *Woodrow Wilson and Colonel House: A Personality Study* (New York: Courier Dover Publications, 1964), 202.

3. David A. Andelman, *A Shattered Peace: Versailles 1919 and the Price We Pay Today* (New York: John Wiley, 2008), 1–2.

4. George and George, *Woodrow Wilson and Colonel House*, 202.

5. George Scott, *The Rise and Fall of the League of Nations* (New York: Macmillan Publishing Co., 1973), 39.

6. *New York Times*, February 28, 1919.

7. Scott, *Rise and Fall of the League of Nations*, 148.

8. "Wilson in Italy: A Photographic Journey," http://woodrowwilsonhouse.org/index.asp?section=news&file=news&ID=113.

9. Andelman, *A Shattered Peace*, 29.

10. George and George, *Woodrow Wilson and Colonel House*, 213.

11. John David Lewis, *Nothing Less Than Victory: Decisive Wars and the Lessons of History* (Princeton, NJ: Princeton University Press, 2010), 191.

12. Ibid., 192.

13. Walter Russell Mead, *God and Gold: Britain, America, and the Making of the Modern World* (New York: Alfred A. Knopf, 2007), 66.

14. Paul Johnson, *Modern Times: A History of the World from the Twenties to the Nineties*, rev. ed. (New York: HarperCollins, 1991), 27.

15. Andelman, *Shattered Peace*, 7.

16. Ibid., 33–41.

17. Ibid., 17.

18. Mark Mazower, *Dark Continent: Europe's Twentieth Century* (New York: Vintage, 1998), 27.

19. Ibid., 28.

20.  Johnson, *Modern Times*, 146.

21.  Mazower, *Dark Continent*, 19.

22.  Emily O. Goldman, *Sunken Treaties: Naval Arms Control Between the Wars* (College Park: Pennsylvania State University Press, 1994), 165.

23.  Erik Goldstein and John Maurer, eds., *The Washington Conference, 1921–22: Naval Rivalry, East Asian Stability and the Road to Pearl Harbor* (London: Routledge, 1994).

24.  Hector Bywater, *Navies and Nations: A Review of Naval Developments Since the Great War* (London: Constable, 1927), 139.

25.  James B. Crowley, *Japan's Quest for Autonomy: National Security and Foreign Policy, 1930–1938* (Princeton, NJ: Princeton University Press, 1966), 25.

26.  Goldman, *Sunken Treasures*, 101.

27.  Bywater, *Navies and Nations*, 220.

28.  Goldstein and Maurer, *The Washington Conference*, 19.

29.  Sadao Asada, "Japan's Special Interests and the Washington Conference, 1921–1922," *American Historical Review*, 67, October 1961, 62–70.

30.  Goldman, *Sunken Treaties*, 44–45.

31.  Larry Schweikart and Lynne Pierson Doti, *Banking in the American West from the Gold Rush to Deregulation* (Norman: University of Oklahoma Press, 1991).

32.  Burke Davis, *The Billy Mitchell Affair* (New York: Random House, 1987); John T. Correll, "Billy Mitchell and the Battleships," *Air Force Magazine*, June 2008, 64–65; U.S. Centennial of Flight Commission, "Billy Mitchell Sinks the Ships," http://www.centennialofflight.gov/essay/Air_Power/mitchell_tests/AP14.htm.

33.  William Mitchell, *Winged Defense: The Development and Possibilities of Modern Air Power—Economic and Military* (Mineola, NY: Dover Publications, 2006).

34.  James P. Tate, *The Army and Its Air Corps: Army Policy Toward Aviation, 1919–1941* (Huntsville, AL: Air University Press, 1968), 39.

35.  "Charles Lindbergh, An American Aviator," http://www.charleslindbergh.com/history/paris.asp.

36.  Modris Eksteins, *Rites of Spring: The Great War and the Birth of the Modern Age* (Boston: Houghton Mifflin, 1989), 243–44.

37.  Quoted in Adam Tooze, *The Wages of Destruction: The Making and Breaking of the Nazi Economy* (New York: Penguin, 2006), 10.

38.  Victoria de Grazia, *Irresistible Empire: America's Advance Through 20th-Century Europe* (Cambridge, MA: Belknap, 2005), 19.

39.  Richard P. Hallion, *Taking Flight: Inventing the Aerial Age from Antiquity Through the First World War* (New York: Oxford University Press, 2003), 233.

40. F. Robert van der Linden, *Airlines and Air Mail: The Post Office and the Birth of the Commercial Aviation Industry* (Lexington: University Press of Kentucky, 2002), 243–70.

41. Ferguson, *War of the World*, 242.

42. Michael Burleigh, *Death and Deliverance: "Euthanasia" in Germany, 1900–1945* (Cambridge, UK: Cambridge University Press, 1994), ix; Robert Jay Lifton, *The Nazi Doctors: Medical Killing and the Psychology of Genocide* (New York: Basic Books, 2000); Steven D. Devitt and Stephen J. Dubner, *Freakonomics: A Rogue Economist Explores the Hidden Side of Everything* (New York: HarperCollins, 2005).

43. Jonah Goldberg, *Liberal Fascism: The Secret History of the American Left from Mussolini to the Politics of Meaning* (New York: Doubleday, 2007), 248–49; Thomas C. Leonard, " 'More Merciful and Not Less Effective': Eugenics and American Economics in the Progressive Era," *History of Political Economy*, 35, Winter 2003, 709–34 (quotation on 707); Diane Paul, "Eugenics and the Left," *Journal of the History of Ideas*, 45, October–December 1984, 567–90 (quotation on 586).

44. H. G. Wells quoted in Michael Freeden, "Eugenics and Progressive Thought: A Study in Ideological Affinity," *Historical Journal*, 22, September 1979, 645–71 (quotation on 656).

45. H. G. Wells, *The New Machiavelli* (New York: Duffield, 1910), 379, and his *Modern Utopia* (London: T. F. Unwin, 1905), 183–84, cited in Goldberg, *Liberal Fascism*, 249.

46. Charles Richard Van Hise, *The Conservation of Natural Resources in the United States* (New York: Macmillan, 1910), 378.

47. Goldberg, *Liberal Fascism*, 260. Through governments by elites, Van Hise contended, diseases and food shortages could be wiped out in a decade, and the defective classes expeditiously eliminated. Daniel Kevles, *In the Name of Eugenics: Genetics and the Uses of Human Heredity* (Cambridge, MA: Harvard University Press, 1986), 68.

48. Paul Weindling, *Health, Race and German Politics Between National Unification and Nazism, 1870–1945* (New York: Cambridge University Press, 1989), 344.

49. Edward Alsworth Ross, *Social Control: A Survey of the Foundations of Order* (New York: Macmillan, 1901), and *Seventy Years of It* (New York: Appleton-Century, 1936), 70; Leonard, "More Merciful and Not Less Effective," 699, 703.

50. Sidney Webb, "The Economic Theory of a Legal Minimum Wage," *Journal of Political Economy*, 20, December 1912, 973–98 (quotation on 992).

51. Royal Meeker, "Review of Cours d'economie politique," *Political Science Quarterly*, 25, 1910, 544.

52. John R. Commons, *Races and Immigrants in America* (New York: Macmillan, 1907), 148–51.

53.  Edward J. Larson, *Sex, Race, and Science: Eugenics in the Deep South* (Baltimore: Johns Hopkins University Press, 1995), 1.

54.  Ibid.

55.  Ibid., 27.

56.  Julius Paul, "Three Generations of Imbeciles Are Enough: State Eugenic Sterilization Laws in American Thought and Practice," unpublished manuscript, Washington, DC: Walter Reed Army Institute of Research, 1965, 256–57; Alexandra Stern, *Eugenic Nation: Faults and Frontiers of Better Breeding in Modern America* (Berkeley: University of California Press, 2005).

57.  Larson, *Sex, Race and Science*, 38.

58.  David A. Valone, "Eugenic Science in California: The Papers of E. S. Gosney and the Human Betterment Foundation," 1996, http://www.amphilsoc.org/mendel/1996.htm#Valone.

59.  Larson, *Sex, Race and Science*, 38.

60.  Ibid., 38, 62.

61.  Weindling, *Health, Race and German Politics*, 342–43.

62.  Ibid., 343.

63.  Ibid.

64.  E. S. Gosney and Paul Popenoe, *Sterilization for Human Betterment: A Summary of Results of 6,000 Operations in California, 1909–1929* (New York: The Macmillan Company, 1929).

65.  Tony Platt, "The Frightening Agenda of the American Eugenics Movement," HistoryNewsNetwork, July 7, 2003, http://hnn.us/articles/1551.html.

66.  Larson, *Sex, Race, and Science*, 25 and passim.

67.  Daniel J. Kevles, *In the Name of Eugenics: Genetics and the Uses of Human Heredity* (Cambridge, MA: Harvard University Press, 1997), 62. American eugenicists mused that American eugenics would produce a population with "a maximum number of Billy Sundays, Valentinos, Jack Dempseys, Babe Ruths, even Al Capones" (ibid., 188).

68.  Albert Gringer, *The Sanger Corpus: A Study in Militancy* (Lakeland, AL: Lakeland Christian College, 1974), 473–88; Kate O'Beirne, *Women Who Make the World Worse* (New York: Sentinel, 2006), 163–64; Grant, *Killer Angel*, 63. Sanger was also intolerant of her fellow radicals. She once labeled Socialist presidential candidate Eugene V. Debs a "silk hat radical" and termed anarchist Alexander Beckman "a hack, armchair socialist." See Larry Schweikart and Michael Allen, *A Patriot's History of the United States from Columbus's Great Discovery to the War on Terror* (New York: Sentinel, 2006), 531.

69.  Lothrop Stoddard, *The Rising Tide of Color Against White World Supremacy*, quoted in Christine Rosen, *Preaching Eugenics: Religious Leaders and the American Eugenics Movement* (New York: Oxford, 2004), 216.

70. Margaret Sanger, *The Pivot of Civilization* (New York: Brentanos, 1922), 108.

71. Stephen Mosher, "The Repackaging of Margaret Sanger," *Wall Street Journal*, May 5, 1997

72. Ibid.

73. Linda Gordon, *Woman's Body, Woman's Right* (New York: Grossman, 1976), 332; Margaret Sanger to Dr. Clarence Gamble, December 19, 1939, quoted in Charles Valenza, "Was Margaret Sanger a Racist?" *Family Planning Perspectives*, 17, January–February 1985, 44–46.

74. Adolf Hitler, *Hitler's Second Book: The Unpublished Sequel to* Mein Kampf, Gerhard L. Weinberg, ed. (New York: Enigma Books, 2006), 20.

75. Burton W. Folsom, Jr., *The Myth of the Robber Barons* (Herndon, VA: Young America's Foundation, 1991), 83–100 (quotation on 83); Harold Evans with Gail Buckland and David Lefer, *They Made America: From the Steam Engine to the Search Engine: Two Centuries of Innovators* (New York: Little, Brown & Company, 2004), 318–33.

76. Evans, *They Made America*, 319.

77. Kevles, *In the Name of Eugenics*, 54.

78. Ibid., 56.

79. Johnson, *Modern Times*, 146.

80. Weindling, *Health, Race and German Politics*, 482.

81. Ferguson, *War of the World*, 1.

82. Ibid., 26–27 (quotation on 27).

83. Ibid., 566.

84. Ibid., 62–63.

85. Mazower, *Dark Continent*, 82–83.

86. Ibid., 79.

87. Ibid., 82.

88. Quoted in Paul N. Hehn, *A Low Dishonest Decade: The Great Powers, Eastern Europe, and the Economic Origins of World War II, 1930–1941* (New York: Continuum, 2002), 47, from Macgregor Knox, "Conquest, Foreign and Domestic, in Fascist Italy and Nazi Germany," *Journal of Modern History*, 56, 1984, 1–57, and Herbert I. Matthews, *The Fruits of Fascism* (New York: Harcourt, Brace, 1943).

89. Mazower, *Dark Continent*, 77.

90. Ibid.

91. "Announcement of Prizes," *Eugenical News*, 13, June 1928, 78-79.

92. Mazower, *Dark Continent*, 82.

93. Ibid., 81.

94. Ibid., 82.

95. Weindling, *Health, Race and German Politics*, 372.

96. Mazower, *Dark Continent*, 88.

97. Ibid., 90.

98. Ibid., 97. Most eugenicists were socialists and radicals, and as such, they opposed war, yet ironically on different grounds from traditional Marxists, who asserted that war caused a higher population of the working classes to be killed. Eugenicists tended to claim that war culled the bravest and the best, sparing the dregs of society, who remained home to father new generations of the indigent.

99. Ibid., 84; Weindling, *Health, Race and German Politics*, 421.

100. Weindling, *Health, Race and German Politics*, 429.

101. Paul Lombardo, " 'The American Breed': Nazi Eugenics and the Origins of the Pioneer Fund," *Albany Law Review*, 2002, 745–824.

102. Weindling, *Health, Race and German Politics*, 515–17.

103. Ibid., 497.

104. Kevles, *In the Name of Eugenics*, 118.

105. "The Frightening Agenda of the American Eugenics Movement," History News Network, http://hnn.us/articles/1551.html.

106. Ibid.

107. Christopher Andrew and A. S. Kanya-Forstner, *France Overseas: The Great War and the Climax of French Imperial Expansion* (London: Thames and Hudson, 1981), 238, 248.

108. Carroll Quigley, *Tragedy & Hope: A History of the World in Our Time* (New York: Macmillan, 1966), 128.

109. Ibid., 147.

110. Ibid., 165.

111. Ibid., 111.

112. Andelman, *Shattered Peace*, 51.

113. Ibid., 104.

114. Ibid., 109.

115. Ibid., 75.

116. Jonathan Derrick, *Africa's Agitators: Militant Anti-Colonialism in Africa and the West, 1918–1939* (New York: Columbia University Press, 2008), 269.

117. Ibid., 279–80.

118. Ibid., 294.

119. Ibid., 60.

120. Johnson, *Modern Times*, 151.

121. Ibid., 15; Robin Bidwell, *Morocco Under Colonial Rule: French Administration of Tribal Areas, 1912–1956* (London: Cass, 1973); Alan Scham, *Ly-*

*autey in Morocco: Protectorate Administration, 1912–1925* (Berkeley: University of California Press, 1970).

122. Lance Edwin Davis and Robert A. Huttenback, *Mammon and the Pursuit of Empire Abridged Edition: The Economics of British Imperialism* (Cambridge, UK: Cambridge University Press, 1988).

123. Hehn, *A Low Dishonest Decade*, 10.

124. Angus Maddison, *The World Economy: Historical Statistics* (Paris: Development Center of the Organization for Economic Cooperation and Development, 2003).

125. E. J. Berg, "Backward Sloping Labour Supply Functions in Dual Economies—the Africa Case," *Quarterly Journal of Economics*, 75, August 1961, 468–92.

126. William G. Beasley, *The Rise of Modern Japan: Political, Economic, and Social Change Since 1850* (New York: St. Martin's Press, 1995); Rachel F. Wall, *Japan's Century: An Interpretation of Japanese History Since the Eighteen-fifties* (London: The Historical Association, 1971); and Rhoads Murphey, *East Asia: A New History* (New York: Addison Wesley Longman, 1997).

127. Johnson, *Modern Times*, 151, 178–79; Quigley, *Tragedy & Hope*, 175, 196–205.

128. Jonathan D. Spence, *The Search for Modern China* (New York: W. W. Norton, 1990).

129. Ibid., 267.

130. Ibid., 271.

131. Quigley, *Tragedy & Hope*, 175–95, passim.

132. Larry Schweikart, *The Entrepreneurial Adventure: A History of Business in the United States* (Fort Worth, TX: Harcourt, 2000), 43.

133. Robert P. Thomas, "A Quantitative Approach to the Study of the Effects of British Imperial Policy on Colonial Welfare," *Journal of Economic History*, 25, 965, 65–68; Peter McClelland, "The Cost to America of British Imperial Policy," *American Economic Review*, 59, 969, 370–78; Lawrence Harper, "Mercantilism and the American Revolution," *Canadian Historical Review*, 23, 1942, 1–15.

134. Hernando de Soto, *The Mystery of Capital: Why Capitalism Triumphs in the West and Fails Everywhere Else* (New York: Basic Books, 2003).

135. Daniel Yergin and Joseph Stanislaw, *The Commanding Heights: The Battle for the World Economy* (New York: Touchstone, 2002), 409–10.

136. William Easterly, *The White Man's Burden: Why the West's Efforts to Aid the Rest Have Done So Much Ill and So Little Good* (New York: Penguin, 2006).

137. Ibid., 273.

138. Ferguson, *War of the World*, 320.

139. E. L. Woodward and Rohan Butler, eds., *Documents on British Foreign*

*Policy, 1919–1939*, 3rd series, vol. 1 (London: H. M. Stationery Office, 1949), 846ff.

140. R. A. C. Parker, *Chamberlain and Appeasement: British Policy and the Coming of the Second World War* (London: Palgrave, 1993), 37.

141. Sally Marks, "The Myths of Reparations," *Central European History*, 11, 1978, 231–55; and her "1918 and After: The Postwar Era," in G. Martel, ed., *The Origins of the Second World War Reconsidered: A. J. P. Taylor and the Historians*, 2nd ed. (New York: Routledge, 1999), 13–37.

142. Marks, "Myths," 254.

143. "The German Hyperinflation," http://www.pbs.org/wgbh/commanding heights/shared/minitext/ess_germanhyperinflation.html.

144. Adam Tooze, *The Wages of Destruction: The Making and Breaking of the Nazi Economy* (New York: Penguin, 2006), 4–6.

145. Undated comments from Hitler's "Second Book," circa 1927, cited in Tooze, *Wages of Destruction*, 11.

146. Ibid., 10.

147. Ibid., 658.

148. Douglas Irwin, *Against the Tide: An Intellectual History of Free Trade* (Princeton, NJ: Princeton University Press, 1997).

149. Mazower, *Dark Continent*, 54.

150. Lansing quoted in Thomas Sowell, *Intellectuals and Society* (New York: Basic Books, 2009), 210.

151. Lansing quoted in Daniel Patrick Moynihan, *Pandemonium: Ethnicity in International Politics* (Oxford, UK: Oxford University Press, 1993), 81–83.

152. Sowell, *Intellectuals and Society*, 211.

153. Eric D. Weitz, "From Vienna to the Paris System: International Politics and the Entangled Histories of Human Rights, Forced Deportations, and Civilizing Missions," *American Historical Review*, 113, December 2008, 1313–43 (quotation on 1315).

154. Mazower, *Dark Continent*, 57.

155. Weitz, "From Vienna to the Paris System," 1319.

156. Ibid., 1329.

157. Ibid., 1331.

158. Ibid., 1334.

159. Peter Balakian, *The Burning Tigris: The Armenian Genocide and America's Response* (New York: HarperCollins, 2003), 43.

160. Bernard Lewis, *The Emergence of Modern Turkey*, 3rd rev. ed. (New York: Oxford University Press, 2002); Vahakn N. Dadrian, "The Documentation of the World War I Armenian Massacres in the Proceedings of the

Turkish Military Tribunal," *International Journal of Middle East Studies*, 23, 1991, 549–76; Guenter Lewy, *The Armenian Massacres in Ottoman Turkey: A Disputed Genocide* (Salt Lake City: University of Utah Press, 2005).

161. See Guenter Lewy, "Revisiting the Armenian Genocide," *Middle East Quarterly*, 12, Fall 2005, 3–12.

162. Mazower, *Dark Continent*, 59.

163. Ibid., 64.

164. Max Boot, *The Savage Wars of Peace: Small Wars and the Rise of American Power* (New York: Basic Books, 2003), 176.

165. Ibid., 177.

166. Ibid., 234.

167. Peter H. Smith, *Talons of the Eagle: Dynamics of U.S.-Latin American Relations* (New York: Oxford, 1996), 63.

168. Victor Bulmer-Thomas, *The Economic History of Latin America Since Independence*, 2nd ed. (Cambridge, UK: Cambridge University Press, 2003), 153, 163–74.

169. Ibid., 53.

170. Ibid., 126.

171. Ibid., 104–6.

172. Ibid., 212.

173. Thomas F. O'Brien, *Making the Americas: The United States and Latin America in the Age of Revolutions to the Era of Globalization* (Albuquerque: University of New Mexico Press, 2007), 114.

174. Ibid., 104.

175. Ibid., 93.

176. Ibid., 113.

177. Victoria de Grazia, *Irresistible Empire: America's Advance Through 20th-Century Europe* (Cambridge, MA: Belknap, 2005), 31.

178. Ibid., 29.

179. Ibid., 161.

180. Ibid., 109.

181. Larry Schweikart and Lynne Pierson Doti, *The American Entrepreneur* (New York: Amacom Press, 2009), 258–64; Roland Marchand, *Advertising the American Dream: Making Way for Modernity, 1920–1940* (Berkeley: University of California Press, 1965); Stephen Fox, *The Mirror Makers: A History of American Advertising and Its Creators* (New York: Vintage, 1985).

182. Schweikart and Pierson, *The American Entrepreneur*, 262.

183. Bruce Barton, *The Man Nobody Knows* (New York: Bobbs-Merrill, 1925).

Laurie Beth Jones wrote a modern version of the book, using terminology tailored to the 1990s, *Jesus, CEO: Using Ancient Wisdom for Visionary Leadership* (New York: Hyperion, 1992).

184. J. Murray Allison, "Continental Advertising," *Advertising World*, May 1927, 17–18 (quotation on 18).

185. De Grazia, *Irresistible Empire*, 262.

186. Ibid., 265.

187. Ibid.

188. Ibid., 267.

189. Ibid., 288.

190. Ruth Vasey, "Beyond Sex and Violence: 'Industry Policy' and the Regulation of Hollywood Movies, 1922–39," in Matthew Bernstein, ed., *Controlling Hollywood: Censorship and the Regulation of the Studio Era* (New Brunswick, NJ: Rutgers University Press, 1999). See also Ruth Vasey's *The World According to Hollywood, 1918–1939* (Madison: University of Wisconsin Press, 1997).

191. Siegfried Kracauer, "Artistisches und Amerikanisches," *Frankfurter Zeitung*, January 1926; Miriam Bratu Hansen, "The Mass Production of the Senses," in Linda Williams and Christine Gledhill, eds., *Reinventing Film Studies* (London: Edward Arnold, 2000), 342–43.

192. De Grazia, *Irresistible Empire*, 284.

193. Paul Mazur, *American Prosperity: Its Causes and Consequences* (New York: Viking, 1928), 7.

194. De Grazia, *Irresistible Empire*, 284.

195. Smith, *Talons of the Eagle*, 83–84.

196. Ibid., 85.

197. Ibid., 109–10.

198. Alan Reynolds, "What Do We Know About the Great Crash Fifty Years Later?" *National Review*, November 9, 1979, 1416–21.

199. Paul Johnson, *Modern Times: A History of the World from the Twenties to the Eighties* (New York: HarperCollins, 1983), 216.

200. James Gwartney and Richard Stroup, "Tax Cuts: Who Shoulders the Burden," *Economic Review*, March 1982, 19–27; and Warren Brookes, *The Economy in Mind* (New York: Universe Publishers, 1982).

201. Paul Johnson, *Modern Times: A History of the World from the Twenties to the Nineties*, rev. ed. (New York: HarperCollins, 1991), 225–27.

202. Thomas B. Silver, *Coolidge and the Historians* (Durham, NC: Carolina Academic Press, 1982).

203. Johnson, *Modern Times*, 329.

204. Calvin Coolidge, "State of the Union Address to Congress," December 4, 1928.

## Chapter 4: The Totalitarian Moment

1. Douglas A. Irwin, *Against the Tide: An Intellectual History of Free Trade* (Princeton, NJ: Princeton University Press, 1997).

2. Lee E. Ohanian, "What—or Who—Started the Great Depression?" NBER Working Paper No. 15258, August 2009.

3. "Hoover's Pro-Labor Stance Spurred Great Depression," University of California newsroom, August 28, 2009.

4. The classic study of this remains Milton Friedman and Anna Jacobsen Schwartz, *A Monetary History of the United States, 1867–1960* (Princeton, NJ: Princeton University Press, 1971).

5. Niall Ferguson, *The War of the World: Twentieth-Century Conflict and the Descent of the West* (New York: Penguin, 2006), 203.

6. Michael Ellman, "Stalin and the Soviet Famine of 1932–33 Revisited," *Europe-Asia Studies*, 59, June 2007, 663–93; Dana G. Dalrymple, *Soviet Studies*, 15, January 1964, 250–84; Joseph Stalin, speech in *Pravda*, January 17, 1933.

7. Tom Standage, *An Edible History of Humanity* (New York: Walker & Company, 2009), 177.

8. Ibid., 179; Dana Dalrymple, "The Soviet Famine of 1932–1934," *Soviet Studies*, 15, January 1964, 250–84; Michael Ellman, "Stalin and the Soviet Famine of 1932–33 Revisited," *Europe-Asia Studies*, 59, June 2007, 663–93.

9. Standage, *An Edible History of Humanity*, 180.

10. Dalrymple, "Soviet Famine of 1932–34," 261.

11. Ibid., 282.

12. Walter Duranty, "Russians Hungry, But Not Starving," *New York Times*, March 31, 1933.

13. Standage, *An Edible History of Humanity*, 171.

14. Ibid., 181.

15. Ibid. Malcolm Muggeridge was one of the few who saw the evidence of famine as incontrovertible. Writing for the *Manchester Guardian*, he observed: "The struggle for bread in Russia has now reached an acute stage. All other questions are superfluous . . . the population is in the most literal sense, starving . . . ." (Malcolm Muggeridge, "The Soviet's [sic] War on the Peasants," *Fortnightly Review* [London], May 1933). See also "The Soviet and the Peasantry, An Observer's Notes," *Manchester Guardian*, 1933; I, "Famine in North Caucasus," March 25, 13–14; II, "Hunger in the Ukraine," March 27, 9–10; III, "Poor Harvest in Prospect," March 29, 9–10.

16. Standage, *An Edible History of Humanity*, 171.

17. Carroll Quigley, *Tragedy & Hope: A History of the World in Our Time* (New York: Macmillan, 1966), 258.

18.  Larry Schweikart and Lynne Pierson Doti, *Banking in the American West from the Gold Rush to Deregulation* (Norman: University of Oklahoma Press, 1991).

19.  Ibid., 105.

20.  Peter Huntoon, "The National Bank Failures in Wyoming, 1924," *Annals of Wyoming*, Fall 1982, 34–44.

21.  Schweikart and Doti, *Banking in the American West*, 105.

22.  Larry Schweikart, *A History of Banking in Arizona* (Tucson: University of Arizona Press, 1982), 203–6.

23.  Tom Messelt, Sr., "Montana's Bank Failures of the Twenties," n.d., pamphlet in the Montana Historical Society; Clarence W. Groth, "Savings and Reaping: Montana Banking, 1910–1925," *Montana: The Magazine of Western History*, 20, Autumn 1970, 28–35.

24.  John G. Sproat and Larry Schweikart, *Making Change: South Carolina Banking in the Twentieth Century* (Columbia, SC: South Carolina Bankers Association, 1990), 68–69.

25.  Olin S. Pugh, *Difficult Decades of Banking: A Comparative Study of Banking Developments in South Carolina and the United States, 1920–1940*, Essays in Economics No. 10, University of South Carolina, March 1964, 61.

26.  Charles Calomiris, "Deposit Insurance: Lessons from the Record," *Federal Reserve Bank of Chicago Economic Perspectives*, May–June 1989, 10–30; "Is Deposit Insurance Necessary? A Historical Perspective," *Journal of Economic History*, 50, June 1990, 283–95, and "Do Vulnerable Economies Need Deposit Insurance? Lessons from U.S. Agriculture in the 1920s," in Philip L. Brock, *If Texas Were Chile: A Primer on Bank Regulation* (San Francisco: The Sequoia Institute, 1992).

27.  Alan Reynolds, "What Do We Know About the Great Crash Fifty Years Later?" *National Review*, November 9, 1979, 1416–21.

28.  *New York Times*, January 23, 1920; William Wright, *Harvard's Secret Court: The Savage 1920 Purge of Campus Homosexuals* (New York: St. Martin's Press, 2005); Lawrence R. Murphy, *Perverts by Official Order: The Campaign Against Homosexuals by the United States Navy* (Abingdon, Oxford, England: Harrington Park Press, 1988).

29.  A number of biographies of Roosevelt exist, including Jean Edward Smith, *FDR* (New York: Random House, 2008); James MacGregor Burns, *Roosevelt: The Lion and the Fox, 1882–1940* (Boston: Mariner Books, 2002) and his *Roosevelt: Soldier of Freedom, 1940–1945* (New York: Mariner Books, 2002); Roy Jenkins and Arthur M. Schlesinger, *Franklin Delano Roosevelt: The American Presidents Series: the 32nd President, 1933–1945* (New York: Times Books, 2003).

30.  Larry Schweikart and Michael Allen, *A Patriot's History of the United States from Columbus's Great Discovery to the War on Terror* (New York: Sentinel, 2004); Burton W. Folsom, Jr., *New Deal or Raw Deal? How*

*FDR's Economic Legacy Has Damaged America* (New York: Threshold, 2009); Amity Shlaes, *The Forgotten Man: A New History of the Great Depression* (New York: Harper Perennial, 2008).

31.  *Schechter Poultry Corp. v. United States*, 295 U.S. 495, 528.

32.  H. W. Brands, *Traitor to His Class* (New York: Doubleday, 2008), 690.

33.  See the discussions in Schweikart and Allen, *Patriot's History of the United States*, (2004 ed.), chapter 16; Larry Schweikart and Lynne Pierson Doti, *American Entrepreneur: The Fascinating Stories of the People Who Defined Business in the United States* (New York: Amacom, 2009), chapter 9; and Stephen J. DeCanio, "Expectations and Business Confidence During the Great Depression," in Barry N. Siegel, ed., *Money in Crisis: The Federal Reserve, the Economy, and Monetary Reform* (San Francisco: Pacific Institute, 1984). Extensive research done on trust in societies has shown a critical relationship between prosperity and levels of trust. Any minimum wage, by arbitrarily affixing value to someone's work, promotes a tiny element of distrust, because it's entirely likely that the employer and government are "lying" to the employee about what that employee truly produces. The wage may be too low, arbitrarily undervaluing the employee, but more likely is usually too high, providing a false sense of value when a lesser value is the reality. In that sense, a minimum wage is akin to a teacher being forced to give all students a B even if the students are failing the course, rather than providing a measure that accurately and honestly reflects performance.

34.  Folsom, *New Deal or Raw Deal*, passim.

35.  Paul N. Hehn, *A Low Dishonest Decade* (New York: Contiuum, 2002), 48–49.

36.  Adam Tooze, *The Wages of Destruction: The Making and Breaking of the Nazi Economy* (New York: Penguin, 2006), 31.

37.  John Maynard Keynes, *The Economic Consequences of Peace* (New York: Old Chelsea Station, 2006).

38.  Sally Marks, "1918 and After: The Postwar Era," in Gordon Martel, *The Origins of the Second World War Reconsidered: A. J. P. Taylor and the Historians* (London: Routledge, 1999); and her "Smoke and Mirrors: In Smoke-Filled Rooms and the Galerie des Glaces Comment, From Armistice to *Dolchstosslegende*," in Manfred Boemeke et al., *The Treaty of Versailles: A Reassessment After 75 Years* (Cambridge, UK: Cambridge University Press, 1998); and her article "The Myths of Reparations," *Central European History*, September 1978, 231–55; Niall Ferguson, *The Pity of War: Explaining World War I* (New York: Basic Books, 2000); Stephen A. Schuker, *The End of French Predominance in Europe: The Financial Crisis of 1924 and the Adoption of the Dawes Plan* (Chapel Hill: University of North Carolina Press, 1976); and Gerhard Weinberg, *A World at Arms: A Global History of World War II* (New York: Cambridge University Press, 2005). See also Etienne Mantoux, *The Carthaginian Peace, or,*

*The Economic Consequences of Mr. Keynes* (New York: Scribners, 1952); and A. J. P. Taylor, *The Origins of the Second World War* (New York: Simon & Schuster, 1996).

39. Tooze, *Wages of Destruction*, 27.

40. A. J. Nicholls, *Weimar and the Rise of Hitler* (New York: St. Martin's, 2000), 160.

41. Walter Goerlitz, *History of the German General Staff* (New York: Praeger, 1953), 272.

42. Ibid., 255.

43. Ibid, 274, 291.

44. Tooze, *Wages of Destruction*, 260.

45. Ibid., 62.

46. Jorg Baten and Andrea Wagner, "Autarchy, Market Disintegration, and Health: The Mortality and Nutritional Crisis in Nazi Germany, 1933–1937," CESIFO Working Paper No. 800, October 2002, http://www.cesifo.de/portal/pls/portal/docs/1/1190050.pdf.

47. Ibid.

48. These and other analyses of Hitler's psyche and anti-Semitism appear in Ron Rosenbaum, *Explaining Hitler: The Search for the Origins of His Evil* (New York: Random House, 1998).

49. Among the more useful biographies of Hitler are Ian Kershaw, *Hitler: A Biography* (New York: W. W. Norton, 2010); Thomas Fuchs, *A Concise Biography of Adolf Hitler* (New York: Penguin, 2000); John Toland, *Adolf Hitler: The Definitive Biography* (New York: Anchor, 1991); and Alan Bullock, *Hitler: A Study in Tyranny* (New York: Harper, 1991).

50. Paul Johnson, *Modern Times from the Twenties to the Nineties*, rev. ed. (New York: HarperCollins, 1991), 135.

51. "Hitler's Cushy Prison Life in the 1920s Revealed," *The Independent*, June 24, 2010.

52. Adolf Hitler, *Mein Kampf*, trans. Ralph Manheim from the 1st edition (Boston: Houghton Mifflin, 1943), 643, 654.

53. Ibid., 606.

54. Adolf Hitler, *Hitler's Second Book: The Unpublished Sequel to* Mein Kampf, Gerhard L. Weinberg, ed. (New York: Enigma Books, 2006), 7.

55. Ibid., 46.

56. Ibid., 29.

57. Rosenbaum, *Explaining Hitler*, passim.

58. Adolf Hitler, *Mein Kampf*, trans. Ralph Manheim (New York: Houghton Mifflin/Sentry Edition, 1943), 300–29.

59. Robert J. Loewenberg, "The Trivialization of the Holocaust as an Aspect of Modern Idolatry," *St. John's Review*, Winter 1982, 33–43 (quota-

tion on 33). Indeed, as philosopher Emil Fackenheim contended, Hitler's proposed goal was not a Christian state devoid of Jews but a Nazi religion worshipping Volk, Reich, and Fuehrer. Emil Fackenheim, *Encounters Between Judaism and Modern Philosophy: A Preface to Future Jewish Thought* (New York: Basic Books, 1973), 217.

60.   Adolf Hitler, *Mein Kampf* (New York: Houghton Mifflin, 1939), 288–89; Loewenberg, "Trivialization of the Holocaust," 39.

61.   Loewenberg, "Trivialization of the Holocaust," 41.

62.   Office of Strategic Services: Research and Analysis Branch, R&A No. 3114.4, "The Nazi Master Plan: Annex 4: The Persecution of the Christian Churches," July 6, 1945, 1, in authors' possession.

63.   Hitler, *Mein Kampf*, 1943 ed., 3.

64.   Tooze, *Wages of Destruction*, 213.

65.   Hitler, *Hitler's Second Book*, 93.

66.   Hehn, *Low Dishonest Decade*, 72.

67.   Tooze, *Wages of Destruction*, 65.

68.   Hitler, *Hitler's Second Book*, 95.

69.   Hehn, *A Low Dishonest Decade*, 124.

70.   Ibid., 39.

71.   Tooze, *Wages of Destruction*, 251.

72.   Ibid., 156.

73.   Ibid., 328.

74.   Ibid., 337.

75.   Ibid., 409.

76.   Ibid.

77.   Ibid., 272.

78.   Frank McDonough, *Hitler, Chamberlain and Appeasement* (Cambridge, UK: Cambridge University Press, 2002), 22.

79.   Hehn, *Low Dishonest Decade*, 124.

80.   Nevile Henderson, *Failure of a Mission* (New York: G. P. Putnam's Sons, 1940), ix.

81.   John David Lewis, *Nothing Less Than Victory: Decisive Wars and the Lessons of History* (Princeton: Princeton University Press, 2010), 208.

82.   Hehn, *Low Dishonest Decade*, 126.

83.   Ibid., 59.

84.   McDonough, *Hitler, Chamberlain and Appeasement*, 24.

85.   Hehn, *Low Dishonest Decade*, 54.

86.   John Gooch, *Mussolini and His Generals* (Cambridge, UK: Cambridge University Press, 2007), 317–28.

87. Correlli Barnett, *The Collapse of British Power* (Greenwich, CT: Pan, 2002), 352–56.

88. James Gregor, *The Search for Neofascism* (New York: Cambridge University Press, 2006), 54.

89. Johnson, *Modern Times*, rev. ed., 321.

90. Hehn, *Low Dishonest Decade*, 174.

91. Hugh Thomas, *The Spanish Civil War* (New York: Harper & Brothers, 1961), 27.

92. Ibid., 40.

93. Alban Butler, Peter Doyle, and Paul Burns, *Lives of the Saints*, New Full Edition, vol. 7 (Collegeville, MN: Liturgical Press, 2000), 171–72.

94. Thomas, *Spanish Civil War*, 46.

95. Stanley Payne, *The Spanish Revolution* (New York: Littlehampton Book Services, 1970).

96. Peter Wyden, *The Passionate War* (New York: Simon and Schuster, 1983), 30.

97. Charles Foltz, Jr., *The Masquerade in Spain* (Cambridge, MA: Houghton Mifflin, 1948), 96–97.

98. Ibid., 96.

99. Thomas, *Spanish Civil War*, 631–32.

100. Raymond Carr, *The Spanish Tragedy* (London: Phoenix Press, 2001), 133–34.

101. Foltz, *Masquerade in Spain*, 347–48.

102. Ibid., 44.

103. Thomas, *The Spanish Civil War*, 621.

104. Lewis, *Nothing Less Than Victory*, 221.

105. Goerlitz, *History of the German General Staff*, 326–27.

106. Ibid., 329.

107. Carroll Quigley, *Tragedy & Hope: A History of the World in Our Time* (New York: Macmillan, 1966), 630–31.

108. Telford Taylor, *Munich, The Price of Peace* (Garden City, NY: Doubleday & Co., 1979), 806.

109. Hehn, *Low Dishonest Decade*, 24.

110. McDonough, *Hitler, Chamberlain and Appeasement*, 52.

111. Ibid., 62.

112. Ibid.

113. Hehn, *Low Dishonest Decade*, 175.

114. Ferguson, *War of the World*, 332–33.

115. Hehn, *Low Dishonest Decade*, 220.

116. Ferguson, *War of the World*, 368.

117. Quigley, *Tragedy & Hope*, 635.

118. Ferguson, *War of the World*, 347.

119. Albert Speer, *Inside the Third Reich* (New York: Macmillan, 1970), 118.

120. "Wallis Simpson, the Nazi Minister, the Telltale Monk and an FBI Plot," UK *Guardian*, June 29, 2002.

121. Charles Higham, *The Duchess of Windsor: The Secret Life* (New York: Mc-Graw-Hill, 1988), 362–63.

122. Jonah Goldberg, *Liberal Fascism: The Secret History of the American Left from Mussolini to the Politics of Meaning* (New York: Doubleday, 2007), 147.

123. Ibid., 147.

124. Ibid., 148.

125. Stanley L. Ganskins, "Bernard Baruch, Exponent of Preparedness," Master's Thesis, University of Cincinnati, 1950, 86.

126. David Clay Large, *Between Two Fires: Europe's Path in the 1930s* (New York: W. W. Norton, 1991), 176–77.

127. Hehn, *Low Dishonest Decade*, 63.

128. McDonough, *Hitler, Chamberlain and Appeasement*, 74.

129. Ibid.

130. Johnson, *Modern Times* (1991), 356.

131. Ibid., 360.

132. Paul Kengor, *Dupes: How America's Adversaries Have Manipulated Progressives for a Century* (Wilmington, DE: Intercollegiate Studies Institute, 2010), 151–59, and on the American Peace Mobilization, 139–59.

133. Johnson, *Modern Times*, 361.

134. Ferguson, *War of the World*, 470.

135. Ibid., 473.

136. Ibid., 471.

137. Ibid.

138. James B. Crowley, *Japan's Quest for Autonomy: National Security and Foreign Policy, 1930–1938* (Princeton, NJ: Princeton University Press, 1966), 6–7; Emily O. Goldman, *Sunken Treaties: Naval Arms Control Between the Wars* (University Park: Pennsylvania State University Press, 1994), 64; Sadao Asada, "The Japanese Navy and the United States," in Dorothy Borg and Shumpei Okamoto, eds., *Pearl Harbor as History: Japanese-American Relations, 1931–1941* (New York: Columbia University Press, 1973); and Gerald E. Wheeler, *Prelude to Pearl Harbor: The United States Navy and the Far East, 1921–1931* (Columbia: University of Missouri Press, 1963).

139. Ibid., 25–26.

140. W. T. DeBary et al., eds., *Sources of Japanese Tradition*, Second edition, Volume 2, abridged, part 2 (New York: Columbia University Press, 2006), 297–98.

141. Crowley, *Japan's Quest for Autonomy*, xiv–xvii.

142. Lewis, *Nothing Less Than Victory*, 238–39.

143. Hugh Byas, *Government by Assassination* (New York: Alfred A. Knopf, 1942), 29.

144. Ibid., 42.

145. Johnson, *Modern Times*, rev. ed., 190.

146. Ibid.; David Bergamini, *Japan's Imperial Conspiracy* (New York: Pocket Books, 1971); James Weland, "Misguided Intelligence: Japanese Military Intelligence Officers in the Manchurian Incident, September 1931," *Journal of Military History*, 58, 445–60; Philip Jowett and John Berger, *Rays of the Rising Sun, Volume 1: Japan's Asian Allies, 1931–1945, China and Manchukuo* (Solihull, England: Helion, 2005); Robert Ferrell, "The Mukden Incident: September 18–19, 1931," *Journal of Modern History*, 27, March 1955, 66–72. In 2006, a Japanese newspaper, *Yomiuri Shimbun*, published the results of a research project that concluded that the militarists alone were responsible but that politicians were "impotent" to stop them.

147. Byas, *Government by Assassination*, 87; Brij Tankha, *Kita Ikki and the Making of Modern Japan: A Vision of Empire* (Folkestone, Kent: Global Oriental, 2006).

148. James L. McClain, *Japan: A Modern History* (New York: W. W. Norton, 2002).

149. Johnson, *Modern Times*, rev. ed., 312; Byas, *Government by Assassination*, 265–67.

150. Byas, *Government by Assassination*, 272.

151. Johnson, *Modern Times*, rev. ed., 313.

152. Ben-Ami Shillony, *Revolt in Japan: The Young Officers and the February 26, 1936 Incident* (Princeton, NJ: Princeton University Press, 1973).

153. Byas, *Government by Assassination*, 43.

154. Ibid., 101.

155. Ibid., 155.

156. Ibid., 245; David James, *The Rise and Fall of the Japanese Empire* (London: Allen & Unwin, 1951), 134.

157. Johnson, *Modern Times*, 188.

158. James, *Rise and Fall of the Japanese Empire*, 136.

159. Kurt Singer, *Mirror, Sword and Jewel: A Study of Japanese Characteristics* (London: Routledge, 1973), 39–40.

160. Marshall, *To Have and Have Not*, 25.

161.   Ibid., 23.

162.   Eliot Janeway, "The Americans and the New Pacific," *Asia*, 39, February 1939, 109–13.

163.   Marshall, *To Have and Have Not*, xi.

164.   Ibid., 41.

165.   Ibid., 124.

166.   Byas, *Government by Assassination*, 153.

167.   Lewis Morton, *The Fall of the Philippines* (Washington, DC: Office of the Chief of Military History, 1953), 34–50.

168.   Marshall, *To Have and Have Not*, 150.

169.   Joachim von Ribbentrop, the Nazi foreign minister, and Nomura both provided a template for "negotiations" that was copied in the 1960s by Yippie leader Jerry Rubin in his confrontations with authorities. Rubin, who drafted many of these early tactics modeled on the results of Germany and Japan, explained: "Satisfy our demands and we go twelve more. . . . All we want from these meetings are demands *that the Establishment can never satisfy*. . . .Demonstrators are never *'reasonable'* [emphasis ours]." Jerry Rubin, *Do It: Scenarios of the Revolution* (New York: Simon and Schuster, 1970), 125, 169.

170.   Marshall, *To Have and Have Not*, 156.

171.   Rear Admiral Kemp Trolley, "The Strange Assignment of USS *Lanikai*," *United States Naval Institute Proceedings*, 83, September 1962, 71–84. Trolley, the commander of the *Lanikai*, which was the only vessel actually dispatched by this order, concluded his mission was as bait to provoke an attack.

## Chapter 5: The Hounds Unleashed

1.     Paul N. Hehn, *A Low Dishonest Decade: The Great Powers, Eastern Europe, and the Economic Origins of World War II, 1930–1941* (New York: Continuum, 2002), ix.

2.     Ibid., 15.

3.     Ibid., 36.

4.     John Wheeler-Bennett, *The Nemesis of Power: German Army in Politics, 1918–1945* (New York: Macmillan, 2005).

5.     Ibid., 133–38.

6.     Hehn, *Low Dishonest Decade*, 66.

7.     Ibid.

8.     John Terraine, *The U-Boat Wars* (New York: Henry Holt & Co, 1989), 220–21.

9.     Herbert M. Mason, Jr., *The Rise of the Luftwaffe 1918–1940* (New York: The Dial Press, 1973), 211.

10. Adam Tooze, *The Wages of Destruction: The Making and Breaking of the German Economy* (New York: Penguin, 2006), 339–41.

11. Ibid., 405.

12. Adolf Hitler, *Hitler's Second Book: The Unpublished Sequel to* Mein Kampf, Gerhard L. Weinberg, ed. (New York: Enigma Books, 2006), 113.

13. Ibid., 113.

14. Ibid.

15. Ibid., 99.

16. Gerhard L. Weinberg, "Hitler's Image of the United States," *American Historical Review*, 69, July 1964, 1006–21.

17. Ibid., 1010.

18. Ibid., 1011.

19. Ibid., 1018.

20. Geirr H. Haarr, *The German Invasion of Norway April 1940* (Annapolis, MD: Naval Institute Press, 2009), 32.

21. Earl F. Ziemke, *The German Northern Theater of Operations 1940–1945* (Washington, DC: Department of Army Pamphlet 20-271, 1959), 51–52.

22. Haarr, *German Invasion of Norway*, 397.

23. Ziemke, *German Northern Theater of Operations*, 110.

24. H. O. Lunde, *Plan Catherine, Hitler's Pre-Emptive War, The Battle for Norway, 1940* (Philadelphia: Casemate, 2009); J. L. Moulton, *The Norwegian Campaign of 1940: A Study of Warfare in Three Dimensions* (London: Eyre & Spottiswoode, 1966).

25. Thomas Powers, *Heisenberg's War: The Secret History of the German Bomb* (New York: Da Capo Press, 2000).

26. Diana M. Henderson, "The Scottish Soldier: Reality and the Armchair Experience," in Paul Addison and Angus Calder, eds., *Time to Kill: The Soldier's Experience of War in the West, 1939–1945* (Random House, AUS: Pimlico, 1997), 21–28.

27. John Williams, *The Ides of May: The Defeat of France May–June 1940* (New York: Alfred A. Knopf, 1968), 74; Martin S. Alexander, " 'No Taste for the Fight?' French Combat Performance in 1940 and the Politics of the Fall of France," in Addison and Calder, *Time to Kill*, 161–76.

28. Brian Bond, *Britain, France and Belgium, 1939–1940* (London: Brassey's, 1990); Joel Blatt, ed., *The French Defeat of 1940: Reassessments* (Oxford, UK: Breghahn Books, 1998); Robert Citino, *Quest for Decisive Victory: From Stalemate to Blitzkrieg in Europe, 1899–1940* (Lawrence: University of Kansas Press), and his *The Path to Blitzkrieg: Doctrine and Training in the German Army, 1920–1939* (Boulder, CO: Lynne Rienner Publishers, 1999); and Karl-Heinz Frieser, *The Blitzkrieg Legend* (Annapolis, MD: United States Naval Institute Press, 2005).

29.   Victoria de Grazia, *Irresistible Empire: America's Advance Through 20th-Century Europe* (Cambridge, MA: Belknap, 2005), 215.

30.   Tooze, *The Wages of Destruction*, 373.

31.   Niall Ferguson, *The War of the World: Twentieth-Century Conflict and the Descent of the West* (New York: Penguin, 2006), 388.

32.   John Strawson, *Hitler as Military Commander* (South Yorkshire, England: Pen and Sword Military Classics, 2003), 108.

33.   This is often called *Auftragstaktik*, completely incorrectly, but German commanders were given a mission and then allowed to handle their commands as they saw fit to accomplish that mission.

34.   William L. Shirer, *The Rise and Fall of the Third Reich: A History of Nazi Germany* (New York: Simon and Schuster, 1990), 720.

35.   Quoted in Martin S. Alexander, "'No Taste for the Fight?' French Combat Performance in 1940 and the Politics of the Fall of France," in Addison and Calder, *Time to Kill*, 161–76 (quotation on 161).

36.   Ibid., 163.

37.   *L'Aurore*, November 21, 1949, quoted Gamelin as saying, "There is no longer any."

38.   Winston Churchill, *Their Finest Hour* (Cambridge, MA: Houghton Mifflin, 1949), 46–49.

39.   Roy Jenkins, *Churchill: A Biography* (New York: Plume, 2001), 615–16.

40.   Ibid., 616.

41.   Churchill, *Their Finest Hour*, 181.

42.   Ibid.

43.   Ibid., 62; http://www.winstonchurchill.org/learn/speeches/speeches-of-winston-churchill/122-their-finest-hour.

44.   Maxime Weygand, *Recalled to Service*, trans. E. W. Dickes (Garden City, NY: Doubleday & Company, 1952), 147.

45.   Horst Boog, Juergen Foerster, et al., *Das Deutsche Reich und der Zweite Weltkrieg, v. 4, Der Angriff auf der Sowjetunion* (Stuttgart: Deutsche Verlags Anstalt, 1983), 262.

46.   Ibid., 281.

47.   Ibid., 633.

48.   Terry Brighton, *The Last Charge: the 21st Lancers and the Battle of Omdurman* (Marlborough, England: Crowood, 1998).

49.   Winston Churchill, *Great Contemporaries* (New York: G. P. Putnam Sons, 1937), 225.

50.   There is some indication that Churchill may have painted the alleged Jack the Ripper—Walter R. Sickert—unaware, and allowed Sickert to paint him! See Patricia Cornwall, *Portrait of a Killer: Jack the Ripper—Case Closed* (New York: Putnam, 2002).

51.  Jenkins, *Churchill*, 484.

52.  Winston S. Churchill, *The Second World War, Volume 1: The Gathering Storm* (Boston: Mariner Books, 1986).

53.  Jenkins, *Churchill*, 528.

54.  Ibid.

55.  Richard Clarke, *Anglo-American Economic Collaboration in War and Peace, 1942–1949* (Oxford, UK: Oxford University Press, 1982); Alan P. Dobson, *U.S. Wartime Aid to Britain, 1940–1946* (London: Croom Helm, 1986); and Albert L. Weeks, *Russia's Life-Saver: Lend-Lease Aid to the U.S.S.R. in World War II* (Lanham, MD: Lexington Books, 2004).

56.  Thomas Mahl, *Desperate Deception: British Covert Operations in the United States* (London: Brassey's, 1999).

57.  Peter R. Mansoor, *The GI Offensive in Europe* (Lawrence: University Press of Kansas, 1999), 5.

58.  Ibid., 16.

59.  Gerhard Schreiber, Bernd Stegemann, and Detlef Vogel, *Das Deutsche Reich und der Zweite Weltkrieg, Volume 3, Der Mittelmeerraum und Sùdosteuropa* (Stuttgart: Deutsche Verlags-Anstalt, 1984), 368.

60.  David Brown, *The Royal Navy and the Mediterranean* (London: Routledge, 2002).

61.  Christopher Buckley, *Greece and Crete 1941* (Athens: Efstathadis Group, 1984), 12; Christian Hartmann, *Halder Generalstabschef Hitlers 1938–1942* (Munich: Ferdinand Schoeningh, 1991), 263.

62.  Edward E. Ericson, *Feeding the German Eagle: Soviet Economic Aid to Nazi Germany, 1933–1941* (Santa Barbara, CA: Greenwood Publishing Group, 1999); Geoffrey Roberts, *Stalin's Wars: From World War to Cold War, 1939–1953* (New Haven, CT: Yale University Press, 2006); Aleksandr Moiseevich Nekrich, Adam B. Ulam, and Gregory L. Freeze, *Pariahs, Partners, Predators: German Soviet Relations, 1922–1941* (New York: Columbia University Press, 1997).

63.  Erickson, *Feeding the German Eagle*, 127.

64.  Ibid.

65.  Barton Whaley, *Codeword BARBAROSSA* (Cambridge, MA: M.I.T. Press, 1973), 1–10; John Waller, *The Unseen War in Europe: Espionage and Conspiracy in the Second World War* (London: Tauris & Co., 1996), 192.

66.  Boog, *Der Angriff*, 270.

67.  David M. Glantz, *Colossus Reborn: The Red Army at War, 1941–1943* (Lawrence: University Press of Kansas, 2005), 247.

68.  Donald Rayfield, *Stalin and His Hangmen* (London: Penguin, 2004), 315. Out of 57 corps commanders, only 7 survived, and 30,000 officers total were killed or imprisoned.

69. Christer Bergstrom, *Barbarossa: The Air Battle: July–December 1941* (London: Chevron/Ian Allen, 2007), 20.

70. Alexander Hill, "Did Russia Really Go It Alone?" *World War II Magazine,* June/July 2008, 62–67.

71. Ibid., 64.

72. M. Harrison, *Accounting for War: Soviet Production, Employment and the Defense Burden, 1940–1945* (Cambridge, UK: Cambridge University Press, 1996), 134; G. F. Krivosheev, ed., *Soviet Casualties and Combat Losses in the Twentieth Century* (London: Greenhill Books, 1997), 252. Alexander Hill provides different math for the tanks around Moscow, arguing that the British contribution approached 40 percent.

73. Hill, "British Lend-Lease," 775.

74. David M. Glanz and Jonathan M. House, *The Battle of Kursk* (Lawrence: University of Kansas Press, 1999), 37; Glantz, *Colossus Reborn*; Alexander Hill, "Did Russia Really Go It Alone? How Lend-Lease Helped the Soviets Defeat the Germans," *World War II Magazine,* July 12, 2008, http://www.historynet.com/did-russia-really-go-it-alone-how-lend-lease-helped-the-soviets-defeat-the-germans.htm.

75. Larry Schweikart, *America's Victories: Why the U.S. Wins Wars* (New York: Sentinel, 2006), 157; S. J. Zaloga and J. Grandsen, *Soviet Tanks and Combat Vehicles of World War II* (London: Arms and Armor Press, 1984), 128, 206; Glanz and House, *Battle of Kursk*, 37–38.

76. Tooze, *Wages of Destruction*, 479.

77. Ferguson, *War of the World*, 443.

78. It is useful to review the distinctions within various divisions and subdivisions of the German High Command in World War II.

(1) The German General Staff or General Staff Corps (or in German simply *Generalstab*) was not a staff at all in the American or British sense: it was a group of specially selected and carefully trained officers from the rank of major upward who filled almost all important command as well as staff positions throughout the Army. To separate them from the normal line officers, they had a red stripe running down the outside of each trouser leg. Regular line, non-*Generalstab* officers could rise to high commands (Rommel and Model come immediately to mind), but they were always paired with a *Generalstab* officer to ensure good liaison (Rommel had Bayerlein, von Mellenthin, and Hans Speidel in turn). The Truppenamt's leadership was made up of General Staff officers, and that was why the Army could be expanded so rapidly. In World War I, von Moltke was a General Staff officer, as was Hentsch, and this is critical to understanding how and why Hentsch would have had the extraordinary power he did during the Battle of the Marne in 1914. Von Moltke was also chief of the Army General Staff. It is important to realize

that the chief of the General Staff made all the appointments and assignments for officers in the German Army, even those at higher ranks than himself.

(2) The Army General Staff and the German General Staff were both headed by the Chief of the Army General Staff (*Chef des Generalstabs des Heeres* or simply *Chef des Generalstabs*). That position was occupied by Colonel-General Franz Halder from 1939 to 1942 after the resignation of Colonel-General Ludwig Beck, who had been in that post from 1935 to 1939. After Halder came Colonel-General Kurt Zeitzler from 1942 to 1944, Colonel-General Heinz Guderian from 1944 to 1945 (March 21), then the last, General der Infantrie Hans Krebs, who committed suicide after Hitler in Berlin. On March 16, 1935, the Truppenamt, which had existed until then to serve as the nucleus of the German Army, formally and simply became the General Staff of the Army.

(3) OKH or *Oberkommando Heers* was the Army High Command, and run by the commander in chief of the Army (*Oberbefehlshaber des Heeres*). In 1935 this was Colonel-General Werner von Fritsch; in 1938, Colonel-General von Brauchitsch, who was dismissed and replaced by Hitler himself in December of 1941. After December 1941, the Army's representative and senior officer in the *Fuehrerhauptquartier* (Hitler's Headquarters) was the chief of the Army General Staff.

(4) OKW or *Oberkommando der Wehrmacht* was the Armed Services High Command. Formerly de facto the war minister's office, a position held by Field Marshal Werner von Blomberg until 1938, it was created into a separate command by Hitler upon Blomberg's dismissal (he married a former prostitute). Hitler himself became *Oberster Befehlshaber der Wehrmacht* at that time (February 1938), and his chief of staff, the only one ever to occupy that post, was Field Marshal Wilhelm Keitel (*Chef der OKW*). This position turned into being Hitler's personal staff, and a new staff organization, the *Wehrmachtfuührungsstab* (Wehrmacht Leader Staff—actually the Wehrmacht Operations Staff) was created to handle the work formerly accomplished by the staff in the Department of National Defense. This staff was initially headed by Generalmajor Max von Viebaln from March 1938 to August 1939, afterward by Colonel-General Alfred Jodl, until the end of the war.

(5) The Kriegsmarine (Navy) High Command was OKM, the *Oberkommando der Kriegsmarine*, commanded by Grand Admiral Erich Raeder from 1935 to 1943, when he was succeeded by Grand Admiral Karl Dönitz for the remainder of the war.

(6) The Luftwaffe (Air Force) High Command was OKL, the *Oberkommando der Luftwaffe*, and there was only one commander, Reichsmarschal Hermann Göring.

From 1939 onward there were four General Staffs, the *Wehrmachtfüh-rungsstab*, the General Staff of the Army, that of the Luftwaffe, and that of the Kriegsmarine.

79.  Boog et al., *Der Angriff*, 572.

80.  Siegfried Knappe with Ted Brusaw, *Soldat: Reflections of a German Soldier, 1936–1945* (New York: Dell Publishing, 1993), 229–34.

81.  G. K. Zhukov, *The Memoirs of Marshal Zhukov* (New York: Delacorte Press, 1971), 40.

82.  Ibid., 354.

83.  Georgi K. Zhukov, *Marshal Zhukov's Greatest Battles* (New York: Harper & Row, 1969), 91; David M. Glantz, *Colossus Reborn* (Lawrence: University Press of Kansas, 2005), 21.

84.  Tooze, *Wages of Destruction*, 403.

85.  David Strauss, *Menace in the West: The Rise of French Anti-Americanism in Modern Times* (Westport, CT: Greenwood Press, 1978), 51.

86.  Erik Goldstein and John Maurer, eds., *The Washington Conference, 1921–22: Naval Rivalry, East Asian Stability and the Road to Pearl Harbor* (Essex, England: Frank Cass, 1994), 113.

87.  U.S. Department of State, *Peace and War: United States Foreign Policy, 1931–1941* (Washington, DC: Government Printing Office, 1983), 94.

88.  Peter Wetzler, *Hirohito and War: Imperial Tradition and Military Decision Making in Prewar Japan* (Honolulu: University of Hawaii Press, 1998), 39; Mark R. Peattie and David C. Evans, *Kaigun: Strategy Tactics, and Technology in the Imperial Japanese Navy* (Annapolis, MD: Naval Institute Press, 1997); H. P. Willmott, *The Barrier and the Javelin: Japanese and Allied Pacific Strategies, February to June 1942* (Annapolis, MD: Naval Institute Press, 1983).

89.  John Costello, *The Pacific War, 1941–1945* (New York: HarperCollins, 1982), 116.

90.  Edward S. Miller, *War Plan Orange: The U.S. Strategy to Defeat Japan, 1897–1945* (Annapolis, MD: Naval Institute Press, 2007), 63.

91.  Iguchi Takeo, *Demystifying Pearl Harbor: A New Perspective from Japan*, trans. David Noble (Tokyo: International House of Japan, 2010), 67. See also the *Daibon 'ei rikugunbu shidohan kimitsu senso nisshi* [Confidential War Diaries of the War-guidance-Section of the Army Division, Imperial General Headquarters], 2 vols. (Keneisha, 1998).

92.  Miller, *War Plan Orange*, 122.

93.  Iguchi proves that contrary to the claims of Robert Stinnett (*Day of Deceit: The Truth About FDR and Pearl Harbor* [New York: Free Press, 2001]), the "Climb Mount Nitaka" message was not broadcast in English. Yamamoto's own biographer notes that "the message was encoded syllable by syllable, using the five-digit random number code," and the original decrypt contains the legend "(M) Navy Trans 4/24/46" meaning that the

translation was not completed until April 24, 1946 (Iguchi, *Demystifying Pearl Harbor*, 145–47).

94. "Pearl Harbor Truly a Sneak Attack, Papers Show," *New York Times*, December 9, 1999, http://www.nytimes.com/1999/12/09/world/pearl-harbor-truly-a-sneak-attack-papers-show.html?pagewanted=2&src=pm.

95. Not only does Iguchi bury the arguments of Robert Stinnett and other "Back Door to War" theorists by proving that Stinnett had critically misunderstood one of his key pieces of evidence—which had not even been translated until 1946—but Iguchi also shows that a new generation of Japanese apologists have risen to take up the "Back Door to War" banner as a means of absolving Japan of the attack. See Iguchi, *Demystifying Pearl Harbor*, 148.

## Chapter 6: Canopy of Freedom

1. Peter R. Mansoor, *The GI Offensive in Europe: The Triumph of American Infantry Divisions, 1941–1945* (Lawrence: University of Kansas Press, 2002).

2. Bureau of the Census, *Historical Statistics of the United States Colonial Times to 1970*, Bicentennial Edition, Vol. 1 (Washington, DC: Government Printing Office, 1975), 131 (Series 29-42).

3. John Morton Blum, *V Was for Victory: Politics and American Culture During World War II* (New York: Harcourt Brace, 1948), 115.

4. Several good biographies of Hughes exist, but none covers all aspects of his life. See Richard Hack, *Hughes: The Private Diaries, Memos and Letters: The Definitive Biography of the First American Billionaire* (Beverly Hills, CA: New Millennium Press, 2002); Peter Harry Brown and Pat H. Broeske, *Howard Hughes: The Untold Story* (New York: Penguin Books, 1996); Donald Barlett and James B. Steele, *Empire: The Life, Legend and Madness of Howard Hughes* (New York: W. W. Norton, 1979); and Terry Moore and Jerry Rivers, *The Passions of Howard Hughes* (Los Angeles: General Publishing Group, 1996).

5. John Heitmann, "The Man Who Won the War: Andrew Jackson Higgins," *Louisiana History*, 34, 1993, 35–40, and his "Demagogue and Industrialist," *Gulf Coast Historical Review*, 5, 1990, 152–62.

6. Ibid.

7. Randall Hansen, *Fire and Fury: The Allied Bombing of Germany, 1942–1945* (New York: NAL Caliber, 2008), 37.

8. Ibid., 23, 25.

9. Ibid., 25.

10. Ronald Schaffer, *Wings of Judgment: American Bombing in World War II* (New York: Oxford University Press, 1985); Michael S. Sherry, *The Rise of American Air Power* (New Haven, CT: Yale University Press, 1989); Stephen L. McFarland, *America's Pursuit of Precision, 1910–1945* (Tuscaloosa: University of Alabama Press, 2008).

11.  Hansen, *Fire and Fury*, 131.

12.  Tooze, *Wages of Destruction*, 603.

13.  Mark Mazower, *Dark Continent: Europe's Twentieth Century* (New York: Vintage, 1998), 187.

14.  Ibid., 205.

15.  Ibid., 192.

16.  Ibid., 193.

17.  Ibid.

18.  William Manchester, *American Caesar: Douglas MacArthur, 1880–1964* (Boston: Little, Brown and Company, 1978).

19.  Donald Knox, *Death March: The Survivors of Bataan* (Boston: Houghton Mifflin, 2002); Manny Lawton, *Some Survived: An Eyewitness Account of the Bataan Death March and the Men Who Lived Through It* (New York: Algonquin Books, 2004), 18.

20.  Franklin D. Roosevelt, Broadcast to the Nation, April 28, 1942, http://www.ibiblio.org/pha/policy/1942/420428a.html.

21.  James H. Doolittle and Carroll V. Glines, *I Could Never Be So Lucky Again: An Autobiography* (New York: Bantam Books, 1991); Paolo Coletta, "Launching the Doolittle Raid on Japan, April 18, 1942," *Pacific Historical Review*, 63, February 1993, 73–86.

22.  Joseph H. Alexander, *Edson's Raiders: The 1st Marine Raider Battalion in World War II* (Annapolis, MD: Naval Institute Press, 2000); Richard Frank, *Guadalcanal: The Definitive Account of the Landmark Battle* (New York: Random House, 1990).

23.  Robert M. Citino, *Death of the Wehrmacht: The German Campaigns of 1942* (Lawrence: University Press of Kansas, 2007), 112.

24.  Erich von Manstein, *Lost Victories* (Chicago: Henery Regnery & Co, 1958), 238.

25.  Citino, *Death of the Wehrmacht*, 114–15.

26.  Horst Boog, Werner Rahn, Reinhard Stumpf, and Bernd Wegner, *Das Deutsche Reich und der Zweite Weltkrieg*, Vol. 6, *Der Globale Krieg* (Stuttgart: Deutsche Verlags Anstalt, 1990), 778.

27.  Michelle Malkin, *In Defense of Internment: The Case for "Racial Profiling" in World War II and the War on Terror* (Washington, DC: Regnery, 2004).

28.  Paul Carell, *Unternehmen Barbarossa* (Berlin West: Ullstein Verlag, 1963), 473.

29.  Boog, *Das Deutsche Reich und der Zweite Weltkrieg*, 783.

30.  Ibid.

31.  Carell, *Unternehmen Barbarossa*, 443.

32.  Ibid., 444; Citino, *Death of the Wehrmacht*, 257.

33. Desmond Young, *The Desert Fox* (New York: Harper & Brothers, 1950), 10.

34. Alun Chalfont, *Montgomery of Alamein* (New York: Atheneum, 1976), 151.

35. Rick Atkinson, *An Army at Dawn: The War in North Africa, 1942–1943* (New York: Henry Holt & Co., 2002), 258.

36. Merle Miller, *Ike: The Soldier as They Knew Him* (New York: G. P. Putnam's Sons, 1987), 463.

37. Sam Moses, *At All Costs: How a Crippled Ship and Two American Merchant Mariners Turned the Tide of World War II* (New York: Random House, 2006); Ernle Bradford, *Siege: Malta, 1940–1943* (South Yorkshire, England: Pen and Sword, 2003).

38. Mansoor, *The GI Offensive in Europe*.

39. Mitchell, "GI in Europe," 309.

40. Charles Royster, *A Revolutionary People at War: The Continental Army and American Character, 1775–83* (Chapel Hill: University of North Carolina Press, 1979), 219.

41. Mitchell, "GI in Europe," 304–16.

42. Mansoor, *GI Offensive in Europe*, 164.

43. Jonathan B. Parshall and Anthony P. Tully, *Shattered Sword: The Untold Story of the Battle of Midway* (Washington, DC: Potomac Books, 2005), 407.

44. Hansen, *Fire and Fury*, 64.

45. Ibid., 129.

46. Ibid., 131.

47. Elke Frohlich, ed., *Die Tagebucher von Joseph Goebbels, Teil II Diktate 1941–1945* (Munich: KG Saur, 1994). See entries for December 23–25, 1943, for example. For the most recent biography of Goebbels, see Toby Thaker, *Joseph Goebbels: Life and Death* (New York: Palgrave Macmillan, 2009). Special thanks to Schweikart's University of Dayton colleague Lawrence J. Flockerzie for his unpublished paper "Joseph Goebbels and the Third Reich at Year's End, 1943," 2011, in Schweikart's possession.

48. Larry Schweikart, "Kursk: A Reappraisal," *Against the Odds*, 2, December 2003, 20–23.

49. Donald L. Miller, *Masters of the Air: America's Bomber Boys Who Fought Against Nazi Germany* (New York: Simon and Schuster, 2006), 254; Richard G. Davis, *Carl Al Spaatz and the Air War in Europe* (Washington, DC: Smithsonian Institute, 1992), 303.

50. Albert Speer, *Inside the Third Reich: The Classic Account of Nazi Germany by Hitler's Armaments Minister* (London: Phoenix, 2003), 468.

51. Tooze, *Wages of Destruction*, 627.

52. Ibid., 548.

53. Ibid., 609.

54. Ibid., 521.

55.  Ibid., 317.

56.  Hitler, *Hitler's Second Book*, 15.

57.  Tooze, *Wages of Destruction*, 549.

58.  Paul Julian Weindling, *Epidemics and Genocide in Eastern Europe, 1890–
     1945* (New York: Oxford University Press, 2000), 257–60.

59.  Ibid., 263. Before the war, Germany had a cremation culture, possessing
     the highest percentage of cremations in Europe, and German "crema-
     tionists [had] a special sense of leadership in the international move-
     ment" for cremation (ibid., 264). In the 1930s they led the call for
     international cremation federations and agreements for the transport of
     ashes. Now sanctioned by Hitler, the movement spread: by 1939, there
     were more than 130 German crematoria, performing almost 100,000
     processes a year—many times that of Britain. Even the Nazified crema-
     tions, though, were obsessively regulated, with all urn sizes standardized
     and to be placed only in designated columbaria, never returned to rela-
     tives. As the historian of disease and cremation in Eastern Europe noted,
     "Freedom of choice in death was not acceptable under Nazism" (ibid.,
     266–68). Thus, even before the first killing camps were up and running,
     the ironic employment of the death ritual of heroic Teutons for "subhu-
     mans" became institutionalized.

60.  Mark Roseman, *The Wannsee Conference and the Final Solution: A Recon-
     sideration* (New York: Picador, 2002), 34. The timing of the shift from
     mass executions of national leadership to the dedicated destruction of
     the Jews is a source of debate among historians. Most put the decisive
     turning point in Hitler's thinking to proceed with the Holocaust (as op-
     posed to merely entertaining it as an option) at September 1941,when he
     ordered mass deportations to camps even while the Soviet campaign
     raged on (ibid., 58–59). See also Philippe Burrin, *Hitler and the Jews: The
     Genesis of the Holocaust* (London: Edward Arnold, 1994).

61.  Richard Breitman, *The Architect of Genocide: Himmler and the Final Solu-
     tion* (New York: Knopf, 1991); Weindling, *Epidemics and Genocide in East-
     ern Europe*, 296.

62.  Weindling, *Epidemics and Genocide in Eastern Europe*, 296.

63.  Ibid., 279.

64.  Ibid., 300.

65.  Roseman, *Wannsee Conference*, 127.

66.  Christopher R. Browning, *The Origins of the Final Solution: The Evolution
     of Nazi Jewish Policy, September 1939–March 1942* (Lincoln: University of
     Nebraska Press, 2004), 16.

67.  Ibid., 111–17.

68.  Peter Padfield, *Himmler: Reichsführer SS* (New York: Macmillan, 1990),
     270; J. Von Lang and C. Sybill, eds., *Eichmann Interrogated* (London:
     Bodley Head, 1982), 9203.

69.  "Protocols of the Wannsee Conference," http://www.ghwk.de/engl/pro tengl.htm.

70.  Browning, *Origins of the Final Solution*, 177.

71.  Ibid., 369. Jurgen Matthaus, who contributed to Browning's book and wrote one of the critical chapters on the timing of the final solution, places the extermination decision by Hitler in "mid-July, during the first peak of victory euphoria," and writes that Hitler "led Himmler and Heydrich to believe he expected proposals concerning the fate of the rest of European Jewry that went beyond the expulsion plans of the previous years" (370).

72.  Roseman, *Wannsee Conference*, 110. For example, Eichmann referred to "business with the engine" at his Jerusalem trial, and did not distinguish between killing via an internal combustion engine or a cyanide technique.

73.  Paul Johnson, *Modern Times: A History of the World from the Twenties to the Nineties* (New York: HarperCollins, 1991), 414.

74.  Nuremberg Document NG-5291, cited in Saul Friedländer, *Pius XII and the Third Reich* (New York: Alfred A. Knopf, 1966), 104.

75.  Ibid., 104–10.

76.  Ibid., 90.

77.  Theo J. Schulte, "The German Soldier in Occupied Russia," in Addison and Calder, *Time to Kill*, 277. Daniel J. Goldhagen (*Hitler's Willing Executioners: Ordinary Germans and the Holocaust* [New York: Vintage, 1997]) argues that everyday Germans were hip-deep in blood, and that an "eliminationist" anti-Semitism constituted a central part of ordinary Germans' existence. Yehuda Bauer (*Rethinking the Holocaust* [New Haven: Yale University Press, 2000]) agrees. See the differing views in Ron Rosenbaum, *Explaining Hitler: The Search for the Origins of His Evil* (New York: Harper Perennial, 1999); Christopher R. Browning, *Fateful Months: Essays on the Emergence of the Final Solution* (New York: Holmes & Meier, 1985), and his *The Path to Genocide: Essays on Launching the Final Solution* (New York: Cambridge University Press, 1992); Lucy Dawidowicz, *The War Against the Jews* (New York: Holt, Reinhart, and Winston, 1975); and Geoffrey P. Megargee, *War of Annihilation: Combat and Genocide on the Eastern Front 1941* (New York: Rowman & Littlefield, 2006).

78.  Ian Kershaw, "German Popular Opinion and the 'Jewish Question,' 1939–1943: Some Further Reflections," in Wolfgang Benz, *Die Juden in Deutschland: Leben unter nationalsozialistischer Herrschaft* (Tubingen: J. C. B. Mohr, 1986), 277, 281, 288. Among those who agree with Kershaw—and thus depart from Goldhagen—are Sarah Gordon, *Hitler, Germans, and the "Jewish Question"* (Princeton, NJ: Princeton University Press, 1984); Saul Friedlander, "Ideology and Extermination: the Immediate Origins of the Final Solution," in Ronald Smelser, ed., *Lessons and Legacies V: The Holocaust and Justice* (Evanston, IL: Northwestern University Press, 2002), 31–48; Friedlander's *The Years of Persecution, Vol. 1, Nazi*

*Germany and the Jews* (New York: HarperCollins, 1997); David Bankier, *The Germans and the Final Solution: Public Opinion Under Nazism* (New York: Oxford University Press, 1992); and Otto Dov Kulka, "'Public Opinion' in Nazi Germany and the 'Jewish Question,'" *Jerusalem Quarterly*, 25, Fall 1982, 121–44 and 26, Winter 1982, 34–45.

79.   Kershaw, "German Popular Opinion."

80.   Samuel A. Stouffer et al., *The American Soldier* (Princeton, NJ: Princeton University Press, 1949), 11:32–35.

81.   Michael D. Doubler, *Closing with the Enemy: How the GIs Fought the War in Europe, 1944–1945* (Lawrence: University of Kansas Press, 1994), 258.

82.   Ibid.

83.   Atkinson, *An Army at Dawn*, 463, referencing a memo, "Comparison of Executions During WW I and WW II," U.S. Army JAG Undersecretary of War, April 22, 1946.

84.   Frank Furlong Mathias, *G. I. Jive: An Army Bandsman in World War II* (Lexington: University of Kentucky Press, 1983); interviews with the author, various dates, 1985–90.

85.   Harry Gailey, *MacArthur Strikes Back: Decision at Buna: New Guinea 1942–1943* (Novato, CA: The Presidio Press, 2000).

86.   Courtney Whitney, *MacArthur: His Rendezvous with History* (New York: Alfred A. Knopf, 1956), 67–68.

87.   Francis Trevelyan Miller, *General Douglas MacArthur: Soldier-Statesman*, rev. ed. (Philadelphia: International Press, 1951), 27. Douglas MacArthur, *Reminiscences* (New York: McGraw-Hill, 1964).

88.   William Manchester, *American Caesar: Douglas MacArthur 1880–1964* (Boston: Back Bay Books, 2008).

89.   E. B. Potter, *Nimitz* (Annapolis, MD: Naval Institute Press, 1976), 10.

90.   John Prados, *Combined Fleet Decoded* (Annapolis, MD: Naval Institute Press, 1995), 317.

91.   Michael Smith, *The Emperor's Codes* (New York: Arcade Publishing, 2007), 143–44; Prados, *Combined Fleet*, 410–11.

92.   David M. Glantz with Jonathan M. House, *To the Gates of Stalingrad* (Lawrence: University Press of Kansas, 2009), 261–65.

93.   David M Glantz, *Zhukov's Greatest Defeat* (Lawrence: University Press of Kansas, 1999), 304–8.

94.   Boog, *Das Deutsche Reich und der Zweite Weltkrieg*, 6:1003–4.

95.   Erich von Manstein, *Verlorene Siege* (Chicago: Henry Regnery, 1958), 334.

96.   Andrei Grechko, *Battle for the Caucasus* (Moscow: Progress Publishers, 1971), 93–194.

97.   Stephen E. Ambrose, *The Supreme Commander: The War Years of General Dwight D. Eisenhower* (New York: Doubleday & Company, 1969), 158.

98. Ibid., 159.

99. Nikolai Tolstoy, *Stalin's Secret War* (New York: Holt, Rinehart & Winston, 1982), 57.

100. Winston Churchill, *The Hinge of Fate* (Cambridge, MA: Houghton Mifflin, 1950), 571–81

101. Douglas E. Nash, *Hell's Gate*, 2nd ed. (Stamford, CT: RZM Publishing, 2005), 298, 403.

102. "Faith Staked Down," *Time*, February 9, 1952.

103. Stephen Ambrose, *Eisenhower*, vol. 1 (Norwalk, CT: Easton Press, 1987), 93.

104. Ibid., 133.

105. Merle Miller, *Ike the Soldier* (New York: G. P. Putnam's Sons, 1987), 333–34.

106. Ambrose, *Eisenhower*, 1:134.

107. Ibid., 1:141.

108. Ibid., 1:151.

109. Carlo D'Este, *Patton: A Genius for War* (New York: Harper 1996). General Donald Bennett, a patient at one of the field hospitals, recalled cheering after Patton slapped one of the soldiers. Bennett, who had suffered from pneumonia and had been moved, could not recall which of the two incidents he had witnessed.

110. Arthur Bryant, *The Turn of the Tide* (New York: Doubleday & Company, 1957), 540–42.

111. John Keegan, *Six Armies in Normandy* (New York: Viking Press, 1982), 49.

112. Bernard Law, Viscount Montgomery of Alamein, *The Memoirs of Field-Marshal the Viscount Montgomery of Alamein, K.G.* (Cleveland: World Publishing Company, 1958), 24.

113. "NARA Staff Favorites: Online Records," http://blogs.archives.gov/online -public-access/?p=150.

114. Keegan, *Six Armies*, 315–16.

115. Alex Buchner, *Ostfront 1944: The German Defensive Battles on the Russian Front 1944* (Atglen, PA: Schiffer Military, 1995), 298–99.

116. Keegan, *Six Armies*, 66.

117. Winston Churchill, *Triumph and Tragedy* (Cambridge, MA: Houghton Mifflin, 1953), 227–28.

118. John S. D. Eisenhower, *The Bitter Woods* (New York: G. P. Putnam's Sons, 1969), 381–82.

119. David Dougherty interview with Fertig, 1961; John Keats, *They Fought Alone* ( New York: Time Life Education, 1990), 441–42.

120. Ibid, 384–85.

121. James Bradley, *Flags of Our Fathers* (New York: Bantam, 2006), 207.

122. Victor Davis Hanson, *Ripples of Battle: How Wars of the Past Still Deter-*

*mine How We Fight, How We Live, and How We Think* (New York: Anchor, 2004), 22.

123. Ibid., 30.

124. Sadao Asada, "The Shock of the Atomic Bomb and Japan's Decision to Surrender: A Reconsideration," *Pacific Historical Review*, 67, 1998, 101–48: Richard B. Frank, *Downfall: The End of the Imperial Japanese Empire* (New York: Random House, 1999); and Robert James Maddox, *Weapons for Victory: The Hiroshima Decision Fifty Years Later* (Columbia: University of Missouri Press, 1995). See also J. Samuel Walker, *Prompt and Utter Destruction: Truman and the Use of Atomic Bombs Against Japan* (Chapel Hill: University of North Carolina Press, 2004), at 131–36, as well as Walker's latest contribution, "Recent Literature on Truman's Atomic Bomb Decision: A Search for Middle Ground," *Diplomatic History*, 29, April 2005, 311–34. Lawrence Freedman and Saki Dockrill, "Hiroshima: A Strategy of Shock," in Saki Dockrill, ed., *From Pearl Harbor to Hiroshima: The Second World War in Asia and the Pacific, 1941–1945* (New York: St. Martin's Press, 1994); Herbert P. Bix, *Hirohito and the Making of Modern Japan* (New York: HarperCollins Publishers, 2000); Tsuyoshi Hasegawa, *Racing the Enemy: Stalin, Truman, and the Surrender of Japan* (Cambridge, MA: Harvard University Press, 2005). Barton Bernstein insisted that the bombs were unnecessary in his "The Atomic Bombings Reconsidered," *Foreign Affairs*, January–February 1995, 135–52, but evidence from inside the Japanese government reveals that the war leadership had no intention of surrendering prior to the bombs.

125. Johnson, *Modern Times*, 426.

126. Ibid.

127. "Speech by Emperor Hirohito," August 14, 1945, http://www.mtholyoke.edu/acad/intrel/hirohito.htm.

128. Rick Atkinson, *An Army at Dawn* (New York: Henry Holt & Co., 2002), 463, referencing an April 22, 1946, memo from the U.S. Army Judge Advocate General to the Undersecretary of War.

129. James Bradley, *Flyboys* (New York: Little, Brown, 2003), 198.

130. Ibid., 173–75.

131. Godfrey Hodgson, *The Myth of American Exceptionalism* (New Haven, CT: Yale University Press, 2009); Donald E. Pease, *The New American Exceptionalism* (Minneapolis: University of Minnesota Press, 2009); Deborah L. Madsen, *American Exceptionalism* (Jackson: University Press of Mississippi, 1998); Andrew Bacevich, *The Limits of Power: The End of American Exceptionalism* (New York: Holt Paperbacks, 2009); Seymour M. Lipset, *American Exceptionalism: A Double-Edged Sword* (New York: W. W. Norton & Co., 1997); and Michael Ignatieff, *American Exceptionalism and Human Rights* (Princeton, NJ: Princeton University Press, 2005).

# INDEX

Abdul Hamid II, 221
Abel, Jean-Baptiste, 203
Abortion, 186, 191, 192
Abraham Lincoln Brigade, 285
Abyssinian (Ethiopian) conflict,
  168, 273–75
Addams, Jane, 112, 117, 118, 180
Adler, Alfred, 62
Adler, Victor, 188
Advertising industry, 230–32
African Americans
  army regiments of, 107–8
  See also Racism
African colonies
  Boer War, 2, 39, 40, 79, 85, 89,
    161, 206, 328
  decolonization policy in, 197,
    202, 203, 204
  economic growth of, 205–6
  local administration in, 212
  wars in, 37, 40
African National Congress
  (ANC), 202
African nationalism, 37, 202
Agricultural collectivization, in
  Soviet Union, 149, 150,
  242–43, 244
Agriculture
  contraction, and bank failures,
    246–47
  New Deal policies, 253
  political influence of, 245
  subsidies, 245–46
Aguinaldo, Emilio, 30, 31, 32
Air power
  in Battle of Britain, 327
  British, 269, 315, 341, 357–59
  and long-range bomber, 174
  Nazi Germany, 258, 267, 291,
    313–14, 327, 383
  in Pacific War, 392–93
  Soviet, 341
  U.S., 315, 358–59, 381–84
  in Western Front, 359–60,
    381–84
  in World War I, 129, 131, 135
  See also Aviation
Aizawa, Sabura, 302
Albania, 165, 275, 335
Alcalá-Zamora, Niceto, 278, 280
Alexander, Harold, 378, 409
Alexander III, Czar, 141
Alexandra, Czarina, 140
Alfonso XIII, King of Spain, 278,
  279
Algeria, 196, 203, 219
Allenby, Edmund, 200
Alsace-Lorraine, 161, 265
*Altmark*, 317

American Association of Retired
  Persons (AARP), 254
American Bankers Association, 248
American Birth Control League,
  185
American Economic Association,
  180
American Eugenics Society, 183,
  195
American exceptionalism
  and ascent to world power, 7–12
  European misunderstanding of,
    5–6
  four pillars of, 4–5, 9, 211, 229
  immigrants' challenge to, 6–7
  and Lindbergh's flight, 176–77
  in postwar world, 423–24
American Relief Administration,
  241
Amiens, Battle of, 137
Amundsen, Roald, 2, 62
Anarchism, Spanish, 279, 282, 283
Anderson, Kenneth, 377
Andreas-Salomé, Lou, 62
Anfuso, Filippo, 275
Angell, Norman, 69–70, 293
Antarctic expeditions, 2, 61, 62
Anti-Comintern Pact of 1936, 296
Anti-Semitism
  and eugenics theory, 181, 188,
    189
  in Europe, 188–90
  of Hitler, 260, 262–64
  Jewish response to, 188–89
  in United States, 187
  See also Jews
Appleton, Thomas, 76
Arab Bureau, 198
Araki, Sadao, 301
Architecture, 64–68
Arctic expedition, 2, 61–62
Ardennes offensive, 412–13
Argentina, 225, 226
Armenians, Turkish massacre of,
  220–22
Arms. See Weapons
Army, U.S. See United States
  Army
Arnold, Henry H. "Hap," 358
Art, 69
Asada, Sadao, 417
Assassinations
  Japanese cult of, 300, 301
  political, 82–83
Astor, William Waldorf, 291
Atatürk, Mustafa Kemal, 221
Atomic bombing of Hiroshima
  and Nagasaki, 417–18,
  419, 421

Auschwitz, 387–88, 389, 390
Australia, 100, 214, 301, 353,
  393–94, 405
Austria
  Dollfuss assassination, 271
  Nazism in, 265
  Nazi takeover of, 286
Austro-Hungarian Empire
  assassination of Franz
    Ferdinand, 81, 82
  and Treaty of Versailles, 155,
    164, 219
  in World War I, 83, 106
Automobile industry, 269, 353
Aviation
  design advances in, 173–74
  Hughes's contributions to,
    354–55
  and Lindbergh's flight, 175–
    77
  See also Air power
Azaña, Manuel, 279, 280

Baker, Newton D., Jr., 128, 136,
  174
Balaclava, Battle of, 38
Baldwin, Stanley, 273, 290, 293,
  329
Balfour, A.J., 249
Balfour, Arthur, 155, 162, 200
Balfour Declaration of 1917, 199,
  200
Ballets, of Stravinsky, 68
Banks and banking
  failures, 246–47
  Federal Reserve System, 8, 118,
    123, 241, 247
  fractional reserve, 248
  regulation of, 253
Barbary pirates, 36
Baring, Maurice, 78
Barnes, Ralph, 244
Barnett, Correlli, 276
Barton, Bruce, 231
Baruch, Bernard, 121–22, 293
Bataan Death March, 363, 366
Batton, Barton, Durstein, and
  Osborn (BBD&O), 230,
  231
Bauhaus school of architecture,
  67–68
Baur, Erwin, 194
Bayonet charge, 75, 92, 129, 131
Beard, Charles, 21
Beatty, David, 110
Beaverbrook, Lord, 327, 342
Beck, Ludwig, 271, 288
"Beer Hall" Putsch, 261, 265

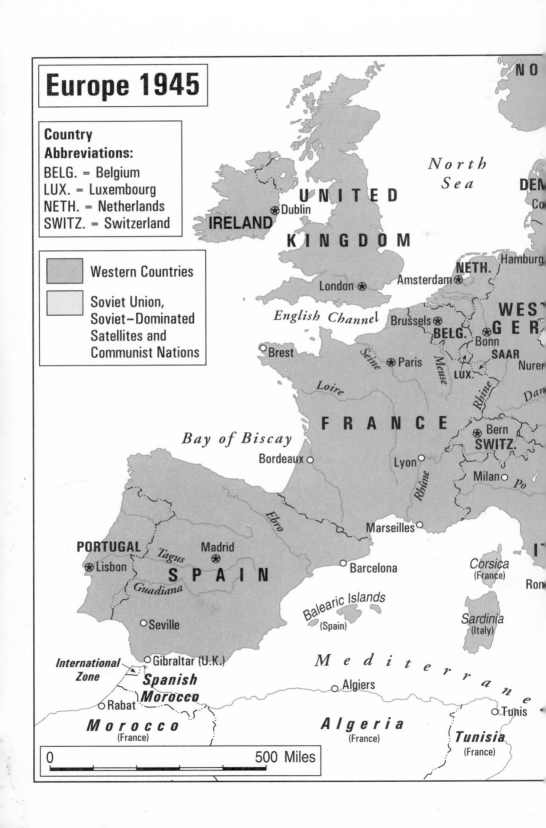

# Europe 1945

**Country Abbreviations:**
BELG. = Belgium
LUX. = Luxembourg
NETH. = Netherlands
SWITZ. = Switzerland

Western Countries

Soviet Union, Soviet–Dominated Satellites and Communist Nations

NO

*North Sea*

DEN
Co

UNITED
Dublin
IRELAND
KINGDOM
London ✪
Amsterdam ✪
NETH.
Hamburg
WEST
GER
Brussels ✪
BELG.
Bonn
SAAR
Nurer
LUX.
Rhine
Dan
*English Channel*
Brest
Seine ✪ Paris
Meuse

Loire

FRANCE
Bern ✪
SWITZ.

*Bay of Biscay*
Bordeaux ○
Lyon ○
Milan ○
Po

PORTUGAL
Tagus
Madrid ✪
SPAIN
Barcelona ○
Corsica (France)
Ron
IT
Lisbon ✪
Guadiana
Rhine
Marseilles ○

Ebro

Seville ○
Balearic Islands (Spain)
Sardinia (Italy)

Gibraltar (U.K.)
*Mediterrane*

*International Zone*
*Spanish Morocco*
Algiers ○

Rabat ○
*M o r o c c o* (France)
*A l g e r i a* (France)
Tunis ○
*Tunisia* (France)

0        500 Miles